HIDDEN ®

Cancún & the Yucatán

HIDDEN®

Cancún & the Yucatán

Including Cozumel, Tulum,
Chichén Itzá, Uxmal and Mérida

Richard Harris

THIRD EDITION

Ulysses Press®
BERKELEY, CALIFORNIA

Published by:
ULYSSES PRESS
P.O. Box 3440
Berkeley, CA 94703
www.ulyssespress.com

ISSN 1098-9005
ISBN 1-56975-292-3

Printed in Canada by Transcontinental Printing

10 9 8 7 6 5 4

MANAGING EDITOR: Claire Chun
PROJECT DIRECTOR: Lily Chou
COPY EDITORS: Summer Block, Lily Chou
EDITORIAL ASSOCIATES: Kate Allen
TYPESETTER: Lisa Kester
CARTOGRAPHY: Pease Press, Ulysses Press
INDEXER: Sayre Van Young
COVER PHOTOGRAPHY: Michael J. Pettypool/HouserStock
  (Pyramid of Kukulcán, Chichén Itzá)

Distributed in the United States by Publishers Group West
and in Canada by Raincoast Books

Write to us!

If in your travels you discover a spot that captures the spirit of Cancún and the Yucatán, or if you live in the region and have a favorite place to share, or if you just feel like expressing your views, write to us and we'll pass your note along to the author.

We can't guarantee that the author will add your personal find to the next edition, but if the writer does use the suggestion, we'll acknowledge you in the credits and send you a free copy of the new edition.

ULYSSES PRESS
P.O. Box 3440
Berkeley, CA 94703
E-mail: readermail@ulyssespress.com

What's Hidden?

At different points throughout this book, you'll find special listings marked with a hidden symbol:

◄ HIDDEN

This means that you have come upon a place off the beaten tourist track, a spot that will carry you a step closer to the local people and natural environment of Cancún and the Yucatán.

The goal of this guide is to lead you beyond the realm of everyday tourist facilities. While we include traditional sightseeing listings and popular attractions, we also offer alternative sights and adventure activities. Instead of filling this guide with reviews of standard hotels and chain restaurants, we concentrate on one-of-a-kind places and locally owned establishments.

Our authors seek out locales that are popular with residents but usually overlooked by visitors. Some are more hidden than others (and are marked accordingly), but all the listings in this book are intended to help you discover the true nature of Cancún and the Yucatán and put you on the path of adventure.

Contents

Maps

OUTDOOR ADVENTURE SYMBOLS

The following symbols accompany national, state and regional park listings, as well as beach descriptions throughout the text.

▲	Camping		Windsurfing
	Hiking		Canoeing or Kayaking
	Swimming		Boating
	Snorkeling or Scuba Diving		Fishing

ONE

Exploring the Yucatán

In Maya legend she is known as Xtabay—the forest goddess whose siren song lures solitary travelers deeper and deeper into the jungle, never to be seen again in the world of civilized mortals. Though some may contend that she is merely primitive superstition, her spirit is very much alive in the Yucatán today. It is the song of Xtabay that inspired the book you are reading right now.

Most travelers begin experiencing the Yucatán in Cancún, a place just about as exotic as Fort Lauderdale and as mysterious as a dozen or so tequila slammers with salt and lime. In Cancún, you don't have to speak Spanish, find your way through a maze of narrow roads, translate kilometers into miles or pesos into real money, learn about ancient history or dine in restaurants where nothing on the menu looks familiar. Most of the time, you don't even need insect repellent. All you need is U.S. currency. Lots of it.

That's why, in less than 30 years, this formerly tiny fishing village has become one of the most popular beach resorts on earth with luxurious highrise hotels like Sheraton, Radisson and Ritz-Carlton providing eery amenity to create vacation paradise. The water is as transparent as glass and so bright blue-green that it seems to possess a Disney World kind of unreality. The beaches are awesome. And it's much closer than Hawaii. What more could you want for your next vacation?

Yet somehow, after a few sunburned, saltwater-soaked days and intoxicating disco nights in this pricey, too-perfect version of Margaritaville, many visitors begin to suspect that there is more. Maybe it's a bus tour to the overcrowded but still haunting Maya ruins at nearby Tulum that starts them daydreaming of other, more distant lost cities overgrown by rainforest. Or maybe it's a wave-runner ride into the mangrove jungle on the far side of the lagoon and a glimpse of a great white heron taking flight that evokes thoughts of more remote places where flamingos and parrots abound. It may even be nothing more exciting than a morning soaking up sun on one of the chaise longues lining the beach for miles that conjures fantasies of other beaches, shell-strewn and empty except for a single set of footprints.

Yes, there it is. Hear it? When you least expect it, whispering in the surf, dancing among the palm trees, floating on the moonlight, you catch the merest hint of melody—the song of Xtabay.

About four million people visit Cancún each year. Two-thirds of them come from the United States, Canada and Europe. About 200,000 people—5 percent—take day trips to the fabulous Maya-Toltec ruins at Chichén Itzá, one of the great wonders of the world. An equal number journey down the Caribbean coast to Cozumel, Tulum or other destinations along Quintana Roo's "Riviera Maya." An estimated 75,000 international visitors—less than 2 percent of those who arrive in Cancún—venture as far as the Yucatán capital city of Mérida, the natural base for exploring Uxmal and other Maya ruins, villages and caves in the Puuc hills of central Yucatán. A small fraction of these travelers find their way to the remote, fascinating wildlife preserves along the Gulf coast near the fishing villages of Río Lagartos and Celestún or walk the 17th-century battlements that protected the colonial city of Campeche from pirate attacks. And only a few hundred international travelers each year make it all the way to the southern part of Campeche state, where Mexico's largest remaining expanse of rainforest conceals some of the most impressive ancient Maya temples to be found anywhere. No matter how far into the Yucatán backcountry you explore, there is always more.

Cancún's most remarkable tourism statistic is this: of the international travelers who arrive in Cancún, more than half have visited before. Few other resorts in the world can make such a claim. While there is no way to know for sure, personal experience leads me to believe that travelers keep coming back because an unshakable fascination and curiosity about what else the Yucatán holds in store tugs at their souls until, as the snow starts to fly in northerly climes, they cannot resist the urge to seek out the places they heard about on their last visit but didn't have time to see.

It is my purpose in *Hidden Cancún & the Yucatán* to share with you the discoveries I've made in 25 trips to the Yucatán over the past 21 years and, more than that, to pass along the know-how and enthusiasm that will help you find your own secret spots. If you would like to share your discoveries with me—and, of course, with the readers of this book's next edition—please drop me a line in care of Ulysses Press or e-mail me at RichardKHarris@earthlink.net.

I hope that you will find in these pages not just another directory of places to stay, eat and sightsee on the Yucatán Peninsula, but, rather, a practical resource on *how* to visit—how to step softly in an ancient culture and a delicate, extraordinary environment. In this region, the tourist trade accounts for a much larger part of the economy than all other industries combined. In fact, in the state of Quintana Roo, tourism accounts for a whopping 94 percent of all local revenue. On the whole, that's good. Tourist dollars have raised the standard of living for thousands of indigenous people while providing a compelling incentive to restore ancient Maya ruins and preserve the natural environment. But as the devastating environmental and social consequences of Cancún's explosive growth show all too graphically, tourism is double edged. It takes considerable sensitivity to recognize the point at which exploration becomes exploitation. Dollars can feed starving villagers, but they can also corrupt ancient ways of life. And most of the snorkelers and scuba divers who have damaged some of the most popular coral reefs beyond repair are undoubtedly nature lovers.

The key to responsible tourism lies in knowledge, in understanding consequences, in knowing when enough is enough—and what to do instead. In this book I have made every effort to present a balanced overview of Yucatán tourism, examining not only established tourist routes but also what the future may hold— the good, the bad, the ugly. I believe that we can work together to make sure it's

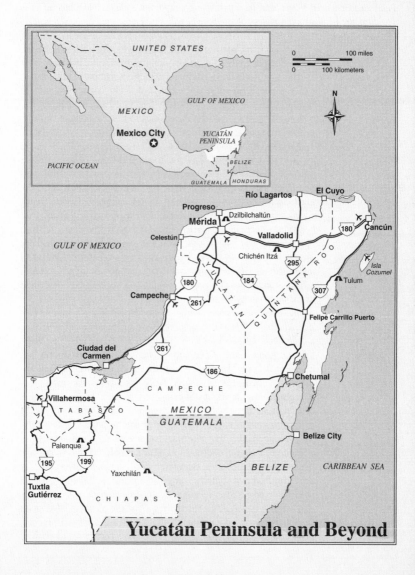

Yucatán Peninsula and Beyond

the good that prevails, for visitors, local residents, the economy and the natural environment.

Bring this book along when you board that jetliner to Cancún. Carry it with you as you head for the beach or pool. Browse through it while you soak up the glorious tropical sunshine. Feel the pull of mysterious places just over the horizon. Armed with the information these pages contain, you may well find yourself without an excuse for remaining long in the land of $200 hotel rooms, high-decibel dance clubs and artificial Maya temples. I'm inviting you to rent a car or buy a bus ticket— and go for it! Xtabay, goddess of the forest, will show you the way.

Where to Go

Whether you are seeking high adventure beyond the edge of the civilized world or want to mix some business with your pleasure, you can do it in the Yucatán. Where you go really depends on what you want to do. The Yucatán possesses stunning natural beauty, fantastic villages and ancient Maya sites, remarkable history and enough exotica to last a traveler a lifetime. It also offers sand, sun and sea—key ingredients for that kick-back-and-relax part of your vacation.

For starters, there's **Cancún**, the world-famous beach resort that has become Mexico's most popular tourist destination and one of the fastest-growing cities in Latin America. If you like Florida's Gold Coast, you'll probably love Cancún—a flashy, trend-swept highrise strip of five-star hotels with beaches as big and beautiful as any in the Caribbean. But even if this doesn't sound like your idea of a good time, you'll probably find yourself there on the first and last days of your Yucatán adventure. Almost all international airline flights to the Yucatán now land at Cancún's airport. Once there, it's easy to head for any other place described in these pages by rental car, passenger bus or ferry. Chapter Six of this book provides information on Cancún's top beach resorts (for which you'll want to make reservations in advance) as well as a couple of budget-friendly alternatives for those who just want to get a good night's sleep and get out of town with money left in their pockets. The chapter also shares insights to help you appreciate Cancún for what it is. Before you think too many disparaging thoughts about this crassly commercial mega-resort city, bear in mind that it will look much more inviting when you return from an expedition into the heart of the Yucatán backcountry. The luxury of a big five-star hotel room with air conditioning and a satellite TV that broadcasts in English, a balcony that overlooks the sea and an elaborate swimming pool complex surrounded by beautiful bodies in bathing suits and a poolside bar make for an irresistible conclusion to your Yucatán adventure.

Thirty years ago, the northern half of the Yucatán's **Mexican Caribbean** coast—now called the Riviera Maya—was unforgiving bush country where common visitors were outlaws and snakes.

Today, much of the coast has been transformed into various resorts, from high-class, all-inclusive vacation complexes to clusters of thatched-roof cabañas on remote beaches. Once you turn off the busy, billboard-lined four-lane superhighway, the boundless, impenetrable jungle protects the coast from the stresses of modern life. The region fulfills just about every dream of paradise. For you perhaps it's the cast-all-your-cares-away mood of Isla Mujeres or the haunting beauty of Tulum, the only Maya city right on the Caribbean Sea. Maybe you're going for snorkeling and scuba diving, unparalleled in these see-through waters. Divers flock to Cozumel for some of the best underwater scenery on earth. Or maybe your idea of heaven is swimming, tennis and golf in the middle of winter.

Much of Chichén Itzá's natural beauty lies underground, in such places as the pre-Columbian ceremonial cave of Balancanché and the stalactite-hung cenote of Dzitnup.

There is much more to the **Quintana Roo Backcountry** than just Cancún and the Riviera Maya. The southern half of Quintana Roo remains mostly wilderness and offers a wealth of little-known natural wonders to explore. Foremost among them is the Sian Ka'an Biosphere Reserve, a federally protected wildlife habitat that fills a large area of coastline and rainforest and includes sheltered bays, deep freshwater cenotes, sawgrass marshes, mangrove and hardwood jungles, islands where birds gather by the hundreds, a unique fishing village that got its start as a pirate's hideaway and, of course, many miles of lonely white beaches. Other great destinations in the backcountry include Cobá, where lofty forest conceals the overwhelming ruins of the Yucatán's largest ancient Maya city, and the obscure, fascinating ceremonial center of Kohunlich, which is only beginning to reveal its strange secrets.

A few hours' journey westward into the Yucatán interior will bring you to **Valladolid** and the world-famous ruins of the Maya-Toltec city **Chichén Itzá**, centerpiece of a region that wears its history like comfortable old clothes. The flat, scrub-choked landscape is liberally scattered with the ruins of ancient Indian temples, colonial churches and plantation haciendas, as well as timeless villages where descendants of the ancient Maya make their homes today. Indians, Spaniards and Mexicans alike have contributed to the deforestation of this countryside over countless centuries, so its fascination lies less in its ecology than in its ruins, reminders of empires that attained awesome heights only to be swept away by time. Maya and Spanish colonial ruins stand side by side in places like the Maya town of Izamal, the ceremonial center turned henequen plantation at Aké and the archaeological site of Dzibilchaltún.

Mérida, capital city of the Yucatán for the last four and a half centuries, offers more comfortable accommodations in all price ranges than are available in other parts of the interior, so it makes a natural home base for exploring more remote parts of the Yucatán. At least half the places described in this book are within day-trip distance of Mérida. More than just a place to find modern lodging, restaurants and nightlife in the ancient world of the Yucatán, Mérida is filled with its own charms. Disregard the semi-industrialized Mexican version of suburbia that sprawls for miles around and focus on the walkable, historic downtown area inside the old city gates. Ride in a horse-drawn carriage down Paseo de Montejo with its stately mansions and monuments or stroll among the galleries of the small but growing arts district. You'll find music and dancing in a city park, a celebration in the central plaza or a stage performance in one of the city's grand old theaters almost every evening. Wander through museums displaying exceptional ancient artifacts and modern folk art from villages around the state.

> Haggle over folk art and tropical fruit in Mérida's bustling public market, the largest in the Yucatán.

The Yucatán's **Gulf Coast** is as different as can be from the international tourist meccas of the Mexican Caribbean. Nature lovers will delight in touring the fecund estuaries tracing the coast along the north and west sides of the peninsula around Río Lagartos and Celestún, where shallow waters teeming with shrimp attract more pink flamingos than any other place in the Western Hemisphere. The port city of Progreso bursts into exuberant life every weekend as the local beach for residents of nearby Mérida; it's certainly not Cancún, but it is the Yucatán's liveliest, funkiest low-budget beach scene. Then there's Sisal, a faded 19th-century seaport turned fishing village, virtually unknown to tourists, where shell-strewn beaches go on for miles.

In the southern reaches of the state of Yucatán lies **Uxmal and the Hill Country**, a nearly uninhabited area that was one of the most important kingdoms in the Maya world a thousand years ago. Uxmal, a popular tourist destination as large as Chichén Itzá but purely Maya in its distinctive, ornate decorative facades carved from limestone, is one of the best-known Maya ruins in the Yucatán, though it receives far fewer visitors than Chichén Itzá or Tulum because it is too far to reach on a day trip from Cancún. This and other Puuc sites such as Kabáh and Labná grow more beautiful with each visit, not only because of ongoing restoration efforts but also because the surrounding forest, destroyed by a fire in the 1970s, is growing back to wrap the ruins once more in lush greenery. Try to visit the ceremonial cave of Loltún, which the ancient Maya believed to be a gateway to the underworld that lay beyond death, and the sadly fallen remains of Mayapán, the ruling capital of the Yucatán in postclassic times.

The route southwest from Yucatán state to Chiapas passes through the Gulf Coast state of **Campeche**, where the capital city of the same name boasts an almost tourist-free atmosphere and a colorful history. The old city is surrounded by stone fortifications erected to defend against pirate attacks. South of town are miles of pure white beaches. A short drive to the east lies Edzná, a large restored Maya ruin that most travelers miss. In fact, the entire state of Campeche is far enough from the major tourist zones of the Yucatán that its magnificent ruins and the deep forest that covers 60 percent of the state often take even seasoned Yucatán travelers by surprise. The crowning glory of Campeche is the Calakmul Biosphere Reserve, which lies in the extreme southern part of the state near the Guatemalan border and is part of a proposed multinational Maya Peace Park. Here, in the vicinity of the solitary village of Xpujil, a wilderness of rainforest conceals fantastic ruins unlike any others in the Maya world. Recently restored, easy-to-drive-to sites like Becán and Chicanná are virtually undiscovered by the tourist industry. If these huge ruins aren't secret enough for you, a guide can take you on a journey that gives "off the beaten path" a whole new meaning: through Mexico's last great expanse of virgin rainforest to the magnificent ruins of Hormiguero, Río Bec and—if you have plenty time and a boundless lust for adventure —the giant lost city of Calakmul, newly opened to the public after a 15-year archaeological project reclaimed it from the rainforest. You can spend all day here trekking from temple to temple where few people have set foot in living memory.

Adjacent to the Yucatán Peninsula are **Tabasco** and lowland **Chiapas**, a land of vanishing rainforest inhabited by the Chol Maya people, distant cousins of the Yucatec Maya. The oil-rich state of Tabasco is worth visiting mainly to see giant stone heads left behind by the mysterious Olmec people who built forest cities thousands of years before the Classic Maya empires began. As this book goes to press, the situation in Chiapas is still unresolved more than eight years after a January 1994 Maya insurgency, as Mexico's president, National Action Party (PAN) leader Vicente Fox, struggles to keep his campaign promise to bring peace between the rebel forces of Subcomandante Marcos, Mexican Army troops and the paramilitary forces sponsored by large landowners. There are still Army checkpoints at highway intersections in Chiapas—in fact, such checkpoints have proliferated all over Mexico in an effort to stem the epidemic of firearms smuggling in this officially gun-free country; but the collapse of Chiapas' tourist economy in the 1990s, exacerbating poverty in what was already Mexico's poorest state, has moved the Army to encourage a more friendly, hospitable attitude toward foreign sightseers. Once more, visitors flock to the ancient site of Palenque, with its elegant architecture, exquisite stone and stucco sculpture, and fantastic jungle setting. A bold side-trip possibility is an expedition overland, by minivan, on foot and by riverboat, to the remote Maya ruins of Bonampak and Yaxchilán.

SAMPLE ITINERARY—ONE WEEK

Day 1   Fly to Cancún. Check into your accommodations in the Hotel Zone or catch the ferry to Isla Mujeres for a more laid-back, lower-cost beach stay. Another inviting possibility is to skip Cancún altogether and head down the Riviera Maya to Playa del Carmen for a friendly, predominantly European ambience and a lively beach scene.

Day 2   Explore Cancún and Isla Mujeres. Try snorkeling, wave-running, parasailing or just sunbathing. Check out Cancún's disco-inferno nightlife. (Or, if you choose to make Playa del Carmen your home base, ferry over to Isla Cozumel for a day of snorkeling, scuba diving on the magnificent coral reefs or riding a motor scooter across the island to outlying ruins and empty, windswept beaches.

Day 3   Rent a car or buy a bus ticket to visit Tulum ruins. If you have a car, continue down the beach into the Sian Ka'an Biosphere Reserve. Spend the night in the vicinity of either Tulum or Cobá.

Day 4   Visit the ruins at Cobá.

Day 5   Visit the ruins at Chichén Itzá. (Motorists can do this without returning to the Riviera Maya or Cancún by following the road north past the Punta Laguna Spider Monkey Reserve to join the main highway midway between Cancún and Chichén Itzá.) If you have a rental car, take a side trip to Balancanché Cave or Cenote Dzitnup. Continue on to Mérida. Stroll the city streets in the evening and take in a concert at the park.

Day 6   Visit the ruins at Uxmal. If you have a rental car, explore neighboring ruins such as Kabáh, Sayil, Labná or Loltún Cave.

Day 7   Return to Cancún and prepare for your flight home the next morning.

SAMPLE ITINERARY—TWO WEEKS

Yucatán off-the-beaten-path (you'll need a car)

Day 1   Fly to Cancún. Catch the ferry to Isla Mujeres for a mellow night by the sea.

Day 2   Take a nature cruise from Isla Mujeres to the bird sanctuary of Isla Contoy.

Day 3   Rent a car and drive to Valladolid. After checking into accommodations there, explore lesser-known attractions such as Cenote Dzitnup and the ruins at Ek Balam.

Day 4   After further explorations in the Valladolid/Chichén Itzá area, drive to Río Lagartos and check into the hotel there. Arrange your boat tour of the nature preserve for the following morning.

Day 5   Tour the flamingo breeding grounds at Río Lagartos. Drive to Izamal; see the cathedral and climb the pyramid. Return to the north coast to spend the night in Progreso.

Day 6   En route to Mérida, stop for a swim in the cenote at Dzibilchaltún National Park. Check into your Mérida hotel, stroll the city streets in the evening and take in a concert at the park.

Day 7   Explore Mérida's museums and public market. Stroll along Paseo de Montejo. Linger in the central plaza or Parque Hidalgo.

Day 8   Drive to Uxmal with a short detour to visit the little known Oxkintoc ruins and Xpukil Cave near Maxcanu. Check into accommodations nearby. Visit the ruins of Uxmal.

Day 9   Explore other hill country ruins including Kabáh, Sayil, Xlapak, Labná and Mayapán. (If possible, schedule this visit for a Sunday to avoid multiple admission charges; admission to all archaeological zones is free on Sundays.)

Day 10   Drive to Campeche, visiting Edzná and perhaps Xtacumbilxunán Cave en route. In the city of Campeche, stroll along the *baluartes* (bulwarks) and take the scenic drive to Fuerte San Miguel overlooking the city.

Day 11   Getting an early start, drive to Xpujil on the edge of the Calakmul Biosphere Reserve. Check into a small hotel there and explore the ruins of Xpujil, Chicanná Becán or more remote jungle sites such as Hormiguero (half-day trip) or Río Bec.

Day 12   Drive the narrow road into the deepest part of the rainforest to see Calakmul, southern Campeche's largest and most important ancient Maya site. Allow all day and plan to spend another night in Xpujil.

Day 13   Head east to the junction with Route 307 near Chetumal, then north to Tulum. Along the way you might want to visit the Maya ruins at Kohunlich, picnic on the shore of Laguna Bacalar (nicknamed the "lake of seven colors") or explore the coast of the Sian Ka'an Biosphere Reserve, following the strands of deserted beach all the way to Punta Allen. Spend the night in a cabaña (luxurious or otherwise) south of Tulum.

Day 14   Visit the ruins of Cobá for a hike or bike ride through the forests that conceal the largest Maya ruin in Quintana Roo. Return to Cancún and check into your hotel there. Rest up for tomorrow morning's plane flight home.

Of course, these itineraries cover mainly "must-sees" among the many fascinating places in the Yucatán that await your discovery. Many visitors will want to modify these suggestions to allow, for example, time to scuba on Cozumel or Chinchorro Reef or to explore the fishing villages of the Gulf Coast. Travelers with additional time may want to spend it exploring deeper into the jungles in the southern part of the peninsula or continuing southeast into Chiapas to visit Palenque and perhaps even Yaxchilán.

▼▼▼▼▼▼▼▼▼▼▼

When to Go

CLIMATE & SEASONS

Like most of the tropics, the Yucatán has just two seasons: rainy and dry. Generally, rain falls and temperatures rise during summer and autumn months, from June to early October. Daily rains can soak inland jungle roads, creating sludge trails that are impassable without four-wheel-drive. Late summer and early fall can also mean hurricane season, particularly along the Caribbean coast. It's not likely that you'll encounter one—they blow in every five to ten years (the most recent was Hurricane Roxanne in October 1995). But if you should, take it seriously: Hurricanes are monsters that take lives and leave paths of destruction. While prices are much lower during these months, when Americans and Canadians are rarely seen, it's surprising to find that coastal areas such as Cancún, the Riviera Maya and Progreso are actually *more* crowded in August than in January. This is partly because European visitors, who typically come in the summer months, account for about ten percent of visitors to the Yucatán and partly because middle-class Mexicans flock to coastal resorts in the summer to cool off. The rainy season in the Yucatán is rarely marked by gray skies for days on end. Instead, mornings are usually filled with sunshine; later in the day, brief, awesome thunderstorms crash their way across the peninsula.

November to mid-April is the high-and-dry season—literally. Prices can shoot up 40 percent or more in response to the crowds rushing here from the United States and Canada to enjoy the idyllic balmy weather and escape the snow. The peak season is January through March. Be aware that *Semana Santa* (Holy Week), the week before Easter, is a major vacation time throughout Mexico. Planes and buses are jammed to capacity and rental cars are scarce. The hotels are packed wall to wall, the beaches towel to towel and the prices sky high. The "shoulder seasons"—April to mid-May and October through November—are pleasantly uncrowded, wonderfully economical and seldom unbearably hot. On the hottest days you'll have to have two swims a day instead of one.

The Yucatán Peninsula is warm year-round, with average temperatures in the 80s. During the summer, the jungles of the interior can be suffocatingly hot and humid, while the Gulf and Caribbean coasts often stay comfortably cooled by tradewinds. If you visit between May and October, you will likely experience *nortes*, nature's quick but tempestuous outbursts of thunder, lightning, wind and rain. They seem to come from nowhere and then disappear into nowhere, leaving a wake of intense blue skies and misty warmth. Winter brings dry weather, but the temperature drops only slightly, staying around a perfect 75°.

CALENDAR OF EVENTS

You may plan your Yucatán visit around a certain holiday or festival to join in the local spirit. As you may already know, Mexicans and Central Americans need no reason to celebrate, though they certainly have many. Writers from Octavio Paz to Alan Riding have described the fiesta as a vital liberation from solitude, stoicism and the restraints of poverty, whether the occasion celebrates a religious or patriotic event, a birthday or a wedding. Mexican holidays are truly wondrous. But plan ahead: remember that because of the festivities, everything else practically shuts down, including government agencies, banks, businesses and professional offices. In other words, if there's a holiday, forget about business and join the party!

Here are the most important events around the Yucatán:

January 1 New Year's Day (*Día del Año Nuevo*), celebrated on January 1 as a national holiday, comes complete with parades, prayers and fireworks. Throughout Mexico, Santa Claus does not give out Christmas presents. Instead, gifts are brought by the Three Kings (*Tres Reyes* or *Santos Reyes*) on January 6. **JANUARY**

Early January The **Day of Kings** (*Día de los Reyes*) marks the Catholic holy day of Epiphany and the end of the month-long Christmas season. In the Yucatán, the biggest celebration of the Day of Kings is in Tizimín (between Valladolid and Río Lagartos), where the Three Wise Men are the town's patron saints. Pilgrims walk there from all over the Yucatán, and religious processions alternate with religious processions in a nonstop ten-day observance starting New Year's Eve.

Early February Candlemas (*Fiesta de Nuestra Señora de Candelaria*), observed as a religious holiday throughout Latin America, marks the midpoint of winter. It is observed in many Mexican towns with dancing, processions and bullfights, a sort of warm-up for the Carnival season. In rural towns and villages around the Yucatán, the holy day is marked by ceremonies to bless seeds, candlelight processions and churches filled with thousands of lit candles. One of the most impressive processions takes place at Tekoh, southeast of Mérida on the way to the archaeological site of Mayapán. **FEBRUARY**

Constitution Day (*Día de Constitución*), a Mexican national holiday, means bank and business closings but no big public celebrations in the Yucatán.

The week before Ash Wednesday Yucatecans indulge in an exuberant **Carnival** leading up to the austerity of Lent. Communities large and small burst into music, dance and fireworks. Mérida has a big parade with colorful floats, similar to Mardi Gras in New Orleans, on Tuesday, the last day of Carnival. The town of Hocabá, a few kilometers off Route 180 midway between Mérida and Chichén Itzá, is known for the elaborate re-enactment of the Spanish Inquisition that it stages during Carnival.

MARCH–APRIL

Mid-March One of the top **Spring Break** destinations, Cancún maxes out with more than 120,000 U.S. students during its busiest week of the year.

The week before Easter Throughout Latin America, **Holy Week** (*Semana Santa*) rivals the Christmas season as the biggest holiday of the year. Everybody travels then. Expect crowds and high prices. It is a time for all-out street parties featuring Passion plays, music and dancing in the plazas, especially in Cozumel, Isla Mujeres and Campeche. There is a general exodus of city folk for the sea or lakeshore, where they picnic and camp. Ticul, south of Mérida near the Maya ruins of the Puuc hill country, celebrates Holy Week with a tobacco festival.

MAY

Early May **Labor Day,** May 1, is a Mexican national holiday. A solemn occasion, **Holy Cross Day** (*Día de Santa Cruz,* May 3) is observed with ceremonies, feasting and crowded town plazas in Izamal, Tekoh and a number of other Maya towns around the region. **Cinco de Mayo** (May 5) celebrates the defeat of the French by the Mexican Army at Puebla in 1862. Neither is celebrated in a very big way in the Yucatán, but banks and many businesses are closed. Cancún's annual **International Gay Festival** takes place the second week of May.

Late May The city of Mérida livens up as it hosts its annual **International Song Festival,** featuring performances of nearly 400 original songs, mostly in Spanish, from a dozen countries.

Late May or early June **Corpus Christi Day** occasions blessings of children all over Mexico.

JUNE

June 1 Día de la Armada (Navy Day) is a big event in Progreso, observed with a festive parade, music and dancing in the streets, and a waterfront fair. Everyone who can find space on a boat sets out to sea for the day, and sailors lost at sea are mourned.

JULY

Mid-July Dancing, fireworks and sporting events are all part of the **Fiesta de Ticul,** a week-long fiesta commemorating the establishment of Ticul, east of Uxmal. **Ciudad del Carmen,** south along the coast from the city of Campeche, honors its patroness, Nuestra Señora del Carmen, with a big citywide fiesta. Another fiesta on the same dates in **Motul,** northeast of Mérida, is known for some of the best folk dancing in the Yucatán.

AUGUST

Mid-August Oxkutzcab, in the center of the peninsula near Loltún Cave, has a lively week-long fiesta beginning August 10 and leading up to **Assumption Day** (*Día de la Asunción*), a Catholic holiday commemorating the Virgin Mary's death and rise into heaven, which is celebrated throughout Mexico on August 15. Izamal has a large religious fiesta in honor of Nuestra Señora de Izamal on Assumption Day.

August 20 The **Fiesta de San Miguel Arcángel** is celebrated in the town of Mani, in the center of the peninsula near Ticul.

September 16 Here and throughout Mexico, parades and fireworks are the bill of fare on **Independence Day**. **SEPTEMBER**

September 27 to October 13 The **Fiesta de Cristo de las Ampollas** (Christ of the Blisters) in Mérida honors a religious relic housed in the city's cathedral and believed by Maya and ladino people alike to have miraculous powers. The annual festival climaxes with a ceremonial procession through the city streets.

October 4 A week of parades and dancing heralds in the **Fiesta de San Francisco de Asís**. **OCTOBER**

October 12 Columbus Day (*Día de la Raza*) is observed throughout Mexico.

October 31 through November 2 Throughout Mexico, the **Day of the Dead** (actually a three-day holiday—*Vispera de Todos Santos*, corresponding to Halloween on the night of October 31; *Todos Santos* on November 1, and *Día de los Muertos* on November 2), blends remembrance of the departed with cheerfully morbid revelry in a unique Indian-Christian tribute to death. Sugar skulls, altars, papier-mâché skeletons and toy coffins fill the streets of Yucatán cities, where strong Indian traditions survive. **NOVEMBER**

November 8 to November 13 The **Fiesta de Tekax** is held in the town of Tekax, south of Mérida in the center of the peninsula, near the ruins of Chacmultún.

November 15 There is a fiesta commemorating the **Día de Santiago**, in Halacho, southwest of Mérida on the Yucatán–Campeche state line.

November 20 The national holiday commemorating the start of the Mexican Revolution of 1910 closes banks and public buildings but otherwise does not cause much of a stir in the Yucatán.

December 8 The **Feast of the Immaculate Conception,** a major religious feast day, draws pilgrims from all over the Yucatán to Izamal. **DECEMBER**

Mid-December The **Feast of Our Lady of Guadalupe,** patroness of Mexico, inspires parades, dancing and music nationwide. Christmas is the holiest of holidays throughout Mexico. The Mexican Christmas season officially begins on December 16, the first night of **Las Posadas,** the Mexican tradition of nightly processions recalling Mary and Joseph's search for lodging in Bethlehem. Nativity scenes are the main form of Christmas decoration, and many towns stage nativity plays. The **Christmas Fair** is the year's biggest community celebration in the city of Campeche.

Late December   Christmas Eve *(Nochebuena)* is a time of holy processions and singing. **Christmas Day** is a national holiday, and the streets are deserted. **All Fools' Day**, on December 28, is similar to April Fools' Day (be careful—in the Mexican version, if someone asks you for something such as your watch or sunglasses and you're foolish enough to hand it over, they don't have to give it back!).

In addition, many small Maya towns hold their own unique observances throughout the Christmas season.

▾▾▾▾▾▾▾▾▾▾▾▾▾
Before You Go

VISITORS CENTERS

To order an information packet about travel in Mexico, call the **Mexican Government Tourism Office**'s nationwide toll-free number. ~ 800-446-3942. For additional information, tourist cards and maps, contact one of the following offices in the United States and Canada:

300 North Michigan Avenue, 4th floor, Chicago, IL 60601; 312-606-9252, fax 312-606-9012; e-mail mgtochi@compuserve.com

10103 Fomdren Street #450, Houston, TX 77096; 713-772-2581, fax 713-772-6058; e-mail mgtotx@ix.netcom.com

2401 West 6th Street, 5th floor, Los Angeles, CA 90057; 213-351-2075, fax 213-351-2074; e-mail 104045.3647@compuserve.com

21 East 63rd Street, 3rd floor, New York, NY 10021; 212-821-8314, fax 212-821-0367; e-mail milmgto@interport.net

1200 Northwest 78th Avenue #203, Miami, FL 33126; 305-718-4091, fax 305-718-4098; e-mail mgtomia@gate.net

999 West Hastings Street, Suite 1610, Vancouver, BC V6C 2W2, Canada; 604-669-2845, fax 604-669-3498; e-mail mgto@bc.sympatico.ca

2 Bloor Street West, Suite 1502, Toronto, ON M4W 3E2, Canada; 416-925-2753, fax 416-925-6061; e-mail mexto3@inforamp.net

1 Place Ville Marie, Suite 1931, Montreal, QB H3B 2B5, Canada; 514-871-1052, fax 514-871-3825; e-mail turimex@cam.org

Many major cities in the United States, Canada and Europe also have Mexican consulates. They can provide general travel information as well as specifics about legal aid and lawyers in Mexico.

PACKING

Pack light! A camera plus whatever else you can fit in your daypack or weekender would be perfect. A couple of freedom-loving Californians I met on a recent trip went even further and started their month-long Mexican journey carrying nothing but belt packs. The less stuff you bring with you, the more stuff you can buy and bring back. There is nothing like lugging 75 pounds of suitcases around in search of a hotel to make one feel absurdly materialistic.

Bring along a minimum of sporty, summery clothing. T-shirts, shorts, swimsuit, sunglasses, a good pair of hiking boots and a bandanna (soak it in water and wear it as a neckerchief or headband for hours of relief from the heat). A flashlight with extra batteries is a must for exploring caves and for those nights when hotel generators shut down early.

If you plan to visit fishing villages or remote Maya towns, you will want to keep your clothing modest so as not to offend the locals. No short shorts, string bikinis, tight tops or other suggestive outfits, though all of these are perfectly acceptable attire in Cancún. Nudity is against the law in Mexico. If you want to sunbathe in the buff, find a very private place to do so. Never visit a church in shorts. Men should always wear a shirt in churches, and women should wear a skirt. Indonesian sarongs are very much in vogue for women travelers in this region. Don a sarong over shorts for instant modesty, use it as a beach towel, wrap things up in it, or wear it with exotic accessories to pass for dressy. It will dry quickly and fold up tiny.

> If you're staying in remote areas, bring a small plastic bottle of liquid detergent, preferably a biodegradable one, to wash both dishes and clothes. Laundry facilities are scarce in the jungle!

Bear in mind that just about anything you neglect to bring along, you can buy in Cancún or Mérida; both places boast just-like-home stores that range from Office Depot to Wal-Mart. When it comes to toiletries, larger towns carry almost everything you'll find in the United States, sometimes at lower prices: toothpaste, deodorant, shampoo, soap, insect repellent, skin creams, shaving cream and batteries. Items like tampons and suntan lotions are also widely available in larger towns. These days, most brand names in Mexican pharmacies and supermarkets look hauntingly familiar. In the late 1980s, when investors were fleeing Mexico, the government legalized foreign manufacturing investment in the country. Many American multinational companies rushed to build factories in Mexico, which allowed them to avoid the stiff tariffs on imported goods. So Mexican-made Colgate toothpaste, for instance, looks and tastes just like in the United States except for the words *Hecho en Mexico* on the package.

Because tourism is a key industry in this area of Mexico, 35mm film is easy to find. As in U.S. tourist destinations, tourist-trap prices prevail in the places where you're most likely to use up all your film and need more. In cities, film and batteries cost only slightly more than in the U.S. You will find especially well-stocked camera stores at Chichén Itzá and in Playa del Carmen and Mérida.

You should definitely pack a first-aid kit. Include aspirin, bandages, cold capsules, vitamins, motion-sickness tablets, calamine lotion or a small bottle of white vinegar (for insect bites), prescription drugs you use, iodine or alcohol for disinfecting wounds, antibiotic ointment, water purification tablets, sunscreen, lip balm and diarrhea medicine.

Anyone with a medical condition should consider wearing a medic-alert tag that identifies the problem and gives a phone number to call for more information. Contact **Medic Alert Foundation International.** ~ P.O. Box 1009, Turlock, CA 95381; 800-344-3226.

LODGING

This book's hotel and restaurant listings range from budget to ultra-deluxe, with an emphasis on unique establishments. Hotels are rated as follows: *budget,* less than $40 a night for two people; *moderate,* from $40 to $80; *deluxe,* from $80 to $120; and *ultra-deluxe,* above $120. The Mexican federal sales tax (called IVA in Spanish-speaking countries) on lodging is 15 percent.

It should come as no surprise that upscale hotels in Cancún and elsewhere along the Caribbean coast—one of the world's premier beach resort areas—charge rates that match their status. In season, rates at these places typically run about $200 a night, though lower room rates can usually be booked through a travel agent as part of a package that includes airfare. Rates drop by about 40 percent during the summer months. What is surprising is that the Cancún area also offers some lower-cost alternatives. You can get a decent room with private bath in any of numerous hotels in downtown Cancún or on Isla Mujeres for $40 or less; you can still find a few cabañas on the beach near the Maya ruins of Tulum in the same price range. In Mérida, rooms are easy to find in all price ranges. You pay about the same price for the same quality of lodging as you would in most medium-size U.S. cities. The city of Campeche offers good selections of both inexpensive (about $15) and expensive ($50–$100) hotels, but hardly any middle-class hotels in between. In the backcountry, virtually all accommodations are low-priced ($25 a night or under) except for resort-style "archaeological hotels" and "ecovillages." Several of the major Maya ruins—Tulum, Chichén Itzá, Cobá, Uxmal— have them within walking distance. These jungle lodges are expensive (though their rates—typically in the $60–$75 range—are much lower than you would pay in Cancún), and in these remote locations the amenities can be a little rustic (for example, their electricity comes from small gasoline-powered generators and may be rationed to a few hours a day), but their location makes the experience of staying there special enough to justify the prices and any mild inconveniences you might encounter. Archaeological hotels let you hike into the rainforest around Cobá to hear it burst into noisy life at dawn, and they let you wander through the abandoned ruins of Chichén Itzá before the first tour bus of the day arrives.

In the Spanish-speaking regions of the Yucatán, away from the jet-set resort areas on the Caribbean, you'll find an amazingly wide range of accommodations, all the way from luxurious *clase internacional* hotels in the capital cities and charming colonial *posadas* (inns), where elegance is affordable if slightly faded, to *casas de huéspedes* (guesthouses) that offer very simple, cheap lodging similar to youth hostels in the United States and Europe but are oriented more toward families.

It's standard practice for hotels in popular resort areas such as Cancún to raise their rates on weekends. During the high season (November to April on the coast, summer in the mountains) and around major holidays like Christmas and Holy Week, many hotels hike their rates *way* up and offer the American Plan (room rates including three meals a day) or the Modified American Plan (dinner and breakfast), ensuring a captive audience for their in-house restaurants. During the off-season, they may switch to the less expensive European Plan (no meals included). Be sure to check when booking hotels in advance.

Reservations are essential during the high season and holidays, when the scramble for rooms can be fierce. Hotels at the archaeological zones are often booked up by bus tour companies months in advance. Confirm your reservation, preferably in writing, before you go. If the hotel reneges (hotels typically overbook during holidays to make sure they are filled if any parties fail to show), make a complaint to the local tourist office and swift action is likely to be taken. Many hotels demand a two-day (but sometimes up to 30-day) cancellation notice before refunding your deposit. Check on cancellation policies at the outset, and remember that cancellation by mail can be fiendishly slow. You can avoid problems and lingering complications by using a knowledgeable, Spanish-speaking travel agent.

CHEAP SLEEPS

Mexicans love to travel, and that includes a lot of people who live far below the poverty line by U.S. standards. There are many very cheap lodgings where you can spend the night for the price of a hamburger. In general, hotel rates in Mexico today are about the same as you would pay in the United States for comparable accommodations. It's just that in Mexico there are more poor travelers who sleep in $3 rooms—the kind with graffiti-scrawled walls, naked lightbulbs hanging from the ceiling, and toilets without seats (presumably for fear that guests would steal them). Those who are willing to sacrifice comfort to save money will have no trouble finding such lodging.

During the April–mid-May and October–November "shoulder seasons," my favorite time to travel in the region, finding a nice room without reservations should be no problem outside of Holy Week (the week before Easter). The hotel information included in this guide should be enough to help you find the kind of lodging you want. If you are arriving in the evening, you'll usually find a few local hotel owners or their representatives hanging around the airport or bus station trying to recruit guests to fill their vacancies. You can take one of these rooms (inspect it before parting with your pesos) to rest up and get oriented, then move to someplace more special the next day.

Throughout this region, tourist areas are sharply defined. If you stray very far off the beaten path, you'll find that rural towns offer only very simple, very inexpensive lodging, often noisy and none too clean, and you will have to ask around (in Spanish) to find it. Reservations are unheard-of in these places.

The Mexican government regulates room rates at all hotels. A notice is posted inside the room's door stating the maximum authorized rate per night. Outside of peak season, you will often find that the rate you are paying is lower than the authorized rate. If it is higher, you can complain to the national tourism agency or at least threaten to do so when you discuss the rate with the hotel manager.

DINING   This book's restaurant listings range from budget to ultra-deluxe, with an emphasis on unique establishments. They are rated as follows: *budget* restaurants usually cost $6 or less for dinner entrées; *moderate* restaurants range between $6 and $12 at dinner and offer pleasant surroundings and a more varied menu than the budget restaurants; *deluxe* restaurants tab their entrées between $12 and $25 and feature sophisticated cuisines, decor and personalized service; and *ultra-deluxe* restaurants are generally priced above $25. Restaurants add a 15 percent IVA (sales tax), and some resorts add a 15 percent service charge on top of that. These ratings are necessarily very approximate because of fluctuating currency-exchange rates and differing demand for tourist accommodations in

BEER AND *BOTANAS*

Outside Cancún and the "Riviera Maya," the Mexican custom of serving *botanas* is common in bars. *Botanas* are free snacks served to all patrons every half-hour or so, different each time. For the price of a few beers or soft drinks, you can feast on such freebies as seafood soup, ceviche, crab claws and tacos.

various parts of the Yucatán. Restaurants listed in this book offer lunch and dinner unless otherwise noted.

Meals tend to be expensive everywhere in Cancún and in resort areas elsewhere along the Caribbean coast; you can expect to pay as much as you would for a comparable restaurant meal in any major U.S. tourist area. In remote resorts, especially those near the major Maya ruin sites, you may find that the only option is your hotel's dining room. In these situations, menu prices are typically quite high—you may spend much more for meals than for your room.

In Mérida, restaurants come in all price ranges—you can dine in elegant surroundings for $50 per person, eat at the food stands above the public market for around a dollar, or subsist on fruits and vegetables from the market for mere pennies. Dining is affordable—$3 to $5 or less—in most backcountry towns that have restaurants, as well as in most seafood restaurants in Gulf Coast fishing villages.

HEALTH & SAFETY

Hospitals, medical clinics, dental offices and other health-care providers, as well as the Red Cross, are located in a number of Yucatán towns. Private facilities are generally better funded, better equipped and less crowded than public hospital emergency rooms. Both public and private facilities require payment in advance. Visits to doctors are relatively inexpensive, and hotels can usually recommend English-speaking physicians. Contact your health insurance carrier before you leave to find out the extent of your coverage while abroad.

For serious medical emergencies, Mexican health care does not measure up to U.S. standards. Mexico has about half as many doctors per capita as the United States. Yucatán residents who can afford it go to Miami or Houston for major surgery. For true emergencies, a San Diego–based service called **Critical Air Medicine** provides air ambulance service to anywhere in Mexico 24 hours a day, every day of the year. ~ Toll-free from Mexico, 95-800-010-0268. There are also air ambulance services that will take you all the way to Houston—for a cost of around $50,000.

AIDS (SIDA in Spanish) is reported to be epidemic in cities and towns along the Caribbean coast, though it is still uncommon in inland cities of the Yucatán and virtually unheard of in rural areas. Most cases here are said to be transmitted through drug use. Take whatever precautions are appropriate for you. Blood plasma may not be screened for the HIV virus. Condoms are not always readily available in Mexico.

Speaking of sexually transmitted diseases, prostitution is legal in areas called *zonas de tolerancia* in Cancún and some other cities. Prostitutes are licensed and must have periodic medical examinations. The bad news is that, while cases of AIDS and syphilis are rare, about one out of twenty prostitutes tests positive for gonorrhea. Caveat emptor.

For a health update on areas you're visiting, contact the **Centers for Disease Control**. ~ 404-639-3311; www.cdc.gov/travel/camerica.htm.

The illness most people encounter is diarrhea, euphemized as *turista* or "Montezuma's revenge," caused by food and drink carrying unfamiliar strains of bacteria. A bout can range from a 24-hour case of mild cramps to an all-out attack with several days of fever, chills and vomiting, followed by a lousy feeling that lingers on for weeks. I have suffered both kinds, and they are truly no fun. But not everybody who visits Mexico gets sick. Those who stay healthy use the best defense: prevention.

> Many Mexicans swear by garlic as the best prevention for *turista*. Juice of the *lima* (Mexican lime) is also a traditional preventative for stomach problems.

Avoid drinking tap water or ice made from tap water (commonly used in restaurants—ask!), and don't brush your teeth with it. Ask if your hotel has *agua purificada* (purified water). Many hotels in Cancún and in the resort areas of the Mexican Caribbean have their own water purification systems. In remote areas, motels and lodges usually provide bottled water in the rooms or will direct you to a grocery store that sells it. These days, virtually every food store in even the smallest towns sells Evian or another international name-brand bottled water. Nevertheless, it can't hurt to bring along a small bottle of water purification tablets just in case.

Eat with discretion. Consume only thick-skinned fruits that you peel yourself, such as oranges and bananas, and vegetables that are cooked through. Nuts with shells, such as peanuts and coconuts, are pretty safe bets, too. Avoid milk products; unpasteurized milk is sometimes served in Mexico. Steer clear of garden salads. Even if the produce was rinsed in purified water, it may have been fertilized (in the fields) with human waste, a common practice in some parts of Mexico.

Raw seafood—especially ceviche—is also renowned for causing *turista*. But it tastes so good. Be aware of the risks and decide for yourself what chances you're willing to take. In fact, there's a risk of diarrhea any time you eat meat, seafood, peeled fruit used in drinks or candies on which flies may have taken their siestas. However, a lot of the food from stalls is delicious and very well prepared. If the facilities look clean and the food is hot off the grill, it's probably okay. Be the judge and take your chances.

Take it easy the first few days, especially with the more piquant varieties of Mexican food. If you sock your system with spicy food and heavy liquor right away, your stomach may seek revenge. Eating jalapeño chicken followed by quesadillas and enchiladas chased by tequila slammers is asking for mucho trouble.

Many people believe in preventive medicine. Some take a slug of Pepto-Bismol before every meal (effective enough, though it has the peculiar side-effect of turning your tongue and stool black); others, a shot of tequila, believing it will extinguish any threatening organisms. The antibiotic Doxycyclin is commonly prescribed as a preventative, although it causes sensitivity to the sun—not a good situation in the tropics.

If you take all the necessary precautions and still get hit with *turista*, several remedies are available. Lomotil, the stopper-upper, is not a cure; it's a morphine derivative that induces a kind of intestinal paralysis. Use sparingly. Stop the dosage as soon as symptoms disappear. The same is true of Paregoric, Kaopectate, Kaomycin, Imodium AD and Pepto-Bismol, which help keep the cramps down. Diodoquin, Mexaform, Streptomagnum and Donamycin are stronger over-the-counter cures available in Mexican drugstores. For diarrhea with a fever, you can take Septra or Bactrim if you are not allergic to sulfa drugs. But remember that prolonged use of any antibiotic is not good for your immune system and can make you more susceptible to other tropical diseases.

Manzanilla (chamomile) tea, popular in Mexico, soothes the stomach and often works wonders. *Yerba buena* (peppermint) tea is also soothing. Papaya restores the digestive tract. Light, easy-to-digest foods like toast and soup keep up your strength. Lots of non-alcoholic liquids—any kind—prevent dehydration. Carbonated water with juice of a *lima* is another popular stomach soother.

Rest and relaxation will help your body heal faster than if you run around sick and wear yourself down. The symptoms should pass within 24 hours or so. A case of *turista* seems to have an immunizing effect—any subsequent bouts you may have will be less severe, and eventually your body will adjust to the foreign water. If you spend a month or more in Mexico and Central America, you may find that you have similar problems with the water back home when you first return—just like Mexican tourists, who suffer from *turista* when they visit the United States.

In rare cases, diarrhea may be a symptom of a more serious illness like amebic dysentery or cholera. See a doctor if the diarrhea persists beyond three days, if your stool is bloody or foamy, or if you have a high fever.

Mosquitoes and Other Pests   Ask anyone who's spent a night in the jungle and they'll tell you: the most ferocious animal is not the jaguar but the mosquito. Mosquitoes protect their territory with a vengeance. The little buzzers are thickest in rainforests, swamp areas and coastal mangrove jungles. They are fewest in the cities and the Puuc hills. The best defenses are long sleeves and pants along with a good repellent.

What works for you may not work for someone else. People who wish to avoid DEET, the active chemical in most commercial mosquito repellents, may want to investigate other methods. Herb shops and health food stores sell good-smelling and more or less effective insect-protection lotions made from oils and herbal essences. Tests have found herbal mosquito repellents made with citronella to be about as effective as DEET but not nearly as long-lasting. Some people swear by daily doses of vitamin B_6 or garlic, others by tobacco smoke. The new electronic mosquito repellent devices, which emit a sound pitched at the high edge of human hearing, are supposed to drive mosquitoes away. I tried them out on a recent trip into the Petén rainforest and emerged from the jungle unbitten.

Campers will find that mosquito netting is more important than a tent or sleeping bag. Hang a mosquito net over a hammock under a palapa in a campground and sleep comfortably (if not exactly privately) in paradise. Whether you're camping or spending your nights indoors, mosquito coils will keep the bugs away while you sleep. In hotel rooms, if mosquitoes are a problem, try turning off all the lights and lighting an electric lantern or flashlight in the closet. Allow a half hour to an hour for the mosquitoes to congregate around the light, then close the door and rest in peace.

For mosquito and other bug bites, lime juice takes the itch out, disinfects your wounds and acts as a repellent, too. Limes (*limones*, not *limas*) are sold in every village. An ointment called *andatol*, sold in pharmacies, also helps reduce itching. Clean bug bites daily, using an antiseptic on bad bites to avoid infection.

Drugs   Marijuana, cocaine, crack and other drugs are widely available and sometimes used publicly up and down the Caribbean coast from Cancún to Chetumal and beyond. Foreign visitors will rarely have access to drugs elsewhere in the Yucatán, though American expatriates in Mérida sometimes deal marijuana to other Americans.

The United States government pays Mexico and other Latin American countries a lot of money to enforce drug laws, and these substances are highly illegal. Possessing, using or exporting any of them can land you in jail, where getting out can take a lot of time and money. The legal system in Mexico operates under the Napoleonic Code, which presumes the accused guilty until proven innocent. Foreigners are not allowed bail or a trial by jury and can be kept in jail for up to 13 months before trial. Prison sentences for possession may run from 7 to 15 years, and there is no parole or other early-release program.

Crime   Travelers from the United States often have a mistaken notion of Mexico as a dangerous place peopled by bandits, leftist guerrillas, brutal or corrupt police, torturers and midnight death squads. This impression has been heightened recently by reports of skyrocketing crime rates in Mexico City—more than a thousand miles away from Cancún. Evil forces may exist; as foreign tourists, we almost never get a chance to find out. You may be surprised to find yourself feeling more at ease in the Yucatán than you do at home. The reason is simple: the crime rate is lower here than north of the border.

The fact is, traveling in the Yucatán today is probably at least as safe as strolling the streets of your own hometown. Thanks to tough laws, the only people who own handguns in Mexico are gangsters and terrorists whom travelers will never meet. Images of *bandidos* are left over from a century ago and have no more present-day substance than the idea of wild Indians on the war-path in the American West.

You may not know that Latin Americans often have the same kind of anxiety about visiting the United States, believing it to be dominated by organized crime and filled with shootings, racial prejudice and promiscuity, a stereotype that comes from American movies and TV. But this notion was confirmed in 1994 when the leading candidate for the Mexican presidency was shot and killed during a speech in Tijuana on the U.S. border—with a gun the assassin had just bought in the United States. Fortunately, gun violence has not spread to the Yucatán—and Army checkpoints at many highway intersections are designed to keep it that way. Be aware that possession of a firearm or ammunition in Mexico is a much more serious offense than drugs.

When choosing a hotel, make sure it's in a safe part of town, preferably one that's frequented by travelers. All hotels recommended in this book are located in safe neighborhoods. As a general rule, downtown areas where there is a lot of activity after dark are safer than outlying neighborhoods of the city. Don't tempt fate by wandering around dark back streets late at night. If you're camping out, avoid lonely roadside stops or isolated beaches unless you're with a group. Stay away from drug deals. In short, exercise the same caution you would use at home. Observe these common-sense precautions and feel fortunate that you are not in New York City, where, unlike in Mexico, every petty criminal carries a gun.

DRIVE SMART

A mild note of caution: Traffic patrolmen in Cancún's Hotel Zone and on the highway between the international airport and downtown have grown increasingly predatory in recent years, stopping both rental cars and taxis on the slightest pretext in hopes of collecting bribes. Take care to be on your best driving behavior when driving in Cancún. Elsewhere in the Yucatán, police harassment is very unlikely.

TRAVELING WITH CHILDREN

Should you bring the kids on a Yucatán adventure? That depends. Lots of Latin American women travel and sightsee with infants in arms, and tourist mothers I've met experienced no problems doing the same. In fact, thanks to the ladino reverence for motherhood, a baby is likely to mean special treatment, attentive service and sometimes lower prices all along the route. Although for some people, traveling by public transportation with an infant could be one too many stressors, it is also true that many travelers find it fairly easy to enjoy the best of both worlds—parenting and adventuring.

Older kids? Take them along, by all means. It's easy in resort areas such as Cancún or Cozumel. As you move deeper into the land of the Maya, it can become more challenging (with children, it's much easier to travel by rental car than by public bus) and more rewarding as well. Ancient temples and pyramids are great for climbing and poking into secret passageways, and the mysteries of vanished civilization they present can tantalize young minds for weeks on end. The jungle holds limitless fascination. You will be amazed at how quickly children can become fluent in Spanish.

> Mexicans adore children and are used to dealing with them in restaurants and hotels, though many hotels do not have cribs or babysitting services.

Remember to get a tourist card for each child. See "Passports & Visas," later in this chapter.

Prepare a junior first-aid kit with baby aspirin, thermometer, vitamins, diarrhea medicine, sunblock, bug repellent, tissues and cold medicine. Parents traveling with infants will want to pack cloth diapers, plastic bags for dirty diapers, and a wraparound or papoose-style baby carrier. If you plan to tour by car with an infant, bring a portable car seat. For children of any age, be sure to bring along toys, books and art supplies to drive away boredom during long trips. Disposable diapers, baby food and medicines are widely available in bigger towns throughout the region.

Pace your trip so your child has time to adapt to the many changes. Don't plan exhausting whirlwind tours, and keep travel time at a minimum. Seek out zoos, parks, plazas, outdoor entertainment and short excursions to amuse your child. Mexico's public markets are more fascinating than museums to many children.

WOMEN TRAVELING ALONE

Feeling less than completely qualified to write on this topic, I interviewed several women who are seasoned Mexico travelers—and received completely contradictory opinions.

One woman, who has blond hair (a turn-on for many Mexican men) and speaks very little Spanish, told me that she finds sexual harassment to be a serious problem in Mexico. "On the first day of a recent visit to Quintana Roo," she says, "I encountered a taxi driver who requested a kiss and a restaurant waiter who gave a discount for '*muy bonitas piernas*' (very pretty legs)! Of course, these incidents may be more annoying than threatening. The best way I found to handle them is to politely say, '*No entiendo*' (I don't understand) and walk away. Most men get the message."

However, another woman of about the same age, who has dark hair and speaks fluent Spanish, says she finds Mexico a comfortable place for women traveling alone: "To avoid problems, dress modestly," she suggests. "Flirting—or forwardness that may be mistaken for flirting—can attract more attention than you expect. But Mexican people are very friendly and like to flirt in a joking way that's not intended to be taken seriously. A light attitude goes a long way. Women travelers in small towns and villages are in a better position to meet local women, who will not speak to foreign men at all but will often invite a gringa to meet their children or see their kitchens." The biggest problem she experienced in Mexico was "fending off horny Germans at Playa del Carmen. It's a popular destination for single Europeans, and they don't go there to be alone."

Bear in mind that incidents of sexual assault against foreign women whose solo sightseeing takes them to isolated places are on the rise all over Mexico and Central America. However, nowhere in the Yucatán is it anywhere near as prevalent as in most U.S. cities.

Torn between the rising tide of feminism in Latin America and the age-old code of machismo, ladino men often behave in unpredictable ways toward North American and European women. The best defense is to travel with one or more companions. Two or more women traveling together or a woman traveling with children will almost never be harassed. Today, many North American and European (as well as many Mexican women) travel independently by temporarily joining up with other woman travelers.

Finally, women travelers agree that away from beaches and major resorts, a lot of unwelcome advances and gropes can be avoided by wearing a brassiere. In the macho Mexican male mind, this particular undergarment is a clue to distinguishing between "good" women (mothers, the Virgin Mary, et al.) and "bad" women (mistresses, streetwalkers, gringo soap opera stars and the like).

GAY & LESBIAN TRAVELERS

Cancún once had a reputation for intolerance, borne of fear that a gay presence might discourage other tourists from visiting the new resort, that manifested as police harassment. Most gay and lesbian visitors headed directly for Playa del Carmen, an anything-goes beach town half an hour's taxi ride down the coast.

In recent years, though, Cancún has lightened up a lot. These days, residents of the Mexican Caribbean have given up being shocked by anything gringo tourists do. Public displays of affection are okay on out-of-town beaches but not in hotel lobbies. Three exclusively gay all-night clubs operate in the downtown area, near a pretty little plaza notorious for cruising. Since 1995, Cancún has celebrated an annual International Gay Festival in early October. For information on this and other aspects of gay travel in the Yucatán, contact festival cosponsor **Arco Iris Services**, a travel agency that specializes in planning gay vacations in Mexico. ~ 1289 University Avenue #154, San Diego, CA; 619-297-0897, 800-765-4370; e-mail arcoiris7@aol.com.

Away from the Caribbean coast, attitudes are much more conservative. Mexico's Catholic, family-oriented society is far behind the United States and Canada in coming to terms with its own gay and lesbian community. This is not to suggest that homosexuality is any less common in Mexico than anywhere else, just that the closet door is still closed, though the knob may be turning. Maya Indians have no longstanding cultural taboos about homosexuality but shun sexual relations of any kind with non-Indians. People in rural villages are offended by public displays of affection or unorthodox dress.

The city of Mérida has a healthy, low-key gay scene focused in clubs and plazas of the Calle 60 arts district.

SENIOR TRAVELERS　The Yucatán Peninsula, and particularly Quintana Roo, is popular among seniors as a vacation and retirement haven. Many older travelers join escorted tours, leaving the planning to others. An agency called **Elderhostel** provides excellent educational programs in the Yucatán Peninsula for seniors ages 60 and up. Programs cover Maya history, folk art and archaeology, and include field trips and instruction from university professors. ~ 11 Avenue de Lafayette, Boston, MA 02111-1764; 877-426-8056, fax 617-426-0701; www.elderhostel.org.

Be extra careful about health matters. Bring any medications you use, along with the prescriptions. Consider carrying a medical record with you—including your current medical status, medical history and your doctor's name, phone number and address. If possible, include a summary of your medical status and history translated into Spanish. Find out whether your health insurance covers you south of the border. Medicare does not, and many private health insurance policies require special riders for temporary coverage abroad.

DISABLED TRAVELERS　Physically challenged travelers can enjoy the Yucatán with proper planning. Most Latin American establishments and transportation systems do not provide special amenities, such as wheelchair access, for people with disabilities. You may want to get help from a good travel agent to track down hotels and other facilities to suit your situation. You may also wish to consult the comprehensive guidebook *Access to the World: A Travel Guide for the Handicapped* by Louise Weiss (New York: Holt, Rinehart & Winston, 1986).

For more information, contact the **Society for Accessible Travel & Hospitality** ~ 347 5th Avenue #610, New York, NY 10016, 212-447-7284, www.sath.org; **MossRehab ResourceNet** ~ MossRehab Hospital, 1200 West Tabor Road, Philadelphia, PA 19141, 215-456-9600, www.mossresourcenet.org; or **Flying Wheels Travel** ~ P.O. Box 382, Owatonna, MN 55060, 800-535-6790, fax 507-451-1685. **Travelin' Talk,** a print and online newsletter published by Access Able Travel Service, provides information for travelers with disabilities. ~ P.O. Box 1796, Wheat Ridge, CO 80034; 303-232-2979; www.travelintalk.net. Persons in wheelchairs will have few problems visiting Chichén Itzá and Tulum, where the terrain is level and most walkways are smooth. Other major sites such as Uxmal and Cobá, as well as most of the less-visited ruins mentioned, have rough, rocky trails or other obstacles that limit wheelchair mobility.

> In Mexico, poor *campesinos* travel as much as the wealthy class, and the demand for budget-travel facilities supports an abundance of low-budget food, lodging and public transportation.

STUDENT TRAVELERS

Despite the astronomical prices for food and lodging in resort areas along the Riviera Maya, all areas of the Yucatán Peninsula offer affordable hospitality for young people traveling on a budget.

You'll find budget rates and fellow students at the following places:

In Cancún, at the **Backpacker Cancun**. ~ Calle Manzano 30; 9-887-7725; www.mexhostels.com. Also at several downtown hotels including both the **Hotel Margarita** ~ Avenida Yaxchilán 41, 9-884-9333, fax 9-884-1324; and the **Cancún Rosa** ~ Calle Margarita 2, Local 10, 9-884-0623, fax 9-884-1294.

On Isla Mujeres, at the lively youth hostel **Poc-Na**. ~ Calle Matamoros 15; 9-877-0090.

At Playa del Carmen, in the wild-and-crazy cabaña-style hippie commune **La Ruina**. ~ Calle 2 Norte; 9-873-0405.

On Isla Cozumel, at several budget hotels in the town of San Miguel, notably the **Hotel Flores**. ~ Avenida Rafael Melgar at Avenida 5; 9-872-1429.

Along the beach between the Tulum ruins and the Sian Ka'an Biosphere Reserve, at any of several funky, thatched-roof cabaña complexes such as the **Cabañas Don Armando**. ~ One kilometer south of Ruinas Tulum; 9-871-2417; e-mail don_armando_mx@yahoo.com. Or, if you bring your own hammock, try the nearby **Camping Santa Fe**, which also has a few basic cabañas. ~ 9-880-5854. There's also **Cabañas Copal**. ~ Five kilometers south of Ruinas Tulum; 9-871-2264.

In Valladolid, at the small, spartan, dormitory accommodations at **Albergue La Candelaria Hostel**. ~ Calle 35 No. 201-F, Parque La Candelaria; phone/fax 9-856-2267; e-mail hostelcande laria@yahoo.com.mx. For low-priced private rooms, try the centrally located **Hotel María Guadalupe**. ~ Calle 44 No. 198; 9-856-2068.

In Pisté (near Chichén Itzá), at the budget-basic **Posada Olalde**. ~ Calle 6 No. 49; 9-851-0086.

In Mérida, dirt-cheap accommodations at **Nómadas Youth Hostel**. ~ Calle 62 No. 433; 9-924-5223; e-mail nomadas1@prodigy.net.mx. Another Mérida hostel is **The Nameless Place**. ~ Calle 57 No. 495; 9-918-4500; e-mail r-espejo@yahoo.com. Dorm-style rooms can also be found at **Hostel Aragon**. ~ Calle 57 No. 474; 9-924-0242, fax 9-924-1122; e-mail hostellingmexico@remaj.com. Or spend a little more to stay where most European student travelers do—at the **Hotel Trinidad**. ~ Calle 62 No. 464; 9-923-2033, fax 9-924-1122; e-mail hostellingmexico@remaj.com.

Near Uxmal, at **Sacbe Hostel**. ~ Route 261; phone/fax 9-955-9795; e-mail sacbehostel@hotmail.com.

In the city of Campeche, in the suburban youth hostel **Villa Deportiva de Campeche**. ~ Avenida Augustín Melgar; 9-816-1802. Or at any of several rundown hotels in the crumbling Spanish colonial buildings of the Old City, such as the **Hotel Campeche**. ~ Calle 8 No. 2; 9-816-5283.

Low-cost lodging is also available in many smaller towns, including Río Lagartos, Celestún, Ticul, Oxkutzcab, Hopelchén and Xpujil.

TRAVELING WITH PETS   If you want to bring a pet with you to Mexico, you need an International Health Certificate for Dogs and Cats (Form 77-043) signed by a U.S. veterinarian verifying that the animal is in good health, as well as a separate certificate stating that the animal has been immunized against distemper and rabies within the last six months (required by U.S. Customs when you reenter the United States). Mexico requires a visa for animals, which must be obtained in advance at a Mexican consulate in the region of the United States where you live. You will need to show the International Health Certificate and pay a small fee ($20).

PASSPORTS & VISAS   United States and most Canadian citizens can visit Mexico without a passport or visa. Citizens by birth must carry proof of citizenship in the form of a certified birth certificate or valid passport. Mexico accepts proof of citizenship in some other forms as well, but these are the only two proofs currently accepted by the U.S. Immigration and Naturalization Service for return to the United States. If you are using a birth certificate as proof of citizenship, you may also be asked to present a photo ID such as a driver's license. A voter registration card is no longer accepted as proof of citizenship.

Naturalized U.S. citizens who do not have a valid U.S. passport must have an original certificate of naturalization or certificate of citizenship. Naturalized Canadian citizens need a passport. All European visitors need passports.

Anyone under age 18 must have proof of citizenship and the following documents: if traveling unaccompanied or with persons other than their parents, a notarized letter of permission signed by both parents or a legal guardian *or* an individual passport; or if traveling with only one parent, a notarized letter of permission from the other parent or legal guardian (or, if applicable, divorce papers, a guardianship document or death certificate) *or* an individual passport. All of these documents need to be authenticated at a Mexican consulate. Foreign students in Mexico are required to have an acceptance letter from the school and a letter certifying that they are financially secure.

Cancún means "bowl of snakes" in the Maya language.

When you enter Mexico, you will receive a Mexican tourist permit (MTP, commonly called a *tarjeta turistica* or tourist card) that you need to keep on your person at all times and surrender when you leave. If you are flying from the United States into Cancún International Airport or another Mexican airport, the airline ticket agent will check to make sure you have proper proof of citizenship; tourist card forms and custom declarations will be handed out aboard the plane—you fill them out and hand them to the Mexican customs and immigration agents before leaving the airport. Tourist cards are free; bribery is no longer common border-crossing practice. Tourist cards can be issued for up to 180 days. (Most American expatriates who live in Mexico, instead of applying for extensions or resident status, keep their paperwork up to date by simply returning to the United States for at least 72 hours every six months and getting a new tourist card.) Multiple-entry tourist cards are also available. They are convenient but not necessary if you are planning to go to Guatemala or Belize and then return to Mexico. To apply for a multiple-entry tourist card, you need two copies of a photo that meets passport standards. The procedure takes longer at the *Migración* desk than simply applying for a new single-entry card when you re-enter Mexico.

MEXICAN CUSTOMS

When entering Mexico from the United States, you will be required to sign a form certifying that you are not importing contraband. Many travelers are surprised to learn that Mexico has a problem with smuggling from the United States. Stiff protective tariffs as much as double the price of goods made in U.S. factories, creating a temptation to circumvent the *Aduana* (Mexican Customs). The gradual implementation of the North American Free Trade Agreement (NAFTA) is expected to eliminate this particular problem as tariffs decrease between now and the year 2009. However, parts of Mexico are currently experiencing an epidemic of crimes committed with illegal firearms, and for this reason customs inspections are becoming tougher, not easier, on those who enter Mexico by car, train or bus. Don't even think of smuggling a gun or bullets into Mexico, where gun control is taken very seriously. The volume of red tape involved in importing a weapon legally is simply not worth it. Smuggling a box of ammunition into Mexico can carry a stiffer prison sentence than smuggling cocaine into the United States!

While rules are more liberal for foreign tourists than for Mexican citizens, you will be required to certify, among other things, that you are not bringing in more than one still camera and one movie or video camera per person, with a maximum of 12 rolls of film each. If your luggage should be inspected by Mexican Customs (which is unlikely), items travelers would be unlikely to use, such as kitchen appliances, will raise official eyebrows. So will more than one of the same item, especially electronics.

U.S. CUSTOMS

Even if you are a resident, the United States can be harder to enter than Mexico. When returning home, United States residents may bring $400 worth of purchases duty-free. The next $1000 worth of items is subject to a 10 percent tax. In case customs officials question the values you declare, save the purchase receipts for goods you buy in retail stores and record your marketplace and street-vendor purchases neatly in a notebook.

Persons over 21 are allowed one liter (or quart) of liquor duty-free.

Sportfish, shrimp and any seafood that can be legally caught in Mexico can be brought across the border. Many other fresh foods are not allowed into the United States and will be confiscated.

Pirata (pirated copies of copyrighted books, records, cassettes, videos and computer programs, as well as clones of trademarked goods such as designer jeans) are produced in Mexico. Bringing these items into the United States is strictly prohibited.

All items made from any part of an endangered species—such as sea turtle, crocodile, black coral or ocelot—are prohibited in the United States and will be confiscated. Vendors of such items usually will not warn you that you can't take them home.

Ancient artifacts, such as pre-Columbian statues or colonial art, cannot be taken from their country of origin and will be confiscated if found in your possession. All archaeological finds are considered national treasures and the property of the country in which they were found.

For more details, write **U.S. Customs Service.** ~ 1300 Pennsylvania Avenue Northwest, Washington, DC 20229; 202-927-

Think Before
You Shoot!

As you visit villages anywhere in this area or stroll through the markets in towns and cities, you will most likely admire the colorful, elaborately handcrafted clothing worn by traditional Maya people and perhaps their exotic facial features, which readily suggest a full range of qualities, from peaceful simplicity to stoic nobility to ancient, mysterious wisdom. It is almost irresistibly tempting to try to capture indigenous people in photographs. It can also be frustrating to try. Many Maya people, especially older women, seem to have a preternatural sense that warns them of tourists with cameras. They may wag fingers at you to warn you not to take their pictures. If you look through the viewfinder you're likely see everyone in the market turning their backs to you. Sooner or later, you're sure to get the message: some traditional Maya people don't want their pictures taken—a taboo that we, as visitors, ought to respect.

For the most part, Yucatec Maya do not have the religious objections about photography that the Highland Maya of Chiapas and Guatemala do. When explorer John Lloyd Stephens was traveling around the Yucatán in the 1840s, he generated a lot of excitement and interest by using his cumbersome, newly invented camera to photograph Maya village leaders. (Unfortunately, the photos never seemed to come out.) Since then, a lot of people who live in the Yucatán have grown sick and tired of tourists who find them picturesque. Photographing a person without consent is an assaultive act. Never do it without asking first.

Remote villagers in the southern part of the peninsula are less likely to object to photography than those who live along main tourist routes. They may look extremely self-conscious as they pose for you. You may even see grown men giggle. Many of these people have never had their pictures taken before. It's up to you as an ambassador of international travel to help them develop a friendly relationship with cameras. No per-photo payment is expected, but when people welcome you into their homes or villages a small gift of money is customary appreciation of their hospitality, and it goes without saying that photography makes a little bit larger gift appropriate. Be sure you record the name and village of anybody you photograph. If your pictures come out, mail copies to the subjects in care of their villages. They make treasured gifts for many villagers who have never seen photos of themselves.

6724; www.customs.treas.gov. Or contact the **U.S. Fish and Wildlife Service.** ~ Department of the Interior, Mailstop 430, Arlington Square, 1849 C Street Northwest, Washington, DC 20240; 202-208-5634. TRAFFIC, **World Wildlife Fund and the Conservation Foundation** has further information. ~ 1250 24th Street Northwest, Washington, DC 20037; 202-293-4800.

To avoid confiscation of prescribed drugs, make sure they are labeled, carry them in their proper containers and bring along a doctor's certificate of prescription. As for contraband drugs, there's a war on. Smart travelers remain neutral. Remember, they search you for drugs when you *leave* the country.

Customs checks at the U.S. border can be stringent or swift, depending on how suspicious you look. To avoid problems, dress neatly, answer the questions in a straightforward manner and declare your purchases.

SHOTS

No inoculations are required to enter Mexico, and international visitors are unlikely to find themselves exposed to any of the tropical diseases that can occasionally occur in rural areas of the Yucatán. If you plan an extended stay in a remote area where public sanitation and health services are lacking, your doctor may recommend tetanus and hepatitis vaccinations and perhaps one for typhoid. For the ultracautious, there is also a new vaccine for cholera, which rarely reaches as far north as the Yucatán; many doctors are loathe to recommend it because of its possible side effects. If you are planning to venture into wilderness areas, especially during or soon after the rainy season, be sure to ask your doctor to prescribe pills to prevent malaria. The pills are taken one per week, beginning a week before your trip and continuing four weeks after your return. By long-standing custom, travelers in tropical areas around the world take their malaria pills on Friday, making it easy to remember and remind one another.

MONEY MATTERS

Currency In Cancún and other Caribbean coast resort areas, U.S. dollars are accepted as readily as pesos, and many prices are posted in dollars. Elsewhere in the Yucatán, everybody who deals with tourists, from hotels and restaurants to small shops and street

MIND YOUR MOOLA

Keep in mind that Maya villages have no banks and that cashing traveler's checks is usually impossible. On market days, there are often money-changers around. At other times, only small-denomination local currency will work.

vendors, will accept U.S. dollars at an exchange rate about ten percent less than you would get at the bank. In this book all prices listed with dollar signs are in U.S. currency.

At the beginning of 1993, the Mexican government changed the currency to "new pesos," written as N$. With its value pegged to the U.S. dollar, new pesos have maintained a stable exchange rate of about ten to a U.S. dollar for a decade. The loosening of trade restrictions under NAFTA means that if Mexican government policy allowed the exchange rate to drop suddenly, prices of American goods in pesos would rise, fueling an inflationary spiral like the ones that devastated the Mexican economy in the 1980s and '90s. Just divide any price in new pesos by ten to translate it approximately into U.S. dollars.

While Mexican currency is easy to figure out, coins are another matter. There are nine different denominations, and sorting them all out can be tricky. It pays to sit down one evening and study the various coins. Those worth less than a peso are made from aluminum and range from the tiny silver-colored centavo to the large, gold-hued 50-centavo piece. Coins worth from N$1 to N$5 are heavier and two-toned, with nickel around the outside and a brass plug in the center. They are not very different in size. The largest-denomination coins—N$10 and N$20—are slightly larger than the others, with brass around a nickel plug. Don't judge coins by their size alone. A N$5 coin is actually smaller (though heavier) than a 50-centavo coin worth one-tenth as much. Take care not to minimize coins when leaving a tip or giving alms. A N$20 coin may be only the size of a U.S. quarter, but it's worth more than US$2! (Note: Prices in this book are given in U.S. dollars unless otherwise specified.)

Changing Money   Be smart and protect your vacation fund by carrying traveler's checks. Even if you get a slightly lower exchange rate or pay a small transaction fee when cashing them, it's worth safeguarding your money. Well-known brands, especially American Express and VISA, are easiest to cash. You will need either a passport or your tourist card and a picture ID to cash them. Canadian and European traveler's checks and currency can pose problems; some banks will not cash them.

Most banks open at 9 a.m., close between 12 noon and 2 p.m., and reopen until 6 p.m., Monday through Friday. They often have specified hours, which vary from bank to bank and day to day, for exchanging foreign money. Despite computerization, Mexican banks are very slow. Cumbersome documentation requirements make every transaction a long, leisurely procedure involving waits in several lines. Tellers type up various papers for you to sign. Allow at least an hour for banking, more if the bank is crowded.

Casas de cambio (currency exchanges) give quicker service and are open longer hours than banks, and their exchange rates are only slightly lower (some *casas de cambio* offer more favorable-looking exchange rates but charge additional transaction fees). Waiting in the long, slow lines at most banks, you'll probably decide that the small extra cost of cashing a traveler's check or exchanging money at a *casa de cambio*—usually about five percent—is well worth it in terms of time saved and aggravation avoided.

Credit Cards   Credit cards are just about as widely accepted in Mexico and Central America as they are in the United States. MasterCard and VISA are the most popular ones; American Express cards are sometimes frowned upon because of their stiff fees charged to merchants. A national bank charge of 7 percent is assessed on credit card transactions, and some hotels assess additional charges.

If you need a financial transfusion while on the road, money transfers can be made via Western Union (*usually* taking one day and costing an arm and a leg) or via any big bank at home through one of its Mexican affiliates (which can take up to five working days). Check before you leave home to see whether your bank offers this service.

You'll find ATMs at banks in Cancún, Playa del Carmen, Cozumel, Mérida and some Maya commercial centers. Your bankcard will work in them just as well as it does back home. Use caution when making withdrawals from a public ATM. Con artists and, less often, robbers have been known to lurk around the machines targeting victims.

Tipping (and Bribery)   While *propinas* (tips) are completely personal, the 15 percent guideline applies in Yucatán restaurants as elsewhere. Tip bellhops, porters, housekeepers and anyone who renders extra service the equivalent of at least 75¢ to $1. Taxi drivers in Mexico do not expect a tip. Gas station attendants deserve one (25¢ to 50¢) if they wash your windows, check your oil or put air in your tires. Children often assault your car at stoplights or outside restaurants, madly cleaning your windows or begging to watch your car for a tip. Musicians often perform for tips on the town plaza. Even a 50-centavo coin is much appreciated.

Though officially frowned upon, the custom of the *mordida* persists in modern Mexico. Literally, the word means "little bite"; in actuality it means bribery of public officials. Mexico has been making serious efforts to eradicate the practice, at least where tourists are involved, because it horrifies many gringos, who are unaccustomed to the practice and fail to understand that public officials in the Third World are woefully underpaid. If you would tip a waiter for giving you the best possible service, then why not reward a traffic cop or border guard for wisely exercising the discretion of his office?

If you find yourself in the position of having to discuss a bribe, never use the word *mordida* or in any way suggest that you are asking the officer to do anything illegal. The very suggestion is highly offensive and could even land you in jail. Sometimes a small bribe is referred to as a *propina* (tip) or as an unofficial *honorario* (fee). More often, if you ask the officer whether there is another way the matter can be worked out, you will hear the following line of reasoning:

"For me to fail to enforce the law would be a serious dereliction of duty and honor. It is for the court, not me, to assess a fine in a case like this. . . . But since you are a visitor in my country, and I like you, if you tell no one, I might let the *delincuencia* pass just this once. Of course, you must understand that in this land it is customary to exchange a favor for a favor. Now that I am doing this favor for you, it would be the right thing for you to give me a *regalo*, a gift. For my wife. The amount is whatever you think is right. . . . Well, a little more than *that*. . . ."

> Bargaining is a kind of universal language. By writing numbers on a pad of paper, you can do it even if you don't speak Spanish.

If the idea of bribery bothers you, pay up anyway and report it to the government tourism office later. Anybody who is in a position to solicit a bribe can also cause interminable delay and hassle if you don't hand over the cash.

The state of Yucatán has a toll-free English-language hotline for tourists to report threats or extortion attempts by police officers and other public officials. ~ 91-800-00-148.

Bargaining   In Mexico, haggling over prices is a tradition that unites Old World and New World heritages. When the Spanish conquerors arrived in the Aztec city of Tenochtitlán (now Mexico City), they found huge marketplaces where food and handmade products were bought and sold in a manner very similar to that used in European cities and towns at the time. Today, Mexico holds onto the custom of bargaining in public markets, though not in retail stores.

Price bargaining can be a lot of fun as long as you maintain a cheerful attitude. It's only natural for market vendors to double or triple their asking prices when they see you coming their way. Just keep things in perspective: your plane ticket to Mexico cost about as much as most vendors earn in six months.

Some people enjoy bargaining. It's an extrovert's game that pays off in savings. Give it a try. Cut the quoted price in half and start bargaining from there. Drift away and watch the vendor call a lower bid. But if you reach a good ballpark figure, don't quibble over nickels and dimes. So the vendor makes an extra 50¢. You undoubtedly got a great deal, too. Everybody wins.

If you feel uncomfortable haggling over prices, you'll probably reach the same result if you simply look at an item with longing and ask, "*¿No me da un discuento?*" (Won't you give me a discount?), then wait patiently. The vendor will do all the work, running through repeated calculations and hypothetical price reductions before naming the bottom-line price.

Bargaining is rare in resort shops, boutiques and in any store that tags the merchandise with fixed prices. In smaller Mexican towns, shopkeepers are more likely to negotiate reduced prices for a quick cash sale. In all small retail stores, it's okay to inquire about discounts when purchasing multiple items.

ELECTRIC VOLTAGE

Electric outlets are the same in Mexico and the United States—110 volts, 60 cycles, compatible with all American portable appliances. If you need to convert appliances from other countries, bring your own adapters.

BUSINESS HOURS & SIESTAS

One of the more famous Latin traditions is the siesta, a midday break lasting two or three hours, when establishments close while workers go home to eat and rest—generally from 1 to 4 p.m. or 2 to 5 p.m. Later, stores reopen until 7 p.m. or so.

TIME

Cancún and the Yucatán Peninsula are on what's called Central Time in the U.S. When Mexico switched to daylight-saving time in 1996, it proved unpopular in tropical lowland areas like the Yucatán, where people do much of their living after dark and don't want to conserve daylight. In fact, in some areas of Quintana Roo people flatly refused to set their clocks forward. Although Yucatecan politicians could not live up to their campaign promises to abolish daylight-saving time, they reached a compromise that shortened the part of the year when it was in effect. Today, all of the Yucatán observes daylight-saving time, but only from the first Sunday in May to the last Sunday in October.

WEIGHTS & MEASURES

Whether you're getting gas, checking the thermometer or ordering a *cerveza* (beer), you'll notice the difference: everything is metric. Mexico is on the metric system, which measures temperature in degrees Celsius, distances in meters, and most substances in liters, kilos and grams.

To convert from Celsius to Fahrenheit, multiply times 9, divide by 5 and add 32. For example, 23°C—the average temperature in Cancún during the winter—equals [(23 x 9)/5] + 32, or (207/5) + 32, or 41.4 + 32, or about 73°F. If you don't have a pocket calculator along (but you probably should), just remember that 0°C is 32°F and that each Celsius degree is roughly two Fahrenheit degrees. Here are some other useful conversion equations:

- 1 mile *(milla)* = 1.6 kilometers *(kilometros)*. 1 kilometer = $^3/_5$ mile.
- 1 foot *(pie)* = .03 meter *(metro)*. 1 meter = $3^1/_3$ feet
- 1 pound *(libra)* = 0.45 kilogram (kilo). 1 kilo = $2^1/_5$ pounds.
- 1 gallon *(galón)* = 3.8 liters *(litros)*. 1 liter = about 1 quart.

Telephone   Calling into Mexico can be a frustrating experience, but recent changes have made the process much easier. Starting in 1999, Mexico revamped its phone number system. Now all phone numbers are seven digits, the same as U.S. phone numbers, preceded by a single-digit area code called a "city code," which is 9 for the entire Yucatán Peninsula, Tabasco and Chiapas. To call into the Yucatán from outside the country, dial 011 (international code), 52 (country code), then 9 (city code), followed by the local number. If you're calling from within Mexico, you dial only the city code and the local number. If you're calling from within city code area 9, just dial the seven-digit local number.

Many establishments in the Yucatán have no phones because of the expense and, in many communities, because it takes literally years on a waiting list to get one installed. For local or long-distance calls, your best bet is usually to ask your hotel manager for assistance in placing the call. You will pay any long-distance charges plus a small fee for the service.

In the Yucatán, you answer the phone by saying "Bueno."

AT&T and some other U.S.-based long-distance companies have special numbers you can dial in Mexico that will connect you with an English-speaking operator and let you charge international calls to your calling card, often at a lower cost than you would pay through the local phone company. Ask your long-distance carrier for a directory of international numbers.

The most economical option is to buy a prepaid long-distance card that works in pay phones marked Ladatel (which stands for Larga Distancia Automática). Many pharmacies, supermarkets and other stores sell the cards. The cost of calling the United States varies with the destination and time of day but is usually under a dollar a minute. You can reach an AT&T operator to make a calling-card call from a Ladatel phone by pressing "01," but you need a Ladatel card to operate the phone.

To phone home without a calling card, go to an old-fashioned long-distance office. They are called *casetas de larga distancia* in Mexico, and they are more common these days in smaller towns than in cities and resort areas. You give your calling information to the person behind the desk and wait until the call goes through, which can take a few minutes or several hours depending on how busy the international phone lines are. Then you take the call in a private booth and talk as long as you want. At the end of the call, you pay cash for it at the desk. These calls can be *very* expensive; it's easy to spend $50 or more on a phone call home.

Even costlier are the tourist phones found in Cancún and other resort areas. They have no dial or number, just a big sign that reads, "Call the USA—credit card or collect." They're easy to find, easy to use, and cost an outrageous $8 to $15 per minute.

For placing calls unassisted, here are some key numbers to remember: long-distance operator: 91; international operator (English-speaking): 98; prefixes for dialing direct to the United States, Canada and Europe: 95 (station to station) and 96 (person to person).

Faxes   Faxes are even more widely used in Mexico than in the United States because international mail is slow and the per-minute cost of long-distance phone calls is much higher than in the United States. In the resort areas and in Mérida, you'll find fax machines at photocopy centers, internet cafés and some pharmacies. In smaller towns, long-distance shops also handle fax and computer transmissions.

E-mail   In downtown Cancún, along the main streets in Isla Mujeres, Playa del Carmen and Cozumel, and in the university district of downtown Mérida, you'll find many internet cafés, where you can rent a computer terminal by the hour, at surprisingly low rates, to send e-mail home and retrieve your messages. The web browser will be a familiar one like Netscape or Microsoft Explorer—but in Spanish—and some punctuation marks are in different places on Mexican computer keyboards, but these little challenges are easily surmountable. The atmosphere runs the gamut from real estate offices and cluttered Internet Service Provider headquarters to clubs where you can surf while sipping *café americano* or herbal "smart drinks." In Cancún there's even an internet bar where you can order a beer or a tequila slammer while you compute. If your regular ISP is a local one back home, ask them in advance to find out how to pick up your e-mail on the road; most have systems that let you do so installed as hidden pages on their own web sites.

Snail Mail   Mail from Mexico to the United States is quite reliable and generally takes less than two weeks to reach its destination. If you want to mail goods to the United States from the Yucatán, you may send items of less than $50 duty-free to a particular address (but not your own) as often as every 24 hours. Mark the parcel Unsolicited Gift—Value under "$50" and enclose a sales receipt.

While on the road, you can receive mail in Mexico at the main post office (*oficina de correos*) in any city via *Lista de Correos* (similar to General Delivery in the United States). Use this address format: [Your Name], Lista de Correos, Name of City, State, Country. The post office holds Lista de Correos mail for only ten days in Mexico, then returns it to the sender. The post office will charge you a small fee, and you will need identification to pick up your mail. For more security, American Express offices hold mail for cardholders and persons carrying American Express traveler's checks.

You can purchase U.S. magazines, newspapers and paperback books in Cancún and other Riviera Maya resorts at newsstands, bookstores and gift shops in big hotels and airports. The *Mexico City News*, a daily English-language tabloid distributed throughout Mexico, is the most widely available English-language publication in Mexico. In Cancún, you can usually find the *New York Times* and the *Miami Herald*, along with other U.S. papers.

English-language Print Media In Mérida and at the Chichén Itzá's visitors center, the Librería Dante bookstore chain carries good selections of books in English, mostly on regional archaeology. In tourist areas, some hotels and cultural centers have trade-in sections of old English-language paperbacks. In gift shops in the Departures building of the Cancún airport you'll find paperback "export edition" of recent bestsellers that have not yet been released in paperback in the United States. They cost 40 percent more than the U.S. cover price, or around $10. In fact, all books from the United States are much more expensive in Mexico. Familiar American guidebooks can cost as much as $45 in Cancún and Mérida.

Transportation

Whether to travel by car or take public transportation is one of the fundamental quandaries of ecotourism. It's an indisputable fact that motor vehicles are inherently bad for the environment, as travelers who visit Mexico City—which has the worst air quality on earth—will immediately see for themselves. Therefore, environmental ethics dictate that public transportation is better. In Mexico, where the majority of the people don't have cars, public transportation—buses, minivan shuttles, taxis and, to a lesser extent, the deteriorating government-monopoly train system—can take you many more places, often in greater comfort, than in the United States, so why not use it? Buses run regular routes on all Yucatán highways, and minivans usually wait at the public market or town plaza to carry people to even the smallest and most remote villages. Traveling without a car can mean no worries about flat tires, fender-benders or the *federales* who patrol the highways.

On the other hand, a rental car provides much greater flexibility. You can go where you want, when you want, without being straitjacketed by limited rural bus schedules. Without a car, many

FLYING FRENZY

Cancún's airport is busy, with about 80 international flights arriving each day. During special events, holidays and the January-through-March high season, make flight reservations at least a month in advance. Conventions, which can descend on Cancún at any time of year, can fill up all flights.

of the places described in this book would be hard to reach. Relying on public transportation to visit rural areas can sometimes leave you stranded overnight in places where there are no hotels or campgrounds. A car lets you search out remote beaches and off-the-beaten-path ruins and cenotes where there is no bus stop for miles. One of the most pleasurable aspects of traveling the Yucatán is the relaxing, carefree feeling you get as you cruise along the traffic-free roads (an aspect, ironically, that will quickly be lost if more people take to the highways of the Yucatán by car). Having traveled the region many times by both car and public transportation, I must admit that, for me, driving makes for a much richer and more enjoyable trip.

As ecotourism develops in the Yucatán, some planners envision a tourist-oriented public transportation system that may include such modes as cable cars and electric-powered narrow-gauge railways to make remote jungle areas accessible without the destructive effects of road building. With the huge investment required to bring these ideas into reality, it may be decades before any such transport can be ready to carry its first passengers.

In the meantime, consider some creative approaches that both minimize environmental impact and maximize freedom. Bicycle touring is a rarely used but feasible possibility. In fact, bicycling has become the primary mode of transportation for villagers in rural Yucatán. Rental bikes are available for day use at all resort areas on the Caribbean coast. It's possible (though not cheap) to air-freight your bicycle from the United States and have it waiting for you at the airport. For extended touring you may want to buy an inexpensive mountain bike in Mexico and resell it at the end of your trip. See Chapter Five for more on Yucatán cycling.

AIR   The best way to get from the United States to the Yucatán is to fly. Commercial airlines fly frequently from the United States and Canada to the international airport at Cancún, with some flights

MAKING TIME

The Yucatán is small enough so that you can drive from any place to any other place in a single day. If you drive, expect to cover more territory than you would by public transportation. If you are merely planning to dip your toe into the rich culture of the Maya world on a sidetrip from Cancún, two or three days will do fine. To explore the region thoroughly, sampling each kind of adventure the Yucatán has to offer, you'll want to take at least two weeks—and even at that, you'll leave wanting more. For some ideas, check out the Sample Itineraries earlier in this chapter.

continuing to Cozumel. You can take **American, United, Continental, Northwest** or either of the two Mexican airlines, **Aeroméxico** and **Mexicana**. The Guatemalan airline **Aviateca** also operates a few international flights to and from Houston, Mérida and Cancún. The more than 90 airliners a day that land at Cancún International also include flights from Canada, Europe and a number of Latin American and Caribbean countries, including Cuba.

Licenciado Manuel Crescencio Rejón International Airport, serving Mérida, is located four miles southwest of the city. The Yucatán state government recently issued a travelers' advisory warning of corrupt customs officials extorting steep bribes from international travelers who fly directly from Mérida, and recommend that tourists arrive in Mexico by way of Cancún. The only international flights that still land at the airport are once-a-week **Aeroméxico** flights from Miami and three-times-weekly **Aviateca** flights from Houston. **Mexicana, Aeroméxico** and **Taesa** all have frequent flights to and from Mexico City. **Aero Cozumel** and **Aerocaribe** offer service between Mérida and the region's other major airports—Cancún, Chetumal, Villahermosa and Tuxtla Gutiérrez. Aeroméxico also serves the small **Campeche National Airport.**

Baggage allowances on international flights are generally the same as on domestic flights—one carry-on item small enough to fit under the seat or in an overhead rack, plus two pieces of check-in luggage. Some Latin American airlines have a weight limitation —typically 88 pounds—on check-in luggage. All airlines allow considerably more baggage than you would want to carry around on this trip.

All Mexican airports have an airport departure tax equivalent to about $6, which must be paid in local currency at the time you check in for a departing flight. This tax is included in the purchase price of a round-trip ticket on most U.S. carriers; to make sure, ask your travel agent when you book your ticket.

When booking your international airline tickets, if you will be taking a connecting flight on your return trip, be sure to allow plenty of time. At the hub airport where you first land in the United States—probably Los Angeles, Dallas, Houston, New Orleans or Miami—you will have to wait for and claim your baggage, clear U.S. Customs, and recheck your bags before boarding your onward flight. Allow one and a half to two hours.

Getting to and from the Airport   Taxis have a monopoly on airport transportation in Cancún and are more expensive than buses. For a trip from the airport to downtown Cancún or the Hotel Zone, expect to pay about $25—less if you opt to share the cab with at least three other passengers. Cab fare to Puerto Juárez (the departure point on Cancún's north side for ferries to Isla Mujeres) is about $5 more. The airport is located far south of the city, so it costs about the same to take a taxi to Playa del

Carmen (the departure point for the ferry to Cozumel) as to Puerto Juárez.

There are several options for getting from Mérida's airport to the downtown area. Besides the many taxi cabs that await arriving passengers, *colectivo* (car) and *combi* (van) shuttles offer lower-cost transportation to most hotels. You can't call these shuttles to pick you up from your hotel, though; they are independent, and most do not have dispatch radios. Taxis are your best bet for getting to the airport from your hotel. A public bus runs between the airport and the downtown *zócalo*.

BUSES

Buses are one of the cheapest modes of transportation in Mexico. Because the majority of Mexicans don't own cars, the bus system is used much more than in the United States, so you can generally get just about anywhere by bus. From the U.S. border, you almost always have to go to Mexico City first, then catch a bus to the Yucatán from there. Depending on where you start from, travel by bus from the border to Mexico City usually takes about 24 hours, and the journey to Mérida takes another 24 hours.

Bus tickets are sold at the stations for cash (local currency only) on a first-come, first-served basis. Avoid bus travel around big holidays (Christmas and Easter) unless you are able to buy tickets well in advance, which can't be done from the United States unless you work through a Mexican travel agency.

Buses are categorized as *primera clase* (first class) or *segunda clase* (second class). Throughout most of Mexico, most first-class buses are more comfortable than those in the United States, with air conditioning, roomy seats and TVs that show Mexican videos—usually loud American action movies dubbed in Spanish—while you travel (carry earplugs). In the inland areas of the Yucatán, first-class buses tend to be more rundown than elsewhere but are adequate, while on the Caribbean coast it is the opposite. Some premium-priced *primera especial* buses are more luxurious than international airline flights, complete with attendants and complementary cocktails.

Second-class buses, the notorious Third World "pigs-and-chickens" kind, are much slower and less comfortable. The lack of onboard restrooms makes second-class buses a dubious choice for long-distance travel. Considering the low cost of first-class bus tickets, budget is seldom a reason to settle for a second-class bus. You will have plenty of opportunity to have funky second-class bus adventures if you plan to visit rural areas of the Yucatán by public transportation.

CAR

Traveling from the United States to the Yucatán by car is a challenging and time-consuming adventure. Not that it's particularly dangerous—it's just demanding. The limited-access four-lane toll

A woman waits with her purchases in the village of Oxkutzcab.

Above: Locals enjoy a game of soccer in front of Hacienda Yaxcopoil, an old henequen plantation converted to a museum.

Below: Brightly painted buildings such as this local store in Santa Elena are common in Yucatecan villages.

highways that now span most of the distance from the U.S. border to Cancún make the trip faster, though the tolls can add up to about the price of a plane ticket. The drive to Cancún from Brownsville, Texas, the closest border crossing, is almost 1500 miles. It can be done in roughly 30 hours of actual driving time. To make the journey comfortably, without arriving in the Yucatán exhausted, allow a week. From El Paso, Texas, it's a 2160-mile trip requiring more than 40 hours of driving; and from San Diego it's 2880 miles—more than 60 hours of driving.

If you are driving to the Yucatán from the U.S. border, plan well ahead for refueling and evening stops. Gas stations in Mexico are a government monopoly, and in much of the country they are few and far between, though this is changing fast. Never pass up an opportunity to fill up. In northern Mexico especially, it can be a long way between towns large enough to have hotels or restaurants. For those with trailers, RVs or motor homes, private campgrounds can be found in most parts of Mexico. The broad open areas adjacent to most village graveyards are sometimes used as overnight RV stops.

Motor Vehicle Requirements   For driving in Mexico, your current driver's license is valid. If you're bringing your own car, you'll need a Mexican car permit and Mexican auto insurance. To obtain a car permit (a special stamp on the owner's tourist card, issued for up to 180 days), you need proof of ownership—the original and a photocopy of a current registration certificate and title. If the title shows a lien against the vehicle or if it is registered in another person's name or a company name, you need a notarized letter from the lienholder or owner authorizing you to take the vehicle to Mexico for a specified time. The owner or driver who has the car permit stamp on his or her tourist card must be in the car whenever it is being driven.

A few years ago, Mexico enacted stringent regulations designed to stanch the flow of stolen cars from the United States to Mexico. Some requirements, such as requiring that visitors post a substantial bond by credit card, discouraged so many tourists

CARPOOL CONSCIOUSNESS

A reasonable compromise between convenience and environmental conscience is to carpool with a group in a van. Whether you make arrangements before you leave home to share your Yucatán expedition with friends or get acquainted with car-less fellow travelers at a youth hostel or hotel en route, a group of four to six people in a VW minibus or the like compares favorably to bus travel in both environmental impact and enjoyment.

that the government suspended the regulations indefinitely. Before traveling to Mexico by car, be sure to check on current requirements by contacting a Mexican consulate in the United States or the **U.S. Embassy** in Mexico City (Paseo de Reforma No. 305, 60500 Mexico, D.F.; 5-211-0042), or reading the U.S. State Department's latest advisory at travel.state.gov/tips_mexico.html.

Auto insurance policies issued in the United States are not valid in Mexico. Purchase motor vehicle liability insurance (and, if you wish, collision/comprehensive coverage) before crossing into Mexico. It is sold by agencies on the U.S. side at all border crossings. Causing an auto accident is a crime under Mexican law, which presumes defendants guilty until proven innocent. This means that if you are involved in an accident that causes property damage, your vehicle will be impounded until you pay the damage and a fine. If any person is injured in the accident, you will go to jail.

Even in the smallest villages there are always informal sites where self-contained RVs can be parked—inquire locally.

If you're driving to the Yucatán from any U.S. border crossing except Brownsville/Matamoros, you will have to go through Mexico City. Be aware that the national capital has restrictions to reduce air pollution by cutting the number of cars in use, and these restrictions apply to foreign motorists as well as Mexicans. If your license plate number ends with a 1 or 2, the car can't be driven within the city limits on Thursday; 3 or 4, not on Friday; 5 or 6, not on Monday; 7 or 8, not on Tuesday; and 9 or 0, not on Wednesday. Everybody can drive on weekends.

There is a fast four-lane divided toll highway between Cancún and Mérida with exits at Valladolid and Chichén Itzá. The road between Cancún and Tulum is presently being widened into a four-lane divided highway, too. All other major routes through the Yucatán are paved, two-lane highways with lots of *topes* (speed bumps) to slow cars down through each tiny roadside village. Careful, there's a reason why each town's speed bump is next to a *llantera* (tire repair shop). When driving these roads, expect to average about 55 kilometers (33 miles) per hour.

Driving after dark can be dangerous. The most common after-sundown hazards are vehicles stopped in the traffic lane without lights and vehicles traveling without lights well after dusk—sometimes considered a display of machismo. Highway shoulders are narrow or nonexistent; watch out for pedestrians, bicyclists and even people sleeping on the roadside.

In Mexico, unleaded gasoline (called *Magna Sin*) is available at all Pemex stations. Gas is sold by the liter and costs slightly more than in the United States. Beware of gas station rip-offs. Dishonesty is rare in most of the Yucatán but standard practice at some stations on major highways all over Mexico. Particularly beware of gas station scams in the truck-stop town of Escárcega, at the intersection of Highways 261 and 186 in southern Campeche. The most common ploy is short change—giving change for a N$50 instead of N$100, for instance, and if challenged, steadfastly denying that you paid with a larger bill. Another is to reset the pump, pouring a little bit more into your gas tank, and claiming that the 15 centavos showing on the pump meter means you owe 150 pesos. Protect yourself by paying in exact change when possible and keeping your eye on the pump meter. Be especially wary when groups of children gather around the driver's side of the vehicle, creating a distraction. Dishonest attendants count on your unfamiliarity with Mexican money, figuring you'll be well down the road before realizing that a Volkswagen Beetle won't hold 150 pesos' worth of gasoline.

Car Rentals   Renting a car eliminates the need for your own insurance and car permits, and it lets you leapfrog over the thousands of miles between your garage and the land of the Maya. Car rentals are widely available in Cancún, Mérida and Campeche. Advance reservations are always wise if you're traveling during the high season.

Anyone 25 years or older, with a credit card, can order a car in advance through one of the international rent-a-car companies and have it waiting in Mexico. To rent a car upon arrival, you will need your tourist card or passport, a driver's license and a major credit card. Take the optional extra insurance that lowers your deductible for damage to the vehicle.

Rental rates are about the same as in the United States. The cost of renting a car is about the same in Cancún as in Mérida, though you'll avoid big traffic and parking hassles by taking the bus or plane to Mérida and renting a car there when you're ready to leave town. Rates start around $35 a day in Mérida for a newish subcompact car such as a Volkswagen Pointer. Also available in increasing numbers are more expensive four-wheel drive vehicles, necessary for the super-rough and rocky roads; Chevrolet Suburbans are the most common. Rental rates for these vehicles are astronomical. Still, a four-wheel-drive is worth considering if you plan to go into the backcountry during the wet season.

Hotel managers like it if you book your rental car through them. They get a commission from the rental agency, and it costs you no more than if you dealt directly with the agency. Larger hotels have travel-agent desks that will help you arrange car rentals or guided tours.

Luxury cruise ships stop at several points along the Quintana Roo coast: Cancún, Cozumel and Playa del Carmen. Companies that serve this area include **Carnival Cruise Lines** (888-227-6482), **Norwegian Cruise Line** (800-327-7030), **Premier Cruises** (800-222-1003) and **Costa Cruise Lines** (800-327-2537).

SEA

Ferryboats run frequently to the two inhabited islands off the Caribbean coast.

Isla Mujeres can be reached by various competing foot-passenger ferries from Puerto Juárez in the north part of Cancún. There are two classes of ferry. The "slow" ferries take about 35 minutes to make the crossing and cost less than a dollar, while the bigger, newer "fast" ferries take 15 minutes and cost about $3. There is also a car ferry from Punta Sam north of the city (though a car is not very useful on Isla Mujeres); take the pedestrian ferry and use the money you save to rent a bike or moped on the island.

Similarly, inexpensive passenger ferries cross to Isla de Cozumel frequently from Playa del Carmen, while much more costly car ferries run from Puerto Morelos. A high-speed hydrofoil ferry runs daily from Cancún to Cozumel and costs about the same as flying.

TAXIS

Taxis in Cancún are readily available at any hour of the day or night all along the Hotel Zone and downtown, as well as at the Punta Juárez ferry dock during the hours when the boats run.

At Chichén Itzá, taxis and tour vans dawdle in the parking lot until about two in the afternoon. They provide local transportation to the bus station in Pisté and also serve the hotels in the area. The taxi drivers will also cheerfully offer to drive you all the way to Mérida or Cancún. That's because they know foreign tourists have lots of money. (The fare is higher than the cost of a car rental.)

In Mérida, taxis and other conveyances are freelance operations charging rates that are regulated by the government. Taxi cabs operate from stands near the *zócalo*, the market, Parque Hidalgo, the Teatro Peón Contreras and other spots around downtown and Paseo de Montejo. Agree on the fare before you ride. *Combis* (VW shuttle buses) fares range midway between buses and taxis. They depart regularly from the busy bus stop area near the public market and take fixed routes to *colonias* (suburban neighborhoods) and outlying villages.

An unusual transportation option in Mérida is the *calesa* or horse-drawn carriage. These are the real thing—charming old open-air buggies that have been on the streets of the city since before there were automobiles. Nowadays they look sort of beat-up and their wheels wobble a bit, but they still take passengers through the city's narrow streets at the same plodding pace as motor vehicle traffic. Rates run slightly higher than those of taxis. Several other towns, such as Izamal and Valladolid, also have horse-drawn carriages. Izamal cabbies take pride in the fact that the calesas there were built by the same carriage-maker as Queen Victoria's (and, by the look of them, around the same time).

Taxis cost less in Campeche than they do in Mérida or Cancún, but can be harder to find when you want one. Major taxi stands are near the *zócalo*, the government palace and the Baluartes and Ramada Inn hotels. However, since the most recent economic recession, the government has raised gasoline prices while freezing taxi fares; as a result, most taxi operators have abandoned Campeche, and visitors may wait all day for a cab there.

Most taxi drivers double as tour guides and will customize an itinerary and negotiate a fair fee. This can be a reasonable option for in-town sightseeing, especially in Mérida and Campeche. Be careful about taxi travel out of town. In Cancún, cab drivers may offer to take you to distant parts of the Yucatán, seemingly oblivious to the fact that, even for a rich gringo, several hundred dollars is a lot of money for a cab ride. Around Cancún's bus terminal, cab drivers are sometimes heard trying to convince international travelers to take a cab instead of the bus to Mérida, a 200-mile trip. Don't do it! The cost will be about ten times as much as the bus fare, twice as much as the airfare.

HITCH-HIKING

Sometimes, such as when you're visiting off-the-beaten-path ruins, local buses or *combis* may stop several kilometers from your destination, making it necessary to hitchhike. Hitching, especially in the big trucks that outnumber cars on Yucatán roads, is a common way for Maya people who live in rural areas to get around, and it is completely safe. (Trucking companies have rules prohibiting women passengers, though.) Locals are often shy about offering rides to gringos, much as you or I might think twice about letting a space alien ride in our vehicles. If you look like a *jipi* (leftover '60s terminology meaning penniless student with a backpack), you'll probably find rides easily enough; if you dress like a tourist and carry a lot of gear, you probably won't. Pemex stations are a good place to ask around for a ride (*un aventón* or, simply, *"un* ride").

TRAVEL AGENCIES & TOURS

All cities and larger towns in the Yucatán have a lot of travel agencies, most of them located in the lobbies of large hotels and in downtown commercial zones. These agencies do a lot more than just sell airline tickets and make hotel reservations. They often serve as clearinghouses for small tour operators and can help you arrange a motorcycle rental, a plane or four-wheel-drive trip to remote ruins, a horseback expedition into the mountains, a jet-boat or rafting trip down one of the region's spectacular rivers or any number of other adventures. Stop in and see what they have to offer. If nothing else, you'll come away with plenty of friendly suggestions to enhance your visit.

Sightseeing tours, whether by boat, tour bus, van or jeep, cost about the same everywhere—$75 for a half-day trip or $125 for a full-day trip for a party of up to four. An individual or couple pays the same price if the guide cannot find other visitors to share the trip. The same rate prevails whether you take a regularly scheduled sightseeing tour or design your own itinerary.

TWO

The Land
and Outdoor Adventures

GEOLOGY The Yucatán Peninsula is divided more or less into three pie-shaped states—Quintana Roo, Yucatán and Campeche. Each has its own distinct terrain and vegetation.

The state of Quintana Roo spans the peninsula's east coast, including the legendary beaches of the Riviera Maya as well as the wild, almost inaccessible shores of the central and southern Caribbean coast where ancient Maya boat canals link large, sheltered bays with sparkling, spring-fed freshwater lakes a few miles inland. Two of the largest bays, along with much of central Quintana Roo's forest wilderness, lie within the boundaries of the Sian Ka'an Biosphere Reserve. Inland, most of Quintana Roo is sparsely inhabited and difficult to travel. Unlike the rest of the peninsula, where the porous limestone soaks away the surface water, the ground in this region consists of slick, greasy-feeling clay so dense that it will not absorb water. As a result, much of Quintana Roo's forest stands in shallow water during the summer months, making it a paradise for wading birds, crocodiles and tapirs but also making it unreachable by either car or boat. Even hiking trails don't last long in this soggy, steamy overgrowth. Despite the rugged isolation, most of the lofty mahogany trees in the Quintana Roo jungle were cut down during the 19th and early 20th centuries. The Maya people who live in scattered villages at the end of narrow, two-track seasonal roads through the forest make their living by tapping sapodilla trees for chicle, the base for chewing gum.

The state of Yucatán includes the peninsula's north coast, which fronts on the Gulf of Mexico. Many visitors prefer the charm of its beaches and small fishing villages to the glitz of Cancún. Also along the coast are three natural parks—Río Lagartos, San Felipe and Celestún—where thousands of pink flamingos nest each year and thousands of human visitors come to watch them. Inland, Yucatán state encompasses the part of the peninsula where most of the population lived from ancient Maya times through the Spanish colonial period and up to the time in the 1970s when Cancún's boomtown economy started luring people eastward. Today, the land is a patchwork of henequen and sugar cane fields, slash-and-burn corn *milpas, cebu* cattle ranches and hard-to-reach stands of second-growth forest some distance from the road. The access problem is not that there is any shortage of foot trails through the woods but that there is virtually no place along the highways to park a car while exploring on foot. Several lesser-known Maya ruins in the region provide parking areas and trails into the forest. The southern boundary of Yucatán state is marked by the Puuc hill country, a thinly populated area with the greatest concentration of ancient Maya ruins on the peninsula. The hills reach a maximum elevation of about 800 feet above sea level—an impressive height overlooking a land that is otherwise as flat as the proverbial hotcake (in Spanish, *jotcek*).

The state of Campeche is mostly hill country, with elevations rising to 1200 feet. Covered in thick scrub and luxuriant forest, the hills surround traditional Maya villages, caves and ancient ruins so impressive that it is surprising that so few travelers make their way over to this part of the Yucatán Peninsula. The west side of the peninsula has little to offer in the way of beaches, though small, little-known resorts stand on a few exceptional strands of the Gulf coast south of Campeche city. Potentially the most exciting attraction in the state is the towering rainforest in the southern interior near the Guatemalan border. The Calakmul Biosphere Reserve, the largest surviving area of primeval rainforest in Mexico, lies nearly roadless at the end of rocky tracks over terrain so hilly that a four-wheel-drive trip there becomes a very slow roller-coaster ride. Hidden in the forest are some of the Yucatán's least-known and most dramatic Maya pyramids.

BEACHES AND REEFS   The Caribbean coast of the Yucatán Peninsula is justly famous for its soft, white beaches, brilliant turquoise water and coral reefs teeming with colorful tropical fish. These, far more than Maya ruins or rainforests, lure millions of visitors to the Yucatán each year. Yet in Cancún and other major resort areas along the peninsula's northeast coast, there is mounting evidence that visitors are loving this piece of tropical paradise to death.

Twenty years ago, Mexico's most popular lagoon was alive with dazzling brain coral, flamboyant fans and schools of fish so thick you couldn't see a snorkeler ten feet away. Then the reef at Parque Nacional El Garrafón died, a victim of its greatest admirers —tourists. Day after day, party boats from Cancún dumped hundreds of snorkelers on the Isla Mujeres reef. And day after day, they stepped on and stole the precious living coral, spreading disease that turned it into a skeleton reef. Somewhere along the line all the fish swam away. Today the undersea national park has been turned over to a private water-park development company in the peculiar hope that boosting commercial tourism with snorkeling tours and dolphin dives can resurrect Isla Mujeres's faded coral wonderland.

Preventing an El Garrafón is as easy as not touching the reef. Even a slight brush from a fin is enough to damage a coral forever. Always anchor in the sand or grass flats, far away from the reef. If you can't see where you're anchoring, send a snorkeler down to check the sea bottom. And no matter how tempted you may be, never take a piece of coral. That small souvenir will destroy in one second what it took nature thousands of years to build.

Cancún made a belated effort to save its small, spectacular, terribly overcrowded natural reefs by providing a manmade alternative—towing hundreds of boat hulks destroyed by Hurricane Gilbert in 1988 to sink them where they're meant to provide not only an ideal fish habitat but also a playground for snorkelers and scuba divers.

Crumbling, lifeless coral reefs and overcrowded beaches lined with high-rise hotels account for only a tiny fraction of the Yucatán's coastline. There are other, equally beautiful beaches where accommodations range from small clusters of thatch-roofed cabañas to free camping on the beach. (Bring your own mosquito netting.) Then, too, there are vast, magnificent living coral reefs that are visited by fewer than a hundred divers a year. Finding and enjoying these places may take a lot more imagination and ingenuity than booking a package deal at a mega-resort development. It takes the kind of information this book is designed to provide.

Most coral reefs are located along the eastern shore of the Yucatán Peninsula, from Cancún and Isla Mujeres south all the way to huge Chinchorro Reef offshore from Chetumal. The largest and most spectacular formations lie off the landward shore of the island of Cozumel, where the almost continuous chain of reefs is the world's second-longest, surpassed only by the Great Barrier Reef of Australia.

DEEP IMPACT

Not far from Alacrán Reef the waters of the Gulf conceal a unique geological feature: the crater left by the largest meteor that ever struck the earth's surface. The impact took place more than 40 million years ago. Many scientists believe that the clouds of steam released when the white-hot meteor plunged into the sea obscured the sun for several years, making it too cool and dark for large, cold-blooded land animals to survive, thus causing the extinction of the dinosaurs. Even though the crater is in water far too deep to be reached by divers, it can tug at your imagination as you gaze out to sea from the north coast.

The only major reef that is not in Caribbean waters is Alacrán Reef, also known by its English name, Scorpion Reef, which is located in the Gulf of Mexico northwest of Río Lagartos.

CENOTES The state of Yucatán has not a single above-ground river. Beneath a thin layer of topsoil, the whole region stands on a sheet of porous limestone. Although during the summer wet season as much rain falls on Yucatán as on the wetlands and soggy forests of Quintana Roo, it quickly drains away through the limestone into subterranean rivers that flow to the sea through caves. The complete lack of surface water makes it doubly remarkable that the most highly developed civilization in pre-Columbian America evolved here. Unlike other parts of the Maya empire such as Chiapas and Guatemala, in the Yucatán the rain god Chaac dominated the ceremonial life of Maya cities. Yucatec Maya communities large and small depended upon Chaac, more than any other god in the Maya pantheon, for their very survival. The ancient people of the Yucatán Peninsula developed various ingenious methods to make up for the lack of water. In Quintana Roo, they paved broad plazas to serve as catchments for reservoirs the size of football fields. In the Puuc hills, they dug *chaltunes*, huge underground cisterns capable of capturing and storing enough rainwater to support whole cities through the dry season. Nevertheless, the greatest number of Maya cities were built in the northern part of Yucatán state, where water was available from *cenotes*, or sinkholes, a geological phenomenon unique to this region.

A cenote is formed when part of the roof of an underground river collapses. Some cenotes, like the popular swimming hole at Dzibilchaltún National Park, are surface-level ponds covered with water lilies; you'd never guess that they're actually hundreds of feet deep. Others, such as the famous sacred cenote of Chichén Itzá, are fully exposed but hard to reach, surrounded by sheer 50-foot cliffs. Still others, like the wonderful Cenote Dzitnup near Valladolid, are cavernous, dripping with stalactites, accessible only by narrow passageways that descend from ground level. Among the hundreds of cenotes that dot the northern Yucatán within a half day's drive of the city of Mérida, about 40 are large enough to have supported ancient cities. Each is unique. To the local people, these major cenotes are as important as the ancient ruins themselves. Few cenotes still serve as reservoirs since windmills now pump enough water to satisfy the meager water needs of the rural villages and plantations. Today they serve both spiritual and recreational needs. Now, as in ancient times, they link the surface world of light and air with a deep, cold, secret underworld that forms the Yucatán's subconscious soul. They are places of magic. If you doubt this, simply follow a dirt track through the forest to one of the cenotes mentioned in this book and discover a cool, delightful place that will make for a lifelong memory. Along the Caribbean coast, scuba diving in cenotes is a fast-growing sport, and you'll find dozens of indigenous Maya people who will lead you to local cenotes for a small fee.

FLORA   **MANGROVES**   The Yucatán coast, like most of the world's tropical seashores, is wrapped in mangrove jungle. The maze of mangroves makes the coast practically impenetrable to humans as well as to many predators, and so it hosts a wondrous variety of birds and sea life. Insects, too. Mangroves and mosquitoes have protected the coastline from development over countless centuries. Maya kings and Spanish conquistadors alike have chosen to locate their main cities inland instead of at the edge of the sea.

Ecotourism is developing on a small scale along the fringes of both Sian Ka'an and Calakmul, though the primitive roads may require high-clearance four-wheel-drive vehicles and may be impassable in the rainy season.

Mangroves reach about 20 feet in height and form dense thickets along muddy saltwater shorelines. Three species grow along the Yucatán coast—red, white and black mangroves. The red, or American, mangrove gets its name from its hard, dense, red-colored wood used in wharf pilings and for fuel. The thick gray bark supplies tannin, used by the Maya in leather tanning. You can recognize the red mangrove by the stiltlike prop roots that reach from its trunk to the ground to provide additional support. The aerial roots form tangles that protect fish and crabs while catching and holding soil sediments, thereby stabilizing and slowly extending the shoreline. They have thick, leathery oval leaves and pale yellow flowers, which make brownish berries that begin to germinate while still on the tree, sending out embryonic roots. When the fruit drops from the tree it floats until it contacts mud, where it immediately begins growth. The white mangrove lives in the squishy muck right along the shoreline and sends breathing tubes up through the mud to help the roots get oxygen. Black mangrove lives on terra firma and grows like most trees.

Though they present a formidable, nearly impassable barrier along much of the coast, the mangrove wetlands are fragile and easily destroyed by hurricanes—or by bulldozers. A century ago, the Florida coast from Palm Beach to Miami Beach looked pretty much like the wildest parts of the Yucatán coast today. Large mangrove jungles are protected from bulldozers in Quintana Roo's Sian Ka'an Biosphere Reserve and Yucatán's Río Lagartos Natural Park, San Felipe Natural Park and Celestún Natural Park.

RAINFOREST   Yucatecans refer to any woodsy area that has not been under cultivation in recent years as *la selva*—the jungle. Swampy mangrove coast, thickets of scrubby trees growing back over played-out cornfields—if it's too thick to walk through without a machete, it's jungle. The rainforest, for which the Spanish language does not have any other word than *la selva*, is something more than mere jungle. It is a place so canopied that sunlight comes through the leaves like a moonlight glow, where rain scatters into a fine mist before it reaches the forest floor, where you can stand on top of an ancient pyramid temple and look out over hundred-foot-tall treetops to see an abundance of orchids, fruits and birds' nests, the domain of creatures that live out their years without ever touching the earth far down in the dim depths below.

The Yucatán has been populated and cultivated for about four thousand years. Slash-and-burn farming was practiced extensively by the ancient Maya and is still the primary farming method today. Because the topsoil is thin everywhere in the Yucatán, between 18 and 36 inches deep with solid limestone beneath, a cornfield created by burning away the jungle only produces crops for three years before its nutrients are exhausted. Then it takes four years of lying fallow, during which thickets of wild tree saplings grow to human height, before the land can produce another year's crop.

Because of this traditional but inefficient farming method, two-thirds of the Yucatán Peninsula has been deforested in the historical past; one-third is under cultivation at the present time, much of it with unprofitable crops such as henequen, for which there is little demand and which are grown and harvested mainly out of habit. In the one-third of the ancient forest that has never been cleared, located across the southern part of the peninsula in Quintana Roo and Campeche, every place that has ever been reached by road has been selectively timbered to harvest valuable hardwoods, particularly mahogany, which will not grow back to full height for a hundred years, if ever.

Yet a small portion of the Yucatán Peninsula still qualifies as primeval rainforest, so hard to reach that scientists have explored it only by helicopter fly-overs and satellite photos. Located along the state line between Quintana Roo and Campeche at the southern end of the peninsula near the Guatemala border, Mexico's largest remaining expanse of virgin rainforest has been protected from exploitation by terrain so steep and rugged that it could not even be mapped, let alone cut for timber or slashed and burned.

In recent years, the most remote and inaccessible part of the rainforest has been protected under rigid UNESCO environmental restrictions as the Calakmul Biosphere Reserve, part of the cooperative three-nation Maya Peace Park conceived by the private, nonprofit La Ruta Maya Foundation and the multinational Organización Mundo Maya. The Maya Peace Park also includes Belize's Río Bravo conservation area and the huge, adjoining Maya Biosphere Reserve in Guatemala. Since Mexico's Instituto Nacional de Antropología e Historia opened the huge site of Calakmul, one of the largest cities in the ancient Maya world, to the general public in 1998, it has become possible to drive a rental car right into the heart of the protected rainforest. Still, access to the biosphere reserve is extremely limited—not by law, which is hypothetical at best, but by the reality that, even today, getting there means hours of narrow, pitted roads with no gas, food lodging or human habitation along the way.

Yet the forest is under siege. About a decade ago, Route 186 became a paved highway through the forest, providing a direct route to Quintana Roo's capital, Chetumal. The jungle highway did not pass through a single village in its more than 150-mile route across the neck of the peninsula, but it provided an artery from which settlement could begin. Today, although the rainforest remains by far the most remote part of the Yucatán Peninsula, settlers are flooding in. The Mexican government has declared the area of Xpujil, where the highway meets the biosphere boundary, open to homesteading.

In 1994, the government, responding to political unrest that resulted in a guerrilla uprising in Chiapas, bulldozed miles of straight gridded roads through the jungle near the edge of the biosphere reserve. Innumerable small dams were built to capture rain water in ponds large enough to last through the dry season, and Chol-speaking Maya people from the forests around Palenque, Chiapas, were enticed with free land to move to the new planned villages. Each spring, the sky darkens with the smoke of more slash-and-burn fires.

While Mexican border patrol helicopters clatter over the rainforest canopy several times a day, there are few rangers on the ground to prevent looting and poaching in the Calakmul Biosphere Reserve. The biosphere has now reached a crossroads that will determine its survival. Government agencies, environmental groups and individuals concerned with saving the rainforest and its ancient treasures have embarked on a campaign to involve the *campesino* newcomers in the protection of the biosphere and its archaeological sites. To succeed, environmentalists must prove to the newly relocated villagers that preserving the rainforest for scientific research and limited ecotourism can pay better, in terms of self-importance as well as hard cash, than unauthorized slash-and-burn farming or even digging among the old ruins for treasures buried in the tombs of ancient kings. It is here in the forests around Xpujil, more than anywhere else in the Yucatán, that a fistful of ecotourist dollars can make an immediate difference between destruction and preservation of the rainforest. Visitors who venture off the main highway cannot help but sense the urgency of the situation.

FAUNA   **SEA CREATURES** Though they look like inanimate rock, the Yucatán's coral reefs are living entities, built gradually over a span of time far longer than all the centuries that have passed since

construction began on the ancient cities of the Maya. The reefs
are the creation of polyps, tiny relatives of sea anemones that grow
hard shells of calcium and live in colonies that combine to form
the fanciful shapes of fan coral, brain coral, elkhorn coral, sting coral and other varieties. The cells
of coral polyps are packed with microscopic single-
celled algae known as *zooxanthellae*. The coral supplies the algae with shelter, and the algae's photosyn-
thesis makes food for the coral. Coral colonies are
sensitive; environmental unbalances can cause them to
expel the algae, weaken, and in some cases starve to death.
This process, known as "bleaching," is destroying reefs
all over the Caribbean, especially where the reefs are heavily used for recreation.

> The fact that coral depend
> on light for their nutrition
> explains why coral reefs
> grow only in shallow
> water and also why
> many coral forma-
> tions grow to look
> plantlike.

One of the most common animals among thousands of species of echinoderms, mollusks, crustaceans and fish that live in the
labyrinths of the reefs, the spiny sea urchin feeds on algae growing on dead reef areas as well as on sea-grass beds that often surround shallow reefs. Urchins are such efficient grazers that they
clear a "halo" around the edges of the reef. Other reef denizens
include bristle worms, giant tube sponges, starfish, coral crabs,
spiny lobsters and caquama turtles.

The spectacle of fish life on the coral reefs along the Quintana
Roo coast is nothing short of fabulous. In this teeming undersea
world, bright-hued tropical fish such as the redband parrotfish,
the four-eye butterflyfish and the queen angelfish dart through the
water's magical blue-green glow in an endlessly dazzling dance
of color and light.

The reefs also host more sinister residents. Great barracudas
flash along the reef like swords as they seize and eat smaller fish
with lightning speed. Other predators include relatively benign
nurse sharks and more aggressive reef sharks. Reaching four feet
in length, moray eels strike at their prey from hiding places within
the undersea forest of coral.

Predators that bite pose far less hazard to snorkelers and divers
than creatures that sting: sea thimbles, sea lice and stingrays. The
first is a tiny, brown, thimble-shaped jellyfish that scoots along the
surface of the water. If you swim along the surface, it will scoot
with you and inflict little bites that later turn into big red welts.
Sea lice also lurk on the surface and bestow measles-looking bite
marks that itch for a week. Unfortunately, sea lice are invisible.
You can avoid sea thimbles by not swimming where you see them.
You can't avoid sea lice, but you can minimize the bites by rinsing
your body in fresh water as soon as you leave the sea. Rinse extra
well underneath your swimsuit—the little guys hang out where
there's clothing. Like sea lice, stingrays are tough to see. The flat,
slippery creatures camouflage themselves in the sand along shal-

low areas and can deliver a wicked puncture with their stingers. Avoid being stung by shuffling away. If you're stung, see a doctor at once.

You'll find the most seashells on the west-facing beaches of the Gulf of Mexico. Common shells include various subspecies of cockles, cones, tulips, figshells, whelks, pen shells and conch shells. The meat of the conch (*caracol* in Spanish, *chac-pel* in Maya) is one of the most widely eaten seafoods along the Yucatán coast. It is grilled as a fillet, with tasty but rather rubbery results, or diced into a spicy ceviche.

BIRDS The Yucatán is gaining international recognition as a birders' paradise. At least 340 species of birds live on the shores and in the forests for at least part of the year. Besides being the place to which many birds from the United States and Canada fly south for the winter, the Yucatán is a vital stopover for birds migrating to Central and South America. In all, the Yucatán Peninsula is full-time or part-time home to at least 600 bird species—more than are found in all of Europe. Bird migrations reach their height in November and mid-March to mid-April. Many islands and mangrove wetlands along the coast are prime birdwatching territory. Even along Cancún's Laguna Nichupté you can expect to see an array of shorebirds and wading birds including cormorants, frigate birds, laughing gulls, brown pelicans, white pelicans, great blue herons, white herons, night herons, green herons, boobies and bitterns. The most popular birdwatching excursion from Cancún is the boat trip to the federally protected wildlife sanctuary of Isla Contoy.

Many ducks from the eastern United States winter in Sian Ka'an Biosphere Reserve, Celestún Natural Park and other coastal wetlands. Although the ducks' presence attracted flocks of *norteamericano* hunters in former times, sport hunting is uncommon

CATCHING CRUSTACEANS

On any night you can look out across the water from any Gulf coast fishing village and watch the ghostly dance of lights as shrimp fishermen lure the shrimp into their nets. Most shrimpers in Yucatán and Campeche do not use large boats like those seen along the U.S. Gulf coast but instead fish from long, narrow wooden motorboats. Shrimp thrive in the waters of the northern Gulf coast, where a shelf extends out to sea for many miles, keeping the water shallow enough so that sunlight can heat it to bathwater temperature. Shrimp is the main seafood—in fact, the main food of any kind—served in fishing villages and ports along the Gulf coast.

in the Yucatán today because of tough gun-control laws and license requirements that tie up would-be hunters in mountains of red tape. (Local residents in rural areas are allowed to hunt birds and small game for food, but only with small-bore .22- or .25-caliber rifles).

The region's favorite bird is the flamingo. In the late spring, when 90 percent of the flamingos in the Western Hemisphere descend on the shallow estuary at Río Lagartos to build their nests in the mud, thousands of Mexicans—as well as a mere handful of *norteamericanos*—come to witness the spectacle. More modest flocks of flamingos can be seen in Río Lagartos and Celestún Natural Parks at any time of year.

In the inland areas of the Yucatán, by far the most frequently seen bird is the black vulture. The presence of these eagle-sized carrion eaters is virtually constant along the region's highways, since their most important source of food is roadkill.

The rainforest in the southern part of the peninsula is full of exotic bird life, ranging from colorful parrots and guacamayas to keel-billed toucans and pileated (or imperial) woodpeckers. A kind of oriole known as an *oropéndola* colonizes the tallest trees in the forest with hundreds of hanging nests. The most unusual of the jungle birds is the ocellated turkey, a colorful ground dweller that resembles a peacock.

REPTILES Several species of sea turtles, especially Kemp's ridley and hawksbill sea turtles, are native to the Quintana Roo coast and have been hunted by the Maya people for meat since ancient times. Many Classic-period Maya artifacts made of sea turtle shell have been found, including hundreds of combs and figurines dredged from the sacred cenote at Chichén Itzá, where they had been thrown as offerings to the gods. Unfortunately, as coastal beaches in Quintana Roo have become more accessible in recent years, the sea turtle population has plummeted to near-extinction. The main reason is that turtle eggs, which are laid by the thousands in beach sand, have traditionally been considered not only a delicacy but also a stimulant for superhuman male sexual prowess. For the last several decades, poachers have been snatching turtle eggs by the truckload for sale on the black market. Before the government undertook any serious effort to protect turtle nesting beaches in the 1980s, the numbers of turtles born along the Quintana Roo coast had declined to less than 2 percent of the levels that existed 30 years before. (Since very little is known about the turtles' adult life in the open ocean, experts cannot say for sure whether their numbers have declined that much or whether they have moved to other, safer breeding areas, but experts suspect the worst.) Today, there is no place on the Yucatán coast where visitors can watch the spectacle of baby sea turtles hatching and racing for the sea. Mexican laws protecting sea turtles and their nesting grounds are very strict, and possession of turtle eggs can mean a long prison sentence, but many people fear that protection has come too late. Private environmental groups in Quintana Roo are trying to restore the sea turtle population through captive breeding programs.

The most common reptile in the Yucatán is the iguana. You will see these large, plant-eating lizards everywhere in rural Yucatán, especially around Maya ruins, where the ancient stone walls are ideal for basking in the sun and the wildlife is protected. They keep growing throughout their lives. Young ones are bright green and have smooth backs. As they change color with age, reach a length of three feet or more and grow comblike serrations down their backs, they take on a primeval aspect that adds to the region's strangeness. Iguana meat is considered a delicacy in the Yucatán. They can be hunted without firearms; they are just slow enough so that, with a little luck, a fast human can catch one. Naturally enough, they taste like chicken.

You are driving along the highway and what looks like a small iguana scoots across the road in front of you like a streak, running upright on its hind legs with its collar flared out like a miniature escapee from Jurassic Park. You have sighted a basilisk. The flared collar acts like a wing, helping the lizard stay upright while running. It can run this way for long distances and even dash across the surface of a pond.

Five species of crocodiles, alligators and caymans inhabit coastal regions of the Yucatán. Most people in Mexico, including wildlife experts, draw no fine distinctions but refer to all of them as crocodiles, or sometimes *lagartos* (lizards), an euphemistic understatement. You may see one just about anywhere. Once, after searching through the wild sawgrass wetlands of Sian Ka'an with my camera for two days and finding plenty of crocodile nests but not a single giant reptile, I returned to civilization and, within hours, spotted a nine-foot alligator basking along the lagoon shore beneath a marina dock in the Cancún Hotel Zone.

Rattlesnakes must have been abundant in the Yucatán a thousand years ago, judging from the prominent role their images played in the art of the Maya cities built in the Puuc region south of Mérida. Today, a rattlesnake encounter is possible, though not very likely, when visiting that region. In the backcountry, walk loudly and try to sound too big to eat. Don't put your hands or feet where you can't see them. The same rules apply in rainforest and wetlands areas, where rattlesnakes are less common but other kinds of poisonous snakes may live. But many travelers in the Yucatán worry more than they should about them. Poisonous snakes are about as common in the Yucatán as they are anywhere in the eastern United States. If you walk around in the countryside every day of your life, a snakebite is about as likely as being struck by lightning. Most snakes in the Yucatán are harmless.

MAMMALS Almost all wild mammals of the Yucatán are nocturnal and are rarely seen even by local people. If you explore very far into the forests of southern Quintana Roo and Campeche, you will probably see their tracks and spoor, but sighting the animals themselves is a highly unusual experience to be treasured.

To the ancient Maya, the jaguar symbolized the forces of darkness and primeval nature. Jaguars were the first gods recorded in stone by Preclassic Maya sculptors. Even earlier in the mists of prehistory, the Olmec people worshipped gods that were represented as half jaguar and half human child. Known in Spanish as *tigre* and often translated as "tiger" by English-speaking guides, the endangered jaguar is now rare throughout its range, which once spanned from Argentina to Texas and the American Southwest. In the Yucatán, jaguars still inhabit the deep rainforest of the Calakmul Biosphere Reserve in southern Campeche. This region is also home to four other species of wild cats—the cougar (*león* in Spanish), the ocelot, the jaguarundi and the margay. Cougars are even rarer than jaguars in this region.

The most common large animals on the peninsula are whitetailed deer, which are found in all parts of the peninsula but especially in the thick scrub of the inland part of the Sian Ka'an Biosphere Reserve, where they are protected from hunting. Venison is a favorite meat among the rural Maya people. It is rarely served in restaurants because it is technically illegal to sell meat from wild animals; however, some small-town restaurants will verbally offer venison as a daily special when available. Other Yucatán mammals that are traditionally hunted and eaten (and surreptitiously served in restaurants) include armadillos and *tepezcuintles*. The latter, known as a paca in English, is so reclusive that it is rarely seen. Among the Maya, it is considered an epicurean delicacy.

Monkeys in the Yucatán are of two species—the spider monkey, which is abundant in the southern jungles, and the howler monkey, which is rarely seen in the region but sometimes heard in

GOOD-LUCK GECKOS

In any hotel room, including the fanciest ones, you are likely to notice a tiny, lizardlike gecko scrambling along the wall, now and then emitting a little clicking noise. Geckos are believed to bring good luck in Yucatec homes, and you're in luck if your room has one. They eat mosquitoes, which the clicking sound attracts. A single tiny gecko can keep a whole room insect-free.

the distance. Its cry is unmistakable. You can usually tell when spider monkeys are around because as they move from limb to limb through the trees, they make crashing sounds. You can also tell when they have been around by the debris of partly eaten fruit at the base of trees. Local guides usually have no trouble locating the monkeys because they frequent certain trees, particularly the sapodilla, or chicle, tree, whose sweet fruit smells and tastes like flan, the Mexican desert custard. Howler monkeys are hard to spot because they are small, black and nocturnal. They crouch at the base of tree branches and sound off with improbably loud, deep roars that make them sound like lions.

Other denizens of Yucatán forests include agoutis, anteaters, coatimundis, raccoons, javelinas, kinkajous and many species of bat. Tapirs are occasionally seen in the seasonally flooded jungle of southern Quintana Roo.

One of the most remarkable animals native to the Yucatán is the West Indian manatee, a large, endangered aquatic mammal that lives on underwater plants along mangrove shorelines, river deltas and estuaries. The northern half of Chetumal Bay has recently been declared a manatee preserve.

INSECTS No survey of Yucatán wildlife would be complete without at least a brief acknowledgment of the insect kingdom. Bugs abound in coastal and jungle areas, and no trip should be without chiggers, sand fleas, mosquitoes and scorpions. Before you cancel your trip, remind yourself that most insect species are not only benign, they're also fascinating—especially in rainforest areas, where watching bugs can be more fun than TV. There are bugs that disguise themselves as vegetation and others that are gaudy in their brilliant hues and elaborate markings. Giant blue dragonflies dance across wetlands and among ancient ruins. Ants —particularly leaf-cutter ants, which can strip a bush of virtually all its leaves in a matter of a few hours and transport the vegetation a fragment at a time along a line that can stretch unbroken along the jungle floor for miles—can be interesting to watch when you realize that an ant colony functions as a single mind, capable of transmitting remarkably complex messages rapidly by leaving trains of scent chemicals called pheromones. Bees are also abundant throughout the Yucatán. Honey was a staple food of the ancient Maya, and beekeeping is an important agricultural industry in many areas today. African "killer" bees have reached the region in large numbers; in many areas you will see traps for them, which look like boxes wrapped in plastic and hung from trees. Regarding scorpions, just remember to shake your shoes out before you put them on in the morning.

Insects—especially mosquitoes, sand fleas and ants—are likely to share your campsite. Locals burn coconut husks to smoke out bugs, but for campers insect repellent, mosquito nets and insect coils are more convenient.

The Yucatán Peninsula has more than 1200 kinds of butter-flies, though it seems that at any given place and time you'll only see uncountable swarms of a single kind. (If you went back a few days later, you'd find a different kind.) According to Maya legend, the souls of the dead become butterflies—and who's to say different? Their colorful wings certainly add an extra touch of magic to the Yucatecan landscape.

▼▼▼▼▼▼▼▼▼▼▼▼▼

Outdoor Adventures

Even if you don't spend a single hour sunbathing on Cancún's legendary beaches, you can count on returning home from the Yucatán tanned to a deep bronze or, if you're less cautious on the early days of your trip, fried to a flaming red. Just about everything there is to do in the Yucatán happens outdoors.

Outdoor recreation in the Yucatán Peninsula falls into two broad categories: resort sports, which require specialized sporting goods, and backcountry adventures, which generally do not. Outside of resort areas, you won't find much in the way of sports equipment for rent in the Yucatán; in fact, the whole idea of personal property rental is unfamiliar to most Mexicans.

In places where tourists come in large numbers, such as Cancún, Isla Mujeres and Cozumel, entrepreneurs have discovered that renting bicycles, scuba equipment, wave-runners, mopeds, golf clubs and so on can be a highly profitable business. If your vacation plans involve fun-in-the-sun activities like parasailing, windsurfing and jet skiing, Cancún or any of a half-dozen other Caribbean beach resorts should loom large in your itinerary. The same is true of scuba diving, except that serious divers who venture beyond the familiar waters of Cancún, Isla Mujeres and Cozumel to the vast, hard-to-reach reefs of southern Quintana Roo can discover new and largely unexplored underwater worlds.

If your plans involve boldly going where no tourist has gone before, look to the Gulf Coast and the interior for hiking, camping, fishing and bicycling possibilities. But keep in mind that backcountry recreation is not the common pastime in Mexico that it is in the United States, so amenities like trail maps, trailheads, campgrounds and bike rentals just don't exist in these areas. Ask at the nearest hotel and you will have no trouble finding a freelance guide who can take you wherever you want to go and outfit you with the equipment you may need.

CAMPING

By no means the organized activity that it is up north, camping in Mexico takes place in a handful of national parks and trailer parks and along scores of peaceful beaches. All beaches in Mexico are public by law, though a good bit of beachfront land is connected to private property—hotels, homes, *ejidos* (communally owned Mexican land)—which the owners may consider off-limits for camping. When in doubt, check with the facility nearest the spot you're interested in.

Many marvelous camping spots lie along the Caribbean coast. Developed resort areas on Cancún and parts of Cozumel are off-limits to campers, but that still leaves miles of beaches to the south, many with palm-shaded campgrounds right on the sea. Of the several beach campgrounds along the Quintana Roo coast where you can pitch your tent for a small fee and enjoy such refinements as restrooms and drinking water, the most popular is Chemuyil, about 111 kilometers south of Cancún. A picturesque assortment of aging American hippies and youthful European backpackers hang out here, sometimes for weeks at a time. A handful of run-down "eco-campgrounds" can be found just south of Tulum along the road to the **Sian Ka'an Biosphere Reserve**; most of these are old tourist cabaña complexes that were never completely rebuilt after the most recent hurricane, though a few boast nice land-scaping and all the amenities you might want. Within the bio-sphere reserve you'll find plenty of remote camping possibilities (but no restrooms).

In the interior, camping options are generally limited to trailer and RV parks, which also accommodate tent campers. You'll find them around **Chichén Itzá** and **Uxmal**, as well as on the outskirts of **Cancún, Mérida** and **Campeche**. Some villages and *ejidos* have built screened, group-sized camping palapas in the forest; travelers can bring their own sleeping bags or hammocks and experience a night alone in the jungle, bug-free.

Many campers in the Yucatán eschew tents and sleeping bags in favor of hammocks and mosquito nets, and many campgrounds offer palapas, thatch-roofed open-air structures under which you can sling your hammock. This hot-weather mode of camping doesn't offer much privacy, but the necessary gear is lightweight and very compact.

Camping supplies and sporting goods can be found in Cancún at **Supermarket San Francisco de Asís** ~ Avenida Tulum next to Mercado Kuhuic; on Isla Mujeres at **Super Betino** ~ Avenida Mor-elos 5, 9-882-0127; on Cozumel at the **Conasupo** ~ Avenida 10 in San Miguel; in Chetumal at **Mercado Lázaro Cárdenas** ~ Cal-zado Veracruz and Segundo Circuito Periférico; in Mérida at **Supermaz** ~ Calle 59 No. 514 and **Deporterama** ~ Calle 59 No. 508, 9-923-6307; and in Campeche at **Superdiez** ~ Area Akim-Pech off Malecón Miguel Alemán near Avenida Francisco Madero.

Organized camping trips into Calakmul Biosphere Reserve—where you can spend the night at the Calakmul Archaeological Zone or in the rainforest near a Maya rubber tappers' village, com-plete with a traditional Maya feast—can be arranged through Expediciones Aventura Maxima. ~ 9-871-6010, fax 9-871-6011 (Xpujil); 9-987-2521 (Mérida).

Mexico's Natural Treasures

More than 3.5 million acres of land on the Yucatán Peninsula is under government protection, including two vast expanses of wilderness set aside as biosphere reserves under an international conservation program and three large *parques naturales* (natural parks) that protect sensitive wetlands along the Gulf coast. More than 30 federal archaeological zones preserve ancient Maya cities and ceremonial sites, while a handful of other unique areas have been designated as Mexican national parks.

Access to these areas varies widely. Easiest to reach are restored Maya ruins such as Chichén Itzá, Uxmal and Tulum, located just off major highways and visited daily by tour buses. These and most of the lesser-known ruins described in this book can be reached via paved roads in a passenger car. Some ruins make good departure points for day hikes into the surrounding forests. Even where the surrounding land has been cleared for agriculture, the outlying areas of the archaeological sites themselves are preserved in their natural condition and often attract abundant wildlife.

At the other extreme, "core areas" of both Sian Ka'an and Calakmul Biosphere Reserves are off-limits to all but biologists, archaeologists and other scientists, who must obtain permission from the Mexican government to perform research in those territories. UNESCO's Man and the Biosphere program, under which these reserves were established, protects core areas for future generations by prohibiting all human use, sheltering them with a buffer zone where local people use the land in nondestructive, usually traditional ways such as chicle tapping and some types of fishing.

Several coral reefs along the Caribbean coast are protected by the government as underwater national parks. Don't expect any visitors centers or ranger-guided tours; Mexico's park system lacks the budget for such things. The national park designation is purely protective. Parque Nacional El Garrafón, off Isla Mujeres; Parque Nacional Laguna Chankanaab, off Cozumel; and Parque Nacional Laguna Xelha, off the mainland coast north of Tulum, are easy to reach for snorkeling and diving, while the largest of the underwater parks, Parque Nacional Banco Chinchorro, is only accessible by an hour-long, privately arranged boat trip from Chetumal.

Boats are also the main mode of travel in the three large *parques naturales* (natural parks, similar to wildlife preserves in the U.S.) along the Gulf coast— Río Lagartos, San Felipe and Celestún. Ecotourism promises to boost the dismal local economies of these villages, so count on being welcomed by local fishers eager to guide birdwatching excursions through the wetlands.

FISHING

Cancún has a reputation as a sport-fishing paradise. Offshore reefs teem with everything from hard-fighting snapper, jacks and barracuda to bluefin tuna (March through May), wahoo (May through September), grouper, kingfish and cobia. Coastal lagoons offer excellent fishing for bonefish and pompano. Marlin and sailfish are also found in these waters. Cancún hosts a sportfishing tournament in early May; it is not uncommon for participants to reel in 30 billfish during the six-day competition. The saltwater fishing season is April through June, and a saltwater fishing license is required. Deep-sea fishing charters are available from charter companies, marinas and fishing lodges at Cancún and other major coastal resorts including Isla Mujeres, Playa del Carmen, and Cozumel. There is a shortage of charter boats in the area, so reservations should be made well in advance. High demand makes the charters costly—typically in the $500- to $800-a-day range.

DIVING

When it comes to underwater sports, few places on earth can match Quintana Roo. The coral reefs that run from Isla Contoy for 250 miles down the Caribbean coast to Belize lure millions of scuba divers and snorkelers each year.

The reefs, though they look like inanimate rock, are actually living colonies of polyps that absorb food from the nutrient-rich Gulf Steam and have slowly grown into a coral jungle as complex as the Amazon. Finger coral, elkhorn, mountainous star, brain coral, purple leaf and orange tube coral, precious black coral with sepia age rings, plus green stinging coral and red fire sponges, which burn when touched, are just a few of the species that bloom to towering heights on the ocean floor. Hewn into breathtaking landscapes, this subterranean jungle is dappled with vivid sea fans, treelike gorgonia, prickly sea urchins, sea whips and lush anemones. Coral crabs skitter sideways like moving shards of reef. Brilliant schools of fish and myriad other sea creatures—gaudy parrotfish, candy bass, turquoise angelfish, flamefish and starfish, spotted scorpionfish camouflaged by the mottled sand, colossal sea turtles and manta rays—ripple by, an astonishing visual symphony, beautiful beyond belief. To dive around these reefs is to enter another world, a silent, blossoming dream, a dazzling hallucination.

Just off Isla Mujeres lies the bizarre Cave of the Sleeping Sharks—the only place in the world where you can stroke a deadly reef shark as it dozes in a stupor brought about by this area's low salinity.

But not all is harmonious beauty. Inside crevices, where you should never poke a prying hand, live moray eels, whose saw-toothed fangs hold decayed food particles that can fatally poison their victims.

Where are the tamer dive sites, you ask? Near Isla Mujeres, Manchones reef provides calm depths for beginning divers. El Dormitorio is a graveyard of 16th-century pirate ships. Cancún shares with Isla Mujeres a group of lovely shallow reefs (40-foot depths), including Cuevones Reef (full of small caves), fish-rich La Bandera Reef and the ornate reef off Punta Nizuc.

South of Cancún, there's fantastic diving around Akumal, where objects from old Spanish galleons have been recovered, and great snorkeling at Xelha, where kaleidoscopic fish eat from your hand. Farther south, some 20 miles offshore from the village of Xcalak, lies the notorious Banco Chinchorro, whose jagged reefs have sent hundreds of ships to an early grave—a diver's happy hunting ground.

As for Cozumel, its riches surpass description. The most popular fishing spots include the shimmering Laguna Chankanaab, La Ceiba Reef with its sunken plane, the precipitous Santa Rosa Wall, Columbia Reef with its mountainous columns and pinnacles, and the mighty Palancar Reef, six miles long and plunging 3000 feet, containing easily a half-dozen kingdoms of labyrinths, caverns and ravines.

For many scuba enthusiasts, a trip to Palancar Reef or one of the other world-class dive areas along the Quintana Roo coast means the experience of a lifetime. Visitors who do not have scuba certifications can glimpse the spectacle of undersea life on the more easily reached coral reefs from a glass-walled sightseeing boat or explore it with nothing more elaborate than swim fins, a face mask and a snorkel.

Strangest of all is to dive a cenote, the region's remarkably deep natural wells. Many are swirled with murky waters, where blind fish wriggle through the darkness. But other cenotes have water as clear as liquid air, making them marvelous for diving. Dive shops can point you to the best cenotes. (Those at archaeological sites are off-limits to prevent looting.)

Dive shops abound along the Quintana Roo coast. Renting snorkeling or diving equipment is easy in any resort area. Scuba divers must have proof of certification (advanced open-water certificate required for the Cave of the Sleeping Sharks and other challenging areas). Those who aren't certified can take resort classes (mini-courses) at the larger hotels. Diving lessons and excursions are not cheap, but if you savor beauty and mystery, skip a few movies back home and catch this show.

Washed by stunning seas, crisscrossed with smooth-flowing rivers **SWIMMING** and pocketed with glassy lakes and cenotes, the Yucatán offers **& SNORKEL-** many wonderful ways to get your body wet. Swimming in this **ING** blessed region is not only rejuvenating; it's a trip back in time. Where else can you plunge down bottomless sinkholes where Maya priests once sought sacred visions? Or float along rivers where thousand-year-old temples line the shore?

Along the east coast, the turquoise Caribbean Sea laps at the edges of Quintana Roo, its offshore waters tamed by coral reefs. Most days, the water is so clear you can drop a quarter into the sea and tell if it lands heads or tails. North and west of the Yucatán Peninsula, the Gulf of Mexico creates a shallow shelf that keeps the often-murky water bathtub-warm for year-round swimming. Add to this hundreds of dreamlike, seemingly bottomless cenotes in the Yucatán interior, and you have a myriad of heavenly possibilities for beating the tropical heat.

Wherever you swim, remember that nature is in charge. In the ocean, conditions can change from good to bad in a matter of minutes. Erratic currents and powerful waves contain hidden pitfalls that can be avoided with a little awareness. Waves can be deceptive. They come in varying sets: one set may consist of seven small waves, followed by seven big ones; or seven big waves followed by one calm swell; or a series of small waves overshadowed by a sudden, big, angry swell. If you get caught in a wave about to crash you onto the shore, try to roll up and tumble with it rather than thrashing against it. Remember that waves grow bigger and more surly during the full moon. Stay alert and never turn your back to the sea.

Snorkeling rentals are expensive, so you'll save money if you bring a mask, snorkel and fins from home.

While the sea is for the most part calm and splendid, swimming can be a bit tricky in some areas. Rip currents threaten open sections of the Caribbean—including the Cancún shoreline from the Hotel Camino Real to Club Med. These sudden, strong currents can be spotted by their ragged-looking surface water and foamy edges. They can drag you out to sea. If you get caught in one, don't panic and struggle against it or try to swim straight for shore; instead, free yourself from its inexorable pull toward the open sea by swimming parallel to the shore until you have escaped the current, then swim in diagonally.

Be careful in waters full of coral reefs. Coral edges are jagged and can make nasty cuts. Consider wearing rubber thongs in the water to protect your feet. Treat any cuts with alcohol and an antiseptic.

Above all, when you go swimming, use common sense in judging safety conditions. Strong surf, steep dropoffs at the tide line, whirlpools and eddies around rocky areas all signal danger. If in doubt, don't go. Avoid swimming alone.

Beware of sunburn, the trickiest ailment of the tropics. Tan slowly and use plenty of sunscreen on sensitive areas: lips, nose, shoulders, even the tops of your feet.

Nude sunbathing is against the law in Mexico. Be discreet. Travelers get away with it on deserted Caribbean beaches along the Cancún–Tulum corridor, where local people are no longer easily shocked by foreign ways. Elsewhere in the Yucatán, Catholic traditions reign, and nudity, or even female immodesty, is considered highly offensive. On the beaches of Progreso and Celestún, frequented mainly by Mexicans from Mérida, it is common to see women bathing fully clad in dresses. Mexican men favor skimpy bikini trunks, but women who wear revealing Cancún-style bathing suits on a Gulf Coast beach can expect disapproving glares from other bathers and perhaps unwanted sexual advances.

Snorkeling equipment can be rented at any dive shop in resort areas but can be hard to come by at more remote beaches.

BIRD-WATCHING

With more than 600 species of birds, the Yucatán has been gaining an international reputation in recent years as one of the ultimate places for birding expeditions. The ultimate birding thrill is to view the flocks of pink flamingos that congregate in Celestún Natural Park and at the nesting grounds in Río Lagartos Natural Park. While some flamingos live in both parks year-round, the best time to see the birds by the thousands is in May and June. Hotel operators and tour guides at both areas are highly knowledgeable about the flamingos and other birds in the area.

Though pink flamingos are rare, other shore and sea birds can be seen in amazing abundance at the bird sanctuary on Isla Contoy, reached by excursion boats from Isla Mujeres and Cancún. You can anticipate seeing cormorants, frigate birds, laughing gulls, great blue herons, white herons, night herons, green herons, white pelicans, brown pelicans, boobies and bitterns. In lesser numbers, these birds are also found in all coastal areas of the Yucatán.

The rainforest of southern Quintana Roo and Campeche is also an incomparable birders' destination. Among the many species found there are *oropéndolas* (a variety of oriole), parrots, guacamayas, keel-billed toucans, pileated (or imperial) woodpeckers and even the rare ocellated turkey, also called the Petén turkey.

WIND-SURFING

The waves along the Caribbean and the Gulf of Mexico generally don't come big enough to support surfing, but they are ideal for windsurfing. Sailboard rentals and lessons are widely available along the Caribbean.

BIKING

Flat terrain makes northern Yucatán a cyclist's dream—if you don't mind the hot climate. You will only find bicycle rental places in the tourist corridor, though.

Even though more people in rural Yucatán ride bicycles than drive cars, the concept of bike rentals is unheard of in this region (well, almost). Rentals can often be arranged informally. Tell your hotel manager or a local travel agent a day or two in advance that you'd be interested in renting a bicycle, and chances are good that someone will want to rent one out to a rich gringo. Bicycle stores, plentiful in cities and many small towns in the Yucatán, sell new, relatively low-priced mountain bikes and are occasionally willing to rent them, too. If you plan to take an extended bike tour of the peninsula, you may want to consider buying a bike from a retail store with an agreement to sell it back at a lower price at the end of your trip.

One of the best routes for long-distance road touring is Route 180 Libre—the narrow old highway (not the new toll freeway) between Mérida, Chichén Itzá and Valladolid. Most big trucks and buses use the freeway, so the old highway is fairly traffic-free as it passes through picturesque Maya villages and woodlands. Several cenotes along the way offer respite from the heat.

If you have your own mountain bike and have a car equipped to carry it, a trip into the Calakmul rainforest south of Xpujil can be the adventure of a lifetime. The Mexican government has recently opened up vast expanses of forest to homesteading on the fringes of the biosphere reserve, and in so doing, they have cleared a network of steep, rocky, unpaved, remarkably wide roads through the jungle—too rough for most passenger cars but ideal for mountain bikes. A bicycle trek to remote Maya ruins such as Hormiguero or Río Bec is feasible. Unofficially, rugged four-wheel-drive roads like these run all the way to the Guatemala border—and beyond, they say, through the Petén rainforest to Guatemala's Tikal National Park. There is presently no legal way to cross the border. Biking through the rainforest on the road to Calakmul would be an awesome experience, though the round trip probably could not be completed in a single day.

For an easier jungle-and-ruins ride, rent a mountain bike at Cobá and pedal along thousand-year-old ceremonial roads through this magnificent Maya site.

HIKING   If you have the urge to take a day hike, beaches are your best bet. For long-distance beach trekking, the sandy, sometimes rocky coastline south from Tulum into the Sian Ka'an Biosphere Reserve is unsurpassed.

The concept of recreational hiking has not yet caught on in the Yucatán interior, where walking is generally viewed as a transportation mode for rural people too poor to afford a bicycle or a bus ticket. The Yucatán backcountry is laced by foot trails, thanks to at least 4000 years of habitation by pedestrians, but there are no real trailheads. Highways have no shoulders, so when you come to an inviting-looking hill or forested expanse while driving in the countryside, there's never a place to park. Trails lead into the backcountry from virtually all villages, but finding them is often not easy. If you ask local people about trails through the forest, your request will usually be met with stunned disbelief, especially if you don't have a definite destination in mind. If your

Spanish is good, children are often happy to help you. (They will expect a tip—and deserve one; ten pesos is less than the price of a Big Mac.)

Because trails are not readily accessible, Maya ruins are key destinations for nature lovers as well as archaeology buffs. The forests surrounding most ruins visited by tourists are usually protected from timber cutting and slash-and-burn farming. Besides the trails used by local villagers, you will often find paths to small temple ruins over an area of several square miles, as well as to ancient Maya quarries that now supply stone for restoring the ruins. While the temple at the end of a trail usually proves to be less than spectacular, the walk through forests teeming with birds and butterflies, overgrown with vines and orchids, is its own reward. The best ruin in the Yucatán for hiking is Cobá, a huge, mostly unexcavated ancient city in the Quintana Roo jungle, where archaeological sites along the shores of several lakes are linked by a series of jungle trails. Other ruins that make especially good places to surrender to the forest's mysterious allure include Edzná and Becán in the state of Campeche.

THREE

History and Culture

Nearer to Jamaica or Miami than to Mexico City, the Yucatán has never been part of mainstream Mexico. Its heritage all the way back to the legends of antiquity has been one of dynamic tension between the local Maya people and various invaders from the outside world. To a civilization already ancient came the Itzá, then the Toltecs, then the Cocom. Then the Spanish conquerors, Christianizers, bringers of the Spanish Inquisition. Indian fighters, revolutionaries, pirates and treasure hunters also made their way to this part of the world. Most recently, gringos have swarmed the beaches and begun to venture into the Yucatán backcountry on newly paved roads in their rented Volkswagen Beetles.

History

▼ ▼ ▼ ▼ ▼ ▼ ▼ ▼ ▼ ▼

THE PRECLASSIC PERIOD (2000 B.C.–A.D. 250) About 4000 years ago the Maya people began farming in the region bounded by the Caribbean Sea on the east, the Gulf of Mexico on the north and west and the Pacific Ocean on the south. They enjoyed a simple, comfortable, tropical way of life. They built thatched-roof huts, slept in hammocks and reaped the bounties of forests rich with fruit and game. From neighboring Olmec people they learned about the calendar and began to calculate time. They erected outdoor shrines and small temples to the *chaacs*, the gods who brought rain. And they grew corn, runner beans and tomatoes, as well as cocoa beans, which were used throughout Mexico and Central America as a form of money.

Spanish explorers applied the Yucatecan tribal name "Maya" to all indigenous people of the Yucatán and Central America, as far south as Panama, so it is uncertain whether the earliest Maya belonged to a single culture or spoke a single language. By the end of the Preclassic period there were three separate language groups: one in the Yucatán; one in the central rainforest that is now lowland

Chiapas, Guatemala, Belize and Honduras; and one in highland Chiapas, Guatemala and El Salvador. Today, the original Maya language has splintered into 26 different, mutually unintelligible languages, most of which are spoken in the Chiapas and Guatemala highlands. While the successive rulers of the Yucatán have spoken many languages, recent translations of ancient hieroglyphs prove that since the dawn of recorded history, Yucatec Maya villagers continued to speak the same language. It is the same language that all the native people of the Yucatán speak today, though in recent years many people who speak Chol, a different Maya language, have moved from Chiapas to homestead in southern Campeche.

The 1993 discovery of the ruins of a large city known as El Pital may provide a missing link between the Maya civilization and the mysterious Olmec people, whose civilization flourished between 1200 and 400 B.C. Other possible Olmec-Maya connections have been unearthed on the Pacific plains of southern Guatemala, leading some scientists to speculate that the Maya may be direct descendants of the Olmec. The jaguar god first appeared in Olmec art and was later revered by the Maya as the symbol of earth and night. Moreover, the Olmecs developed a crude form of writing and the foundation of the calendar system later used by the Maya and other Mexican cultures.

Exactly who the Olmec were is one of the great mysteries of New World archaeology. No Olmec burial remains have ever been found, and their dwellings were swallowed up by swamplands millennia ago. We know them only through their art: sculptured altars, finely carved jade jewelry, cone-shaped clay pyramids and, strangest of all, giant heads carved from volcanic boulders that weigh as much as eight tons and were somehow transported to Olmec towns from sites more than 50 miles away.

At least one large Maya city, Dzibilchaltún, developed in the Yucatán during the Preclassic period. Over an area that spans 19 square miles, excavations beneath later structures at Dzibilchaltún reveal foundations and artifacts dating back as far as 800 B.C.

THE CLASSIC PERIOD (A.D. 250–900) The civilization known to modern archaeologists as the Classic Maya blossomed suddenly, seemingly out of nowhere, around the time of the Roman Empire's decline. The Maya began to build huge, exquisitely ornamented temples and palaces in the form of "stepped" pyramids. Even more significant, they began erecting stelae, stone monuments carved with hieroglyphs that recorded the history of Maya nobility. This was one of the most important moments in pre-Columbian times because it saw the introduction of the only true written language ever developed in the Americas before European colonialists arrived. It was a complex, versatile writing system similar in principle to Chinese.

The Maya hieroglyphs were instrumental in the spread of civilization—and are particularly fascinating today—because Maya tribes who spoke different languages could read the same written language. This remarkable fact is explained by the modern theory that Mayan hieroglyphs evolved from the hand sign language that let members of different tribes talk face-to-face. The same sign language, experts believe, came north to the Indians of the United States along the same trade routes that brought corn north from the Maya world.

An intriguing mystery of the Olmec is that their artwork depicts two distinct races: one with slender faces and beards much like those of the Semitic races in biblical times, the other with features that might be African or Polynesian.

Maya writing consisted of about 1500 hieroglyphic elements, some of them phonetic and others pictorial. Scholars today do not know whether peasant farmers could understand the inscriptions carved on stone stelae and temple walls or whether reading and writing were the exclusive province of the ruling elite. The prevailing theory today is that many Mayan peasants could read but not write, and that hieroglyphic stelae were erected to be viewed by the common people as well as future generations.

It may be that the scientific and cultural achievements of the Classic period had been evolving for millennia before artists began recording them in stone for future generations. Astronomers may have grounded their calculations in natural landmarks long before they built elaborate observatories in accordance with cosmic alignments. Because so few artifacts remain from that distant time, modern scholars may never know for sure.

Many theories have been advanced to explain why the Maya civilization blossomed from an unremarkable farming culture into the glory and splendor of the Classic period. For instance, the Church of Latter-day Saints, founded in 1830, about the same time the ancient Maya civilization was being "discovered," initially believed that the Maya were members of the Lost Tribes of Israel who had learned to build pyramids in the time of the Egyptian pharaohs. Their guiding document, the *Book of Mormon*, chronicles the lives of the Lost Tribes in the New World. Other 19th-century theorists speculated that Maya civilization sprang into existence as the result of contact with ancient Egyptians, Phoenicians, Cambodians or even the people of lost Atlantis. More recently, out-of-the-mainstream theorists cite ancient Maya sculptures as proof that travelers from outer space visited earth long ago.

Asians, Atlanteans, gods from outer space—none of these theories has been proven false. But all share a common, unspoken premise: that "mere Indians" could have achieved such feats of architecture, astronomy and art only with outside help. The truth may be even more amazing: perhaps a single insight of genius on the part of an American Indian individual whose identity remains unknown may have inspired a burst of creative energy that spread throughout a region larger than Greece or Italy to shape human accomplishment over a span of nearly seven centuries. The catalyst may have been a fundamentally new way of understanding time. It may have come from the invention of the Maya "long count" calendar, which enabled priests to visualize enormously large time spans and make predictions thousands of years into the future. This new perspective may have made permanence important, inspiring the creation of architecture, art and writing in stone, designed to last into the distant future—as it has.

The Classic period lasted much longer than the timespan between Columbus' first landfall in the so-called New World and the present day. Although it was once thought that the great Maya civilization began in the Yucatán, archaeologists now agree that it spread from the southern rainforests to the relatively primitive people of the north late in the Classic era. This golden age of massive, ornate, brightly painted architecture, exquisite works of art, and astounding advances in mathematics and astronomy dawned in Cholan Maya cities such as Tikal in the Petén rainforest of northern Guatemala and spread west to Yaxchilán and Palenque in the Chiapas lowlands before reaching the Yucatán. The greatest city on the eastern Yucatán Peninsula through most of the Classic period was Cobá. In the north it was Izamal, which monopolized the lucrative salt trade and built the most massive pyramids in the Maya world. In the south it was Calakmul, which rivaled Tikal for control of the rainforest.

Around 800, as the Classic period neared its close, Uxmal—the most phenomenal community in the ancient Maya world—rose to dominate the central and western Yucatán Peninsula. During the Classic era Uxmal was one of several ceremonial and administrative centers of roughly equal size and importance, including Kabah, Sayil, Labná and Xlapak, among others. Between these centers lay thatch-hut neighborhoods inhabited by approximately 250,000 people—by far the largest city in the Maya world, as large as any European city at that time. Uxmal took over control of the whole Puuc hill region near the end of the Classic era.

Though it is one of the most often visited and thoroughly studied ancient Maya cities, Uxmal remains enigmatic. Its elaborately sculptured facades reveal practically nothing of the hieroglyphic history found at other sites of the same era; instead, the art of Uxmal is laden with mythological images and abstract symbols, the meanings of which are only partially understood. Instead of history, legends about Uxmal have lived on in the oral traditions of Maya people in nearby villages. For example, we are told that Uxmal served as a sort of university from which knowledge of Maya arts and sciences was disseminated throughout the region. That sounds plausible, but we are also told that the great pyramid at Uxmal was built in a single night by a dwarf magician, even though this "thrice-built" pyramid was obviously built a level at a time over a period of centuries. Clearly, many of these stories need to be taken with a grain of salt. In fact, although archaeologists have a clear picture of Uxmal's later history in Postclassic times, its earlier history remains completely unknown.

According to scholars who analyze pre-Columbian thought processes, the world view of the Maya was so different from that of traditional Western civilizations—ancient Egypt, Greece, Rome and medieval Europe—that any parallels drawn between the cultures are likely to be misleading. At the beginning of the 20th century, H. G. Wells wrote in his masterwork, *The Outline of History*: "It is as if the Maya mind had developed along a different line from that followed by the Old-World mind, had acquired a different twist to its ideas, was not, indeed, by Old-World standards a strictly rational mind at all. . . ."

Recent investigations into Maya thought, based on expanded understandings of Maya hieroglyphs, archaeoastronomy and symbolism, reveal that Maya priests, far from suffering from the crippling mental aberration Wells imagined, subscribed to a philosophy that people of European descent find hard to comprehend. The concept of duality—true/false, form/substance, mind/body— was foreign to Maya thought. Time and space formed a unified whole. Science and religion were one and the same. Early accomplishments mirrored cosmic purposes. The individual merged with the infinite.

It's no wonder that modern travelers experience a sense of awe upon visiting a ruin from the Classic period, for the more we learn about the ancient Maya, the more we realize that theirs was a world of surpassing strangeness. We ponder lesser riddles—how they achieved such flawless and intricate stone carvings without metal tools; how they derived astronomical formulas unknown to Western science until the 20th century; whether or not they practiced human sacrifice. Yet what we feel when confronting artifacts left behind from a culture that evolved in directions alien to our own is itself the fundamental mystery.

The Maya of the Classic period were ruled by lords who claimed authority through legendary god-king ancestors. The throne was passed down from father to son. Each region had its lord, and each lord lived in a palace flanked by temples at the center of the city. He employed priests, scientists, artists and warriors to govern the common people, who lived in huts scattered across a broad agricultural zone on the outskirts of the city. Most of the Yucatán and the Petén were under cultivation at the time.

Social classes were rigidly divided. The nobility flattened the skulls of their children, a procedure started at birth, to distinguish them from the masses. Some experts suggest that this practice

may have altered not only their appearance but also the function-
ing of their brains. Knowledge was probably passed along in
teacher-student relationships, but whether common people could
gain admittance to the "universities" and thus join the ruling class
through education is not known.

Most of the major Maya sites had been occupied for hundreds
of years before the reigning lords of the Classic period transformed
them into elaborate ceremonial centers. In many areas, a single lord
supervised the construction of the great plazas and pyramids we
see today, burying the older, smaller temples within them. Building
these pyramids meant quarrying stone blocks that weighed as much
as 65 tons each, transporting them despite the lack of wheels or
beasts of burden, and hauling huge volumes of earth to fill them
in. One can only wonder if these astounding feats, like the pyramids of Egypt, were accomplished by conscripted labor or, like
the Gothic cathedrals of France, through religious devotion.

The Classic Maya civilization, from beginning to end, was set
in stone, the most permanent of nature's building materials. As a
result, bas-relief sculptures, hieroglyphic inscriptions and astronomical alignments detailing this cultural epoch have survived
more than a thousand years of weathering and plant growth. Much
of the long-forgotten stonework of the Maya has been discovered; much more has yet to be found; little is understood.

THE POSTCLASSIC PERIOD (A.D. 900–1511) Just as no one
knows what triggered the flowering of Maya civilization, no one
knows what caused its collapse. In fact, less is known about the
centuries that followed the carving of the final hieroglyphic date
on the last stone stela than about the years that went before. Most
scientists speculate that the Classic period ended simultaneously
throughout the Maya world with the abandonment of many of the
great ceremonial centers, especially in the Petén, giving rise to the
idea that ancient Maya civilization "collapsed" because of some
cataclysmic event—war, disease, famine or environmental disaster.
The currently favored theory is that a long drought put an end to

ROYAL TREATMENT

Many Maya leaders attained great wealth and flaunted it. They ate meals
smothered in chocolate sauces made from the cocoa beans that among
the lower classes served as money. They wore headdresses graced by
the plumes of quetzales, macaws and other forest birds, which were
also traded as money. Their jewelry and masks were fashioned from
jade, the most precious commodity in the Maya world. Unlike the
people of central Mexico or Peru, however, the Maya had no gold
or other precious metals.

the Classic period throughout the Maya world. Core samples from the lakebed of Laguna de Chicnancab show that coincidental with the end of the Classic period, the Yucatán experienced a drought that lasted several decades; without rain, the cenotes, reservoirs and cisterns that supplied water to Maya communities and cornfields would have run dry after 18 months.

The Maya people themselves may never have detected a decline in their civilization, or perhaps they recorded the fall of the Maya empire in books that were later lost to posterity. After the last inscription was carved on a stone monument, Maya priests wrote in books, a major new technology that allowed for the recording, in portable form, of much more voluminous and detailed information. These priests, as well as the masses, may have seen Postclassic Maya society as more modern and efficient, and the great ceremonial centers as just plain old-fashioned.

On the Yucatán Peninsula, the Postclassic period was a time of cultural collisions and sweeping changes. As the Classic civilization collapsed, other groups moved in to seize control of the region. Some were semibarbaric Maya tribes who had lived on the fringe of mainstream civilization during the Classic period. Others were invaders from distant lands.

Among the most influential newcomers were the Itzá. Originally related to the builders of Tikal and other cities in the central rainforest, these seagoing Maya merchants had been traversing the coast of the peninsula in canoes for centuries from a home port at Chakanputún (now the town of Champotón) on the Campeche coast, trading in commodities such as salt and dyes. With the collapse of the Classic Maya civilization, they moved inland to build some of the most impressive cities of the Yucatán, including Chichén Itzá. The new Itzá seaport, whose ruins were discovered in 1985, was located on Isla Cerritos in the mouth of the Río Lagartos.

Itzá is commonly translated as "water witches," though the word probably derived from their worship of Itzamna, the god of knowledge, who gave the Maya their calendar, mathematics, astronomy and the art of writing.

Soon after the Itzá moved into northern Yucatán, their civilization began to show influences from the Toltecs, the dominant civilization of central Mexico. They built Chichén Itzá into a magnificent ceremonial center patterned on Tula, the Toltec capital. Realized by master Maya sculptors and architects, Chichén Itzá abounds with distinctly non-Maya art reminiscent of the ancient cities that existed at the same time some 750 miles to the west, on the far shore of the Gulf of Mexico. With the Toltec influence came the worship of Quetzalcóatl (known among the Maya as Kukulcán), the Plumed Serpent god, whose image appears throughout Chichén Itzá. They also brought more fearsome images, such as the reclining Chac-Mool figures used as sacrificial altars.

Experts disagree about whether the warlike Toltecs actually invaded the Maya world, seizing control of Chichén Itzá from its Maya rulers, or whether the Itzá were merely influenced by the Toltecs as both cultures expanded their commerce; evidence is strong that around A.D. 1000 Toltec trade networks extended not only eastward to the Yucatán Peninsula but northward to the Anasazi cities of New Mexico and Arizona. Many pots and other artifacts found at Chichén Itzá appear to have been manufactured by Toltecs in central Mexico; metal objects such as gold disks and copper bells also appeared during this period and may have been imported from as far away as Panama.

With the Toltec influence also came the practice of human sacrifice. While Classic Maya sculptures show that some of the more warlike rulers made a habit of executing their enemies in public, there is little or no evidence that they practiced human sacrifice for religious purposes, and mass sacrifices such as those staged by the Aztec in later centuries were probably unknown among the Maya. Toltec artwork at Chichén Itzá shows that athletes were sacrificed in connection with ball games; some religious altars are also thought to have been used for sacrifices; and there are persistent (though dubious) tales of virgins sacrificed to the gods of Chichén Itzá's sacred cenote. According to other legends, however, the priest-king of the Quetzalcóatl cult came to Chichén Itzá after being banished from Tula because he was opposed to human sacrifice. Like so much of ancient Maya life, the question of human sacrifice remains a mystery.

The Itzá/Toltec rulers occupied Chichén Itzá for about 200 years. Then for unknown reasons they abandoned the city, though they continued to use its temples for ceremonial purposes. Moving southward, they built a new city called Mayapán—a crude imitation of the glory that was Chichén Itzá—surrounded by a castle-like defensive wall. A clan of Itzá known as the Cocomes ruled Mayapán and quickly spread in power until they controlled all of northern Yucatán. With a larger population than the agricultural productivity could feed, Mayapan thrived on tribute payments from other cities, which they enforced by taking lifelong hostages from the other rulers' families.

In the 15th century, yet another barbarian Maya clan from the western outlands came to power in the Yucatán. The Xiu Maya first occupied Uxmal and Mani, then, finally, in 1450, staged a palace coup in Mayapán. Although they succeeded in overthrowing the central authority of the Yucatán, they were unable to govern their empire effectively. The Yucatec civilization deteriorated into an unimpressive scattering of rival fiefdoms ruled by local caciques. Mayapán continued to be the nominal capital of the Yucatán until the arrival of the next wave of invaders, the Spanish, who looted the city and destroyed much of it.

CLOSE ENCOUNTERS (A.D. 1511–19) The first Europeans ever to set foot on Mexican soil were a small group of shipwreck survivors who, in 1511, found themselves hopelessly stranded in the area of present-day Cancún. Most of the group were put to death by the local tribal chief, but two men—Jerónimo de Aguilar and Gonzalo Guerrero—lived to assume unique roles in Yucatán legend. From abject slavery, the two men gained acceptance within the tribe, making their homes among the Maya for eight years. Guerrero married a Maya woman and raised a family.

Meanwhile, in 1517, conquistador Francisco Hernández de Córdoba "discovered" the Yucatán while exploring the western Caribbean for the Spanish colonial government in Cuba. Believing that the Yucatán was an island, like Cuba, Hispañola, Jamaica and all other Caribbean lands then known, Córdoba tried to sail around its perimeter and map it. He followed the Gulf coast as far as Champotón, about 32 miles south of the site of modern-day Campeche, where the coastline veers west. At that point, finding no quick sea route back to the Caribbean, Córdoba and his men landed to forage for supplies and were attacked by Maya warriors. The few survivors miraculously made their way back to Cuba in a small boat, carrying with them the standard cities-of-gold tales that sprang from the imaginations of so many early Spanish explorers. In this case, the stories were completely false. Aside from the lack of gold in the Yucatán, Córdoba's men never saw any of the great cities that actually did exist in the peninsula's interior.

A second expedition, led by Juan de Grijalva, set out in 1518 to search for the fabled golden cities of the Yucatán. Grijalva's ships followed the shoreline even farther west, to the Tabasco coast, but were finally forced to turn back because hostile Maya tribes would not let them land to search for food or fresh water. Grijalva's discovery, that the Yucatán was part of a much larger landmass, inspired the governor of Cuba to send out a larger expedition under the command of Hernán Cortés. This third expedition would lead to the conquest of Mexico.

Cortés' 1519 expedition made its first landfall at the island of Cozumel, where they met the Spanish castaways Aguilar and Guerrero, who told them that the Maya people had no gold. With that information, Cortés decided—in violation of his orders from the Cuban governor—to bypass the Yucatán and head west, seeking his destiny in unexplored seas. He rescued Aguilar, but Guerrero chose to stay among the Maya.

For nearly 20 years, Aguilar would serve as scout and interpreter on expeditions whose purpose was to conquer the Yucatán. Simultaneously, Guerrero rose to become a top military adviser to the Maya rulers who resisted the Spanish invasion. He was eventually killed in battle by his former countrymen.

THE SPANISH CONQUEST (A.D. 1526–44)   Francisco de Montejo, a young Spanish noble who had served as a lieutenant to Cortés in his conquest of the Aztecs, applied to the king of Spain for an appointment as adelantado of the Yucatán. His request was granted in 1526. The position of *adelantado*, which roughly translates as "one who advances" the interests of the Spanish crown, gave Montejo the authority to take military control of the region, to spread the Catholic faith, and to exploit the land and its people for personal profit. The appointment was for life, and whatever wealth he gained through the conquest could be passed down to his heirs. Montejo's problem was the thousands of Maya warriors who had no intention of sharing their homeland with either Montejo or the king of Spain.

Montejo first attempted to conquer the Yucatán from an outpost that he established in 1527 at Xelha on the Caribbean coast. Many of his soldiers fell victim to malaria and were unable to repel attacks by the local Maya. Abandoning Xelha, he took his remaining forces to establish another colony at Chetumal, but the Maya again drove them off.

In 1528, Montejo returned with a larger army and invaded the peninsula from the other side, establishing a fortress colony at Campeche. The Maya, instead of using the guerrilla tactics that had proved so effective on the east coast, attacked en masse with an army of 20,000 warriors. Despite their vastly superior troop strength —the Maya outnumbered the Spaniards by 800 to 1— Montejo's soldiers, with their armor, horses, steel swords, crossbows, cannons and attack dogs, soundly defeated the Maya, who fought on foot with wooden spears and stone-tipped arrows. To consolidate Spanish control of the peninsula, Montejo's son led another army to establish a second colony in the north among the ancient ruins of Chichén Itzá. But the Maya stood their ground at Chichén Itzá, surrounding the settlement. Only a few Spaniards—including Montejo the Younger—escaped the ensuing massacre. Meanwhile, news of the conquest of the gold-rich Inca empire in Peru inspired Montejo's soldiers to desert, and in any case Montejo was on the brink of bankruptcy. Once again the conquistador was forced to abandon his campaign to conquer the Yucatán.

For five years Montejo participated in expeditions to other parts of Central America. But in 1536, warfare broke out between the Cocom and Xiu Maya, and a devastating plague of smallpox weakened the armies of both tribes. Montejo, his son and his nephew mounted a third military campaign in the Yucatán. By persuading the Xiu people to pledge allegiance to Spain in exchange for Spanish help in defeating the Cocom, the Montejo clan gained control of the peninsula. They re-established Champotón

> According to the Maya calendar, the next apocalypse is scheduled for December 23, 2012.

and Campeche in 1540, built their new capital at Mérida in 1542, and established Spanish strongholds at Valladolid, Zací and Chetumal in 1544. Even though the Cocom Maya launched the largest attack in Maya history against Mérida, with an army 60,000 strong, the Montejos defeated them in this final battle.

Although Francisco de Montejo was soon to be stripped of his authority as *adelantado*, the Montejos' descendants remained the richest family in the Yucatán throughout the Spanish colonial era and remain a powerful family in Mérida even today. Many things in the region bear the Montejo name, from Mérida's poshest boulevard and biggest downtown bank to a popular brand of beer.

THE MISSIONARIES (A.D. 1545–1600)   Franciscan friars, whom the king of Spain had charged with the duty of converting the Mexican natives to Catholicism, built missions in Campeche and Mérida in 1545. Their first attempts to spread the faith among the Maya were thwarted when a tribe of Itzá Maya from the eastern forests swept across the peninsula in a lightning-fast uprising, during which they killed every Spaniard in the Valladolid area, slaughtered the settlers' livestock and even cut down the fruit orchards. Once again, Montejo's army put down the revolt, driving the surviving Itzá deep into the Petén rainforest and putting an end to organized Maya resistance for three centuries.

> Day-to-day ministry and spiritual guidance was generally left in the hands of trusted Maya converts—who often doubled as priests of the Maya religion in secret.

With the Spanish military conquest of the Maya complete, the Franciscans moved into the towns and villages throughout the Yucatán Peninsula. The Franciscans' first act was to complain to the king of Spain about the brutality used by Montejo's army against the Indians. In the same kind of drama that had already stripped other conquistadors, including Columbus and Cortés, of their dictatorial powers in the New World, the Spanish royal court took away Francisco de Montejo's authority as *adelantado*. Although the Montejos remained in the Yucatán as large landowners, the real power devolved to the Franciscan brothers, who initiated an ambitious plan to capture the hearts and minds of the Maya people and create a Catholic utopia in the Yucatán forests. The effects of their missionary efforts are still very much alive today in Maya towns throughout the region.

Rounding up villagers from a wide area and relocating them to new missions patterned after Old World Spanish communities, the early missionaries established most of the towns that exist in the Yucatán today. The priests not only required the Maya to be baptized and to worship in the Catholic manner but also restructured every aspect of Maya life in the Spanish image. The Maya practice of slavery was abolished; instead, the Maya themselves became virtual slaves of the missionaries.

Most of the missions were built on the sites of former Maya ceremonial centers. Chinked limestone churches with grandiose facades were built on the sites of ancient temples, using facings stripped from the old temples as building materials. Unwittingly, the priests were following a 2000-year-old Maya tradition of building newer, larger temples over old, outmoded ones.

Within a few years there were 22 major missions and more than 180 *visitas*, village chapels where traveling priests performed baptisms and marriages; but only about 60 Franciscan brothers operated all of the missions. Glorying in their success at converting tens of thousands of heathens to Catholicism, the Franciscans failed to recognize the strange, hybrid folk religion that was taking hold in the mission communities.

The first evidence of secret pagan ceremonial rites among the Maya converts was discovered in 1562. Unfortunately for the Indians, the new king of Spain had recently declared the Spanish Inquisition, a widespread and brutal policy aimed at suppressing all forms of religious heresy throughout Spain's global empire through terror, torture and execution. Diego de Landa, the first bishop of the Yucatán, ordered his priests to search the land for evidence of idolatry and to arrest every Indian suspected of indulging in such practices, obtaining confessions by any means necessary. Landa's brief, fearful inquisition climaxed on July 12, 1562, in the town of Mani, when he publicly burned every Maya codex found by his priests. Although it's often said that Landa destroyed "thousands" of Maya texts in his auto-da-fé, witnesses' accounts place the number at only 14 to 20. Modern-day experts believe that libraries at cities such as Mayapán and Uxmal contained thousands of codices, but that they remained hidden until the bark pages disintegrated; small, indecipherable fragments of such books have been found at several sites, but only four ancient Maya books are known to have escaped the bishop's bonfires.

The older, pre-Inquisition generation of priests who operated many of the missions condemned Landa's fanaticism. On their complaints he was brought back to Spain to stand trial, a process that took ten years. During that time, as penance for destroying the books and other items used by Maya shamans, the Pope ordered Landa to write his study of Maya culture, *Relación de las Cosas de Yucatán*, including an account of preconquest Maya history as described to him by his improbable companion, a cacique of the Cocom Maya clan. Thus, ironically, the same man who destroyed the sacred libraries of the Maya also created the only ethnological account of the Maya people at the time of the Spanish conquest.

Landa was finally acquitted by the pro-Inquisition Spanish courts and allowed to return to the Yucatán, where he continued his bishopric until his death six years later at the age of 55. His

Relación de las Cosas de Yucatán lay unknown in a musty church archive for nearly three centuries. It was rediscovered and made public during the renewed fascination with the Maya culture that followed John Lloyd Stephens' explorations in the 1840s. Translated into 20 languages, Landa's book has been in print continuously from that time to the present day. A 1937 English-language translation by American anthropologist William Gates is available under the title *Yucatán Before and After the Conquest* (New York: Dover, 1978).

Soon after Landa's death, Maya scribes who had learned the European alphabet transcribed *The Books of Chilam Balam,* recording the oral traditions of a visionary cult known as the "Jaguar Priests," whose claim to fame was that they had accurately predicted the arrival of the white men from the east. Until epigraphers cracked the code for interpreting Maya hieroglyphs in the 1970s, *The Books of Chilam Balam* served as the best source of information—and misinformation—on 500 years of postclassic Maya history. These records are hard to interpret, however, because the basis of Maya prophecy was that history is cyclical and literally repeats itself on the same days of each *katun,* or cycle of roughly 256 years. This makes it impossible to know whether any particular event was ancient history, recent history or future prediction. Muddling the historical value of the texts even more is the fact that many Maya leaders intentionally falsified their dynastic histories for political purposes. Unfortunately for Maya buffs, almost all translations of these books are out of print today, though they can be found in many anthropological libraries.

UNDER SPANISH RULE (A.D. 1600–1820) After the early years of turmoil brought by the military conquest and forcible religious conversion of the Yucatán, the history of the region was characterized by more than two centuries of tropical torpor during which virtually nothing happened at all. There was no gold to attract fortune seekers. Even the farmland was so poor that few Spanish settlers were interested in it. Factions of the clergy, seeking to wrest

GODS IN DISGUISE

Among the Indians the strange, new Catholic holy figures were regarded as ancient Maya gods in disguise. The Virgin Mary was seen as a manifestation of Ixchel, the moon goddess of the Itzá people; Jesus Christ was similarly identified with the Toltec-Maya plumed serpent god Kukulcán. Saints and archangels became local gods and rain-bringers. The striking resemblance between the Christian cross and the traditional tree of life symbol of the Maya religion was not lost on the new converts, and some groups secretly practiced a new form of human sacrifice—crucifixion.

control of the missions from one another devised endless plots so arcane and convoluted as to be historically meaningless. The Maya were generally allowed to govern their own villages and day-to-day religious life. Spanish colonists, numbering only a few thousand, made their homes almost exclusively in the towns of Mérida, Campeche, Valladolid and Chetumal. The local economy consisted of nothing more than a handful of medium-size sugar cane plantations.

Although uneventful compared to the periods of sweeping change that preceded and followed it, the Spanish colonial era had its own problems. By far the worst was piracy. Privateers—pirates such as the "British sea dogs," "French sea wolves" and "Dutch sea beggars" who were commissioned by nations at war with Spain, as well as criminal pirates who owed allegiance to no one—preyed on the galleons that carried silver and other treasures of the New World back to the king of Spain. Only 30 percent of the wealth that left Mexico reached its destination; the other 70 percent was plundered by pirates. Not only were Spanish ships robbed and sunk, the pirates and privateers also laid siege to Spanish cities. One of the hardest hit was Campeche, on the Yucatán's western Gulf coast, where looting and rape occurred with depressing regularity well into the 18th century.

Among the most famous pirates and privateers who pillaged the Yucatán coast was Francis Drake, who robbed Spanish ships of more than $9 million in treasure and was rewarded for his atrocities when Elizabeth I dubbed him a knight of the realm and sent him back to sea to defeat the Spanish Armada. Although Drake is viewed as a hero in English and American history books, he is still remembered in Yucatecan legend as *El Draque*, a semimythical bogey man invoked to frighten children. Drake's successor as the terror of the Spanish Main, Henry Morgan, was so successful at stealing gold and silver and sharing it with the British crown that he was rewarded with an appointment as governor of Jamaica, whereupon he retired from piracy.

By the beginning of the 1700s, England had become a colonial power in its own right and no longer supported piracy against the Spanish. After that, pirates of the Caribbean attacked Spanish and English ships alike. The most notorious pirate of the era, Edward Teach (better known by the nickname "Blackbeard"), made his headquarters on the Quintana Roo coast for more than a decade, stealing cargos of tobacco from British merchant ships and selling them to Dutch merchants. Today, descendants of Blackbeard's crew still inhabit the remote village of Punta Allen (named after his pirate ship), a little more than 100 miles south of Cancún.

Three other scourges have plagued the peninsula from ancient to modern times: famine, epidemic and revolution. In 1648, a plague of yellow fever wiped out half the Maya population of the

Yucatán. Without enough able-bodied Indians to work the fields, starvation swept the land. Many missions were abandoned to local Maya *cofradías*, or lay religious brotherhoods. The *cofradías* reinstated the Maya ancient rituals but with the thinnest veneer of Christian symbolism overlaying them. In time these leaders formed a new ruling elite among the Maya and, in some cases, became wealthier than the most successful Spanish plantation owners.

In 1761, a Maya revolutionary known by the assumed name Canek (after a famous preconquest Itzá warlord) incited angry demonstrations around the small town of Sotuta, protesting new taxes and the taking of Maya farmland for Spanish cattle ranches. Although the "Canek Rebellion" involved little violence and no bloodshed, the threat of an Indian uprising provoked a sudden, brutal counterinsurgency campaign by Spanish soldiers, Canek was arrested and taken in chains to the capital at Mérida, where he was drawn and quartered in the town plaza.

Conditions returned to normal. The Maya grudgingly paid the taxes and surrendered the ranchland. The Spaniards dismissed the rebellion as an isolated event instigated by a lone madman. They failed to recognize the deep, brooding anger of the Maya people that would resurface a century later in the War of the Castes.

INDEPENDENCE AND REBELLION (1821–46) The chain of events that led to Mexican independence from Spain was complex and tumultuous. The end of Spanish colonialism was brought about by political turmoil thousands of miles away in Spain, along with brief and often bloody uprisings against church and state in various parts of Mexico. In the Yucatán, revolutionary violence broke out in 1820 in the form of anticlerical riots. Mission churches were looted, church property was seized by local politicians, and priests and nuns were driven from the peninsula.

In 1821 Spain surrendered its colonial holdings in the New World under an agreement called the *Plan de Iguala*, which created a single nation spanning the continent from Oregon to Panama. The new nation was to be a constitutional monarchy, ruled by an elected Mexican legislature under the authority of the king of Spain, if he wished, or a prince of any other royal family whom he designated. The constitutional monarchy lasted for less than a year before it was swept away by a military coup—the first of many; in the next 100 years, Mexico would suffer exactly 100 coups, revolutions, assassinations and other violent changes of government.

The Yucatán, like the rest of Mexico and Central America, found itself newly independent and in political disarray. The Catholic clergy was outlawed throughout Mexico, and nowhere were the consequences more sweeping than in the Yucatán, where political opportunists rushed in to grab up the farmlands previously owned by the missions. As the Franciscans were driven out, nearly all churches were abandoned to the Maya *cofradías*, who continued to operate them without benefit of clergy. At the same time, the church laws protecting the Indians were abolished, the Maya elite were stripped of their own landholdings, and the entire Indian population was conscripted into virtual slavery.

Political disputes quickly arose between the newcomers, who wanted the Yucatán to be part of the newly formed Republic of Mexico, and the old-guard leadership of the peninsula, who wanted to form their own independent nation. In 1840, revolution broke out as the separatists tried to secede from Mexico and form an alliance with the newly independent Republic of Texas. A deal was struck whereby Yucatán would share the cost of creating the Texas navy and together the two new nations would control the Gulf of Mexico.

Though Texas won its war for independence, the Yucatán lost. General Santa Anna, already infamous for the massacre of the Alamo's defenders in Texas, subdued the rebellion in the Yucatán. He accomplished his victory partly by training a huge militia of Maya men who proved all too enthusiastic about taking up arms against their oppressors. After the rebellion, Santa Anna divided the peninsula into three triangle-shaped territories (now states)—Yucatán, Campeche and Quintana Roo—to decentralize the power of local politicians. The Maya militia remained, armed and dangerous.

THE "DISCOVERY" OF THE ANCIENT MAYA (1838–42)   Into the midst of the revolutionary turmoil sweeping the Yucatán and Central America strode John Lloyd Stephens, one of the most colorful gringo adventurers ever to head south of the border, and his sidekick, illustrator Frederick Catherwood.

Stephens, the son of a New York congressman, had studied to become a lawyer, but after a short time in practice he developed a profound distaste for the profession. Claiming to suffer from nervous exhaustion, he closed his practice and embarked on a long journey to Greece, Turkey and the Holy Land, a part of the world that

SHEDDING NEW LIGHT

John Lloyd Stephens was the first writer to put forth the revolutionary theory that the ancient Maya cities had been built, not by Egyptians, Atlanteans or Israelites, but by the same Indians who still lived in the region. He even speculated that future explorations might reveal a "lost city" inhabited by Maya people who still followed their ancient way of life.

few Americans of the time knew much about. On that journey he cultivated an interest in archaeology and wrote a travel book about ancient ruins that earned him modest fame and fortune.

In 1837, upon hearing wild rumors about ancient cities lost in the jungles of Central America, Stephens planned an expedition to see them for himself. Through his father's political contacts he was able to secure an appointment as U.S. ambassador-at-large with two ambitious missions: to identify a political leader—*any* political leader—with whom the United States could establish diplomatic relations in Central America, and to chart a route for a proposed canal linking the Atlantic and Pacific Oceans.

Neither of Stephens' official missions came to much. The canal route he charted through Honduras was later rejected in favor of the present Panama Canal location, and none of the warring leaders Stephens met in his diplomatic capacity ever succeeded in unifying Central America under one leader. But his explorations of Maya ruins created a worldwide sensation. His book *Incidents of Travel in Central America, Chiapas and Yucatán* became a bestseller in the United States and Europe. Both it and its sequel, *Incidents of Travel in Yucatán*, have stayed in print for more than 150 years and still make for entertaining reading. Today, bookstores and curio shops throughout the Maya world sell reproductions of Catherwood's illustrations.

> The Secret City of Chan Santa Cruz was the closest thing to the "lost city" that John Lloyd Stephens had written about.

Actually, most of the Maya ruins Stephens visited were already well known to scholars and travelers. His unique contribution to Maya studies was that he captured the public imagination with his tales of ancient, mysterious ruins deep in the jungle and kindled enthusiasm for future archaeological explorations. Stephens' "discoveries" would certainly have inspired a frenzy of archaeological expeditions in the Yucatán except that soon after his books were published, war swept the peninsula, halting all exploration for more than 50 years.

THE WAR OF THE CASTES (1847–1901)   According to Yucatec Maya prophecy, 1847 was expected to bring the end of the world. In Maya tradition, the world ends and a new one is created at regular intervals that can be predicted on the calendar.

The ancient prophecy began to fulfill itself in July of that year, when a Maya unit of irregulars deserted from the Mexican Army and ran amok in the streets of Valladolid, terrorizing non-Indian residents. The government response was swift and harsh. Soldiers conducted house-to-house searches of the Maya villages in the area, burning and looting as they went. The Indians were forced to assemble in the Valladolid plaza and watch the execution of a man accused of conspiracy in the riot. The incident triggered the War of the Castes (from the Spanish word *casta*, meaning "race").

It was the longest and most devastating Indian war in the history of the Americas.

All the Maya soldiers in the Yucatán deserted, taking their weapons with them, to form small, disorganized bands that would eventually unite under the leadership of two Maya chiefs, Jacinto Pat and Cecilio Chi. Declaring their intention to drive every non-Indian man, woman and child out of the Yucatán, they swept through the countryside, burning churches and sugar plantations, killing any Spaniard they saw. The climax came in March 1848, as the Maya rebels seized Valladolid and put the entire non-Indian population of the town to death. Within two months, every "foreigner" in rural Yucatán had either fled the country or been murdered, and the last two Spanish strongholds—the cities of Mérida and Campeche—were under siege.

Then, with victory nearly in their grasp, the Maya abandoned their offensive. As the rainy season arrived, they returned to their villages to plant corn. Mérida and Campeche were saved. Many Maya retreated into the roadless jungle of Quintana Roo.

Hostilities between the Mexicans and the Maya continued for 60 years. Maya war parties raided outlying settlements. The Mexican Army slaughtered the Maya people whenever they could be found. Maya raiders captured and enslaved Mexicans foolhardy enough to travel through the Yucatán forests by road. Mexican politicians granted Cuban sugar barons the right to establish plantations throughout the northern Yucatán and use Maya slaves to work the fields.

The sugar cane plantations did not last long before the soil was depleted. Famine and a deadly influenza epidemic, along with massacres by both the Indians and the Army, devastated the Yucatán's population, which fell from about 500,000 in 1847 to 200,000 in 1900. Nearly all the survivors were ladinos. The Maya population was estimated at no more than 300. They were believed to be on the verge of extinction—and not a minute too soon as far as the Mexican government of the time was concerned.

Unknown to the Mexicans, the descendants of the Maya fugitives who had fled into the Quintana Roo forests in 1848 had built a capital city called Chan Santa Cruz, where about 10,000 Maya people still lived. There they had reverted to the ancient Maya religion, worshipping the "Speaking Cross" (the traditional Maya "tree of life" cross, not a Catholic crucifix) and practicing a form of visionary prophecy known as "night writing." The existence of the capital had remained a secret for generations because no Mexican who entered the Quintana Roo jungle was ever seen again.

In 1901, the Mexican Army discovered the existence of Chan Santa Cruz and attacked it in force, slaughtering or scattering the occupants and destroying the city. (It was rebuilt in the 1930s to become the present-day settlement of Felipe Carrillo Puerto.) With the fall of the Maya capital, the War of the Castes came to an end. Ladino and Maya residents in the Yucatán distrust each other even in modern times. Virtually all Yucatec Maya living today are descendants of either sugar plantation slaves or the free people of Chan Santa Cruz.

IN THE WAKE OF DEVASTATION (1901–68) During the late 19th and early 20th centuries, land in the Yucatán was free for the taking, and most of those who took it were planters out to make their fortunes growing henequen (also called sisal after the Gulf Coast port from which it was shipped), the best natural fiber for making rope. Indians performed the dreadful labor required to make rope: chopping the thick, hard, sharp, three-foot-long leaves of the plant and beating them against boards studded with nails to shred them into rope fiber. Before the advent of tourism, the plantations generated more wealth than any other industry in the history of the Yucatán.

Several of the most significant figures in the Yucatán during the early 20th century were archaeologists from the United States who, with the end of the War of the Castes, finally had their chance to explore the tantalizing ancient world John Lloyd Stephens had unveiled 60 years before. Two such men, Edward Thompson and Sylvanus Morley, characterized the emerging roles of Americans in the Yucatán.

In 1901, Edward Thompson, the U.S. consul to Mérida, bought the ranch on which the unexcavated ruins of Chichén Itzá were located for $500 and proceeded to dredge the bottom of the sacred cenote for treasure. His efforts over several summers yielded an amazing array of artifacts that had apparently been thrown into the cenote as offerings to the rain god, Chaac. The items included jade jewelry, metal and rubber balls, pottery, wooden and wax figurines, mirrors, sandals and incense. Some of the objects came from as far away as Panama and perhaps Colombia, hinting at a trade empire far more extensive than had been thought. Most of Thompson's loot was sent to Harvard University, in whose museum it remains today. Alongside Thompson's original dredge, now on display in the huge, modern visitors' center at Chichén Itzá is a plaque in Spanish that condemns Thompson for stealing Mexico's treasures and Harvard for refusing to return them.

Sylvanus Morley, an archaeology student at Harvard soon after the university's museum received Thompson's treasure trove, published so many popular accounts of the Maya world in the *National Geographic* and elsewhere that he, as much as John Lloyd Stephens, deserves credit for making the world aware of the ancient Maya legacy in all its majesty and mystery. After poking around in the unexcavated ruins of Tulum in Quintana Roo, Uaxactún in Guatemala, and Copán in Honduras, Morley presented the Carnegie Institute with a comprehensive proposal for it to fund an unprecedented restoration project at Chichén Itzá.

Academic archaeologists of the time reconstructed ruins on paper based on what they found while digging exploratory trenches and studied artifacts they found along the way. Then they filled the trenches, reburying the ancient temples for future generations of scientists. They had no scientific interest in unearthing the ruins, let alone rebuilding them. Morley, however, proposed a 20-year plan to restore one of the great Maya ceremonial centers to a semblance of its former grandeur and invite tourists to come see it for themselves. The public interest that a Maya ruin would generate, Morley believed, would result in more funding for archaeological digs. Chichén Itzá was selected because it was the easiest Maya ruin for visitors to reach. The charge is often made that in his passion to restore the ruin, Morley did not take enough time to analyze evidence that might have told scholars more about the true history of the enigmatic city; as a publicity coup, however, the restoration of Chichén Itzá succeeded beyond Morley's wildest imaginings.

Sylvanus Morley, an early 20th-century archaeologist with an interest in the Yucatán, is said to have inspired the movie character Indiana Jones.

Morley used his early archaeological expeditions as a cover for espionage activities he performed for U.S. Naval Intelligence during World War I. Later, after he had established himself at Chichén Itzá, Maya leaders came to ask his help in convincing Queen Victoria to form an alliance with the Maya to drive the Mexicans out of the Yucatán once and for all. A "Speaking Cross" prophet had foreseen that a foreigner who knew how to read ancient hieroglyphs would lead the Maya people to freedom from Mexican oppression. Morley could not help them with Queen Victoria, since he was not British and, besides, she was dead, but he did serve as the leading spokesperson for the Yucatec Maya from 1923 until his death in 1948. It is largely thanks to Morley's role in mediating between the Indians and the outside world that Maya people in the Yucatán today regard gringos in a friendly, positive manner.

The leading political heroes of the region are President Lázaro Cárdenas (grandfather of present-day opposition leader Cuauhtémoc Cárdenas II) and his land commissioner, Felipe Carrillo Puerto. In the 1930s, they implemented a plan that gave half the land in Quintana Roo, as well as large tracts throughout Yucatán and Campeche states, to Maya communities under the *ejido* system of communal ownership. Their statues appear in public parks and plazas all over the Yucatán.

With World War II the development of stronger, cheaper synthetic rope fibers spelled the end of the henequen era. Ruins of lavish haciendas such as those at Yaxcopoil, Aké and Bella Flor dot the northern Yucatán landscape today. Many henequen fields have run wild and are reverting to thorny jungle, while others are tended and harvested by descendants of Maya slaves who eke out a small living from the fiber. Many of the majestic mansions that henequen money had built along Paseo de Montejo in Mérida were lost to foreclosure and bankruptcy. After the end of World War II, the economy of the peninsula collapsed until the Yucatán became the poorest region of Mexico. Thousands of Maya villagers starved to death as famine settled over the land once more.

By the 1950s, the Yucatán Peninsula was still such a wild and empty place that for several years before the 1959 Cuban revolution, Fidel Castro operated his guerrilla training camp on the Quintana Roo coast near the site of modern-day Cancún. Although Castro's soldiers numbered several thousand, the secret camp escaped official notice until after the revolution.

THE "CANCÚN MIRACLE" (1968 TO THE PRESENT) In 1968, the Mexican tourism development agency FONATUR performed a computer analysis to determine the best place to develop a mega-resort that would surpass even Acapulco, the reigning beach resort of the day. In retrospect, it seems obvious that the best place for an international resort would be the closest point to the east coast of the United States. At the time, though, the results of the study astonished everyone. Quintana Roo was not even a state then, only an undeveloped federal territory. The only community in the area was Puerto Juárez, a tiny fishing village with about 500 residents.

Rumor has it that the late Don Luis Echeverría Alvarez, president of Mexico during the early development of Cancún, made a fortune unparalleled in the annals of Latin American political corruption by helping his cronies buy Cancún land cheap and then resell it to international resort developers for huge sums. If the rumor is true (and it probably is), the people of the Yucatán certainly got their money's worth. Construction on the bridges that link Cancún Island to the mainland began in 1970, and the first resort hotel opened in 1974.

As Cancún's tourist industry has flourished in the Caribbean sunshine, more than $3 billion corporate and government dollars have been invested in creating the resort city. Today, tourist revenues exceed $4 billion a year. People have flocked not only from the Yucatán countryside but also from Tabasco, Veracruz and Mexico City to find work in the hotel and restaurant industry, and Cancún's population has grown to about 800,000—nearly ten times the entire population of Quintana Roo a generation ago. The per-capita income is the highest in the country, and the unemployment rate is the lowest.

In the 1980s, owing to an oil glut at a time when the nation had borrowed heavily against future oil revenues, Mexico's economy plunged into a terrible depression. Unemployment rates were more than twice as high as they had been in the United States in the depths of the Great Depression, and inflation peaked at 400 percent a year. Despite the nation's agony, Cancún and the Yucatán continued to prosper as the Mexican peso became so nearly valueless in foreign exchange that bargain-basement prices (in dollars) brought international visitors to Cancún in record numbers. Even the destruction of Cancún's Hotel Zone by Hurricane Gilbert in 1988 failed to slow the area's explosive growth. All the existing resorts were remodeled and reopened, and 61 more luxury hotels—two-thirds of the total—have been built along Cancún's beach strip since the hurricane.

At the end of 1994, an even worse financial crisis laid waste to Mexico's economy. Hardest hit was the Mexican middle class, the mainstay of Cancún's summer tourist business. Yet an increase in international tourism due to favorable currency exchange rates offset the loss of summer business, so the local economy of Cancún and the Caribbean coast was virtually unaffected by the recession (though less touristed places such as Campeche were devastated by it). In October 1995, Hurricane Roxanne left a swath of destruction across the peninsula from Tulum to Campeche; damage to Cancún and other major tourist centers on the Caribbean coast was repaired almost instantly, and the effect on tourism was hardly noticeable.

> There are three times more Maya today than the total American Indian population of the United States.

The past 15 years have seen most of the peninsula's roads paved, and even the most remote Maya villages now have electricity. Most villagers own not only shoes but also bicycles or *triciclos* (three-wheeled bikes with small truck beds on the front), and color TVs—a standard of living that would have been unthinkable a few years ago. To earn money for these things, Maya men leave home for months to work on road-building projects or Cancún construction sites. Young Maya people who can pass tough academic achievement tests leave the family cornfields to study at free national universities, mostly around Mérida. The most popular and potentially lucrative fields of study are not medicine, law or architecture but English, hotel and restaurant management and a uniquely Yucatecan college major called "Turismo."

The Maya people are by far the largest indigenous group in North America. Besides the Yucatán, they inhabit the nearby Mexican state of Chiapas (see Chapter Twelve) as well as Belize and Guatemala. The Yucatán has a higher percentage of native people than any other part of Mexico. Despite four and a half centuries of brutal warfare, famine and epidemics that have brought their race to the brink of extinction several times, today the Maya people number 20 times more than the Navajo, the largest Indian tribe in the United States.

Culture

PEOPLE

Although Cancún and the Riviera Maya have attracted a huge influx of workers from other parts of Mexico over the past 20 years, at least half of the Yucatán Peninsula's population still live traditionally in small villages and towns and speak the Yucatec Maya language at home. The future of the Yucatán, like its heritage, belongs to them.

To any knowledgeable traveler in the Yucatán, it must seem nothing short of miraculous that the Yucatec Maya have survived in the wake of forces that have reduced their numbers to fewer than 5000 at least three times. Equally miraculous, they have kept their culture distinct and separate from that of their ladino neighbors over a span of centuries. Even today, the Yucatec Maya's culture has less in common with modern Mexico than with the ways of their pyramid-building ancestors who lived during the time of the Roman Empire.

The character of modern Yucatán constantly reflects the delicate, at times uneasy, balance between Maya and ladino ways. More than 90 percent of ladino Mexicans, the vast majority of the Mexican population, are of mixed Indian and Spanish blood and tend to view their Indian ancestry with pride, yet paradoxically treat modern-day Indians as inferior. Indian laborers perform the most menial labor and are paid much lower wages than ladinos. Though not immediately obvious to outsiders, there is widespread discrimination against Indians in public transportation, restaurants and other facilities. *Indígenas* can gain access to the mainstream culture, with its social and economic advantages, by attending school and adopting ladino attitudes and social ways, but this assimilation comes at the expense of their Maya heritage. Maya language and folkways are not taught in Mexican schools—not even at the Universidad Mayab (Mayan University) north of Mérida near the ruins of the ancient Maya capital at Dzibilchaltún. Yet somehow, perhaps because of the Maya's isolation, resilience and history, their traditions remain very much alive in this new millennium.

A note on terminology: In Spanish colonial Mexico, although there were no taboos against interracial marriages, the system of *castas*, or racial classes, divided the population into 16 separate categories. For instance, there was a special category for a person born of a black mother and a father of Spanish descent who was born in Mexico. Today, the caste system is simplified, but words referring to race or culture can pose questions of political correctness. To avoid giving offense, follow these guidelines:

In English, we often use the term *Indian,* which most American Indian tribes prefer to *Native American.* But in Spanish, always use *indígena* (or, in the Yucatán, *Maya*)—never *indio,* which is a highly offensive racial slur. Many rural areas are inhabited by both Maya and mestizo villagers; country people irrespective of race are called *campesinos.*

The mainstream culture in Mexico, derived from Spanish colonial tradition, is called *ladino*. It is essentially the same as what is called the Latino, Hispanic or Chicano culture in the United States. A *mestizo* is a ladino person of mixed Spanish and Indian ancestry.

The polite word for someone from the United States or Canada is *norteamericano* (North American). Some Mexicans object to this terminology on the grounds that their country is also part of North America, contending that the correct word is *gringo*. Gringo originated during the Mexican War as a pejorative term loosely meaning "rich white honky," but today it is generally not intended as an insult; instead, it has come to mean "tourist." Applying the word to oneself (*"Lo siento. Soy gringo."*) will excuse just about any social blunder.

CUISINE

Yucatán has the most distinctive regional cuisine to be found anywhere in Mexico. Chicken *(pollo)* and pork *(puerco)* are its mainstays. One of the most common regional dishes is *pollo pibil*, chicken marinated in a sauce of achiote, Seville orange and spices, then barbecued in banana leaves. The same dish made with pork is called *cochinita pibil*. Another dinner entrée served just about everywhere is *pocchuc*, pork fillet cooked in a tangy sauce of Seville orange and pickled red onions. *Puchero,* a stew made of chicken, pork, carrots, squash, cabbage, potatoes, yams and bananas, is traditionally served on Sundays in Yucatecan homes. Another typical Yucatec meat dish is *longaniza*, a spicy sausage that resembles hard salami.

> Street vendors often peel mangoes, skewer them on wooden sticks through the soft spot at one end of the seed, and sell them on the street as refreshments.

Turkey *(pavo)* is by far the most common meat served in Yucatec Maya households. Most small restaurants prefer chicken to turkey, partly because a turkey's size makes it less practical for cooking individual orders and partly because turkey has traditionally had a reputation in this region as a peasant meat, less classy than chicken. The turkey dish most commonly seen in restaurants is *pavo escabeche*, strips of turkey marinated in a spicy sauce and served with pickled onions. In smaller towns, tacos are made with grilled, shredded turkey. At home, Maya women cook a soupy stew using chunks of turkey with the bone left in.

For lighter fare, the best bet is *sopa de lima*, a soup made with chicken, fried tortilla pieces and a slice of lime. (The large, sweeter Mexican lime, or *lima*, is not the same fruit known in the United States as a lime, which Mexicans call a *limón*.) Yucatecan tacos, called *salbutes* or *panuchos* depending on how the tortilla is cooked, are made with shredded turkey, pickled onion and avocado. A popular vegetarian dish is *papadzules*, chopped hard-boiled eggs rolled up in tortillas and served in a pumpkin-seed sauce. *Frijol con puerco*, a standard meal in many Yucatec homes, is made from black beans and slivers of pork; smothered in chunky grilled tomato sauce and garnished with radish, cilantro and onion, it is served over rice.

While most restaurants in the Yucatán also serve *norteamericano* breakfasts, such as bacon and scrambled eggs or hot cakes (*hot ceks* or *jotceks* in Spanish), the regional breakfast specialty is *huevos motuleños*—fried eggs served over tortillas spread with refried black beans and topped with tomato salsa, peas, diced ham and shredded cheese. Another common Yucatec breakfast is a *plata de frutas* (fruit plate), usually made with *sandía* (watermelon), *piña* (pineapple), *melón* (cantaloupe) and papaya, often served with a side order of black beans and tortillas. *Chilaquiles* is a breakfast casserole of yesterday's tortillas stir-fried with slivered chicken, onions and spices and topped with crumbled *queso ranchero*, a hard, white cheese.

Campeche has its own distinctive cuisine, which originated in just a few restaurants but has spread throughout much of Latin America. It starts with *campechanos*—square, spicy puff-up bar snacks—and drifts into such entrées as *ceviche campeche*, a toss of raw, marinated shrimp and octopus, or *pan de casón*, soft tortillas filled with shredded baby shark meat. A seasonal Campeche specialty is *pibipollo* (not to be confused with *pollo pibil*), a chicken-tamale pie that Maya people traditionally share with their bygone ancestors during their prolonged Day of the Dead celebration.

Aside from chilies, another vegetable that is common in the Yucatán is jicama, a potatolike tuber with an unobtrusive flavor and a crunchy texture similar to that of water chestnuts. Street vendors sell plastic cups of jicama, sliced into long strips and seasoned with lime and ground red chili.

Whether you're strolling among the vendors at a public market or slowing down for a speed bump marking a village along the highway, someone is almost certain to offer to sell you some fruit. *Chinos* (oranges) and *limas* (Mexican limes) are grown in groves throughout the Yucatán interior. Other common fruits include many you probably won't find in your local supermarket back home. There are *ciruela maya* (a small, round, green plum), *mamey* (a large fruit, brown outside, orange inside, that tastes like a sweet potato and has a texture similar to an avocado's), *sapodilla* ("custard apple," the fruit of the chicle tree, looks like a brown crabapple, tastes like dessert custard) and many varieties of mango. The most common are the pale, firm mango manila and the juicy, reddish mango indio. Several varieties of bananas are sold throughout the region, from finger-length, very sweet yellow bananas to *plátanos*—hard, green jumbo bananas that are sliced into strips and fried.

Hot Stuff

The ghastly looking green sauce in little bottles set on most restaurant tables is *salsa habanera*. It is made from the *chile habanero* (the Maya name for it means "crying tongue"). The *habanero* comes in red, green or yellow; it looks small and innocent but is way hotter than a *jalapeño*. Mexican men sometimes eat a *habanero* to demonstrate their machismo. Serious chile connoisseurs on both sides of the border rank *habaneros* on a par with great sex. The sauce comes in either green or red (equally hot, but the red contains fully ripened peppers with a somewhat different taste) and is about as piquant as tabasco sauce. In some restaurants you may have to ask for *salsa habanera* at your table, since it is commonly assumed that gringos don't like spicy foods or sauces.

At least 15 different varieties of chilies are commonly used in cooking and sold in public markets. Contrary to common belief, chilies are *not* peppers; Columbus mistook them for peppers because their piquant taste reminded him of the sought-after black pepper of India, and the name stuck (along with the misnomer *Indian* for the people who had been cultivating the chilies for centuries). Mexicans can distinguish the flavors of different chilies as easily as gringos tell the difference between vanilla and chocolate. Among the most common Mexican varieties are *chile poblano,* a mild-flavored, dark green chili that is often stuffed. Dried *poblano,* called *chile ancho,* is commonly used in moles and salsas. The blazing-hot little red or green chile de árbol is also used in hot sauces and sometimes served whole in restaurants (to be diced into tiny bits and sprinkled on food). *Chipotle*, a smoked *jalapeño*, adds a distinctive taste to some salsas.

In coastal areas, of course, nearly all food is seafood. As you visit fishing villages along the Gulf coast, it is not unusual to find that the entire menu consists of *camarones* (shrimp) prepared in a dozen or more different styles. Particularly along the Caribbean coast, other widely available fresh-catch seafood includes *langosta* (spiny lobster), *jaibas* and *cangrejos* (types of crab), *caracol* (conch), *pulpo* (octopus) and *calamar* (squid), as well as *huachinango* (red snapper), *sierra* (mackerel), *tiburón* (shark) and barracuda. The most typical seafood dish in the Yucatán, ceviche is any kind of raw seafood diced with tomato, onion, garlic, lime juice and chilies. Conch is the favorite ceviche ingredient in the Yucatán; octopus, mackerel and shark are also good.

All familiar-brand Mexican beers are widely available in the Yucatán. Those brewed in the region include light Cerveza Montejo and two dark beers, *León Negro* and *Negro Modelo*. As for other alcoholic beverages, the regional favorite is *xtabentún*, a strong, sweet honey-and-anise liqueur. While claims that it was the nectar of the ancient Maya god-kings are probably exaggerated, since they had no distilling process back then, there's some evidence to support the traditional Maya belief that it is an aphrodisiac; try it and find out for yourself.

LANGUAGE Of course you'll get more out of a Latin American trip if you speak fluent Spanish. But what if, like most people who live in the United States, you don't? Many people who have never studied Spanish worry more than they ought to about traveling to Mexico. One of the fundamental lessons foreign travel teaches is that people can communicate even though they don't know a word of each other's languages. Words help, but it's your tone of voice, the expression on your face, and gestures or sign language that often count for more when it comes to making yourself understood.

In the parts of the Yucatán where international visitors come in large numbers, English is the key to a good job in the tourist industry, and it is widely taught in secondary schools and colleges, so many people you will meet as a visitor will speak at least a little English. But that is less the case as you venture away from tourist areas. Some residents of Campeche city study English at the university, but as you travel to other parts of Campeche state, few locals speak any English at all.

Even in bilingual areas like Quintana Roo's *Corredor Turístico*, people will relate to you better if you attempt to speak Spanish, no matter how poorly. It pays in smiles if you study for your trip by practicing a few useful phrases like "*¿Cuanto vale esto?*" (How much is this worth?), "*La cuenta, por favor*" (The check, please), "*¿Tiene usted un habitación para la noche?*" (Do you have a room for the night?) and "*¿No habría modo de resolver el pro-*

blema de otra manera?" (Isn't there some other way to resolve the problem?). You'll find these and many others in any of the Spanish phrasebooks sold in U.S. bookstores. I like the *Berlitz Latin American Spanish Phrase Book & Dictionary* (Berlitz, 1998), which contains regionalisms of both Mexico and other countries. Spanish-language instructional cassette tapes can help you learn Spanish pronunciation, which is much more straightforward than that of English.

One hint: Ask questions that can be answered with a yes or no, with one word or with a number. It can be very frustrating to ask for directions and receive a cheerful reply so long, fast and complicated that you can't make sense of it. Better to ask questions like "Is this the right way to_____?" "How many blocks?" "On the right or left?"

Many people who have studied Spanish in school find themselves helpless when it comes to actually communicating in Mexico. Once you've learned it, Spanish vocabulary stays stored in the deep recesses of the mind, but it's often hard to bring it to the surface after years of disuse. Before you leave for Mexico, you may find that a few weeks using aids such as cassette tapes can help attune your ear and tongue to the language. A painless way to tune into Spanish is to spend your TV-viewing hours watching Spanish-language cable channels or rented Spanish videos. The Mexican motion-picture industry is undergoing a renaissance these days with internationally acclaimed films such as *Como Agua Para Chocolate* (*Like Water for Chocolate*), well worth watching repeatedly in Spanish with or without the English subtitles. Most U.S. video stores can order Mexican films and Spanish-version videocassettes (subtitled or dubbed) of almost any popular Hollywood film. Some DVD movies contain both English and Spanish versions on the same disk.

Many rural people in the Yucatán speak a patois of Maya and Spanish as their primary language. Although anthropologists say that *maya puro* ("pure Maya") is no longer spoken anywhere, even Mexicans who have lived in the Yucatán for generations find the native dialect almost impossible to understand. Resources for learning Yucatec Maya are few. The most complete book currently available is the *Itzah Maya–Spanish–English Dictionary* by Charles Hofling et al. (University of Utah Press, 1997), a 900-page tome that is designed for scholars rather than travelers and costs $75 in paperback. More accessible and affordable, *Maya for Travelers and Students: a Guide to Language and Culture in Yucatán* by Gary Bevington (Austin: University of Texas Press, 1995) and its companion audiotape, *Spoken Maya for Travelers and Students* by Fernando Ojeda (Austin: University of Texas Press, 1995) show how the Maya language works and teach a vocabulary of more than 3000 words. Or you can just strike up conversations with Maya vendors and craftspeople and ask them to teach you a few phrases. For starters, *Bixabol boxkauol ek* (pronounced "Bish-a-BOL bosh-ka-WALL eck") is a formal way of saying "hello."

Be sensitive if you try to talk with indigenous people in their own language, though. Unlike Spanish-speaking Mexicans, who are positively impressed when visitors try to speak their language, some Maya people are offended when outsiders try to speak Maya. This attitude has its roots in 19th-century slavery, when the language barrier between Spanish and Maya speakers was almost absolute and the only non-Indians who spoke Maya were field overseers. Today, some indigenous people—especially hotel and restaurant workers in Cancún and along the Riviera Maya—take such pride in their ability to speak Spanish or English that they resent visitors who seem to assume they are uneducated Maya-speakers.

FOUR

Cancún

For most visitors to the Yucatán Peninsula, a stop in Cancún is inevitable. About 90 jetliners a day arrive at Cancún's international airport, most of them from Miami, Houston and other U.S. cities. Today there are only a few international flights to Mérida, and most of them go there only three or four times a week and cost significantly more than flights to Cancún. Compared with driving your own vehicle (1550 kilometers from Brownsville, Texas, or 2232 from El Paso) or enduring a grueling three-day bus trip, there's no question that a direct flight to Cancún is the quickest and easiest way to go.

Seasoned travelers like to say with disdain that Cancún isn't *really* Mexico, but in truth Cancún is a place as uniquely Mexican as Las Vegas, Nevada, is American. Like Las Vegas, Cancún is a newly built city in the midst of a formerly unpopulated wasteland, with no reason for its existence other than resort fun—flashy, gaudy, steeped in money and dubious taste, and one of the fastest-growing cities around.

As recently as 30 years ago, Cancún was practically unpopulated—a fishing camp with about 500 residents in the surrounding area. Quintana Roo was so unpopulated that in 1974 it became the last territory in Mexico to attain statehood. Then in 1968, as the result of a computer survey (so the story goes), the Mexican government's tourism development agency "discovered" the 14-mile-long barrier island known as Isla Cancún ("Bowl of Snakes" Island). With its remote location, as isolated from the rest of Mexico as if it were a pristine Caribbean island, yet closer to the major population centers of the U.S. East Coast than almost any other tropical beach you can visit without a passport, Cancún had the potential to surpass all of Mexico's existing beach resorts, even Acapulco and Puerto Vallarta, and rival any in the world.

Promoting the idea of a mega-resort on the Caribbean coast of the Yucatán, the government persuaded some 80 international hotel chains to invest more than $3 billion in just 25 years. The result is an amazing cavalcade of world-class resorts, now known as the *Zona Hotelera,* or Hotel Zone, that lines the slender strip of Cancún now attracts more international visitors than all other Mexican resorts combined and boasts 90 luxury resort hotels and a total of more than 27,000 rooms. Tourism never slows down very much. During the winter months, the city caters almost exclusively to English-speaking visitors from the United States and Canada who come to escape the snow and ice back home. In the summer, European travelers join the hordes of middle-class Mexican vacationers who descend on the beaches to escape the sweltering heat of the interior. International business conventions keep things going between seasons.

Cancún is a transcultural city, where English is heard as much as Spanish, where U.S. dollars are spent as easily as Mexican pesos, where every resident is a newcomer. Whether your plans involve a quick visit to Chichén Itzá or a month-long exploration into remote jungles, Cancún can serve as a glitzy base camp for your journey into the land of the Maya. Strategically located at the junction between the highway that leads south along the Caribbean coast of Quintana Roo, with its legendary reefs and beaches, and the highway that leads west into the strange world of the Maya, Cancún is a playground for grownups, where wet and wild days of snorkeling, sailboarding or sunbathing lead into nights fuzzy with margaritas and a disco beat.

For the adventurous, Cancún is the gateway to the Yucatán Peninsula and a world of adventure. A day trip from Cancún can take you to the mysterious jungle-cloaked ruins of Cobá or the offshore bird sanctuary of Isla Contoy. On a two-day excursion, you can visit the stately old Spanish colonial capital of Mérida, swim in an underground cenote once believed to be sacred or see the flamingo breeding grounds on the remote coastline of Río Lagartos. And by taking an extra week in tandem with your Cancún beach resort stay, you open your journey to a wealth of possibilities ranging from the sites of magnificent, rarely visited ancient cities to coral reefs breathtaking in both size and abundance of sea life and to the distant, brooding majesty of Mexico's last great rainforest.

▼▼▼▼▼▼▼▼▼▼
Hotel Zone

Unless you have reservations at one of the 90 luxury resorts that line the Hotel Zone, you probably don't belong in Cancún for longer than it takes to make transportation connections to more folkloric reaches of the peninsula. Resorts are virtually the only industry in this city of nearly half a million people, generating economic prosperity on a scale previously unknown in the Yucatán.

SIGHTS
The Hotel Zone occupies a narrow, 17-kilometer-long island with only one thoroughfare—Paseo Kukulcán, a busy four-lane divided highway that becomes a congested city street toward the north end of the island. Paseo Kukulcán connects to the mainland by bridges at both ends. The south bridge is five kilometers from Cancún International Airport on the mainland, while the north bridge is four kilometers from downtown Cancún and the bus station.

The entire length of Cancún Island has only one street—Paseo Kukulcán (aka Kukulcán Boulevard)—and it is entirely lined along the beach side with large, expensive resort hotels, many of them at the end of long drives flanked by acres of verdant lawns and lush

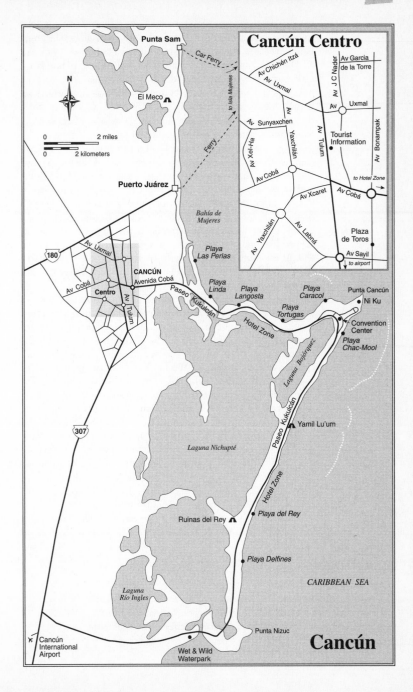

Punta Sam

Car Ferry

to Isla Mujeres

El Meco

Ferry

N

0   2 miles
0   2 kilometers

Puerto Juárez

Bahía de
Mujeres

180
Av Uxmal

CANCÚN
Avenida Cobá

Av Cobá

Centro

Av Tulum

Paseo Kukulcán

Playa
Las Perlas

Playa
Linda

Playa
Langosta

Hotel Zone

Playa
Tortugas

Playa
Caracol

Punta Cancún

Ni Ku

Convention
Center

Playa
Chac-Mool

Laguna Bojórquez

307

Laguna Nichupté

Paseo Kukulcán

Yamil Lu'um

Hotel Zone

Ruinas del Rey

Playa del Rey

Playa Delfines

Laguna
Río Ingles

CARIBBEAN SEA

Cancún
International
Airport

Punta Nizuc

Wet & Wild
Waterpark

Cancún

Cancún Centro

Av Chichén Itzá

Av Uxmal

Av J C Nader

Av Garcia
de la Torre

Av   Uxmal

Av
Sunyaxchen

Av Xel-Ha

Yaxchilán

Av Tulum

Tourist
Information

Av Bonampak

Av Cobá

Av Xcaret

Av Cobá

to Hotel Zone

Av Yaxchilán

Av Labná

Plaza
de Toros

Av Sayil

to airport

tropical landscaping. Don't look in the Hotel Zone for taco stands or local handicrafts. There are none. You *will* find Denny's, Domino's Pizza, KFC, Burger King, Pizza Hut and your choice of McDonald's locations, as well as Planet Hollywood, a Hard Rock Café and plenty of imported designer beachwear with startling price tags and T-shirts that say "Cancún" in imaginative ways. This blatant Americanness not only makes first-time vacationers from the United States and Canada feel "safe" but also offers wealthy Mexicans a taste of north-of-the-border style.

To get a good feel for the scope of the tourist industry in Cancún, hop into your rental car or aboard one of the inexpensive shuttle buses that constantly run up and down the Hotel Zone, and cruise the length of this island strip along its only street, Paseo Kukulcán, aptly named for the Maya sun god. Though bounded on the side away from the sea by **Laguna Nichupté**, a broad lagoon that is about two miles across in places, the island, shaped like the number 7, almost touches the mainland at each end. At the south end, crossing the bridge takes you to the airport road and Route 307, the main highway to Tulum, Felipe Carrillo Puerto and Chetumal.

Just off the tip of the island, known as **Punta Nizuc**, is Cancún's local diving reef. This underwater fantasyland of coral formations teems with colorful fish, not to mention snorkelers by the hundreds and yellow, glass-sided Sub See Explorer sightseeing boats reminiscent of the "Twenty Thousand Leagues Under the Sea" submarine ride at Disney World. The base of operations for snorkelers is **Paradise**, a floating manmade island with a restaurant, a gift shop and sunbathing decks. AquaWorld water sports center operates both the "island" and the boats that take you there, as well as scuba-diving expeditions to other parts of the reef. The newest addition to the recreation complex is the Rocket, a two-person cage suspended slingshotlike from two towers that are more than 100 feet tall; when the hook that holds the cage to the ground is released, you hurl high into the sky for a brief blast of weightlessness. ~ Paseo Kukulcán, Km. 15.2; 9-848-8326; www. aquaworld.com.mx, e-mail info@aquaworld.com.

Also at Punta Nizuc, located at the mainland side of the bridge to Cancún Island, **Wet & Wild Waterpark** (formerly called Parque

Nizuc) has water toboggans, a 180-foot-tall rollercoaster water slide, a wave pool and other features common to Wet'n Wild water parks everywhere. The park also features Cancún's only swim-with-dolphins program and a snorkeling area stocked with sting-rays, nurse sharks and colorful tropical fish. ~ Paseo Kukulcán, Km. 25; 9-881-3000.

If Cancún is your first or only chance to dive the coral reefs of the Mexican Caribbean, Punta Nizuc will prove memorable enough. If you have seen Cozumel's Palancar Reef or Chetumal's Chinchorro Reef, you will find this one disappointing. Despite strictly enforced "look but don't touch" regulations, daily crowds of vacationers have exacted their toll on the delicate underwater landscape. The hundreds of wrecked boats that still litter the coast from the 1988 hurricane have been dragged to a heap off Punta Cancún (the elbow at the other end of the island) to create an ar-tificial reef, providing a new habitat for fish that live in the pro-tection of the coral reefs and creating an area for snorkeling and diving. Diving at Punta Nizuc is now restricted in hopes that peo-ple will explore these shipwrecks and leave the natural reef to re-cover from the inevitable impact of too many tourists.

Search hard enough and you'll find patches of "real" Mexico even in the Hotel Zone. One poignant reminder is **Ruinas del Rey**, the remains of a Maya ceremonial center dating back to the Post-classic era, set picturesquely among the palm trees on the lagoon side toward the south end of the island. Though about as archaeo-logically boring as a Maya ruin can be, the temples around Cancún are a reminder—the first of many you'll discover as you further ex-plore Mexico's Caribbean shores—of the vast reach of the Maya coastal trade empire, which once spanned from the Bay Islands of Honduras to the salt beds of Yucatán's north coast. The largest site in the Cancún area, del Rey consists of two plazas surrounded by temples and ceremonial platforms, all built between A.D. 1300 and 1400. The ruins are named for a sculpture of a human head found in the main temple when the site was excavated in 1975–76; on scant evidence the sculpture is reputed to be the image of a Maya king (*rey* in Spanish). According to one exotic legend, the tiny openings in the ruins show that they were occupied by *aluxes*, bewitched Maya pygmies who stood about 18 inches tall. Ruinas del Rey has recently been incorporated into the Hilton Resort complex, and the ancient foundations, columns and platforms are now virtually surrounded by a golf course. At the entrance is a re-created Maya village, and sound-and-light shows are presented nightly. Admission. ~ Paseo Kukulcán, Km. 17; 9-881-8000.

Another minor Maya temple, with a smaller annex not quite attached to it, **Yamil Lu'um** stands on the highest point of Cancún, next to the Sheraton at Km. 12.5. Yucatec Maya for "Hilly Land,"

Text continued on page 106.

Three Days and Two Nights in Cancún

Drive to the airport an hour early, leave your car in long-term parking, check in, present your proof of citizenship, pass through the metal detector and board the plane. Before you know it, you're flying high above the Gulf of Mexico while filling out the Mexican visa and customs paperwork your flight attendant hands out. Soon you descend into a jungle of greenery with the blue, blue Caribbean in the distance. Deplaning, you walk single-file to the immigration area, where agents check your proof of citizenship again and stamp your tourist card. Next, pick up your luggage and clear customs (a process that's usually easier than filling out the paperwork), change some dollars into pesos, and you're there—an exotic Latin American country! (So how come everybody's still speaking English?)

DAY 1 • Check into your beachfront resort hotel. In your room, immediately change into a swimsuit and sandals and step outside to admire the view from your balcony. Almost every room in the Hotel Zone has fantastic vistas of the sea's turquoise shallows and azure depths as well as of the swimming pool and swim-up palapa bar complex directly below you. Feeling self-conscious about your body? This is a good time to scope out some of your fellow guests and notice that they, too, have just escaped from sitting behind desks in chilly northern climates. The occasional golden-tanned hardbody you may see is probably on the hotel payroll. You could probably relax on your balcony for the rest of the day, but hey, this is your vacation. Time's a-wastin'! Head for the beach.

• One way to end your afternoon is in air-conditioned comfort at one of the clubby cigar bars you'll find in many Cancún resort hotels. Sure, tobacco is disgusting and bad for you, but these are Cohibas—Cuban cigars, illegal in the U.S., hand-rolled (so the legend goes) on the thighs of *cubano* virgins. See whether they taste any different from Dutch Masters.

• Once the sun sets or your stomach growls (whichever comes first), head out to dinner at one of those typical Cancún restaurants where, while waiting for the entrée, you can gulp a dozen or so tequila slammers while a waitperson puts a saucepan hatlike on your head and bangs on it with a spoon, then chase it with a huge, bright, fruity concoction containing enough alcohol to paralyze a buffalo.

- After dinner, head for a giant disco like **La Boom** or **Dady Rock**. Hop from club to club up and down Paseo Kukulcán. There's plenty of time to check them all out—most stay open until dawn.

DAY 2
- After about 90 minutes of sleep, awaken with a furious sunburn and a feeling as if bees were living in your head. You may question whether another day on the beach is really such a good idea, but hey, you're on vacation, right? Maybe this is the time to rent some water-sports equipment and try your choice of sailboarding, jet-skiing, scuba diving or parasailing.

- Later in the day, when your skin has turned so crimson that people are starting to stare, there's only one option left: go shopping. Be astonished at how much silver jewelry can fit into a single retail mall, and how much it costs even at "50% off." If your friends back home aren't sufficiently impressed by your suntan, a copy of your next Visa statement is sure to knock their socks off!

- It's your vacation, you're in wild-and-crazy Cancún, and the nighttime is the right time to paar-TEEE! Or not. Maybe the human body, mind and spirit can endure only so much tequila and technopop before your survival instinct starts whispering, "Don't you wish you were back home watching *The Beach* on video instead?" In this moment of lucidity, phone down to room service for dinner. Pull up a chair on your private balcony, slather yourself with some kind of soothing sunburn cream and let the gentle evening breeze cool your tortured skin. Now's the time to remember that you brought along this book—*Hidden Cancún & the Yucatán*. Get it out. Open it up. Notice that less than ten percent of the book is actually about Cancún. Skip past the Cancún chapter and spend a few quiet hours reading up on the fascinating, exotic world that lies just beyond the big-resort tourist zone. Let your imagination fly.

DAY 3
- Check out of your Cancún hotel. Rent a car. Hit the road. Mystery and adventure await. *Now* you're on vacation!

Yamil Lu'um consists of a fair-sized Postclassic (A.D. 1200–1500) temple with a smaller annex typical of the mysterious little structures found all the way up and down the coast from Punta Juárez to the Sian Ka'an Biosphere Reserve. Fragments of the tiny, badly deteriorated temple of **Ni Ku** can be seen on the grounds of the Camino Real hotel on Punta Cancún. There are two more temples at the Pok-Ta-Pok golf course that date back to the 14th century.

HIDDEN ► Serious Maya ruins enthusiasts may wish to drive or take a taxi to the site of **El Meco**, where a partially collapsed temple stands atop a 40-foot-tall pyramid, the tallest architectural structure in northern Quintana Roo. Fragments are all that remain of stone-and-stucco serpent-head sculptures that once ornamented the pyramid and other temples and the platforms surrounding it. The site is undergoing restoration, and the Instituto Nacional de Antropología e Historia has recently declared it open to the public. Admission. ~ Six kilometers north of Cancún on the highway between Puerto Juárez and Punta Sam.

As you drive or ride along the busy thoroughfare of the Hotel Zone, it may seem hard to believe that the primeval wilderness of the Quintana Roo coast lies only a few miles away. Yet much of the mainland side of Laguna Nichupté remains undeveloped. Narrow channels winding through mangrove jungles teeming with egrets, herons, turtles and occasional alligators lead to secluded spots such as **Laguna Río Ingles**, where freshwater springs near the shore offer a different kind of snorkeling experience. Aqua-World offers two-hour "jungle tours" of the lagoon on wave-runners, the nautical equivalent of a motorcycle, which are easier than a motorboat to maneuver through the mangrove maze. ~ Paseo Kukulcán, Km. 15.2; 9-848-8326; www.aquaworld.com.mx, e-mail info@aquaworld.com.

Of course, the main focus of activity along Cancún's Hotel Zone is the almost unbroken chain of a dozen sparkling white beaches that trim the windward side of Isla Cancún, lapped by the picture-perfect turquoise waters of the Caribbean. If you were to begin walking up the beach from one end of the island at dawn, it would be afternoon before you reached the other end. Most of the beaches are quite narrow, though, partly because of 1988's Hurricane Gilbert, but mostly because the hotels were built too close to the water. All beaches are public by law. If you are not a guest at one of the beachfront resorts, finding a place to park can be tricky at some beaches. And it's easy enough to reach the beach through the lobby of any hotel, but security guards try to keep nonguests from entering the hotel grounds from the beach, so returning to your car can be tricky. For more information, see the "Beaches & Parks" section of this chapter.

In a fiercely competitive retail atmosphere, Cancún's malls strive to be as much theme park as shopping center. The most striking example is **La Isla Shopping Village**, which features MayaVentura, an elaborate maze packed with passageways, game challenges, mysterious pseudo-ancient temples and a high-energy soundtrack. La Isla also has its own aquarium and movie theater multiplex. ~ Paseo Kukulcán, Km. 12.5; www.mayaventura.com.mx.

International convention trade keeps the Hotel Zone jumping right through the off-season. The **Cancún Convention Center** has 40,000 square feet of conference and exhibit space, with another 65,000 square feet of retail shop space. The ground floor of the convention center houses the city's only museum, the Instituto Nacional de Antropología e Historia's **Museo Arqueológico de Cancún**, with stelae from the ruins at Cobá and displays of artifacts from Tulum, Kohunlich and other ancient Maya sites in Quintana Roo. ~ Paseo Kukulcán, Km. 9; 9-883-0305.

> It is best to arrive on an early flight, leaving plenty of time to search for a place to spend the night or, if worst comes to worst, to get out of town.

The island's elbow, where Paseo Kukulcán veers suddenly west toward the mainland at Km. 8.5 near Punta Cancún, is known as **La Glorieta** in Spanish or "The Hub" in gringo. Marked by a lofty free-form monument in the center of a traffic roundabout, this is Cancún's upscale commercial center, lined with chic shopping malls, nightclubs and restaurants. Continue west on Paseo Kukulcán and you will be on your way to downtown Cancún, Puerto Juárez, Punta Sam (where ferries leave for Isla Mujeres) and the main highway to Mérida.

LODGING

Few resorts in the world can touch Cancún's hotel scene. Some 88 hotels parade along the sea, their grounds boasting fantasy landscaping and pool areas that are works of art. Guest rooms offer every creature comfort imaginable, and hotel nightclubs lure a jet-set crowd.

The Mexican government points proudly to the 85 percent of Cancún hotel units that are rated five-star, which means not only that the hotels live up to a high standard of luxury but also that they are above the laws that regulate room rates in hotels of lower stature. From about a week before Christmas to early April, a room in a Cancún resort hotel costs around $200 a night (the rest of the year, rates run about 30 percent lower).

Relatively few people pay full rate, however, since a high percentage of Cancún's hotel rooms are block-booked in advance by "four-day-and-three-night" tour packagers in the United States. If you plan to spend more than one night in Cancún on your trip, these combination airfare-and-hotel offers are worth looking into, since the room prices are typically a fraction of what you would pay if you booked your room directly. Most packages let you postpone your return flight for several weeks as you explore the rest of the peninsula. Some let you split up your Cancún days, staying at a resort the night you arrive and the night you leave, and some also include a discount rate on a car rental.

Beginning at the island's south end, closest to the airport and farthest from shopping and nightlife, the first hotel you come to is **Club Med**. This 429-room resort on the most remote point of Isla Cancún is typical Club Med, which started on the Riviera and has spread around the world. If you're looking for a quiet place to lie on the beach away from the tequila-soaked fun-in-the-sun scene at the far end of the island, all-inclusive rates make this hotel a bargain—especially for water-sports enthusiasts. Waterskiing, sailing, windsurfing and snorkeling are included in the lodging rate, as are all meals. An action-packed, sports-oriented activity schedule runs the gamut from basketball to ping-pong. There is an additional charge for scuba rentals or lessons. No children under age 12. Air conditioning. ~ Punta Nizuc; 9-885-2900, fax 9-885-2290, or 800-258-2633 in the U.S.; www.clubmed.com. ULTRA-DELUXE.

The chic **Westin Regina** has 293 rooms, with a choice of either the sea or lagoon exposure. The rooms are spacious, with colorful, contemporary furnishings, and some have balconies. Facilities include *five* outdoor pools, plus tennis courts, a fitness center, a water sports marina and a boat dock. Air conditioning. ~ Paseo Kukulcán, Km. 20.8; 9-885-0086, fax 9-885-0666, or 800-228-3000 in the U.S., 800-524-5405 in Mexico; www.westin.com, e-mail westin@sybcom.com. ULTRA-DELUXE.

The **Royal Solaris Caribe** has 500 light, airy rooms and suites with decor that strives for a Mediterranean villa look—everything glaringly white. The guest units are built around a swimming pool and health club fronting on a broad, soft beach. This is a sporty place, where you can rent anything from a pedal boat to a sea kayak or sailboard. There are tennis, basketball and volleyball courts, a lively disco, seven restaurants, four bars and a full slate of daily activities. Air conditioning. ~ Paseo Kukulcán, Km. 19.5;

LAST-MINUTE LODGING

Arriving in Cancún without reservations is an invitation to adventure. Cancún's hotels operate at more than 90 percent of capacity year-round. Even in the depths of the rainy season, Cancún's international reputation as a convention city frequently fills the hotels with businesspeople. But even in the busy winter months, last-minute vacancies do come up. Commission agents for some hotels and condominiums hang around the airport watching for people who don't seem to know where they're going and rent rooms at surprisingly low prices—under $50 in winter or $40 in summer—for a first-rate room in a highrise.

9-885-0600, fax 9-885-0354; www.clubsolaris.com.mx, e-mail referido@clubsolaris.com.mx. ULTRA-DELUXE.

The **El Pueblito Beach Hotel** offers the least expensive accommodations in the southern part of the Hotel Zone. Located across the boulevard from Ruinas del Rey, the hotel has 240 guest rooms and suites. The decor is plain and simple, like a standard midrange businesspersons' motor inn in the United States; most units have balconies overlooking a swimming pool or the sea. The hotel has five swimming pools, plus a waterslide. Air conditioning. ~ Paseo Kukulcán, Km. 18.3; 9-885-8800, fax 9-885-0731; e-mail pueblito reservations@acnet.net. MODERATE.

The **Hilton Cancún Beach & Golf Resort** offers Cancún's largest golf course, a long stretch of "private" beach—actually, all beaches in Mexico are public property, but this one can only be reached through the hotel with its watchful security guards—and a huge ballroom overlooking the Caribbean. There are also seven swimming pools plus outdoor jacuzzis, tennis courts and water sports equipment. Each of the 426 huge, ultramodern guest rooms and suites has a large terrace with a sea view. The hotel seems to have been designed for business-and-pleasure travelers, with meeting facilities, secretarial service and such in-room amenities as three phone lines and a personal computer connection. Air conditioning. ~ Paseo Kukulcán, Km. 17; 9-881-8000, fax 9-881-8080, or 888-594-2483 in the U.S.; www.hiltoncancun.com, e-mail reservations@hiltoncancun.com. ULTRA-DELUXE.

The **Gran Oasis Resort** has a central eight-story pyramid that houses the reception area, restaurants, a lounge and 232 guest rooms. The pyramid is connected by air-conditioned walkways to four long buildings parallel to the beach that contain another 792 guest rooms, half of them with views of the water. Facilities include eight levels of swimming pools, a complete spa, a nine-hole executive golf course and a full range of organized activities from beach volleyball to bingo. Decor is simple and contemporary; all rooms have balconies, but only the more expensive ones have sea views. Air conditioning. ~ Paseo Kukulcán, Km. 16; 9-885-0867, fax 9-881-7006. ULTRA-DELUXE.

A lofty, thatched palapa roof that must surely be the largest in the Yucatán covers the vast lobby of the **Fiesta Americana Condesa**. Glowing with Miami Beach–style pastel hues on rough-textured stucco, the towers that house the 502 guest rooms and suites in this palatial hotel stand apart from one another, separated by a labyrinth of walkways and hanging bridges around and over the free-form, multilevel pool with its swim-up palapa bar. The rooms are bright and large, and most overlook the pool area to the beach and sea beyond. Air conditioning. ~ Paseo Kukulcán, Km. 15.5; 9-881-4200, fax 9-885-1729; www.fiesta americana.com. ULTRA-DELUXE.

The **Meliá Cancún** has, quite simply, Cancún's most smashing lobby. Footpaths wind through lush gardens, streams and gazebos inside this soaring, glass-crowned atrium, and thousands of vines and flowers pour from overhead balconies. It would be enough to spend all day in the lobby, but why not try the cool blue swimming pools out back? Just past the pools, a patch of sand is one of Cancún's few topless beaches—one reason Europeans favor this hotel. Each of the 450 oversized rooms features plush carpets, contemporary decor and balconies overlooking the lagoon or sea. Air conditioning. ~ Paseo Kukulcán, Km. 16.5; 9-881-11-00, fax 9-885-1963, or 800-336-3542 in the U.S.; www.solmelia.com. ULTRA-DELUXE.

From the boulevard, the **Marriott Casa Magna Cancún** looks like a plain-Jane, but behind the facade is architectural majesty. Massive columns support a 44-foot dome over a lobby with arches, curving windows and a cupola; myriad pale blue ponds shimmer across the landscape. Wrought-iron chandeliers and Victorian furnishings decorate the lobby, hinting at the hotel's corporate clientele. The 452 rooms and suites, all with sea or lagoon views, offer more luxury with their marble floors, stuffed chairs and amenities such as hair dryers and ironing boards. Air conditioning. ~ Paseo Kukulcán, Km. 14.8; 9-881-2000, fax 9-881-2071, or 800-327-0200 in the U.S.; www.marriott.com, e-mail cancunmarriott@infosel.net.mx. ULTRA-DELUXE.

Reigning as the most elegant of Cancún's resort hotels, the **Ritz-Carlton** has a lobby that gleams with polished marble and stained glass. All 365 guest rooms and suites have balconies overlooking the sea and the hotel's lush gardens. The rooms are among the most spacious in the hotel zone and feature such touches as plush robes, separate bathtubs and showers, and phones in every room. Recreational amenities include two heated swimming pools, three lighted tennis courts, and a health club complete with exercise gym, sauna, jacuzzi, steam room and massage service. ~ Paseo Kukulcán, Km. 14; 9-885-0888, fax 9-885-1039, or 800-241-333 in the U.S.; www.ritzcarlton.com, e-mail mmaya@rc-cancun.com. ULTRA-DELUXE.

The **Casa Turquesa** has the distinction of being the smallest hotel on Isla Cancún. All 32 guest units are lavish suites designed to cater to European royalty and rock stars, with overstuffed furniture, large plants and that solid feel of fine quality. Each suite has a private balcony or patio with its own outdoor jacuzzi and a view past the quiet, private pool area to the sea. Air conditioning. ~ Paseo Kukulcán, Km. 13.3; 9-885-2924, fax 9-885-2922, or 800-634-4644 in the U.S. ULTRA-DELUXE.

Sheraton Resort and Towers is a huge, 471-unit complex with its own beach. The hotel offers classes in everything from aerobics to scuba diving. The spacious, bright-colored guest rooms feature a choice of sea or lagoon view. Built in the shape of three pyramids, the hotel overshadows a small but genuine Maya site on the grounds. Called Yamilum, the temple marks the highest point on Cancún. Nearby, in a grove of coconut palms, hammocks offer a shady, relaxing retreat. Air conditioning. ~ Paseo Kukulcán, Km. 12; 9-883-1988, fax 9-885-0244, or 888-625-5144 in the U.S.; www.sheraton.com. ULTRA-DELUXE.

Though still pricey, the **Flamingo Cancún Resort** is one of the more affordable lodgings in the Hotel Zone. Instead of lavishly landscaped grounds, it has the endless array of silver jewelry shops at the Flamingo Mall across the street and more shopping and restaurants all around—including a McDonald's. The 219 guest rooms surround the hotel's swimming pool, and the wide, white beach is washed by a crystal sea. Air conditioning. ~ Paseo Kukulcán, Km. 11; phone/fax 9-883-1544; e-mail flamicun@grool. prodigy.net.mx. ULTRA-DELUXE.

Perched on a limestone bluff overlooking a narrow, secluded beach is the **Hyatt Cancún Caribe**, a sloping, Maya-style hotel whose terraces overflow with brilliant flowers. Designed in a daring crescent shape for wide-angle ocean views, the hotel relies not on extravagance but on understated elegance to create a chic, intimate ambiance. The 201 guest rooms and suites are warmly adorned with amber tile floors, tropical prints and oak furniture. Most have seafront balconies; beach-level rooms have spacious garden terraces. Palapa bars peek out from the pool area, and a generous swath of beach couldn't be more ideal for sunning. Peacocks stroll free on the hotel grounds. Four restaurants, including the excellent Blue Bayou, provide yet more allure. Air conditioning. ~ Paseo Kukulcán, Km. 10.5; 9-848-7800, fax 9-883-1514, or 800-228-9000 in the U.S.; cancun.hyatt.com, e-mail hyattcc@cancun.com.mx. ULTRA-DELUXE.

One of the oldest hotels on the island, and one of the few bargains left, is the **Hotel Aristos**. The 245 guest rooms are clean and cool, with tile floors and colorful utilitarian furnishings.

AUTHOR FAVORITE

My favorite Cancún resort is the **Ritz-Carlton**, where I was once privileged to spend a couple of complimentary nights while writing an article for the hotel chain's magazine. Surrounded by bigger, taller, more crowded hotels, the Ritz-Carlton radiates the kind of classiness I could easily get accustomed to. Of course, when I'm paying my own way, I opt to stay elsewhere—like Isla Mujeres or Playa del Carmen. See page 110 for more information about the Ritz-Carlton.

Half the rooms face the lagoon and cost more. The others face the street and are noisy. Facilities include a swimming pool, tennis courts and water sports equipment rentals. Air conditioning. ~ Paseo Kukulcán, Km. 9.8; 9-883-0011, fax 9-883-0078; e-mail aristos@cancun.com.mx. DELUXE.

Beautiful people check into **Krystal Cancún**, a place low on glamour but high on energy. Set on a thin stretch of cream-colored beach, the sandstone-and-glass buildings feature 322 tan-toned rooms comfortably appointed with queen-size beds, rattan furniture and pastel decor. The real draw is the chic young crowd that gathers poolside during the day and at the hotel's wildly popular disco at night. Other amenities include a weight room, sauna, whirlpool and tennis courts. Convenient to shopping malls and restaurants. Air conditioning. ~ Paseo Kukulcán, Km. 9.4; 9-883-1133, fax 9-883-1790, or 800-231-9860 in the U.S. ULTRA-DELUXE.

The **Hyatt Regency Cancún** enjoys the privileged position of being right on the tip of Punta Cancún. Flanked by the sea on three sides, the 14-story, cylindrical 298-room hotel features a soaring lobby crowned with glass and balconies strung with flowering vines. Outside, the swimming pool meanders through lush foliage and a glass-walled gymnasium sits near the sea. Activities (wet-T-shirt contests, men-versus-women volleyball) are geared to a young crowd. Air conditioning. ~ Paseo Kukulcán, Km. 9.3; 9-848-7800, fax 9-883-1514, or 800-228-9000 in the U.S.; cancun.hyatt.com, e-mail hyattreg@cancun.com.mx. ULTRA-DELUXE.

Next door, the similarly spectacular **Camino Real** is laid out like a country club and boasts a natural seawater pool fed by the Caribbean and a gently sloping pyramid design that meshes with sun and sand. The usual assortment of bars, restaurants, nightspots, sea sports and swimming pools is enhanced by lush interior gardens. The 381 guest rooms have real native charm, with festive furnishings and balconies opening to the sea. One of the first and finest hotels on Cancún when it was built in 1975, the Camino Real remains one of the most elegant. Air conditioning. ~ Paseo Kukulcán, Km. 9; 9-883-0100, fax 9-883-1730, or 800-722-6466 in the U.S.; www.caminoreal.com/cancun, e-mail crc unin@mail.caribe.net.mx. ULTRA-DELUXE.

At the action-packed hub of the Hotel Zone, the **Fiesta Americana Coral Beach** is the largest and most luxurious of three Cancún hotels operated by this top-ranked Mexican hospitality chain. Curving coral buildings trimmed with emerald balconies and dripping with ferns embrace a lavish pool area complete with bridges, waterslides, swim-up bars and a heart-shaped island for sunbathing. Marble floors, stylish archways and soaring potted palms make the lobby ultrasleek but not overdone. The 602 marble-floored rooms are tropically decorated and feel like suites with their separate sitting areas and terraces overlooking the sea.

Next Stop, Cuba

Cohiba, Montecristo, San Luis Rey.... Connoisseurs browse among legendary brands of Cuban cigars in the humidor in the Ritz-Carlton Cancún's Grill Room bar. Then they set fire to their selections. Cuban cigars enjoy a forbidden-fruit allure because for 40 years it has been illegal to import them into the U.S. It has also pushed their prices *outside* the U.S., in Cancún cigar bars and tobacconist shops like La Casa del Habano in the Plaza Flamingo mall and La Casa Verde downtown, up to US$25 to $50 per cigar.

Cuban cigars first came to Quintana Roo's shores in the 1950s, clenched in the jaws of Fidel Castro, who used the swamps and sandbars of the then-unpopulated coast as a secret training ground for his revolutionary army and a staging area for smuggling guns into Cuba. Ironically, it was Castro's revolution, more than any other single factor, that transformed Cancún into one of North America's largest megaresorts.

Before the revolution, Cuba with its glitzy nightclubs, casinos and tropical beaches was the choice destination for an astonishing 95 percent of all international tourism in the Caribbean. Soon after the revolution, the same economic embargo that declared Cuban cigars contraband also prohibited U.S. tourists from visiting Cuba. Other winter tourist destinations close to the U.S. East Coast, such as Nassau and Cozumel, faced water supply limitations that restricted resort development. Both the Mexican government and hotel investors realized that the time was right for a new Caribbean mega-resort on an unprecedented scale, and that Cancún was the ideal place for it.

In the 1990s, Cancún became the gateway for an estimated 22,000 U.S. vacationers per year who visited Cuba despite the travel ban. Technically, the embargo does not prohibit *going* to Cuba, only spending money there. So Cancún travel agencies arrange package tours that include a Cuban tourist visa (which doesn't show up on your U.S. passport), prepaid hotel/restaurant vouchers, and air fare on one of the flights that leave Cancún for Havana several times daily. Once visitors arrive in Cuba, they discover that they *can* spend U.S. dollars there, and even use charge cards issued by U.S. banks.

Caution: Since 2001, the Bush administration has been trying to crack down on U.S. citizens traveling to Cuba by putting U.S. undercover agents in the Cancún airport to watch passengers who deplane from Cuba. The maximum penalty that can be imposed for violating the embargo is $55,000. Check with a local travel agency about current U.S. enforcement activities. For more information on visiting Cuba, contact **Caribbean Tropical Tours**, Avenida Xpuhil 3-A, Suite 277, SM 27, Cancún 77506, Quintana Roo; 9-880-8160, fax 9-880-8144. Or try **Viajes Divermex**. ~ 9-884-5005, fax 9-884-2325.

There are 13 restaurants and bars, indoor tennis courts with stadium seating and a health club. Air conditioning. ~ Paseo Kukulcán, Km. 9.1; 9-881-3200, fax 9-881-3349, or 800-343-7821 in the U.S.; www.fiestaamericana.com, e-mail coralbus@cancun.rce.com.mx. ULTRA-DELUXE.

Located near the heart of Cancún's shopping district, the original **Fiesta Americana Cancún** is smaller than its sister hotels—281 guest rooms and suites, making it one of the more intimate hotels on the island—and strives to present a romantic, honeymoon-hideaway ambiance. The exterior epitomizes the pseudo-Italianate "Mexican Riviera" architectural flourishes that were in vogue during Cancún's early development, while the rooms are some interior decorator's bold statement in white walls and smoky glass with only the subtlest embellishments of muted color. Air conditioning. ~ Paseo Kukulcán, Km. 8.7; 9-883-1400, fax 9-883-2502; www.fiestaamericana.com. ULTRA-DELUXE.

The **Holiday Inn Express Cancún** has 120 rather plain guest rooms and some of the most reasonable prices in the Hotel Zone. True, it has neither a beach nor a restaurant, but a free shuttle bus can take you downtown or to the off-premises beach club. The hotel adjoins the Pok-Ta-Pok golf course on an island linked to the Hotel Zone by a short causeway, with views of bigger resort hotels over the placid waters of Laguna Bojórquez. Accommodations surround a pretty central courtyard with a swimming pool and two artificial waterfalls. Guests enjoy tennis privileges at Pok-Ta-Pok, as well as discounts on green fees. Air conditioning. ~ Paseo Pok-Ta-Pok No. 21 y 22; 9-883-2200, fax 9-883-2532, or 800-465-4329 in the U.S.; www.ehi.com. DELUXE.

HIDDEN ►

Located on one of the island's few quiet side streets, on the shore of Laguna Nichupte and just a few minutes' walk from the beach, the convention center and the huge Plaza Caracol shopping mall, the **Imperial Laguna Cancún** offers one of the best bargains in the Hotel Zone. Big resorts nearby dwarf this modest place with its three-story buildings surrounding a courtyard and pool. All of the 52 accommodations are suites, making this an appealing choice for families. Rooms have cable TV and balconies overlooking the swimming pool. Air conditioning. ~ Calle Quetzal No. 11 (near Paseo Kukulcán, Km. 7); 9-849-4270, fax 9-849-5200, or 800-544-3005 in the U.S.; www.hotelimperialcancun.com. MODERATE.

Villas Tacul consists of 61 motel-style units and 14 individual casitas with two to five bedrooms each. A good choice for families and groups, the casitas may be reserved months in advance. The feel is traditionally Mexican, with Spanish colonial–style furniture, big wooden doors and wagon-wheel chandeliers. Facilities include a swimming pool, a bar, two tennis courts and a private stretch of beach. Air conditioning. ~ Paseo Kukulcán, Km. 6; 9-883-0000, fax 9-883-0349; e-mail vtacul@cancun.rce.com.mx. ULTRA-DELUXE.

The laidback little **Carrousel Cancún** is situated on one of Cancún's widest, whitest beaches. This hotel offers 160 guest rooms and suites, all with ocean views overlooking Bahía de Mujeres. Facilities include a swimming pool, tennis court and jacuzzi. Air conditioning. ~ Paseo Kukulcán, Km. 3.8; 9-883-0388, fax 9-883-2312. ULTRA-DELUXE.

One of the few hotels fronting on the lagoon side of the island, **Club Las Velas** offers unusually private accommodations. The 285 guest units are scattered along quiet walkways through shady, landscaped grounds reserved for guests only. This is an all-inclusive hotel—the room rate covers not only meals but also water sports equipment and unlimited drinks—with a three-night minimum stay. A full schedule of activities, from aerobics and water polo to board-game tournaments and Spanish lessons, is available to guests at no additional charge. Air conditioning. ~ Paseo Kukulcán, Km. 3.5; 9-883-2222, fax 9-883-2118, or 800-223-9815 in the U.S. ULTRA-DELUXE.

Still technically in the Hotel Zone but on the mainland side of the bridge, along Playa las Perlas, are a series of condominium-style hotels with three-star ratings. Unlike the major resorts that line most of the Hotel Zone, the room rates at these places are government-regulated in pesos rather than U.S. dollars, meaning that they rent at bargain rates—under $100 in peak season and as low as $60 at other times of year. Typical of the breed is the **Barceló Club Las Perlas**. The 194 rooms are comfortable though slightly frayed around the edges, and most but not all have balcony views of the sea or the lagoon. Rooms have satellite TV, minibars and phones, not to mention full bathtubs instead of just showers, a luxury in Mexican hotels of any price range. There are two swimming pools, a poolside bar and a restaurant on the premises. Air conditioning. ~ Paseo Kukulcán, Km. 2.5; 9-848-9100, fax 9-848-

A FAMILY AFFAIR

The all-inclusive **Beach Palace** goes all out to make families feel at home. Here, the young set can join in *Camp de Chamacos* (Camp for Kids), with fun activities like body painting and diving for fake jewels. Parents delight in the family-size suites with marble floors, whirlpool tubs, kitchenettes and separate sleeping nooks for the kids. The hotel is relatively small, with 200 guest rooms and suites. Three swimming pools, tennis court, fitness center and multiple restaurants (including a family-style deli) round out the amenities. Air conditioning. ~ Paseo Kukulcán, Km. 11.5; 9-883-1177, fax 9-885-0439, or 800-346-8225 in the U.S.; www.sunrisepalace resorts.com, e-mail info@sunrisepalaceresorts.com. ULTRA-DELUXE.

9110; www.clublasperlas.com, e-mail booking@clublasperlas.com.
MODERATE TO DELUXE.

DINING

Cancún has not yet earned much of a reputation for fine dining, and Hotel Zone restaurants tend to be overpriced. At most of Cancún's Hotel Zone restaurants, you pay top dollar for catchy themes, splashy decor and food that's sometimes intriguing but rarely superb. Authentic Mexican cuisine is conspicuous by its absence. There are large numbers of seafood restaurants and, for some reason, Italian restaurants.

The ebullient **Carlos 'n Charlie's** is a sprawling waterside restaurant, open and carefree, casting the glow of its yellow lanterns upon Laguna Nichupté. Less manic than some of the other restaurants in this nationwide chain, C 'n C's serves the same humorous "Peep, moo, splash, crunch, slurp" menu of fine selections, from French onion soup to barbecued ribs. A lively disco-bar is attached. ~ Paseo Kukulcán, Km. 4.5; 9-883-0846; www.carlosandchar lies.com. MODERATE.

An array of international favorites, from McDonald's to some of the city's best European specialty restaurants, clusters around the busy hub of the Hotel Zone at Km. 8. At the glitzy Plaza Caracol you'll find the romantic, award-winning **Casa Rolandi**. The splendid, grottolike room serves Swiss-Italian cuisine and fresh seafood with style. Try the black ravioli stuffed with shrimp or the fish baked with squid and shrimp in parchment paper. There is also an elaborate salad bar. ~ Paseo Kukulcán, Km. 8; 9-883-2557. MODERATE.

Also in the Plaza Caracol, **Iguana Wana** is a big, contemporary café specializing in "vacation cuisine"—buckets of peel-and-eat shrimp, vegetarian fajitas, fresh seafood soup and some of the best ceviche you'll find in any Cancún shopping mall. The café also features live music in the evening, and TVs in the bar show sports videos constantly. ~ Paseo Kukulcán, Km. 8; 9-883-0829. BUDGET TO MODERATE.

Vegetables—steamed, stir-fried, juiced or wrapped in an omelet—are the specialty at **100% Natural**. The restaurant also

DINING WITH GYPSIES

Overlooking a lagoon view, **Gypsy's** serves paella and other Spanish-style seafood dishes. The restaurant is set in a palapa decorated with bullfighting capes—your first hint that the real attraction at this popular restaurant is not the food but the entertainment. Dramatic, foot-stamping flamenco shows by the Carmen Reyes Gypsy Ballet are presented twice nightly. ~ Paseo Kukulcán, Km. 10.5; 9-883-2120. DELUXE.

serves fruit salads, chicken and seafood, as well as a few menu items such as hamburgers and fried eggs for those who would rather eat greasy than healthy. The restaurant's Plaza Terramar location is open 24 hours a day. ~ Plaza Terramar, Paseo Kukulcán, Km. 8.5; 9-883-1180. There are also two other 100% Natural locations: Kukulcán Plaza ~ Paseo Kukulcán, Km. 13, 9-885-2904; and downtown ~ Avenida Sunyaxchén No. 62 y 64, 9-884-3617. Both are open until 11 p.m. The downtown location hosts an ecology forum on Thursday nights—the best opportunity in town to make contact with environmentally minded locals and visitors. BUDGET TO MODERATE.

El Mexicano, located in La Mansión–Costa Blanca shopping mall in the heart of the Hotel Zone, may well be the most expensive Mexican restaurant in Mexico. The menu features creative versions of dishes representing different regions of the country, such as *carne asada* (roasted strips of marinated beef) and the chef's specialty, *empanxonostle* (a seafood-stuffed pastry). The food here is "delicately seasoned." The fixed-price dinner includes the "Birds of Paradise Tropical Show," with Caribbean music and dancing, at 10 p.m., as well as a complimentary glass of champagne. (Additional drinks, not included in the dinner price, are expensive.) ~ Paseo Kukulcán, Km. 8.5; 9-883-2220. ULTRA-DELUXE.

For a truly elegant Italian restaurant, consider Augustus Caesar in La Mansión–Costa Blanca Commercial Center. Opened in 1977, it is one of Cancún's oldest fine-dining establishments, yet the decor is fresh and contemporary. A beautiful stonework floor and pink tablecloths nestled amid an abundance of potted palms set the atmosphere. Veal scallopini is the house specialty, though guests who care about animal rights might look farther down the menu to the selection of succulent pasta dishes. ~ Paseo Kukulcán, Km. 8.5; 9-883-3384. DELUXE.

In the same shopping center is Pacal, a gourmet "Maya" restaurant that offers traditional dishes like *sopa de lima* (lime soup), *cochinita pibil* (pork steamed in banana leaves) and *pavo escabeche* (turkey in an onion and orange sauce), along with others whose authenticity is more questionable, like *dzo'on*, a New York–cut steak in tomato and herb sauce. You'll also find some wholly original specialties that might best be categorized as "Maya fusion cuisine," such as *ya'hax* (duck over a fried green tomato and peanut base) and conch carpaccio in hibiscus vinaigrette. ~ Paseo Kukulcán, Km. 8.5; 9-883-2184. DELUXE.

Strangely enough, until recently the distinctive cuisine of the Yucatán was almost impossible to find in Cancún. The first Maya restaurant to open was the downtown location of Los Almendros, a spinoff from the famous little restaurant of the same name in the Maya town of Ticul in the center of the peninsula that was the first restaurant to serve some of the dishes now considered "traditional." It quickly became so popular in Cancún that a new, more upscale Los Almendros location was opened in the Hotel Zone. The recipes for menu items like lime soup, *poc chuc* (pork barbecued in a distinctive sauce) and *pollo pibil* (chicken cooked in banana leaves) have retained their authenticity in the transition from Maya village to megaresort. ~ Club Nautico 1, Paseo Kukulcán, Km. 9; 9-883-3093. DELUXE.

Located in the Forum by the Sea shopping and entertainment complex, the **Santa Fe Beer Factory** is part of Mexico's only microbrewery chain. The ultracasual atmosphere, which features bigscreen music videos, has little if anything to do with Santa Fe style. Neither does the food—a conventional, gringo-oriented selection of steaks, pizza, pasta and salads along with a few Mexican choices such as quesadillas. Still, the service is speedy and the beer is fresh from the brewing vat. ~ Paseo Kukulcán, Km. 9; 9-883-4469. MODERATE.

When it comes to atmosphere, few restaurants can touch **Bogart's**. Beautifully appointed with colored fountains, dreamy Moroccan columns and keyhole arches, the place is straight out of the movies. The bill of fare is not Moroccan but Continental, with dishes such as "three wishes" (lobster served with three different sauces) and rack of New Zealand lamb provençal. ~ Hotel Krystal Cancún, Paseo Kukulcán, Km. 9; 9-883-1133. DELUXE TO ULTRA-DELUXE.

The Krystal Cancún's other dressy eatery, **Hacienda el Mortero**, is fashioned after an 18th-century colonial house, complete with barrel-tile roof, sand-colored stucco and cannons lining the eaves. A mariachi band makes merry while you feast on Yucatecan *sopa de lima* (chicken soup simmered with onions and slices of Mexican lime), butterflied shrimp with cactus and chilies, and other regional dishes. ~ 9-883-1133. DELUXE.

You'll find surf-and-turf and sushi side by side at the informal **Chockos & Tere Lobster House** and **Campay Sushi Bar**, both under the same management. The specialty at Chockos & Tere is a lavish seafood platter for two. Campay is a traditional Japanese-style sushi bar with authentic decor. Besides sushi, the restaurant features a tepanyaki grill, where the food is prepared right at your table. ~ Paseo Kukulcán, Km. 9. Chockos & Tere: 9-883-1156; Campay: 9-883-1151; e-mail partycenter@cancun.novenet.com. mx. MODERATE TO DELUXE.

Lorenzillo's serves seafood fresh from the Caribbean and the Gulf of Mexico in a seafront dining room at the Hotel Continental Villas Plaza. The decor—rough beams, plank floor and nautical memorabilia including a full-size ship's wheel and dinghy—is intended to make you feel as if you were dining on an old-fashioned sailing vessel at sea, though some may find the ambience more appropriate to a theme park than to an upscale restaurant. The

seafood is exceptional. Soft-shell crab and stone crab are specialties, as is seafood-stuffed filet mignon. ~ Paseo Kukulcán, Km.
10.5; 9-883-1254. DELUXE.

The big **Planet Hollywood,** with its international-style pseudo-
glamor and movie memorabilia designed to keep reminding you
that the place is owned by Arnold Schwarzenegger and friends,
somehow fits into the Cancún experience perfectly. The menu fare
is a medley of "California-style" cuisine—creative, contemporary
renditions of Italian and Asian dishes as well as health-conscious
and just plain self-conscious nouveau dishes. Try the mango and
chipotle shrimp with pine nuts on a bed of curried fettuccine; or,
if you prefer, go for the cheeseburger. It turns into a trendy disco
late in the evening. ~ Paseo Kukulcán, Km. 11; 9-883-2995. DELUXE.

A longtime Cancún favorite that has recently been relocated
from downtown to the Hotel Zone, **La Dolce Vita** enchants with
flickering candles, lacy tablecloths and attentive waiters who
speak in deep husky tones. No dish disappoints, from the lob-
ster-studded fettuccine and grilled chicken breast with porcini
mushrooms and sun-dried tomatoes to the rigatoni swimming in
chorizo, mushrooms and chili peppers. The Mediterranean ambience is pure romance. ~ Paseo Kukulcán, Km. 14.6; 9-885-0150.
DELUXE.

SHOPPING

During Spanish colonial times, the mines of central Mexico produced more silver than has ever been found in any other region of
the world. Ever since large-scale silver jewelry making was revived
in Taxco, Guerrero (in the mountains near Acapulco), during the
1930s by an American entrepreneur employing cheap local workers, silver has become the material of choice for artisans in modern Mexico. To see for yourself how big the silver jewelry industry
has grown, take a dizzying stroll through any of Cancún's shopping malls, which seem to be filled almost entirely with jewelry

GLOBAL SHOPPING

Cancún and all of Quintana Roo is a free-trade zone, where imports from
other nations are sold duty-free. That means international visitors can avoid
the extremely high protective tariffs Mexico has traditionally imposed on
imports, while Mexican vacationers in Cancún may have to pay duty on
excess purchases when they leave Quintana Roo. With the implementation of NAFTA and other international trade agreements, the free-trade
status is less and less important to Cancún's economy. Still, it is often
cited to explain why French perfume, Cuban cigars, Indonesian wood
carvings and Japanese electronics are easier to find in Cancún than
anything traditionally Yucatecan.

stores. Most stores carry the work of craftspeople in far-off Taxco, and you can expect to pay *at least* as much as the same piece would cost in the United States. Cancún is *the* most expensive resort in Mexico, the place where the country's finest jewelers and fashion designers sell their creations. You can spend a fortune.

Still the plushest shopping arena, the air-conditioned, twin two-story malls, **Plaza Caracol I** and **Plaza Caracol II**, make for the most pleasant place to shop—clean and polished, a fusion of white marble and tinted skylights, run with American efficiency. The 200 shops within feature everything from Kmart quality to Polo and Gucci. Try **Face** for elaborate masks, earrings and necklaces; **Keko Tassia** for upscale Mexican designer dresses; and **Mordo** for leather boots, luggage and fashion belts. ~ Paseo Kukulcán, Km. 8.5; 9-883-1038.

Near Plaza Caracol is **Plaza Lagunas**, which alongside chic shops such as Calvin Klein and Ellesse also has an impressive array of imported American fast-food franchises. ~ Paseo Kukulcán, Km. 8.5; 9-883-1266. Next door, pink **La Mansión–Costa Blanca** is an outdoor villa-style shopping center selling beachwear, designer clothes, Maya replicas and leather. And, of course, jewelry. It also houses some of the Hotel Zone's finer restaurants. ~ Paseo Kukulcán, Km. 8.5; 9-883-0888.

The closest thing you'll find in Cancún to a Mexican-style arts-and-crafts *mercado* is the **Coral Negro Flea Market**. Sixty-five small shops feature clothing, jewelry and *artesanía* from all over Mexico. The prices, selection and authentic atmosphere can't compare with the wonderful public market in Mérida, or even the arts-and-crafts stalls at Chichén Itzá, so keep your souvenir money in your pocket if you're planning to venture into the Yucatán interior. But if Cancún is as far as you're going, the "flea market" is worth checking out. ~ Paseo Kukulcán, Km. 9.5; 9-883-0758.

At **Plaza La Fiesta**, across from the convention center, the large Mexican jewelry and handicraft market is great for last-minute shopping. ~ Paseo Kukulcán, Km. 9; 9-883-2116.

A sort of combination shopping mall–theme park, the **Forum by the Sea** lures shoppers with dining, nightclubs, live entertainment and even its own beach. Famous-name designer outlets stand side by side with the local Harley Davidson dealership. ~ Paseo Kukulcán, Km. 9; 9-883-4425.

Art aficionados should check out the works by Sergio Busta-mante, one of Mexico's premier artists, at the **Hyatt Cancún Caribe**. ~ Paseo Kukulcán, Km. 10.5; 9-883-0044.

You will recognize **Flamingo Plaza** by the giant Gold's Gym filled with muscled bodies pumping iron. Situated lagoon-side, Flamingo also boasts a more balanced selection of shops than most of the other malls. Next to international designer boutiques such as Guess?, Bally and Pelletier Paris, you'll find a dozen quality Mexican handicrafts shops and more T-shirt places than any other mall in the Hotel Zone. ~ Paseo Kukulcán, Km. 11; 9-883-2945. Wanna buy some contraband, *meester*? At **La Casa del Habano**, they sell fine Cuban cigars (which you still can't bring back to the United States). ~ 9-885-2929.

Cancún's largest shopping mall, **Plaza Kukulkán** has more than 300 shops and a new Fashion Gallery featuring international designer clothing. The mall also has entertainment facilities that include bowling alleys and a laser game arcade. ~ Paseo Kukulcán, Km. 12.5; 9-885-2200.

The newest and showiest of Cancún's shopping malls, **La Isla Shopping Village** mixes shops and boutiques with unique features such as an indoor aquarium, a multiscreen movie theater, a gaming arcade, a marina and a "riverwalk" by the lagoon. ~ Paseo Kukulcán, Km. 12.5. If contraband Cuban cigars aren't quite daring enough for you, you can buy (but not bring back to the U.S.) eastern European absinthe, the psychoactive liqueur made infamous by French Impressionist painters a century ago, at **Super Gourmet Deli**. ~ Locations at Plaza La Isla, Plaza Kukulkán and Forum by the Sea; 9-885-3904.

NIGHTLIFE

From the deafening discos and laid-back palapa bars to mini-symphonies in hotel lobbies, Cancún really lights up the night. Clubs overrun the Hotel Zone, where every big hotel has its lobby bar and disco. Ciudad Cancún, too, sizzles after dusk. Expect to pay dearly for drinks ($4–$6). Cover charges are up to $15 in many top nightspots.

The Mediterranean-modern **La Boom** is the most famous of all Cancún discos. A big, round, revolving dancefloor housed inside a big white building by the lagoon, La Boom glints with exposed girders, carpets, mirrors and videos. The club is named for its most spectacular novelty lighting effect—a simulated nuclear blast. Stay here long and you'll see it over and over. For even more sightseeing thrills, check out the rowdy, thoroughly chauvinistic Friday-evening bikini contests, which rank among Cancún's hottest after-dark events. Cover. ~ Paseo Kukulcán, Km. 3.5; 9-883-1152.

CANCÚN BY NIGHT

For a different perspective on Cancún by night, hop aboard one of the many available specialty cruises, such as AquaWorld's **Cancún Queen Dinner Cruise**, a paddlewheel riverboat that embarks each evening with a cargo of steak and lobster, live entertainment and plenty of boat drinks. ~ Paseo Kukulcán, Km. 15.2; 9-885-2288; www.aquaworld.com.mx, e-mail info@aquaworld.com.mx.

Palapa-style **Carlos 'n Charlie's**, with its elevated dining and pier-side dancing along Laguna Nichupté, is a Cancún institution. Great for people watching. ~ Paseo Kukulcán, Km. 5.5; 9-883-0846. Next door and part of the same chain, found from here to Mazatlán and Puerto Vallarta, **Señor Frog's** is a wildly popular place featuring live reggae or world beat music nightly. ~ Paseo Kukulcán, Km. 9.5; 9-883-1092.

Azucar Bar Carabeño, adjoining the Hotel Camino Real, caters to the tastes of Latin American jet setters with big-band salsa featuring top musicians from all over the Caribbean. For performers from places like Cuba and Haiti, a gig in Cancún spells success and pays more per week than they could make back home in a year. This is a dressy place in the Latin American manner; women who don't wear high heels may feel . . . well . . . short. Cover. ~ Punta Cancún; 9-883-1755.

Cat's Reggae Club in the Cancún Convention Center also features live Caribbean musicians. Cover. ~ Paseo Kukulcán, Km. 9; 9-883-1910.

For glamour and special effects, no other disco can touch **Christine**. A forest of plants under glass extends around the periphery, and overhead the ceiling is crusted with spinning, blinking, rolling spotlights as well as lasers and video screens. Popular and expensive. Cover. ~ Hotel Krystal Cancún, Paseo Kukulcán, Km. 9; 9-883-1133.

Perhaps the flashiest nightclub complex in the Hotel Zone is **Dady'O** and **Dady Rock**, two adjoining clubs under the same management, with entrances on opposite sides of the same building and separate cover charges. Dady'O is a dressy, high-tech European-style disco with a laser lightshow, minimalist styling and electronic everything. Dady Rock is a back-to-the-'50s rock-and-roll hamburger bar that boasts an "incredible party atmosphere." The same management runs the T-shirt-and-jeans danceclub **Ma'ax'o** up the road at La Isla Shopping Village, where the music is international with a Caribbean flair. A free shuttle takes partiers between these three clubs. Cover. ~ Paseo Kukulcán, Km. 9.5; 9-883-3333; www.dady-o.com.

Cancún's largest nightclub, **Cocobongo**, boasts 8000 square feet of dancefloor in the Forum by the Sea entertainment and shopping complex. The entertainment mixes rock and pop disco with short live-music sets, punctuated with occasional cascades of balloons from the ceiling. The action lasts until dawn. Cover. ~ Paseo Kukulcán, Km. 9.5; 9-883-0592.

The only legal wagering in Cancún is found at **Caliente Sports World**, one of the largest locations of the conglomerate that holds a monopoly on gambling operations throughout Mexico. Big-screen TVs simultaneously show satellite feeds of up to 12 sporting events—hockey, football, baseball, soccer, boxing, horse and dog racing—whatever games are being broadcast at the moment from anywhere in the world. Bets are placed by means of a high-tech electronic wagering system. The sports book is open from 1 p.m. to midnight. ~ Fiesta Americana Cancún, Paseo Kukulcán, Km. 8.7; 9-884-2546.

Whatever you do, don't miss the outstanding **Ballet Folklórico de Cancún**. Not to be confused with impostors claiming to be Cancún's "original" folk ballet, this authentic performance is pricey but worth it. A fabulous Mexican buffet supper precedes the performance as a live band entertains. The show presents indigenous dances from 11 regions of Mexico, with colorful costumes, high energy, humor and finesse. ~ Cancún Convention Center; 9-881-0400.

Another Mexican folkdance performance, *Cantos y Danzas de México*, is presented Monday through Friday evenings at the **Teatro de Cancún**. Also performed here on an ongoing basis is a music and dance show called *Caribbean Traditions*. Tickets are available at the door until 15 minutes before showtime. ~ Paseo Kukulcán, Km. 4; 9-849-7777.

PLAYA DELFINES The first beach on the island north of Punta Nizuc, located opposite the Ruinas del Rey, starts with softly vegetated dunes sloping down into thick, virgin sand that runs along the turquoise sea. This and other east-shore beaches facing the Caribbean have some dangerous currents. Be sure to check the colored flags along the beaches for current swimming conditions before taking the plunge. Though flanked on both ends by hotels, this long, unspoiled beach will give you a clue about how Cancún looked before the tourist buildup. Not for long, though. ~ Paseo Kukulcán, Km. 18.

BEACHES & PARKS

PLAYA CHAC-MOOL This fabulous walking beachfronts an almost unbroken wall of hotels and condos. It stretches uninterrupted for about five miles. Its sugary white sand gives you little white slippers as you step out of the crystal tide. The water burns so intensely green it appears to be dyed. Up on a sandy dune, a

AUTHOR FAVORITE

My favorite place to get sand between my toes is *not* in Cancún (as you'll see in the chapters that follow). But when I'm in Cancún, my favorite walking beach is **Playa Delfines** (Dolphin Beach), flanked by wild sand dunes instead of big resorts. When there's enough breeze off the sea to make choppy waves that discourage bathers, this beach can seem as remote and secluded as any you'll find on the Riviera Maya. See above for more information.

reproduction of the god Chac-Mool surveys the scene. ~ Paseo Kukulcán, Km. 13.

PLAYA CARACOL 🏊 🎣 The safest beaches for swimming—Caracol, Tortugas, Langosta and Las Perlas—touch the gentle Bahía de Mujeres. Beginning with a rustic picnic shelter and a fishing pier, Playa Caracol is a quiet, satiny beach within easy walking distance of the busiest commercial center in the Hotel Zone. It loops gently along Bahía de Mujeres to the Hotel Camino Real and a small lighthouse. This is the most easterly beach on the bay before the island makes its 90-degree turn around Punta Cancún and rolls south along the Caribbean. Take the Punta Cancún turnoff from Paseo Kukulcán, proceed around the *glorieta* past the Hyatt Regency and turn into the parking lot past the "Archaeological Information" kiosk. ~ Paseo Kukulcán, Km. 8.5.

> Camping is prohibited on all Cancún's beaches.

PLAYA TORTUGAS 🏊 🎣 Lovely and undeveloped, with powdery white sand, this beach could almost be in some backcountry fishing village. A few palapas and a bamboo lifeguard stand shade the sand. Watch for the marked turnoff from the main boulevard. ~ Paseo Kukulcán, Km. 6.

PLAYA LANGOSTA 🏊 🎣 This sandy cove curves out to a small, rocky point and widens into a fuller, softer beach at the feet of the Hotel Casa Maya. This part, scattered with palapas, is protected by a small jetty. ~ Paseo Kukulcán, Km. 5.

PLAYA LAS PERLAS 🏊 🎣 Playa Las Perlas is the most westerly beach, the first you hit coming from Ciudad Cancún, and one of the most natural beaches in the area. The hard-packed sand, tinted with shadows of surrounding trees, makes a tranquil picnic ground. A pier leads out over the exquisite water. ~ Paseo Kukulcán, Km. 2.5.

Downtown

Cancún Centro, the not-very-old downtown area of the city, lacks the color and exotica you'll find in Mérida and other Yucatán cities. Still, for sheer strolling enjoyment, there's no place in town like downtown, where international vacationers go to look for "the real Mexico." With its cobbled sidewalks, grassy medians, crowded shopping stalls, colorful awnings and lively sidewalk cafés, the place is like a nonstop fiesta. Kids with kid-size pushcarts peddle icies on the *zócalo*, and mariachi music pours from open windows.

SIGHTS

Downtown is a four-by-eight-block area bounded by Avenida Tulum, the main street, and three other streets named after Maya ruins—Avenida Uxmal, Avenida Cobá and Avenida Yaxchilán. U-shaped streets go in from these main avenues to a central plaza.

The little back streets change name and direction, but it's hard to get lost because all side streets turn around and lead back to one of the four avenues with Maya names.

Downtown Cancún is easy to reach from the Hotel Zone on one of the low-cost shuttle buses that run constantly. Bus stops are everywhere, and you'll never have to wait more than five minutes. Taxis are also readily available but much more expensive. By car, just follow Paseo Kukulcán; downtown is four kilometers west of the bridge from Cancún Island to the mainland.

Oddly, there is not much to see downtown. A modernistic Catholic church squats at one corner of the *zócalo*, a sun-baked expanse of pavement presided over by a statue of Francisco Madero, the enormously popular revolutionary leader who became the first democratically elected president of Mexico in 1911—and was executed following a coup two years later. The time-honored custom of hanging out in the plaza is little in evidence here; except on Sundays after church, the locals generally hang out on the beach.

Besides the T-shirt shops that seem to fill every inch of storefront space along Avenida Tulum, there are several reasons to visit downtown. A number of fun restaurants are found here, along with small hotels that offer rooms at a fraction of Hotel Zone rates. The downtown bus depot presents opportunities to be transported to the real Mexico in air-conditioned comfort at any hour of the day or night. Less than $15 (the price of a chef's salad in many Hotel Zone restaurants) will take you all the way to Mérida.

One of the more popular activities away from the Hotel Zone is the Wednesday bullfight at the **Plaza de Toros**, a small arena where matador meets beast in true Spanish tradition. Four bulls die each week, beginning at 3:30 in the afternoon, and the intermission features folk dancers. Tickets, priced in the $30 range, are available at hotels and travel agencies. In most parts of Mexico, bullfights are held only during annual festivals, so this may be your best chance to witness the spectacle that has been a part of Mexican culture for centuries. However, if outrageous animal-rights violations offend you, save your money. ~ Avenidas Bonampak and Sayil; 9-884-8372.

Cancún's least expensive lodging can be found in the downtown area, several miles from the beach. Inexpensive shuttle buses run constantly between downtown and the Hotel Zone, making beach access no problem. A downtown hotel room makes sense if you are arriving in Cancún late in the evening or planning an early-morning departure. (Otherwise, the same room rate buys fishing-village charm and beaches you can walk to on Isla Mujeres, a short taxi-and-ferry trip away. See Chapter Five.)

One of the best bargains downtown is **Hotel Margarita**. This four-story hostelry has 99 modern rooms with balconies, televisions

LODGING

and two double beds. You also get a swimming pool and a good restaurant. Air conditioning. ~ Avenida Yaxchilán 41; 9-884-9333, fax 9-884-1324. BUDGET TO MODERATE.

Slightly more expensive but still one of the best money savers in town is the charming white pseudocolonial **Hotel Novotol**. The fancier rooms, with air conditioning, televisions and phones, cost the most. The cheaper rooms out back behind the parking lot are lovely lodgings with red-tile floors, fans, brightly tiled baths, dark wood trim and comfortable beds. There's also a charming lobby café. Rooms have either air conditioning or ceiling fans. ~ Avenida Tulum 75; 9-884-2999, fax 9-884-3162. MODERATE.

One of the best midrange downtown hotels is the **Hotel-Suites Caribe Internacional**. The glassy, six-story hotel contains a lobby bar, poolside restaurant, hibiscus-filled garden and 80 attractive, rooms with tile floors and marble showers. Air conditioning. ~ Avenida Yaxchilán 36; 9-884-3999, fax 9-881-3850. MODERATE.

Another good bet downtown is the **Mexhotel Centro**, a three-story place tucked away from the street behind a small shopping mall across from Perico's restaurant. Not for honeymooners, the 80 cozy guest rooms have two double beds each. The walled interior courtyard has palm trees, a pool and a touch of Old Mexico ambience. Guests are also entitled to use the pool and beach facilities at the Mexhotel Resort, located a long bus ride away near the south end of the Hotel Zone. ~ Avenida Yaxchilán 31; 9-884-3888, fax 9-884-3478. MODERATE.

On a quiet side street off Avenida Uxmal, within walking distance of the bus depot, the **Cancún Rosa** offers clean, attractive, affordable guest rooms with TVs—no satellite dish, so no English-language stations. The 22 rooms have tiny windows and are pleasantly cool, if a little bit dark. As with all downtown hotels in this section, the accommodations are nothing special by Cancún standards but verge on the luxurious when compared to lodgings

AUTHOR FAVORITE

I'd love to claim that my favorite place to stay in Cancún is the elegant Ritz-Carlton, but my pocketbook disagrees. Instead, when I spend the night in Cancún, I usually pick a downtown lodging like the **Hotel Plaza Caribe**, then take the bus to the Ritz, sit in the lobby and bask among the rich and famous for free. The grounds here are completely secluded from the urban environment outside. Surrounding its interior patio and pool are 140 clean, small, cheerful rooms with phones (on the blink at times), carpeting and marble washbasins. Air conditioning. ~ Avenidas Tulum and Uxmal; 9-884-1377, fax 9-884-6352. MODERATE.

almost anyplace else in the Yucatán. Air conditioning. ~ Calle Margarita 2, Local 10; 9-884-0623, fax 9-884-1294. BUDGET.

DINING

For restaurants with more personality, lower prices and often better food, head for downtown Ciudad Cancún. You'll find good seafood, steaks and traditional Mexican fare in all price ranges. However, despite the international selection of restaurants in Cancún, the famous regional cuisine of the Yucatán Peninsula is hardest to come by.

In modern Mexico you may notice that traditional fast-food *taquerías* are quickly being replaced by pizza parlors as the favorite places for locals to eat out. In Cancún, it seems, locals prefer famous-name American chain establishments like **Pizza Hut**. ~ Avenida Tulum 25; 9-887-3836. For the best in town, try **Rolandi's Pizzeria**, located near the *glorieta* intersection where the avenue from the Hotel Zone meets Avenida Tulum, the main downtown street. Operated by the same family as the spiffy Swiss restaurant in the Hotel Zone, Rolandi's bakes its pizzas in wood-fueled ovens and itemizes its wide assortment of toppings, including shrimp, on three-foot-tall, four-language wooden menus carried to your table by a waitperson fluent in whatever language you're overheard speaking when you walk in. ~ Avenida Cobá 12; 9-884-4047. MODERATE.

You can find almost any kind of "back-home" food in Cancún. So you're on vacation in this, like, practically foreign country and suddenly you get this craving for lox and bagels. Hey, anything can happen, right? Or maybe a corned beef on rye would do wonders for a temporary case of culture shock. If so, the place you should go is **Super Deli**. You'd never know you're in Mexico. Besides operating its New York deli–style café, the establishment sells gourmet food items imported from the United States, Canada and Europe. ~ Avenidas Tulum and Cobá; 9-884-1122. MODERATE.

The refreshingly clean, minimalist, air-conditioned **Cafetería Pop** has an American-style directness and a lengthy menu of breakfasts, sandwiches and Mexican plates. The proprietor, Jorge Zaldumbide, speaks English and is a fine Cancún resource. ~ Avenida Tulum 25; 9-884-1991. BUDGET.

You'll find authentic Maya food at the downtown Cancún location of **Restaurant Los Almendros**. I'm not suggesting that it's the kind of food indigenous Yucatecans normally eat at home; the Maya diet consists almost entirely of corn. "Traditional" Maya cuisine derives from foods eaten on special feast days, and almost all the Maya dishes served in restaurants were invented at the original roadside eatery called Los Almendros ("the almonds") in the central Yucatán town of Ticul before large-scale tourism came to the region. The owners opened several Los Almendros restaurants around the peninsula before starting the first Maya restaurant in Cancún. It was an instant hit here. Stop in for dinner and find out why. ~ Avenidas Bonampak and Sayil; 9-887-1332. MODERATE.

A newer downtown restaurant that serves Yucatecan food, **El Venado** ("the deer") trades on the reputation of another regional restaurant "chain," Faisán y Venado, found in several less touristy areas. Like its small-town counterparts, it does not actually serve venison despite its name, but it does serve versions of traditional Maya dishes such as lime soup, *pollo pibil* and *pavo escabeche*, tempered for what Mexican restaurateurs presume are American tastes. ~ Avenida Uxmal 23; 9-884-4369. MODERATE.

For choice seafood, check out **El Pescador**. This nondescript little indoor-outdoor joint on a side street, cramped with scarlet tables, serves great fish and shrimp. One drawback: many time-share condominiums offer coupons for free dinners at El Pescador; hence, long lines. ~ Calle Tulipanes 28; 9-884-2673. MODERATE.

If that's the case, get your seafood fix nearby at **Bucaneros**, which gets high marks from locals. No wonder, considering the seafood is extra fresh and delightfully prepared, and the grotto atmosphere couldn't be more romantic. Cozy booths and oil lamps create a perfect ambience for dishes such as creamy lob-ster bisque, rich bouillabaisse and snapper *lizianne* (sautéed with tomato sauce and white wine). ~ Paseo Kukulcán 88; 9-884-2280. DELUXE TO ULTRA-DELUXE.

Rosa Mexicano ranks as one of Cancún's finest authentically Mexican restaurants. Colorful crepe-paper decor changes with the season, making the restaurant feel as if a party is about to start, while soft candlelight, live easy-listening music and a junglelike

AUTHOR FAVORITE

When I think of all the meals I've eaten in Cancún, the one that stands out as the best is **La Habichuela**'s *cocobichuela*, a coconut stuffed with curried shrimp and lobster and accompanied by tropical fruits. The dinner alone would be memorable, but the setting—a lush tropical garden courtyard that re-creates the mystery of a Maya temple—doubles the pleasure of the experience. Accurate reproduc-tions of stone monuments and bas-reliefs are everywhere, along with a few authentic Maya pieces. The Pezzotti family has been operating La Habichuela, one of Cancún's longest-established restaurants, since 1977. It started in a small house dating back to the days when Can-cún was a fishing village and has sprawled, expanding constantly with new construction. Steak and seafood selections with a Caribbean flair are the specialities. ~ Calle Margarita 25; 9-884-3158. DELUXE.

courtyard whisper romance. Dinner entrées include *pollo almendro* (roasted chicken in almond sauce) and *pescado veracruzano* (fish fillet smothered in a spicy tomato sauce). ~ Claveles 4; 9-884-6313. DELUXE.

Perico's offers something of the gaudy old Mexican rambunctiousness. Live marimba music bounces off the yellow globe lights and makes the thick walls of the quasi-colonial building vibrate. Dancers in big sombreros shimmy among the pigskin tables. Rubber masks of celebrities are available for patrons uninhibited enough to wear them. You may see Bill Clinton and Margaret Thatcher drinking from lewd-shaped glasses at the packed bar. The party atmosphere is fueled by the house specialty drink, the Pancho Villa, a Pepto Bismol–pink concoction in an 18-inch-tall glass, containing enough alcohol to serve it flambé. Lunch or dinner choices range from juicy shish kebabs to filet mignon. ~ Avenida Yaxchilán 61; 9-884-0821. MODERATE.

SHOPPING

If the Hotel Zone is awash in amazing quantities of silver jewelry, the regional specialty downtown is T-shirts, which come in all kinds from in-your-face booze-and-sex slogans to occasional masterpieces of illustration.

Clothing and jewelry shops in Ciudad Cancún charge as much as the shopping malls of the Hotel Zone. Avenida Tulum, the main drag, is the hub of the shopping action. One of the better spots is **Sybele**, a classy department store featuring fine clothing for the whole family. ~ Avenida Tulum 109; 9-884-1181.

Aggressive shopkeepers beckon at the **Plaza Centro** and **Pancho Villa Market**. For jewelry, check out **Artes Casa Maya** in Plaza Centro or venture upstairs to **La Siesta**, which features Guatemalan and Central American arts and crafts. **Cultura Maya** in Pancho Villa, stalls 20 and 59, is operated by Efrain Herrera, who speaks Maya and sells hand-painted vases from Ticul. ~ Between Avenidas Tulum and Nadar.

Another downtown find is the aromatic Alondra Lore's complete **UltraFemme**, with its more than 100 quality cosmetic lines. You'll also find soaps and beauty accessories. ~ Avenida Tulum 111; 9-884-1402.

Mercado Municipal de Artesanías Ki Huic, Cancún's oldest crafts market, has always been an overpriced circus disguised as a Mexican-style public market, but as the city's tourist-based economy has prospered, the quality of a lot of the goods sold here has improved. You'll find an occasional treasure, though no bargains. Stalls sell silver jewelry, horsewhips, blankets and lace tablecloths in an open-armed aura that feels so Mexican, so much the bargainer's bailiwick. Shop around, or you will be stung. One of the better shops is **Artesanías Xochimilco** (9-884-1137), with artistic chess sets, Maya statues and elegant boxes in marble, lapis lazuli and jade. Another is **Artesanías Cielito Lindo** (9-884-4511), featuring cases of loose gems. ~ Avenida Tulum. Nearby, **Plaza Mexico** also specializes in Mexican arts and crafts. ~ Avenida Tulum.

Plaza Bonita, a neighborhood public market, is about the only place in the downtown area geared more for locals than tourists. While little out of the ordinary in the way of arts and crafts is to be found here, this is where you'll find the best buys in practical items such as hammocks and plastic squeeze bottles. ~ Avenida Yaxchilán near Avenida Uxmal; 9-884-6212.

The main place where locals shop these days, however, is the big **Wal-Mart Supercenter**, where you'll find both Mexican and imported goods of every description, from blue jeans and hair dryers to books and antibiotics, at the same prices you'd pay in the United States—and lower than anywhere else in Cancún. ~ Avenida Cobá 2; 9-884-0808.

Works by local painters and sculptors—American expatriates as well as Mexican artists—are exhibited for sale at **La Casa de la Cultura**, located behind Wal-Mart. ~ Prolongación Avenida Yaxchilán 21; 9-884-8364.

NIGHTLIFE Order a cocktail in Cancún and you get preposterous proportions. Three-pound watermelons hollowed out and filled with three pints of liquor. Whole pineapples spiked with half a dozen potions. Margaritas served in vessels the size of punch bowls. And glasses of beer so tall they come in their own wooden stands. To check out the big beer scene, stroll the sidewalk bars in Ciudad Cancún. Make no mistake: all of these places were conceived with the tourist trade in mind. Many have quaint old traditions—sometimes several months old—such as the alleged custom of gulping down 12 tequila slammers while a couple of waiters jiggle your head. The better part of valor may be to sip something slowly and watch other patrons use two hands to chug their two-foot-tall beers (one is almost always enough).

A block behind the main drag stands tropical colonial-style **Perico's**. With a marimba band, a Day of the Dead motif, an animated bar complete with saddles for stools and dancing in the aisles, there's never a dull moment. ~ Avenida Yaxchilán 71; 84-48-84.

Cancún's gay scene is restricted to the downtown area. The city's two exclusively gay and lesbian discos are located close together on Avenida Tulum. They are **Picante** ~ Avenida Tulum 20, no phone; and **Disco Karamba** ~ Avenida Tulum 9 at Calle Azucenas, no phone. Both are large, loud and open 'til dawn. Though mainly straight earlier in the evening, nearby **Risky Times** often gets cruisy around three in the morning. ~ Avenida Tulum at Avenida Cobá; 9-884-7503. Pretty little **Parque Palapa** is the city's most active—and sometimes predatory—cruising spot after dark. ~ Calle Margarita, off Avenida Uxmal. A kinder, gentler gay men's bar is the soft-spoken **Picante**. ~ Cancún Galerías, Avenida Tulum.

Most local residents can't afford to patronize downtown nightspots very often. Instead, locals of all ages can be found any weekday evening at **Fun Place** in Plaza Bonita, Cancún's biggest video game arcade. ~ Avenida Yaxchilán near Avenida Uxmal.

Another "hidden" form of local entertainment can be found in Cancún's *zona de tolerancía*, nicknamed "**Plaza 21.**" Prostitution is legal in Mexico, but only in combination bar-brothel establishments in "tolerance zones" like this one on the city's outskirts. Taxi drivers know where to find it. It is well-policed and crime-free, but despite regular health examinations, gonorrhea is common. ~ Carretera a Merida, Km. 21.

Outdoor Adventures

FISHING

Most big-game fishing is catch-and-release, to insure that billfish remain abundant in the waters of the Mexican Caribbean. Favorite varieties of smaller fish for eating are barracuda and *huachinango* (red snapper).

Cancún's mind-boggling variety of facilities for lagoon fishing and deep-sea fishing includes big-game fishing tours on yachts operated by **AquaWorld**. ~ Paseo Kukulcán, Km. 15.2; 9-848-8326. **Aqua Fun** also offers daily fishing tours. ~ Paseo Kukulcán, Km. 16.5; 9-885-2930. **Aqua Tours** offers deep-sea fishing excursions. ~ 9-883-0400. The specialty at **Asterix Noviera** is nighttime party fishing; in the daytime, the boats are for rent. ~ Carlos 'n Charlie's dock; 9-886-4847. In addition, many independent fishing charters sail from Puerto Juárez and other Cancún docks. These charters can be arranged through the lobby travel agency at any major hotel. *Note:* Fishing charter rates are much higher in Cancún than on Isla Mujeres or Cozumel.

DIVING

In Cancún, a good place for diving instruction is **Manta Divers**. ~ Paseo Kukulcán, Km. 6.5; 849-4050. **Aqua Sports** offers a full

AUTHOR FAVORITE

I thought I'd tried everything—gone scuba diving among sharks, snorkeling in cenotes and sightseeing in submarines along coral reefs—until the day I tried a BOB (Breathing Observation Bubble) and mingled with schools of bright yellow and glowing blue fish. The BOB is an electric-powered underwater vehicle you ride like a jet ski; it has a bubble helmet with a clear faceplate like an astronaut's, fed by a scuba tank, which lets you breath normally without an air hose or regulator. A 45-minute trip costs $75. Not in the same league as diving with sharks, of course, but way cool nonetheless. ~ 9-892-4102

selection of reef dives around Cancún and beyond, as well as cave dives, short courses and certifications. ~ 9-887-3414; www.cancun-aquasports.com. Equipment and lessons are also available at **Aqua Tours**. ~ Paseo Kukulcán, Km. 6.25; 9-883-0400.

Good snorkeling areas include the shallow reefs off **Punta Nizuc**, the southern tip of Cancún Island, where AquaWorld operates **Paradise**, a manmade deck where snorkelers can relax between plunges; there are fins and goggles for rent, and each passenger on the the boat trip to the "island" receives a free snorkel. ~ 9-848-8326. Freshwater jungle springs along the mainland edge of Laguna Nichupté are also good snorkeling areas.

There are also several options for visitors who want to experience the undersea world without getting wet. Among them are the **Atlantis Submarines** (Embarcadero Playa Linda; 9-883-4963) and **Sub-See** semi-subs (9-885-2288).

WIND-SURFING

In Cancún, nearly every beach has a marina offering windsurfing lessons. Most windsurfing is done along the north-shore beaches of the Hotel Zone and at the southern end of Laguna Nichupte. The premier windsurfing school is at the **Hotel Camino Real**. ~ Punta Cancún; 9-883-0100. Many hotels offer sailboard rentals for guests and have qualified instructors. You'll also find board rentals at **Windsurfing Cancún**. ~ Playa Tortugas; 9-884-2023. **Club de Vela** has a reputation as the place to stay if you're into windsurfing. ~ Paseo Kukulcán, Km. 3.5; 9-883-2222.

BOATING

Although many local people travel up and down the Caribbean coast on *cayucas*, or dugout canoes, there are no established canoe rental places. However, Cancún offers an amazing range of equipment for other water sports: waterskis, jet skis, wave-runners, parasails, paddleboats, speedboats, airboats and sea kayaks. Check out the possibilities at **AquaWorld** ~ Paseo Kukulcán, Km. 15.2, 9-848-8326; **Aqua Fun** ~ Paseo Kukulcán, Km. 16.5, 9-885-3260; or **Asterix Noviera** ~ Carlos & Charlie's dock, 9-886-4847. Sea kayak rentals are also available at almost all hotels along Paseo Kukulcán. For waterskiing and parasailing, try **Club Caribe** ~ 9-883-0311; or **Club Lagoon** ~ 9-883-0222.

BIKING

Open-air entrepreneurs rent both bicycles and inline skates at most of Cancún's shopping plazas, especially Plaza Caracol. Automobile traffic makes the Hotel Zone a scary place to ride, but many cyclists enjoy the wide, paved path lined with palm trees and condominiums that parallels Paseo Kukulcán between the Hotel Zone and downtown.

GOLF

Designed by Robert Trent Jones, the 18-hole **Pok-Ta-Pok Club de Golf Cancún** is set on the island that separates Laguna Nichupté from Laguna Bojórquez near the elbow of Cancún's Hotel Zone. It has cool breezes and wraparound sea views, as well as a pro shop, showers and bar. The green fee is around $30. (By the way, the name of the club comes from *pok-ta-pok*, the high-speed sport that was played in ball courts all over the ancient Maya world.) The ruins of two small Maya shrines dating back to the 14th century stand right on the golf course. ~ Hotel Zone, off Paseo Kukulcán at Km. 7; 9-883-1230; e-mail poktapok@sybcom.com.

The **Hilton Cancún Golf Resort** has a public, 18-hole par-72 golf course with green fees $10 to $15 higher than at Pok-Ta-Pok. ~ Paseo Kukulcán, Km. 18; 9-881-8000 ext. 8305. The **Melía Cancún** has a nine-hole course that is open to nonguests for a fairly steep green fee. ~ Paseo Kukulcán, Km. 15.5; 9-881-1100. The 36-hole **Mini Golf Palace**, the only putt-putt golf course on the Mexican Caribbean coast, is lavishly landscaped with artificial waterfalls, rivers, a lagoon and phony Maya temples. ~ Cancún Palace Hotel, Paseo Kukulcán, Km. 14.5; 9-885-0867.

Pok-Ta-Pok Club de Golf Cancún also has tennis courts. ~ Hotel Zone, off Paseo Kukulcán, Km. 7; 9-883-0871; e-mail poktapok@ sybcom.com. You'll find other courts at most resorts in Cancún's Hotel Zone.

TENNIS

▼ ▼ ▼ ▼ ▼ ▼ ▼ ▼ ▼ ▼ ▼

Transportation

AIR

Cancún International Airport, the largest airport on the Yucatán Peninsula and the second-busiest in Mexico, is located in a broad jungle clearing 15 kilometers south of downtown Cancún and five kilometers west of the southern tip of the hotel zone. Aeroméxico, American, Aviateca, Continental, Mexicana, Northwest and United fly into Cancún from major cities in the United States, Mexico and Canada.

TAXIS

Taxis provide the main transportation between the Hotel Zone and the airport. Rates are regulated but not cheap. Expect to pay a little over US$20 a person to get from the airport to either the Hotel Zone or downtown. There are also a few *combis*, or van shuttles, that carry passengers for about $8 each. Along Paseo Kukulcán, taxis outnumber all other vehicles, and you'll almost always find a free one within hailing distance.

CAR RENTALS

A rental car is not necessary for getting around Cancún; valet parking can cost as much as taking a taxi. If you're planning to venture beyond Cancún, you'll find desks for three dozen major rental chains at Cancún International Airport, including **Avis** (9-886-0222, or 800-331-1212 in the U.S.; www.avis.com), **Budget** (9-884-0204, or 800-527-0700 in the U.S.), **Hertz** (9-887-6604, or 800-654-3131 in the U.S.; www.hertz.com) and **National** (9-886-4490, or 800-227-7368 in the U.S.; www.nationalcar.com).

PUBLIC
TRANSIT

Shuttle buses that run up and down Paseo Kukulcán constantly, from 6 a.m. to midnight, make it quick, easy and inexpensive to reach any place in the Hotel Zone, and to get anywhere there from downtown. Riding a public bus costs only five pesos, or about US50¢. Privately operated shuttles also cruise the Hotel Zone and cost much more. You can tell the difference because the public buses have the fare painted on the front.

▼▼▼▼▼▼▼▼▼▼▼▼▼▼▼▼▼▼▼▼▼▼

Addresses & Phone Numbers

Angeles Verdes ("Green Angels"—roadside assistance) ~ 9-884-2950

Canaco-Servitur (Cancún Chamber of Commerce) ~ Avenida López Portillo; 9-884-4315

Cruz Roja (Red Cross) ~ Avenida Yaxchilán 2; 9-884-1616

Delegacion Regional de Servicios Migratorios (Mexican Immigration Office) ~ Avenida Náder at Avenida Uxmal; 9-884-1404

Emergency Number (similar to 911 in U.S.) ~ dial 060

Hospital Americano ~ Calle Viento 15; 9-884-6133

Internet Café ~ Avenida Tulum at Avenida Mexicana; 9-887-3167

Policia ~ 9-884-1913

Procuraduría del Consumidor (Consumer Protection Agency) ~ 9 y 11 Avenida Cobá; 9-884-2634

Quintana Roo State Tourism Office ~ Avenida Tulum 26; 9-887-8229

Total Assist (English-speaking emergency room) ~ Calle Claveles 5; 9-884-1092

United States Consulate ~ Plaza Caracol II; 9-883-0272

FIVE

The Mexican Caribbean

The stretch of Route 307 that hugs the Caribbean coastline from Punta Sam, the Isla Mujeres car ferry dock just north of Cancún, to the magical Maya ruins at Tulum, about 145 kilometers to the south, has experienced a sweeping transition from jungle backcountry to resort mecca. Known until recently as the *Corredor Turístico*, this area was romantically re-nicknamed the *Riviera Maya* or, for English-speaking visitors, the Mayan Riviera, and the new name caught on so well that now it's used more commonly than individual town names along this stretch of the coast. The transition began in the aftermath of Hurricane Roxanne, which struck this part of the coast in October 1995, smashing fishermen's boats, snapping phone and power lines, and ripping apart the thatched roofs of small, picturesque tourist lodgings and local fishermen's huts. Faced with expensive repairs and plunging land prices, the Mexican government decided the time was right to open up the mostly pristine coastline to international resort development. Today, Cancún-style international resorts and gated condominium communities are completed or under construction on almost every beach between Cancún and Tulum; the few natural beaches tucked away along the coastline cost hefty admissions to get in. (Yes, the beaches themselves are public property by law, but getting to them through the dense forest means using a privately owned road.)

The narrow little ribbon of highway between green walls of jungle has been replaced by a four-lane freeway as far as Playa del Carmen. Any "hidden" mystique associated with this stretch of the Caribbean coastline is spoiled by the many unsightly billboards that line the highway, promoting Riviera Maya resorts, dive shops and commercial attractions, along with official looking highway signs announcing things like "Palenque—1285 km. Club Akumal Caribe—22 km." (Not to single out this resort; they all seem to have bought into the promotion.)

Take time to explore and discover the diversity that makes this stretch of the Caribbean coast unique. The highway, Route 307, is rarely more than a quarter of a mile from the sea, but for much of the trip all you see is dense forest. For a

135

vista of the Caribbean, you must take one of the short side roads that lead east to hideaway beaches, Maya ruins, cabaña hideaways, resort hotels and even theme parks. Many of these roads have become driveways for hotels and ultra-exclusive residential developments, and some have guards at the gates. International visitors are usually allowed to use these roads for beach access, especially if they also stop in at the hotel for a meal or a drink; remember, the beaches themselves are public, even though you may have to cross private property to reach them. (Locals complain that security guards are less tolerant toward Mexicans, putting some of their favorite beaches off-limits.)

On the other side of the highway, the forest reaches westward practically forever. No road or village breaks the stillness of this jungle, which is uninhabitable in the rainy season because the clay earth turns as slippery as grease and accumulates shallow water that stands for months, breeding mosquitoes. It also provides a vast expanse of safe nesting for herons and other wading birds, which you see just about anywhere you look as you drive down Route 307.

Playa del Carmen, the largest town on the Riviera Maya, is a great vacation alternative to Cancún, offering good lodging values in all price ranges, including many budget-priced small hotels within a block or two of the beach. The atmosphere is friendly, with a European flair, and the fabulous coral reefs of Cozumel are just a quick ferry ride away.

Isla Mujeres

A speck of land ringed with water the color of apple jade, Isla Mujeres is the jewel of the Yucatán. Incredibly, though it lies only five miles from Cancún, the island has so far managed to maintain a faraway feel. Low jungle bush, brambly bougainvillea and banana plants still claim much of the land. Narrow crumbling roads wend up and down hills, and bristly thatched roofs peek out of the brush. And, at every glance, there is the dazzling green sea.

The island's big action occurs every midday, when hundreds of Cancún daytrippers come to snorkel and shop. Most arrive on one of the double-decker party boats that embark from Cancún's Playa Linda.

If rum-infused hordes are not your idea of fun, catch the public ferry from Puerto Juárez, in the north part of Cancún city. The big, modern, touristy "fast boat" takes passengers across Bahía de Mujeres to the village on the north end of Isla Mujeres in about 15 minutes, and has shipboard entertainment by a little Mexican band. But take the older, funkier "slow boat" and let the breathtaking cruise across the shallow blue-green bay take a full 35 minutes! It's also possible to take a car ferry to Isla Mujeres from Punta Sam, 12 kilometers north of Cancún, but Isla Mujeres is small enough that a car is an unnecessary headache there.

Traveling on your own, you can arrive before the crowds (a must for snorkeling), rent a moped or bicycle and really explore the island. Isla Mujeres is only about five and a half miles long and has only a few roads, so it's easy to get around.

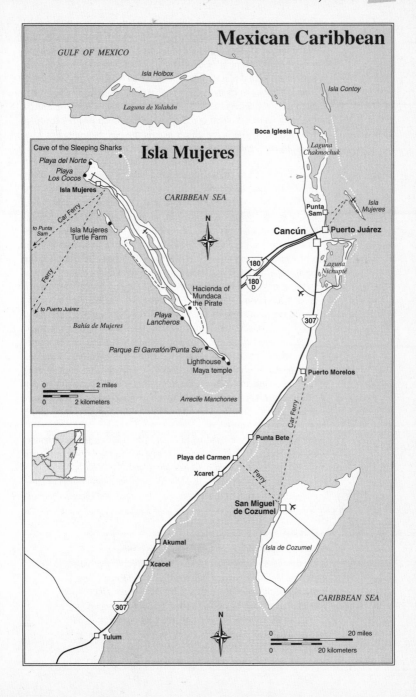

Mexican Caribbean

GULF OF MEXICO

Isla Holbox

Laguna de Yalahán

Isla Contoy

Boca Iglesia

Laguna Chakmochuk

Isla Mujeres

Cave of the Sleeping Sharks

Playa del Norte

Playa Los Cocos

Isla Mujeres

CARIBBEAN SEA

Car Ferry

to Punta Sam

Isla Mujeres Turtle Farm

Ferry

N

Punta Sam

Isla Mujeres

Cancún

Puerto Juárez

to Puerto Juárez

Hacienda of Mundaca the Pirate

180

Laguna Nichupté

180 D

Playa Lancheros

Bahía de Mujeres

Parque El Garrafón/Punta Sur

307

Lighthouse Maya temple

Arrecife Manchones

0   2 miles

0   2 kilometers

Puerto Morelos

Car Ferry

Punta Bete

Playa del Carmen

Ferry

Xcaret

San Miguel de Cozumel

Akumal

Isla de Cozumel

Xcacel

CARIBBEAN SEA

307

N

0   20 miles

0   20 kilometers

Tulum

If your Yucatán travels take you to any of the genuine fishing villages along the Gulf coast (see Chapter Nine), you will find that they are not at all like Isla Mujeres. In fact, Isla Mujeres has more hotels, restaurants, T-shirt shops, street vendors and sports-equipment rental places than all the towns on the Gulf coast combined. Thanks to its proximity to Cancún, Isla Mujeres has managed to parlay its fishing-village quaintness into a bustling tourist industry. Yet the charm is real and has not been lost. In contrast to Cancún, whose lights glitter across the bay at night, Isla Mujeres' tourist trade is still small-scale and refreshingly human.

SIGHTS

Drop by the **Casa de la Cultura** for a look at what local residents do for fun and self-expression. Every morning and evening, the cultural center comes to life with music, dance and art classes. You might see Isla Mujeres women of all ages belly dancing or practicing a Hawaiian hula. The cultural center also provides exhibition space for the island's sizable artist colony, made up of U.S. and Canadian expatriates as well as Mexicans. In addition, the center operates an English-language book exchange, inviting you to trade in your unwanted paperbacks instead of leaving them in your hotel room. ~ Avenida Guerrero; 9-877-0307.

At the south end of the island, Parque Nacional El Garrafón (see "Beaches & Parks") has traditionally been one of the most popular snorkeling spots in the Mexican Caribbean. Management of the park, now renamed **Parque El Garrafón/Punta Sur**, was turned over in 1999 to the private company that manages the Laguna Xelha and Xcaret environmentally oriented theme parks. El Garrafón is undergoing a major facelift. Today, besides snorkeling, there's a swim-with-the-dolphins program; relandscaping is underway. Admission.

Along the main road to El Garrafón, notice the **Shell House**, a local landmark. The contemporary, white two-story residence is built in the shape of a giant conch shell.

Just as today's visitors use Isla Mujeres as a scenic stopover, the ancient Maya rendezvoused here on their way to Cozumel to wor-

AUTHOR FAVORITE

My favorite spot on Isla Mujeres is not the beach, the reef, the shopping district, or the ruins of the Maya temple or the pirate's mansion. After the last of the tourist "booze cruises" leave, the small fishing-village atmosphere returns, romantic and vibrant, to the big central **zócalo**, which serves as everything from a basketball court to a dance pavilion. This kind of authentic small-town exuberance is rarely encountered anywhere around Cancún.

ship Ixchel, goddess of fertility and the moon. Ixchel got her own **temple** on Isla Mujeres, the remains of which lie at the southern-most tip of the island, just past the old lighthouse. Climbing the gnarled, rocky path to the temple, it's easy to see why the Maya chose this spot. The island's most spectacular locale, and the high-est point in the entire Yucatán region, it is a bluff that pokes boldly into the sea, its sides deeply carved by eons of wind and water. Recently restored after it collapsed during Hurricane Gilbert in 1988, the dramatic setting has remained a fitting testament to the world that was. The land's-end cliffs that drop down to the sea once made an ideal location for ancient astronomers—some ex-perts believe one of the functions of the temple was as an obser-vatory—and today it's a perfect spot from which to watch the sun set over distant Cancún. Except for the sun-wrinkled light-house watchman, you're apt to be the only one here. Now the tem-ple is being restored as part of Parque El Garrafón/Punta Sur.

Hundreds of years after the Maya had moved on, pirates fell prey to Isla Mujeres' bewitching scenery and charm. Among the rogues who supposedly hid out here was privateer and smuggler Jean Lafitte. In 1841, during his exploration of the Yucatán, John Lloyd Stephens encountered a man on Isla Mujeres who claimed to have been Lafitte's prisoner for two years.

Near the south end of the island lie remnants of the island's illustrious pirate past—the **Hacienda of Mundaca the Pirate**. The ruins, a rotting house and arched well that once watered the es-tate, are wrapped in a tangle of low, dense vegetation. According to local legend, notorious Spanish pirate Fermín Mundaca fell in love with an 18-year-old island beauty and quit his pirating to build a hacienda and fabulous tomb for himself to impress her. For a while it worked. Then she jilted him and eloped with a penni-less man. Mundaca slowly went mad. Near the house, a crum-bling tombstone with his epitaph says it all: "What I am, you shall be; what you are, I was." In truth, Fermín Mundaca was not ex-actly a pirate. He was a slave trader who sold Maya laborers to Cuban sugar growers in the early 19th century, when a British embargo put an end to the importation of slaves from Africa. A pathway meanders through lush gardens that have run wild for nearly two centuries, and the hacienda has been partly restored as part of Parque El Garrafón/Punta Sur. Admission. ~ Off Carretera al Garrafón, across from Playa Lancheros, Parque El Garrafón/ Punta Sur.

A small **zoo** has recently been added next to Mundaca's ha-cienda. Here you'll find wildlife native to the Quintana Roo jun-gle, including spider monkeys, crocodiles, boa constrictors, trop-ical birds and even a jaguar. Admission. ~ Parque El Garrafón/ Punta Sur.

If it's underwater wonders you seek, you might also check with one of the dive shops in the fishing village and find out about special snorkeling or diving spots. For instance, the Manchones reef provides calm depths for beginning divers, and **El Dormitorio**, a graveyard of 16th-century pirate ships, offers adventure for more experienced scuba enthusiasts. Perhaps the ultimate thrill dive off Mexico's Caribbean coast is the **Cave of the Sleeping Sharks**. At a depth of about 66 feet, the cave is actually an undersea cenote where freshwater flows out of a subterranean river. Scientists believe the reef sharks gather in the cave because parasites that fasten themselves to sharks cannot tolerate the salt-free environment and leave to find a new home. Another theory is that the higher oxygen content of the freshwater acts as an intoxicant on the sharks' tiny brains. It certainly makes them docile. Nevertheless, sharks are sharks, and this dive involves risking your life.

On a tiny peninsula separated by a lagoon from the rest of the island, the **Isla Mujeres Turtle Farm** protects three species of sea turtles that have traditionally nested on the beaches here. A baby turtle's chances of survival were never great, since sea birds would try to gobble them up during their dash from nest to surf, and the situation was aggravated as humans raided the nests for turtle eggs. For decades, adult sea turtles were tethered at El Garrafón as a tourist attraction while kids had their photos taken sitting on the big beasts' backs. All that changed, though, when Mexico joined the United States in declaring the turtles to be endangered species. Today, the Mexican government operates this hatchery designed to restore the area's sea turtle population. The turtle eggs are removed from their nests on the beach (the mother turtle never returns to the nest after laying her eggs) and hatched in pens that protect them from predators. The hatchling turtles are raised in saltwater tanks until they're a year old, at which time they are released into the open sea by Isla Mujeres school children. ~ Sac Bajo.

LODGING

Despite its tiny size, Isla Mujeres has a lot to offer in the way of lodging. Travelers suffering from Cancún burnout come here seeking a slower pace and a less-expensive place to sleep, and they find it.

Because the island offers no car rentals (only bicycles and mopeds), taxis are expensive. If you need to be near the action, low-key though it is, choose a hotel in town. If total escape is your goal, plant yourself at the southern end of the island.

The three-story stucco **Posada del Mar** resembles a plain motel but is ranked among the island's better lodgings. The 30 big white rooms enjoy bright views of the village beach and lighthouse, with phones, balconies and American-style furnishings; there are also 12 individual bungalows. A lovely pool, garden and restaurant-bar add to the relaxation. Air conditioning; ceiling fans. ~ Avenida Rueda Medina 15; 9-877-0212, fax 9-877-0266, or 800-544-3005 in the U.S.; www.posadadelmar.com, e-mail hotel@posada delmar.com. BUDGET TO MODERATE.

Near the *zócalo* stands the **Hotel Isleño**. Molded cement forms the closets and bedstands in the small white rooms, decorated by little more than cute overhead lamp-fans. There are several rooms per shared bath and some rooms with kitchens and private baths. Ceiling fans; some rooms have air conditioning. ~ Avenidas Madero and Guerrero; 9-877-0302, fax 9-877-0114. BUDGET.

On the village's shops-and-restaurants pedestrian street, **El Mesón del Bucanero** has a dozen rooms and suites, each individually configured and tastefully decorated in Caribbean island style. All rooms have cable TV, and some have refrigerators and bathtubs. Set around a pretty courtyard behind Bucaneros restaurant, this little hotel offers all the privacy and charm of a Mexican hacienda inn just minutes' walk from the beach, the ferry dock and the best shopping in town. Air conditioning; ceiling fans. ~ Avenida Hidalgo; phone/fax 9-877-0210; www.bucaneros.com, e-mail bucanero@prodigy.net.mx. MODERATE.

The **Hotel Rocamar** was a favorite hippie hangout in decades past. The three-story hotel overlooks the sea from its vantage point just uphill from the town plaza. Its three floors, lined in stone railings decorated with seagull motifs, contain 15 slightly funky, very homey guest rooms. The ones with balconies are a seabreeze heaven. The sea theme appears everywhere—in seashell lamps, giant fishhooks holding up the dressers and polyurethane washbasins inset with shells and seahorses. Ceiling fans. ~ Avenidas Guerrero and Bravo; phone/fax 9-877-0101; e-mail roca mar@mjmnet.net. MODERATE.

Of the many low-cost hotels on the island, the cheapest is **Poc-Na**, a pleasant youth hostel with neither age limits nor curfew. Located just a short walk from Playa Los Cocos, the rambling hostelry contains mixed dormitories with woven-hemp bunks and small communal baths. There's an extra charge for sheets,

LOOKING FOR LODGING?

Except for Mexico's peak vacation times—the Christmas season, Holy Week and summer weekends—you can usually find a place to stay on Isla Mujeres without making advance reservations. Local promoters armed with loose-leaf binders full of information on hotels, restaurants and motorbike rentals descend on each arriving passenger ferry, ready to help you find a place to stay in the price range of your choice.

towels, pillow and mattress. The restaurant on the premises serves breakfast only. Ceiling fans. ~ Calle Matamoros 15; 9-877-0090, fax 9-877-0059. BUDGET.

Several remarkably inexpensive small hotels with clean, modern rooms and private baths are located away from the beach in the middle of the village. (Remember, nowhere in town are you more than four blocks' walk from the beach.) The **Hotel Francis Arlene** has 26 rooms in a rambling two-story building around a small concrete courtyard used for guest parking in the unlikely event that one of the guests has a car on the island. All rooms have refrigerators and balconies or patios, and some have cooking facilities. Some rooms have air conditioning. ~ Avenida Guerrero 7; phone/fax 9-877-0310, fax 9-877-0861. BUDGET.

For bungalows right on the island's nicest beach, check in at **Hotel Cabañas María del Mar**. Included among the 56 rooms are five roomy cabañas with outdoor patios, plus eight smaller rooms in this garden-filled compound. The cheerful rooms include carved beds, little refrigerators and hammock-slung patios. The hotel has a small swimming pool and offers boat and motor scooter rentals. Some rooms have ceiling fans. ~ Avenida Carlos Lazo 1; 9-877-0179, fax 9-877-0213, or 800-223-5695 in the U.S.; www.cabanasdelmar.com. MODERATE.

Set on picturesque Playa del Norte, the pretty, pink-washed **Nautibeach Playa Norte** satisfies those travelers who need plenty of space. Accommodations in this nearly new 35-unit condominium complex feature two bedrooms, a kitchenette and terraces or balconies overlooking the sea. A swimming pool and an excellent French-Caribbean restaurant round out the amenities. Jungle landscaping creates an aura of seclusion, though the center of town is just a five-minute walk. Air conditioning. Not all of the condos available for rent are under the same management; the following contact information is for the Canadian couple that manages 20 of the units. ~ Avenida Rueda Medina; contact Joyce and Bob, 9-888-0033, fax 9-888-0034; www.nautibeach.com, e-mail joyce@nautibeach.com. DELUXE TO ULTRA-DELUXE.

Located near the east end of Playa del Norte, **Na-Balam Beach Hotel** enjoys a private location within walking distance of town.

ISLAND CHARM

With its crayon-colored sloops and narrow, cobbled, balcony-lined lanes, the town at the north end of Isla Mujeres, where the ferry docks are located, epitomizes travel fantasies of a charming Mexican fishing village. The island's hotels, restaurants and shops are concentrated here.

Each of the 32 spacious suites has a sitting area and either a king-size or two double beds. The palm-shaded grounds surround a swimming pool, and there are hammocks for guests' use. Air conditioning. ~ Calle Zazil-Ha 118; 9-877-0279, fax 9-877-0446. DELUXE TO ULTRA-DELUXE.

Punta Norte, the triangular peninsula at the east end of Playa del Norte, is the site of several newish luxury hotels, including the three-story **Hotel Playa la Media Luna**. Each of the 18 bright-colored guest rooms has a balcony or patio with an ocean view. Rooms offer your choice of a king-size bed or two double beds. There's a swimming pool. Air conditioning. ~ Half Moon Bay; 9-877-0759, fax 9-877-1124, or 800-833-5971 in the U.S. DELUXE TO ULTRA-DELUXE.

Nearby, the **Hotel Secreto** offers similar amenities to those at Media Luna for about the same rates. The difference is one of style. The decor in these 18 guest rooms is very white. Walls, curtains, bedspreads and contemporary furniture—all are white, white, white in dazzling contrast to the bright blue sea and sky outside the windows. Some rooms have canopy beds. There is an outdoor living room area under a broad, shady portal overlooking the swimming pool. ~ Punta Norte; 9-877-1039, fax 9-877-1048; e-mail reserv@hotelsecreto.com. ULTRA-DELUXE.

Midway down the island, a manmade channel provides boat access to Laguna Makax, a mangrove-sheltered lake that has been transformed into a yacht basin. Here, the **Marina Puerto Isla Mujeres** offers some of the most luxurious accommodations on the island. The 25 suites and two-bedroom casitas are scattered around spacious, palm-shaded grounds. All units are sparely furnished in Scandinavian natural-wood style, and the casitas have patios with jacuzzis and full kitchens with dishwashers. There is a swimming pool on the grounds, and a water taxi carries guests to a private beach club on the seashore nearby. The marina has a gourmet deli and bicycle, motor scooter and jet ski rentals. Air conditioning. ~ Puerto Makax; 9-877-0330, fax 9-877-04-85, or 800-400-3333 in the U.S. ULTRA-DELUXE.

At the south end of the island stands the **Hotel Garrafón de Castilla**, a bright pink three-story complex surrounded by palms, lawn and shade trees. The 12 rooms are simply and tastefully furnished in hues of pink and gold; each has a minibar and a private balcony or patio with a view of the Cancún skyline that's sure to make you glad you're here instead of across the water. The attractions of Parque El Garrafón/Punta Sur are a short walk away, and guests have the use of the hotel's private beach club nearby. It's a long trek into town, but on request the managers will have a moped or golf cart waiting for you when you arrive. Air conditioning. ~ Carretera Punta Sur, Km. 6; 9-877-0107, fax 9-877-0019. MODERATE.

Also located near El Garrafón and the southern tip of the island, **Casa de los Sueños** offers some of the classiest accommodations on Isla Mujeres. All nine units in this modernistic bed-and-breakfast inn have bright contemporary furnishings and balconies with views of Cancún across the water. Amenities include a swimming pool and seaside meditation spaces, as well as free use of bicycles, snorkeling gear and sea kayaks. Adults only; no smoking. ~ Carretera al Garrafón; 9-877-0651, fax 9-877-0708, or 800-551-2558 in the U.S. ULTRA-DELUXE.

When the Rolandi family, longtime Cancún restaurateurs, set out to create an ultraexclusive small hotel, they chose to do it not in Cancún but rather on Isla Mujeres. The result, **Villa Rolandi**, is nothing short of spectacular. Bronze sculptures, white pillars, polished stone floors and vaulted ceilings set the tone of hushed elegance in the lobby. The 29 suites, brightly decorated with contemporary Mexican artworks, feature one king-size or two queen-size beds and big marble bathrooms with showers, water jets, steam, and amenities such as hair dryers and terrycloth robes. Guests enjoy private seafront balconies with their own jacuzzis. Other facilities at the hotel include a dock on Laguna Makax, where a private yacht carries guests back and forth to Cancún, plus a swimming pool, a beach and an exercise center. Air conditioning. ~ Laguna Mar, Carretera Sac-Bajo; 9-877-0700, fax 9-877-0100; www. villarolandi.com, e-mail hotel@villarolandi.com. ULTRA-DELUXE.

DINING

For breakfast or lunch, it's hard to beat **La Cazuela**, a café near the town plaza that features tables on two patios overlooking the sea as well as a small indoor dining room. The house specialty is the *cazuela*, similar to a soufflé made in a Mexican clay dish of the same name. Also on the menu are traditional Mexican and American breakfasts, fruit plates, salads, sandwiches, giant glasses of fresh fruit and vegetable juices, and some of the best espresso and cappuccino in town. ~ Avenida Bravo, next to Hotel Rocamar. BUDGET.

The **Restaurant Miramar**, next to the ferry pier, is a good place to absorb the rhythms of local life. Palapa-roofed and hemmed with a red balcony railing, it's like a backwater stop for gondolas. Some of the island's tastiest seafood is served here, including lobster, succulent garlic shrimp, *sopa de lima* and fish tacos. ~ Avenida Rueda Medina Sur. BUDGET TO MODERATE.

Just off the plaza, **El Sombrero de Gomar** is a popular place to meet fellow travelers. Its hacienda-style patio and indoor dining room are decked out in striped serape tablecloths, twirling fans and painted tiles. A cool screen of foliage shelters tables from the dust and sun. Good meals, including fresh seafood and meats, are served. ~ Avenida Hidalgo; 9-877-0142. BUDGET.

At night, **La Peña** offers a breezy seaside picnic ambience under a palapa alive with Latin music. Savory pizza (vegetarian to seafood) is the house specialty. There's also chicken, chow mein and conch. ~ Avenida Guerrero 5, adjacent to the plaza. BUDGET.

Bucaneros, a comfortable, wood-paneled restaurant in the heart of town, serves fresh seafood, central Mexican food and traditional Maya dishes. The house specialty is freshly caught *huachinango* (red snapper) or other fish fried whole. ~ Avenida Hidalgo between Madero and Abasolo; 9-877-0210; e-mail bucanero@prodigy. net.mx. MODERATE.

Strolling around the village is great fun any-time—*except* from noon to 3 p.m., when Cancún daytrippers jam the streets.

Ciro's Lobster House is one of the island's classier seafood houses, with an Americanized wood-paneled look and live music. The food, from shrimp curry to lobster thermidor, is outstanding. ~ Avenida Matamoros 11. MODERATE.

Zazil-Ha, the eatery at the Na-Balam Beach Hotel, is a restaurant in three parts sharing the same kitchen. The main Restaurant Zazil-Ha exudes tropical ambience from its huge palapa roof, skylights and the plants-and-seashells decor. The menu presents and interesting selection of Maya and vegetarian dishes, along with homemade bread and exotic snacks. (Strangely, though this is one of the best vegetarian restaurants on the island, the chairs are upholstered with pigskin.) The outdoor Snack Bar Zazil-Ha also leans toward heart-healthy fare with fresh salads, fruit plates and a juice bar; if eating healthy is not a priority while on vacation, there are also cocktails, hamburgers and Mexican-style snacks. The same selection is served at the beachfront Palapa Bar as well. ~ Calle Zazil-Ha 118, Playa Norte; 9-877-0279; www.nabalam.com, e-mail nabalam@cancun.com.mx. BUDGET TO DELUXE.

The island's much-touted house of French haute cuisine is **Maria's Kan Kin Restaurant.** Though the food may be pretty ordinary as fancy French restaurant fare goes, in atmosphere this softly lit garden establishment does excel. Sharks' jaws and seashells dangle from the palapa roof. Hand-painted burlap menus offer king crab, lobster, shrimp and coconut mousse. Everything is priced (or, to be more accurate, overpriced) in dollars. ~ Carretera al Garrafón; 9-883-1420 in Cancún. MODERATE TO DELUXE.

You'd expect **Casa Rolandi,** the dining room at Villa Rolandi, the elegant little inn run by Cancún's first family of fine Italian restaurateurs, to be exceptional—and you'd be right. The atmosphere is so full of Old World charm that the sea through the big arched windows might easily be mistaken for the Mediterranean if it weren't for the bigger-than-life skyline of the Cancún hotel zone across the water. Romantic live music sets the mood for sunset and a gourmet meal featuring dishes such as medallions of lamb or shrimp-filled black ravioli in cognac sauce, which combines Swiss and northern Italian cuisine with local fresh-caught seafood. ~ Laguna Mar, Carretera Sac-Bajo; 9-877-0700, fax 9-877-0500; www.villarolandi.com, e-mail hotel@villarolandi.com. ULTRA-DELUXE.

The Rolandi family also operates a branch of its famous **Rolandi's Pizzeria** in town. ~ Avenida Hidalgo 110, Laguna Mar; 9-877-0429. MODERATE.

SHOPPING The village is packed with shops where prices tend to be more reasonable than in either Cancún or Cozumel. You'll find handicraft and gift items from all over Mexico, as well as an amazing array of Guatemalan goods. Since Guatemala's currency is weak against the Mexican peso as well as the U.S. dollar, in the past few years it has become very profitable to buy handwoven clothing and accessories and bring them to Mexico to sell as souvenirs to international tourists.

When the party boats arrive from Cancún, watch how the guides usher tourists into certain big, expensive jewelry shops. The shops pay them a commission on each purchase.

At the other end of the jewelry spectrum, street vendors display their wares—such stuff as coral jewelry and bead necklaces—atop low stone walls near the ferry dock. The most unusual items are pendants and earrings made from sharks' teeth, often with designs incised on them. Most of the jewelry sold by street vendors is locally (or at least regionally) made, while most jewelry in retail shops comes from other parts of Mexico, particularly Taxco, Guerrero.

If you're around on Sunday afternoon, head for the central plaza, where locals offer their works for sale in the **Gran Fería** open-air arts and crafts show.

Nearby, along the pedestrian plaza, **Paulita's** has crisp white woven dresses with colorful sashes. ~ Avenida Morelos. **La Sirena** has a big inventory of masks, Maya figures, T-shirts, blankets and papier-mâché items. ~ Avenidas Hidalgo and Madero; 9-877-0223.

Down the street you're apt to observe an artist at work chipping designs in limestone at **Casa del Arte México**. Besides these superb carvings, there are Maya temple rubbings, images in obsidian and quartz, and batik clothing. ~ Avenida Hidalgo 6.

While printed and silk-screened Isla Mujeres T-shirts are everywhere you look, only at **Casa Isleño II** will you find T-shirts handpainted by local artists. ~ Avenida Guerrero 3; 9-877-0265.

For quality contemporary paintings and sculptures by Mexican artists, visit the **Martin Good Gallery**, located out of town next to the Casa de los Sueños. ~ Carretera Garrafón; 9-877-0651.

On weekends, enjoy the live music and dancing on the *zócalo*. A funky hangout where you can meet the locals is the **Calypso Disco**, just past the Posada del Mar near the lighthouse. Cancún it ain't; in small-town Mexico, anything with a dancefloor is called a disco.

NIGHTLIFE

The best place to watch the sunset—and later listen to hot island sounds—is a palapa bar called **Las Palapas**. ~ On Playa del Norte near the end of Avenida Rueda Medina. **Pinguino** in the Hotel Posada del Mar has live music most nights. ~ Avenida Rueda Medina 15; 9-877-0212.

PLAYA DEL NORTE 🏊 The main beach adjoining the village begins near the docks and wraps around a point. The sand is white and so soft you can sink to your knees in it. Lined with hotels, Playa del Norte is often as lively as any beach in Cancún. ~ Located adjacent to the village of Isla Mujeres.

BEACHES & PARKS

PLAYA LOS COCOS 🏊 Isolated by expanses of limestone pitted with tidepools, this serene stretch of velvety sand and azure sea is Isla Mujeres' most beautiful beach. In fact, it ranks among the best swimming and sunning spots on the whole coast. The only thing lacking is shade. Unlike other areas the island's international set can sometimes be caught bathing topless or tanning bottomless here. ~ Located on the northwest shore near the Nautibeach.

Leave your tent and camping gear behind when you visit Isla Mujeres: Camping is prohibited on all of the island's beaches.

PLAYA LANCHEROS 🏊 A secluded white-sand beach along the Caribbean side of the narrow spit that separates Laguna Makax from the sea, Playa Lancheros has a protected section for gentle swimming. Large cat sharks frequent the area, though local youths who like to chase them for fun swear the sharks are docile and harmless. Northward along the spit are two smaller and more secluded strands, Playa Pescador and Playa Mexico. ~ Located east of Carretera al Garrafón at the north end of the national park.

PARQUE EL GARRAFÓN/PUNTA SUR 🏊 🤿 This underwater land-and-sea park boasts see-through emerald waters that are a magnet for snorkelers. Although as many as a thousand snorkelers a day have damaged the reef's coral beyond the possibility of reclaiming it by natural means, ambitious re-landscaping efforts are underway both above and below the water. Dazzling schools of colorful tropical fish make El Garrafón a spectacular place to swim and dive. On dry land, the national park has grassy hills and complex of shops and restaurants, as well as a mostly rocky beach, a small zoo and a museum with mediocre aquarium exhibits. Admission. ~ Located 7 kilometers from the village on the southwest end of the island.

▼▼▼▼▼▼▼▼▼▼
Isla Contoy

If Cancún is the antithesis of ecotourism, Isla Contoy is the epitome. Tiniest of all the Mexican Caribbean islands, it is inhabited not by humans but by a fantastic array of birds. From common pelicans and egrets to ibis, strange brown boobies and flamboyantly colored roseate spoonbills, Isla Contoy is a birder's dream. This national wildlife refuge, a one-and-a-half-hour boat trip from Cancún (less from Isla Mujeres), is also a sunbather's paradise. Sugar-white beaches, almost always deserted, line the sliver-shaped island. Snorkelers will find plenty to explore offshore.

SIGHTS

Trips to Isla Contoy can be arranged in Cancún at any major hotel's travel desk or on Isla Mujeres by contacting **Contoy Express**. ~ Avenida Rueda Medina Norte; 9-877-0816.

A dock and pavilion featuring a display of indigenous marine life constitute the park station on the island's leeward side. Here you can also climb up to the top of the park tower to take in a panoramic view of both the isle and sea.

HIDDEN ►

A portion of the area known as Yalahau, situated at the northeast tip of the Yucatán Peninsula, on the mainland parallel to Isla Contoy, was set aside in 1994 as the **Yum Balaam Biosphere Reserve**, the peninsula's newest UNESCO protected area. An untamed, biologically rich region of tropical forest, *tintale* (swamp forest) and savannah, it is home to spider monkeys, crocodiles and even jaguars. Most interesting to biologists, however, are the many unique plants that have been found here, including a new wild species of vanilla, a new species of acacia, and a new genus of nitrogen-fixing algae. The name Yalahau, Maya for "where the water is born," refers to the hundreds of spring-like microcenotes that feed the swamps and wetlands. Environmental activists in Quintana Roo are lobbying to have the whole area, including Yum Balaam, the privately owned El Eden Ecological Reserve and other uninhabited lands adjoining the two, set aside to form a much larger Biosphere Reserve covering 500,000 acres, to be called Yalahau.

There is no reliable road access to Yum Balaam. At present, the area is only accessible on tours, which are offered by **Yum Balaam, A.C.**, located in the village of Kantunilkin in northwestern Quintana Roo, about 70 kilometers from Cancún: take the old Route 180 libre and turn off at the village of Vincente Guerrero, bearing north. The nonprofit group of conservationists and biologists who formed El Eden Ecological Reserve in 1990, sometimes offers overnight tours to its research station through travel agents located in Cancún. ~ Avenida Adolfo Lopez Mateos s/n, Kantunilkin, Quintana Roo 77500, Mexico; phone/fax 9-887-5088.

South of Cancún, Route 307 is a four-lane divided highway that follows the standard tourist route as far as Playa del Carmen. Though lined with far too

The Riviera Maya: Cancún to Playa del Carmen

many billboards, it's a big improvement over the narrow two-lane highway between walls of jungle scrub that used to make for a frustrating drive because of long lines of slow tour buses that travel between Cancún and Tulum. (You can still expect to get caught behind tour buses if you continue south of Playa del Carmen.)

Travelers interested in the region's fauna should take time to visit **Croco Cun**. Much more than the Florida-style alligator farm that the cutesy name suggests, Croco Cun is actually the best zoo of regional wildlife in the Yucatán. Crocodiles are the featured attraction; an endangered species called the morolette reproduces here under a privately funded captive breeding program, and the offspring are released in coastal habitats. Other animals on exhibit include monkeys, white-tailed deer, javelinas and even boa constrictors, all native to the surrounding forest. Guides open cages

SIGHTS

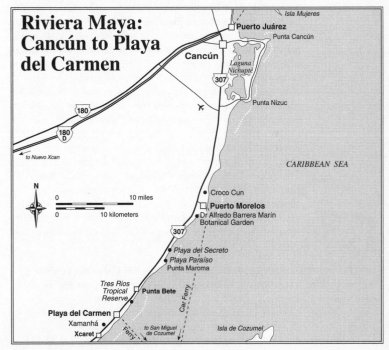

and let human visitors in or animals out—including crocodiles, which they say are well-fed and prefer to eat chickens, not people. Admission. ~ Route 307, Km. 30; 9-884-4782.

When you consider that **Puerto Morelos** is a mere 36 kilometers south of Cancún, it is nothing short of a miracle that the small fishing village remains so simple and authentic, with an inviting central park and attractive public beach. Aside from the flora-and-fauna parks mentioned above, the town's main claim to fame is that a car ferry to Cozumel leaves from here—a much longer and more expensive trip than the passenger ferry from Playa del Carmen. Though overshadowed by more famous dive spots nearby, Puerto Morelos has a fascinating coral reef studded with shipwrecks just 1640 feet out from the beach.

Not far past the Puerto Morelos turnoff, the **Dr. Alfredo Barrera Marín Botanical Garden** displays trees, bromeliads and other flora native to the forests of the Yucatán Peninsula, labeled with small plaques in Spanish. A lovely nature trail leads past one of the insignificant little Postclassic Maya stone buildings that line the Quintana Roo coast. Admission. ~ Route 307, Km. 38.

The newest of the commercial nature parks along the Riviera Maya, **Tres Rios Tropical Reserve** occupies a section of coastline between Punta Bete and Playa del Carmen. A winding estuary cuts through the mangrove jungle that contains trails, lagoons and eight cenotes. This is one of the few places along the Riviera Maya coast where cenotes flow at ground level instead of underground, making them easily accessible to wildlife; over 100 bird and animal species wander through the park, including macaws, ocelots, raccoons and coatimundis. The mazelike topography allows for a wide range of outdoor sports in an area of just 370 acres. You can go hiking, biking, snorkeling, scuba diving, canoeing, sea kayaking or horseback riding, and relax in between on the beach with its hammocks and beach chairs. There's also a pricey palapa restaurant. Admission. ~ Route 370, Km. 63; 9-887-8077, 800-714-3643; www.tres-rios.com.

About 68 kilometers south of Cancún, **Playa del Carmen** gets my vote as the hottest spot on the Caribbean coast. For years, this

AUTHOR FAVORITE

sights

If you could stroll with me down **Playa del Carmen's** beach and back up the parallel Avenida 5 shops-and-cafés pedestrian street, you'd see for yourself why this is my favorite resort town on Mexico's Caribbean coast—friendly, sociable, international and sexy. Jet-setters happily rub elbows with young backpackers in the liveliest, friendliest scene on the Riviera Maya. So who needs "sightseeing attractions"?

picturesque fishing and sunbathing village surrounding the port where the passenger ferries push off for Cozumel was a Continental secret. The only town near a beach where women could sunbathe topless and the one most accepting of gay and lesbian activities, it developed a reputation among Europeans as a swinging-singles hideaway. But despite its white, palm-edged beaches that stretched in both directions as far as the eye could see and its pedestrian main street lined with open-air cafés that burst with energy from sunset late into the night, few American travel agents acknowledged Playa del Carmen's existence.

Then in the early 1990s the Barbachano family, for three generations the most prominent figures in the Yucatán tourist industry, started an exclusive mega-resort, a sort of mini-Cancún which they called Playacar, on the south edge of town. It grew into a complex of brick-paved streets and million-dollar vacation homes that is now larger than the town itself and has sprouted several five-star luxury resorts. In the process, Playa del Carmen received so much publicity that it has become Quintana Roo's "in" beach town and the self-proclaimed capital of the Riviera Maya.

In less than a decade, Playa del Carmen has grown from a fishing village of fewer than a thousand people to a busy little city of 30,000, complete with traffic congestion and parking problems. You only experience these when arriving or leaving, though. The visitor-oriented part of town includes the beach and Calle 5, the long pedestrian-only street lined with small hotels, cafés and shops. It is still very European for much of the year but the town gets crowded with wealthy *norteamericanos* from January to mid-March, when gringo college students briefly transform it into Fort Lauderdale South. The close proximity of budget-priced palapas, moderate little beach hotels and big, expensive resorts makes for an unusually diverse café crowd. During busy times, you have to walk farther up or down the endless beach before you can lie on the beach without proper bathing attire. Besides tourism, Playa del Carmen's economy thrives thanks to the Volkswagen plant just north of town.

Playa del Carmen is also the site of **Xamanhá**, several groups of late Postclassic Maya buildings that formed the northern boundary of the settlement at Xcaret during the period A.D. 1200–1500. Then, as now, the village was the departure point for boats headed for Cozumel. The ruins are similar in appearance to the temples and ceremonial platforms of Tulum but on a smaller scale. There is public access to a pair of structures (one of them almost completely collapsed) near La Ruina Campground, a few blocks north of the plaza, and to a series of other ruins in poor condition north of there. Two others are on an Army base south of the plaza; with permission, they can be viewed at a distance but not photographed. The largest and best preserved of the Xamanhá ruins are south of town, along a private road on the grounds of a condo-minium complex called Villas Playacar. You must stop and obtain permission from a gate guard before entering.

Nearby at Playacar resort, **Xaman Ha Aviary** is open to the public. The huge sanctuary is home to 30 native bird species including flamingos, toucans, ibis, storks and parrots. Admission. ~ Playacar resort.

LODGING

Puerto Morelos has a few small hotels that cater mainly to divers, as well as a few bigger resorts being built along the beach on the outskirts of town. The most affordable lodging is at the no-frills **Posada Amor**, south of the ferry dock. The 20-room establishment has thin mattresses on concrete beds, mosquito netting and some private baths. Ceiling fans. ~ Puerto Morelos; 9-871-0033. BUDGET.

Room rates are about the same at the beachfront **Hotel Ojo de Agua**, where you'll find 20 no-frills rooms. There's also a swimming pool with palm trees and a sea view. Fishing, diving, snorkeling, windsurfing and kayaking equipment rentals are available. Air conditioning; ceiling fans. ~ Avenida Javier Rojo Gomez, Puerto Morelos; 9-871-0027, fax 9-871-0202. BUDGET.

In the same category, **Hotel Inglaterra** has 14 rather small rooms. All have ceiling fans and private baths, and some have kitchenettes. The hotel has a rooftop sundeck with a sea view. Some rooms have air conditioning. ~ Avenida Niños Héroes 29, Puerto Morelos; phone/fax 9-871-0418. BUDGET.

On the edge of town, **Rancho Libertad** stands surrounded by banana trees and palms just a few steps from the beach. The small cabaña complex strives for the kind of "away-from-it-all" ambience that visitors used to find up and down the Quintana Roo coast before megaresort development took over. The reception area is a big palapa with a sand floor. Guest accommodations are in Yucatán-style thatch-roofed huts with beds suspended from the ceiling beams by ropes. Staying here, it's hard to believe that you're just half an hour from Cancún and a few minutes from the airport. ~ Puerto Morelos; 9-871-0781; www.rancholibertad.com, e-mail rancholibertad@prodigy.net.mx. MODERATE.

At the other end of the Puerto Morelos lodging spectrum, the Mediterranean-style **Caribbean Reef Club** is an all-inclusive, clothing-optional vacation complex for adults only—one of the few nude resorts in Mexico. The 30 luxury condominium units feature kitchenettes, microwave ovens and satellite TV. Set on a long strand of remote beach, the lodge has a swimming pool and giant hot tub by the sea. Non-motorized water sports equipment is available for guests' use at no additional charge. Air conditioning. ~ Villa Marina, Puerto Morelos; 9-871-0191, fax 9-871-0190, or 888-522-6286 in the U.S.; www.caribbeanreefclub.com, e-mail info@caribbeanreefclub.com. ULTRA-DELUXE.

One of the very best places to stay in Quintana Roo is at charming, secluded **La Posada del Capitán Lafitte**. Just an hour's drive from Cancún but worlds away from the crowded resort city, the Capitán Lafitte is an escapist's beachside paradise. Tucked about one and a half kilometers off the main highway down a dirt road, the hotel rests under low palms and magenta bougainvillea. Its 62 stone-and-wood cabañas with private terraces face the turquoise sea. The deceptively simple, sandy grounds contain a dive shop, a pool, a restaurant-bar and a palapa gameroom with television. The all-inclusive rate covers breakfast, dinner, taxes and tips. Some units have air conditioning; the rest have ceiling fans. Three-night minimum stay required. This and the other two resorts at Punta Bete are managed by the same organization, the Turquoise Reef Group, based in Evergreen, Colorado. ~ Carretera Tulum, Km. 62, Punta Bete; 9-873-0214, fax 9-873-0212, or 303-674-8735, 800-538-6802 in the U.S.; www.mexico holiday.com, e-mail info@turqreef.com. ULTRA-DELUXE.

Also located at Punta Bete are two other, quite different lodging facilities. The **Shangri-La Caribe** has 50 palm-thatched cabañas spread along the beach. The emphasis here is on water sports. It has a dive shop and sailboard rentals on the premises as well as a pool. ~ Punta Bete. Reservations are made through La Posada del Capitán Lafitte or the Turquoise Reef Group: 800-538-6802 or 303-674-8735 in the U.S.; www.mexicoholiday.com, e-mail info@turqreef.com. ULTRA-DELUXE.

Not far away, on an even more secluded beach, the **Kai Luum Camptel II** is a cross between a campground and a chic bed-and-breakfast establishment. The 29 rustic camping cabañas come complete with tents and hammocks. There is no electricity, but gourmet meals are served in a central palapa dining area. All meals are

---

POLLY WANTS A VACATION

Like some whitewashed haven for shipwrecked souls on a half-forgotten isle, the **Blue Parrot Inn** rests among the palms with a semi-Mediterranean laziness. Its 45 rooms run the gamut from funky little beachfront bungalows to modern, refurbished duplexes. You will also find a dive shop, a restaurant and a terrific castaway bar frequented by some of the most interesting expatriates and colorful characters on the whole coast. What more could you want for a relaxed beach vacation? Ceiling fans, some air-conditioned rooms. ~ Six blocks north of the plaza, on the beach, Playa del Carmen; 9-873-0083, fax 9-873-0049, or 888-854-4498 in the U.S.; www.blueparrot.com. MODERATE TO DELUXE.

included in the guest fee. Unlike most campgrounds, there are real beds and daily maid service. No children allowed. ~ Punta Bete. Reservations are made through the same organization as La Posada del Capitán Lafitte or the Turquoise Reef Group: 800-538-6802 or 303-674-8735 in the U.S.; www.mexicoholiday.com, e-mail info@turqreef.com. ULTRA-DELUXE.

The pretty beachfront town of Playa del Carmen offers both unique little tropical inns and gleaming new resort hotels clustered in a resort development area called Playacar just south of town. Opened in 1991, the **Continental Plaza Playacar** is draped picturesquely along the sea, a striking sight for arriving ferry passengers. Its sand-colored buildings wend along a pretty beach and a fantasy swimming pool with swim-up palapa bar. Gleaming white tile, designer draperies and ethereal shades of blue and green give the 185 rooms an ultramodern look. If you don't mind the price tag, this place offers a blend of first-class resort amenities and away-from-it-all seclusion. Air conditioning. ~ Route 307, Km. 62.5, Playa del Carmen; 9-873-0100, fax 9-873-0105, or 800-784-1180 in the U.S.; e-mail hcpply@sidek.com.mx. ULTRA-DELUXE.

Puerto Morelos is the main seaport for imported goods sold in the tourist shops of Cancún and Cozumel.

The **Allegro Resort Playacar** bills itself as an "ecotourism resort" but caters to the package-tour crowd. An employee drives you to your room, one of 300 guest units in flexible two-story fourplexes, in a golf cart. Each level has two guest units with a living room in between, so that a regular room converts easily into a one-bedroom or two-bedroom suite. The big, modern fourplexes are designed to resemble jungle lodge bungalows—a huge, cynical knockoff of the intimate backcountry lodges found around Palenque and Tikal and in many parts of Belize. All have satellite TV showing American cable networks, but the in-room phones can only call within the hotel complex; guests are cut off from communication with the outside world. Also on the premises are an organized activities pool, a relaxation pool, a lighted tennis court, a combination basketball/volleyball court, a children's play area, cafeteria-style and full-service restaurants, three bars, and rental agencies for cars, bicycles, sailboats, kayaks, sailboards, boogieboards and snorkel gear. You have to wear a picture ID clipped to your clothing at all times while on the resort grounds. Air conditioning. ~ Route 307, Km. 62.5, Playa del Carmen; 9-873-0340, fax 9-873-0348. ULTRA-DELUXE.

But if it's a big, self-contained resort you want, why leave Cancún? Small, friendly hotels are what make Playa del Carmen different. In fact, there are now more hotels in Playa del Carmen than there are in Cancún's Hotel Zone, with new ones sprouting up each season—but most have fewer than two dozen guest rooms.

epresentative of the colorful wildlife abundant throughout the Yucatán Peninsula, the toucan found in the rainforests of southern Quintana Roo and Campeche.

Above: This stretch of beach along Laguna Chankanaab, one of the many strands found on Cozumel's shores, offers palapas for sun worshippers.

Below: Serving as a gateway to the Yucatán Peninsula, Cancún is best known for its white sand beaches, highrise hotels and party atmosphere.

One of the longest-established hotels in town, the slightly worn, colonial-style **Hotel Molcas** building features a swim-up bar, a boutique and a popular waterfront restaurant. The 41 guest rooms have tiny balconies, dark Spanish furniture and little Tiffany lamps. Ask for a room toward the back; the hotel's location, a block uphill from the ferry dock, makes for pedestrian pandemonium, but only during the daytime. Air conditioning. ~ Calle Juárez, a block uphill from the ferry terminal, Calle 1 at Avenida 5, Playa del Carmen; 9-873-0070, fax 9-873-0138. MODERATE.

For those short on funds, the 24-bed **Urban Hostel** offers the simplest possible accommodations in a palapa dormitory two blocks from the beach, with a small vegetarian restaurant on the premises. There's little privacy but lots of fun. ~ Avenida 10 between Calles 4 and 6. BUDGET.

Posada Copa Cabaña, with four rooms and three cabañas, all sparkling clean and set in a quiet garden, is a real find. Its touches include nice tile baths and a dive shop. Ceiling fans. ~ Calle 5, five blocks north of the plaza and one block from the beach, Playa del Carmen; 9-873-0218. BUDGET.

The **Albatros Royale** features an eye-catching blend of desert-hued stucco and dramatic palapa roofs. Colorful Mexican blankets, and tile floors give each of the 31 guest rooms a cozy feel. The sea lies a few steps out the front door. Ask for a room on the upper floor; the vaulted palapa ceilings are extra-special. Ceiling fans. ~ Calle 8, five blocks north of the plaza, on the beach, Playa del Carmen; 9-873-0001, fax 9-873-0002, or 800-538-6802 in the U.S. MODERATE.

Surrounded by a remnant of natural forest just half a block from the beach, the **Treetops Hotel** offers a choice of rustic individual bungalows with ceiling fans and mosquito nets (some with full kitchens) or air-conditioned rooms with king- or queen-size beds and refrigerators. All ten units have private patios or balconies, and there's a swimming pool. ~ Calle 8 off Avenida 5, Playa del Carmen; phone/fax 9-873-0351; www.treetopshotel. com, e-mail treetops@prodigy.net.mx. BUDGET TO MODERATE.

◄ HIDDEN

Centrally located along the Calle 5 pedestrian walk a block from the beach, **Hotel Delfin** has 14 simply furnished rooms with private baths and refrigerators, including some with sea views. No frills, but location and low rates make this little hotel a great choice for budget travelers. ~ Avenida 5 at Calle 6, Playa del Carmen; phone/fax 9-873-0176; www.hoteldelfin.com, e-mail hotel delfin@worldnet.att.net. BUDGET.

Another centrally located budget option along the pedestrian walk, the **Posada Freud** offers simple, nicely rustic rooms on the ground floor and nicer mid-range rooms with refrigerators, balconies and hammocks on the second floor, as well as one big, ultra-deluxe-priced penthouse suite . Don't expect such amenities as phones, TV or air conditioning, but the 12 guest units offer private baths and hot water. Use of bicycles is included in the room rate. Ceiling fans. ~ Avenida 5 between Calles 8 and 10, Playa del Carmen; phone/fax 9-873-0601; www.posadafreud.com, e-mail reservations@posadafreud.com. MODERATE.

Two blocks inland from the north end of the beach, the **Hotel Zanzibar** is a small hotel impeccably run by European owners. Its strange architecture, incorporating castlelike crenelated towers and palm-thatched palapas, encloses a tropical garden with a barbecue area, as well as private terraces and a rooftop garden with views of the jungle and the sea. The nine rooms range from small and simple accommodations to studio suites with kitchens and a large penthouse. Guests enjoy full privileges at the Playa Tulum Beach Club two blocks away. ~ Calle 26 between Avenidas 5 and 10, Playa del Carmen; phone/fax 9-873-0990; www.hotelzanzibar. com, e-mail info@hotelzanzibar.com. MODERATE.

HIDDEN ► Six blocks from the beach, **Mom's Hotel** offers some of the nicest budget accommodations in town. Colorful artworks decorate the white walls of the 20 rooms, accented with natural wood trim and floral-print bedspreads. All have private baths, and some have refrigerators. There's a swimming pool in the central courtyard, as well as protected parking, bicycle rentals and internet access. The American owners are particularly friendly and helpful in offering sightseeing advice and arranging sailing and scubadiving excursions. Ceiling fans; some rooms have air conditioning. ~ Avenida 30 at Calle 4, Playa del Carmen; phone/fax 9-873-0315. BUDGET.

DINING The place to eat in Puerto Morelos is **Los Pelicanos,** a palapa restaurant serving fresh-from-the-sea lobster, shrimp and conch as well as whatever fish the locals have just brought in. You will soon see where the restaurant got its name: lots of pelicans hover around the restaurant and nearby boat docks, hoping humans will toss some food their way. ~ On the waterfront, Puerto Morelos. MODERATE.

In Playa del Carmen, the longest-established restaurant in town is **La Tarraya**, located on the sand with lively views of the ferry dock, basketball players, sunbathers, souvenir shoppers—the whole scene. Naturally enough, seafood is the specialty; in fact, the family that runs the restaurant does its own fishing and prepares what it catches with special spices in traditional Maya style. ~ On the beach between Calles 2 and 4, Playa del Carmen. BUDGET.

Across the plaza, the friendly indoor/outdoor **Las Mascaras Pizzaria**, with its delicious thin-crusted wood-oven pizzas and homemade pastas, bills itself as Playa del Carmen's "only *real*

Italian place." Two to try: lasagna layered with shrimp and squid à la romana. Fresh fish and happy hour from 1 to 7 p.m. are daily specials. ~ Avenida Juarez, Playa del Carmen; 9-873-0177. BUDGET TO MODERATE.

Along Avenida 5, the two dozen or so indoor/outdoor restaurants make comparison simple with photos, example dishes and even fresh seafood on ice, displayed alongside multilingual menus. Several restaurants have menus in German, French and Italian—but not in English—reflecting the European influence in this resort town. Just stroll up and down the ten-block pedestrian walkway until your taste buds light up. The reasonable **Restaurant-Bar Pez Vela** is a wild and crazy palapa stop for breakfast. T-shirts hang over the bar like faded flags, while salsa music rings out. The tourist special is Texas-type chili con carne. Lunch and dinner fare includes seafood and a range of traditional Mexican dishes. ~ Avenida 5 Norte and Calle 2, Playa del Carmen; 9-873-0999. BUDGET TO MODERATE.

You'll find outstanding vegetarian cuisine at the **Sacbé Café**, a friendly, laidback little place along the pedestrian walkway. The changing menu features variations on Mexican and international dishes. All ingredients are fresh, and the service is often so unhurried that you may suspect those fruits and veggies are grown while you wait. ~ Avenida 5, Playa del Carmen. BUDGET TO MODERATE.

Vegetarians and other health-conscious diners will find a choice of Playa del Carmen restaurants to suit their tastes. For instance, check out **Sabor**, a shady patio café and juice bar that offers tantalizing *platillos*, or vegetable plates. ~ Avenida 5 between Calles 2 and 4, Playa del Carmen. BUDGET.

Don't judge the hole-in-the-wall **Media Luna** by its rustic, backpacker-hangout appearance. It may come closer than any other Playa restaurant to mastering contemporary fusion cuisine. Fresh seafood, produce and homemade pasta go into the kitchen, and daily specials come out with a teaspoon of Mexican tradition, a dash of Asian flair and a hint of Italian panache. Crêpes are a breakfast specialty. The menu also includes sandwiches, salads

STEPPING OUT IN THE RIVIERA MAYA

Oddly enough, Playa del Carmen has hardly any expensive restaurants. If your plans call for an extra-special dinner, your best bet is **La Parrilla**, a romantic third-floor restaurant overlooking the pedestrian walkway. *Parrilla* means grill, and the specialties of the house are steak and lobster. Among lower-priced entrées, the generous portions of fajitas stand out. ~ Avenida 5 at Calle 8, Playa del Carmen; 9-873-0687. MODERATE TO DELUXE.

and stir-fries. ~ Avenida 5 between Calles 8 and 10, Playa del Carmen. MODERATE.

At **Yaxché**, waiters in spotless white guayabaras serve Maya specialties like *pollo pakal* (chicken smothered in sour orange, onion and chile *xcatik* sauce), *pescado tikin xic* (fish grilled in achiote and orange sauce and served on a banana leaf) and *epazote* shrimp. ~ Calle 8 between Avenidas 5 and 10, Playa del Carmen. MODERATE TO DELUXE.

Toward the north end of Avenida 5, **Ristorante Italiano Da Gabi** features fresh seafood and hand-rolled pastas that have been pleasing Italian (and other) visitors since the days when Playa was a small fishing village. A shady garden provides a peaceful romantic setting for dishes such as sautéed calamari and fettuccine with shrimp and mussels. Bountiful breakfast buffets, featuring eggs, beans and rice and fresh-squeezed juice, are morning highlights. ~ Calle 12, off Avenida 5, Playa del Carmen; 9-873-0048; e-mail dagabi@hotmail.com. BUDGET TO MODERATE.

SHOPPING

You can pick up curios at small shops around the plaza in Playa del Carmen. Most people head for the obvious—a shopping mall called **Mercado de Artesanías Xaman Ha**, where 14 shops sell silver, dresses, blankets, hats, serapes, jewelry and T-shirts. Just across from the plaza, **Toucan Curios** stocks embroidered bags and beachwear.

Playa del Carmen begins jumping at sundown along Avenida 5, which is lined with happy-hour restaurants and bars. You'll hear four or five languages and an international mix of music.

For authentic Maya and Mexican folk art, one of the best places in town is **Telart,** which carries an outstanding selection of handwoven textiles including native clothing, tablecloths, bedspreads and rugs, as well as a more limited stock of ceramics and paintings. ~ Avenida Juárez 5, Playa del Carmen; 9-873-0066.

You won't need a tour guide to shop your way along Avenida 5, where almost all the gift shops and boutiques in town are located. You'll find lots of handicrafts (batik is a local specialty) and beachwear. There are surprisingly few Cancún-style silver jewelry stores, though a stroll along Avenida 5 could easily give you the impression that the main regional folk-art medium is the T-shirt.

NIGHTLIFE

Cocodrilos, upstairs across from the plaza, is a hot place to dance to Latin rhythms, live or recorded. ~ Avenida 5 at Calle 2, Playa del Carmen.

Equally popular for its mix of Latino and international dance music is **Captain Tutix's**, a club in the shape of a wooden pirate ship. ~ On the beach at Calle 4. Next door, **La Raya** features techno music and all-night rave parties. ~ On the beach.

Look for live Caribbean island and salsa music at **Calypso**, a big upstairs palapa where the dancing goes on all night and is packed to the rafters on weekends. ~ Avenida 5 between Calles 4 and 6.

The huge upstairs cocktail lounge in the **Diamond Allegro Playacar** features karaoke nightly, making it one of the liveliest places in the Playa del Carmen area if you're into that sort of thing. ~ Route 307, Km. 62.5, Playa del Carmen.

The **Bar Hernán Cortés** is a small but swank air-conditioned tavern featuring black leatherette chairs, conquistador decor and an elevated television broadcasting the latest in sports. ~ Hotel Molcas, Calle Juárez near the ferry terminal, Playa del Carmen.

Everyone should have a drink at the **Dragon Bar** at the Blue Parrot Inn. Set outdoors on the beach, the ship-shaped watering hole has swings for seats and crazy characters for patrons. The island music is great, too. In 1996 *Newsweek* magazine named the Dragon Bar "one of the top 10 bars in the world." ~ Six blocks north of the plaza, Playa del Carmen; 9-873-0049.

PLAYA MORELOS 🏊 🐟 The beach at Puerto Morelos is short and wide, with dazzling white sand and a scattering of shade palapas. It's as public a beach as you'll find on the Mexican Caribbean. Not only do sunbathers share it with local fishermen, but they may feel like they're basking right on the main street of town. A spectacular coral reef suitable for snorkeling and scuba diving lies about a quarter of a mile offshore. ~ Located at the end of the road into Puerto Morelos, 26 kilometers south of Cancún.

▲ The beach is too exposed for comfortable camping, though transient construction workers sometimes sleep there.

PUNTA MAROMA AND PUNTA BETE 🏊 🐟 Bordered by coconut palms, a gleaming white beach extends for three miles along the bay between these two rocky points occupied by resort hotels. Near the midpoint of the beach, a cenote-fed river flows into a crystal-clear sea ideal for swimming and snorkeling. On the north side of Punta Maroma are two other beautiful beaches, **Playa del Secreto** and **Playa Paraíso**. About 10 kilometers apart, both are lined with private houses and are at the end of gated private roads. ~ Punta Bete can be reached from the mile-long road to La Posada del Capitán Lafitte, about 50 kilometers south of Cancún.

▲ Free camping is not allowed on any of these beaches, but there is an expensive campground with palapas and solar electricity at Xcalacoco, just south of Punta Bete.

PLAYA DEL CARMEN 🏊 One of the liveliest beaches in the Yucatán, the section of Playa del Carmen that begins north of the ferry dock is surprisingly clean and attractive considering the throngs of fishermen, soccer-playing kids, beachcombers and sun worshippers that use it. Some of the small hotels along the beach

BEACHES & PARKS

rent lounge chairs and water-sports equipment. It is hard to continue following the beach south of the ferry dock because of a jumble of slippery rocks, though it is possible to swim around this obstacle that keeps the riff-raff away from the stretch of beach fronted by the luxury resorts of Playacar. ~ The north half of the beach is easily reached from any place in the town of Playa del Carmen, 60 kilometers south of Cancún; the south half can be reached via the private roads of Playacar once you talk your way past the security guard.

▲ Although camping is technically legal on the north half of the beach, it isn't actually done because of lack of privacy and possible safety risks.

▼▼▼▼▼▼▼▼▼▼▼▼

Isla de Cozumel

To the Maya, the island of Cozumel was a shrine, a place whose rugged beauty and mystique inspired sacred ceremonies to sensuous gods. As early as A.D. 900, Maya women from across the Yucatán made pilgrimages here to worship Ixchel, goddess of fertility. They arrived by the hundreds in dugout canoes, praying that the island's potent warmth and windy spirit would stir their wombs.

Today's pilgrims come from all over the world to indulge in Cozumel's heady mix of silky beaches, gemlike waters and kaleidoscopic coral reefs. Mexico's largest island, the 28-mile-long coral cay is still largely wild and windswept, clothed in shaggy jungle and mangrove swamp. It predates Cancún as the Mexican Caribbean's prime getaway and remains the finest diving site in the country. Despite its international popularity, Cozumel can make you feel like you have left civilization—or found it.

Inhale the tangy sea breeze as you ride a water-jet ferry across the 22 miles of sea that lie between Playa del Carmen and Cozumel. Most passengers spend the trip indoors, in seating areas where TVs show Latin American music videos from port to port. Instead, stand out on the deck, where saltwater spray tingles your face as the big, fast boat slices through the turquoise waves.

SIGHTS

The hub of activity is **San Miguel de Cozumel**, Cozumel's only town, located on the northwest side of the island. The town surrounds what may be the most elaborate *zócalo* in Mexico, a large plaza landscaped with palms, fig trees, terraces and statuary ranging from a gold-painted bust of Mexican hero Benito Juárez to a contemporary fountain sculpture that's part conch shell and part female nude, as well as twin Mexican flags so expansive they're the first thing you see as the ferry approaches the island. Pick a shady bench and people-watch. By day, hordes of cruise-ship passengers and day trippers pack the surrounding tourist shops. After sundown, locals reclaim the plaza in a relaxed social scene that spills over onto the *malecón*, the seawall promenade that runs the length of San Miguel's waterfront.

Located along the plaza, the Palacio del Gobierno houses the **Delegación Estatal de Turismo**, which provides visitor information. ~ Avenida 5 Sur; 9-872-0972. Also, check with the **Cozumel Chamber of Commerce**. ~ Avenida 20 Sur; 9-872-0583.

On the *malecón* several blocks north of the *zócalo* is the island's museum, **Museo de la Isla de Cozumel**. A pleasant refuge from the sometimes oppressive afternoon heat, the Museo de la Isla de Cozumel fills four dimly lit galleries in a big, pink colonial-style building on San Miguel's seafront boulevard. Landlubbers can get an idea of what they're missing as they marvel at the realistic life-size re-creation of a coral reef teeming with tropical fish.

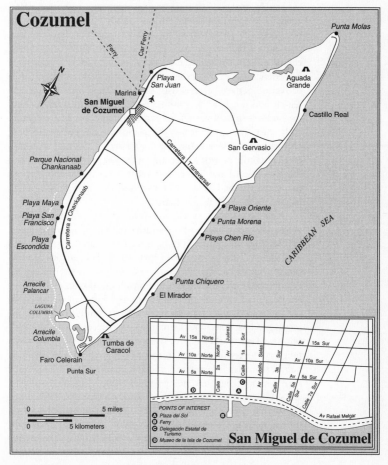

Cozumel

Punta Molas

Ferry

Car Ferry

Playa
San Juan

Marina
**San Miguel
de Cozumel**

Aguada
Grande

Castillo Real

Parque Nacional
Chankanaab

Carretera Transversal

San Gervasio

Playa Maya

Playa San
Francisco

Carretera a Chankanaab

Playa
Escondida

Playa Oriente

Punta Morena

Playa Chen Río

CARIBBEAN SEA

Arrecife
Palancar

LAGUNA
COLUMBIA

Punta Chiquero

El Mirador

Arrecife
Columbia

Tumba de
Caracol

Faro Celerain

Punta Sur

0   5 miles
0   5 kilometers

Av 15a Norte		Juárez	Salas		Av 15a Sur
Av 10a Norte	Norte	Av 1a			Av 10a Sur
Av 5a Norte	2a	Calle	Av Adolfo	3a	Av 5a Sur

Av Rafael Melgar

POINTS OF INTEREST
Ⓐ Plaza del Sol
Ⓑ Ferry
Ⓒ Delegación Estatal de
   Turismo
Ⓓ Museo de la Isla de Cozumel

San Miguel de Cozumel

Other exhibits include a jungle waterhole diorama, Maya artifacts from San Gervasio and other sites around the island, and memorabilia from the days when San Miguel was the only port on the Mexican Caribbean. In the rear courtyard is a reconstructed Maya house with typical furnishings. Admission. ~ Calle 6 Norte and Avenida Rafael Melgar; 9-872-1475.

A different kind of museum that's well worth a visit is the **Pax Museum of Musical History, Culture & Indigenous Peoples**. Attached to a music-themed gift shop, the museum exhibits nearly 800 antique musical instruments from 37 countries, as well as a large collection of dance masks and video documentaries of field recordings made at Indian ceremonies in various parts of Mexico. ~ Avenida Benito Juárez at Calle 15; 9-872-5269.

San Miguel de Cozumel has as many motor-scooter rental agencies as scuba outfitters. An easy-riding Honda scooter is the perfect vehicle for exploring the undeveloped countryside. A narrow, paved highway crosses the island and follows the mostly empty eastern shoreline, eventually looping back to Cozumel. Experience the exhilaration of gliding alongside mile after mile of picture-perfect beaches with no windshield between you the sea air and sunshine. A complete circuit of Cozumel takes about four hours—plus time out for sand and surf. It's best to get an early start and travel around the island in a clockwise direction, visiting San Gervasio before the oppressive heat of midday settles on the island's interior and spending the hot part of the day along the always cool and breezy east coast. Start by traveling across the island via the **Carretera Transversal**, which originates in San Miguel as Avenida Benito Juárez.

A side road off the Carretera Transversal leads inland to **San Gervasio**, once a Maya administrative center and now the largest ancient ruin on Cozumel, though far less impressive than other sites such as Tulum, Cobá and Chichén Itzá. The remains of 11th-century temples and palaces surround the lost city's central plaza. Follow the restored section of the *sacbé,* or limestone-paved ceremonial road, through the giant stone archway that was once the city's entrance, and you'll soon come to the temple of Ixchel, the moon goddess, where in ancient times women came from throughout the Maya world for fertility rituals. Side trails from the *sacbé* take you deeper into the tall forest where, in the steamy shade of palms, strangler figs, poisonwood and gumbo limbo trees, you're sure to spot big iguanas, many species of birds, and perhaps even a boa constrictor draped motionless over a tree limb. When San Gervasio was excavated in the 1970s, archaeologists found a mysterious mass grave containing more than 50 bodies. Since some Spanish beads were found among the burials, most experts believe the people died in a smallpox epidemic that decimated Cozumel's population soon after the first Spaniards arrived. Admission.

Cozumel's Undersea Paradise

The sleepy little fishing village of San Miguel de Cozumel was transformed forever in 1961, when underwater explorer Jacques Cousteau produced a TV documentary that revealed the spectacular chain of coral reefs that lay offshore. Within five years, Cozumel became the world's most popular diving destination, a distinction it still holds three decades later.

A wide diversity of formations offers thrilling diving for everyone from novices to advanced scuba enthusiasts. They include shallow reef dives, deep reef dives, wall dives and cave dives. Outfitters run dive expeditions to about 30 destinations. Here are some of the best:

Palancar Reef, the best-known Cozumel dive area, is a three-and-a-half-mile-long queen reef about a mile offshore. It includes shallow (20 to 40 feet) and deep (40 to 90 feet) areas and drops off in a sloping wall to depths of over 3000 feet. Palancar is such a diverse area that it would take 20 to 30 dives to fully explore; just to get an idea of its many facets takes six dives. All areas of Palancar except the wall are suitable for novices.

Columbia Reef is a popular beginner's dive—a vast sea garden of diverse coral formations teeming with tropical fish and crustaceans, it is one of Cozumel's shallowest reefs. The outer edge of the reef drops off in a spectacular wall with gigantic coral pinnacles over 90 feet tall, interspersed with tunnels and caverns.

Paradise Reef lies only 200 yards from shore and is the only reef on Cozumel that can be reached swimming from the shore. It is known for abundant marine life, including crabs, lobsters, angelfish, yellowtails and moray eels, as well as the splendid toad fish, a species found only in Cozumel waters. This is the island's most popular night dive.

Santa Rosa Wall begins at 50 feet and plunges in a sheer dropoff for more than half a mile. The wall is covered with huge sponges, coral overhangs and caverns. Groupers and other large fish congregate, expecting divers to feed them. Not for novices.

Torments Reef is another popular intermediate dive, with blue valleys of sand between colorful coral heads. Large morays are common here.

At 90 to 120 feet, the legendary **Chun Chakab** site is so difficult to find that even the most expert divers rarely get there. Because of this, it is one of the best preserved coral reefs anywhere. Many advanced divers working for Cozumel dive shops claim the pristine **Virgin Wall** site is their favorite because strong currents make it impossible to take large tour groups there.

No fewer than 40 ruins testify to Cozumel's importance as a trading center in ancient times. Unfortunately, thanks to neglect, ravages of time, and hurricanes, most of the sites are poorly preserved or impossible to reach. Other minor ruins in the early stages of excavation dot the whole northern tip of the island. A 14-mile sand track, only suited for jeeps and too sandy in some spots for easy travel by motor scooter, squiggles north of Santa Cecilia along empty beach to **Punta Molas**. You pass the small altar and vaulted fortress of the Maya ruin **Castillo Real** along the way. Out at the point, a lighthouse shares sea winds with **Aguada Grande**, circular ruins of buildings on platforms.

The name *Chankanaab* means "small sea" in Maya, referring to the Parque Nacional Chankanaab's blue lagoon full of parrotfish, barracuda, sergeant majors, octopi and other colorful specimens.

The road continues to the antique **Faro Celerain** lighthouse at Punta Sur, land's end. The tallest structure on the island, the lighthouse offers an incomparable, though wildly windy, view when someone is around to let you climb up to the top—which is often now that the surrounding area has been transformed into the new **Punta Sur Ecological Reserve**. The lighthouse now contains a museum of navigation, which traces the evolution of trade on the Mexican Caribbean from ancient Maya times to the present. Trucks take you around the park to see some of the 214 bird species that inhabit the reserve, or you can rent an electric golf cart and explore on your own. (Watch out for giant iguanas and the occasional alligator.) There's also a tiny Maya ruin called **Tumba de Caracol**, a conch-shaped temple dating back to A.D. 1200 that resembles a Disney mini-ruin crowned by a small square cupola. It's much too small even for the petite Maya. (Could it be another haunt of the *aluxes*, those legendary Maya pixies?) Its most unique feature is the conch shells embedded in the lower part of the outside wall that sound in an eerie moaning chorus when the wind blows. At the end of the road is one of the nicest white-sand beaches on the island, rarely crowded because of the reserve's $10 admission fee and the rough road. You can also take a boat ride on nearby Laguna Columbia. Admission. ~ Punta Sur.

Midway between Punta Sur and San Miguel on the road along the west coast of the island, **Parque Nacional Chankanaab** has a dazzling abundance of sea life as well as coral formations that are strictly protected in an attempt to revive them. The Riviera Maya's "eco-park" frenzy has reached this once-tranquil setting, bringing a show that features trained sea lions and tropical birds as well as a swim-with-the-dolphins program and miniature golf. Visitors may not swim in the lagoon but can snorkel in the even more resplendent sea or roam through the park's botanical gardens, which contain more than 2000 species of plants from all over the world. The small but lovely manmade beach has full facilities. An "archaeological trail" through the jungle is lined with 60 replicas of Maya and Olmec structures. Other trails meander through a botanical garden with tropical plants from 22 countries. ~ About nine kilometers south of San Miguel off the coastal road.

Fancy hotels, many with scuba-diving packages built into their prices, line the leeward side of the island. Some of the finest rooms on the island, for instance, await at the **Paradisus Cozumel**, an all-inclusive beachfront highrise north of town. All carpeted, with lovely sea views and balconies, the 149 rooms have rich tapestry touches: wallhangings, brocade chairs, burlap-shaded lamps. The grounds include two pools, a restaurant, shops and tennis courts. Air conditioning. ~ Punta Norte; 9-872-0411, fax 9-872-1599, or 800-336-3542 in the U.S; www.paradisuscozumel.net, e-mail paradisus.cozumel@solmelia.com. ULTRA-DELUXE.

A relatively small, affordable hideaway amid the big hotels along Playa San Juan north of town, **Sol Cabanas del Caribe** is one of Cozumel's oldest resorts and somewhat rustic. The 48 smallish rooms have no phones or TV, but they do have air conditioning. There's a swimming pool with a palapa bar beside it and a soft sand beach with plenty of chairs and tables. Guests snorkel around the hotel's restaurant, which extends out over the water; the kitchen staff regularly chums the water with seafood scraps so there is usually an abundance of tropical fish. ~ Carretera Costera Norte, Km. 5.1; 9-872-0017, or 866-231-9330 in the U.S. MODERATE TO DELUXE.

The more modest inns are mostly in the village of San Miguel. Prefer a sea view? The most reasonable waterfront hotel with a sea view is the whitewashed **Hotel Vista del Mar**, right on the *malecón* in town. All three floors have lounging areas, and its 26 ample, bright rooms with compact refrigerators and balconies are so breezy the air conditioning is hardly needed. There's a swimming pool. Air conditioning. ~ Avenida Rafael Melgar 45, San Miguel; 9-872-0545, fax 9-872-0445. MODERATE.

A nice compromise between luxury and affordability is the **Mesón San Miguel**. It's the classiest hotel in the village but the price is working class. Right on the *zócalo*, its easygoing lobby with rattan furniture and spacious, attractive restaurant set the tone for the 97 rooms. Airy and casual, with terraces overlooking the square, the rooms have carpets and phones. Air conditioning. ~ Avenida Benito Juárez 2, San Miguel; 9-872-0233, fax 9-872-1820. MODERATE.

In a lodging scene dominated by large name-brand resort hotels, it's a rare treat to discover a little place like the **Tamarindo Bed and Breakfast**, presently the island's only B&B inn. In a residential area five blocks from the plaza and four from the water, flower

◄ *HIDDEN*

LODGING

gardens and an upstairs terrace offer plenty of peace, quiet and homelike atmosphere. The five guest rooms—only two of them air-conditioned—blend modern furnishings with rustic accents. Amenities include a massage room, bicycle rentals, scuba-equipment rinse tank and storage, and a communal kitchen. The proprietress, a native of France, gives "continental breakfast" a whole new meaning. ~ Calle 4 Norte 421, San Miguel; 9-872-3614, fax 9-0872-6190; e-mail tamarind@cozumel.com.mx. BUDGET.

Look for Old Mexico atmosphere and a full range of room configurations at the **Hacienda San Miguel Hotel and Suites**, featuring architecture reminiscent of a colonial hacienda nestled among fountains, gardens and shade trees behind wrought-iron gates. Accommodations range from motel-style "studio suites" to split-level two-bedroom townhouses with kitchens and dining rooms. All units have TVs and continental breakfast served in-room. Air conditioning. ~ Calle 10 Norte 500, San Miguel; 9-872-1986, fax 9-872-1648; www.haciendasanmiguel.com, e-mail info@haciendasanmiguel.com. MODERATE.

An anomaly among Cozumel hotels, **Plaza Las Glorias** is on the beach and within walking distance of town. Fashioned as a Mediterranean villa and painted the prettiest shade of peach, it is one of the island's brightest and best hostelries. Besides the pool overlooking the ocean, this 171 suite, top-of-the-line facility offers several restaurants and bars and a dive shop. Air conditioning. ~ Avenida Rafael Melgar, Km. 1.5, San Miguel; 9-872-2000, fax 9-872-1937, or 800-342-2644 in the U.S.; e-mail hplgcoz @sidek.com.mx. ULTRA-DELUXE.

A nice, reasonably priced divers' hotel, the **Casa del Mar** has 98 small rooms and 85 suites, all with amenities that include TV. An inner courtyard ablaze with tropical flowers surrounds a shallow swimming pool. A walkway over the main road takes you to the beach at La Ceiba, a more costly waterfront resort under the same management as Casa del Mar. The affiliated Del Mar Aquatics offers dive packages guaranteed to make you glad you saved money on a roof over your head to spend it on underwater adventuring. Air conditioning. ~ Costera Sur, Km. 4, San Miguel; 9-872-1900, fax 9-872-1855, or 800-435-3240 in the U.S.; www.casadelmarcozumel.com, e-mail casamar@cozumel. com.mx. MODERATE TO DELUXE.

Built by divers for divers, the **Scuba Club Cozumel** offers all-inclusive room, meals and dive-trip packages. Fondly remembered by scuba old-timers as the Galapago Inn, one of Cozumel's original dive resorts, this 55-room Spanish Colonial–style hotel has a freshwater pool and an in-house dive center. It fronts on a limestone shoreline with a manmade beach. The rocky shelf drops off into 15-foot-deep water, providing an interesting wall for snorkeling, shallow diving and night diving. The surrounding area is full of crevices and small caves to explore. Divers enter the water from piers and emerge through a tunnel. Dive boats go to major reef sites daily. The rooms have white stucco walls, tile floors and sliding glass doors opening onto spacious terraces complete with scuba-gear drying racks. This place has a large following of return guests, so make reservations well in advance. Air conditioning. ~ Avenida Rafael Melgar, Km. 1.5, San Miguel; 9-872-0663, or 800-847-5708 in the U.S.; www.scubaclubcozumel.com, e-mail info@scubaclubcozumel.com. ULTRA-DELUXE.

The **Presidente InterContinental Cozumel** has a splendid beach property. The hotel has a breezy, outdoor restaurant and sits next to a perfect snorkelers' cove. The 253 big, brightly colored rooms offer sea views and large bathrooms. Air conditioning. ~ Carretera a Chankanaab, Km. 6.5, San Miguel; 9-872-0322, fax 9-872-1360, or 800-468-3571 in the U.S.; www.interconti.com. DELUXE TO ULTRA-DELUXE.

Luxury ecotourism is the goal of the **Allegro Cozumel Resort**, a 300-unit clone of the huge palapa resort across the water at Playa-car. Located near the island's southern tip, this is the farthest resort from town and one of the closest to Palancar Reef. Rental scooters and bicycles, as well as dive gear, are available. There are two pricey restaurants and a nightclub on the premises. Air conditioning. ~ Carretera a Chankanaab, Km 16.5, San Miguel; 9-872-3443, fax 9-872-4508. ULTRA-DELUXE.

DINING

Enjoy a cool drink or hot meal at the open-air **Plaza Leza**. Its umbrella-shaped outdoor tables provide the best vantage point for people-watching on the plaza, while the raised interior is top heavy with Spanish-style furniture and travel posters. Mexican dishes dominate the menu. The Spanish omelets and coconut ice cream with Kahlúa are tops. ~ Calle 1 Sur 6, San Miguel; 9-872-1041. BUDGET TO MODERATE.

If you're in the mood for a different genre of seafood, check out the **French Quarter**, an air-conditioned second-floor New Orleans –style restaurant run by Louisiana expatriates. The food is authentic, the portions are large. A seafood specialty platter includes butterfly shrimp, stuffed prawns, catfish strips, crawdad tails and

LOBSTER AND LAFITTE

You can feast on lobster while gliding along the Cozumel coast on a dinner cruise aboard the **Jean Lafitte**, a replica pirate ship that sets sail every evening at 7:45 p.m. There's live Caribbean music, and the ticket price includes all the margaritas you can drink. ~ Puerto de Abrigo, Avenida 25 No. 8; 9-872-0399 or 9-872-5973.

frog legs. The Cajun-style lobster is also exceptional. ~ Avenida 5, south side of the plaza, San Miguel; 9-872-6321; e-mail cozumel frqtr@yahoo.com. MODERATE TO DELUXE.

The oldest restaurant on Cozumel, **Casa Denis** serves Yucatecan and Caribbean food such as grilled grouper with beans and rice and *empanadas* with a wide assortment of fillings. The walls of the restaurant, which occupies an old-fashioned wooden house, are covered with photos of celebrities who have eaten there over the years, including Jackie Onassis. ~ Avenida 1 Sur 132, San Miguel; 9-872-0067. BUDGET.

Pizza Guido's (formerly Pizza Rolandi) has a romantic garden patio where guests can listen to classical music while enjoying a pitcher of sangria, homemade pastas, thin-crusted pizzas baked in a wood-fired oven and attentive service. Ask for the pizza-crust garlic bread. ~ Avenida Rafael Melgar 23, San Miguel; 9-872-0946; e-mail donguidoczm@hotmail.com. BUDGET TO MODERATE.

At the city museum, the **Restaurant del Museo** offers a standard selection of American and Mexican dishes for breakfast and lunch. While the food is well prepared, what's really special about this place is its rooftop location, which offers a sea view, sea breezes and a welcome respite from the traffic noise below. ~ Avenida Rafael Melgar and Calle 6 Norte, San Miguel; 9-872-0838. BUDGET TO MODERATE.

HIDDEN ▶

It takes a little searching to find **La Veranda**, tucked behind the Zermatt Bakery on Calle 4 Norte, three blocks northeast of the plaza, but the food and atmosphere are worth the walk. There's outdoor seating on the restaurant's namesake veranda or below in the shady garden patio; the indoor area is divided into conversation pits with sofas and low tables. The fare ranges from seafood platters and Mexican standards to a curious combination of Caribbean and Asian influences. Try the shrimp curry, the fish filet in mango sauce, or Jamaican jerk chicken with rice. ~ Calle 4 Norte, San Miguel; 9-872-4132. MODERATE.

AUTHOR FAVORITE

Just me, the salt air and the wind in my face as I ride my rental motor scooter along the all-but-deserted east coast of Isla de Cozumel, where the threat of devastating storms like 1995's Hurricane Roxanne discourage development. When I feel the need for a break from motor-scooting, I stop for a beer and *botanas* at one of the little beachfront palapa seafood restaurants like **Mezcalito's**. Not all of Cozumel's thrills lie underwater. See page 170 for more information.

Believed by many to be the island's best, **Pepe's Grill** is a smart, slightly snobbish upstairs-downstairs restaurant on the *malecón*, shimmering with candlelight and live piano music. Such flaming specialties as shrimp jovial and brandy-laced drinks light up the aisles like a magic show. Exotica such as tomato stuffed with baby eels and conch chowder share menu space with delicious Mexican meals and meats. Dinner only. ~ Avenida Rafael Melgar and Calle Adolfo Salas, San Miguel; 9-872-0213. DELUXE.

Pancho's Backyard serves heaping helpings of familiar Mexican dishes. The margaritas are cold, the plates are handmade and mariachis make you feel like you're really south of the border. ~ Calle 8 at the waterfront, San Miguel; 9-872-2141. MODERATE.

A find is the family-run **La Choza** at the corner of Calle Adolfo Salas and Avenida 10 Sur. A palapa room with crude wooden chairs, this eatery caters to the locals and serves the best Mexican food in town. At least one Yucatecan dish is whipped up daily, though the rest of the day's entrées depend on what the cook has in mind. Ask for the daily special. ~ Avenida Rosado Salas 198, San Miguel; 9-872-0958. MODERATE.

The rich, dark-wood **Morgan's**, all in imported pine, resembles a West Indies townhouse, with lush island melodies lilting inside and comfortable veranda and patio outside. Named for English pirate Henry Morgan, this chic, air-conditioned restaurant presents a treasure chest of entrées, from flaming crêpes to Spanish *zarzuela* (seafood in tomato stew) to conch fillets. ~ Avenida 5 and Avenida Benito Juárez, San Miguel; 9-872-0584. MODERATE.

The back streets of town hide a number of small, local eateries that serve Yucatecan-style seafood just like Maya mamas used to make (and sometimes still do). Try, for example, **El Moro**, ◄ HIDDEN
with its large menu of traditional Maya dishes served in a clean, bright atmosphere of formica tabletops and orange walls. The specialty here is *empapelado*, fish slow-cooked in paper with herbs. Also popular is the *pollo Ticuleño*, chicken breast in spicy tomato sauce with peas and cheese. ~ Avenida 75 between Calles 2 and 4, San Miguel; 9-872-3029. BUDGET.

Another great local place is **El Turix**, which has a changeable bill of fare featuring daily specials that often include delicious paella. ~ Avenida 20 Sur between Calles 17 and 19, San Miguel; 9-872-5232. BUDGET TO MODERATE.

Organically grown natural foods are served at **Naturalia**, including both international dishes and imaginative Mexican-style specialties. For breakfast, you might want to try Aztec eggs, scrambled with tomato, onion, serrano chile and nopal cactus. Lunch or dinner might be a Greek salad or a Thai pita filled with teriyaki stir-fried vegetables and chicken slices. Simultaneously small and spacious, the restaurant has glass-topped wrought-iron tables set far apart and big picture windows. ~ Avenida 20 No. 132, San Miguel; 9-872-1862. BUDGET TO MODERATE.

An outstanding gourmet restaurant, **La Cocay** (Maya for "the firefly") is set at the edge of a small hilltop park with a view of the cathedral. The decor is simple and romantic, with soft live music and low lighting, and as for the food . . . the chef creates a new menu once a month with innovative entrées such as sesame-encrusted tuna on a bed of Thai noodles or baked breast of chicken with a coating of nuts and tamarind. The deep, dark chocolate desserts are legendary. Reservations are essential. ~ Avenida 17 Sur 1000, San Miguel; 9-872-5533. DELUXE.

Ernesto's Fajitas Factory may be Cozumel's most distinctive eatery—an open, round palapa on the roadside, the counter ringed in stools that are usually crowded with fajita fans. Fajitas are rolled tacos filled with stir-fried onions, peppers and meat or chicken. You can also order all-American breakfasts, nachos and hamburgers. (By the way, fajitas actually come from the United States, too; owner Ernesto learned about them in his native Texas and claims that his was the first restaurant in Mexico to serve them.) ~ Avenida Rafael Melgar 141, San Miguel; 9-872-1154. MODERATE.

HIDDEN ►

Half the pleasure of dining at **Restaurant Playa Bonita** is getting there. Located on Cozumel's remote eastern shore, the simple little restaurant has a beautiful undeveloped beach all to itself. Watch the crashing waves from the shade of a palm-thatched palapa on the sand as you enjoy a seafood cocktail, ceviche or shrimp *al mojo de ajo* (in garlic sauce) and a cold Mexican beer with lime. Here as in virtually all Cozumel restaurants, seafood reigns supreme—even though fishing is banned to protect marine life on the reefs. All that lobster, shrimp, conch, red snapper and barracuda is imported from the mainland. ~ Playa Bonita. MODERATE.

Another ideal destination for a motor scooter excursion to the wild and windblown Caribbean side of the island is **Mezcalito's**. You can't miss it—it's one of the few buildings out there. The big, rustic palapa restaurant specializes in grilled shrimp and other seafood, sometimes including small, succulent lobster tails and tall, cool afternoon drinks. (Careful—it's a long drive back to town.) ~ Punta Morena. MODERATE.

SHOPPING

Shopping in San Miguel de Cozumel is terrific, if touristy, thanks to the hordes of cruise-ship passengers that descend on the town each day looking for ways to spend money. Starting at the *zócalo* where it faces the *malecón*, several megashops and narrow minimalls are catchalls of crafts.

Shoppers are reminded constantly that Cozumel is a duty-free port. This means real bargains for Mexican visitors, since Mexico imposes huge tariffs on European imports and lower but still substantial ones on U.S.-made goods. Whether North American visitors get better deals at duty-free shops than they would at home is questionable. Only a few types of goods—perfume, watches, jewelry, china, crystal, sweaters, linens, camera equipment, leather goods and liquor—are taxed significantly when they enter the U.S. For these items you may find lower prices in Quintana Roo's free-trade zone; but remember, you'll still have to pay the same U.S. duty on items you bring home in excess of the $600-per-person exemption. Above all, *don't* buy anything in a duty-free shop that was imported from the United States; these are intended for European shoppers and always cost more than stateside. If this kind of shopping sounds irresistible, you'll find one of the widest selections of luxury items at **Pama Duty Free**, such as crystal by Lalique, Swarovski and Waterford, jewelry from Cartier and Majorica, Tagheuer watches and Chanel, Giorgio Beverly Hills and Carolina Herrera perfumes. ~ Avenida Rafael Melgar Sur 9; 9-872-0090. The new duty-free store in town, so large that it calls itself a department store, is **Prococo**. ~ Avenida Melgar 99; 9-872-0791.

Tucan carries a wide selection of curio-priced *artesanía* from all regions of Mexico, including pewter, talavera pottery, blown glass, papier-mâché, onyx and traditional clothing. ~ Avenida 8 Norte at the waterfront; 9-872-1586. **Los Cinco Soles** is a restored colonial mansion full of surprises, from wooden puzzles and papier-mâché fruits to a back gallery full of temple rubbings and antiques. ~ Calle 8 at the waterfront; 9-872-2040. You'll find works by local artists, including paintings, jewelry and art glass, at **Galeria Azul**. ~ Avenida 10 near Avenida Rosado Sales. *Artesanía* from all parts of Mexico is sold at **Indigo**. ~ Avenida Rafael Melgar; 9-872-1076.

For inexpensive souvenirs that are authentically Mexican and, in many cases, edible, visit **Puro Chile**. Here you'll find an amazing variety of dried and packaged chiles—chile poblano, chile de arbol, chile habañero, chile serrano and dozens of others—as well as chile-motif gift items including ceramic table decorations and strings of Christmas tree lights. ~ Avenida Juarez at Avenida 10; 9-872-4544.

◆◆

PAINTED BLACK?

Cozumel is known for a type of black coral found nowhere else in the world. It is a rarity these days, since environmental protection laws prevent coral harvesting, so many of the stores around town that advertise it are actually selling coral that has been imported from the Philippines and dyed black. One place where you can still find examples of the genuine item is **Plaza del Sol**, which also deals in silver and gold jewelry, antique coins and loose gems. ~ Avenida Rafael Melgar 15; 9-872-1468.

Unicornio carries one of the largest selections of Mexican arts and crafts in town, including ceramics, wool tapestries, malachite carvings, handmade etchings, and papier-mâché. ~ Avenida 5 Sur 2; 9-872-0171.

Original, colorful and often surrealistic papier-mâché sculptures, ceramics and jewelry by renowned artist Alexander Flores are sold exclusively at **Galería Alexander**. ~ Avenida 5 Sur near Calle Salas; 9-872-4720.

Cozumel's **municipal market** is located on Avenida Rosado Salas, five blocks from the waterfront.

NIGHTLIFE   The after-dark scene on Cozumel ranges from spirited sports bars and lively discos to cozy waterfront palapas. The proximity of everything creates a neighborly atmosphere.

The hot spot downtown is **Carlos 'n Charlie's**, maybe the best in the chain. Noisy and crazy, with a volleyball court, beer-guzzling contests and gobs of great graffiti, it doesn't skimp on either atmosphere or drinks. ~ Punta Langosta Shopping Center, on the waterfront by the pier; 9-872-0191.

Within staggering distance up the street is **Coco Wook**, a technopop disco cloaked in artificial rainforest greenery; it's guaranteed to bring out the Eurotrash in its patrons. The trancedancing continues until dawn. ~ Avenida Rafael Melgar, across from the pier; 9-872-0316.

The disco king is **Neptuno**, across from the Restaurant Acuario. The room heats up with videos, laser lights and a late happy hour, and is often filled with a young international crowd on the prowl. ~ Avenida Rafael Melgar; 9-872-1537.

Like just about every major resort destination on earth, Cozumel has a **Hard Rock Cafe** full of rock-and-roll memorabilia and party-minded tourists. Dance music starts at 10 p.m. ~ Avenida Rafael Melgar on the north side of the plaza; 9-872-5271.

In the conspicuous waterfront location where Cozumel's Planet Hollywood used to be, **Kiss My Cactus** serves up live music nightly with bands ranging from rock to salsa and reggae. ~ Avenida Rafael Melgar 161; 9-872-5799.

Also among the new wave of San Miguel hot spots is **Cafe Salsa**, with nightly live Latin music from 10:30 p.m. on. ~ Avenida 10 between Calles Juarez and 2. Then there's **Viva Mexico**, with deejay dance music all night long. ~ Avenida Rafael Melgar; 9-872-0799.

BEACHES & PARKS   **PLAYA SAN JUAN** Also known as Playa Azul, this friendly, family-oriented beach stretching across the northern hotel strip from the Paradisus Cozumel hotel to Puerto Abrigo. Its best section fronts the Hotel Playa Azul. Here, windsurfers skim the soft waves, shade trees rustle and tiny black-and-yellow birds flit down to the local restaurant and perch on your chair. ~ Located toward the northwestern end of Cozumel; turn off the paved road at Hotel Playa Azul.

▲ To protect the offshore reefs from pollution, camping is not permitted on Cozumel's west coast beaches

PLAYA MAYA 🏊 🍴 This quiet sandy beach, with a few palapa umbrellas and plastic reclining seats in the sand, lacks the sizzle of the more popular spots but instead exudes a feeling of dreamy relaxation. Backed by low-lying jungle, the beach forms scallops around soft points to the south. The sand is scattered with white coral and broken conch shells. ~ Located about 15 kilometers south of San Miguel; take the marked turnoff from the main coastal road.

PLAYA SAN FRANCISCO 🏃 🏊 🍴 Cozumel's most popular beach is anchored by one of the island's oldest restaurants, the San Francisco Beach Club, where you can enjoy lunch or an early dinner under a palapa. The splendid beach, which runs along the crystal-clear sea, is where narcissistic, bikini-clad sunbathers sip piña coladas. Beach activities here include wave-runners that you can rent and snorkeling trips to Columbia Reef. ~ Located 15 kilometers south of San Miguel, just past Playa Maya.

PLAYA PALANCAR 🏃 🏊 🍴 This busy beach with palapas, water-sports equipment rentals and a refreshment stand is actually the south end of Playa San Francisco. The two are connected by three miles of undeveloped beach that is ideal for long, dreamy walks far from the crowds. Palancar Reef, one of the most popular and spectacular scuba destinations, lies offshore, and dive boats often make a stop at this beach on the return trip from the reef. ~ Located 20 kilometers south of San Miguel.

PLAYA ESCONDIDA 🏃 🏊 In a hushed jungle at the end of a bumpy road, this stretch of sand flows out of the shadows and wanders for several miles along limpid and motionless water. Tin-and-thatched shacks half-buried in shoreline vegetation send little smoke signals into the air as fish sizzle on outdoor grills. More

CORAL OF COZUMEL

Cozumel is unique in that, although the main natural beaches are on the east side of the island, all resort development is on the rocky western shore. This is because the island's main attraction is the chain of fantastic coral formations just off the landward side of the island that together form the world's second-longest coral reef, surpassed only by the Great Barrier Reef of Australia. Since the waters surrounding the island are part of an underwater nature park, shore fishing is not permitted.

a sanctuary for natives than tourists, this may be Cozumel's best escapist beach. ~ Located about 24 kilometers south of San Miguel along the coast road; look for the marked turnoff.

HIDDEN ▶ **PLAYA ORIENTE** 🏃 This unmarked beach is the northernmost of the beautiful white-sand beaches that line the windward shore of the island, separated by outcroppings and flat shelves of gray limestone. Although idyllic for sunbathing and beachcombing, this and other east coast beaches face the open ocean, and the crashing surf creates undertows that make swimming dangerous. ~ Located where the Carretera Transversal meets the coast.

▲ Camping is permitted on east coast beaches.

Just past Punta Chiquero, pause at El Mirador and gaze out from the rocky lookout point to the surging Caribbean.

PUNTA MORENA 🏃 Punta Morena winds down from a small settlement of huts and palms where fishermen gather to barbecue fresh fish. Seaweed and interesting rock formations lie along the beach. One sculpted rock, reached by a little wooden bridge, is called Copa de Piedra (stone cup). An overhanging grotto with a sandy floor, called Cueva del Amor (Cave of Love), is reached by crude rocky stairs. ~ Located along the windward coast road at Km. 45.

HIDDEN ▶ **PLAYA CHEN RÍO** 🏃 Located in a cove protected by a wall of rocks, this crescent of sand slides along the somnolent turquoise water. Very quiet and private, with a few palapa umbrellas for shade. ~ Located along the windward coast road at Km. 42.

PLAYA BONITA (PUNTA CHIQUERO) 🏃 This is the most beautiful beach on Cozumel's eastern coast, perhaps on the entire island. Protected by a tousled green headland, the sugar-white shore clings to a sheltered cove, then ventures south for half a mile or so along the open sea. Cages holding parakeets dangle from the eaves of the quaint thatched-roof restaurant, and playful coatimundis nuzzle their pointy noses into your sandals for attention. A small beach club nearby rents sailboards. ~ Located off the windward coast road at Km. 37.

▲ This is a favorite camping beach.

The Riviera Maya: Playa del Carmen to Tulum

Back on the mainland, Route 307 narrows and continues south from Playa del Carmen toward Tulum in a straight line between solid walls of greenery. Every few kilometers, a small road runs eastward into the vegetation a short distance to the seashore. Down these roads the kind of tropical beaches you've daydreamed about still exist—but many have become the private domains of big resorts, sometimes with golf courses and commercialized "nature" theme parks built around Maya ruins.

Six kilometers south of Playa del Carmen, a marked turnoff leads to **Xcaret**. Anyone who knew Xcaret before 1991 will lament its fate: the development of an $8.1 million tropical amusement park. This once-secluded cove sheltering bold, brilliant fish and phantomlike waters has been dynamited and dredged to make way for a 1700-foot "underground river trip" for snorkelers. Most of the fish are gone, and the dolphins have been corralled into the lagoon so humans can swim with them ($90, first-come, first-served; if you want to swim with the dolphins, you must get there at least an hour before the park opens). Pink-and-blue "folk" buses designed just for Xcaret deliver Cancún daytrippers by the hundreds and sometimes thousands. There are botanical gardens, cenotes, a petting zoo, a small archaeological museum, a seafood restaurant, a bar, a water-sports center and a souvenir shop. Promoters call the transformed Xcaret "Nature's Sacred Paradise" and charge US$40 a person to enter it; snorkel rentals and swimming with the dolphins cost extra. The park also incorporates several recently restored Maya temples of an ancient town now referred to as Xcaret but originally known as Polé. Discovered by American anthropologists on a 1926 expedition, the Postclassic Maya town was a key mainland outpost for the people who inhabited Cozumel between A.D. 1200 and the early 1500s. In size it was second only to Tulum. The modern restoration work looks somehow too picture-perfect; the same can be said for just about everything in this overland-scaped "eco-archaeological" park. Admission. ~ Carretera Tulum, Km. 72; 9-881-2400 in Cancún, fax 9-881-2424.

Beyond the Calica ferry and cruise ship dock is a place that's sure to satisfy the tropical beach fantasies of those who find the Disneyish landscaping of Xcaret a little uncomfortable. **Paamul**, a few kilometers to the south, offers a little slice of Caribbean coastline less retouched by commercialism. This small, mellow, rocky crescent beach with its offshore reef (see "Beaches & Parks" below) has been a favorite of snowbirds and scuba enthusiasts ever since the owners transformed it from a coconut plantation to a beach getaway in the 1970s. Facilities on the beach include an RV park with full hookups, a row of brightly painted concrete-block beachfront rooms and an exceptional seafood restaurant and bar. There's an excellent dive shop right on the beach. Admission. ~ Carretera Tulum, Km. 85.

The most glaring example of industrial tourism development along the coast south of Cancún is **Puerto Aventuras**, billed as "the new Maya civilization." Right. This slick mini-city sprawls along 980 acres and boasts 30 tennis courts, a 230-slip marina, a championship golf course, a shopping mall, numerous bars and restaurants, and 2000 hotel rooms and condos. With its ersatz Mexi-Mediterranean architecture and flawless Disneylike design, it looks about as Mexican as the Eiffel Tower. New? Sure. Civilized? Perhaps. But Maya? Well, not exactly. ~ Carretera Tulum, Km. 91.

HIDDEN ►

One of the last undeveloped inlets along the Riviera Maya lagoon, **Yalku**, just north of Akumal, is a Y-shaped cove. Only about six feet deep, its vivid green, mirror-smooth, crystal-clear water is an ideal place to observe coastal marine life such as starfish, sea urchins, parrotfish and queen triggerfish. Submarine caves and fish that nibble from your hand add to Yalku's appeal as a marvelous swimming, snorkeling and diving hole. A crude, small stone shrine surrounded by a crumbling stone wall is reached via a short foot trail that begins at the parking area. When the shrine was discovered in the 1950s, it contained an altar with a stucco figure of an ancient Maya god. Located north of Akumal, the beach is reached via a dirt road from the Akumal parking area. Admission. ~ Carretera Tulum, Km. 96; 9-856-3178, fax 9-58-6-3977.

Akumal, the first resort area on the Quintana Roo coast (more than a decade before Cancún was conceived), got its start as a base for scuba divers salvaging treasure from the 18th-century Spanish wreck of the *Mantanceros* on the reef a mile offshore. Magazine and television coverage of the project combined with Americans' fascination with the then-new sport of scuba diving to lure the adventurous down unpaved jungle roads to the little palapa village, and the rest is history. Today, Akumal is well on its way to becoming an "I remember when" beach colony. Most of Akumal was flattened by Hurricane Roxanne in October 1995, and developers rushed in to grab bargain-priced beachfront real estate. Today, the resurrected Akumal is taller and squarer than the original, with big, blocky condominium complexes springing up to frame the beach around the sheltered bay in a series of new "suburbs" such as Jade Beach and South Akumal. But the swimming is sublime, and dive shops offer gear, lessons and trips to offshore reefs. Artifacts from the wreck of the *Mantanceros* can be seen in the CEDAM Museum on the waterfront. (CEDAM, the name of the nonprofit group established for the salvage operation, stands for Conservation, Ecology, Diving, Archaeology and Museums.)

HIDDEN ►

On the beach said to be where shipwrecked sailors Jerónimo de Aguilar and Gonzalo Guerrero washed ashore in 1511, becoming the first Europeans to set foot on what is now Mexican soil, stands a **bronze statue of Guerrero**, dressed as an Indian, with his Maya wife and children—the first mestizo family. He refused to return to the Spanish world eight years later when "help" arrived in the form of a naval expedition led by Hernán Cortés. Aguilar expressed gratitude for his rescue from the *indigenes* by volunteering as a scout for the Spaniards, while Guerrero, content in his role as a Yucatecan family man, became the Spaniards' mortal enemy and acted as chief military adviser to the Maya, helping forestall the Spanish conquest of the Yucatán for 30 years. No monument commemorates Aguilar.

The Riviera Maya's newest "eco-park," **Aktun Chen** is the first dry cave system in Quintana Roo to be opened to the public. Soft lighting in the large vaults of the cave showcases elaborate crystal formations, limestone curtains and more than a thousand stalactites and stalagmites, as well as a pristine cenote pool. Knowledgeable guides lead tours around not only the easy paved pathways of the cave but also the 1000 acres of surrounding jungle with its abundant wildlife. ~ Route 307, Km. 100; 9-892-0662; www.aktunchen.com.

A little farther south, the crystal lagoons at **Laguna Xelha** attract everyone who ever wanted to don mask and flippers. Sometimes called "the world's biggest natural aquarium," Xelha was one of the Yucatán's major attractions long before it was converted into a commercial "eco-park." Its setting is the largest freshwater creek on Mexico's Caribbean coast, flashing with rainbows of fish. Environmental protection and ecotouristic exploitation strike a delicate balance in this labyrinthine waterway through the mangrove forest. Tubing or snorkeling down the inlet takes you past several cenotes and a cave once inhabited by the

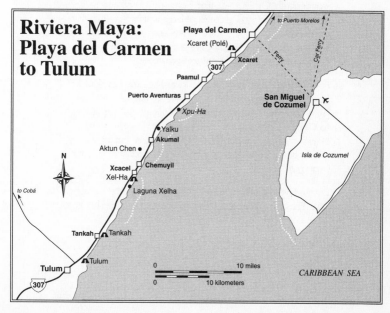

Riviera Maya: Playa del Carmen to Tulum

CARIBBEAN SEA

Text continued on page 180.

Mother Nature's
Theme Parks

Travelers who can remember the olden days (10 or 15 years ago, when Mexico's Caribbean coastline was dotted with idyllic, hidden natural areas where, after a hair-raising all-day expedition along narrow, unpaved jungle roads, you could pitch your tent and enjoy your own private piece of paradise) are likely to be shocked at the way things have changed.

Today, as a result of the Mexican government's odd ideas about ecotourism, just about all the most picture-perfect places along the coast have been converted into "eco-parks." Multimillion-dollar improvement projects have cosmetically tamed nature. Yet commercialization may be the only way to save these natural wonderlands. Other areas that were not turned into parks have become the exclusive grounds of large luxury hotels. In fact, one commercial eco-park—Xpu-Ha—recently went out of business and was taken over by Cancún's largest hotel chain, which developed it into an ultra-deluxe "eco-resort."

For many tourists, these eco-parks provide the best—or at least easiest—opportunity to experience natural flora and fauna they would never see if they confined their vacations to Cancún's Hotel Zone. Here's a summary of the Riviera Maya's major eco-parks. (Prices change often, and admission usually costs more when it is included as part of a bus tour package.)

Located 54 kilometers from Cancún near Playa del Carmen, 370-acre **Tres Rios Tropical Reserve** is set in an area that attracts an abundance of wildlife. Horseback riding is the favorite activity; others include hiking, biking, scuba diving, canoeing, kayaking and sunbathing. *(page 150)*

On Cozumel Island, **Parque Nacional Chankanaab** began as a nature preserve, but recently has taken on the character of a theme park. Activities include a seals-and-dolphins performance and self-guided hikes along jungle trails with reproductions of Maya temples, as well as botanical gardens. Dolphin swimming is available. *(page 164)*

Situated 74 kilometers from Cancún, **Xcaret** was the original eco-park. Developed in 1991 at a cost of more than $8 million, it became the blueprint for other parks on the Riviera Maya. Activities include snorkeling and exploring the botanical gardens, a small Maya ruin, and a hands-on zoo. *(page 175)*

Aktun Chen is located 107 kilometers from Cancún and centers around a large cave with delicate curtainlike limestone formations. Tours take visitors not only through the cave but also through the surrounding jungle teeming with wildlife. *(page 177)*

A long-established "natural aquarium" 122 kilometers from Cancún, **Laguna Xelha** had deteriorated badly under government management before it was renovated and converted to a commercial attraction. Activities include tubing and snorkeling; bubble helmets are available. *(page 177)*

Maya. As at other nature parks along the Caribbean coast, Xelha now offers a swim-with-the-dolphins program. The cost is substantial, and reservations should be made far in advance. From where you enter the park, the first lagoon is closed to swimmers but the shallow seaside lagoon swarms with snorkelers exclaiming over the streaks of fish. There are several restaurants and places to rent snorkels or diving gear. The park also has a small zoo. Admission. ~ Route 307, Km. 122; 9-884-9422; www.xelha.com.mx.

Some archaeologists point to the Xel-Há's Aztec warrior mural on the Los Pájaros building as proof that the Aztec trade empire, headquartered at the site of modern Mexico City, reached all the way to the Yucatán in the last days before the Spanish arrived.

Across the highway from the lagoons, the **Xel-Há ruins** are gradually being dug out of the jungle. When Route 307 was built in the 1970s, it sliced through the middle of these Maya ruins; since then, the surviving structures have been consolidated with stones saved from the buildings that were damaged beyond repair. Experts now believe that Xel-Há was the seaport that served the large city of Cobá (see Chapter Six) farther inland. The first Spanish settlement in Quintana Roo was established here in 1627. Of greatest archaeological importance are two faint frescoes depicting birds, located in a building called **Los Pájaros** (The Birds), and a third mural on the same building, so hard to see that it was not noticed until 1982, depicting an apparently Aztec warrior in ceremonial costume. Nearby lies a leaf-strewn cenote. The small admission charge is separate from that for the Xelha nature park across the highway. ~ Route 307, Km. 122.

Also cut in half by the highway, the Maya site of **Tankah** is believed to contain some of the oldest structures on the Caribbean coast, dating back to the Terminal Classic or Early Postclassic period around A.D. 900 or 1000. This site is thought to have been the area's major population center, with Tulum a few miles down the coast serving primarily as a ceremonial center and perhaps a fortress offering protection against invaders. At least 45 ancient buildings have been found at the site, but only one, designated Structure 12, is easily reached. It contains badly damaged fragments of murals. Across the road, a foot trail that is often too overgrown to travel without a machete leads to Structure 44, containing the remains of murals that depicted Maya gods and strange figures that are either costumed dancers or mythological lizard people. ~ Route 307, Km. 129.

LODGING   Cabañas Paamul has nine beachfront cabañas alongside the largest RV park on the Yucatán Peninsula. The cabañas have hot water and 24-hour electricity. Furnished in rattan, they have tile floors and private baths. Air conditioning; ceiling fans. ~ Located

4 kilometers north of Puerto Aventuras on Playa Paamul; phone/fax 9-875-1051; e-mail paamulmx@yahoo.com. MODERATE.

The biggest time-share game south of Cancún, **Puerto Aventuras Resort** offers 309 hotel rooms. The pseudo-Mexican planned community, with its golf course, tennis courts, marina and chic shops, could be anywhere. Accommodations are ultramodern and cushy, featuring soft pastel decor and wall art made with Cancún sand. Each room has a kitchen with microwave. (A word of caution: the Puerto Aventuras time-share salespeople, who work at locations along Route 307, may say anything to lure you here for a high-pressure sales pitch. Just say no and don't go.) Air conditioning. ~ Off Route 307, seven kilometers north of Akumal; 9-873-5100, fax 9-873-5102, or 800-451-8891 in the U.S.; e-mail info@puertoaventuras.com.mx. ULTRA-DELUXE.

Staying at the new **Xpu-Ha Palace** just south of Puerto Aventuras is like spending the night in one of the "eco-parks" that have proliferated along the Riviera Maya. In fact, Xpu-Ha was one of those mostly natural theme parks until it was bought out by Quintana Roo's largest hotel chain. Most of the park features have been retained by this all-inclusive resort, including snake, bird, crocodile and deer habitats and naturalist tour guides who will take you through the mangroves and jungle. One of the two beaches is on a sheltered inlet where manatees are sometimes spotted, and a long, narrow cenote offers cave-diving access. Water sports are all nonmotorized and include kayaking, sailing and snorkeling. Guest rooms are scattered throughout the jungle in clusters of eight thatch-roofed fourplexes, each facing outward away from the others to create an illusion that the resort is much smaller and more secluded than its size—464 units—would suggest. The rooms have jacuzzis, minibars, satellite TV, phones and balconies. Breakfast, lunch and dinner at your choice of three on-site restaurants (Mexican, Italian and Asian) included. Air conditioning. ~ Route 307, Km. 93; 9-875-1010, or 877-505-5005 in the U.S.; www.xpu-ha-palace-resorts.com. ULTRA-DELUXE.

The scenic, away-from-it-all beach community of Akumal is an oasis of quaint bungalows and hotels. In the center of Akumal "action," offering the most character for the least money, is the **Club Akumal Caribe**. Rooms are in a beachfront hotel and a sprinkling of villas. The three-story hotel demonstrates real Mexican flavor in its white stuccoed walls, arched doorways trimmed in pink, and tile floors that shine like glass. Each room overlooks the sea and Z-shaped pool and has a kitchenette stocked with purified water. A few steps away in the sand, the villas are tucked in a tangle of brilliant bougainvillea and palm trees. Though slightly smaller and more rustic than the hotel rooms, the villas do have beds so comfortable you'll forget you are away from home. Air conditioning; ceiling fans. ~ Carretera Tulum, Km. 104; 9-875-9012, or 915-584-3552, 800-351-1622, fax 915-581-6709 in the U.S.; www.hotelakumalcaribe.com. DELUXE.

Down the beach, the **Hotel Akumal Cancún** has 91 rooms, all with sunny terraces. Also featured are a disco-bar, restaurants, a dive shop and tennis. Air conditioning. ~ Carretera Tulum, Km. 104, Akumal; 9-872-2453. MODERATE.

Remote, picturesque and luxurious, **Villas Flamingo** is a five-minute drive farther down the beach on a windswept crest of Half Moon Bay. Architecturally stunning, the pink Moorish Mediterranean villas are decorated with domes and arches, clay-tiled awnings, pillared terraces and a stairway that curls like a serpent's tail. The four apartment-size units—each with two floors—have kitchens, living rooms and one to three spacious bedrooms. A fish-filled lagoon provides splendid snorkeling. Managed by the Club Akumal Caribe. Air conditioning. ~ Carretera Tulum, Km. 104; 9-875-9012, or 915-584-3552, 800-351-1622, fax 915-581-6709 in the U.S.; www.flamingos-akumal. com. MODERATE TO ULTRA-DELUXE.

Half Moon Bay is rimmed with low-slung condominiums built in recent years. The **U-Nah-Kin** has contemporary beachfront condo units equipped with satellite television. If bookings are slow, the owners may make you a budget-priced deal. Air conditioning. ~ For reservations, call 409-935-4475 in Georgia. DELUXE TO ULTRA-DELUXE.

Just south of Akumal, on its own private beach, **Adventure Akumal Vacation** presents an all-inclusive, modern beach resort with high energy and an appealing dive program. Each room bears a plaque with the name of a Mexican diver, and the diving focus is clear in the well-equipped dive shop. The hotel is a play-ground of rusty ballast balls, ships' ropes and horns, nets and shells around its pool, restaurant and bar. Rates include all meals, cocktails and water sports. Air conditioning. ~ Route 307, Km. 107; 9-875-9099, fax 9-875-9098; adventure-akumal.com. DELUXE TO ULTRA-DELUXE.

Midway between Xel-Há and Tulum, the little **Tankah Inn** offers five spacious ground-floor rooms with the sea practically licking at their doorsteps. The inn is designed with divers in mind—a pristine, rarely visited reef that lies just offshore, and dive packages for all skill levels can be arranged. What's for dinner changes nightly, but you can safely bet it will be fresh seafood. ~ Carretera Tulum, Km. 127; 9-874-2188, fax 9-871-2092; e-mail tankahdiveinn@mailcity.com. DELUXE.

DINING

Akumal offers several fine restaurants. The best is the Club Akumal Caribe's newly rebuilt open-air **Lol-ha (Flor de Aqua)**, where colorful piñatas and hammocks dangle from a soaring palapa ceiling. This, and a perennial breeze rustling its potted plants, make Lol-ha a relaxing place to dine. For breakfast there's bacon and eggs; for dinner, an extensive lineup of seafood, meat, chicken and make-your-own tacos. The attached **Pizzeria Lol-ha** is a cozy glass-walled room serving good Italian pies and the latest American sports on television. No lunch. ~ Playa Akumal. MODERATE.

The name *Akumal* is Maya for "Place of the Turtle," after the thousands of sea turtles who used to bury their eggs on the beach.

A brief stroll from Lol-ha, **Restaurant Zacil** sits under a cavernous palapa roof alive with spinning fans. Its circular glass walls look out to the beach, inviting fine views of the sea. You can choose from caesar salad, steak, chicken and a seafood plate. ~ Playa Akumal. MODERATE TO DELUXE.

In the middle of town, **La Cueva del Pescador** is owned by local fishermen and serves the fresh catch of the day. The sand-floored restaurant offers indoor and outdoor seating and a romantically candlelit atmosphere after dark. ~ Central Akumal. MODERATE.

For breakfast, lunch or picnic fixings, the **Turtle Bay Bakery & Café** offers an array of homemade breads, pastries and desserts as well as a gourmet dining menu. ~ Central Akumal, across from the beach. BUDGET TO MODERATE.

In the small village of Tankah, nine kilometers south of Xel-Há, good home-style Mexican food is served at the **Casa Cenote Restaurant,** so named because it is located across the road from Cenote Tankah, one of the largest cenotes on the Yucatán Peninsula. ~ Route 307, Km. 127. BUDGET TO MODERATE.

The resorts here have limited shopping. Akumal has two shops selling crafts and clothes near each other right on the beach. At the entrance to Xelha is a row of crafts shops offering beachwear and blankets.

SHOPPING

A sprinkling of sleepy beach bars barely keeps the coast awake at night. Everyone gathers around the **Snack Bar Lol-ha** for drinks, day and night. The big beachside palapa bar attracts some of the most unusual people you're likely to find in your travels. ~ Playa Akumal.

NIGHTLIFE

During the winter high season, enough people fill the Hotel Akumal Cancún to enliven its **Disco Arrecife.** Really just a palapa bar, it features dancing in the sand. ~ Route 307, Km. 104, Akumal.

PLAYA PAAMUL 🏃 🏊 🦐 This rocky, palm-lined beach has an intimate feel despite the presence of a small cabaña resort and the largest RV park in the Yucatán. Marvelous breezes sweep across the aquamarine cove, whose creamy blue waters are darkened by offshore reefs. Rocky platforms intrude upon the cottony sand,

BEACHES & PARKS

but the area is all the more pleasant because it is tucked between two protective points. Camping is allowed. ~ Located about 24 kilometers south of Playa del Carmen; take the marked turnoff from Route 307, then follow the dirt road about one and a half kilometers to the beach.

▲ The **Paamul Caribbean Paradise,** a privately owned RV park on the beach, has 190 sites with full hookups.

PLAYA AVENTURAS Beautiful in its own right, the beach at Puerto Aventuras has no palm trees and is somehow a little lacking despite its smattering of palapa shelters. Backed by the lowrise hotel and time-sharing complex at its northern end, the beach moves beyond a protecting point of land into a wilder open area that is quite empty and isolated. A pier near the hotel accommodates boat traffic. Little globs of petroleum sometimes wash ashore from passing oil tankers and can blacken your feet. ~ Leave Route 307 at the turnoff for Hotel Aventuras Akumal or Puerto Aventuras.

Tulum

The name *Tulum* means "City of the New Dawn," perhaps because of the fantastic sunrises that bathe the buildings. Created in honor of Kukulcán, god of the planet Venus and alter ego to the Toltec plumed serpent deity Quetzalcóatl, the architecture reveals obvious Toltec influences in its platforms and sloping terraces and balustrades fashioned as feathered rattlesnakes. Though Tulum lacks the grand pyramids of earlier cities such as Chichén Itzá and Uxmal, its stylized designs and unparalleled seaside setting more than make up for them.

A fabled fortress by the sea, Tulum is the Maya world's most visited site and surely one of the most disarming. Silvery temples and columns gather on a rocky bluff lashed by transparent green waves and skirted by an apron of white beach. The salt-beaded limestone walls set amid steamy jungle along the pounding sea have a brooding feel.

In 1913, after the end of the 64-year War of the Castes between the Maya and the Spanish, the School of American Research in Santa Fe, New Mexico, chose Tulum as the first major Maya site to be studied because it could be reached by sea. Sylvanus Morley, the real-life American archaeologist who is said to have inspired the film character Indiana Jones, was put in charge of the expedition. To get to Tulum, he hitched a ride to Isla de Cozumel on a Mexican Navy gunboat and then cross over to the mainland in a rented fishing boat with five armed guards. He stayed just long enough to discover evidence that Maya priests still visited Tulum regularly for religious ceremonies. Morley left after a few hours, reported to his sponsors that "serious work can only be done when there is no danger of attack," and did not return to Tulum until a peace treaty was signed with the Maya three years later.

As recently as the 1960s this crude and slightly crooked walled city, dating back to A.D. 1200, three centuries after the fall of the Classic Maya empire, could be reached only by boat. But the construction of paved Route 307, the backbone of the Riviera Maya, has put these ruins on the map in a big way. Hundreds, often thousands, of Cancún daytrippers pour out of as many as 80 tour buses a day. Clad in swimsuits and armed with cameras, they spill across the ruins, jockeying for good photo angles—a sight that would horrify the ancient residents of this sacred city. Today the entrance to the ruins is a grandiose combined visitors center and shopping mall near the main highway. From there, visitors can hike the last hot kilometer to the ruins or pay a few dollars extra to be driven in a shuttle.

Around midday you're sure to find throngs of tourists standing in line to get a look at the temples. A better plan is to spend the night in a cabaña a few miles down the coast and see the silent ruins bright and early, before the hordes arrive. Tulum is not large and can easily be seen in two hours. The walled compound contains 60 buildings, thought to be about 10 percent of the original city. Multilingual tour guides abound, and they're expensive (about $25 per hour), so if you hire one, it's best to share him or her with other visitors. Finding the other visitors will be your job. With luck, you can join a group tour in progress and then just tip the guide. Most guides are locals. Their stories, while perhaps not entirely accurate, are told with great enthusiasm.

In its heyday, **Tulum** (admission) was home to only a few hundred permanent residents, most of them seafaring Putún Maya—relatives

SIGHTS

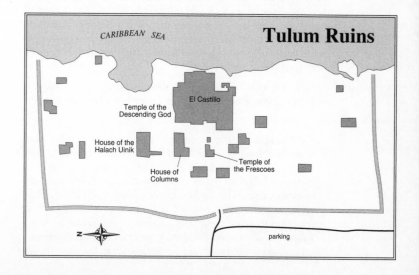

CARIBBEAN SEA

Tulum Ruins

El Castillo

Temple of the
Descending God

House of the
Halach Uinik

House of
Columns

Temple of
the Frescoes

parking

A Stroll through Tulum

The most accessible of the Yucatán's pre-Columbian ruins, the archaeological zone of Tulum deserves a stroll first thing in the morning or late in the afternoon, when you can sense the strangeness of these ancient stone structures perched above the sea free from elbow-to-elbow tour-bus crowds. Here's a temple-by-temple tour of the site.

TEMPLE OF THE FRESCOES   As you walk through the entrance gate in the ancient stone wall that surrounded the city, the trail will lead you into the midst of the site's main concentration of temples. Although not the largest, this temple is considered the most important to archaeologists—an observatory that reveals the Maya genius in measuring days. Using its perfectly placed columns and porticoes to measure the size of the sun's and moon's beams, ancient people figured hours of day and night. Inside the temple is another amazing find: paintings and murals whose colors and ornamented figures still quite vividly portray the Maya zest for life in flowing pictures of tropical flowers and fruits and through depictions of local farming and offerings of food, including maize, to the gods. Unfortunately, barriers have been erected to keep visitors from entering the temple, but a strong flashlight and binoculars or a telephoto lens can give you a good look.

HOUSE OF COLUMNS   Walk around the Temple of the Frescoes, past the badly eroded Stela 2, to this L-shaped royal residence, also called the Great Palace because it was the city's largest dwelling. Indeed, its rooms and galleries are spacious despite the building's flat roofs. Although Maya buildings typically had vaulted roofs, flat roofs were popular in Tulum. Unfortunately, their design brought them tumbling down much sooner than vaulted roofs.

HOUSE OF THE HALACH UINIK   A short stroll north of the palace is an archaeoastronomer's dream. Inside a columnar solar sanctuary, myr-

of the Itzá people who conquered the northern Yucatán Peninsula in the Postclassic era. The major population center was Tankah, a few miles to the north; set on the highest point along the entire coastline, Tulum served as a ceremonial center, observatory and lookout where raiders and traders could be spotted while still far up the coast. Its 20-foot-thick walls often provided temporary refuge for those escaping from warring tribes. Legend has it that Tulum was also the official starting point for funeral processions, which, accompanied by impassioned singing and praying, de-

iad drawings and sculptures proclaim the intricacies of solstices and equinoxes. A pair of plumed serpents arch together to show the daily journey of the sun. Again, as with all Tulum structures that contain artwork, barriers prevent visitors from entering.

TEMPLE OF THE DESCENDING GOD   Turn east and walk toward the sea to see this temple's sculptured facade, the trademark of the Putún Maya who built these structures. The "Diving God" seen here, depicted with his feet in the air, head pointed down and body encased in plumed phallic symbols, is a fitting deity for divers. The figure is the subject of a mysterious phenomenon that occurs each morning: as the sun emerges from the horizon, its first rays illuminate his feet; then, for one fleeting moment, the entire image of the descending god is lit by the rising sun.

EL CASTILLO   Gracefully powerful despite a thousand years of hurricanes, Tulum's castle looms atop the only rocky promontory in Quintana Roo. Built in two phases, the edifice is crowned by a temple whose columns are wrapped in carvings of plumed serpents, symbols of Kukulcán. In front of the temple rests an altar that may have been used for sacrifices. In ancient times, the Castillo held the secret of safe passage through the jagged reefs that guard Quintana Roo's shoreline. High in this castle by the sea are two small windows that, when illuminated by lanterns, send beams of light across the water. At precisely the spot where both beams can be seen is a natural opening in the reef. Recently, the Mexican government has prohibited visitors from climbing the castle to help preserve what's left of this marvelous building.

PLAYA TULUM   Archaeologists have identified at least 50 other structures in Tulum, most of them small and not very interesting—skip them and instead take time to relax on the curve of beach at the foot of the jagged cliff on which the Castillo looms. It may be only a minuscule patch of sand, but thanks to its spectacular setting, this beach is sure to linger in your memory for years to come. Go early or late to avoid crowds.

parted in canoes for the trip around the Yucatán Peninsula to the royal Maya burial ground on the island of Jaina, on the Campeche coast.

Besides its compelling surroundings, Tulum enjoys another distinction: it was one of the few Maya cities still inhabited when the Spanish arrived in 1518. The expedition, led by Juan de Grijalva, encountered brilliant red, white and blue buildings stretching so far down the coast that Tulum appeared as big as the Spanish city of Seville. Approaching by ship, the conquistadors were no doubt most overwhelmed by the sight of the lovely **Castillo** looming atop the highest promontory on the entire Quintana Roo coast. Built in two phases, the castle is crowned by a temple whose columns are wrapped in carvings of plumed serpents, symbols of Kukulcán. In front of the temple rests an altar thought to have been used for human sacrifices. In ancient times, the Castillo held the secret of safe passage through the jagged reefs that guard Quintana Roo's shoreline. High in this castle by the sea are two small windows that, when illuminated by lanterns, send beams of light across the water. At precisely the spot where both beams can be seen is a natural opening in the reef. Recently, the Mexican government has prohibited visitors from climbing the castle to help preserve what's left of this marvelous building. At the foot of the jagged cliff on which the Castillo looms, **Playa Tulum** may be only a minuscule patch of sand, but thanks to its spectacular setting, this beach is sure to linger in your memory for years to come. Go early or late to avoid crowds.

LODGING   If you just want to see the ruins, the **Hotel Acuario** has 15 rooms, mini-refrigerators, hot water, marble floors, televisions and a pool. Ceiling fans. ~ Route 307, Km. 131, at the turnoff to the ruins; 9-871-2195, fax 9-871-2194; e-mail hotel-acuario@yahoo.com. mx. BUDGET TO MODERATE.

Just south of the ruins, at the intersection with the Coba road, is the actual **pueblo of Tulum**, a drab eye-blink off the highway, with a few stores, a taco shop and a palapa-roofed church that blends Maya and Catholic traditions. A handful of no-frills motels has sprung up around the crossroads. One of the more attractive, the **Hotel Riviera Tulum** has a dozen spic-and-span guest rooms with private baths and hot water. Copies of Maya fresco paintings decorate the walls. Ceiling fans. ~ Crucero Ruinas Tulum. BUDGET.

To reach Tulum's hotel zone, turn left (east) at the Tulum crossroads and go for about three kilometers to a T-intersection with the coast road. The road to the south, Carretera Boca Paila, follows a long spit of land along the Sian Ka'an Biosphere Reserve (see Chapter Six). From the intersection to the biosphere boundary you'll find accommodations in all price ranges. The road to the north was originally the entrance to the Tulum archaeological site; today it's a dead-end road lined with hotels.

Nowhere along the Riviera Maya has seen such dramatic change as this hidden stretch of coast road, a lost world of primitive, strangely idyllic thatched-roof beach bungalows with communal restrooms until Hurricane Roxanne scoured the shoreline clean in 1985. Big money rushed in at that point to rebuild some of the formerly rustic resorts, while others toppled from neglect.

One of the best (and priciest) bungalow complexes is **Maya Tulum**. This unique, tropical-style hamlet is truly an oasis. Innovative vegetarian and seafood cuisine is prepared in a modern, hygienic kitchen with its own water-purification system and served in a large thatched-roof dining room. In the 35 spacious, round, stone cabañas, beds suspended from the ceiling let you blissfully float the night away beneath your mosquito net. A few have private baths with hot water. Meditation, yoga, massage, dance and reflexology sessions are available, as are healing experiences with a Maya shaman. The large, circular meditation hall doubles as a presentation space for workshops of up to 150 people. ~ Carretera Boca Paila, Km. 7; 9-871-20-94, or 888-515-4580 in the U.S.; www.mayantulum.com, e-mail maya@mayan tulum.com. DELUXE.

One of the first lodgings in the Tulum area, **Cabañas Ana y José** was little more than a cluster of a dozen or so Yucatán-style huts when the 1995 hurricane destroyed it. Today the property has been refurbished and expanded to include 15 comfortable, tastefully decorated rooms and suites in two-story duplexes surrounding a swimming pool and sun deck. There's an exceptional Mexican seafood restaurant and 24-hour electricity, a rarity in these parts. The beach is just a few steps away through a garden of palms and flowers. ~ Carretera Boca Paila, Km. 7; 9-887-5470, fax 9-887-5469; www.anayjose.com. DELUXE.

One of the nicest small luxury cabaña clusters south of Tulum is **Zamas,** which has 15 thatched-roof stucco cabañas designed in "rustic-chic" style with gentle curves and soft hues to blend into the surrounding beach and fan palms. Inside, by contrast, the bungalows' interiors sparkle with bright-colored furnishings and Mexican tiles. There's no pool, but the sandy beach is one of the best around. Solar-electric and wind generators provide full-time electricity. ~ Carretera Boca Paila, Km. 5; 9-871-2067, or 800-538-6802 in the U.S.; e-mail zamashotel@cs.com. MODERATE TO DELUXE.

AUTHOR FAVORITE

The first time I visited **Maya Tulum** (then called Osho Oasis), my fellow guests included a famous TV personality and several network executives who chose this hideaway for retreats because it was impossible to reach by phone. Now the place has conference facilities for 150 and cell phones work here. Yet it's still one of the most idyllic places to stay on the entire Caribbean coast. See above for more information.

Offering accommodations similar to those at Zamas, the newest of the small, secluded lodgings in the Tulum hotel zone, **Villa Tulum** has 18 guest rooms in a split-level arrangement around the swimming pool and palapa dining area. Each room has a living area, full bathroom and closet, hot water and 24-hour electricity. Air conditioning. ~ Hotel zone; 9-871-2418, fax 9-871-2419; www.hotelvillatulum.com, e-mail reservations@villatulum.com. MODERATE TO DELUXE.

When visiting Tulum, be sure to use your mosquito net, and shake out your shoes before you put them on in the morning to avoid rude surprises.

As you continue farther south toward the Sian Ka'an Biosphere Reserve (and away from Tulum), the cabaña clusters generally show a sad state of disrepair. Several, billing themselves as "eco-camps," offer bare-bones palapas along with shared baths and a food stand; bring your own amenities such as sheets, mosquito netting and fresh water. The last one down the road, and the bottom of the line, is **Camping Santa Fe**, where for less than the price of a Big Mac you can unfurl your bedroll right on the beach, bask in the Caribbean moonlight, and scratch sand flea bites for the next few days. ~ Carretera Boca Paila, Km. 6.

DINING   **El Paraiso** feels like the end of the world. Propped up on a pretty, deserted beach, the big, round, concrete-floored restaurant is wrapped in jalousie windows to catch the constant sea breezes. Pork chops, fried chicken, broiled grouper and hefty breakfasts of hotcakes and *huevos rancheros* are featured on the mainly American bill of fare. ~ Located about three kilometers south of Tulum toward Boca Paila; 9-872-3636. BUDGET.

Most other restaurants are located in cabaña resorts along the coast road. For finer dining, locals enthusiastically recommend **¡Que Fresco! Restaurante** (the name means "How fresh!"—a pun, since besides "fresh ingredients," *fresco* also means "open-air") in Zamas. Fresh seafood—the daily catch typically includes huachinango (red snapper), grouper and lobster—is served in imaginative salsas such as tomatillo-avocado, pumpkinseed and chipotle. The restaurant also features a full menu of Italian selections ranging from four-cheese gnocchi to wood-fired pizzas. ~ Carretera Boca Paila, Km. 5; 9-871-2067, fax 9-871-2067; e-mail zamas@compuserve.com. MODERATE TO DELUXE.

Another good restaurant in the Tulum hotel zone, **SianKa'an** in the Villa Tulum offers regional cuisine with an emphasis on seafood and a menu that changes according to the daily catch. A palm-thatched roof, bright, eclectic Mexican decor and a view of the swimming pool create the ambience. ~ Hotel zone; 9-871-2418. MODERATE TO DELUXE.

SHOPPING   Like many other ancient Maya sites, Tulum is a paradox. Right at the entrance to this age-old complex is modern-day capitalism.

The recently completed entrance to Tulum is like a shopping mall, with about 60 stores selling everything from T-shirts to pricey carved wooden masks. Silver, onyx, blankets, hammocks, machetes in elaborately tooled leather sheaths—the full lineup of tourist trade goods can be found here. You park your car at the entrance, a full kilometer from the ruins, and either walk or pay to take a shuttle. If you walk to the ruins, you'll meet blanket and trinket vendors who were selling their wares at the ruins long before the new commercial complex came along.

PLAYA TULUM ⚓ Wider than it is long, this small pocket of pristine sand lies between two limestone cliffs with temples on top. The turquoise water is fine for swimming. Seems like hardly any visitors realize you're allowed to play in the water and languish on the sand here as on any other public beach, but you are. In fact, it's an exquisite setting for sunbathing—if you don't mind thousands of bus tourists staring down enviously at you from the rims of the cliffs. ~ Located within the Tulum archaeological zone.

BEACHES & PARKS

▼▼▼▼▼▼▼▼▼▼▼▼

Outdoor Adventures

On Isla Mujeres, sportfishing can be arranged through **Sociedad Cooperativa de Transportación Turística de Isla Mujeres**. ~ Avenida Rueda Medina at Calle Madero; 9-877-0036. Anthony Mendillo, captain of the charter boat **Keen M**, specializes in saltwater flyfishing trips. ~ 9-877-0759.

FISHING

On Cozumel, fishing trips can be arranged through **Albatross Charters**. ~ 9-872-7904, or 888-333-4643 in the U.S. There's also **Ocean Tours**. ~ Calle 5 Sur 25; 9-872-1379. Several dive operators also arrange fishing charters on the side.

In Playa del Carmen, sportfishing boats operate out of the marina located just north of town. You can arrange a fishing trip through **Arturo's Dive Shop** ~ Calle 8, half a block from the beach and five blocks from the plaza; or **Aqua Ventures** ~ Avenida 5 at Calle 2, phone/fax 9-873-0969. In Puerto Aventuras, **Captain Rick's** offers half-day and all-day sportfishing trips. ~ 9-873-5195. Playa Chemuyil's dive shop, directly on the beach, also offers trips.

Before booking your dive, be sure to ask about the size of the group—during peak season some outfitters run "cattle dives" with as many as 40 people per trip.

DIVING

On Isla Mujeres, diving instruction and gear are provided by **Bahía**. ~ Avenida Rueda Medina 14; 9-877-0340. Among the most popular dives is Los Manchones, a beautiful coral reef at a relatively shallow depth of 30 to 50 feet below the water's surface. **Mexico Divers** offers trips to the Cave of the Sleeping Sharks. ~ Avenida Rueda Medina at Avenida Madero; 9-877-0131.

You'll find gear and lessons in Playa del Carmen at **Arturo's Dive Shop** ~ Calle 8; and **El Oasis** ~ Calle 4.

Cozumel, one of the world's top scuba diving destinations and site of legendary Palancar Reef and many other living coral reefs (see sidebar below), has 40 dive shops with trips for every taste and skill level, including shallow reef dives, deep wall dives, sunset and night dives and nitrox dives. Some of the best dive shops are **Cozumel Equalizers** ~ Acolfo Rosado Salas 72, 9-872-3341; **Dive Paradise** on the waterfront ~ Avenida Rafael Melgar 601, 9-872-1007; **Deportes Acuáticos** ~ Avenida Rafael Melgar at Calle 8 Norte, 9-872-0640; **Blue Bubbles** ~ Calle 5 Sur 298, 9-872-1865; and **Fantasía Divers** in front of the Fiesta Americana Sol Caribe ~ Carretera a Chankanaab, 9-872-0700. **Buzos del Caribe** has three locations on the island. ~ 9-872-1080.

In Akumal, dive shops line the main road; try **Kapaalua Dive Shop**. ~ Playa Akumal. The most popular sport in town these days is cenote and cave diving. A special course is required, and participants must already have an open-water certification. For a cenote experience in the Akumal area, head for **Dos Ojos Dive Center**. ~ Route 307 south of Xelha; 9-876-9967, fax 9-871-2091; e-mail dosojos@cancun.rce.com.mx. Dos Ojos cenote intrigues with surreal limestone formations splashed with light and color. The center also offers snorkel tours down a semi-submerged underground river, no experience required.

OTHER WATER SPORTS

On Isla Mujeres, check at **Water Sports Center Tarzan** for sea kayak rentals and Hobie Cat sailing lessons. Ask for Tarzan himself; this local character is an excellent instructor. ~ Playa Los Cocos; 9-877-0036.

In Playa del Carmen you can rent sea kayaks at the **Allegro Resort Playacar**. ~ Route 307, Km. 62.5; 9-873-0341.

On Cozumel, sailboard rentals are available at: **Sol Cabañas del Caribe** ~ Playa San Juan, 9-872-0072; **Hotel Fiesta Inn** ~ Carre-

---

DIVER'S DELIGHT

To find out why underwater enthusiasts consider Cozumel the finest divers' destination in the Western hemisphere, book a trip to **Palancar Reef** with EcoCozumel or any of the 40 other scuba outfitters on the island. The largest in a chain of coral reefs that runs the entire length of the landward shore, Palancar has such an amazing diversity of formations that it takes at least six dives to get an idea of its scope. Expect to see angels, triggers, yellowtails and other colorful tropical fish darting among the coral heads, as well as octopi and big green moray eels in the many undersea caves and canyons.

tera Chankanaab, Km. 1.7, 9-872-2900; and the **Hotel Stouffer Presidente** ~ Carretera a San Francisco, 9-872-0322.

On Isla Mujeres, head for **Rent Me Sport Bike**, where you'll find durable old "newspaper bikes" for rent. ~ Avenida Juárez and Calle Morelos. Also among the dozen or more bike rental places around town is **Rentadora La Isla.** ~ Avenida Juarez 11. Bicycling is second only to moped riding as a favorite way to reach El Garrafón and other sights around the island.

BIKING

    Bicycling is also a great way to explore Cozumel. Rentals are available at many hotels and independent dealers such as **Rubens** ~ Calle 1 Sur and Avenida 10, 9-872-02-58; and **Rentadora Cozumel** ~ Avenida 10 Sur 172, 9-872-1503.

South of Cancún, the big **Rancho Loma Bonita** has more than 150 horses in its stables. Organized trail rides on the beach and into the jungle are available. Guide service, lunch and drinks are included in the tour price. ~ Carretera Cancún–Tulum, Km. 49, near Puerto Morelos; 9-887-54-65.

RIDING STABLES

    Horseback riding is also one of the myriad outdoor sports available at **Tres Rios**, a nature park just north of Playa del Carmen. ~ Route 370, Km. 63; 9-887-8077, or 800-714-3643 in the U.S.; www.tres-rios.com.

    Much of Cozumel's interior is covered with lush jungle. Although you can't reach the wilderness by road, several small ranches along the Carretera Transversal and the windward coast road offer horses for rent. Trails that have been used by the locals for centuries penetrate the depths of the forest. Four-hour guided jungle tours on horseback can be arranged at **Rancho Buenavista**. ~ Near Punta Chiquero; 9-872-1537.

Tennis and golf are practically unknown in the ladino and Indian cultures, so elsewhere in the Yucatán nearly all tennis courts and golf courses are found at or near luxury tourist resorts. Most of these places offer equipment rentals as well. Newly opened in 2001, the 18-hole **Cozumel Country Club** golf course was designed by Jack Nicklaus and has cart and club rentals. ~ Carretera Costera Norte, Km. 6.5, Cozumel; 9-872-9570, fax 9-872-9590. The **Playacar Golf Club** also has an 18-hole course with club and cart rentals; intended primarily for use by guests at the all-inclusive Playacar Golf Resort, the course is open to the public, but the green fees for nonguests are very expensive. ~ Paseo Xaman Ha, Playacar; 9-873-0624. The 9-hole golf course is the main attraction at **Puerto Aventuras Resort**. ~ Route 307, Km. 96, Puerto Aventuras; 2-23-00. The resort also has tennis courts, as does the **Allegro Resort Playacar** at Playa del Carmen. ~ Route 307, Km. 69, Playacar; 9-873-0341.

TENNIS & GOLF

Transportation

CAR

There's a car ferry to Isla Mujeres from Punta Sam, 12 kilometers north of Cancún, but the island is small enough that a car is unnecessary there.

A car ferry to Cozumel leaves from Puerto Morelos once a day, at 5 a.m., returning at 9:30. To confuse things even more, on certain days, when the ferry carries fuel trucks, no foot passengers are allowed aboard. There's also a second ferry at a more reasonable hour on Tuesday only, but it often carries fuel trucks and is therefore prohibited from taking passenger cars; and, owing to a curiously antiquated regulation, no women drivers are allowed on any of the ferries! Call 9-872-0916 in Cozumel for current schedule. There is also a twice-daily car ferry between San Miguel de Cozumel and the international shipping dock at Calica south of Playa del Carmen; its schedule seems designed to accommodate Cozumel visitors taking short trips to the mainland to visit Xel-Há. The fact is, though, it's easier and more economical to rent transportation on Cozumel than to take a car there on the ferry.

The drive from Cancún to Playa del Carmen, 68 kilometers south on Route 307, takes less than an hour on a fast divided highway. It's a slower 39 kilometers from Playa del Carmen south to Akumal on a two-lane paved road, and another 24 kilometers from Akumal south to the ruins of Tulum.

AIR

Some Continental Airlines flights from the U.S. to Cancún continue to **Aeropuerto Cozumel**, located several miles east of San Miguel; the fares are the same to either destination. In addition, there are daily flights from Cancún to Cozumel on AeroCozumel, Mayair and Mexicana.

TAXIS

Oddly, cab fares from Cancún International Airport to Playa del Carmen are high—upwards of US$40—but the trip from Playa del Carmen back to the airport costs only half as much, or about the same as the cab fare from Cancún's hotel zone to the airport.

CAR & SCOOTER RENTALS

In Playa del Carmen, you'll find car rental offices at numerous locations along Calle Juarez, such as **National Car Rental**. ~ Hotel Molcas; 9-873-0360. Or try **Julia Car Rentals**. ~ Calle 6 near Avenida 20; 9-873-0556. Cozumel has several places to rent standard transmission Volkswagen Beetles and four-wheel-drive vehicles. Try **Rentadora Aguila**. ~ Avenida Rafael Melgar 685; 9-872-0729, fax 9-872-3285. Or there's **National Interrent**, with three additional locations around town. ~ Avenida Juarez 10; 9-872-3263.

On Isla Mujeres, you'll find motor scooters and golf carts for rent at Avenida Hidalgo 19; 7-00-19. On Cozumel, there are dozens of locations with motor scooters for rent, such as **Rentadora Marlin**. ~ International Pier, with additional locations on

the main plaza and at the Coral Princess Hotel; 9-872-1586 or
9-872-3675.

BUS

Luxury, first-class and second-class buses run south on Route
307 from Cancún's downtown bus terminal to Playa del Carmen
and points beyond. Some buses also stop at Puerto Morelos, and
bus drivers will let you off anywhere along the highway, though
if you get off at a beach far from civilization, you may have trouble getting a ride back.

Any of the 14 buses that run daily from Playa del Carmen
south to Tulum and Chetumal will let you off at Akumal. Not
all express or first-class buses will stop to pick you up there, though
all second-class buses stop there. It's easy to catch one of these
less comfortable buses to Playa del Carmen or Tulum and take a
first-class bus from there.

All first- and second-class buses between Cancún and Chetumal stop at the village of Tulum, where shuttles wait to take sightseers to the ruins. Besides the almost hourly bus service up and
down the coast, there are two buses a day to and from Mérida
by way of Cobá.

BOAT

Passenger ferries make almost 50 trips to Isla Mujeres and back
daily, with the first departure from Cancún at 6:30 a.m. (from
Isla Mujeres, 6 a.m.) and the last return boats from both Cancún
and Isla Mujeres at 9 p.m. The "fast boat" crosses Bahía de Mujeres to the village on the north end of Isla Mujeres in about 15
minutes and costs just over $3. The older "slow boat" takes a
full 35 minutes and costs about $1 a person (compared to $45
for the party boat!).

Isla Contoy is located 32 kilometers north of Isla Mujeres.
Boats leave for Isla Contoy from Cancún, Cozumel and Isla Mujeres. Prices for the excursion are much lower from Isla Mujeres
than from the other resorts—about $40. While the boats do vary
greatly in size and speed, the fares are virtually the same for all
boats. To purchase tickets, in Isla Mujeres contact the Sociedad

ANGELS ON WHEELS

Angeles Verdes (Green Angels), the Mexican government's free roadside
assistance patrols, go up and down Route 307 daily and also patrol the
paved roads on Cozumel. When traveling around Cozumel by car or
motor scooter, bear in mind that there are only two gas stations on
the island—both on Avenida Juárez in San Miguel.

Cooperativa Turística (Avenida Rueda Medina; 9-872-0274); in Cancún, contact the travel agent desk in any of the numerous hotels.

Cruzeros Maritimos de Caribe runs passenger ferries between Playa del Carmen and Cozumel. Big, fast jet boats such as the *México* and the *Cozumeleño* make the crossing in 30 minutes and charge about $8 one-way. Smaller, older boats such as the *Xel-Ha* take as much as 75 minutes and cost as little as $3. Schedule information (which changes constantly) is not available by phone, and there are no reservations. Just show up at the ferry docks. During daylight hours you shouldn't have to wait more than an hour for the next departure. In peak season the wait can be lengthy, though, so get your tickets before heading off to eat lunch or explore Playa del Carmen. Buy only a one-way ticket instead of the slightly more economical roundtrip ticket to avoid having to wait for a particular boat when you want to return to the mainland. ~ 9-872-1508. A **Maratima Chankanaab** car ferry leaves daily from Puerto Morelos to San Miguel de Cozumel, departing before dawn, and returns to the mainland in the midmorning, with a second crossing at a more reasonable hour on Tuesday only; it costs about $40. ~ 9-871-0088. The same company also runs a car ferry that sails between its home port of San Miguel and the Calica dock just south of Xcaret twice daily. ~ 9-872-0827.

▼▼▼▼▼▼▼▼▼▼▼▼▼▼▼▼▼▼▼▼▼▼▼

Addresses & Phone Numbers

Air ambulance (Cozumel) ~ 9-872-0912

Centro de Salud (Cozumel) ~ Avenida 21 at Calle 11; 9-872-0140

Centro de Salud (Playa del Carmen) ~ Calle Juárez; 9-873-0134

Cruz Roja (Red Cross—Cozumel) ~ 9-872-1058

Cruz Roja (Red Cross—Playa del Carmen) ~ 9-873-1233

Emergency number ~ 060

Municipal Tourist Information Office (Isla Mujeres) ~ Avenida Medina 15 at Calle Juárez; 9-877-0098

Policia (Cozumel) ~ 9-872-0092

Policia (Isla Mujeres) ~ 9-877-0082

Policia (Playa del Carmen) ~ 9-873-0291

Recompression chamber (Cozumel) ~ Calle 5 off Avenida Rafael Melgar; 9-872-3070

Tourist Information Office (Cozumel) ~ Plaza del Sol; 9-872-0972

Internet access (Cozumel) ~ CoffeeNet, Avenida Rafael Melgar 798; 872-6394

Internet access (Playa del Carmen) ~ Cyberia, Calle 4 between Avenidas 10 and 15; 9-873-2159

SIX

Quintana Roo Backcountry

To escape the tourist crowds of the resort region, head south or west from Tulum. Beyond the tourist zone of Cancún, Isla Mujeres and Cozumel is a different Quintana Roo—a land of swampy coastline where sea birds perch by the hundreds on tiny islands of mangroves and crocodiles glide along canals made by Maya sea traders seven centuries ago.

As soon as Cancún and the Riviera Maya began exploding into a burst of tourism that would radiate out across the Yucatán Peninsula—just ten years after Quintana Roo was promoted from territorial status to statehood—a vast area of the coastline was set aside as the Sian Ka'an Biosphere Reserve. The area is similar to the Florida Everglades but contains a wider array of natural habitats, from trackless beaches, cenotes and unspoiled coral reefs to deep inland jungle where spider monkeys and boa constrictors reign. Protected by reefs and mosquitoes, the central coast has remained so pristine that the United Nations Educational, Scientific and Cultural Organization (UNESCO) has designated much of it a World Heritage Site.

From Tulum, at the south end of the tourist corridor recently renamed the Riviera Maya, lonely roads through boundless, empty forests lead to once-colossal cities. Cobá was the largest city on the eastern Yucatán Peninsula during the Classic Maya period (A.D. 250–900). Muyil, one of the longest-lived Maya cities, was occupied continuously for more than 15 centuries. Farther south lies the edge of the Petén rainforest, which sprawls across parts of Quintana Roo, Campeche, Chiapas, Belize and northern Guatemala. There at the edge of the forest stand the ruins of Kohunlich, a recently excavated site where discoveries suggest the existence of more archaeological treasures to be found in a hundred other sites hidden throughout this largely unmapped land.

The ancient Maya ruins of central and southern Quintana Roo are very different from those of the northern Yucatán Peninsula and Chiapas. These centers were influenced by Tikal, Guatemala, in the Maya Biosphere Reserve south of Quintana Roo and Campeche and adjoining the Calakmul Biosphere Reserve (see Chapter

Eleven). After the mysterious collapse that ended the Classic Maya civilization, large inland cities like Cobá and Kohunlich were abandoned while waterfront settlements like Tulum rose to dominate a coastal trade empire that extended all the way around the Yucatán Peninsula from the Bay Islands of Honduras to the Gulf coast near Campeche.

Three routes lead into the Quintana Roo backcountry from Tulum. The first, unpaved, follows the shoreline south along a narrow coastal spit for several hours' drive to the unique little fishing village of Punta Allen, located in the heart of the Sian Ka'an Biosphere Reserve. A second road from Tulum, this one paved, runs northwest to the ancient Maya site of Cobá. The third route—south on Route 307—takes you to the final native capital of the Maya world, which lasted into the 20th century, and then continues to Quintana Roo's little Caribbean-style capital city, Chetumal, a good base for excursions to places like the colorfully idyllic Laguna de Bacalar and the ruins of Kohunlich.

Access to just about any area in the southern Quintana Roo rainforest, except around the major Maya ruins of Cobá, Muyil and Kohunlich, is only possible with local cooperation. People in this area have not benefited much from the tourist dollars flowing in a hundred miles or so to the north. In the poverty-stricken Maya villages of southern Quintana Roo, where the only cash-generating industry is tapping the sapodilla trees for chicle to sell for chewing gum, local people hope their pollution-free environment with its abundant bird and animal life can draw the kind of ecotourist trade that has transformed neighboring Belize. Anywhere you go, locals are waiting to help you find someplace to eat or sleep and somebody to show you the wonders of the forest.

Sian Ka'an Biosphere Reserve

Sian Ka'an Biosphere Reserve was created by presidential decree on January 20, 1986, following the guidelines of UNESCO's international Man and the Biosphere program. In 1987, UNESCO declared Sian Ka'an a World Heritage Site. Mexico is quite proud of the reserve and envisions it as a focal point of future ecotourism development. At present, though, access to the reserve is limited. Comparison with the Florida Everglades shows that inaccessibility is a virtue.

Small Maya temples dot the mangrove islands along the edge of the bay. One mysterious temple, barely larger than a telephone booth, has steps leading down below water level to the shallow bottom and therefore may have been a place where ancient navigators prayed before setting out onto the open sea.

SIGHTS   The boundaries of the **Sian Ka'an Biosphere Reserve** protect a 1.3-million-acre coastal wilderness that looks a lot like Florida's Everglades National Park and is even more remarkable in the diversity of habitats it contains. One difference is that Sian Ka'an has not been overrun by tourists. Another is that, unlike the Everglades, there is no present threat to Sian Ka'an's water supply. One-third of the reserve contains tropical forest, another third is

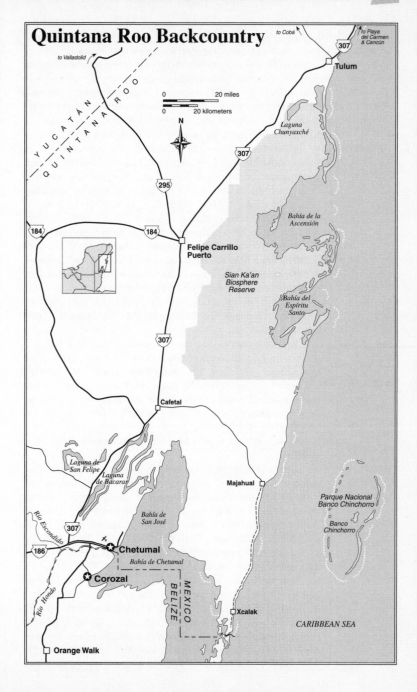

Quintana Roo Backcountry

to Cobá

to Playa
del Carmen
& Cancún

307

Tulum

to Valladolid

0   20 miles
0   20 kilometers

N

307

Laguna
Chunyaxché

295

184

184

Felipe Carrillo
Puerto

Bahía de la
Ascensión

Sian Ka'an
Biosphere
Reserve

Bahía del
Espíritu
Santo

307

Cafetal

Laguna de
San Felipe

Laguna
de Bacarar

Majahual

Parque Nacional
Banco Chinchorro

Banco
Chinchorro

Río Escondido

307

Bahía de
San José

Chetumal

186

Bahía de Chetumal

Corozal

M
E
X
I
C
O

B
E
L
I
Z
E

Río Hondo

Xcalak

CARIBBEAN SEA

Orange Walk

savannah and mangrove jungle, and the rest is water, including the large, wild bays **Bahía de la Ascensión** and **Bahía del Espíritu Santo**. Along the coast, extending northward almost to Tulum, is the longest coral reef system in the world. The reefs guard both bays against entry by ships and so have helped protect the area from development for 500 years. There are also large, cenote-fed freshwater lakes inland from Bahía de la Ascensión, connected to the sea by canals cut through the tall-grass savannah 800 years ago by ancient Maya mariners and kept clear by local fishermen to this day.

The general public is not allowed into the core area of Sian Ka'an, including both bays. Five-hour guided tours into the area are organized by **Amigos de Sian Ka'an**, a nonprofit environmental group affiliated with The Nature Conservancy. The tours leave from Cabañas Anna y José south of Tulum on Monday, Tuesday, Thursday and Friday mornings. Proceeds from the tours supports research that includes studies of traditional Maya medicinal plants and of bats as indicators of environmental health. Amigos de Sian Ka'an also publishes a bilingual checklist of birds of the Yucatán— 366 species, all of which can be found within the Sian Ka'an Biosphere Reserve. ~ Avenida Cobá 5, Plaza América local 50, 2o piso, Cancún; 9-884-9583; mailing address: Apartado Postal 770, Cancún 77500, Quintana Roo, México; fax 9-887-3080; e-mail sian@ cancun.rce.com.mx.

On your own, the most interesting way to visit Sian Ka'an is to drive the rugged road down the narrow, 57-kilometer-long spit of land south of Tulum. The road jounces along beside slender, empty threads of palm-lined beach and, after about an hour's drive, midway down the spit, plunges into shaggy rainforest around the outpost of **Boca Paila**. A few fishing lodges and private homes dot the coast in this area. Built before Sian Ka'an was declared a reserve, these places are still occupied but closely monitored for environmental impact.

HIDDEN ►

The road then leads to **Punta Allen**, one of the Yucatán's most unique and picturesque villages, perched on the tip of the spit where it juts out into Bahía de la Ascensión. The road is unpaved and not always passable in a passenger car, so it's a good idea to inquire at the ranger's hut (if it is open) or at one of the little cabaña hotels south of the Tulum ruins. During the rainy season it is completely impassable; from June to mid-October the residents of Punta Allen can reach the mainland only by boat.

Punta Allen consists of funky Caribbean-style clapboard homes and a soft beach slanting down into the bathwater-warm waters of the bay. The village is inhabited by an odd mix of Mexican fishing families and American expatriates who enjoy living on this near-island where tourism is still an occasional phenomenon. Someday Punta Allen may turn into a bustling little vacation spot with the commercialized quaintness of Isla Mujeres, but for now this place conjures up romantic fantasies. You could string a hammock between two palm trees on the beach and lose a month or two.

Punta Allen claims as its founding father none other than Edward Teach, better known as the pirate Blackbeard. In the early years of the 18th century, Teach employed spies on the waterfronts of the Virginia and Carolina seaports to learn about tobacco shipments to England. He would then rob the British ships and, according to local legend, flee to his hideout in Bahía de la Ascensión, far from the jurisdiction of the British navy. There he would ren-

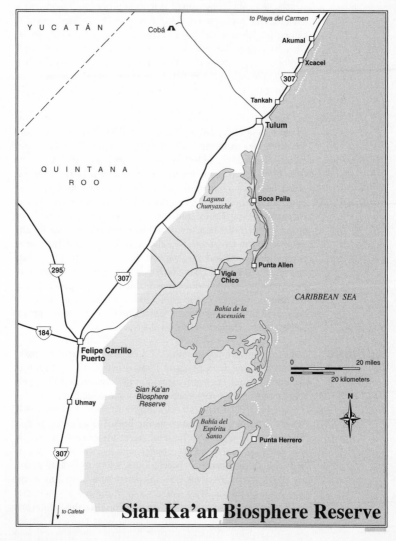

Sian Ka'an Biosphere Reserve

dezvous with Dutch merchant ships who were eager to buy tobacco and wouldn't ask too many questions about where it came from. The pirate concealed his ship in a sheltered cove behind the long spit, where pursuing vessels could not follow without knowing Blackbeard's secret passageway through the reefs that block the entrance to the bay. The village that grew up on the tip of the spit was named after Blackbeard's ship, the *Allen*.

Over the decades, the tiny village became populated mainly by castaways who made their living by salvaging ships that struck the treacherous reefs. Later, as improved navigation made sea disasters less common along this coast, the village turned to fishing for lobsters and other bounty of the reefs. Today, Punta Allen fishermen "harvest" lobsters for export to the United States. Ecological regulations of Sian Ka'an Reserve allow local fishermen to take only lobsters that have reached a certain size.

From Punta Allen, the only way back to the mainland is the way you came.

HIDDEN ►

Two unpaved roads enter Sian Ka'an Biosphere Reserve from its western boundary along Route 307. The more-used one runs 58 kilometers from the town of Felipe Carrillo Puerto to a tiny mainland village called **Vigía Chico**, across Bahía de la Ascensión from Punta Allen. Some Punta Allen residents park trucks on the mainland, boating across the bay and then driving into Felipe Carrillo Puerto for supplies. A rougher road enters the reserve midway between the Muyil ruins and Felipe Carrillo Puerto. Some long-distance foot trails are maintained through mainland Sian Ka'an's thick forest, a little-used area that provides habitat for almost every animal, bird and reptile species found in the Yucatán. Entry restrictions have been changing frequently, depending on government funding. When money is available to pay rangers, parts of the reserve are open to the public; when it runs short, the roads are closed to all but local residents. Check in first at the ranger station where either road enters the reserve.

LODGING

Cabaña beach lodgings south of Tulum (see Chapter Five) make a good base for daytripping to Punta Allen. Only a handful of accommodations are available within the reserve, and biosphere regulations prevent construction of any more facilities.

The Boca Paila area offers lodging in the form of a few small, expensive fishing camps, such as the **Boca Paila Fishing Lodge**. This expensive mecca for bonefishing in the nearby lagoon has nine large, attractive stucco cabañas with electricity and private baths, all facing a heavenly beach. Rates, which include all meals, are startlingly high—over US$300 per person per night in the spring peak season. Designed to preserve the resort's character by discouraging non-fishermen, the rates are less shocking when you consider that they include a fishing boat and experienced guide all day, each day of your stay. A seven-night stay is required in the high season. Ceiling fans. ~ Carretera Boca Paila; for reservations (required), 9-872-5944, fax 9-872-0053, or 800-245-1950 in the U.S.; www.bocapaila-lodge.com. ULTRA-DELUXE.

For visitors out to experience the natural environment in ways other than catching fish, a better spot for escaping into your personal tropical paradise is **Caphé-Ha**. Accommodations, in two mosquito-screened cabañas with solar electricity are refreshingly rustic. The American hosts can provide snorkeling gear and ecologically sensitive guided birding or nature trips by boat. Rates include breakfast and dinner. ~ Carretera Boca Paila; for reservations (required), call 9-921-3404 in Mérida, or fax 610-912-9392 in the U.S. DELUXE TO ULTRA-DELUXE.

There's only one place to stay in Punta Allen—the 12-room **Cuzan Guest House**. Guest accommodations are Maya-style huts with shared baths and thatched-roof wooden cabañas with private baths and front-porch hammocks. The innkeepers are full of information on birding and snorkeling and can arrange low-cost fly-fishing trips as well as wonderful overnight boat tours of the Sian Ka'an Biosphere Reserve that include remote beaches, islands and Maya ruins for about $75 a person. ~ Punta Allen; for reservations, write Apdo. Postal 24, Felipe Carrillo Puerto 77200, Quintana Roo, Mexico; 9-834-0358, fax 9-834-0292; www.flyfishmx.com, e-mail fishcuzan@aol.com. BUDGET TO MODERATE.

DINING

Several lodgings in the areas of Tulum and Boca Paila have dining rooms and are happy to serve meals to nonguests, though most have limited hours of service and higher prices than you'd pay in places with more dining options. Boca Paila Fishing Lodge and Caphé-Ha all serve exceptional meals at deluxe prices.

In Punta Allen, the place to eat is **Restaurant Candy**, a palapa and courtyard where local fishermen lounge over bottles of beer on hot afternoons. Diners seated at long wood-plank tables can feast on fresh lobster, conch ceviche, barracuda or whatever else

AUTHOR FAVORITE

Fancy restaurants are fine with me, but I must confess that one of the best dinners I've had in Quintana Roo was a fresh barracuda steak with lobster on the side under gently waving palm trees at the funky little open-air **Restaurant Candy** in Punta Allen, a true fishing village where cooking seafood is the local form of folk art. See above for more information.

the fishermen may have caught that day. ~ Punta Allen. BUDGET TO MODERATE.

BEACHES & PARKS

SIAN KA'AN BEACHES 🐚 🦅 The empty, palm-fringed beaches along the Caribbean shore of the Punta Allen Peninsula offer visitors a glimpse of what Cancún Island must have looked like before anyone lived there. Without the artificial widening that has been done on Cancún's beaches, those along the road to Punta Allen are narrow and often steep, littered with palm trunks and a beachcomber's daydream of detritus from past tropical storms. Currents can be treacherous in any but the calmest water, and there are no warning signs. On the plus side, you're almost sure to have the beach all to yourself wherever you choose to pull your vehicle over to the roadside. Seabirds are abundant, and tide-pools in the occasional limestone shelves contain assorted marine-life surprises. The best spot for swimming is the sheltered beach on the lagoon side of Punta Allen village. ~ The beach is virtually unbroken along the 57-kilometer unpaved road from Tulum to Punta Allen.

⚠ Camping is permitted along the Caribbean shoreline, though few travelers take advantage of it because of the exposed locations and lack of fresh water or other facilities.

Cobá

Cobá, which means "Ruffled Water," was an apt name for this city built on the shores of five broad, shallow lakes. Spread across 80 square miles, an area of shallow lakes intertwined with ancient limestone roads and engulfed in undergrowth, Cobá is believed to be the largest ancient Maya site in the eastern Yucatán. It's certainly one of the most fascinating. A mind-boggling 20,000 structures testify to Cobá's greatness as a center of commerce, worship and community life in the Classic period. At one time, archaeologists believe, some 40,000 people lived here in a city that covered 27 square miles. A network of trails linking the various excavated and restored ruins presents an exceptional opportunity to hike in the tall jungle. Cobá is away from the tour bus routes so you'll feel as if you have the place to yourself.

Situated about 40 kilometers northwest of Tulum (not far off the paved two-lane road that runs between Tulum and Nuevo Xcan), past jungle hamlets and hidden cenotes, Cobá is slowly being resurrected from the forest. Less than ten percent has been excavated, yet it is possible to spend days exploring the broad causeways, shady leaf-floored paths, hidden caves and temples that reach high above the treetops. The soaring pyramids and intricate stelae found here testify to Cobá's status as one of the grandest cities of the ancient Maya world. Half-buried vaults and walls around every bend in the trail give visitors a genuine sense of discovery and adventure.

During Cobá's heyday, from A.D. 600–900, thousands of small houses were sprinkled throughout the area, and at least 20 plazas provided social and ceremonial centers for an elite stratum of Maya society. At least 45 *sacbés* (Maya for "white roads," so named because they were cobbled with limestone) radiated in absolutely straight lines through the jungle from Cobá to satellite settlements. One of these ancient Maya highways, the longest known *sacbé* in the Classic Maya world, can still be traced through the forest for nearly 100 kilometers to the town of Yaxuná, near Chichén Itzá. (A section of the *sacbé* has been cleared where it crosses Route 295, midway between the two sites, about 23 kilometers south of Valladolid near the village of Tixcacalcupul; watch for the "Mirador" sign.) Some experts believe the Yaxuná-Cobá *sacbé* continued eastward all the way to the coastal port of Xcaret. But the usefulness of paved roads was limited in ancient times since the Maya had no wheeled vehicles or pack animals; most archaeologists believe that the roads were used primarily for ceremonial processions or pilgrimages. One of the many Maya mysteries is how these limestone-stucco roads were paved so flawlessly that after 1400 years they are smoother than the highway that brought you here. One theory is that the builders used giant circular stones, some 12 feet in diameter and weighing several tons, as steamrollers are used today. Such stones have been found here, but experts dispute whether they were roadbuilding

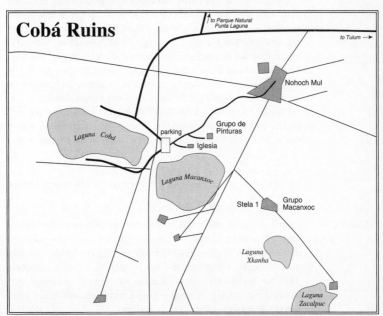

Cobá Ruins

to Parque Natural Punta Laguna

to Tulum →

Nohoch Mul

Laguna Cobá

parking

Grupo de Pinturas

Iglesia

Laguna Macanxoc

Stela 1

Grupo Macanxoc

Laguna Xkanha

Laguna Zacalpuc

WALKING TOUR
Exploring Cobá

Bigger than Chichén Itzá and older than Tulum, the ancient city of Cobá is the ultimate Maya archaeological site in the Mexican Caribbean. It's easy to drive there from Cancún, Playa del Carmen or Tulum. Visiting Cobá also involves more hiking than most other sites, but it's through lush rainforest. Here's what to expect:

GRUPO DE COBÁ A single pathway leads from the ticket-seller's shack near the parking lot directly into a tropical forest so thick you can't see the first set of buildings, called simply the Grupo de Cobá, until you're practically climbing them. Largest of the structures is the **Iglesia**, a pyramid with rounded corners and superimposed platforms. At 78 feet in height, it is the second-tallest temple at Cobá. Carefully climb the steep, crumbling steps for a magnificent jungle panorama. Back at ground level, slip through the vaulted rock tunnel that heads off south from the Iglesia. A little way past the main group, a side track leads a short distance off the main *sacbé* to a fair-sized ball court that has recently been restored.

NOHOCH MUL Farther along the main *sacbé*, you come to three forks in the road. Turn left to take the half-mile hike through the forest to Cobá's most striking site, the 140-foot Nohoch Mul temple. It is one of the tallest pyramids in the Yucatán, far surpassing those at Chichén Itzá and Uxmal. Similarities to the steep pyramids at Tikal have led some experts to believe that the Nohoch Mul pyramid was designed to rival the magnificence of that city deep in the rainforest of northern Guatemala. The front face of the pyramid has recently been excavated and sufficiently restored to make climbing it relatively easy, and a chain down the center of the stairway offers a handhold. When you finally reach the top, you'll find a small, squat temple like those at Tulum, complete with a Tulumlike diving god figure over the doorway—evidence that Putún

equipment or something more stationary like altars or performance stages.

SIGHTS Nearly a dozen major trails and myriad smaller ones lead to marked ruins at **Cobá** (admission; free on Sunday)—some of them little more than heaps of rubble, others hidden treasures with elaborate sculptures and traces of brightly painted murals. The distance you have to walk to see all the ruins in a single visit is daunting. Luckily, a local entrepreneur rents mountain bikes where the trail forks off to the Cobá group. This may be the best

Maya, seafaring cousins of the Itzás, used Cobá as a ceremonial site long after the city had been abandoned by its original residents. The view from the summit reveals Laguna Cobá and the Iglesia pyramid surrounded by a green jungle that seems to go on forever.

GRUPO DE PINTURAS   Back on the main sacbé, another turnoff takes you to the Grupo de Pinturas, or group of paintings, named for the murals painted in a riot of colors at the top of a four-tiered pyramid surmounted by a little temple where a thatched roof protects the fading artwork and inexplicable Postclassic inscriptions.

DOS LAGUNAS   From the main *sacbé*, a right fork leads between the site's two largest lakes, **Laguna Cobá** and **Laguna Macanxoc**. (You won't get much of a lake view, but you will encounter lots of the mosquitoes that breed there, so bring insect repellent.)

GRUPO MACANXOC   One of the most fascinating sights at Cobá is the Grupo Macanxoc, located in a dark, secluded grove. The small temples at Macanxoc are in poor condition, but there are several elaborately carved stelae. **Stele I** bears on both sides the likeness of a queen who is believed to have ruled Cobá between A.D. 653 and 672—one of the few woman leaders commemorated in Maya art. Another of the Macanxoc stelae is inscribed with the "long count" date for the start of the current Maya era—3188 B.C. This date has enabled archaeologists and others to see how other Maya inscription dates translate to our calendar, and in particular to determine that the current Maya era will end on December 23, 2012. Maya people, then as now, believe that time is made up of cycles within cycles, and their prophetic tradition is based on the idea that exactly the same events repeat at the same points in the cycle. Now, hardly a decade before Maya tradition says the world will start over and the same things that took place 5200 years ago will happen all over again, it's not too early to contemplate the profound implications. And there's no more appropriate place to give the question serious thought than among the mysterious stelae of Macanxoc.

opportunity you'll ever have to pedal along 1200-year-old paved roads through lofty tropical forest to the temples and palaces of an ancient lost city—don't pass it up.

Plan to visit the site as early or as late in the day as possible: Cobá is far beyond the reach of sea breezes, so the afternoons can be numbingly hot. Those fortunate enough to be staying at the nearby Villa Arqueológica Cobá can do their jungle trekking in the morning and late afternoon and take time out for a shady midday siesta under a ceiling fan. Multilingual guides are usually available near the entrance to the archaeological zone.

Spider monkeys used to be common throughout Quintana Roo's forests, but hunting and habitat destruction by logging have eliminated the monkey population in most areas. The one place you're likely to spot some in the wild is **Parque Natural Punta Laguna,** a nature preserve created by resident Maya activist Serafio Canul with help from the Mexican environmental group Pronatura, 19 kilometers north of Cobá off the paved road to Nuevo Xcan. The small lakeside archaeological site, originally a satellite community of Cobá, has a band of spider monkeys living in a cave beside a lake; you can often spot some of them feeding in the trees where the trail bends at the bottom of the path to the lakeshore. One of the Canul family, who live beside the road to the preserve and act as caretakers, can take you on a tour into the rainforest, then out in a boat to see the cave and a single intact Maya temple.

If you continue north past Punta Laguna, you'll drive through the forest for another hour before reaching Route 180, the main highway Cancún–Mérida highway, at Nuevo Xcan, a Maya town situated on the state line between Quintana Roo and Yucatán.

LODGING

To truly immerse yourself in the mood of Cobá, stay at **Villa Arqueológica Cobá**. Parked at the entrance to these fascinating ruins, this is the most remote of a series of luxurious jungle lodges operated by Club Med at major Maya ruins around the Yucatán (but without the somewhat silly organized activities and megaresort feel found at more civilized Club Med locations). It's also the only hotel for miles around. The setting is at the edge of Laguna Cobá, a placid mirror of a lake that shifts moods with the weather and makes the stone terrace in front of the hotel a romantic place to be at any hour. The charming two-story villas are a splendid choice for Mayaphiles and those who appreciate comfort on their jungle expeditions. There's a library well stocked with books and videos on the Maya world, as well as 40 guest rooms designed with real local flavor: handwoven blankets, red tile floors and white stucco walls worn to a perfect Mexican patina. The lodge also offers a good restaurant, swimming pool

sights

AUTHOR FAVORITE

One reason I like to visit the archaeological zone of **Cobá** whenever I can—sometimes driving directly there after my arrival at Cancún International Airport—is that it's the only place I know of where you can rent a mountain bike by the hour and pedal along ancient ceremonial roads in the shade of a rainforest canopy to the pyramids of one of the Maya world's largest cities. See page 206 for more information.

and tennis court. Room rates are quite reasonable, and meals aren't as overpriced as you might expect at a jungle lodge. Air conditioning. ~ For reservations, phone/fax 9-874-2087, or 800-258-2633 in the U.S. MODERATE.

The only other lodging at Cobá, **El Bocadito** has eight very plain rooms, each with two double beds and a private bath. Ceiling fans provide scant relief from the jungle heat. Arrive early—it fills up by mid-afternoon in winter. Room rates are rock-bottom, though recently young European youth-hostelers have recommended against this place. ~ Cobá. BUDGET.

DINING

A few tiny restaurants provide dining near the ruins entrance. **El Bocadito**, translated as "Little Mouthful," has sandwiches and meat dishes that, though average tasting, will boost your energy for climbing pyramids. The quaint eatery also serves up indigenous ambiance with its ragged thatched roof, red tile floors and jungle bouquets set on linen tablecloths. ~ Cobá Ruinas. BUDGET.

More small restaurants stand beside the driveway to the Villa Arqueológica Cobá. **Nicté-Ha**, for instance, serves a selection of classic Mexican breakfast, lunch and dinner specialties that changes according to the ingredients available on a particular day. The results are reliably tasty. ~ Carretera Cobá. BUDGET.

If you're seriously craving a good meal or just want to mingle with Cobá enthusiasts, dine at Club Med's **Villa Arqueológica Cobá**, located near the ruins entrance. Archaeologists, Mayaphiles and other experts trade stories in this spacious, formal dining room. To match the conversation, the international cuisine features a choice of chicken, beef or seafood dishes. MODERATE TO DELUXE.

SHOPPING

Several clusters of *artesanía* vendors' huts lie along the road to Cobá, and there are more near the Villa Arqueológico Cobá and the ruins parking lot. Woodcarving is the distinctive local art form. Painted wooden jaguars in an amazing variety of sizes and positions seem to be unique to this area. You can often watch the artisans at work.

Tulum to Chetumal

If you drive south of Tulum on Route 307, the highway skirts the western boundary of Sian Ka'an Biosphere Reserve. Few tourists make it down this way, since most of the trip from Tulum to Chetumal is a long, uneventful drive through flat, featureless forest. The curious traveler, however, can find a few little-known sightseeing highlights along the way.

SIGHTS

About 27 kilometers from Tulum are the ruins of **Muyil** (admission), also known as Chunyaxché. This city, one of the largest on the coast of Quintana Roo in its day, was occupied from about

◀ *HIDDEN*

A.D. 1–1550. The long period of occupancy resulted in an accumulation of architectural styles that makes the site feel like a blend of Cobá and Tulum. Most structures that now stand on the site date from the late Postclassic period. While the buildings are architecturally similar to the temples of Tulum, Maya enthusiasts will be struck by their resemblance to those at the Guatemalan site of Tikal, the center of a great Classic Maya empire from A.D. 600–900. This was a city of tall, decorative roof combs atop steep, lofty pyramids long before 14th-century residents built a Tulum-style wall around the city and erected new temples atop crumbling, already ancient pyramid mounds.

The most imposing of the many structures at Muyil is **El Castillo**, an unrestored Classic-era pyramid temple that rises nearly 50 feet in height. Only traces of an ancient stairway remain, and climbing the pyramid is prohibited. Its steep sides were destabilized by Hurricane Gilbert in 1988 and could collapse. A network of *sacbés*, or ceremonial roads, once ran from El Castillo to other groups of buildings at Muyil. One of these *sacbés* has been traced all the way to Cobá, about 50 kilometers to the north. By water, the city was linked with Tulum and Cozumel by a series of lagoons and manmade canals, some of which still exist in the Sian Ka'an Biosphere Reserve.

Most archaeological efforts at Muyil have focused on a temple known only as **Structure 8**, a high, squat ceremonial platform with a partially collapsed temple on top. The exterior of the platform has been cleared of the centuries' accumulation of dirt and plant overgrowth, though two massive trees growing out of the ruin were left standing and give a vivid picture of the temple's antiquity: after centuries of use, the temple was abandoned before these forest giants sprouted from the ground. Simple murals are faintly visible on the interior walls of the temple. Within the platform lies buried an older temple that scientists have excavated, but it is not open to the public. In the earth beneath the platform is an ancient cave that may have been used for ceremonies by the first residents of Muyil nearly 2000 years ago.

Though Muyil was discovered in the 1920s, archaeological work has been under way there only since 1987. Its proximity to the *Corredor Turístico* and the more famous ruins at Tulum and Cobá make it a good candidate for future restoration.

Ninety-six kilometers south of Tulum, the town of **Felipe Carrillo Puerto** (pop. 50,000) is known to travelers mainly as a place to stop for gas and perhaps lunch en route to Chetumal. Small streets lined with Maya huts surround the roadside town center, where you'll find the Pemex station, the best restaurant and a handful of nondescript shops. If you stop there, children flock around to sell you peeled oranges, chewing gum or an abundant local fruit known as *ciruelas mayas*—Mayan plums. The small-town plain-

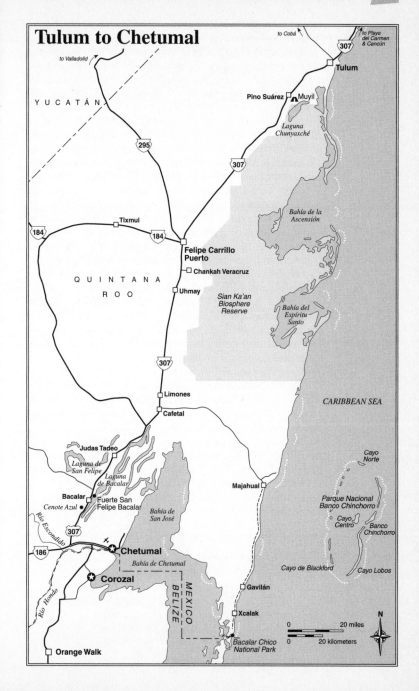

Tulum to Chetumal

to Cobá

to Playa del Carmen & Cancún

307

Tulum

to Valladolid

Y U C A T Á N

Pino Suárez   Muyil

Laguna Chunyaxché

295

307

Tixmul

184

184

Felipe Carrillo Puerto

Chankah Veracruz

Bahía de la Ascensión

Q U I N T A N A   R O O

Uhmay

Sian Ka'an Biosphere Reserve

Bahía del Espíritu Santo

307

CARIBBEAN SEA

Limones

Cafetal

Judas Tadeo

Cayo Norte

Laguna de San Felipe

Laguna de Bacalar

Majahual

Parque Nacional Banco Chinchorro

Bacalar

Fuerte San Felipe Bacalar

Cenote Azul

Bahía de San José

Cayo Centro

Banco Chinchorro

Río Escondido

307

186

Chetumal

Bahía de Chetumal

Cayo de Blackford

Cayo Lobos

Corozal

M E X I C O
B E L I Z E

Gavilán

Río Hondo

Xcalak

0   20 miles

0   20 kilometers

N

Orange Walk

Bacalar Chico National Park

ness of Felipe Carrillo Puerto belies its fascinating place in history as Chan Santa Cruz, the last capital of the Maya empire.

Through all the centuries of Spanish colonial rule, the *conquistadores* never succeeded in penetrating the dense forests on the east side of the Yucatán Peninsula. Any native settlements in this forbidding land were unknown to them. In 1848, following the first terrible massacres of the War of the Castes between Maya people and Mexicans, the Army slaughtered or enslaved every Maya Indian it could find. Half a century later, the Mexican government declared the Maya race virtually extinct. But it was wrong. Thousands of Maya rebels and their families had withdrawn to the safety of the uncharted forests to escape the violence in the north.

Chan Santa Cruz, one of many scattered Maya villages, had risen to prominence in 1850, when it had been the site of a miracle. A cross carved in a tree by a local cenote began speaking to local prophets, urging the people to fight on and drive the Mexicans from the peninsula. A cult of *Cruzob* (People of the Cross) continued to receive prophecies by means of "night writing" and conveyed the commands of the gods to the more than 10,000 Maya people living in the forest that surrounded the town.

The war between the Maya and the Mexicans amounted to a half century of sporadic, vicious skirmishes. All during this period the federal army thought that the Maya war parties raiding the countryside were merely Indian slaves who had run away from sugar-cane plantations, and that there were no more "wild" Maya people in the Yucatán.

The *Cruzob* built the last non-Christian Maya temples in the Yucatán at Chan Santa Cruz. The massive **Balam-Na** (Jaguar House), built in 1856 to house the Speaking Cross, borrowed from the architecture of Spanish mission churches in earlier centuries but had no towers or bells. Constructed by non-Indian slaves captured in raids on haciendas in the north, it was the headquarters of the revolutionary *Cruzob* cult for 45 years. The town was wiped out by the Mexican Army in 1901 and not resettled until the 1930s. Today, the temple is an austere Catholic church in the center of Felipe Carrillo Puerto where priests minister to the Maya people.

THE ORIGINAL SPEAKING CROSS

A historical curiosity can be found on the northwest edge of Felipe Carrillo Puerto, where a small, round-vaulted chapel housed the original Speaking Cross from 1850 to 1856. Only the stone shell remains today, but historians who have reconstructed the original temple on paper say that a secret pit hidden by the altar let a priest speak to the people in the name of the Speaking Cross.

Its interior is absolutely plain. Only a bare wooden cross, spiritual successor to the Speaking Cross of times past, adorns the echoing interior.

Mexican politician Felipe Carrillo Puerto, for whom the town was named, was the architect of a sweeping land-reform plan in the Yucatán during the 1930s. He gave the Maya people *ejido* land, owned by the federal government but used communally by the villagers. The system lasted nearly 60 years until, in 1992, the Mexican government conveyed ownership of all *ejido* lands to the villagers, who were then free to choose whether to keep their communal structure or subdivide the land and distribute it to individual owners. Most *ejidal* villagers in southern Quintana Roo have elected to keep their landholdings communal. The Maya people of the Quintana Roo forests face two choices: one, lease timber rights to large-scale forest products operations or two, preserve their forests intact, continue to eke out a meager living by traditional means such as chicle-tapping and develop ecotourism as a way to improve their standard of living.

Almost 100 percent Maya, the population of central Quintana Roo is growing fast. Not only do the Maya share in the population explosion that has created Mexico's continuing national crisis; the government has also begun opening forest lands west of Felipe Carrillo Puerto for homesteading. Alongside the traditional inhabitants of old Yucatec Maya villages such as Chankah Veracruz and Tixcacal Guardia, Chol Maya relocated from the Palenque area, Tzotzil and Tzeltal Maya exiled from their villages in the Chiapas highlands and even Guatemalan refugees come to the Felipe Carrillo Puerto area for free land and a new life. More roads into the jungle wilderness appear almost daily.

The Mexican government recently formed the Fideicomiso Costa Maya, or Maya Coast Trust, a regional development program designed to develop tourism along the 130-kilometer stretch of Quintana Roo's southern coastline from Punta Herrero in the Sian Ka'an Biosphere Reserve south to the remote divers' destination of Xcalak, almost within shouting distance of the Belize border. This nearly unpopulated shore is being made more accessible by paved roads, and eight new developments have been authorized. All are described as "ecotourism projects," but in Mexico the word *ecoturismo* can mean a lot of different things. At least two of the proposed projects include 18-hole golf courses, while a third would have its own marina. The Costa Maya plan, according to its boosters, would attract $1 billion in new investment and generate 30,000 jobs. One of the real estate brokerages that is busily selling beachfront lots around Majahual sloganizes that this coast is "like the Riviera Maya was 30 years ago." That's probably true, too, so put this area on your "see it before it's gone forever" list. It's hard to imagine this remote stretch of coastline becoming a resort mecca; right now there are no telephones and no public water system, they say a Pemex station will be completed one of these days, and hotel operators have to make their own electricity using solar or wind power. But then, 40 years ago it was probably at least as hard to imagine that anyone would ever spend the night on Cancún Island.

Just south of the village of **Limones**, 66 kilometers south of Felipe Carrillo Puerto, a paved road runs east to the peninsula bordering the eastern side of Bahía de Chetumal and the tiny coastal village of **Majahual**, a 58-kilometer jungle drive that takes a little more than an hour. You must clear an Army checkpoint at Majahual because from here the road leads to the border and the small channel—narrow enough to swim across—that separates the peninsula from the resort island of Ambergris Cay, Belize.

HIDDEN ▶

At the tip of the peninsula, 58 kilometers south of Majahual on a good, recently paved road, is the tiny village of **Xcalak**, which had 1200 inhabitants before it was destroyed by a hurricane in 1958; today, the figure has slowly grown to 300 people, most of whom live in small wooden houses built on stilts to withstand tropical storms. Along the coast for several miles in both directions from Xcalak lie scattered roadside food vendors, palapa lodges and rustic dive resorts. Today, visitors to this hard-to-reach area are limited to a small but growing number of scuba enthusiasts in search of the ultimate dive. This is the departure point for scuba and snorkel trips to Chinchorro Reef, the spectacular coral atoll 22 miles offshore.

HIDDEN ▶

Travelers who do not turn off toward Xcalak but instead stay on Route 307 southbound soon come to **Laguna de Bacalar**, a 36-mile-long lake that stretches just east of the highway between Cafetal and Chetumal. It's also known as Lago de Siete Colores (Lake of Seven Colors) because of the crystal-clear, placid water's contrasting bands of brilliant green and blue that shimmer like strips of satin. The original Maya name meant "Where the Rainbow Is Born." This is the second-largest lake in Mexico (only Lago de Chapala, in Jalisco, is larger). Wild orchids and coconut palms, along with a few private vacation homes and a couple of lodges, dot the lakeshore. The constant breeze across the lake has given Laguna de Bacalar a reputation as one of the most exotic places on earth to go windsurfing. A *balneario*, or bathing resort, 46 kilometers south of Cafetal, provides bathroom facilities, a restaurant and pier. Little open-air restaurants line the shore. Watch for the character of this quiet hideaway to change with the construction of a recently approved all-inclusive "ecological resort" called Club Las Velas Gold, a spinoff from the Club Las Velas in Cancún. The plan envisions 296 guest rooms (many more than exist on the entire peninsula at this time) and an 18-hole golf course.

Fuerte San Felipe Bacalar, a fort built in 1729 to fend off pirate attacks, peers out from a hillside near the *balneario* and contains a small museum of regional artifacts. A little way south of the fort is the turnoff to **Cenote Azul** (admission), a cenote in the forest that is said to be the largest in the world. Scuba diving is permitted in the virtually bottomless cenote, which is also a popular local swimming hole.

Accommodations in Felipe Carrillo Puerto are basic. Few tourists spend the night here, and lodging is geared toward truck drivers. The best choice is the budget-priced **Hotel Faisán y Venado**, with 21 slightly threadbare but functional rooms, some with TVs. Some rooms have air conditioning. ~ Avenida Juárez; 9-924-0043. BUDGET. The smaller, more austere **Hotel San Ignacio** has 12 rooms with rates way down toward the low end of the budget range. ~ Avenida Juárez; 9-924-0122. BUDGET.

LODGING

Just south of Majahual on the beach road, the **Maya Ha Resort** is an all-inclusive establishment designed with divers in mind. The 18 guest accommodations are in separate villas, each with a private bath and patio; all front the beach except four that are secluded in the trees on the beautifully landscaped grounds. The central building, containing an air-conditioned restaurant, bar and game room, is shaped like a three-story Maya pyramid. There's also an outdoor pool. Most guests choose from one of the "dive packages," which give each person a voucher for every day of their stay. The vouchers can be used for dive trips to Chinchorro Reef or for land-based activities such as Maya ruin tours. A hotel van can take guests to and from the Cancún airport (four hours away) for $50 per person. ~ Reservations: 2206 Forest Bend, Austin, TX 78704; 512-443-2977, 877-443-1600, fax 512-443-2978; www.mayaharesort.com, e-mail info@mayaharesort.com. ULTRA-DELUXE.

Ten kilometers north of Xcalak is **Rancho Cielos Azules**, a small luxury inn set right on a broad, pristine beach. There are

AUTHOR FAVORITE

A massage on the shore of a still lake, a jacuzzi soak under the stars, a hammock in front of a comfortable cabaña—these are a few of the things I look forward to at **Rancho Encantado**, on the shore of idyllic Laguna de Bacalar. As if that weren't enough, the resort also has a special permit to guide tours to magnificent, little-known Maya ruins (such as nearby El Resbalón, where archaeologists are uncovering and restoring three spectacular hieroglyphic staircases) that are off-limits to the general public. See page 216 for more information.

four guest rooms—two with private baths and two others that share a bathroom—brightly decorated in contemporary style with dark wood and leather furnishings set off by white or beige walls. Sliding doors open to a balcony or patio directly on the beach. Guests have kitchen privileges, and the inn has a few commodities that are taken for granted elsewhere but rare in these parts: reliable hot water and its own 110-volt wind-and-solar electric system, as well as a rainwater collection system and a new LP gas-powered refrigerator. ~ Carretera Majahual–Xcalak; 9-967-7174, fax 9-967-6050; members.aol.com/cazules/xcalak/homex.html, e-mail mediakzar@aol.com. ULTRA-DELUXE.

Along the edge of the reef at Parque Nacional Banco Chinchorro lie five centuries of shipwrecks, from Spanish galleons to modern cargo vessels. At least 30 wrecks are in plain view on the surface and an estimated 200 are located below.

Farther south on the Carretera Majahual–Xcalak, the **Costa de Cocos Dive Resort** has the area's most attractive accommodations in six immaculate, stucco-walled cabañas with tile floors, private baths and modern handcrafted furnishings. Moderate to deluxe rates include all meals (continental breakfast is served at the resort; you must go to a restaurant in the village for your free lunch and dinner). Dive packages, including not only food and lodging but also scuba equipment and boat transport to Chinchorro Reef, run in the ultra-deluxe range. ~ Xcalak; for reservations, call 800-961-6181 in the U.S. or fax 9-831-0110; www.costadecocos.com, e-mail cdcdavidrandall@aol.com. DELUXE.

In the village of Xcalak, **Sandwood Villas** offers four two-bedroom, two-bath beachfront villas with living room, dining area, and fully equipped kitchen. Amenities include hot-water showers, 24-hour electricity and daily maid service. Guests have the use of a 23-foot *panga*, a canoe and sea kayaks. There is a restaurant on the premises. ~ Xcalak; 9-831-0034, or 952-898-1667 in the U.S.; www.sandwood.com, e-mail asanders@isd.net. DELUXE.

Also located in the village, the **Hotel Tierra Maya** has six guest rooms with balconies where guests can lie in hammocks and gaze out to sea. Palms along the beach frame the view, and the lush forest behind the hotel makes for exceptional birdwatching. The American owners go out of their way to ensure guests a laidback, comfortable stay. ~ Reservations: 812 Garland Avenue, Nokomis, FL 34275; 941-627-3888, 800-480-4505, fax 941-627-0089 in the U.S.; www.tierramaya.net, e-mail fantasea@xcalak.com. MODERATE.

On the shore of Laguna de Bacalar, about 42 kilometers north of Chetumal, **Rancho Encantado** pioneered the concept of ecotourism in southern Quintana Roo when it opened in the early 1980s. The owners have a long-term vision for this place and keep improving it year by year, making it the kind of secret Caribbean hideaway dreams are made of. Accommodations are in eight individual casitas with tile floors, hardwood ceilings and furniture handcrafted of mahogany and rattan. Each one has a separate living room and bedroom, a kitchenette, and a patio porch facing onto a carefully groomed lawn and gardens. Fresh fruit can be picked from the orchards. Continental breakfast, lunch and a four-course dinner of freshly caught seafood are included in the rates. The owners also organize environmental and archaeological tours throughout the region, including trips to several Maya ruins that are closed to the public except by permit. ~ Laguna de Bacalar. Reservations: P.O. Box 1256, Taos, NM 87571; 505-758-9790, 800-505-6292, fax 505-716-2102 in the U.S.; www.encantado.com, e-mail reservations@encantado.com. DELUXE TO ULTRA-DELUXE.

Also found on Laguna de Bacalar is the quiet **Hotel Laguna de Bacalar**. Rising three stories, it reveals a turquoise-and-white facade nestled among shade trees and reflecting the jeweled sheen of the lagoon. The spacious, pale blue guest rooms, freshened by breezes and expansive terraces, have shell lamps. A shimmering pool, patio-bar and restaurant overlook the water. Ceiling fans. ~ Route 307, Cenote Azul turnoff; for reservations, call 9-832-3517 in Chetumal. DELUXE.

DINING

Except for a few tiny *taquerías* and pizza joints on Felipe Carrillo Puerto's don't-blink-or-you'll-miss-it main street, the only restaurant in town is **Restaurant Faisán y Venado**, diagonally across from the Pemex station. The famous restaurant of the same name near Tulum is a spinoff of this eatery. The Felipe Carrillo Puerto location is bright and pleasant. Despite the restaurant's name, which means "pheasant and deer," the menu no longer offers venison; Mexican law now prohibits serving wild game in restaurants. Instead, the bill of fare features traditional Maya dishes such as *pavo escabeche*. ~ Avenida Juárez; 9-834-0043. BUDGET.

Elsewhere, dining options are pretty much limited to the handful of resorts in the Xcakal and Laguna de Bacalar areas. As the only sit-down eateries around, these resorts' dining rooms will usually serve nonguests for a fairly steep price. Budget-watchers will find a few street vendors who sell fried fish and fish tacos along the beach in Xcakal; the problem is, they shut down around 5 p.m.

Near Laguna de Bacalar, **Restaurante Cenote Azul** presents a daily-special seafood menu that may be less than spectacular but is just about the only dining option along the highway between Felipe Carrillo Puerto and Chetumal. The setting overlooking the Yucatán's largest cenote, along with the restaurant's menagerie

Text continued on page 220.

Tourism & the Environment

*I*nspired by the development of environmental tourism in Costa Rica and Belize, the Mexican government has seized on the concept of ecotourism to attract tourist dollars to economically depressed southern Quintana Roo. *Ecotourism* means environmentally and socially sensitive pleasure travel. It is based on the idea that protecting ecosystems and the traditions of indigenous cultures can go hand in hand with appropriate kinds of economic development, especially tourism.

Conservationists' experience in Central America over the past 20 years has shown that the keys to protecting rainforests, ancient ruins, coral reefs, wetlands and endangered species are local people and tourist dollars. If local villagers learn to depend on visiting sightseers for a living, they no longer have an incentive to burn the forest for food or hunt jaguars and crocodiles for the price of their skins. They are less likely to loot pre-Columbian ruins if they can get paid to guide tourists there for picture taking instead.

In Mexico, the ecotourism concept is still quite new, and neither the government nor local tourism promoters seem to have a clear idea of what to do with it. The Mexican federal agencies in charge of tourist development are geared to work with multinational corporate investors on big, expensive projects that will employ hundreds of people. They have had little success at encouraging small people-to-people tourist enterprises.

One government-sanctioned effort at ecotourism is in operation at Tres Garantías, an *ejido* (village using communal land) of Maya chicle tappers in the rainforest of southern Quintana Roo. The people of the *ejido* have voted to set aside more than half of their forest as a wilderness providing habitat for spider monkeys, boa constrictors, crocodiles, coatimundis and jaguarundis, as well as tourists who come to stay in their jungle lodge. So far, the lodge consists of a single large camping palapa enclosed with mosquito netting. Located in the heart of the forest, several miles' exciting ride from the village in the back of a pickup truck, it has an elevated wood floor and a picnic table. Maya women bring you meals. Guests provide their own hammocks or sleeping bags. Based on a plan that has proven successful at Maya villages in Belize, the camp is a pilot project that may expand to as many as a dozen other chicle-tapping *ejidos* throughout the wild southern forest of Quintana

Roo. To realize this dream, they say, they need international investors who will put up the money to build more camping palapas—and buy a fleet of all-terrain vehicles so guests can roar around the jungle, presumably watching for wildlife. It is widely believed that gringos never eat chili peppers or walk anywhere. ~ Reservations: 2-98-02 in Chetumal.

To fully enjoy and contribute to the environment of the Yucatán, please observe this short environmental code of ethics:

1. **Do not disturb wildlife or natural habitats.** Stay on trails, avoid using machetes and collecting plants or wildlife. Coral reefs are especially sensitive and should never be touched. Bird nests should be viewed from a safe distance with binoculars, and nesting sea turtles should be observed only with a trained guide. Do not feed monkeys or other wild animals; feeding by humans alters their diets and behaviors. Raccoons, who normally live alone, become pack animals when fed and spread diseases that kill them. The stomach fluids of deer who eat human foods change so they can no longer digest leaves or other wild food sources, and they starve to death during the off-season.

2. **Do not litter.** If you'll be in remote areas, take along a sack to carry out your garbage. Just one food wrapper or aluminum can is all it takes to ruin a remote beach or little-known ruin for the next visitor. Many kinds of trash—plastic six-pack holders, for instance—can be deadly to wildlife.

3. **Be conscious of helping local communities.** Use the native tour guides—they are the best—and patronize locally owned lodges, restaurants and markets. Buy souvenirs from native craftspeople; Maya villagers make marvelous handicrafts. Make sure your economic impact benefits the local population.

4. **Be culturally sensitive.** Remember that you are a guest in the Maya world. Make an effort to learn basic customs and follow them. Try to communicate in Spanish whenever possible. Don't judge Mexico by hometown standards. Respect local tradition and bear in mind that some gringo tourist habits may be offensive to village people.

5. **After your trip, write to government agencies and nonprofit environmental groups.** Whether in Spanish or English, compliment places where you saw ecotourism principles applied successfully, and if you observed problems, suggest changes or improvements.

of exotic birds, is worth the stop even if you're not hungry. ~ Route 307. MODERATE.

BEACHES
& PARKS

XCALAK BEACHES 🏊 🐟 🏄 🏕 The coast from Majahual to Xcalak is lined with strands of sandy Caribbean beach, though many of them are shadeless and littered with storm debris. The nicest beach area is Playa de Cocos, fronted by the Costa de Cocos Dive Resort just north of Xcalak. The resort has sea kayaks and sailboards for rent. ~ From Route 307 at Cafetal, a paved road runs 58 kilometers east to Majahual, where an unpaved road continues down the coast for another 58 kilometers to Xcalak.

▲ Camping is unrestricted along the Majahual–Xcalak coast.

PARQUE NACIONAL BANCO CHINCHORRO 🐟 Until recently, this huge, oval-shaped reef spanning almost 200 square miles of ocean 22 miles offshore was virtually impossible for travelers to reach. It was known to only a few lobster fishermen, who would venture out to the reef for several days at a time, spending the night in shacks propped above water level on rickety-looking stilts. Now shellfish harvesting is restricted on the reef. The central area of the living coral reef, which some divers call the last untouched reef in the Caribbean, lies as little as three feet below the water's surface, protected from the ocean's force by a barely sea-level atoll of mangrove-covered islands. The only large island, Cayo Centro, in the middle of the reef, is so densely covered with mangroves that it is impossible to land there. The only place to beach a boat is a tiny sand island that supports a lighthouse. Outside the fortress of mangrove-clad atoll, coral-clad underwater cliffs plunge 3000 feet straight down into the ocean depths. ~ Visitors can get there on dive boats from either of the two resorts between Majahual and Xcalak.

BACALAR CHICO NATIONAL PARK 🏊 🐟 🏕 This undeveloped park on the north end of Ambergris Caye, Belize, along the Mexican border, is only about ten miles south of Xcalak. Covering about 41 square miles, it takes in sandy sea floors and canyons of coral, rock ledges and caves prowled by enormous grouper, lagoons and mudflats, and chunks of island with lush ridge forest, exposed limestone boulders, sinkholes and dry savanna that provide habitat for jaguars and pumas. Snorkeling and diving are exceptional, as is sea kayaking among the crocodile-infested mangrove channels. More loggerhead and green sea turtles nest here than anywhere else on the Caribbean coast. There are seven Maya archaeological sites in the park, though only one has been cleared of overgrowth. ~ The park is only accessible by sea. Although there is no formal immigration process for visitors from Xcalak, new arrivals should check in and present their passports at the ranger station located about a mile south of the Belizean border.

Located 74 kilometers south of Cafetal, Chetumal, the capital of Quintana Roo at the edge of Belize, is probably Mexico's nicest border town. On the north

Chetumal Area

shore of the mouth of the Río Hondo, which defines the border between Quintana Roo and Belize, the town is slowly casting off its former isolation and its shady past as a smugglers' haven by developing into a modern free port where imports of all sorts of foreign goods and exports of hardwoods from the nearby jungle pass through. Chetumal's 95,000 inhabitants include many white-collar government workers and other educated professionals who give the city a corporate edge and create a daily hustle and bustle downtown. The city has a large Lebanese ethnic minority but few Maya residents. As the state capital, Chetumal prospers on state-tax revenues from Cancún, far to the north, but sees few tourists.

Opened in 1998, Chetumal's **Museo de la Cultura Maya** features fewer stone sculptures but lots more high-tech multimedia gimmickry than other archaeological museums in the region. One highlight is a flight simulation featuring bird's-eye views of major Maya sites across the Yucatán, Belize, Guatemala and Honduras.

SIGHTS

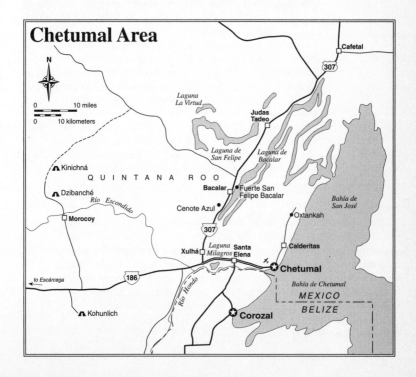

Chetumal Area

Other exhibits vividly demonstrate the complexities of Classic Maya society and religion. Admission. ~ Avenida de los Héroes between Avenidas Colón and Gandi; 9-832-6838.

Across Avenida Gandi from Museo de la Cultura Maya is the **Mercado Nuevo**, or new market, where fresh produce, fish, raw meat and other foodstuffs and merchandise are offered for sale. A block down Avenida de los Héroes is the **Mercado Altamarino**, also known as the Mercado Viejo or old market, a raucous bazaar. Both markets cater to the needs of local people and Belizean visitors, not tourists. Don't expect much in the way of curios or *artesanía*, but besides fresh produce, you'll find lots of *plásticos* (cheap, colorful bowls, baskets and just about anything else that can be made from polyethylene), *norteamericano*-style clothing, much of it bearing counterfeit designer labels, and such curiosities as dozens of kinds of live songbirds.

Across Avenida de los Héroes from the Mercado Nuevo stands the Centro Cultural de las Bellas Artes, housing the **Museo de la Ciudad**. This tiny museum would be utterly unimpressive except for the marvelous model of Chetumal as it appeared in the 1920s. The wooden storefronts and many old-fashioned houses are exact miniature reproductions copied from old photographs. The model was built entirely by a local artisan named (no kidding) Luís Reinhardt McLiberty. Admission. ~ Avenida de los Héroes 68.

Take an eight-block walk south along **Avenida de los Héroes**, the city's original main street. There's low-budget shopping galore, but very little of the old-time Caribbean architecture McLiberty memorialized in his model. Chetumal seems as newly built as downtown Cancún. Most of the downtown area was destroyed by Hurricane Juanita in 1955 and quickly rebuilt in concrete. Keep an eye out and you'll spot a few older historic buildings here and there.

Avenida de los Héroes passes the **Palacio del Gobierno**, or State Capitol, the largest building in the city that isn't a hotel. Then you arrive at the waterfront, where a pleasant *malecón* curves along Boulevard Bahía, following the contours of the bay. A *balneario,*

LOST AND FOUND

Little publicized and least visited of the restored Maya sites in Quintana Roo, Kohunlich presents a long-forgotten world, half-consumed by Edenic forest, brushy hills and the cohune palms that give the ruins their name. The ruins lay hidden by dense jungle until 1967, when a hunting dog led local villager Ignacio Ek to a looters' dig that had unearthed a huge temple mask. He reported it to local authorities, and the Mexican government quickly declared it an archaeological zone. Ek was made caretaker of Kohunlich, a position he held until his death in 1991 and passed on to his son, Francisco Ek.

or bathing resort, northeast of the square provides swimming facilities but no beach. In a town full of statues, the most arresting is the **Alegoría de Mestizaje**, a sculpted Indian woman, Spanish man and their children, representing the first *mestizos*. ~ Avenida de los Héroes near Avenida Mahatma Gandhi.

The city of Chetumal forms a largely imaginary dividing line between the Bahía de Chetumal, which curves south through Belize to the point of Ambergris Cay, and the Bahía de San José, which reaches north into the jungle heartland parallel to Laguna de Bacalar. The northern half of Bahía de San José has been set aside by the government as the **Chetumal Manatee Refuge**. Travel agencies in the city's better hotels can arrange boat excursions to the refuge, where endangered West Indian manatees gather in the bay to take advantage of its thick underwater vegetation and mix of freshwater and saltwater.

Newly opened to the public after a 1997 restoration project, the archaeological zone of **Oxtankah** served as a major Maya seaport for at least 12 centuries. Archaeologists believe it was the seat of a kingdom once governed by Gonzalo Guerrero, one of the two castaways who were the first Spaniards to set foot on the Mexican mainland in 1511, who became a Maya military leader and led the resistance against the *conquistadores*. Impressive stairways surround a central plaza and cenote at this medium-sized site. There are also ruins of a Spanish church believed to have been the oldest church in the Maya region. Admission. ~ Located 16 kilometers north of Chetumal. Take the Carretera Calderitas, which turns off Route 307/186 just west of Chetumal, through the village of Calderitas and continue about five more kilometers on the paved road that follows the shore of Chetumal Bay.

Pretty and peaceful **Laguna Milagros**, little sister of Bacalar, lies about 12 kilometers west of Chetumal off Route 186. Little restaurants fringe its grassy, palm-shaded shores.

Few visitors stay long in Chetumal, preferring to see the real wonder of southern Quintana Roo: **Kohunlich** (admission). The ruins are reached via Route 186, the nearly deserted highway that crosses the southern limits of the Yucatán from Chetumal to the big highway junction at Escárcega, Campeche, 270 kilometers away. Outside of Chetumal, farms hug the highway but soon become smaller and more scattered as the forest begins to close in. The turnoff to the marvelously obscure ancient Maya site of Kohunlich lies 61 kilometers west of Chetumal, and from there it is a 10-kilometer trip down a side road to the ruins.

Kohunlich was built over a long timespan, with older temples dating back to the Early Classic period (A.D. 300–600) buried beneath larger, later structures built in Late Classic times (A.D. 600–900). The architecture of Kohunlich is Río Bec style, similar to the sites around Xpujil (see Chapter Eleven) just 58 kilometers to the west. The rough stone structures of Kohunlich were stuccoed over with layers of the thick, sticky clay that underlies most of southern Quintana Roo. The temples were almost certainly covered with stucco sculptures that have been washed away by centuries of tropical storms. Not only the buildings were covered with clay; the central **Great Plaza** and a series of reservoirs downhill were also paved to form a giant water catchment that channeled runoff from summer rains into an artificial lake to sustain the community through the dry season.

Small though it seems, the city of Chetumal has more people than the entire nation of Belize, with shopping to match.

Deep in the palm forest stands Kohunlich's crowning glory, the Early Classic **Pyramid of the Masks**, where six huge, impeccably detailed and remarkably humanized sculptures of Kinich Ahau, the "Sun-eyed Lord," line both sides of the pyramid stairway. The masks were part of the highly ornamented stucco facade of an early temple that was buried within a larger, round-cornered pyramid similar to the one at Uxmal, protecting them from the elements for more than 1400 years. A thrill for any Mayaphile, the masks stand about six feet high, their bulging tongues, handlebar mustaches and saucer eyes forming a haunting image in the dim light filtered through protective thatch roofs. The eyes of the masks contain the hieroglyph *kin,* meaning sun, day or time.

Exploration of the Kohunlich archaeological site is still in its early stages. A 1991 dig found royal burials at the foot of another temple platform here, and a satellite survey has disclosed about 200 mounds similar to the Pyramid of the Masks hidden by the surrounding jungle. Today we can only speculate as to what additional wonders they may contain.

HIDDEN ►

If Kohunlich gets your imagination racing, there's an even more undiscovered Maya site nearby. To reach the ruins of **Dzibanché**, follow a paved road marked to Morocoy, which turns northward off Route 307 less than a kilometer east of the road to Kohunlich. The pavement deteriorates before the road reaches the village of Morocoy, 30 kilometers from the highway. Not far beyond the village, a potholed hard-surface road to the right is marked to Dzibanché. The Classic-era city was inhabited from about A.D. 300 to 900 and covered 26 square miles. There are two main pyramids, at least one of which contains two mysterious royal tombs. One of the tombs has been excavated but is not open to visitors. Several smaller temples are also of special interest. The Temple of the Lintels still contains the original carved wood lintels (the horizontal beams across the tops of doorways) some of which date back almost 1300 years—a rare discovery in the Maya world. Another structure, the Building of the Captives, is festooned with hieroglyphs and has a big monster mask beside its staircase. Though archaeologists only began studying this site in 1993, restoration is in full swing, and by the time you visit you may find it cleaned up to join the ranks of "new" ancient ruins.

A marked side road that branches off the Dzibanché road takes you to the site of **Kinichná**, which has been partly excavated but not restored. This unique site consists of a single acropolis that was among the most massive structures in the southern Yucatán. It was built over a span of more than 600 years, and the differences in stonework between levels are striking. The ground-level platform, dating to around A.D. 100, is not tall but covers a vast area. On top of it is a tall, classic-style pyramid flanked by smaller temples. From the top of this pyramid, a very steep stairway takes you up to another pyramid, on top of which is a temple that contained two royal tombs. Admission.

Returning to the main highway and continuing westward on Route 307 will bring you to a series of other archaeological sites including Xpujil, Chicanná and Becán near the highway and Río Bec, Hormiguero and Calakmul deeper in the forest.

Unless you're a fan of hot, bustling cities, you probably won't want to stay long in Chetumal. For those who do need a bed for the night, there are several low-cost, no-frills hotels. No matter what time of year you visit, Chetumal is steamy, so go for a room with air conditioning.

LODGING

The best place to hang your hat is the somewhat classy **Hotel Los Cocos**, where visiting politicians stay. The peaceful interior garden, with its swimming pool and gardens dotted with white furniture, gives respite from the city. Good sized, the 80 guest rooms have been redone with tirol (textured) walls, contemporary decor, televisions, phones, small terraces and seating areas. It's not what you'd call fancy, but maids do leave candies on your pillow when they turn down the bed in the evening, and a full complement of bath amenities is provided, including tiny bottles of imported French cologne. Air conditioning. ~ Avenida de los Héroes 134, Chetumal; 9-832-0542, fax 9-832-2360. MODERATE.

A pleasant alternative is the reasonably priced **Hotel Caribe Princess**, a few blocks off the main drag. Its ugly concrete-molded exterior belies a comfortable, friendly interior of plain rooms with carpets, phones and balconies. Air conditioning. ~ Avenida Alvaro Obregón 168, Chetumal; 9-832-0520. BUDGET.

The **Hotel Holiday Inn Puerta Maya** looks strangely out of place with its stark modern facade wedged between chaotic storefronts. Inside, things brighten up in the lush atrium decorated with fountains and a swimming pool. The 61 rooms are sterile but thankfully clean, with servibars and televisions. Air conditioning. ~ Avenida de los Héroes 171, Chetumal; 9-835-0401, fax 9-832-1676. DELUXE.

If all you desire is a simple room with small private bath, TV and a double bed, you'll find it at the 20-room **Hotel Nachancún**, located within walking distance of the public market and the Museo de la Cultura Maya. Air conditioning. ~ Calzada Veracruz 379; 9-832-3232. BUDGET.

The most unusual lodging in the area is **Campamento La Pirámide,** a single large, screened camping cabin with a palapa roof located several miles from the village of Tres Garantías in the heart of primary rainforest, part of a Maya chicle-tapping *ejido* owned by the people of Tres Garantías. The daily rate, $100 a night for up to four guests, includes transportation from Chetumal and meals prepared and served by local Maya women. There's no furniture except a large table, so you need to bring your own sleeping bag or hammock. The people of the *ejido* are looking for outside investors to help expand this humble beginning into an ecotourism resort. Their success or failure may well determine the future of the region: a dozen other *ejidos* in the region are facing imminent decisions about whether to preserve their forest lands in hopes of attracting visitors or to cut them down for timber and so are closely watching the progress of this pilot project. ~ Tres Garantías. Reservations: Avenida Carmen Ochoa de Merino 143, Chetumal; 9-832-9802. BUDGET TO MODERATE.

In an entirely different price range from La Pirámide, the **Explorean Kohunlich** is owned and operated by the Fiesta Americana chain, which runs megaresorts all over Mexico and Latin America. Secluded in the rainforest near the Kohunlich ruins, the Explorean resembles the luxury jungle lodges found in many parts of Belize but rarely in Mexico. Its eight palm-thatch luxury cabañas are patterned after traditional Maya homes, built using local construction methods and materials and decorated with regional furniture and handcrafts. Far less rustic than they appear at first glance, these "huts" come with air conditioning and satellite phones. There are also a colorful garden terrace, a pool and a dining room where gourmet meals are served. Nature and archaeology tours, as well as all meals, are included in the room rate. Three-night minimum stay. ~ Carretera Kohunlich; 5-201-8333 in Mexico City, or 877-397-5672 in the U.S.; www.explorean.com, e-mail contact@explorean.com. ULTRA-DELUXE.

DINING   Chetumal offers a myriad of dining choices at reasonable prices. Start with **Restaurant La Ostra,** off Avenida Héroes near the "Agua Potable" tower. Air conditioned and clean, it serves typical Mexican dishes and a hearty breakfast. ~ Calle Efraím Aguilar 162, Chetumal; 9-832-0452. BUDGET.

A pleasant spot for breakfast or evening coffee, **Café Pérez Quintal,** adjacent to the Government Palace, is an open-air café facing the tree-filled Parque Central. Here you'll find delicious omelets, seafood, sandwiches, fruit salads and meat entrées. ~ Edificio 7 de Deciembre 4 at Calle 22 de Enero, Chetumal. BUDGET.

For pizza you can't go wrong at popular, attractive **Sergio's Pizza**, where the excellent service is second only to the crisp crust. Air conditioned and as sparkling as an English bistro, it's adorned with beautiful stained glass, wood-paneled walls and bottles of pricey liquor lining the bar. Sergio's also has a salad bar, cheese fondue, barbecued ribs and a respectable wine list. ~ Avenida Alvaro Obregón 182, Chetumal; 9-832-2355. BUDGET TO MODERATE.

Next door, same ownership, is the modern and elegant **María Restaurante**, a splendid room with open kitchen, polished tile floors, beamed ceilings and wooden tables and chairs. It serves the best pasta in Chetumal, as well as delightful bean soup, churros, tacos, seafood, steaks and giant goblets of sangria. ~ Avenida Alvaro Obregón, Chetumal; 9-832-0491. BUDGET TO MODERATE.

You can watch your chicken baking through the window of **Pollo Brujo**. Choices include baked, roasted or barbecued chicken wrapped in a steamy tortilla. ~ Avenida Alvaro Obregón 208, Chetumal; 9-832-2713. BUDGET.

A traveler's friend is the **Super & Restaurant Arcadas**. Open 24 hours, it attracts a local crowd and feels like a sidewalk café with its open walls, ceiling fans and breezy ambiance. A large selection of Mexican-style sandwiches is on hand; menus are available in English. ~ Corner of Avenida de los Héroes and Calle Zaragoza, Chetumal. BUDGET.

SHOPPING

Much of the clientele of Chetumal's retail trade is made up of Belizeans who cross the border for the day to buy things that can't be found in Belize City or Belmopan. There is not much tourist trade. Unless you plan to stock up on Danish ham, Planter's Peanuts or imported calculators, most of the import shops along Avenida de los Héroes won't interest you. But the **Mercado Nuevo** (new market) and the nearby **Mercado Altamira**, commonly called the Mercado Viejo (old market), probably will, especially on Sunday. Everyone who hasn't skipped off to one of the blue lagoons is here, fingering mounds of gaudy plastic jewelry or listening to cheap, pirated cassettes of Mexican hits. Clothing, hammocks,

AUTHOR FAVORITE

As an avid snorkeler, I've never seen an undersea sight as amazing as **Chinchorro Reef**, a huge sheltered ring of coral just a few feet down that swirls with colorful tropical fish and weird crustaceans. The reef is a long boat ride from shore—and the shore where the boats start out is an even longer drive from anyplace that tourists often visit—and the experience is worth every minute of the trip. See page 228 for more information.

dolls—a vibrant variety of sweet nothings—make for a good spree. ~ Avenida de las Héroes near the Museo de la Cultura Maya.

NIGHTLIFE   It's slow. If you're in the mood for dancing, you can try crowded **Antares Disco**, but if you're over 30 you'll feel every inch an old-ster. All the teens in town congregate here. Cover. In the same building, **La Mancha** features a live band, singers, a clever emcee and lots of zest, energy and color. The entertainment begins at 11 p.m. and continues until sunup. ~ Boulevard Bahía near Calle Esmeralda, Chetumal.

Switch Bar in the Hotel Holiday Inn Puerta Maya mixes live Latin tunes and music videos in a mature environment where you can converse without shouting. ~ Avenida de los Héroes 171, Chetumal; 9-832-1100.

Outdoor Adventures

FISHING   South of Tulum, at Boca Paila, two fishing camps feature bonefishing in the flats of Bahía de la Ascensión: **Boca Paila Fishing Lodge** (9-832-0053) and **Pez Maya Fishing and Beach Resort** (9-832-0411).

DIVING   The Majahuil–Xcalak coast offers some of the least-known and most spectacular coral reef dives in the Caribbean. There are good scuba waters that can be reached from shore without a dive boat, but the main event is **Chinchorro Reef**, 22 miles offshore. This large, ring-shaped reef submerged just three feet below the sea's surface is said to be the last virgin reef in the Caribbean. Dancing and crawling with abundant marine life, it is surrounded by sheer 3000-foot dropoffs that make for dramatic wall dives. Dive arrange-ments can be made at dive resorts around Xcalak or through **Aven-turas Chinchorro**. ~ 812 Garland Avenue, Nokomis, FL 34275; 941-488-4505, 800-480-4505.

OTHER WATER SPORTS   The waters around Xcalak also offer exceptional sea kayaking and windsurfing. Kayaks and sailboards can be rented at **Costa de Cocos Dive Resort**. ~ Xcalak.

Transportation

CAR   An unpaved road (passable only in the dry season) runs 57 kilometers from the Tulum area south through the Sian Ka'an Biosphere Reserve to Boca Paila and Punta Allen. Inquire locally about road conditions before driv-ing this road in a passenger car. During the rainy season it is com-pletely impassable; at that time the residents of Punta Allen can reach the mainland only by boat. Another unpaved road leads into the reserve from Felipe Carrillo Puerto, 58 kilometers to the tiny fishing village of Viglia Chico, where boat passage across Bahía de la Ascensión to Punta Allen can often be arranged with a local fisherman.

Cancún–Mérida Route 180 crosses the Quintana Roo–Yucatán state line at the Maya town of Nuevo Xcan. Cobá is 43 kilometers from either Tulum or Nuevo Xcan, but the road is much easier to find from the Tulum end.

Route 307 veers inland as it continues southward from Tulum through Felipe Carrillo Puerto. The turnoff to the southern Caribbean coast is near Limones.

Route 307 ends where it meets Route 186, the highway that crosses the base of the Yucatán Peninsula from Escárcega, Campeche, by way of the Xpujil archaeological zone. Chetumal is just 19 kilometers east of this intersection.

AIR

Aerocaribe operates daily flights from Cancún, Cozumel and Mérida to Chetumal's little international airport.

CAR RENTALS

Car rentals are available in Chetumal from Continental Rent-a-Car (Holiday Inn; 9-832-1100 ext. 191) and Aventura Maya (Hotel Los Cocos, 9-832-0920). Both agencies will provide complimentary airport pickup and drop-off service.

BUS

There is no bus service to Punta Allen or other points in the Sian Ka'an Biosphere Reserve.

Buses stop at Cobá several times daily en route to Tulum and Playa del Carmen and, in the opposite direction, to Valladolid and Mérida.

There is no regular bus service to Majahual, Xcalak or other points on the southern Caribbean coast, but *combis* (VW bus shuttles) meet buses that stop at Cafetal and provide transportation to the dive resorts along the coast.

Second-class buses will stop at Laguna de Bacalar on request, though first-class direct and express buses won't. *Combis*, found around the public market in Chetumal, make the trip to Bacalar and back routinely.

Chetumal has frequent connections from all major population areas of the Yucatán. There are five first-class and seven second-class buses a day from Cancún, 15 first-class and eight second-class buses from Mérida, and two first-class buses from Campeche.

▼▼▼▼▼▼▼▼▼▼▼▼▼▼▼▼▼▼▼▼▼▼▼

Addresses & Phone Numbers

Cruz Roja (Chetumal) ~ Avenidas Héroes de Chapúltepec and Independencia; 9-832-0571

Hospital General (Chetumal) ~ Avenida Andres Quintana Roo 399; 9-832-1932

Policia (Chetumal) ~ 9-832-1500

State Tourism Office (Chetumal) ~ Prolongación Avenida de los Héroes; 9-835-0860

SEVEN

Valladolid and Chichén Itzá

The toll highway linking Cancún and Mérida is a fast, dull trip through a landscape just starting to overgrow the scars of road-building. Piles of limestone boulders dumped at intervals in the center median have been spray-painted in different gaudy hues; otherwise, there's not much to see. Instead, why not take the older, much slower free highway that parallels it? You'll see more and save the outrageously high toll on the new freeway.

The old highway was once a hellish little road packed with trucks and buses careening and crashing over the ubiquitous *topes*, those slow-down-or-die speed bumps in the road at every village and hut. Now, since all the big commercial vehicles started using the new toll road, the old highway offers the pleasure of cruising on a traffic-free paved road through expanses of low, thick forest, home to wild boar, white-tailed deer, wild turkeys, ducks, rabbits and the most often-seen wildlife in the Yucatán interior—vultures and iguanas. The landscape is scattered with big trees and roadside clusters of oval, white, thatched-roof huts festooned with brilliant red bougainvillea, vivid against the deep green surroundings.

As visitors travel west across the Yucatán Peninsula in search of adventure-filled days and romantic tropical nights under a Maya moon, it doesn't take long to realize that they're not in Kansas anymore. Or Cancún, either. Towns like Nuevo Xcan and Chemax introduce a world where things happen at a slower pace. Maya women, in white embroidered dresses that miraculously always seem to look spot-less, stroll through the village streets. Children chase turkeys or sit by the roadside watching with big eyes as tourists drive by. Old men trudge along the highway carrying loads of firewood on their backs.

White churches with grand facades built from the rubble of Maya temples reach above the treetops and can be seen for miles around from the tops of pyramids. With the awesome church and monastery of Izamal as its center, a network of Spanish colonial churches came to include just about every town and village between Val-ladolid and Mérida in a sweeping missionary effort that spanned two and a half centuries. Today, virtually all Yucatec Maya people are devoutly Catholic, and Izamal's church is still the most majestic on the peninsula.

Throughout the Yucatán you'll see stately old plantations that now stand abandoned and overgrown, a new generation of old ruins. Until the mid-20th century, this was a wealthy region where a handful of plantation owners exploited the Indian population to produce most of the world's henequen (*sisal*), a fiber that comes from large yuccalike plants and was used to make rope. As synthetic fibers replaced henequen after World War II, the big plantations shut down and the rural people of the region returned to subsistence sharecropping. The Yucatán remained the poorest region of Mexico for decades until the development of Cancún brought tourist dollars to the region in the 1970s. Aside from tourism, the largest industry in this part of the Yucatán is limestone quarrying. The cement produced from the limestone is the same substance that the ancient Maya used to stucco and sculpt the facades of their temples.

Each year, North Americans and other visitors are drawn to the Yucatán in ever-increasing numbers to see the great Maya ruins. Chichén Itzá, strongly influenced in its day by newcomers from central Mexico, recalls in its art the Toltec traditions of military might and human sacrifice. Although Mayapán, for centuries the greatest capital of the Yucatán, has vanished almost completely (other ceremonial centers such as Ek Balam and Aké remain unknown to all but a few visitors), Chichén Itzá now attracts hundreds of thousands of international visitors, and millions of Mexicans, each year.

Walking among the ruins of a once-great civilization, one may wonder how a simple farming culture suddenly flowered into a great empire that produced magnificent pyramid temples, elegant works of art, libraries and an advanced calendar system and developed amazingly precise knowledge of astronomy. Or why, after six centuries, it suddenly ended, to be replaced by a militaristic system of feudal city-states ruled by warlords.

Even though the Classic Maya civilization flourished just a few hundred miles from what is now the United States and ended only a few centuries ago, we know much less about it than we do about ancient Egypt, Greece or Rome. Many clues were intentionally destroyed by European invaders, and many others were lost to the jungle and the ravages of time. Today, experts armed with computers are devoting millions of hours to unlocking the secrets of the ancient Maya. New discoveries and new theories are revealed every year. New mysteries appear faster than the old ones are solved. As for us curious amateurs, we approach the great Maya ruins of the Yucatán with boundless curiosity and an overwhelming sense of awe. We come away trying to explain their existence with scientific theories or with old legends or simply with our innermost spirits.

Legends about the ancient Maya abound in this region of the Yucatán. Chichén Itzá, Mayapán and Uxmal (see Chapter Ten) came complete with detailed histories that are still recounted today even though modern-day archaeologists tell us these histories are mostly fictional. While I set out several such legends in this chapter, it's best to consider their sources before taking them too literally. Some were recorded in Spanish by 16th-century monks, others in the 19th century by American explorers gathering material for travel books some 600 years after the heyday of the semimythical League of Mayapán (see "Chichén Itzá," later in this chapter). Some came from the prophecies of Maya spiritual leaders seeking to foment revolt against the Spanish, and some from 20th-century archaeologists trying to generate public interest and funding for projects in the Yucatán. But while these legends may contradict much of what archaeologists now believe about the Maya, they speak volumes about the centuries of cultural clashes that have shaped the Yucatán we know today.

▼▼▼▼▼▼▼▼▼▼▼▼

Valladolid

Valladolid is the first major town you come to after crossing from Quintana Roo to the state of Yucatán on Route 180. This quiet colonial town of 100,000 people was founded by upper-crust Spaniards in 1543. It bore the brunt of the Yucatecan War of the Castes: in 1847, Maya warriors massacred the town's non-Indian residents, triggering the Maya people's violent but futile struggle for independence from Mexico.

SIGHTS   Some of the oldest church buildings in the Yucatán are here. The massive **Church of San Bernardino de Siena** (c. 1552) and adjoining **Ex-Convent of Sisal** are six blocks west of the *zócalo*, behind thick fortified walls that defended them against frequent Indian attacks during the War of the Castes. All of the church's art and ornamentation were looted during that war and a later Indian uprising in 1910, leaving the interior simple and austere to this day. The resident statue of the Virgin of Guadalupe is believed to work miracles.

In recent years, Valladolid's fortunes have brightened as its location, 90 minutes from Cancún and just 29 miles from Chichén Itzá, has made for a steady stream of tourist traffic through the center of town. Most visitors still find little reason to stop in Valladolid, though for economy-minded travelers it does offer the best budget lodging prospects in the Chichén Itzá area.

As is true of virtually all colonial cities on the Yucatán Peninsula, a pre-Hispanic Maya center formerly existed on the site of modern-day Valladolid and was destroyed to provide building materials for the Spanish settlement. The ancient name was Zací, and its water supply was the **Cenote Zací**, located in a park three blocks east of Valladolid's main plaza. The cenote is a huge pool, formed when part of an underground river's roof collapsed. Its green waters plunge to nearly 400 feet within a stalactite-studded cavern that you enter via a narrow, slippery stairway. Boys dive for tips from the overhanging precipice. Swimming is allowed but the fuzzy, gooey growths of algae in the cenote make it a not very appealing idea. Admission. ~ Calle 36 between Calles 39 and 37.

HIDDEN ►   Not far from Valladolid, the ruins of **Ek Balam** (admission) rank among the most impressive in the northern Yucatán; yet tourism is almost unknown here. Until recently, Ek Balam has received little attention from either sightseers or scientists because . . . well, let's face it, Chichén Itzá is a hard act to follow. Although scientists who were restoring Chichén Itzá noticed the wreckage of Ek Balam in the 1920s, archaeological excavation did not begin

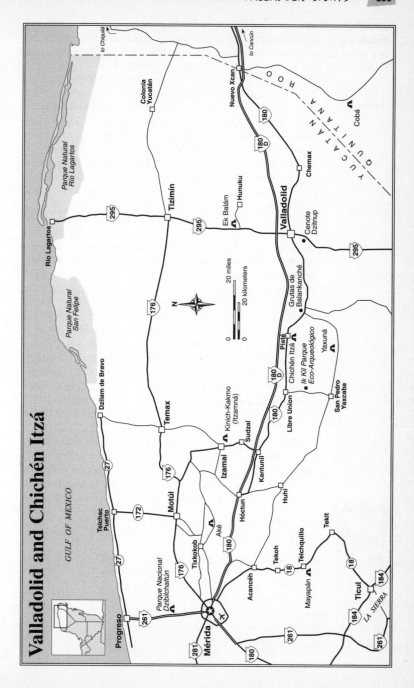

Valladolid and Chichén Itzá

until quite recently. If you'd dropped by Ek Balam in the mid-1990s, you'd have seen unnaturally steep hills covered with mature trees, tumbled stones, scattered fragments of sculptures and not much else. Since then, several international teams of archaeologists have undertaken the restoration of different structures surrounding the city's central plaza. Today, this ignored site has been restored to the point where it'll knock your socks off.

Ek Balam represents one of the fundamental mysteries of the Classic Maya civilization: why we know so little about it. Covering more than four square miles, Ek Balam was clearly a major city in the region, yet experts have found no reference to it in hieroglyphic inscriptions at other Maya sites. Most of the structures found here date from A.D. 700 to 1000, but carbon dating reveals that smaller temples stood on the same site as early as 100 B.C. A double wall nearly a mile in circumference surrounds the center of the ancient city. Experts believe the wall was symbolic of the town's independence and was not actually needed to defend against attacks. A 16th-century Spanish account tells of a legendary Maya lord named Ek Balam (Yucatecan for "Black Jaguar") who founded a city named Tiquibalon somewhere in the region, but based on pottery studies, archaeologists don't think this was the same place. The curious may also wonder what relationship the city of Ek Balam had with the Chilam Balam, the "Jaguar Priest" cult of visionary shamans whose collected prophecies, the *Books of Chilam Balam*, provide insights into pre-Columbian Mayan spirituality.

The entrance to Ek Balam skirts **Las Gemelas** (The Twins), the only structure here that has been given a name. The pair of identical buildings shares a platform south of the main plaza with a gracefully curved base reminiscent of the main pyramid at Uxmal. An amalgam of exquisite architectural design and crude stonework that was once covered with stucco and paint, the twin four-room buildings are thought to have been used as a palace, but the significance of their strange look-alike symmetry remains a mystery.

Rounding the corner of Las Gemelas, you come face-to-face with Ek Balam's largest structure on the north side of the plaza.

sights

AUTHOR FAVORITE

I've gone swimming in the sea, in tropical lagoons and in luxury resort pools complete with swim-up bars all over the Yucatán Peninsula, but I've never—repeat, *never*—found a body of water that could match the thrill of **Cenote Dzitnup**, the "bottomless" subterranean swimming hole near Valladolid. Admission. ~ Located just off Route 180 on a marked side road seven kilometers west of Valladolid.

Known only as **Structure 1**, it is 558 feet long, covers an area larger than a city block and reaches a height of about 100 feet—considerably more than Chichén Itzá's Pyramid of Kukulcán. Several temples on different levels of the tiered pyramid open out onto the central plaza, but strangely, they are reached by different stairways, so you must descend from one temple before climbing to another. Palm-thatched roofs erected to protect restored stucco ornamentation on the pyramid's facade help us see how it may have looked during its heyday, when most temples had palapa roofs like these. Once you reach the summit of this immense pyramid, you may be able to see the Nohoch Mul pyramid of Cobá rising from the forest almost 37 miles away.

Stelae—stone monuments carved with hieroglyphic inscriptions and bas-relief sculptures of gods, leaders or heroes—have been unearthed recently at Ek Balam and may one day provide answers to this lost city's mysteries. Today, other large temples flanking the sides of the plaza remain untouched and overgrown by forest, providing a strange before-and-after juxtaposition. ~ From Valladolid, follow Route 295 north, toward Tizimín, for 23 kilometers to the junction with an unpaved road that goes east (right) toward the village of Hunuku. Watch for a paved and well-marked road (once an ancient Maya *sacbé*) that turns off to the left and continues for about another kilometer to the ruins.

The best accommodations in Valladolid are at the **Hotel El Mesón del Marqués**. This colonial hotel on the *zócalo*, a hacienda in the 18th century, lost none of its cool, thick-walled magic in its transition to an inn. In addition to its 34 old-fashioned, yellow-walled rooms with beamed ceilings and heavy wooden furniture there are 39 guest rooms. Most rooms at the Hotel El Mesón del Marqués have bathtubs, a rare luxury in Mexican hotels. The windows in the old section open onto a balcony overlooking the pool. At the entrance is a garden, fountain, lovely gift shop and colonial restaurant. ~ Calle 39 No. 203; 9-856-3042, fax 9-856-2280; e-mail marques@chichen.com.mx. MODERATE.

LODGING

A swimming pool fills the inner courtyard of the **Hotel María de la Luz**, giving the refurbished colonial building the aspect of a modern motel. The 30 guest rooms with TVs do little to dispel that perception. Located on the west side of the plaza, it is under the same management as El Mesón del Marqués. Air conditioning or ceiling fans. ~ Calle 42 No. 193; 9-856-1181, fax 9-856-2071. BUDGET.

The inexpensive **Hotel San Clemente**, located on the corner of the plaza in Valladolid, has 64 guest rooms, some with TVs, as well as a swimming pool, restaurant and bar. Some rooms have air conditioning. ~ Calle 42 No. 206; 9-856-2208. BUDGET.

Even more affordable is the **Albergue La Candelaria Hostel,** where you'll find basic dorm rooms with four bunk beds each. Located just off the pretty little Parque Candelaria, the hostel has lockers, shared baths, kitchen and laundry facilities, internet access and a TV room with videocassette documentaries about the Yucatán. ~ Calle 35 No. 201-F; phone/fax 9-856-2267; e-mail hostelcandelaria@yahoo.com.mx. BUDGET.

DINING

The **Restaurant María de la Luz,** just off the lobby of the hotel of the same name, serves Yucatecan lunches and dinners in the same price range as that at the Hostería del Marqués. For some reason, more people seem to eat lunch here and dinner around the corner at the del Marqués. Poolside seating is available. ~ Calle 42 No. 195; 9-856-1181. BUDGET TO MODERATE.

Another exceptional Valladolid restaurant, **Casa de los Arcos,** one block east of the *zócalo*, serves regional cuisine such as *pocchuc* (pork fillets served with an orange-and-onion sauce) and *pollo pibil* (chicken barbecued in banana leaves). A combination plate offers samples of the most popular Yucatecan dishes. The two dining rooms are spacious but rather plain, while the pretty courtyard dining area is inviting in the evening. ~ Calle 39 between Calles 38 and 40; 9-856-2467. MODERATE.

BEACHES & PARKS

CENOTE DZITNUP 🏊 Here's a unique subterranean beach—a sandy limestone shelf on the brink of the best freshwater swimming hole on the Yucatán Peninsula. Cool and crystalline, the pool glows soft blue where the sun streams through a small hole in the cave ceiling a hundred feet above, then fades into blackness in the depths of a cavern dripping with limestone curtains and crystals. Legend has it that the cenote is bottomless, and it might as well be; its depth has never been measured. Absolutely irresistible on a hot Yucatán afternoon. Admission. ~ Located just off Route 180 on a marked side road seven kilometers west of Valladolid.

AUTHOR FAVORITE

In a region where decent restaurants are few and far between, I consider the **Hostería del Marqués** a real find—affordable, atmospheric, colonially charming in a peeling-paint sort of way. The decor is as luxurious as it gets in Valladolid, and the service is first-rate. It's the best place to sample the Maya-Spanish fusion cuisine distinctive to Valladolid (such as chicken in a tangy tomato sauce), and the lobster (fresh from Río Lagartos) is to die for. The restaurant is located in the Hotel El Mesón del Marqués, facing the main plaza. ~ Calle 39 No. 203; 9-856-2073. BUDGET TO MODERATE.

Each year three million people visit Chichén Itzá, the best known of all ancient Maya ruins. Located just off the main highway midway between Cancún and Méri-

▼▼▼▼▼▼▼▼▼▼▼▼
Chichén Itzá

da, the ruins can be reached by car or bus from either city in about two hours.

One of the world's great archaeological wonders, Chichén Itzá is the most completely restored site in the Yucatán. After persuading the Carnegie Institute to fund the rebuilding of the ruins so that visitors could see for themselves what archaeologists had previously been able to envision only on paper, scholar-adventurer Sylvanus Morley spent 20 years of his life—from 1924 to 1944—supervising the project. His original idea was that the restoration would boost public interest in the Maya civilization and generate funding for other archaeological projects in the area. The plan succeeded. Each year Chichén Itzá has the same number of visitors as the Parthenon or Stonehenge, and its success has inspired extensive restoration projects at many other Maya sites in Mexico, Guatemala, Belize and Honduras.

Chichén Itzá was founded in A.D. 495 and later taken over by the Itzá Maya people, who originated far south in the Petén rainforest and migrated up the Caribbean and Gulf coasts to the northern Yucatán. An academic debate still rages over whether the Itzá were part of the faraway Toltec culture when they arrived in the region or were later conquered by Toltec war parties. In either case, the Itzá Maya spoke a different language and were regarded by the Yucatec people as a different race, and their invasion of the northern Yucatán was a pivotal point in Maya history. Conflicts between the Yucatec and Itzá people shaped the peninsula's culture for more than 500 years. The name *Itzá* is often translated as "Water Sorcerers," referring to priests who divined the wishes of the gods from the waters of cenotes (limestone sinkholes). One of these is the famous sacred cenote at Chichén Itzá, which was used for ceremonies and, some say, human sacrifices.

Early Maya people occupied the original community of Chichén Itzá for about 200 years. In A.D. 692, they abandoned the site. About 300 years later, in A.D. 998, the Itzás—who may or may not have been the descendants of the city's original inhabitants—returned to Chichén Itzá. According to legend, the place became a part of the powerful, perhaps mythical, triumvirate of Postclassic Maya cities known as the League of Mayapán, which reigned supreme in the Yucatán until A.D. 1204, when it was destroyed by civil war. The Itzá people then retreated into the Petén jungle for the final time.

The art and architecture of Chichén Itzá looks more like Toltec cities of central Mexico, 992 miles away, than any other site in the ancient Maya world. Massive limestone carvings of the plumed serpent god are known to the Maya as Kukulcán (the namesake of Cancún's tourist strip) and to the Toltec as Quetzalcóatl. How the plumed serpent god came to the Yucatán is a subject of endless speculation. The conventional theory—that the Maya people of Chichén Itzá were conquered by invading Toltecs—is a variation on one of the Yucatán's most familiar legends.

Every Mexican schoolchild knows the story of Quetzalcóatl, the Plumed Serpent, a mythical godlike leader who taught the indigenous people of Mexico all their arts and sciences. Quetzalcóatl first appeared in Teotihuacán Toltec legend as a leader much like Britain's King Arthur. The founder of the Toltec civilization, he fell into disgrace for violating his own laws and set himself on fire, vowing, as he rose to become the planet Venus, that he would be back one day.

Thereafter, the Toltec head priests of this cult were given the title *Quetzalcóatl*. One of them, a messiahlike figure named Ce Acatl Topiltzin, proclaimed himself the second coming of Quetzalcóatl and became king of the Toltecs in A.D. 968, reigning for decades and building the Toltec capital of Tula. Finally, his opponents deposed him and drove him from the city. The second Quetzalcóatl sailed away into the east on a raft of snakes, vowing, like his namesake, that one day he would return.

This time, Quetzalcóatl's raft carried him straight across the Gulf of Mexico to a Yucatán beach. By coincidence, the Maya people were also expecting the return of the Plumed Serpent, whom they knew as Kukulcán. Topiltzin-Quetzalcóatl-Kukulcán became the king of the Itzá Maya. He revived and rebuilt the ancient capital at Chichén Itzá, where massive sculptured stone heads representing the Plumed Serpent were placed throughout the city in his honor. (Later, his enemies deposed him once more. He went to Uxmal, where he committed suicide and was buried under the Pyramid of the Magician—or so the story goes. No burial has been found there.)

The new generation of archaeologists are challenging both the hoary old legend and the conventional scientific theory that Chichén Itzá was first built by the Itzá Maya and later conquered by the Toltecs. Many believe that the Itzá Maya had previously mixed with the Toltecs before founding the city. Others theorize that in its heyday, Chichén Itzá had established trade relations with the Toltec city of Tula, hundreds of miles to the west on the far side of the Gulf of Mexico.

SIGHTS   Chichén Itzá (admission plus parking fee) is unique among Maya ruins. Its meticulously restored structures feature many columns and warrior images, inviting comparison with ancient Rome. Here, too, stands the largest blood-sport stadium ever built in pre-Hispanic America. Elaborate bas-reliefs and sculptures memorialize warriors of old, while carved stone murals, still bearing traces of paint after a thousand years, depict gruesome scenes of human sacrifice. The features that form Chichén Itzá's awe-inspiring, somewhat macabre character are uncommon in other archaeological sites in the Yucatán.

At the entrance to the Chichén Itzá ruins area is a large, modern **visitors center** featuring a relief map that gives you an overview of the ruins as they must have looked in ancient times, with the large structures stuccoed and brightly painted and their roofs intact. There is also a museum that has preserved some of the site's best sculptures. As at all Mexican archaeological zones, admission is free on Sunday and the ruins are extremely crowded then.

Chichén Itzá is one of a very few sites where sculptures and artifacts are displayed in a museum adjoining the ruins. Visitors to Maya ruins are sometimes disappointed to learn that the best statues, stelae and bas-relief carvings have been removed to museums in other parts of the world. (Indeed, very rarely will you find artworks left in place among the ruins because they will eventually be destroyed by acid rain.) At the museum you'll find photographs documenting early archaeological expeditions and excavations at the site. Look at a photo that shows the condition in which the Pyramid of Kukulcán was discovered, and you will get

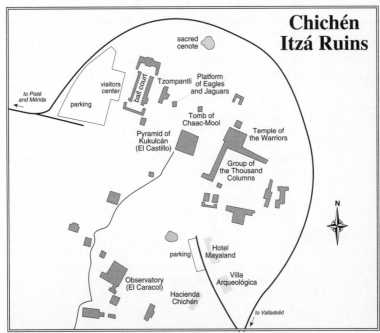

Chichén Itzá Ruins

some idea of the years of painstaking tree chopping, digging and sifting and the endless organizing of chunks of rubblelike pieces of a giant puzzle that went into restoring the ruins to the condition in which we see them today.

Here's something to wonder about as you view the finely detailed sculptures in the Chichén Itzá museum and among the ruins: in the natural environment of pre-Hispanic Yucatán, limestone was the hardest substance known. The Maya had no metal tools. How did they achieve the smooth, delicate stone carvings that have endured over the centuries? Some archaeologists doubt that this sculptural work could have been done by chipping stone against stone. They suggest that the Maya people may have used a solution from some forest plant to soften the limestone so it could be worked more easily. As logical as this theory sounds, no one has yet discovered any substance in the Yucatán forest that softens the stone. How the ancient artists carved limestone remains one of the many mysteries that still surround the ruins at Chichén Itzá.

The pathway from the visitors center leads directly into the heart of the Northern Group, the main cleared and reconstructed area of Chichén Itzá. Straight ahead, the first structure to catch your attention is the **Pyramid of Kukulcán**, also called **El Castillo**. This magnificent stepped pyramid, purely Toltec in its design, rises to a height of 79 feet. The main stairway, flanked by giant stone serpent heads, faces the path to the sacred cenote. Only two of the four sides have been fully restored, so that future archaeologists can look at the other two sides and see the condition in which the pyramid was originally found. The facade of the temple at the top is adorned with a giant mask of Chaac, the Maya rain god, as well as representations of the plumed serpent Kukulcán or Quetzal-cóatl. The pyramid was built over an earlier, lower temple mound, and a narrow interior passage that runs beneath the north stairway, open to the public during limited hours, leads up into the older temple in the heart of the pyramid, where you'll find a Chac-Mool altar (see description of Temple of the Warriors, below) and a throne in the shape of a red jaguar with jade eyes and spots.

Every year at the spring equinox (March 20) and the autumn equinox (September 21), at about 3 p.m., a strange phenomenon

TOUR TIME

Chichén Itzá is the top guided-tour destination in the Yucatán; in fact, tour buses usually outnumber private cars in the archaeological zone's parking lot. To appreciate this ancient ceremonial center free from polyglot throngs of fellow tourists, it's best to visit before 10 a.m., when the buses start rolling in.

can be seen on the balustrade of the north staircase on Chichén Itzá's Pyramid of Kukulcán. The shadow of the pyramid's northwest edge aligns precisely with the balustrade to cast an undulating pattern of light that joins the serpent head at the base of the stairway to become the body of the serpent descending the pyramid. On these days, many thousands of spectators come to Chichén Itzá to witness the event—travelers from around the world as well as Yucatán Maya people, who come to lay hands on the statues of the Plumed Serpent as a way of gaining personal power. The equinox phenomenon is one of the best-known examples of the ancient Maya people's sophistication in astronomy and proves that they planned this giant structure according to precise calculations of the sun's path. Today, hundreds of scientists devote their careers to studying the relationships between Maya structures and celestial bodies.

The **Temple of the Warriors**, due east of the Pyramid of Kukulcán, originally had a roof made of wood and stucco. While it, too, contains rain god and plumed serpent figures, the temple was apparently dedicated to Chac-Mool, the semireclining, humanlike sculpture at the top of the steep stairway. Rarely seen in Maya culture, Chac-Mool is found more often in central Mexico, where in later centuries he was associated with human sacrifice. With his distant, perhaps psychopathic countenance, this mythical being held a bowl ready to receive from the priests the heart ripped still beating from the sacrificial victim. No direct evidence that the same kind of ritual was practiced at Chichén Itzá exists, however, and many experts contend that this Chac-Mool may have been used as a place to leave other types of religious offerings or to hold an oil torch.

Another unusual feature of this temple is the altar located toward the back, supported by 19 "Atlantean figures"—statues that support altars. The name comes from Atlas, the Greek Titan who carried the heavens on his shoulders, and bears no relation to the mythical kingdom of Atlantis. The many unique Atlantean figures found here and elsewhere at Chichén Itzá were each individually designed. The figures wear many different kinds of apparel and appear to have different racial characteristics. Whether they represent real persons or whether their designs reveal some inexplicable Maya awareness of humankind's incredible diversity is unclear.

The Temple of the Warriors was named for the grid of some 200 square columns that stand in rank and file at the foot of the main stairway. Each is carved in low relief, with a different Toltec warrior on each side. On some of the columns traces of the paint that once brought them to life can still be seen. The warriors' eyes were originally inlaid with pearlescent shells. More rows of columns fill the colonnades on the west side of the temple, bringing the total to 1000 columns, which probably once supported a thatched roof. Many archaeologists believe that the colonnades were used as a public marketplace, while others think they housed small chapels or shrines.

A long *sacbé*, a causeway that was paved with limestone in ancient times, leads to the **sacred cenote**, a large natural sinkhole fed by an underground river, which provided the main water supply for the city of Chichén Itzá. The circular cenote is about 197 feet in diameter, with a sheer vertical drop of 73 feet from the rim to the surface of the water. The water itself is about 57 feet deep, with a layer of muck at the bottom that is too deep to measure.

In 1901, Edward Thompson, the United States consul to Mérida, bought the ranch on which the unexcavated ruins of Chichén Itzá were located for $500 and proceeded to dredge the bottom of the sacred cenote for treasure. His efforts over several summers yielded an amazing array of artifacts that had apparently been thrown into the cenote as offerings to the rain god Chaac. The items included jade jewelry, metal and rubber balls, pottery, wooden and wax figurines, mirrors, sandals and incense. Some of the objects came from as far away as Panama and perhaps Colombia. Most of Thompson's loot was sent to Harvard University, in whose museum it remains today. Thompson's original dredge is on display near the restrooms at the Chichén Itzá visitors' center, alongside a plaque in Spanish that condemns Thompson for stealing Mexico's treasures and Harvard for refusing to return them. Even today, some Maya people who make pilgrimages to Chichén Itzá throw small fetishes or figurines into the cenote as prayer offerings for rain.

Besides artifacts, Thompson's dredging operations turned up the bones of 50 human beings, giving rise to the legend that virgins were sacrificed in the sacred cenote. The tale provides a popular motif—pagan priests preparing to hurl a beautiful young woman into the murky deep—for restaurant murals and kitsch tourist art all over the Yucatán. There is little, if any, truth to the sensationalist legend. Most of the skeletons found in the cenote were those of young children, who may have fallen in and drowned by accident over the five centuries that Chichén Itzá was inhabited. Some sort of religious ceremonies undoubtedly took place on the brink of the sacred cenote, since there is a sweat lodge of the type used by ancient Maya priests for ritual purification, but many archaeologists doubt that human sacrifice was involved. Why, they ask, would the people intentionally pollute their water supply with corpses?

The **Ball Court** at Chichén Itzá is the largest in the Maya world. While other Maya ball courts, such as the ones that have been restored at Uxmal and Palenque and the eight smaller courts in unexcavated areas of Chichén Itzá, are similar in area to tennis courts, this one is longer than a football field—545 feet from end

Song of the Pyramids

You might think that all the secrets of the pyramid of Kukulcán, one of the most extensively studied ancient structures in North America, would have been revealed long ago. Yet the more we learn, the more mysterious it becomes.

For instance, archaeoastronomers have noted that not only do the number of steps in the pyramid's four stairways add up to 365, the number of days in a year, but the number of terrace segments on each face of the pyramid total 18, the number of months in the Maya calendar. It was recently discovered that the diagonal axes of the pyramid's northwest and southwest corners point precisely toward the rising point of the sun at the summer solstice and its setting point at the winter solstice.

Archaeologists from the University of Guadalajara and the University of Washington have shown that the pyramid of Kukulcán, as well as other great pyramids from Palenque, Chiapas, to Uaxactún, Guatemala, were located in alignment with *trazos* ("traces")—invisible, mystical energy lines that spanned the Maya world, embodying the same geomancy principle as the "ley-lines" said to connect Britain's ancient Druid stone circles and the *lung-mei* ("dragon paths"), which, according to Chinese feng-shui, link the world's sacred mountains. Although there is no scientific proof that *trazos* actually existed, there is ample evidence that Maya architects believed they did—and designed the pyramids accordingly.

Most recently, acoustics expert David Lubman discovered that when you stand at the foot of the pyramid's frontal staircase and clap your hands, the result is a long, drawn-out echo that drops in frequency. Sonograms show that the echo is identical to the cry of the quetzal, a Central American bird that ancient Maya people believed was a "messenger of the gods." Thus, Lubman claims, the echoing stairway was the world's first sound recording.

Weird, huh?

to end, with goal rings 20 feet above the ground. No one knows for sure why this court was built on such a grand scale, but playing the Maya ball game here must have been difficult. Some archaeologists suggest that the game provided a substitute for war, and that this ball court may have been the site of a kind of ancient "Superbowl" where disputes between the city-states of the Yucatán Peninsula were settled. The bas-relief sculptures located along the side walls depict players of one team holding the severed, gushing head of an opposing team member. (Those who contend that human sacrifice was not practiced at Chichén Itzá suggest—unconvincingly—that the beheadings depicted here may have been merely symbolic.)

Adjacent to the ball court, the grim **Tzompantli** (Wall of Skulls) is a low platform, similar to sacrificial platforms found in the Toltec cities of central Mexico, covered with carvings of hundreds of human skulls. It also has sculptured panels of armed warriors and eagles devouring human hearts, as well as another panel that shows a winning ball team decapitating the loser, like the ones in the ball court. All these clues suggest that the Tzompantli was where sacrifices were carried out in connection with the ball games. Right next to the Tzompantli, the **Platform of Eagles and Jaguars** is exquisitely decorated in motifs associated with a powerful military order from the Toltec city of Tula.

The Northern Group also includes a number of lesser structures, some of them completely ruined and unreconstructed. One of them, the **Ossuary**, a collapsed temple on a burial mound about 33 feet high, has an opening in its center that descends into a natural cave beneath the mound.

The Central Group is generally believed to be older than the Northern Group. Most buildings in this group, such as the Nunnery and the Temple of the Deer, are typical of Maya ruins found elsewhere in the Yucatán and show much less Toltec influence than do the structures in the Northern Group. Recently, some archaeologists have found evidence that the structures in both groups were actually built around the same time, suggesting that more than one subculture may have occupied or used Chichén Itzá simultaneously.

The most remarkable structure in the Central Group is the **Observatory**, also called **El Caracol** (The Snail) because of the spiral form of its inner stairway. This round tower was designed to track celestial movements. The partially crumbled upper room, which is not open to the public, contains windows aligned with the positions of the setting sun at the equinoxes and the summer solstice, as well as others marking the four cardinal directions. Archaeoastronomers have also found sightlines between other windows and doorways in the building relating to cycles of the moon and the planet Venus. A human face peering out of the jaws of a serpent, the Maya symbol for astronomers, is a common motif in sculptures throughout Chichén Itzá and shows the reverence in which stargazers were held.

In the woods beyond the Central Group, trails lead to various sites in the South Group, which consists of about 15 structures in an advanced state of ruin. The largest is the **Temple of the Tree Lintels**, reminiscent of the architectural style of Uxmal. Nearby, at the **Temple of the Initial Series**, hieroglyphs on a doorway lintel represent a date corresponding to the year A.D. 879, the only "long count" Maya calendar date found at Chichén Itzá. In another crumbled structure, the **Temple of the Phalluses**, giant stone phallic monuments typical of a Gulf Coast fertility cult and found in several rooms are quite unusual in either a Maya or Toltec ceremonial center.

As large and impressive as Chichén Itzá is, the structures we see at this site are only a sampling of what lies hidden in some four square miles of land still overgrown with jungle. Every hill around the ruins is actually a manmade mound or unexcavated ruin. Much is left for future generations of archaeologists to unearth. Future digs may reveal answers to some of the puzzles that surround Chichén Itzá. More likely, though, they will disclose still more mysteries to tantalize our imaginations.

When you leave Chichén Itzá, be sure to tour the **Grutas de Balankanché**, or you'll miss one of the most mysterious places of worship in the Chichén Itzá area. Local guides take small groups down into the electrically lit corridors of these caves, which narrow into passageways so tight and twisting you have to writhe through like a snake. Suddenly a wondrous chamber opens up. A massive stalagmite rises from the floor like a mystic tree; its leaves, sparkling stalactites, encrust the ceiling. All around the chamber's base, carved faces stare up from Maya pots, which are

◆◆◆

A TEMPLE FOR STARGAZERS

Although experts disagree on how much of El Caracol was built by early Maya people and how much reflects later Toltec influence, there is no doubt that this was one of the most important structures at Chichén Itzá, where religion and the science of astronomy were inseparable. The large incense burners in the shape of human heads placed all around the edges of the observatory platform indicate that major ceremonies were held here. Celestial movements provided Maya priests with their only accurate measure of the flow of time, the essence of Maya religious beliefs. This observatory may have helped make Chichén Itzá one of the most important cities in the Yucatán.

believed to be thousand-year-old offerings to the gods who lived in the cave. Another crouch-down passageway leads to an underground pool as still as glass, with more pots peering out of the crannies, one even sitting on its own small island in the water. The oxygen gets thin very fast, so the tour does not last long. Check the current schedule at the display in the Chichén Itzá visitors center and arrive punctually. A regional botanical garden surrounding the parking area and cave entrance building provides a pleasant, peaceful environment in the event you have to wait for your tour. Tours in English and Spanish alternate hourly. ~ About eight kilometers east of Chichén Itzá off Route 180.

HIDDEN ►

New on the horizon, the Maya site of **Yaxuná** went all but unnoticed until recently. New digs by the foremost Maya archaeologists have revealed the site to be much larger and older than was previously realized. The ancient city dates back to Preclassic times, and its monumental buildings include the tallest Maya pyramid ever built north of El Mirador in the Petén rainforest along the Guatemalan border, as well as a large acropolis and ball court. The site is best known for the longest known *sacbé,* or ceremonial road, which ran precisely straight through the jungle to Cobá, 100 kilometers away. A defensive outpost called **Xcan Ha** stands alongside another *sacbé* that runs north to connect Yaxuná with Chichén Itzá. The public is welcome, though the site is still undergoing restoration. ~ Follow the Carretera Popolá south from Pisté for 20 kilometers, through the village of Popolá, to the intersection with the narrow, paved Carretera San Pedro Yaxcabá–Ticimul, and watch for the Yaxuná turnoff on your left.

The Grutas de Balankanché, shut up for more than 500 years, were discovered in 1959 by a tour guide.

HIDDEN ►

If you have plenty of time on your hands to explore the Chichén Itzá area in depth, you may want to take a side trip to check out the new **Ik Kil Parque Eco-Arqueológico**, a privately owned eco-park adjoining the practically unknown Maya ruin from the time of Chichén Itzá's height. It can be found at Rancho San Isidro, about nine kilometers south of Route 180 on a road that turns off at Libre Unión. Only one structure has been cleared at the site, and if there are any other ancient buildings in the area, they are concealed by vegetation. The view of the flat surrounding landscape from the summit of the imposing Ik Kil pyramid, which rises about 79 feet to a temple on top, is worth the climb. The crumbled temple once supported a large roof comb, a decorative stone superstructure built on the roof that added to the structure's height. Only tumbled-down rock fragments remain to show the hieroglyphs that once decorated the stone lintels over the temple doorways. The pyramid was built over two older temples, and vaulted passages from the center of the crumbled stairways lead into the as-yet-unexcavated interior, adding an air of mystery. Ik Kil also has a nicely landscaped cenote with waterfalls for swimming. Admission. ~ Route 180, Km. 122; 9-851-0000; www.ikkil.com.

If you go to Ik Kil, be sure to continue south on the paved road for another nine kilometers to the magnificent Spanish colonial church at the fading village of **San Pedro Yaxcaba**. The huge three-towered church's fanciful, Moorish-looking facade is right out of 16th-century Spain. The interior contains elaborately decorated folk shrines to the saints. Nearby is the beautiful blue-green **Yax-caba Cenote**. Beside the cenote stands an abandoned colonial-era mansion known as the **House of the Wizard**, though the original owner was actually a merchant.

Just outside Chichén Itzá, several "archaeological hotels" offer the closest thing in the area to real luxury. Until recently, it was an easy walk from these hotels to the ruins, but the gate between the hotel road and the archaeological zone is now permanently locked, and shuttle buses take guests to the main entrance. Top of the line—and closest to the ruins—is the **Hotel Mayaland**. The guest rooms in the main hotel building, which dates back to 1923, are spacious and most have balconies. The rustic Yucatán-style huts set alongside bougainvillea-shaded footpaths amid 100 acres of lush grounds cost more and have no air conditioning, only ceiling fans, but do offer plenty of comfort and character. All 95 guest units have showers, telephones and satellite television. The hotel has a large swimming pool, a bar and several restaurants. Other amenities include horse rentals and tennis courts. A new spa facility offers massages, facials, reflexology and yoga and tai chi sessions. Air conditioning in hotel, ceiling fans in huts. ~ Chichén Itzá; 9-851-0027, fax 9-851-0129, or 800-235-4079 in the U.S.; www.mayaland.com. DELUXE TO ULTRA-DELUXE.

LODGING

The **Hacienda Chichén**, on the same road as Mayaland, is under the same management and offers slightly lower rates. This was originally the site of a Spanish colonial hacienda built in the late 1500s, using stones from outlying temples of Chichén Itzá. The hacienda was burned during the War of the Castes in the mid-1800s, and its ruins became a slave market where Maya war parties rendezvoused with people from the forest tribes of Quintana Roo to sell European captives. Fifty years later, U.S. Consul Edward Thompson bought the abandoned house and its land, which included the archaeological zone of Chichén Itzá, for $500. Thompson was later deported for looting the site and smuggling the spoils out of Mexico to Harvard University's museum, and the hacienda was seized by the Mexican government. Archaeologist Sylvanus Morley built the cottages that serve as guest rooms today and used the hacienda as a base of operations during his 20-year restoration project at Chichén Itzá. The 26 rooms are large, airy and simple, with no televisions or phones. There is, however, a swimming pool surrounded by tranquil gardens. Ceiling fans. ~ Chichén Itzá; phone/fax 9-851-0045; for reservations, call 9-924-2150 in Mérida, fax 9-924-5011, or 800-624-8451 in the U.S. MODERATE.

The **Villa Arqueológica** is one of a chain of hotels managed by Club Med that are located at ancient ruins all over Mexico. The 40 guest rooms, though small, are fairly luxurious. There are no double beds. Tennis courts and a pool are surrounded by pretty gardens. The public areas of the hotel display an impressive collection of Maya sculpture and artifacts, and there is an extensive library of books on Maya archaeology, about half of them in English. Air conditioning. ~ Chichén Itzá; 9-851-0034, or 800-258-2633 in the U.S. DELUXE.

Located two kilometers east of the Chichén Itzá archaeological zone, the **Hotel Dolores Alba** offers 40 small, clean rooms with private baths in an attractive country house surrounded by gardens. There are two swimming pools, one of them with a natural limestone bottom. The management can provide transportation to the ruins; you will have to take a taxi back. Rates are in the budget range, but meals for two in the hotel dining room can set you back more than the cost of the room, and no other restaurants are close by. ~ Route 180, Km. 122; 9-858-1555; www.doloresalba.com, e-mail asanchez@sureste.com. BUDGET.

The Pirámide Inn boasts a genuine Maya burial mound—a reminder that the site of modern-day Pisté was part of the greater Chichén Itzá metropolitan area a thousand years ago.

Just down the highway, about four kilometers west of Chichén Itzá, the **Pirámide Inn** is my favorite among the numerous motels in the town of Pisté. Most of the 40 rooms are dark but pleasant, with satellite television offering a limited number of U.S. channels. The grounds surrounding the swimming pool are nicely landscaped with palms and flowering plants as well as a small shrine, a model of a Maya pyramid and an artificial waterfall. Explore the back streets of town and you will find other small Maya sites dating from ancient times. On the second floor above the lobby is an extensive and fascinating display of photos and maps, developed over the years by the Explorers' Club, covering most major archaeological sites of the Yucatán as well as some in Chiapas, Guatemala, Honduras and Belize. Air conditioning. ~ Route 180, Pisté; 9-851-0115, fax 9-851-0114; www.piramide inn.com. BUDGET TO MODERATE.

The most luxurious accommodations in Pisté are at the **Hotel Chichén Itzá**, one of a regional chain of modern, upscale hotels and motor inns. The 44 cheery rooms feature warm pink-and-orange decor and fancy wall tiles. A restaurant and bar adjoin the nice, private swimming pool surrounded by a lush lawn with palms, banana trees and tropical flowers. However, the location cannot compare to similarly priced lodgings within walking distance of the ruins. Air conditioning. ~ Route 180, Pisté; 9-851-0022, fax 9-851-0023; www.hotelchichenitza.com, e-mail info@hotelchichenitza.com. DELUXE.

Ik Kil, located at the "eco-archaeological park" of the same name, rents simple rooms in modern, thatch-roofed casitas scattered around the landscaped grounds. Each has two double beds with mosquito netting and not much else (except the idyllic setting). ~ Route 180, Km. 122; 9-851-0000; www.ikkil.com. BUDGET TO MODERATE.

Cafetería Ruinas, small cafeteria-style restaurant in the visitors center complex at Chichén Itzá, serves *sopa de lima* and luncheon entrées ranging from hamburgers to *pollo pibil*. ~ MODERATE.

DINING

For a more luxurious intermission from exploring the ruins of Chichén Itzá, try a restaurant in one of the hotels within walking distance of the ruins. They are located outside the south gate, west of the Observatory. While the main dining room at Mayaland is historic and full of rustic elegance, the menu is more interesting in the restaurant at the Villa Arqueológica, which offers a full range of French, Maya and Mexican menu selections. Both hotel restaurants are in the deluxe price range.

In Pisté, the gaudy **La Fiesta** caters mainly to bus tour groups. The typical Yucatecan cuisine served here—*sopa de lima, cochinita pibil, pescado à la veracruzana*—is well prepared and the service is efficient, but the most notable feature of this restaurant is its murals. Two walls are painted with the artist's concept, based loosely on temple art, of each major god in the Maya pantheon. Another wall is decorated with a lurid portrayal of an attractive young woman, presumably virginal, about to be sacrificed in Chichén Itzá's sacred cenote. ~ Route 180. MODERATE.

Authentic regional food costs less at **El Carrousel**, under a huge thatched roof in the center of town. Decor is utilitarian, and the tablecloths are Mexican blankets. The *pollo pibil* here is excellent. The restaurant's clientele mostly consists of daytrippers from Cancún or Mérida, so it closes early in the evening, before the traditional Mexican dinner hour. ~ Route 180. MODERATE.

The **Puebla Maya**, across the highway from the Pirámide Inn, seats patrons in a Disneyesque atmosphere of Maya hut replicas around a central pool landscaped with hundreds of potted plants. Mariachi musicians stroll among tables full of bus tour passengers. The surroundings may be overly cute, but the buffet-style breakfast, lunch and dinner are bargains. ~ Route 180. MODERATE.

You can't go far wrong at **Los Arcos**, the bright, modern restaurant in the Hotel Chichén Itzá, where Maya women dressed in traditional *huipiles* serve touristy versions of standard

Text continued on page 252.

Experiencing
Yucatán's Haciendas

There are more than 300 Spanish colonial haciendas within a 50-mile radius of Mérida. Most of these grand (and sometimes grandiose) manor houses were originally more modest homes of cattle ranchers, built in the 1500s and handed down through generations until, in the mid-1800s, Maya freedom fighters sacked the ranches during the War of the Castes. After the Indian uprising subsided, a new breed of entrepreneurs took over the haciendas and converted the pastures into sisal fields. The *sisal*, or henequen, plants produced fiber used to make the finest rope available at the time. The plantation owners exploited Maya slave labor and made enormous amounts of money, which they used to turn their houses into ostentatious showplaces. Their lifestyle lasted until the late 1930s, when land reform measures turned the land over to the Maya people who lived there. The former plantation owners moved away, often leaving the great haciendas to collapse from disrepair.

In 1997, the Yucatán state government started a historic restoration program that offers financial incentives to individuals and companies who rehabilitate the haciendas. While some have become private residences of the wealthy, both Mexican and foreign investors are rescuing others and turning them into bed-and-breakfast inns. For motorists, inns like this provide a welcome alternative to staying in Mérida, where virtually all lodgings are located in the congested downtown/Paseo Montejo area where a car is a liability. Here's a sampling of the best in various price ranges.

HACIENDA KATANCHEL   Considered the cream of the crop of hacienda inns, this elegantly refurbished mansion surrounded by 650 acres of forest and gardens has 21 air-conditioned indoor-outdoor "pavilion" rooms and 20 spacious suites, as well as a "niñas" room with four single beds and two bathrooms; some rooms have private plunge pools. The hacienda offers spa services such as facial and body treatments. The dining room ranks among the Mérida area's finest restaurants, with appetizers such as squash mousse in lime sauce, entrées like grilled boneless chicken breast in bougainvillea sauce, and a long international wine list. ~ Located 26 kilometers east of Mérida on Route 180; 9-923-4020, fax 9-923-4000, or 888-882-9470 in the U.S.; www.hacienda-katanchel.com, e-mail hacienda@mail.mda.com.mx. ULTRA-DELUXE.

HACIENDA SAN PEDRO   More than four centuries old, this hacienda was one of the first in the Yucatán. It's also one of the closest to Mérida, located in a small pueblo just two kilometers outside the city; you can taxi to the city center for $5. The main house, containing the guest accommodations, features lofty ceilings, tile floors, colonial arches and wrought iron. The old *sisal* fiber factory nearby has been converted into attractive dining and sitting areas. Each of the nine large suites has a separate bedroom, comfortable chairs and tables, and satellite TV; some have hide-a-beds. The tasteful decor blends colonial wood and contemporary floral patterns. A continental breakfast is included in the room rate, and guests have kitchen privileges. Bicycles are available for guests' use. ~ Located two kilometers from Mérida on Route 180; 9-988-0542, fax 9-988-0572; www.haciendaholidays.com, e-mail hacienda holidays@hotmail.com. MODERATE.

HACIENDA SAN ANTONIO CHALANTE   The roof of this grand old mansion had collapsed long before an American archaeologist and his innkeeper partner bought the near-ruin in 1997. Since then they've performed wonders of restoration. The main house contains three guest rooms, including an impressive master suite, as well as dining and sitting rooms. The overseer's house and two workers' houses add six more guest rooms, each with a private bath. The site of a collapsed family chapel has been transformed into a meditation garden. The location, at the small village of Sudzal, is close to Izamal and within easy day-trip distance of major ancient sites including Chichén Itzá, Dzibilchaltún and Mayapán. ~ Located on the Carretera Kantunil–Izamal road, ten kilometers north of Route 180; phone/fax 9-954-0287; www.macanche.com/hacienda.htm, e-mail izamal@ wohlmut.com. BUDGET TO MODERATE.

Yucatecan dishes such as *poc chuc* and *pollo pibil.* ~ Route 180, Pisté; 9-851-0022. MODERATE.

Hacienda Xaybe'h, the restaurant in front of Ik Kil Parque Eco-Arqueológico, also has serving staff in traditional dress, and its food is traditional as well. House specialties include *papadzules*—chopped hardboiled eggs rolled in soft tortillas and smothered in a pumpkin seed sauce. Another typical local dish is *panuchos,* similar to north-of-the-border chicken tacos containing refried beans; if you don't want the beans, ask for *salbutes.* The restaurant's decor is a pink, ersatz elegant re-creation of fin-de-siecle hacienda style. ~ Route 180, Km. 122; 9-851-0000. MODERATE.

SHOPPING   The visitors center complex at Chichén Itzá has a camera shop, a fine jewelry store and a branch of Librería Dante, the Yucatán's major bookstore chain, which carries a large stock of books about the Maya, including many in English, French, German and Japanese.

Since a Maya groundskeeper at Chichén Itzá first noticed the equinox phenomenon in the 1940s, a whole new field of study, called archaeoastronomy, has emerged.

Across the parking lot from the visitors center is a big **open-air market** filled with curio stands. Vendors seduce, cajole and implore tourists (*"Sprechen sie Deutsch?* No? You speak English, my friend? Come see what I have for you—almost free!"*) to examine their wares, which range from many, many T-shirts to Chac-Mool keychains and ashtrays to regional products like hammocks, Panama hats and colorful machine-embroidered white *huipiles* of the type that Maya women wear throughout the Yucatán. Prices and selection are nowhere near as good as you will find in Mérida but better than in Cancún.

NIGHTLIFE   A **Sound and Light Show** is presented at Chichén Itzá twice nightly —one show in Spanish and the other in English—every night of the year. Check for times at the visitors center or any hotel in the area. Upgraded for more sophisticated audiences in recent years, the show blends archeological theory, pageantry, mythology and misinformation about ancient Chichén Itzá. The special lighting effects are impressive, and the show is certainly the most exciting thing going on around here after dark.

Izamal

Izamal (pop. 40,000) embodies both the collision and synthesis of cultures that shaped the Yucatán and offers some of the best glimpses of what life may have been like in both ancient Maya and Spanish colonial times. In the centuries before the Itzá invasion, Izamal controlled the trade in salt, one of the most valuable commodities in the ancient world. Centuries later, when the Spanish *conquistadores* arrived, four massive pyramid platforms with temples on top still surrounded the central plaza. They are thought to have been painted yellow, as the whole town center is today. The oval, thatched-roof homes of the city's residential areas probably looked much the same as today. Most of the structures surrounding the central plaza were built with stones from the ancient ceremonial center.

Izamal is easiest to reach by turning north from Route 180 Libre at Kantunil, midway between Chichén Itzá and Mérida, and driving 18 kilometers to Izamal. Several more circuitous driving routes make their way from northeastern Mérida through successions of Maya villages to Izamal; the road through Tixkokob lets you make a short detour to visit Aké en route.

The first sight that greets every visitor arriving in Izamal is the magnificent **Iglesia de Izamal y Convento de San Antonio de Padua.** The grandiose church complex was the largest in the Yucatán when it was competed in 1561 and still is today. It was built by Fray Diego de Landa, who would later become the notorious instrument of the Spanish Inquisition in the Yucatán, imposing Catholicism on the Maya people through fear, torture and destruction. Landa chose Izamal as the site of the first great missionary church in the Yucatán because of the huge pyramids there; if the ancient temples were already sacred, attracting pilgrims from all over the peninsula, presumably the new mission could inherit the same sanctity. Landa ordered the destruction of the ornate temples atop the town's four pyramids and used the stones from them to build his church on the largest, called the House of Heads and Lightning, converting the ancient pyramid into an unmistakable demonstration of the power and majesty of the Catholic faith. Franciscan monasteries were constructed on other platforms. A rather diabolical-looking statue of Fray Landa stands at street level on the south side of the church complex.

The most striking feature of the church and monastery complex is its huge atrium, the open lawn surrounded by a shady covered walkway, which serves as a public gathering place on church feast days. The largest church atrium in the world, it covers the entire top of the ancient Maya pyramid platform—9600 square yards—an area larger than a football field. A long, stepped ramp where the original pyramid stairway used to be ascends about 18 feet (about two stories) from the level of the town plaza to the atrium and church entrance. It is a gradual climb, designed for Maya pilgrims who still practice the penance of ascending the stairway on their knees. As you near the top, you are greeted by an image of the Virgin Mary on the front of the church that appears to rise in the east like the moon, vivid blue surrounded by bright yellow. Switchback walkways up the north and south sides of the church were built later so that Spanish members of the congregation would not have to share the same stairs with common Indians.

SIGHTS

In 1558, while building the church, Fray Landa brought a
"black madonna"—a statue of the Virgin Mary carved from dark
wood and venerated by the Indians—from Guatemala, where it
had already gained a reputation for miracles. Over the centuries,
the Virgin of Izamal reigned as one of the two most sacred religious icons in the Yucatán. (The other was the Christ of the Blisters
statue at the Mérida cathedral.) The virgin was carried to other
areas of the Yucatán in formal processions to intercede in famines
and epidemics. She was destroyed in an anticlerical riot in 1829,
but it was soon discovered that Landa had brought a twin carving
from Guatemala at the same time, storing it in a secret room where
it stayed for almost three centuries as insurance against just such a
disaster, and the black madonna cult of Izamal continued, as it does
to this day. The virgin can be seen in the chamber behind the
main church. A terrace outside this chamber provides a good view
of the flying buttresses that support the back side of the church,
which extends over the edge of the old pyramid. The terrace outside Fray Landa's secret room commands the only view in town
of the great Maya pyramid a few blocks away.

HIDDEN ▶   The **Pyramid of Kinich-Kakmo**, also called the Pyramid of
Itzamná, was one of the largest structures in the ancient Maya
world. It is the third-largest pyramid in Mexico. Its base covers an
area of over 43,200 square yards and rises nearly 56 feet above
street level; it is over four times as large as the pyramid base on
which the church was built. Yet the town is arranged so that the
pyramid cannot be seen from the plaza. To reach it, follow Calle
28 two blocks west of the *zócalo*, turn north on Calle 27 and
watch for a narrow alleyway between two buildings, inconspicuously marked with a "Zona Arqueológica" sign. Someone may
or may not be there to charge admission; the ticket booth is
tended mainly when tour buses are in town. Walk up the alleyway,
and you find yourself on a broad stairway that climbs by levels.
When it finally seems that you've reached the top of the stairs, you
emerge onto a broad, parklike area atop the pyramid base. At the
far end of this expanse is the upper pyramid, another 59 feet high.
At the top are a wooden cross and a plain pole where people lay
flower offerings. The view reveals the bare tops of three other,
smaller pyramids rising above the town and makes the grandiose
church look insignificant. Viewing the pyramid from the church
and the church from the pyramid shows how Izamal's architecture embodies the battle that raged here for the hearts and minds
of the Maya people. Admission.

About nine kilometers down a well-marked side road from the
village of Tixcokob, which lies 34 kilometers west of Izamal on
one of several possible back routes into Mérida, are the unique
ruins of **Aké**, rarely visited even though they are only about 35 kilometers outside of the capital city. The main Maya ruins, which date

back to the Early Classic Period (A.D. 250–600), were surrounded by a defensive wall and connected to Izamal by a 32-kilometer *sacbé* that ran straighter than any modern road in the area. Two of the 25 major structures at the site have been cleared and partially restored. The most striking is Structure 1, also called the Palace, a long pyramid with a stairway of huge stone blocks that stretches 164 feet across its face and with 36 massive stone columns on top. The nearly 15-foot-tall columns once supported what was probably a thatched roof. Across the ceremonial plaza, a pyramid that is taller—nearly 66 feet—but not as wide provides a good vantage point for taking pictures of Structure 1.

Amid the ruins of ancient Aké stand the more recent ruins of a 19th-century henequen hacienda that was built on a ceremonial platform between two pyramids. The palatial house has long been abandoned, but local Indians still use the machinery to harvest and process nearly worthless henequen fiber. If you're lucky, you may have a chance to see the machines with their studded moving belts shredding the huge, hard, sharp leaves of the henequen plant into rope fiber.

Also worth a visit is the cemetery at **Hóctun**. A time-honored custom throughout the Yucatán is for people's status in life to be reflected in the size of their burial crypts, which range from plain, foot-tall markers to enormous houses adorned with spires and statues of angels. Hóctun has the most spectacular such graveyard I've seen. Children often hang around this and other cemeteries, ready to tag along after visitors in hopes of a tip. ~ On Route 180 about 25 kilometers southwest of Izamal.

AUTHOR FAVORITE

No other place in the region gives me a sense of the enduring flow of Maya culture like Izamal, a city that has been inhabited continuously for at least 2000 years. Now at last I can spend the night there in comfort thanks to **Macan Ché**, an affordable little inn that is an attractive alternative to Mérida's congested streets. Macan Ché offers 12 cottages in a garden setting, each decorated in a different theme—from Mexican and Southwestern to African and even Olde English. Facilities include a pool, exercise room and bikes; guests can horseback ride at the owners' private ranch outside of town, which also has three more guest cottages and a backpacker camping area. The same owners also operate the Hacienda San Antonio Chalante in the neighboring village of Sudzal. ~ Calle 22 No. 305, Izamal; 9-954-0287, fax 9-954-0287; www.macanche.com, e-mail izamal@wohlmut.com. BUDGET TO MODERATE.

LODGING   Until recently, Izamal was almost exclusively a daytrip destination, often visited briefly en route between Chichén Itzá and Mérida. Facilities for overnight visitors were minimal. There are two hotels in town, both on the north side of the plaza, in crumbling old colonial buildings. The **Hotel Kabul** is basic at best, with spacious rooms and amazingly high ceilings from which bare lightbulbs dangle on 12 feet of wire and sway back and forth in the breeze from the glassless windows. ~ Calle 31; 4-00-08. BUDGET.

It's the kind of place where the toilets don't have seats, but if you want to spend the night in Izamal and catch the sunrise from the top of the pyramid, you'll probably choose this place after comparing it to the other choice, the even less expensive **Hotel Canto**. ~ Calle 310. BUDGET.

DINING   Izamal has four restaurants and several pushcart *taquerías*. The **Restaurant Wayané Né** features authentic village versions of regional dishes such as *poc-chuc* and *pollo pibil*. This simple restaurant is located south of the church behind the statue of Fray Landa. ~ Glorieta Diego de Landa. BUDGET.

Several blocks west of the plaza, near the base of Izamal's large pyramid, the attractive **Restaurante Kinich Kakmó** offers a similar Yucatecan menu. ~ Calle 27 No. 299 between Calles 28 and 30; 9-954-0153. BUDGET. So does the **Tumban-Lol**. ~ Calle 24.

Ceviche and other seafood are often included in the bill of fare at **El Puerto de Manzanillo**. ~ Calle 31 No. 303.

SHOPPING   Izamal has a small *parador turístico* (handicrafts market), where you'll find some local handwoven *huipiles*, old photographs of Maya subjects and other attractive items amid the Guatemalan imports. ~ On Calle 31 between Calles 22 and 24, three blocks north of the *zócalo*.

Hecho a Mano, a shop established by a *mexicano* and a *norte-americano* in partnership, is one of the best places in the Yucatán to buy folk art, handcrafts and photos of the region and its people. ~ Calle 31 No. 323; 9-954-0344.

▼▼▼▼▼▼▼▼▼▼
Mayapán

Mayapán is absolutely unique among Maya sites. No other city like it has been found anywhere in the Maya world.

Although more "history"—whether accurate or fictitious—is connected with Mayapán and its remarkable two-century reign over the entire Yucatán Peninsula, this lost city's very existence remains inexplicable.

What has puzzled the experts most is Mayapán's location, alone on the dry side of the Sierra de Ticul, the Yucatán's hill country. With poor soil and almost no rain, farmers around Mayapán could not have grown nearly enough corn to feed the city. Archaeologists believe Mayapán must have depended on tributes from other cities. Many think that the warriors of Mayapán, the first in the region to use bows and arrows, conquered other wealthy cities such as Izamal in wars, taking hostages to insure payment of tribute. But Mayapán's supremacy may also have been spiritual or economic. The site contains more shrines and family altars than any other Maya city in the Yucatán, and artifacts found there include such rare trade goods as obsidian from Central Mexico and turquoise from the American Southwest.

Travelers take note: The ruins of Mayapán are not to be confused with the village of Mayapán 40 kilometers to the south.

Mayapán was shunned until recently by archaeologists, who dismissed its architecture as decadent and its rulers as brutal warlords responsible for the decline of Maya civilization. Surprisingly for such an important site, Mayapán was not restored until the late 1990s. Before that, no sign marked the turnoff from the highway, and the few visitors who got there found only overgrown mounds and tumbled rocks. Today, though, the entrance is well marked, the main structures are painstakingly restored and the entrance welcomes visitors with bright red bougainvillea flowers.

It's as if Mayapán was viewed by archaeologists as something of an embarrassment, not the kind of project you'd want to risk your academic career on. Restoration of Mayapán finally began very recently and is still going on, driven less by scientific curiosity than by its location, less than an hour's drive from Mérida in an area that previously saw very few tourists.

SIGHTS

Twenty kilometers southeast of Mérida on Route 18, the small town of **Acancéh** is one of many Yucatán settlements that have been inhabited more or less continuously since the Classic Maya era. What makes this town unusual is the large **Pyramid of Acancéh**, which stands between storefronts on the main street, facing out on the dusty plaza. Stripped of most of its stone facing, the pyramid remains one of the tallest and most imposing landmarks in town. Another ancient structure, the **Temple of the Stucco Facade**, is located two blocks away. Fragments of a stucco frieze, adorned with hieroglyphs and images of magical animals, can still be made out on the front of the temple. Both structures date back to the Early Classic period.

◄ *HIDDEN*

From Acancéh continue for another 20 kilometers south on Route 18 to reach the a recently paved road into **Mayapán** (admission), the Postclassic Maya capital of Yucatán. The turnoff is well marked with a big green-and-white freeway-style sign.

Entering the parklike central plaza of this city, which once covered two-and-a-half square miles and contained more than 2000 residences within a castlelike stone wall, visitors are confronted by the strangest aspect of Mayapán: the structures are unmistakably copies of the architecture at Chichén Itzá—in minia-ture. There's a smaller version of Chichén's famous **Castillo** pyra-mid, a scale model of Chichén's round **Observatory**, a reproduc-tion of Chichén's **Group of Thousand Columns**, all crammed close together to fit inside the city walls. Original sculptures decorating the temples are crude, but artwork from older Classic-era Maya sites was brought here and installed in the facades of Mayapán buildings. Notice the striking Puuc-style Chaac (rain god) mask on the long Acropolis across the trail from the Castillo pyramid. It's as if the rulers sought to recapture the fallen grand-eur of Chichén Itzá in a limited space—much the way America's tourist industry does when it re-creates New York and Paris in the form of Las Vegas hotels and Japan and Morocco as Epcot Center pavilions.

The site has a total of six excavated temples as well as sev-eral residential structures thought to have been palaces for the royal family. In fact, given the grandeur of the palaces and the relative modesty of the temples here, one might suspect that the rulers of Mayapán were more interested in building palaces than religious structures. But what Mayapán's temples lack in size, they make up for in number: more family altars and shrines have been found here than at any other ceremonial center in the Maya world.

Another baffling aspect of Mayapán is that the entire walled city was jam-packed with houses—about 3600 of them, housing an estimated 11,000 people, in an area of only 1.6 square miles. No other Maya site had anything close to this residential density. Unlike in other cities, the homes were so close together that there were no streets or city blocks, only narrow, labyrinthine walk-ways between the walls of the huts. One theory is that the pop-ulation huddled inside the walls for protective reasons; but many archaeologists believe Mayapán's surrounding wall was sym-bolic and not actually needed for defense. In fact, the evidence for Mayapán's warlike reputation is rather thin; its government was overthrown at least twice, but both times were revolts from within, not assaults from outside the walls.

Which brings us to Mayapán's "history." A legend recorded by explorer John Lloyd Stephens in 1841 describes how Maya-pán conquered Chichén Itzá in a war that bears suspicious simi-larities to the Trojan War in Homer's *Iliad*. According to the leg-end, young Hunac Ceel, a member of the Cocom dynasty of Itzá Maya, joined a religious pilgrimage to the sacred cenote at Chi-chén Itzá, where he hurled himself into the water seeking a vision and resurfaced to announce that the gods had declared him lord of Mayapán and ruler of the Yucatán. Ceel formed the League of Mayapán, a three-way alliance between Mayapán, Chichén Itzá and Uxmal that rose to become the most powerful force in the

Touring the centro in a calesa (horse-drawn carriage) is popular in the colonial city of Mérida.

Above: Uxmal is considered by many to be the finest, most Mayan site in the Yucatán.

Below: A detail of the Temple of the Jaguars at Chichén Itzá.

Postclassic Maya world. The alliance was cemented by exchanging members of the three cities' royal families as lifelong hostages.

Archaeologists give no credence to this tale but have determined that Mayapán was built by the Itzá Maya—the same group that inhabited Chichén at the time—between A.D. 1224 and 1244. Despite at least two revolutions that put new leadership in control of the city, Mayapán reigned as the capital of the Yucatán for more than two centuries and was still an important ceremonial center when the Spanish arrived. As the saga continues, Lord Hunac Ceel's daughter, Sac-Nicte, fell in love with Canek, the young lord of Chichén Itzá, while she was a hostage there. Unfortunately, Sac-Nicte was pledged to marry the older, wealthier lord of Uxmal. Canek attacked the wedding celebration and carried Sac-Nicte off to share a honeymoon exile in the Petén, never again to be seen in the Yucatán. (A different version of the tale has Sac-Nicte hurling herself into Chichén Itzá's sacred cenote—the original sacrificial virgin.) This outrage started a war that put an end to the League of Mayapán, as the combined armies of Uxmal and Mayapán wiped out the Itzá armies and drove the surviving residents of Chichén Itzá deep into the forest. Later, the Itzás would take their revenge by totally destroying the city of Mayapán, but Chichén Itzá would never be reoccupied.

No food or lodging is available in Mayapán's immediate vicinity. The closest accommodations are in Mérida (Chapter Eight) or Ticul (Chapter Ten).

Experts dismiss the legends as bunk, of course. They believe that the Itzá people built Mayapán after abandoning Chichén Itzá. According to stories recorded by 16th-century Spanish historians from Maya oral tradition, Hunac Ceel and his heirs, the Cocom clan, ruled over the Yucatán without major wars for nearly two centuries. Their main rivals were the Xiu clan, another Itzá family that had reinhabited the ancient ceremonial center at Uxmal. By the 15th century, because of commerce and politics, many Cocomes and Xiu were living in each other's cities. The Xiu living in Mayapán organized a revolution, overthrowing and exiling the Cocom rulers. But the Xius were never able to consolidate their influence around the peninsula, and as Mayapán's power waned, strife within the Xiu family brought about another rebellion in A.D. 1441. At that time, it is said, Mayapán was destroyed completely, leaving only heaps of rubble where great pyramids and palaces once stood. (But consider the source: Spanish conquistadores often feared idols of non-Christian gods and made a practice of defacing the temples at important Maya sites. This may have happened at Mayapán, since there is historical evidence to suggest that the city was still one of the most important ceremonial centers in the Yucatán at the time the Spanish arrived.)

Dzibilchaltún

Another good short excursion into the countryside from Mérida takes you to a site that was formerly one of the most important cities in the Maya empire, then continues north to Yucatán state's main seaport. Drive 17 kilometers north of Mérida on Route 261, a continuation of Paseo de Montejo also known as the Mérida–Progreso Highway. Located about seven kilometers east of the highway on a marked, paved side road that runs past the small Universidad del Mayab campus is Parque Nacional Dzibilchaltún. The city of Dzibilchaltún was one of the largest on the Yucatán for much of the period from 800 B.C. to A.D. 1250. Many experts believe it served as the peninsula's capital city in the early Classic period, probably because it held a monopoly on the salt trade, which it later lost to Izamal. Archaeologists have identified the foundation mounds of more than 6000 residential structures on the 7.4-square-mile site. The name *Dzibilchaltún* means "Place of Inscriptions on Flat Stones." Several of the stelae, or sculptured monument stones, found in the park are on exhibit in the park's new Museum of the Maya. Restoration of four major temple complexes began here in 1993–94, and visitors who haven't been here for a few years will find it spiffed up almost beyond recognition.

SIGHTS

Parque Nacional Dzibilchaltún (admission) preserves all that's left of a site the Maya people occupied continuously for over 2000 years. Stop at the park's outstanding new **Museo de los Mayas**, which contains artifacts and interpretive exhibits; visitors who don't read Spanish will find this multilingual museum more informative in many ways than Mérida's Museo de Antropología e Historia.

The park entrance trail intersects a long, straight *sacbé* that runs in both directions. If you turn right, the first large structure you will notice as you walk along the dirt trail into the ruins area was not built by the Maya. It is an old **Spanish mission church** built between 1590 and 1600 of stones that were salvaged from ancient Maya temples. You'll recognize the church by its large round arch, an idea that Maya architects never thought of. Today the church ruins have crumbled enough to blend in with the much older Maya ruins that surround it.

Across the *sacbé* from the church is a four-tiered temple pyramid known only as **Structure 36**, topped by the ruins of another Spanish chapel. Past that is **Structure 38**, a broad platform with several small, restored temples around a small plaza on top; much larger temples stood here in earlier periods of Dzibilchaltún's history. Across the *sacbé* and beyond the Spanish church is **Structure 44**, a recently restored palace that was one of the longest structures in northern Yucatán—more than 430 feet long. From the exterior, it looks like a set of stone football bleachers topped by columns that once supported palapa roofs. Inside are three large chambers with 35 entrances.

A little way past Structure 44 is the most popular spot at Dzibilchaltún, the sacred cenote called **Xlacah**. Shallow enough to wade among the water lilies at the east end, 131 feet deep at the west end, it is a well-used local swimming hole where Maya kids from miles around congregate on hot days (which, in this region, means most days). Archaeologists who dredged the bottom of this cenote found some 30,000 artifacts that had been thrown into the water over the centuries, probably as offerings to the god of rain. Many are on exhibit in the museum at the site's entrance. Unlike at Chichén Itzá, no human skeletons were found in this cenote.

Turning around and following the long *sacbé* back east past the entrance trail, you'll come to the **Temple of the Seven Dolls**, the first structure to be restored at Dzibilchaltún and one of the most important to archaeologists. It has a stairway leading up to a square towerlike temple with a unique pyramidal roof comb. Also unusual in Mayan architecture, it has windows next to two of its four doors. In the museum you can see the dolls that were found in the temple and gave it its name. Each doll has a different physical defect, suggesting that the temple may have been used for healing ceremonies.

To archaeoastronomers, the most remarkable aspect of the Temple of the Seven Dolls is that the doorways were arranged to mark important calendar dates: The rising sun casts its rays precisely through the eastern door to the threshhold of the western door on the spring and fall equinoxes (about March 21 and September 21), while the moon does the same on the first full-moon night after March 21 (the paschal full moon, or last full moon before Easter Sunday).

No food or lodging is available near Dzibilchaltún. Both Mérida (Chapter Ten) and Progreso (Chapter Eleven) are within a half-hour's drive.

AUTHOR FAVORITE

Getting off the beaten tourist path makes me feel like a real explorer, and nowhere more so than **Rancho Konchén de los Pajaros**, a private nonprofit nature reserve teeming with birds, fox anteaters, margay cats and pygmy deer. You can rent a bike or horse to explore the back trails, and there are even budget-rate stone Maya huts with hammocks where you can spend the night. ~ Libramiento Dzemul-Xtampu, Km. 1.5. There's no phone, so reservations can only be made via internet: www.konchen.org.

Transportation

CAR

Two highways, both designated **Route 180**, run between Cancún and Mérida. The limited access **Route 180 Cuota** (toll road) is fast, smooth and shockingly expensive; the toll is almost as much as a day's car rental charge. There is an exit from the toll freeway at Valladolid. Route 180 has an exit at Pisté, the town near Chichén Itzá.

Motorists can also get there on the free **Route 180 Libre**, which runs right along the edge of the archaeological site at Chichén Itzá, close enough so that from the road you can see the temple atop the Castillo pyramid rising above the treetops. This narrow, old two-lane highway takes a lot longer than the toll road, mainly because of the speed bumps designed to slow traffic to a crawl through populated areas. It offers a more picturesque, traffic-free trip, and it's free.

Forty kilometers southeast of Mérida, the ruins of Mayapán (not to be confused with the present-day village of Mayapán, about 50 kilometers away) are located west of **Route 18** near the village of Telchaquillo.

The turnoff to Dzibilchaltún from **Route 261**, the Mérida–Progreso Highway, is 15 kilometers north of Mérida.

AIR

Tour planes operated by Aerocaribe fly from Cancún to Pisté every day. ~ Cancún International Airport; 86-00-83.

BUS

Buses run between Cancún and Mérida constantly—about 25 per day in each direction. All second-class and many first-class buses stop at Valladolid. There are several competing bus lines, so the best plan is to visit the bus terminal the day before and shop and compare for the most convenient departure time. ~ On Calle 69 at Calle 68.

Most first-class and all second-class buses from Cancún and Mérida stop at Pisté, a few kilometers from Chichén Itzá. Several competing companies operate out of the central terminal at each city, with varied schedules and fares. Even on first-class buses, fares to Chichén Itzá are surprisingly inexpensive. At Pisté, taxis and shuttle vans are available to take you to the ruins.

Four buses go from Mérida's central bus terminal to Izamal. Fares are very low. ~ Located on Calle 69 at Calle 68. Sometimes you can also find a *combi* (VW microbus shuttle) headed for Izamal from the loading area near the public market in Mérida. ~ Bounded by Calles 56, 65, 54 and 59.

There is no regular bus service to the vicinity of Mayapán. *Combis* (VW shuttle vans) run between Ticul and Acancéh once in a while and can get you *to* Mayapán, though you may wait hours for another one to come along later and pick you up.

Frequent buses between Mérida and Progreso will drop you off and, usually, pick you up at the spot where the Dzibilchaltún road turns off the main highway; there is no public transportation on the road to the site. The hot five-kilometer walk can seem much longer than it really is.

▼ ▼ ▼ ▼ ▼ ▼ ▼ ▼ ▼ ▼ ▼ ▼ ▼ ▼ ▼ ▼ ▼ ▼ ▼ ▼
Addresses & Phone Numbers
Clinica Promesa (Pisté) ~ Calle 14 No. 50; 9-851-0005
Police (Piste) ~ 9-851-0097
Hospital S.S.A. (Valladolid) ~ Calle 41; 9-856-2883
Policia (Valladolid) ~ 9-856-2100

EIGHT

Mérida

Mérida has long carried the nickname *La Ciudad Blanca* (The White City). Just as Izamal, Mérida's one-time rival, has been painted yellow since ancient Maya days, many other Yucatecan communities painted their town centers a uniform color. This was not only for tradition's sake, but because paint was once hard to come by. Mérida was a city of whitewashed buildings until the 1930s, when more colors of paint became available. Today, Mérida is tropical pink, green and gold, with often peeling paint; it's a bright, multi-hued city of buildings with architecture that speaks of antiquity. Cancún's complete opposite, Mérida proudly wears its patina of age. In the narrow streets and cheerful plazas, visitors sense the vital heritage that binds Mérida to a bygone era, soon after the time of Columbus, when Spain ruled the continent.

The capital of Yucatán since colonial times and still the peninsula's largest city, Mérida makes an ideal base camp for exploring ancient cities and Gulf Coast fishing villages. It is within daytrip distance of both Chichén Itzá and Uxmal, the two most magnificently restored Maya ceremonial centers in the Yucatán, and a number of lesser-known archaeological sites, as well as the great cathedral at Izamal, the beaches of Progreso and Sisal, and the birders' paradise around Celestún. After a hot day among the ruins, Mérida, with its gracious restaurants, dignified old colonial hotels and lively streets, is a welcome sight. Less than one-tenth as many international visitors come to Mérida as Cancún, but tourism is one of the city's most important industries. (The other is production of cement and concrete blocks from the peninsula's seemingly limitless supply of limestone.)

So, is Mérida still worth visiting? You bet! The downtown plazas come alive after dark. Lovers stroll. Street vendors sell them roses. Floodlights illuminate architectural embellishments that date back to the time of Don Quixote.

Today Mérida, like other cities around Mexico, is being transformed by an unprecedented population explosion. This gem of a colonial capital, its streets created centuries before the automobile, now has more than its share of traffic congestion, parking problems and air pollution. A municipal historic restoration project is sprucing up the many colonial-era buildings, patching cracks and applying fresh coats of tropical-hued latex paint. Nevertheless, downtown Mérida has grown far more crowded than those who laid out its once-tranquil plazas and claustrophobically narrow streets ever intended. The experiences of strolling the city's streets and exploring its public markets can be as sublime as ever; but arriving in Mérida in a rental car may well stand out as the most frustrating moment of your vacation.

Only two contiguous areas of the city have hotels, and finding them is easy enough. The downtown (*centro*) area, where all but the most expensive lodgings are located, can be found by following the brown street signs that show the way to the Zona Hotelería, the historic district and the folk-art market. Whichever side of the city you're arriving from, simply follow the street numbers in the general direction of Calles 60, 61, 62 and 63. (These streets form a square surrounding the central plaza—see the explanation of Mérida's unusual street numbering system below.) Paseo Montejo, a boulevard that runs north from downtown to become the highway to Dzibilchaltún (see Chapter Seven) and Progreso (see Chapter Nine).

The problem is what to do with your car when you arrive. Most hotels have off-street parking arrangements for their guests, but they may be several blocks from the hotels themselves. When you get into the city, grab any parking space you can find (there are no parking meters—and almost no empty spaces), lock your gear in the trunk and start walking. When you check into your hotel, the desk clerk will tell you where to park for the night.

A better strategy for many travelers is to take the bus from Cancún to Mérida and rent a car there. Rental rates are significantly lower in Mérida than in Cancún, and you don't have to worry about the vehicle until you're ready to leave the city.

Visitors can also stay in one of the growing number of hacienda inns that are being opened in the countryside around Mérida (see Chapter Seven) and taxi in to the city.

Downtown Mérida

Downtown Mérida has more Spanish colonial architecture than any other place in the Yucatán, protected by some of the most rigid historic preservation regulations in Mexico. Historic churches, palaces, theaters and mansions await around every street corner. But taking in a checklist of sightseeing highlights is not the way to a memorable visit in Mérida. The best way to experience the magic that makes this one-of-a-kind city so special is by lingering on benches in the busy plazas, plunging into the clamor of the public market and enjoying an evening stroll along stately Paseo Montejo.

Central Mérida is easy to navigate once you catch on to its unusual street-numbering system. Even-numbered calles (streets) run north and south, with the street numbers increasing as you go west. Odd-numbered calles run east and west, with the street numbers increasing as you go south. Most places give their addresses in the form Calle 57 x 58 (that is, the corner of 57th and 58th streets) or Calle 57 between Calles 58 and 60. Street address numbers, used for receiving mail but not very helpful in locating the place, are sometimes given but are more often nonexistent. When used, they always follow the street number, as in Calle 57 No. 421.

Central Mérida was made for walking. In fact, being without a car is an advantage during a stay in Mérida because all streets in the downtown area are one-way and very narrow. It is not safe to park a car on the street overnight. Guarded off-street parking lots are small, privately operated and not very expensive. Don't even think of driving a car downtown on Sunday, when throngs of people crowd the plaza area for the weekly Mérida a Domingo celebration and many streets are closed to vehicular traffic.

SIGHTS   Start your walking tour of downtown Mérida at the **Plaza de la Independencia**, the central *zócalo*, which is bounded by Calles 60, 61, 62 and 63. In Latin America, the plaza serves an important social purpose: it's *the* place one goes to meet people. Visitors and residents alike hang around on its long, long benches and people-watch. You can, too. If you're willing to try out your Spanish, you'll find plenty of locals, not all of them selling anything, happy to converse with you. Strolling mariachi bands play in the late afternoon as lovers whisper on *confidenciales*, the S-shaped loveseats unique to Yucatecan parks.

The plaza was formerly the ceremonial center of a Postclassic Maya city called T'ho. Mérida was founded in 1542 by Francisco de Montejo under a charter from the king of Spain granting him the exclusive right to exploit the Yucatán Peninsula at his own expense. Montejo ordered the pyramids and temples of T'ho destroyed; then he used some of the ancient stones to build his home, **Casa de Montejo**, located on the south side of the plaza. Experts cite the mansion as one of the Western Hemisphere's finest examples of the ornate Plateresque architectural style, a distinctive type of 16th-century Spanish architectural decoration blending Gothic, Renaissance and Moorish elements. Carved by craftsmen from the early Spanish colonial capital of Santo Domingo, Hispañola, the sculptural work on the facade (what's left of it) evokes a vision of the dim past as vividly as carvings on a Maya temple. Flanking the grand doorway, stone *conquistadores* in armor stand on the heads of conquered Indians beneath the Montejo coat of arms, the centerpiece of a facade that also features stone lions, wild beast-men and grotesque faces. Walk in and enjoy the lavishly landscaped patio while imagining how the grandees lived at the time when Spain was growing fat on Mexico's riches. Montejo was summoned to Spain to face charges of atrocities against the Maya people less than two years after the house was completed. He never returned to Mérida, but the Montejo family continued to live in the house for 279 years, until 1828. The Montejo name is still prominent in Mérida on everything from the city's most exclusive boulevard to a popular local brand of beer. The mansion had fallen into a sad state of decay before it was refurbished as bank offices in 1984. It is open to the public during banking hours and on Sunday. ~ Calle 63.

Built on the exact site of the main temple in ancient T'ho, the **Mérida Cathedral** looms over the east side of the plaza. Designed to double as a fortress against any native people who might resent the Spanish presence, it was constructed between 1561 and 1598 from the stones of the Maya temple. The oldest Catholic cathedral on the American mainland, it is considered one of Mexico's finest Spanish colonial buildings. High above the massive wooden doorway, a coat of arms displays the Mexican eagle and serpent symbols, replacing the Spanish kings' heraldic eagles that originally decorated the escutcheon but were destroyed soon after Mexico won its independence from Spain. Mérida's most wretched beggars huddle in the church's entranceway. Give alms if you are so inclined. ~ Calle 60.

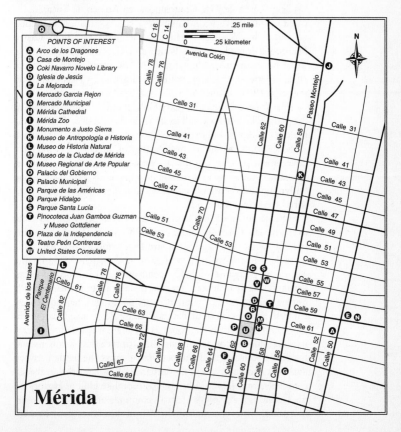

POINTS OF INTEREST
- **A** Arco de los Dragones
- **B** Casa de Montejo
- **C** Coki Navarro Novelo Library
- **D** Iglesia de Jesús
- **E** La Mejorada
- **F** Mercado Garcia Rejon
- **G** Mercado Municipal
- **H** Mérida Cathedral
- **I** Mérida Zoo
- **J** Monumento a Justo Sierra
- **K** Museo de Antropología e Historia
- **L** Museo de Historia Natural
- **M** Museo de la Ciudad de Mérida
- **N** Museo Regional de Arte Popular
- **O** Palacio del Gobierno
- **P** Palacio Municipal
- **Q** Parque de las Américas
- **R** Parque Hidalgo
- **S** Parque Santa Lucía
- **T** Pinacoteca Juan Gamboa Guzman y Museo Gottdiener
- **U** Plaza de la Independencia
- **V** Teatro Peón Contreras
- **W** United States Consulate

Mérida

The interior of the cathedral is not as sumptuous as you might expect from its huge size. Most of the gold and great art was lost when revolutionary mobs looted and burned the church in 1915.

Legend says the Cristo de las Ampollas was carved from a flaming tree that remained unscorched. It became an object of cult worship in the early 1600s when it survived a fire that destroyed the church at Ichmul (south of Chichén Itzá), unscathed except for a few blisters.

The most venerated object in the cathedral is **Cristo de las Ampollas** (Christ of the Blisters), a black Christ crucifixion figure in its own shrine along one side of the cathedral. The presumedly inflammable crucifix was brought to the cathedral in Mérida for safekeeping in 1645 and kept there until 1915, when revolutionaries proved that it really would burn. Even though the Cristo de las Ampollas you see in the church today is only a copy, it is revered by many faithful of Maya and Spanish ancestry alike. The annual festival honoring this relic lasts for 17 days (September 27–October 13) and climaxes with a ceremonial procession through the city streets.

The **Museo de Arte Contemporaneo Ateneo de Yucatán**, located next to the cathedral, exhibits a large permanent collection of works by Yucatecan painters, including Fernando Castro Pacheco, Fernando García Ponce and Gabriel Ramirez Aznar. There's also an outstanding display of Yucatecan embroidery and eight galleries of changing exhibits. Admission. ~ Pasaje de la Revolución 1907 x Calles 60 y 58; 9-928-3236.

The **Palacio Municipal** (City Hall) stands on the west side of the plaza. The third city hall to stand on the site since 1542, it was built in the 1850s, and from its clock tower to its Grecian columns it shows off the Romantic architecture of the era. Here the local government posts its last quarter's financial statements, showing how much it received in taxes and how the funds were spent, along with photographs of public events and projects the city has sponsored recently. ~ Calle 62.

On the north side of the plaza, the **Palacio del Gobierno** is the executive headquarters of the state of Yucatán. Mural-size paintings, some as large as 432 square feet, symbolically depict the struggle between Spanish conquerors and ancient Maya for the Yucatecan body and soul. The peninsula's most respected artist, Fernando Castro Pacheco, created the murals in the early 1970s as part of a series of 27 contemporary paintings intended to present fresh interpretations of Yucatán's cultural heritage. Maya mythology and Spanish cruelty loom as the main themes of the paintings that line the courtyard, while the triptych that wraps around the grand staircase to the upper floor depicts the battle between darkness and light within the Indian soul as described in the sacred Maya text *Popul Vuh*. The ballroomlike Hall of History on the second floor displays Castro's paintings of people and events in Yucatán history, including the War of the Castes, Fray Landa's burning of the Maya books, Mexican politicians and Cuban sugar planters selling the Maya people into slavery, and British pirates capturing Belize. The high doorways and balconies of the Hall of History afford a fine view of the Plaza de la Independencia. ~ Calle 61.

Half a block east of the Palacio del Gobierno, across the street from the side of the cathedral, is the small **Museo de la Ciudad de Mérida**. Models, drawings and photographs trace the history of Mérida from its Maya roots to the 20th century. This is also the best place to see sculptures and other artifacts from the Maya city of T'ho, which stood on this spot for centuries before falling prey to the Spanish Conquest's version of urban renewal. Admission. ~ Calle 61 between Calles 60 and 58; 9-961-2258.

The **Mercado Municipal** (Public Market) begins two blocks east and two blocks south of the Plaza de la Independencia. Mérida used to have five separate markets in the adjoining district, some for produce, meat and fish; others for handicrafts and household goods. As the city's population boomed, the several markets sprawled together into a somewhat disorganized maze of vendors' stalls, hole-in-the-wall retail shops and colorful crowds filling several blocks. Take a look at the exotic selection of tropical fruits offered for sale: *ciruela Maya, manililla, mamey, lima, mango indio, sapodilla* and papayas the size of watermelons. Of all the mouth-watering fruits sold at the Mercado Municipal, the most popular ones these days are red and golden delicious apples. Formerly all but unavailable in tropical Mexico, apples are now imported from the U.S. and considered a delicacy. Here, too, lots of fresh flowers and live birds are sold. Visit the meat department and turn vegetarian. There is a tourist-oriented *artesanía* section on the second floor of the main market, along with an array of food stalls. ~ Bounded by Calles 56, 65, 54 and 59. Another arts-and-crafts market, the **Mercado Garcia Rejon**, is nearby. ~ Calles 65 and 62.

A block north of the central Plaza de la Independencia, **Parque Hidalgo** is a busy little plaza full of sidewalk café tables and flanked by a movie theater, a bookstore and two fine old hotels. This plaza is a popular gathering place for foreign travelers as well as for hawkers selling hammocks and Panama hats. There are two **statues** in the park: one of the heroic Father Hidalgo, who launched Mexico's War of Independence, and one of General Cepeda Peraza, who fought with Benito Juárez against Porfirio Díaz in 1873. ~ Calles 60 and 59.

Across Calle 59 from Parque Hidalgo rises the old **Iglesia de Jesús,** where Mérida's aristocracy congregates for masses and weddings. It dates back to 1618. All of the stones used in its construction were salvaged from an ancient temple, and some in the church walls on the Calle 59 side still show traces of Maya carvings; inside, a room at the rear of the church contains exhibits of Spanish colonial art and artifacts. It is also commonly called Iglesia del Tercer Orden (Church of the Third Order), referring to a lay order of Franciscan monks who occupied the church when the Jesuits were expelled from Mexico in 1767. Adjoining the church on the other side, the peaceful little **Parque La Madre** features a marble replica of a mother-and-child sculpture by Lenoir; the original stands in the Luxembourg Gardens in Paris. Copies of other mother-and-child sculptures are found in virtually every town in the state of Yucatán. Part Virgin Mary, part Ixchel the moon goddess and part everybody's mom, wife and/or daughter, the ubiquitous madonna is yet another aspect of the Yucatán's unique spirit. ~ Calles 59 and 60.

Also across from Parque Hidalgo, the **Pinocoteca Juan Gamboa Guzman y Museo Gottdiener** presents a well-kept, starchy collection of old Yucatecan and European oil paintings, with a more contemporary sculpture gallery attached. Admission (free Saturday and Sunday). ~ Calle 59 between Calles 58 and 60.

From Parque Hidalgo, sightseers face a choice: continue strolling up Calle 60 with its galleries and shops for about six blocks to where it joins Paseo Montejo near the Museo de Antropología e Historia, or walk six blocks east through the narrow old streets to the Museo Regional de Arte Popular. While both museums are worth taking the time to see, they do not combine well into a single walking tour.

La Mejorada, a church built by Franciscan brothers in 1621 on what was then the eastern edge of the city, served for over two centuries as the Catholic center for study of Maya language and culture. Abandoned when the Franciscans were banished from Mexico in 1861, the old church became an Army barracks and later a decrepit, collapsing empty building. In recent times it was taken over by the Universidad de Yucatán, whose staff has renovated the old church with its impressive dome as office and classroom space for its architecture school. It's open to the public on a variable schedule. ~ Calles 59 and 50.

Located behind the church, the **Museo Regional de Arte Popular** pays tribute to the wild Mexican imagination in displays of handiwork by *indígenas* (native people) of the 32 Mexican states. Situated in a vast, decrepit-looking old colonial building with 20-foot-high ceilings, the museum also displays maps showing local folk arts and crafts of various villages throughout the Yucatán Peninsula. The museum shop offers a selection of fine artesanía, including beautifully embroidered women's dresses priced in the hundreds of U.S. dollars. ~ Calles 59 and 50.

A block south of La Mejorada and the folk art museum is the **Arco de los Dragones**, or Dragoons' Gate, so called because the adjoining building used to be an Army barracks. The gate was one of 11 that controlled passage into and out of the walled city of Mérida in the 1700s. Although the city outgrew its old fortress walls, in 1849 they saved the city when it came under siege by Maya revolutionaries during the War of the Castes. ~ Calle 61 between Calles 50 and 52.

Calle 60 is the center of downtown Mérida's arts district, thanks to the presence of the city's finest hotels as well as the **Teatro Peón Contreras**, a half-block-long cultural center of Italian design, full of fin-de-siècle flourishes, across Calle 60 from the Parque La Madre. The theater, named for a local poet, stages many theater and dance performances. During the morning hours you can climb the majestic Carrara marble staircase and enter the theater to marvel at its many levels of balconies and box seats and its frescoed dome. ~ Calles 60 and 57. The Yucatán tourist office is located at the corner of the theater facing the park.

The plaza officially named Parque Los Héroes but universally known as **Parque Santa Lucía** was a slave market and a terminal for horse-drawn carriages in centuries past. Today it features informal art exhibitions. Mérida's municipal government has been presenting La Serenata Yucateca, a free program of orchestral music and Yucatecan folk dancing, in this park every Thursday evening for nearly 30 years. **Iglesia de Santa Lucía**, facing the park, dates back to 1575 and served as a church for blacks and mulattos. Until 1821, its churchyard contained the municipal cemetery. ~ Calles 60 and 55.

Coins and currency are the focus of the **Coki Navarro Novelo Library** near Parque Santa Lucía. In addition to a collection of old and foreign money, the library has books on the subject in English and Spanish. Chronically short-staffed, this privately financed library is open erratic hours. If you find it closed, drop by later. ~ Calle 55 No. 510 A, upstairs.

Nine blocks southwest of the *zócalo* you'll find the tiny 18th-century **Ermita de Santa Isabel**, where pilgrims stayed en route from Campeche to view the holy relics of northern Yucatán's churches in the 18th and 19th centuries. Still used as a travelers' chapel by the faithful who come here to pray for safe journeys, the

◄ HIDDEN

AUTHOR FAVORITE

sights

Top on my list of sights to see around downtown Mérida are the **murals by artist Fernando Castro Pacheco** inside the Palacio del Gobierno. They offer a powerful Yucatán history lesson in any language—and it seems like a good idea for government officials to see paintings of horrific uprisings against oppression as they arrive at work in the morning. ~ Calle 61.

Ermita de Santa Isabel has a walled garden full of Maya sculptures. If you walk there along Calle 64, you will pass through an ornate old gate, one of two remaining entrance gates into the walled colonial city. ~ Calle 66 between Calles 77 and 79.

LODGING   Inconspicuously situated on a quiet downtown side street midway between Parque Hidalgo and the Museo Regional de Arte Popular, the **Calinda Panamerica Merida** is one of the plushest hotels in Mérida. The front part of the hotel includes a vast tiled court-yard lobby dating back to the turn-of-the-20th-century Porfirio Díaz era. The ornate opulence of that bygone era is kept alive in the hotel's common area, which features Corinthian columns that were imported from Europe. In stark contrast is the modern, nondescript highrise building behind the old part of the hotel, where the 114 guest rooms are located. There is a fine restaurant, as well as a bar and a nightclub that has fiestas on weekend nights, folk-dancing performances on other nights. Other guest facilities include a swimming pool and gift shop. Rooms, though lacking any hint of the colonial charm that the front lobby seems to promise, are big and have every amenity, including room service and satellite television with most U.S. cable networks. Air conditioning. ~ Calle 59 No. 455 at Calle 52; 9-923-9111, fax 9-924-8090, or 800-624-8451 in the U.S. DELUXE.

Centrally located on artsy Calle 60 near Parque Hidalgo, the **Misión Mérida** (the sign over the door says "Hotel Mérida") is a complete resort in a hacienda package, with a lobby/bar, restau-rant, pool, disco and shops set amid potted plants, beamed ceilings, fountains, urns and columns. The Spanish influence disappears in the 153 carpeted, contemporary rooms with demure color schemes, phones, satellite televisions and lovely views of the town. An im-pressive piece of Maya sculpture from the ancient city of T'ho, which stood where downtown Mérida is located today, was dis-

BARGAIN-PRICED ELEGANCE

Just on the other side of the movie theater from the Hotel Caribe, facing Parque Hidalgo, stands the **Gran Hotel**, Mérida's oldest hotel, dating back to 1894. Restored in historic style, this hotel offers one of the city's most affordably elegant lodging bargains. The 30 guest rooms have lofty ceilings and palace-size wooden double doors that open out onto spacious sitting areas decorated with 19th-century antiques, overlooking a central tropi-cal deco courtyard full of columns and plants. Rooms have TVs, phones and private baths. Some rooms have air conditioning. ~ Calle 60 No. 496; 9-924-7622, fax 9-924-7672. MODERATE.

covered by workers digging the foundation for this modern 11-story hotel. It is now on display near the front entrance. Air conditioning. ~ Calle 60 No. 488 at Calle 57; 9-923-9500, fax 9-923-7665. DELUXE.

Next door to the Misión Mérida, the **Casa del Balam** was formerly the mansion of the Barbachano family, pioneers in developing the Yucatán's tourist industry back in the 1930s. Today it is one of the city's most elegant vintage hotels. Wrought iron, fancy tilework and a courtyard fountain accent the colonial flavor of the common rooms, while the 54 guest rooms have been renovated to the highest standards of contemporary comfort. Amenities include a pool, sun deck, restaurant, two bars and a gift shop. Air conditioning. ~ Calle 60 No. 488 at Calle 57; 9-924-8844, fax 9-924-5011, or 800-624-8451 in the U.S.; e-mail balam@differ entworld.com. ULTRA-DELUXE.

The most offbeat and entertaining hotel in Mérida is the **Hotel Trinidad Galería**. It's in the same artsy-ritzy neighborhood as the Misión Mérida and Casa del Balam but in an extremely different price range. Rooms here are windowless and dark. Fans and private bathrooms make them a bargain. Some rooms have phones, and there are a none-too-clean swimming pool and a wildly overgrown central courtyard. The lobby, courtyard and common rooms are decorated with an amazing array of paintings, sculptures and found objects, including broken mannequins and colonial-era statues painted in bright colors. A life-size cutout of Charlie Chaplin stands beside the homemade fountain to greet guests as they enter the lobby, where the walls are filled with art by resident painters. Ceiling fans. ~ Calle 60 at Calle 51; 9-923-2463, fax 9-924-2319. BUDGET.

A more conventional, equally affordable hotel in the same area, the **Hotel Santa Lucía** has a swimming pool and offers amenities including color TV. Some of the plainly furnished rooms overlook a central courtyard with a fountain, while others have shuttered windows that open onto interior hallways. Air conditioning or ceiling fans. ~ Calle 55 No. 508; 9-928-2672, fax 9-924-6233. BUDGET.

Posada Toledo, a longtime favorite among Yucatán travelers in the know, is also the former home of a prominent Mérida family. It is smaller than the Casa del Balam—just 20 rooms and not nearly as luxurious—but its quiet, homelike feel makes it special. Guest accommodations are on two and a half floors surrounding a romantic tropical courtyard that overflows with flowering plants. Be sure to look at your room first. The quality of the guest quarters varies from room to room a lot more than the rates do, from high-ceilinged, antique-filled suites with spectacular decor to small, dark rooms devoid of charm. No television. Some rooms have air

Text continued on page 276.

Once and Future Transportation

etting there is a big part of the excitement when you choose one of the new modes of tourist transportation that is being introduced in Mérida and the Yucatán. Because both excursion-train and passenger-ship travel are operating on a trial basis, you'll want to check in advance to verify their current status before planning your vacation around them.

TRAINS

In the late 1990s, the Mexican government shut down its subsidized train system and offered to sell its rolling stock and rail routes to local governments or private companies. In most cases, the move spelled the end of Mexico's slow, decrepit, but very cheap passenger train service. The state of Yucatán bought the portion of the national rail system that linked Chiapas, Tabasco, Campeche and northern Yucatán with Mérida. In 2000, the state began operating a refurbished luxury excursion train, the Blue Train, from Mérida to Izamal (see Chapter Seven) and back. The scenic trip among old henequen plantations and past Maya villages lasted about 90 minutes each way and ran daily, on weekends, or on Sundays only, depending on the time of year, and cost about US$25. Because of the decline in tourism following the September 11, 2001, terrorist attacks in the United States, the Blue Train shut down—but may start running again. Check its current status at the tourist office in Mérida's Teatro Peón Contreras or at your hotel desk.

In early 2002, the state of Yucatán began using the former Blue Train's rolling stock for a much more ambitious project, the **Espreso Maya Train**. Carrying up to 128 passengers in coach class and 128 more in deluxe class, the air-conditioned train makes two-day (one-way) trips from Mérida to Palenque (see Chapter

Twelve), including a tour of Uxmal (Chapter Ten) and an overnight stop in Campeche city (Chapter Eleven). The return trip can be made on another train or by air or bus. Trips each direction run approximately once every two weeks except during September, and cost about US$500 (coach) to $700 (deluxe, including meals). Five-day excursions, including side trips by bus to other Maya sites, are also available. ~ 866-684-3019 in the U.S.

SHIPS

For several years there have been rumors of a new ferry between Tampa, Florida, and Progreso, Yucatán, the seaport near Mérida. Originally scheduled to start service in late 1999, the ferry became mired in regulatory permit problems, but as this book goes to press it appears definite that the first Yucatán Express will depart Tampa for Progreso in November 2002. Operated by a Canadian-based cruise line, the "ferry" is actually an eight-deck luxury liner, the *Scotia Prince*, also used for cruises between Maine and Nova Scotia during the summer months. It has sleeping accommodations for 1100 passengers and can carry 200 cars or motor homes. Shipboard amenities on the 36-hour trip include fine dining, entertainment and casino gaming. Departures are scheduled from Tampa on Fridays and Tuesdays. After a six-month trial, the cruise line hopes to expand service to include a stop at one of the new cruise-ship docks being opened near Cancún and Playa del Carmen. Roundtrip passenger fares cost significantly more than flying from Florida to Cancún but about the same as a three- or four-day cruise to the Bahamas; taking your car costs about the same as renting a compact car for ten days. ~ 800-514-3935, or 866-466-3935 in the U.S.; www.yucatanexpress.com, e-mail holidayinfo@yucatanexpress.com.

conditioning. ~ Calle 58 at Calle 57; 9-923-1690, fax 9-923-2256; e-mail hptoledo@finred.com.mx. BUDGET TO MODERATE.

Nearby, the larger **Hotel Maya Yucatán** has 80 clean, modern guest rooms with cheery folk-art-and-flowers decor and cable TV. A large swimming pool fills the courtyard area, and there's just about every commercial facility you could want in a hotel, including a restaurant, lobby bar, nightclub, travel agency and tobacconist, as well as a guarded parking lot. Air conditioning. ~ Calle 58 No. 483 between Calles 55 and 57; 9-923-5395, fax 9-923-4642, or 800-812-0088 in the U.S.; www.hotelmayayucatan.com, e-mail info@hotelmayayucatan.com. MODERATE.

The best-located of Mérida's youth hostels, **The Nameless Place** is an old colonial home two blocks from the *zócalo*. It has one large co-ed dorm opening onto a central patio. The 12 single and double beds are stacked three-high. Amenities include shared baths with hot water, kitchen and laundry facilities and internet access, and the cost is under $6 a night. There are also two private rooms with separate baths. ~ Calle 57 No. 495 between Calles 58 and 60; 9-918-4500; e-mail espejo@yahoo.com. BUDGET.

Farther from the center of things, the larger **Nomades Youth Hostel** has 35 beds in separate men's and women's dorms, as well as private rooms, in a historic house in a safe neighborhood. The shared baths have 24-hour hot water. Other amenities include kitchen privileges, lockers, a cable TV room and internet access. ~ Calle 62 No. 433 at Calle 51; 9-923-2033, fax 9-928-1697; e-mail nomades1@prodigy.net.mx. BUDGET.

The delightful old **Hotel Caribe** occupies a balcony-laced colonial-style building overlooking Parque Hidalgo. The building was originally a 17th-century Catholic college, but there's nothing austere about the accommodations today. The beam-ceilinged lobby, where a suit of armor is on display, opens into a courtyard restaurant. The 53 comfortable rooms and suites have tiled floors, phones, simple furnishings, TVs and balconies. Rooms have either air conditioning or ceiling fans. ~ Calle 59 No. 500; 9-923-6963, fax 9-924-8733; www.hotelcaribe.com.mx, e-mail reservaciones@hotelcaribe.com.mx. MODERATE.

Two blocks west of the *zócalo*, the elegant little **Misión de Fray Diego** is a 17th-century colonial residence converted into a hotel. The 26 rather austere guest rooms and suites, each with two double beds, open onto a lovely central courtyard with a fountain. Accommodations are designed with business travelers in mind: rooms have large desks and extension phones, and there's a business services center. Other amenities include a swimming pool and off-street parking. Guests are entitled to courtesy green fees at one of Mérida's two golf clubs. ~ Calle 61 No. 524 between 64 and 66; 9-921-0599, fax 9-923-7397, or 866-639-2933 in the U.S.; www.lamisiondefraydiego.com, e-mail res@la misiondefraydiego.com. DELUXE.

"Gay-owned and straight-friendly," the **CasaRamos59** offers three apartments (with seven more in the planning stages) on a daily, weekly or monthly basis. In a hundred-year-old residence, the accommodations are simply and tastefully decorated, mostly in white, with archway windows. Privacy is paramount. ~ Calle 59 No. 541 between Calles 66 and 68; 9-928-3626; www.casa ramos59.com. MODERATE.

Sister hotel to the smaller low-priced lodging of the same name at Chichén Itzá, the **Dolores Alba Mérida** has expanded from a colonial-era residence to a 95-room hotel with two court-yards and one of the cleanest swimming pools in town. The clean, modest rooms open onto open-air sitting areas sheltered by arcades. The guest rooms have private baths. The hotel has guarded off-street parking. The location is close to the main pub-lic market. Air conditioning; ceiling fans. ~ Calle 63 No. 464; 9-928-5650, fax 9-928-3163; www.doloresalbalcom, e-mail info@ doloresalba.com. BUDGET TO MODERATE.

DINING

A leisurely breakfast spot is the outdoor **Cafetería El Mesón** in front of the Hotel Caribe in Parque Hidalgo, a popular gathering place for international travelers. Enjoy an omelet, an enchilada or a fruit salad at an umbrella-shaded wrought-iron table while you try to resist the moneychangers and hammock and Panama hat ven-dors who work the park day and night. ~ Calle 59 No. 500; 9-924-9232. MODERATE.

Also at Parque Hidalgo, **El Patio Español** in the Gran Hotel presents traditional Spanish dishes such as paella Valenciana as well as Yucatecan regional cuisine in an atmosphere that takes full advantage of its Spanish colonial architecture to create an Old World ambience right out of Don Quixote. ~ Calle 60 No. 496; 9-924-7730. MODERATE.

The classic coffeehouse and hangout for locals and foreign visitors alike is bustling, high-ceilinged **Café Express**. The service can be slow and the surroundings noisy; nevertheless, it's a de-

LIBROS EN INGLÉS

One of the best places in Mérida to find out more about Yucatecan culture and events, the **Mérida English Library** was started in 1999 by a group of *norteamericano* expatriates. It now has a sizable collection of English-language books, as well as videos, audiotapes and computers. The library also serves as a meeting place for visitors and English-speaking locals alike, with a community bulletin and a game room featuring backgam-mon, and hosts many social events. ~ Calle 53 No. 524; phone/fax 9-923-3319.

lightful spot to nurse a coffee, watch the people pass in the Parque Hidalgo across the street or write postcards under the whirling ceiling fans, the Express also has good food, from yogurt to *pavo escabeche* to *pollo pibil*. ~ Calle 60 No. 502 at Calle 59; 9-921-3738. BUDGET.

A great little semivegetarian café in downtown Mérida is **Amaro**. Set in a sunny, white, open-air courtyard away from the street noise, this restaurant was formerly the Ananda Maya, an East Indian run vegetarian eatery that catered to a clientele of international travelers with its health-conscious, vegetarian dishes. Now under new management, the restaurant seems bent on keeping the old clientele but broadening its menu into the mainstream. While you can still get some vegetarian stir-fry and pasta dishes as well as beverages made with *chia* and aloe vera, the menu emphasizes more conventional Yucatecan and Mexican food. ~ Calle 59 No. 507 between Calles 60 and 62; 9-928-2451. BUDGET.

Dine inside in an air-conditioned colonial salon or outside on a starlit patio at **Portico del Peregrino**, a sweet old-fashioned restaurant near the university. Selections on the international menu include seafood *zarzuela*, beef fillet in mustard sauce and baked eggplant, as well as Yucatecan specialties. ~ Calle 57 No. 501; 9-928-6163. MODERATE.

La Belle Epoca, upstairs in the Hotel del Parque, serves regional and international cuisine such as chateaubriand with béarnaise sauce, eggplant parmesan and grilled beef à la Yucateca in a lavish atmosphere of ornate 19th-century elegance. ~ Calle 60 No. 497; 9-928-1928. DELUXE.

If you're ready for a break from regional cuisine, dip into some zesty Italian cooking at charming **La Casona**. Occupying a fine old restored house with a lush interior garden near Paseo Montejo,

AUTHOR FAVORITE

I first discovered there was much more to "Mexican food" than my gringo tastebuds had realized when I sampled the *pollo ticuleño* (breaded chicken in a special sauce) at **Los Almendros** more than 20 years ago. Even today the unique flavors have lost none of their appeal for me, and the best place to enjoy them is still the restaurant run by the family that "invented" Yucatecan cuisine and *poc-chuc*. One of Mérida's finest regional restaurants, Los Almendros is a higher-priced, big-city spinoff of the little eatery in the Maya town of Ticul, some 37 miles south of Mérida. The spacious, air-conditioned, cheerful, turbulent restaurant buzzes with employees in regional costumes. Menus include photos and translations of all selections. ~ Calle 50 No. 493 between Calles 57 and 59; 9-928-5459. MODERATE.

La Casona serves homemade pasta, steaks, seafood and soups. Try the manicotti, osso buco or spinach calzone. ~ Calle 60 No. 434; 9-923-9996. MODERATE.

Mérida has a large Lebanese subculture, and some of its finest restaurants feature cuisine from Lebanon. **Alberto's Continental Patio** serves specialties such as shish kebab, hummus, tabbouleh and fried *kibbee*, as well as other choices ranging from spaghetti to sea bass, in a beautiful white colonial building erected in 1727 over the rubble of a Maya mound. Old statues, lamp-lit eaves and a courtyard full of antiques give it the air of an enchanted monastery. ~ Calle 64 No. 482; 9-928-5367. DELUXE.

The Yucatán is less than 400 miles from Cuba, so Cuban expatriates are a major influence in both the art and restaurant scenes around Mérida. A good, authentic Cuban restaurant in the downtown area is **El Tucho**. The air-conditioned restaurant features specialties like roast suckling pig, sleeping black beans, green banana fisticuffs and Mojitos cocktails. ~ Calle 60 No. 482 between Calles 55 and 57; 9-928-2858. MODERATE.

SHOPPING

Souvenir and gift items typical of the Yucatán include *guayaberas* (pleated men's dress shirts), *huipiles* (beautifully embroidered native dresses), hammocks (the world's best and brightest) and Panama hats, available all over Mérida. With a little negotiating, prices are much better than in Cancún or around Chichén Itzá. In the *zócalo* and Parque Hidalgo, hat and hammock sellers of all ages are drawn to foreign travelers like flies to honey. The two main retail shopping districts are the public market area and the shops, galleries and boutiques north of the *zócalo* along Calle 60.

The **Mercado Municipal** is the nucleus of a rambling four-block area bursting with bohemian madness. Hammock vendors will attach themselves to you like long-lost friends. Children will dog your footsteps and beggars will put demands on your generosity. Mosquito coils, toothbrushes, bouquets of radishes and pyramids of grapes swell the outdoor aisles. The indoor stalls are packed with *huaraches*, sombreros, guitars and exquisitely embroidered *huipiles,* as well as exotic items like live two-inch-long scarab beetles bedecked with costume jewels (people wear them). A maudlin local fairy tale, which any beetle vendor will be happy to share with you, says that the first *maquech* was a Maya prince who asked to be transformed into a beetle to stay close to the heart of a forbidden princess. Unfortunately, to this day nobody has figured out how to change the beetle back into a prince. U.S. Customs will not allow you to take one of these little guys home. ~ Calles 65 and 56.

Two large gift shops among many in the bazaar are **Curios Lucy** ~ Calle 56; 9-923-7491 and **Bazar de Artesanías Mexicanas** ~ Calle 56. Besides locally made items, numerous shops sell clothing and rugs from the state of Oaxaca and silver from Taxco, in Guerrero. These and other items that are not made in the Yucatán are quite expensive, often costing as much here as they would in the United States. Taxco silver costs more in the market than it does in retail stores along Calle 60.

One of the embroidered white *huipiles* (often called "hipiles" —pronounced EE–pee–lays—among the Maya) that the village women wear might make a great souvenir or gift. Maya women have worn these dresses ever since the Church came along in the 1500s preaching modesty. Modern Mérida women would not be caught wearing *huipiles,* which are viewed as low-class, countrified garb. Back in the United States, though, these dresses become stunning. Commercial *huipiles* are usually made of synthetic fabrics and embroidered with a sewing machine. Fine hand-embroidered, 100 percent cotton *huipiles* can be found if you search diligently. They cost much more.

> It seems amazing that there could be buyers for all the hammocks in Mérida's *mercados*, but they are not just for the tourist trade. Hammocks are the main item of furniture in every Yucatecan hut, and more people possess hammocks than own shoes.

For men, *guayaberas,* four-pocket dress shirts decorated with elaborate double stitching and lots of little buttons that don't fasten to anything, are the tropical equivalent of a coat and tie. A *guayabera* will satisfy the dress code in the fanciest restaurants in the Yucatán. Unless you live in Miami, however, you may not have much occasion to wear it back home.

A quieter place to browse is the government-run **Casa de los Artesanías,** which gathers Christmas ornaments, ceramic devils, painted urns, straw bags and crafts from all over Mexico under one roof. ~ Casa de la Cultura de Mayab, Calle 63 No. 503; 9-928-6676.

Visitors who buy hammocks from street vendors are likely to overpay. The municipal market is the place to get the best hammocks. Village people all over the Yucatán spend their days weaving hammocks and sending them to the Mérida marketplace for sale. The two factors that determine a hammock's quality are its size and the thickness of the strands. The cotton ones are cheaper, but nylon is finer. One of the best places to buy hammocks is **Tejidos y Cordeles Nacionales,** a cooperative shop with 10,000 hammocks to choose from. ~ Calle 56 No. 516-B; 9-921-3368. Two other good hammock stores are **El Hamaguero** ~ Calle 58 No. 572 and **El Campesino** ~ Calle 58 No. 543, both between Calles 69 and 71. The shops, which are also family factories, have rooms where you can try the hammock before you buy. Bargaining is in order at both stores.

Shops along Calle 60 range from blatantly tourist-oriented curio shops to fine art galleries. Selections of quality folk art and *traje* clothing from all over Mexico can be seen at **Artesanías**

Mexicanas ~ Calle 60 No. 443-2; 9-928-6186 and **Perla Maya** ~ Calle 60 No. 485; 9-928-5886. **El Paso** has bright batik blouses, handblown glass and wooden *santos* (statues of saints). ~ Calle 60 No. 501; 9-921-2828. Next door, snazzy **Galería Mexicana** stocks exquisite vases and smashing jewelry, along with toys, books and art postcards. ~ Calle 60 at Calle 59; 9-924-5211. Up the street, colonial-style **Fernando Huertas** shines with unusual jewelry, sculptures and women's fashions displayed in antique armoires. ~ Calle 59 No. 511; 9-921-6035. **Guayaberas Jack** has good-quality *huipiles*. The shop also carries cool, stylishly tailored *guayaberas*. ~ Calle 59 No. 507; 9-928-6002. For a good *jipi* hat, try **Becal Panama Hats**. ~ Calle 60 No. 527-A; 9-927-9896.

Mexico Lindo, next door to the hotel Casa de Balam, dazzles with Taxco silver jewelry. ~ Calle 60 No. 486; 9-923-5043. A fascinating antique shop featuring colonial furniture, clocks and mirrors, with a few museum-quality pieces, is **Antiguedades Imporio**. ~ Calle 60 No. 455 at Calle 51; 9-921-0126. Across the street, the **Galería Manolo Rivero** showcases modern art from all over the world. ~ Calle 60; 9-921-0935. For the best in local art, search out **Galería de Arte**, which exhibits paintings, engravings and sculptures by Yucatecan artists. ~ Calle 53 No. 502, between Calles 60 and 58.

On Parque Hidalgo, a **Librería Dante** store has a great selection of maps and books on the Yucatán's ancient Maya sites available in English, Spanish and other languages. This and almost all other bookstores in the Yucatán are owned by the region's largest publishing house, Editorial Dante, which puts out everything from college textbooks to tourist-oriented comics. ~ Calle 60 at Calle 57; 9-924-9522.

The **Plaza Internacional**, located near Parque Hidalgo, is the best example of a new trend: historic district gentrification, where old mansions are converted to fashionable off-street shopping malls. Inside this grandiose 17th-century residence are boutiques, galleries and shops, as well as a free art exhibition in the corridors, tourist services such as a long-distance telephone shop and a currency exchange, and shaded tables in the central courtyard, where you can sample the mostly American-style fast food or just rest your feet. ~ Calle 58 at Calle 59; 9-924-8060.

Mérida's municipal government sponsors nightly entertainment in public places around the city. All weeknight performances are free and start at 9 p.m. year-round. The biggest event of the week is on Sunday, from 9 a.m. to 9 p.m., when the streets surrounding the Plaza de la Independencia are closed to motor vehicles. Concerts ring out from the adjoining municipal buildings as street theater and sidewalk vendors fill the city center with a festive atmosphere. Don't miss the **bazaar** in Parque Santa Lucía,

NIGHTLIFE

where artisans and local cooks show off their talents to visitors. ~ Calles 60 and 55.

Every Monday night, the plaza in the **Palacio Municipal** on the west side of the *zócalo* is the scene of a regional *vaquería*, a Mexican cowboy fiesta with traditional dress and dancing that recalls the era of the great haciendas. ~ Calle 62.

On Tuesday, a **Musical Memories concert** features the big-band music of Glenn Miller and Benny Goodman with a Mexican accent in Parque Santiago, in front of the Rex movie theater. ~ Calles 59 and 72. Another popular Tuesday-night event is the **Ballet Folklórico de la Universidad de Yucatán**, which performs at the Teatro Peón Contreras. Admission. ~ Calles 60 and 57.

Scarab beetles, called *maquech,* have been decorated and used as jewelry by the Maya since ancient times.

On Wednesday, the **Casa Cultural de Artesanías** hosts string quartets and piano concertos. ~ Calle 63 between Calles 64 and 66.

Thursday evening's event, **La Serenata Yucateca**, is the most popular of all the city's concerts, drawing a large crowd of both locals and visitors to view outstanding Yucatecan folk-dancing performances. It has been held in Parque Santa Lucía weekly since 1966. ~ Calles 60 and 55.

When Friday night rolls around, the central courtyard at the University of Yucatán becomes the romantic setting for the **University Students' Serenade**, blending chorale music with lots of youthful public displays of affection. ~ Calles 57 and 60.

On Saturday, the public event is a 6 p.m. mass held in English at **Santa Lucía Church**, directly across from the park of the same name. Later on Saturday evening, people pack the discos. ~ Calles 60 and 55.

Mérida has a fairly sophisticated nightclub scene. Soak yourself in sentiment at **El Trovador Bohemio** near Parque Santa Lucía. The piano bar features singers of the Mexican moonlight-and-roses genre, Mérida's forte. El Trovador is very dim and crowded, with professional performances. Cover. ~ Calle 55 No. 550; 9-923-0385.

Livelier nightlife can be found along Calle 60, where **El Tucho** presents Cuban-style nightclub shows with lavishly costumed dancers and hot salsa music. Entertainment starts late in the evening, and there is a hefty cover charge. ~ Calle 60 No. 482; 9-928-2858. **Pancho's** has the kind of atmosphere that might make you think you're back in Cancún, with its gaudy decor, pricey drinks, endless party atmosphere and waiters in sombreros (ask nice and you can wear one, too), but the club presents some of the hottest Latin dance bands in the downtown area and there's no cover charge. ~ Calle 59 No. 509, between Calles 60 and 62; 9-924-7465.

The **Café Peón Contreras** in the pedestrian-only street at the side of the Teatro Peón Contreras, serves up espresso, cappuccino and latté made with real Cuban coffee, as well as pastries and live guitar music. This place livens up when the theater lets out. ~ Calle 57 at Calle 60.

Visitors who venture to the outer suburbs of Mérida soon realize that only in the downtown area is tourism an important industry. On the outskirts, you can't help but notice the city's *real* economic mainstay—quarrying limestone and converting it into cement. Fortunately, it doesn't take long to drive from the city center to open countryside.

Beyond Downtown Mérida

Early in the 20th century, Mérida's economy did not depend on either tourists or cement, but on rope. Wealthy plantation owners who grew and exported most of the world's supply of sisal for rope-making built grand mansions along the Paseo Montejo, creating an elegant boulevard to rival those of European capitals. In those days, the full extent of the city was within walking distance from the *zócalo*. Today, although its grand facades share the street with modern commercial development, the paseo still makes for pleasant walking and reflection on yet another of the bygone eras that make up Mérida's long history. If that's not enough to quench your urge for urban exploring, take a *calesa* or taxi ride to the city's largest park and see how local families enjoy themselves.

SIGHTS

Just past the Parque Santa Ana, a seven-block stroll or an entertaining horse-drawn taxi ride north from the main plaza, Calle 60 bends into the broad **Paseo Montejo**, named for the city's founder. This grand boulevard, with its sidewalk cafés and roundabout monuments, was inspired by the Champs-Élysées and was once lined with French-style mansions, the spoils of rich henequen landowners who tried to give Mérida a Parisian accent. Sadly, many of these little castles are being replaced by modern construction, while others are becoming bank buildings. Banks along Paseo Montejo are easier to find and usually much less crowded than those downtown. Where this boulevard intersects Avenida Colón, the **Monumento a Justo Sierra** honors the turn-of-the-20th-century scholar and supreme court justice whose philosophical writings helped inspire the Mexican Revolution. About a mile west on Avenida Colón, a sculptural tour de force, the **Parque de las Américas**, covers four square blocks, with a different landmark at each corner. The park is planted with trees from every nation in the Americas. Two blocks farther north on Paseo Montejo, the **Monumento a la Patria** (Monument to the Nation) presents a magnificent sculpture-in-the-round by Rómulo Rozo depicting the history of Mexico, Maya style.

At the south end of Paseo Montejo, the **Museo de Antropología e Historia** is housed in the spacious, high-ceilinged Palacio Cantón, a former governor's mansion, and displays the finest collection of Maya artifacts in the Yucatán. The two-story museum provides a wonderful introduction to the archaeological mysteries of the Yucatán and Chiapas. Exhibits, which cover all facets of pre-Hispanic Maya life, include sculptures, stelae and murals removed from various ruins, as well as pottery and other artifacts discovered during their excavation, before-and-after historical pictures of several restored ruins, and photos and models of little known Maya sites. You'll learn about the complex Maya calendar system and see replicas of pages from the few Maya books that survived the Spanish invasion. You'll also find information about many lowland Maya sites and see firsthand many of the finest sculptures that were discovered at these ruins. There are even exhibits describing Maya beauty practices, such as setting precious stones in their teeth and flattening the craniums of newborn babies. The exhibit captions are in Spanish, but freelance English-speaking guides may approach you as you enter the museum. A good bookstore sells museum guides in English, French, German and Japanese. Admission. ~ Paseo Montejo and Calle 43; 9-923-0557.

A moderate taxi or *calesa* trip from downtown, **Parque El Centenario** and the free **Mérida Zoo** are located on Mérida's west side along Avenida de las Itzaes, the *periférico* that becomes Route 180 south to Uxmal and Campeche. Most of the city's largest park is filled with playground equipment, fanciful statues and shady trees under which parents rig their hammocks to relax while the kids play. There are refreshment stands and a miniature train. The zoo, though small and old-fashioned, has lions and tigers, as well as regional wildlife such as the tapir and the tepezcuintle, a greenish-furred, cat-sized nocturnal rodent native to the Yucatán jungle and hunted by Maya villagers for its meat, which is considered a delicacy. You'll also find an impressive collection of sheep and goat species from around the world. The centerpiece of the zoo is a big, wooded walk-in aviary full of regional birds. Nearby, the **Museo Interactivo de Historia Natural** displays plant and animal exhibits in a 19th-century mansion. The highlight of this small, free museum is an impressive collection of butterflies, beetles and other insects of the Yucatán. ~ Calles 59 and 84.

sights

AUTHOR FAVORITE

I like to ride in **calesas**, old-fashioned horse-drawn carriages that used to be commonplace in most Mexican cities but now roll on only in Mérida. It's not just the romance of the ride, but also the stately pace, stacking up buses, trucks and taxis for blocks and reminding me that once in a while, time *can* stand still.

Unless you know someone who lives in Mérida, about the only time you'll have occasion to visit the suburbs is when you head out of town. The suburbs, called *colonias*, range from poverty-ridden barrios on the city's west side to prosperous northern and northeastern neighborhoods of large new houses whose yards burst with flowers. Travelers heading for Chichén Itzá take Calle 65 east; it becomes Route 180 eastbound. Those going to Dzibil-chaltún and Progreso follow Paseo Montejo north; it becomes Route 261 northbound.

The Maya town of **Umán**, 17 kilometers south of Mérida on Route 180, is Mérida's major suburb, with a population larger than all the other indigenous villages surrounding the city combined. Most of the Maya vendors in Mérida live here. Until recently, any time you left Mérida going south, whether you planned to take Route 281 westbound to Celestún, Route 261 toward Uxmal or Route 180 toward Campeche, you would find yourself in Umán, where the three highways divide at the town plaza. Aside from its Maya residents, the town's main attraction is its huge, late-18th-century church, crowned by a drum-shaped upper story that has 16 stained-glass windows and a broad dome. As impressive as the exterior architecture of this fortresslike church may be, the interior is very plain except for a wooden pulpit hand-carved with images of Saints Matthew, Mark, Luke and John.

Traffic congestion has became so bad in recent years that a new bypass route has been built around Umán for motorists driving to Uxmal or Campeche. So if you don't want to visit Umán, turn east from Avenida de los Itzaes onto the Anillo Periférico freeway; the bypass is clearly marked.

LODGING

The tallest building in Mérida until a few years ago, the **Holiday Inn** has a pool, tennis courts and one of the most upscale discos in town, as well as clothing boutiques and other pricey shops off the lobby. All 193 rooms have minibars and satellite TV with the most popular English-language cable networks from the U.S. In fact, if you stay here you might forget that you're not in the United States. Because of its distance from downtown, the Holiday Inn is a viable option only if you have a car or, better yet, lots and lots of small bills for taxi fares. Air conditioning. ~ Avenida Colón 498 at Paseo Montejo; 9-925-6877, fax 9-925-7755. ULTRA-DELUXE.

Today, the city's tallest building is the 17-story **Hyatt Regency**. This gleaming edifice, with its curvilinear lobby of gleaming brass and polished stone, looks so shiny and clean that you may feel uneasy about marring it with fingerprints or footprints. Part of the reason is that the lobby, like the 304 rooms, stands empty much of the time. Designed to meet the standards of international businessmen and political VIPs, the Hyatt opened in 1994, just months before the Mexican economy plunged into its deepest recession

Discovering Mérida's Wilderness

In the early 1990s, when Mérida's population started exploding and industrialization began its southward sprawl, local environmentalists persuaded the municipal government that archaeological and natural treasures on the city's outskirts were in grave danger of being lost forever. The city fathers responded by creating Reserva Ecologica Cuxtal, a 26,500-acre protected area just off the Anillo Periférico freeway south of town. Spend a day driving through the reserve to experience Mérida's wilderness. From beginning to end, the drive around the reserve is about 70 kilometers long and takes about two hours plus stops.

RESERVA ECOLOGICA CUXTAL   Reserva Ecologica Cuxtal contains seven large *henequén* haciendas dating back to the 19th century, as well as more than a dozen minor Maya archaeological sites and seven cenotes. It also encompasses several small Maya villages, ranging in size from 200 to 600 inhabitants descended from former plantation workers. The villagers depend on farming for their livelihood. Also within the reserve is the city's water treatment plant. Wildlife in the forest includes white-tailed deer, armadillos, boa constrictors, iguanas and a great diversity of bird life. To reconcile preservation, population and public utilities, the city prohibited further development in the reserve and set aside a network of forested greenways that preserve bird and animal habitat while linking all the haciendas and archaeological sites. Most of the haciendas are open to the public, and many are used by the local Maya as modern-day "ceremonial centers" for traditional fiestas. Reaching the reserve is easy. Three mostly unpaved roads enter it from the Periférico Anillo, the freeway that rings the city. For the most comprehensive driving tour, take Calle 42 south from the city, and across the *periférico*.

in 50 years. It was seized by creditors under Mexican bankruptcy law before it had been open a year, but today it seems to have regained a solid financial footing, largely by charging. Cancún-like room rates to visiting businessmen and politicos. The Hyatt's greatest virtue is its magnificent rooftop pool, aglow in the evening with starry skies and city lights. Air conditioning. ~ Calle 60 No. 344; 9-942-0202, fax 9-925-7002, or 800-228-9000 in the U.S.; www.hyatt.com. ULTRA-DELUXE.

The **Fiesta Americana Mérida** is the city's largest and most expensive hotel. Opened in January 1995, less than two weeks after the Mexican economy plunged into economic crisis, the hotel continued to limp along through the recession in the hope that

HACIENDA SAN ANTONIO TAHDZIBICHÉN   Just 14 kilometers south, this stately hacienda dating back to 1873 is marked by a brick-red Maya-style arched gateway. The front of the residence is a portico supported by graceful Moorish columns, looking out over an expansive, immaculately trimmed lawn and surrounded by tall shade trees. The traditional feast day here is the Fiesta de San Antonio de Padua, celebrated on June 13 with parades, dancing and other festivities.

HACIENDA SAN PEDRO CHIMAY   Continue on the same road until it forks. Take the left fork, and soon the tall smokestack of the hacienda's sisal factory with its strangely shaped top comes into view. This was one of the first *henequén* plantations in the Mérida area, started in 1852. Today it is beautifully restored and remains under private ownership. The Fiesta de San Pedro is celebrated here each June with processions and dances. The road forks here. Take the unpaved fork to the south (right) toward the little farming village of Tekit de Regil.

HACIENDA SAN NICOLÁS DZOYAXCHE   The road leaves the park boundaries for a few kilometers. Turn right (west) at the intersection in Tekit de Regil and you're on your way back into the reserve. The road turns south at the reserve boundary; turn right (west) again and you'll almost immediately find yourself at the enigmatically beautiful Hacienda San Nicolás Dzoyaxche, where the reserve's visitor facilities are located. The approximately 500 people who live around this southernmost hacienda offer an array of outdoor activities including horseback riding, hiking, camping and swimming in Cenote Dzonot-Ich. Tent camping is permitted nearby.

HACIENDA SAN IGNACIO TESIP   Continue west from San Nicolás Dzoyaxche until you reach the village of Molas. Turn right (northeast) and you'll come to hacienda San Ignacio Tesip, remodeled and brightly painted in red, white and gold against a backdrop of broad green lawn and trees. Then, after passing the water treatment plant, the route returns you to the fork in the road that took you into the reserve in the first place.

Mérida would some day see enough wealthy visitors to fill the 350 highest-priced rooms in town, and gradually that wish has come true. The nine-story hotel is dwarfed by the skyscraper Hyatt Regency across the street, but it fills a city block. The architecture is styled after the Bella Epoca elegance of Paseo Montejo mansions, but on a massive scale. The rooms are modern and exceptionally large, with king-size beds and separate sitting areas, and such amenities as robes and computer data ports; some have jacuzzis. Facilities include a pool, a sauna, steam and exercise rooms, a tennis court and computer rentals. Air conditioning. ~ Paseo Montejo 451; 9-942-1111, fax 9-942-1112. ULTRA-DELUXE.

Restoring one of the most elegant mansions of Mérida's glory days, the new **Villa Mercedes** has 84 rooms decorated in Bella Epoca style. Originally built in 1903, the hotel remained the private residence of one of the city's most prominent families until 1998. The ornate mosaic floors and massive pillars that grace the reception area have been restored, and stained glass windows and Art Nouveau details have been recreated from the builders' original drawings. Facilities include a restaurant, bar, swimming pool and meeting rooms. Air conditioning. ~ Avenida Colón 500; 9-942-9000, fax 9-942-9001; www.hotelvillamercedes. com. ULTRA-DELUXE.

Offering somewhat lower rates than the Holiday Inn, the very attractive **Montejo Palace** couldn't be better located on the city's classiest boulevard, a block from the anthropology museum. What this hotel makes up for in location, it lacks in character. It's a pretty ordinary hostelry in a city full of hotels that ooze colonial charm. The 90 guest rooms and suites have white walls, traditional Spanish-style furniture and balconies overlooking the courtyard. Facilities include a swimming pool, a rooftop nightclub and room service. It is possible to walk to the downtown *zócalo* from here, though you may be worn out by the time you get there. Taxis and *calesas* wait beside the museum. ~ Paseo Montejo 483; 9-924-6046, fax 9-928-0388. MODERATE TO DELUXE.

Casa Mexilio is a unique B&B inn concealed in a pleasant residential neighborhood on Mérida's west side, four blocks from the parque central and five from the bus terminal. Developed by

AUTHOR FAVORITE

If money were no object, my favorite place to spend the night in the Mérida area would be the **Hacienda Xcanatún**, just north of the city. One of the oldest haciendas in Yucatán, Xcanatún dates back to the mid-1700s and was expanded to its present mansion-like size in the early-20th-century henequen boom. The plantation was abandoned in 1980, then reduced to ruins by hurricanes. Saved by the state of Yucatán's historic hacienda restoration project, Xcanatún's main house and other major structures have been rebuilt. There are six large suites in the main house and four in the old machine building, which also houses a restaurant and bar. Fountains and pools grace the beautifully landscaped grounds. Guest rooms feature private verandas and jacuzzis. Air conditioning. ~ Tablaje Rustico Catastral 13667, Xcanatún (from Mérida, take the Prolongación Montejo north toward Progreso, turn right at the pedestrian bridge at Km. 12 and follow the signs); phone/fax 9-941-0213; e-mail hacienda@ xcanatun.com. ULTRA-DELUXE.

a partnership of Mexican and *norteamericano* innkeepers, it features extravagant decor blending elements from around the world: French tapestries, oriental rugs and dark, massive, rustic furniture. The five rooms have loft sleeping areas. A central sitting room has a TV, hammock and small library. To make reservations from the U.S., call the Turquoise Reef Group (800-538-6802), an agency based in Colorado that also arranges stays at remote lodges in Quintana Roo's Sian Ka'an Biosphere Reserve. ~ Calle 68 No. 495; 9-928-2505, or 800-538-6802 in the U.S.; www. mexicoholiday.com/destinations/mexilio, e-mail info@turqreef. com. MODERATE.

Hidden away in Colonia Itzamna, a quiet residential neighborhood north of downtown, the **Tranquilo Guest House** has simple rooms and an ultra-mellow atmosphere. The small bed and breakfast offers gourmet vegetarian meals, meditation and yoga sessions and workshops on stress reduction led by the owner, an expatriate psychologist from Canada. ~ Calle 58 No. 301-A between Calles 25 and 27; phone/fax 9-927-9634; e-mail mexicanretreat@ gmx.net. MODERATE.

◀ HIDDEN

DINING

The east side of Paseo Montejo is lined with restaurants of every description, though their numbers are dwindling. Many of the restaurants change hands (and names) often. An old standby that has occupied the same location since 1973 is **Leo Restaurant**, a grill with tables outdoors on the sidewalk surrounded by a jungle of potted palms. Charbroiled beef, pork and chicken are the specialties. ~ Paseo Montejo 460; 9-927-6514. MODERATE.

At the other end of the Paseo Montejo hotel zone, two big, informal restaurants are the busiest in the area. **Sanborn's**, located in the department store of the same name on the ground level of the huge Fiesta Americana hotel, is somewhat upscale and designed with serious shoppers in mind. The international menu features sandwiches, salads and delicate portions of seafood or chicken, and it's probably the cleanest-looking café in the city. ~ Paseo Montejo 451-C; 9-925-2522. MODERATE.

Directly across the street from Sanborn's is Mérida's only **Vip's**, a location of the nationwide café chain that is Mexico's homegrown equivalent to Denny's, or maybe Bob's Big Boy, with hefty sandwiches, lots of fried stuff, but also traditional Mexican fare with intriguing touches such as a wide choice of hot chile salsas and other condiments. ~ Paseo Montejo 444; 9-927-5479. BUDGET TO MODERATE.

Follow Paseo Montejo north toward the outskirts of town to find **La Tablita**. *Tablitas*, this restaurant's specialty, are multiple-course grilled platters designed to be shared by two to four people. For instance, one spread includes a pound of barbecued ribs, a beef fillet, a giant shrimp shish kabob, a baked potato, a baked onion, vaquero bean soup, salsa and four beers for about $35. ~ Prolongación Paseo Montejo 358; 9-944-1256. BUDGET.

For one of the most elegant and atmospheric dining experiences Mérida has to offer, take a drive past the outskirts of town to Hacienda Xcanatún, where the **Casa de Piedra** restaurant specializes in a unique brand of Yucatecan-Caribbean-international fusion cuisine. Besides beautifully presented versions of traditional standbys like *poc-chuc* and *sopa de lima,* the menu features creative dishes such as quails marinated in achiote sauce and sautéed chile-tamarind chicken breast over mango and jicama salad. The ambience is as romantic as anything Mérida has to offer (and that's romantic indeed). ~ Off Cerretera Progreso, Km. 12; 9-941-0213. ULTRA-DELUXE.

NIGHTLIFE   Several nightclubs offer tourist-oriented Maya shows with extravagant costumes and mock sacrificial rituals. The most elaborate is at **Los Tulipanes**. This pricey supper club under a giant palapa roof has its own cenote, where a human sacrifice is simulated. Nightly performances on a gaudily lit stage come with mediocre dinners; order the minimum. The dances are slick and flashy. There's a big cover charge. ~ Calle 42 between Calles 45 and 47; 9-927-2009.

Many of the hotels located along Paseo Montejo have popular nightclubs. Among the most active live music clubs is **La Hach** in the Hotel Fiesta Americana. ~ Avenida Colón at Paseo Montejo; 9-942-1111. Just a few dance steps away is the chic discotheque **Vatzya**. ~ Avenida Colón between Calle 60 and Paseo Montejo; 9-942-1111.

Farther north, **Romanzas** features live salsa bands nightly. The cover charge is expensive for men and less (free on Wednesday night)

WHERE'S THE BEEF?

The northern part of Paseo Montejo seems to be lined with *taquerías* that also serve steaks. Their menus are almost identical, with such specialties as *arrachera tampiqueña* (a thin-sliced skirt steak smothered in a pepper, tomato and onion salsa), as well as chicken, shrimp, pork chops and chorizo sausage served mixed-grill style or in rolled soft tacos. A long-time favorite is **La Parrilla Taquitos**, a comfortably contemporary place with slowish service and smallish handmade tables, warm wood trim and ceramics decorating the walls. ~ Prolongación Paseo Montejo 87; 9-944-3999. BUDGET TO MODERATE. Locals swear by the nearby **Las Jirafas**, across from the Audi dealership near the Monumento a la Patria. ~ Calle 60 No. 327 at Avenida Colón; 9-925-3082. BUDGET TO MODERATE.

for women. ~ Avenida Pérez Ponce 118; 9-926-5280. Another hot salsa hangout, **Video Bar La Jungla,** is still farther north. Cover. ~ Prolongación Paseo Montejo 382. Both of these clubs cater to partons who are young, local and prosperous.

Feel like taking a chance with your vacation budget? The only game in town is **Quiniela Race and Sports Book,** where you can bet on greyhound and thoroughbred races, basketball and soccer games and watch the action on a bank of television screens. ~ Prolongación Montejo at Calle 17; 9-926-7074.

Outdoor Adventures

About 16 kilometers north of Mérida heading toward Progreso, the **Club Golf La Ceiba** has an 18-hole golf course with pro shop and club-house. The club also has tennis courts. ~ Route 261, Km. 14.5; 9-922-0071. Other Mérida-area tennis courts can be found at both the **Club Campestre de Mérida** ~ Calle 30 No. 500, 9-944-2526; and the **Holiday Inn** ~ Avenida Colón 498 at Paseo Montejo, 9-925-6877.

GOLF & TENNIS

Transportation

In the Yucatán, all roads lead to Mérida, which is located at the hub where nine major roads to different parts of the state converge with **Route 180**, the main highway that connects the capital city with Cancún, Valladolid, Chichén Itzá, Campeche and central Mexico. Umán is 17 kilometers south-west of downtown Mérida; to get there, follow Avenida de las Itzaes out of town.

CAR

Mérida International Airport is about four miles southwest of the city. Few international flights land there these days. Both Continental Airlines and the Guatemalan airline Aviateca fly there from Miami and Houston three times a week. There is frequent air service from Cancún and Mexico City on Aeroméxico, and Mexicana provides service to and from Mexico City and Havana, Cuba. Other airlines that connect Mérida with destinations on the Yucatán Peninsula and in Central American countries include Aerocaribe, AeroCozumel, Aviacsa and Taesa.

AIR

There are a handful of rent-a-car agencies at the Mérida airport, including **Executive Car Rental** (Airport, 9-946-1387), **National** (Airport, 9-946-1394) and **Hertz** (Airport, 9-946-1355). A down-town rental office may prove more convenient for travelers who plan to see Mérida on foot and then rent a car to head for the back-country. Downtown agencies include **Kimbila Car Rental** (Calle 58 No. 485; 9-923-9316), **Uxmal Rent a Car** (Calle 57 No. 496 between Calles 57 and 58; 9-928-7050), **Balam Car Rental** (Calle 60 No. 486 upstairs; 9-924-2483) and **Veloz Rent a Car** (Calle 60 No. 488; 9-928-0373).

CAR RENTALS

PUBLIC TRANSIT Buses run constantly to and from Mérida's central bus station, the Unión de Camioneros del Yucatán, six blocks south and west of the main downtown plaza. There are actually two separate bus stations—first class (Calle 70 No. 555; 9-923-8391) and second class (Calle 69 No. 544; 9-921-9150), but they are adjacent to one another; the separation simply means they have different entrances and waiting rooms. Nearly two dozen buses a day connect Cancún with Mérida, while more than a dozen others arrive daily from Campeche, Palenque, Veracruz and Mexico City. There are also daily buses from most other towns around the Yucatán Peninsula. Visiting the bus station for schedule and fare information is easier than calling because of the many competing bus lines. Buses to and from Progreso have a separate terminal (Calle 62 No. 524; 9-928-3965).

Combis (VW microbus shuttles) provide transportation to suburban colonias and nearby villages in the Mérida area from the vicinity of the public market downtown.

▼▼▼▼▼▼▼▼▼▼▼▼▼▼▼▼▼▼▼▼▼▼▼▼

Addresses & Phone Numbers

Cruz Roja (Red Cross) ~ Calle 68 No. 583; 9-928-5391

Emergency number ~ 060

Municipal Tourist Information Center ~ in the Teatro Peón Contreras, Calle 59 Between Calles 62 and 64; 9-924-6547

Centro Médico de las Américas (English-speaking hospital) ~ Calle 54 No. 365; 9-926-2111.

Policia ~ 9-925-2555.

United States Consulate ~ Paseo Montejo 453; 9-925-5011

Internet access ~ Cofy Net, Avenida 1 No. 360 at Calle 60 and Prolongación Montejo; 9-944-7441

NINE

The Yucatán Gulf Coast

If you're searching for the last undiscovered beach in Mexico, Yucatán's Gulf coast is a good place to look. There's very little in the way of major resort development or fancy restaurants along the 350-mile coastline from Holbox to Sisal. There's hardly anything to shop for, unless you want to buy a fish or two. Wooden boats instead of sunbathers' chaise longues line the wide, white beaches. It's a good place to put your mosquito repellent to the test, but if solitude on shell-strewn beaches and world-class bird-watching among the shallow estuaries and mangrove jungle sound good to you, the Gulf coast is the place to go.

A road follows the coastline for only a desolate 41-mile stretch of hurricane-battered beach east of Progreso, the largest town on the north coast. Elsewhere, the only places where you can reach the coast by car are at the end of long routes from the main highways of the interior. A handful of small fishing villages—Chiquilá, Río Lagartos, San Felipe, Sisal and Celestún—are located at the ends of those routes and are departure points for boat expeditions to wild areas along the coast.

Thanks to persistent lobbying by the Mexican environmental group Pronatura and the U.S.-based Nature Conservancy, the Mexican government has designated three large coastal areas as natural parks, a protected status similar to federal wildlife refuges in the United States. A key motivation for creating the parks was to boost the economies of nearby fishing villages. Though accommodations in these villages are basic and large-scale development is neither desirable nor likely in the foreseeable future, local residents are eager to participate in the dream of eco-tourism by rolling out the red carpet for the occasional gringos who succeed in discovering their little towns.

Isla Holbox

The easternmost fishing village on the Gulf coast, tiny Holbox is situated at the tip of a barrier island of the same name, longer and wider than Isla Cancún and almost as close to the mainland at its eastern end, on the north coast of

Quintana Roo. An insignificant destination in the grand scheme of Yucatán tourism, Isla Holbox is made for the few adventuresome visitors who seek deserted beaches far from the madding tourist crowd to the south and who don't mind putting up with less than comfortable sleeping accommodations. To reach Isla Holbox, take Carretera Kantunilkin, which turns off Route 180 a few kilometers east of Nuevo Xcan, on the state line between Quintana Roo and Yucatán. Follow this paved road north for 73 kilometers, all the way to the grubby little fishing village of Chiquilá on the coast.

SIGHTS

HIDDEN ►

Isla Holbox's **beaches** are known particularly for a major nesting site of the green sea turtle. In the hatching season, from August to early September, local biologists monitor the turtle-egg sites and occasionally take interested visitors along on their nighttime expeditions. The rest of the year, Isla Holbox is mainly a sportfishing area for pompano, barracuda and shark.

LODGING

About a kilometer from town, **Xcaloc Resort** offers lodging in nine pretty palapa bungalows right on the beach. Guests have a choice of a king-size bed or two double beds. Each bungalow has tile floors, mosquito netting, a private bath and a porch with chairs and a Maya hammock. There's a swimming pool as well as a restaurant on the premises. ~ Isla Holbox; 9-920-2772, fax 9-925-9047. MODERATE.

Nearby, the Swiss-run and very European **Villas Delfines** has eight spacious palapas with private baths, ceiling fans and porches with hammocks and views of the pristine white-sand beach. The gourmet restaurant on the premises is the best place on the island to eat—and the priciest. ~ Isla Holbox; 9-884-8606, fax 9-884-6342, or 800-555-8842 in the U.S. DELUXE.

In addition, some local residents rent out small individual cabañas in their yards. If you bring a hammock and mosquito netting, camping on the beach may be your best bet.

DINING

Several small food stands wait along the Holbox waterfront. Specialties are fish tacos, seafood ceviche, lobster pasta and fish fried whole, head and all. Aside from the fresh-caught seafood, the only sustenance you'll find on the island is bread, beer and Coca-Cola.

BEACHES & PARKS

ISLA HOLBOX BEACHES 🕺 🛶 ⏬ The island offers nearly 16 miles of white-sand beach with lots of seashells, extending the entire length of the north shore. The water offshore is shallow and warm, though it can be murky at times.

▲ Beach camping is permitted.

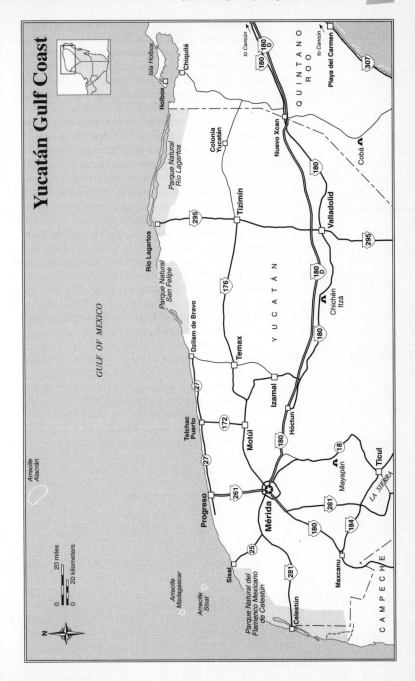

Yucatán Gulf Coast

GULF OF MEXICO

Arrecife Alacrán

20 miles
20 kilometers

N

Arrecife Madagascar

Arrecife Sisal

Parque Natural del Flamenco Mexicano de Celestún

Sisal

Celestún

Progreso

Telchac Puerto

27

261

25

261

Mérida

184

180

Maxcanú

CAMPECHE

Dzilam de Bravo

21

172

Motúl

Izamal

Hoctún

180

Mayapán

18

261

Ticul

LA SIERRA

Parque Natural San Felipe

Río Lagartos

Parque Natural Río Lagartos

176

Temax

Y U C A T Á N

295

Tizimín

Colonia Yucatán

295

Valladolid

180
D

Chichén Itzá

180

Nuevo Xcan

180

Cobá

180 180
to Cancún

180
to Cancún

Playa del Carmen

307

Q U I N T A N O
R O O

Isla Holbox

Holbox

Chiquilá

to Cancún

▼▼▼▼▼▼▼▼▼▼▼▼
Río Lagartos

Río Lagartos (pop. 3000) is a small fishing village in a swampy region of lagoons. The name means "Lizard River," referring to the alligators and crocodiles that used to be abundant in the area and are still spotted occasionally. Upon reaching the remote little town, many visitors are first struck by its bleakness. As you enter the town, the highway becomes a wide main boulevard with a massive concrete monument in the middle and, along the sides of the street, decrepit fishermen's shacks built on the muddy shore of a shallow, foul-looking lagoon.

If you're coming from Cancún or Mérida, where tourist hustlers seem to be waiting for you at every turn, your first impulse in Río Lagartos may be to brush off the teenage welcoming committee that approaches your car as you slow for the speed bumps on the way into town. But give these guys a chance. They are part of an organized community effort to make your visit to Río Lagartos as enjoyable and hassle-free as possible. They will help you find your way around town, locate places to eat and sleep, and arrange tours of the natural park. The people of Río Lagartos display a lot of enthusiasm about the idea of ecotourism, and since the village averages fewer than a dozen visitors a day, you merit VIP treatment just by finding your way there. To reach Río Lagartos by car, take Route 295 north from Valladolid through Tizimín to Río Lagartos, a distance of 103 kilometers.

SIGHTS

Parque Natural Río Lagartos surrounds the town and the coastal wetlands for 47 miles to the east, all the way to the Yucatán state boundary. Río Lagartos is not a typical river; it seems more like a shallow lagoon separated from the Gulf of Mexico by a sandy barrier island three times as long as Isla Cancún. The island itself is technically a peninsula because the east end is tenuously attached to the mainland by a slender, jungle-covered strand, and Río Lagartos is technically a river and not a lagoon because freshwater from several cenotes and *ritos* (intermittent creeks) flows westward to the sea. The flow causes the *río* to "breathe"; that is, it contains more freshwater during the wet season and when the tide goes out, and more saltwater during the dry season and when the tide comes in. This phenomenon means an exceptional diversity of birds and sea life. It also causes salt crystals to extrude up through the beach sand at **Las Coloradas**, forming a natural white crust of salt that has been mined since ancient Maya times, when it was one of the region's most precious commodities and the basis for the wealth of Dzibilchaltún, Izamal and Chichén Itzá. The saltworks don't make an especially scenic stop—lots of machinery piling the sea salt into a huge mound and trucks hauling it away—but you might want to take a look at the nearby shoreline, where natural mineral deposits tint the water in hues of pink, lavender and crimson.

The big attraction in this wildlife preserve area appears from April through early July, when the mudflats blush with hordes of pink flamingos. To see them, hire a boat in town (easily arranged through the youths who wave you down as you drive along the waterfront). The two-hour trip takes you through marshlands as soupy green as a Louisiana bayou, rich with ducks, herons, pelicans, white ibis and egrets. Big, prehistoric-looking horseshoe crabs poke their way along the bottom just inches beneath the boat's keel. Guides know where to look for crocodiles, though not always where to find them. Finally you enter **Orilla Emal**, the muddy shallows where as many as 10,000 fluorescent-pink flamingos nest and feed, gracefully taking wing just before you get close enough for a great photo. During the rest of the year you are likely to see flocks of hundreds rather than thousands. The best time to view them is early morning or late afternoon.

The main flamingo nesting grounds, located on the mainland side of the river north of the Las Coloradas saltworks, are forbidden to tour boats because tourists and guides in the past have too often disturbed the nests. Since time immemorial, this area has been the nesting grounds for virtually all the flamingos in the entire Caribbean, drawn here by the warm, shallow, not-too-salty water that makes shrimp abundant and catching them easy. In the wake of Hurricane Gilbert, however, fewer and fewer flamingos have been nesting at Río Lagartos. There has been a slow, steady movement to more remote breeding grounds to the west,

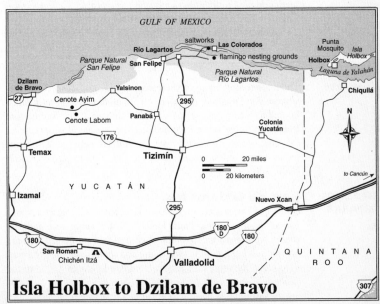

Isla Holbox to Dzilam de Bravo

HIDDEN ▶   necessitating the creation of a second park area, **Parque Natural San Felipe**, along the hard-to-reach coastline between the fishing villages of San Felipe and Dzilam de Bravo. Boat tours to this area are not promoted as a matter of course but can easily be arranged. Half-day tours cost about $20 per person for a minimum of four people or a flat rate of $80 for the boat, which can carry up to eight passengers.

LODGING   The only hotel in Río Lagartos—and the largest building in town—went out of business in 1996 and reopened in 2000 under new management. As this book goes to press, only the bottom two floors of the hotel are open for business, though four or five more stories could be opened if demand justified it. There's no phone (here or anywhere else in Río Lagartos), but there's no need to call ahead for reservations either. ~ Río Lagartos. BUDGET.

A few locals rent out backyard huts, and the teens who greet visitors entering the town can point you in the right direction. The most established of these makeshift tourist hotels is **Cabañas Los Dos Hermanos**, on the waterfront two blocks east of the road into town. There is also the very basic **Hotel San Felipe** in the center of the nearby fishing village of San Felipe.

Visitors who prefer more formal accommodations can stay 52 kilometers south of Río Lagartos in the Maya town of Tizimín. **Hotel 49**, located just off the plaza, offers 14 plain, clean rooms with mattresses on concrete slabs and louvered windows that seem designed to let in as much noise as possible. Ceiling fans. ~ Calle 49 No. 373, Tizimín; 9-863-2136. BUDGET.

Twice as far away, Valladolid (see Chapter Seven) is a reasonable base for a day trip to Río Lagartos if you don't mind visiting in the heat of the day.

DINING   There are several palapa-style restaurants located along the waterfront in Río Lagartos; the bill of fare at all of them is pretty much limited to shrimp, beer and tropical atmosphere. The **Restaurante Isla Conty** is my preference because the owners also operate an informal tourist information service and can help make arrangements with guides. ~ Calle 19 No. 134, Río Lagartos; 9-862-0000. BUDGET.

BEACHES & PARKS   **PLAYA RÍO LAGARTOS** 🏃 🦆 This five-mile stretch of beachcomber's heaven is not on the mainland but on the narrow peninsula across the water at Punta Holohit. The beach is drab and narrow in some places, broad and shell-packed in others. There are no facilities here, but the swimming and shell collecting are great. ~ To reach the area, take a boat from Río Lagartos across to the "island."

▲ Camping is permitted and is very private.

PLAYA SAN FELIPE 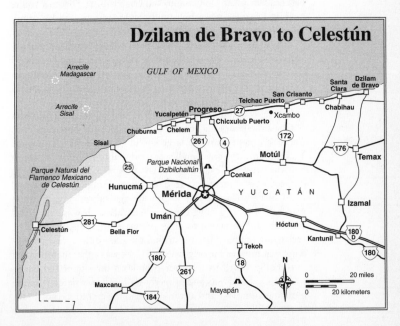 The Gulf-side village of San Felipe, which sees even fewer tourists than Río Lagartos, has no mainland beach. However, an island beach is accessible by a ten-minute boat trip. The crumbly, thin sand curves around a soft point where the shallow water is a gorgeous reminiscence of the Mexican Caribbean. There are no facilities. The sand here is uncomfortable for camping, and there is no shelter. Swimming, however, is excellent and ideal for children. ~ To get there, take a boat to the island from the main pier at the village of San Felipe, 10 kilometers west of Río Lagartos.

Heading westward from Río Lagartos you'll pass through the typical agricultural landscape of cane fields and cebu cattle ranches that one finds in the tropics.

Progreso Area

Dzilam de Bravo is a gathering place for pink flamingos. Boat trips to Parque Natural San Felipe can sometimes be arranged here, though at other times you may not see a soul in town.

Both routes westward from Río Lagartos veer inland around the impassable wetlands of Parque Natural San Felipe. Better road conditions are found on the main highways: Route 295 south for 50 kilometers to Tizimín, then Route 176 for 82 kilometers west to Temax, then a paved but unnumbered secondary road north for 25 kilometers to Dzilam de Bravo. A considerably shorter but not much faster backroad route goes south from San Felipe, turn-

Dzilam de Bravo to Celestún

Arrecife Madagascar

GULF OF MEXICO

Arrecife Sisal

Santa Clara   Dzilam de Bravo

San Crisanto

Telchac Puerto

Yucalpetén   Progreso   27   Xcambo   Chabihau

Chuburna   Chelem   Chicxulub Puerto   172

Sisal   261   4

Parque Natural del Flamenco Mexicano de Celestún

Parque Nacional Dzibilchaltún

Motúl   176   Temax

25   Conkal

Hunucmá   Mérida   Y U C A T Á N   Izamal

Celestún   281   Umán   Hóctun   180 D

Bella Flor   Kantunil   180

Tekoh   180

261   18   N

Maxcanu   184   Mayapán   0   20 miles

0   20 kilometers

ing east at Panabá. The route is unpaved and rough for about 20 kilometers between the tiny village of Yalsihon and the twin cenotes Labom and Ayim, one on each side of the road across from each other. It joins the road from Temax a few kilometers south of Dzilam de Bravo.

SIGHTS

HIDDEN ►

Dzilam de Bravo is the final resting place of buccaneer Jean Lafitte, whose grave is on the beach. From Dzilam de Bravo, Route 27 follows the beaches and wetlands of the coast for 41 miles to Progreso, passing through several small, nondescript fishing villages— Santa Clara, Chabihau, San Crisanto, Telchac and Chicxulub— along an increasingly vivid blue Gulf. These are very poor communities, bypassed by economic development. You'll find hurricane-battered concrete-block shacks; a few small restaurants, food stores and cantinas; a lighthouse or two; and broad, sandy beaches strewn with sun-bleached skiffs. Between the villages the road runs among former coconut plantations, where rows of leafless palms stand dead from a mysterious disease that has been attacking coconut palms throughout the Caribbean and as far north as Florida in intermittent epidemics for about 15 years. Though this stretch of coast may be weathered and economically depressed, it is also refreshingly empty and undiscovered by tourists. Swimming, windsurfing and fishing are good, though you must bring your own equipment. Skiffs can sometimes be rented on the beaches. The best beaches are at San Crisanto and Chabihau. You'll know you're nearing Progreso when half-built condominiums and RV campgrounds begin to appear.

The classy beach resort development of Nuevo Yucatán is situated beside the forlorn little fishing village of **Telchac Puerto**, 34 kilometers east of Progreso and 30 kilometers west of Dzilam de Bravo. The development has an unfinished look, a growing sprawl of condominiums, and the huge Paraíso Maya.

HIDDEN ►

There were almost no ancient Maya settlements along the north coast of the peninsula, probably because of the hurricane risk. The sole exception is the large site of **Xcambo** (also known as Xtampu), located on a small side road that turns off to the south midway between Telchac Puerto and Progreso. This town was an outpost of the great salt trading cities—Dzibilchaltún, Izamal and Chichén Itzá—farther inland. Besides salt mining, Xcambo may have been a fishing center where the catch was salted and sun-dried for shipment to other population centers. Since 1999, archaeologists have been restoring the site—quite a feat considering that most of the original stonework was either incorporated into the Spanish Mission church built on the site or scrounged by locals to build huts and property walls. The six-tiered pyramid mound is climbable and affords views of the gulf to the north, the resort developments to the west and the wetlands of Laguna

Rosada to the east. A little more than a kilometer away, along the shoreline, are man-made limestone ponds used in ancient times to evaporate sea water for salt.

Ever since Hurricane Gilbert scoured the north coast in 1988, the flamingos of Río Lagartos have gradually colonized new breeding grounds to the west. In most of these areas, such as San Felipe and Celestún, you have to take a boat tour to see the flamingos. Not so at **Uaymitún**, where a colony of several hundred of the big ◀ HIDDEN pink birds has taken up residence in the wetlands just offshore. A 20-foot-tall observation tower and a pair of binoculars let you watch the flamingos to your heart's content. The caretaker will even lend you binoculars if you didn't bring any along.

Progreso (pop. 40,000) is the main resort area serving Mérida and the state of Yucatán. Besides the coast route described above, it can be reached easily via Route 261, a 33-kilometer trip from Mérida that takes half an hour and passes Dzibilchaltún (see Chapter Seven). In recent years, Progreso has become the fast-growing capital city's backyard beach, and this once-sleepy town now jumps with fun seekers daily during the summer and on weekends year-round. It's as different as can be from the international resort scene of Cancún. Here, just about everybody who comes to play in the waters is Mexican. English is hardly ever spoken (or understood). Most women wear modest attire on the beach, and many even go swimming in long dresses. There are hardly any shops selling T-shirts or curios.

The nearly two-mile-long **Puerto Progreso** causeway that extends out into the Gulf is a pier that used to be the main shipping port for the Yucatán, where items such as honey, cement, henequen products and fish were exported to the world, and imports, primarily corn, were brought in. In recent years, much of the shipping trade has shifted a few miles west to the newer, sheltered harbor of Yucalpetén, which is also home to the area's fishing fleet. The state of Yucatán has been trying to promote Puerto

AUTHOR FAVORITE

My imagination is piqued anew by each Maya archaeological site I visit because each site has its own distinctive personality and unique mysteries. In the case of **Xcambo**, the virtually unheard-of ruins near Telchac Puerto, the question to ponder from the summit of the central pyramid is why such a large city was situated on the most hurricane-prone stretch of coastline in the Yucatán. (Nearby ancient salt ponds hold the answer.) See page 300 for more information.

Progreso as a cruise-ship destination, but except for the new Yucatán Express ferry (see Chapter Eight) there have been no takers—probably because of competition from new cruise-ship docks being opened near Cancún and Playa del Carmen. At the far end of the pier, the water reaches only about 20 feet in depth. You can drive or walk as far as the port authority building, just over one-half mile from shore.

The wide beachfront *malecón* is Calle 19, which is as low as street numbers go in Progreso (lower odd-numbered streets are in the neighboring resort towns of Yucalpetén and Chelem). Progreso's lively *zócalo* is located six blocks inland from the waterfront on Calle 80 (the street that marks the west end of the *malecón*) between Calles 31 and 33, one block east of the road to the pier. The public market on Calle 80 between Calles 25 and 27 is open daily.

Most of the beach area west of Progreso is filled with vacation homes belonging to wealthy Mérida residents. These places are used mostly in the summer, and many owners rent them out from September through May at surprisingly reasonable rates. Any traveler who is planning a long stay in the Yucatán during the winter months would do well to investigate renting one of these vacation homes. (This requires an advance scouting trip or a local contact.) Progreso is almost as conveniently located as Mérida to serve as a base for exploring the peninsula.

LODGING

Near Telchac Puerto, the **Hotel Reef Yucatán** caters to a mainly Canadian clientele, with 150 spacious guest rooms on three floors. Guest rooms have one king-size or two queen-size beds and balconies or terraces with views of the sea, the pool, or the hotel's gardens. Each room is softly lit, with warm cream-colored walls and bright Mexican textile accents, and has satellite TV and a direct-dial phone, as well as intriguing decorative touches such as limestone sinks made by hand in Ticul. There are two pools, tennis courts and a spa. The rate includes all meals, drinks, sports equipment, stage shows and cultural guest speakers. Bicycles are available for guests who wish to take the easy ride to the nearby ruins of Xcambo. The resort is family-oriented and offers supervised children's activities. ~ Route 27, Km. 32; 9-917-4100, fax 9-917-4086, or 800-000-7333 in the U.S.; www.reefyucatan.com, e-mail reservaciones@reefyucatan.com. DELUXE.

If you want to stay longer than just a day, Puerto Progreso offers a growing number of sleek, modern, expensive resort facilities along with older budget-priced inns full of character. There is not much in the way of mid-range accommodations. Every hotel in town is booked solid during the summer season, and rates shoot sky-high. In the winter, when most international travelers visit the

The Last Buccaneer

The most colorful historical figure to set foot on the Yucatán Gulf Coast was probably Jean Lafitte (1780–1826), the last great pirate on the Spanish Main. Leading a band of Cajun outlaws, Lafitte appeared out of nowhere in 1811 to take control of Barataria Bay on the Louisiana coast. With a small flotilla of stolen ships, he plundered Spanish merchant vessels under the dubious legal authority of a privateer charter from the faraway Republic of Cartagena, a Colombian port city that had declared its independence from Spain that year. When Cartagena was reconquered by the Spanish, the U.S. Navy seized Lafitte's ships, but he and his men took refuge in the maze of swampy islands and bayous around the bay.

Lafitte's fame is based on a single incident at the end of the three-year-long War of 1812, when the United States and Britain clashed over control of the Mississippi River. The British offered Lafitte a Navy commission and £30,000 if he and his men would help attack New Orleans. Instead, Lafitte sent the details of the British plan to U.S. general Andrew Jackson along with an offer to fight on the American side in exchange for a full pardon. In the Battle of New Orleans, he and his shipless pirates fought for the first and last time on dry land—and became heroes as an artillery unit. Ironically, after the bloody battle was over, both sides discovered that the War of 1812 had actually ended two weeks earlier.

Lafitte received his pardon, but his attempts at legitimate business ended in dismal failure. Stealing more ships, he sailed to Galveston Island, Texas, where he established an outlaw colony that grew to more than 1000 men and returned to plundering Spanish ships and smuggling African slaves into the United States. One of his lieutenants, Jim Bowie, went on to become a Texas hero at the Alamo.

In 1821, some of Lafitte's followers started attacking U.S. ships. Alerted that the Navy was coming to arrest him, Lafitte and his hand-picked crew loaded his favorite ship, *The Pride*, with supplies and treasure, and vanished for good—apparently retiring to a life of leisure on the uninhabited Yucatán coast. He is reputed to have buried a fortune in plunder somewhere along the Gulf coast. Whether or not Lafitte's gold lies buried near Dzilam de Bravo, his body certainly does. You can still find his grave on the beach.

Lafitte was immortalized in a 19th-century romantic novel, *The Buccaneer*. The 1938 movie version, starring Clark Gable as Lafitte, was improved upon in a historically accurate 1958 remake starring Yul Brynner that is available on video.

Yucatán, room rates drop 50 percent or more, and if you arrive on a weekday, you'll have your choice of hundreds of vacancies.

The **Hotel Progreso** is in the center of downtown Progreso, a block from the *zócalo* and five blocks from the beach. Although budget-priced, this hotel is surprisingly comfortable, with recently refurbished rooms and nice bathrooms that offer a refreshing change from the decrepit plumbing of so many budget accommodations in the Yucatán. ~ Calle 29 No. 142, Progreso; 9-935-0039. BUDGET.

There are only two hotels along the beachfront *malecón*, and both are good choices. Wrapped in an aura of tropical decadence, the three-story **Tropical Suites** offers clean rooms, some with balconies, as well as apartments with kitchenettes and hammocks. ~ Calle 19 (*malecón*) No. 143, Progreso; 9-935-1263. BUDGET.

One of the nicest bed and breakfasts in the area is the new **Casa Quixote**, a restored two-story mansion near the beach with columns, a balcony extending the length of the house and a mansard roof. There are three guest rooms in the main house and a suite in the former carriage house. All are decorated in muted gray and white tones. Air conditioning. ~ Calle 23 No. 64; 9-935-2909. MODERATE TO DELUXE.

Top of the line in the Progreso area is the **Hotel and Beach Club Sian Ka'an**, which has just eight suites in four thatched-roof stucco luxury duplexes right on Playa Yucalpetén, the area's most exclusive beach. The suites are thoroughly Mexican, with handmade furniture and folk-art decor from all over Mexico. ~ Calle 17, Yucalpetén; phone/fax 9-935-4017. MODERATE TO DELUXE.

Also in Yucalpetén is the much larger **Fiesta Inn Mérida Beach**, a two-story stucco complex with a lively pool area next to the beach, tennis courts, a marina and bicycles for rent. The 88 guest

AUTHOR FAVORITE

The salty smell of the sea breeze, the bobbing lights of fishing boats far out on the water, and the lovers strolling along the *malecón* at the edge of the beach all blend to make evenings in Puerto Progreso, as viewed from the broad colonial-style balcony of the **Real del Mar**, one of my favorite kinds of tropical night. The front unit of this nine-room hotel is a spacious two-room suite, which catches wonderful sea breezes and costs a little more but still falls within the budget range. The big second-floor balcony is furnished to create sitting areas for guests and has a view of the malecón, the beach, the pier and the vast gulf. ~ Calle 19 (*malecón*) and Calle 23, Progreso; 9-935-0798. BUDGET.

rooms—modern and bright, strikingly decorated in a blue-green and peach color scheme—have satellite television and private balconies. ~ Calle 19 No. 91, Yucalpetén; 9-935-0300. DELUXE.

Beach camping is allowed in the Progreso area. Sleeping in a hammock or truck bed is best; sleeping bags on the sand are a bad idea because the beach crawls with crabs after dark.

In Puerto Progreso, an assortment of seafood restaurants lines the *malecón* (Calle 19). Progreso and the other towns along the north coast have a distinctive seafood cuisine. Local specialties include *espedregal*—fish fried whole and smothered with a salsa made from *chile xcatic*, a yellow, jalapeño-like pepper unique to the region. Another favorite dish is *pescado tikin-xic*—grouper baked in banana leaves with *achiote* sauce. Also common is *sopa de calamar*—squid soup.

DINING

Try the big seafront **Capitán Mariscos**, with its central skylight, draped fishing nets and outdoor patio. The restaurant closes early in the evening. ~ Calle 19 (*malecón*) No. 136, Progreso; 9-935-0639. MODERATE.

At the other end of the *malecón* is another good bet for fresh seafood. **Le Saint Bonnet** caters to a mainly Mexican crowd with tantalizing catch-of-the-day fish fillets served in garlic sauce or tangy *salsa veracruzana*. This restaurant burned to the ground in 2000 but was rebuilt almost immediately—like new and more popular than ever. ~ Calles 19 (*malecón*) and 78, Progreso; 9-935-2299. MODERATE.

Sol y Mar has been a waterfront institution in Progreso for generations, catering to a mixed clientele of dock workers and beachgoers. Over the years it has taken on an air of respectability and a flair in presentation, but it still serves fish ceviche, *botanas* (snack-size helpings that come free with drink orders) and other Mexican seafood favorites at prices Mexican families can afford. ~ Calles 19 (*malecón*) and 80, Progreso. BUDGET TO MODERATE.

Just off the *zócalo*, **El Cordobés** is where long-lost gringo dropouts and local Mexican families go to eat or just sip beverages in the shade. The menu is a hodgepodge of standard Yucatecan and Mexican fare, and the decor is as plain as can be, but this is the best people-watching spot in town. ~ Calle 31 No. 150, Progreso. BUDGET.

Many of the area's better restaurants cluster along the beach at Chelem, a 14-kilometer drive west of Progreso. **La Terracita** serves a varied surf-and-turf menu. This is one of the few places in the area where you can get a steak (*bistek*), though it takes a ravenous red-meat craving to face the thin, leathery slabs that Mexicans know as beef, which come from rugged, free-ranging zebu cattle that have not been shot full of hormones or fattened in feedlots like American cattle. A better bet is the ceviche. ~ Carretera a Chelem; 9-935-4173. MODERATE.

BEACHES & PARKS

PLAYA PROGRESO 🏖️🏄 This is a clean, white beach scattered with small shells and lapped gently by emerald-green, often surfless, shallow water. You can wade out into the Gulf of Mexico practically beyond sight of land and still stand on the sea floor. It offers pretty sand, shaded here and there by a solitary palm tree and backed by Puerto Progreso's quaint ten-block *malecón*. The beach is good for picnicking. The swimming is very pleasant, with clear, calm water most of the year. Windsurfing is good. The beach continues eastward for about seven kilometers to the village of Chicxulub. ~ Located along the *malecón* (Calle 19).

PLAYA YUCALPETÉN 🏖️🏄🚤 Playa Yucalpetén is a white beach with small shells and very shallow, emerald-green water. The swimming is very pleasant. Yucalpetén's tidy patch of sand has a *balneario* (bathing resort) with restrooms and showers. Speedboats and waterskiers from the nearby marina streak the blue-green waters. The beach is good for picnicking, but camping is prohibited. Windsurfing is good. Anglers can rent boats at the marina in Yucalpetén. ~ Seven kilometers west of Progreso along the Coast Road; take Route 261 west from Puerto Progreso for 13 kilometers.

PLAYA CHELEM 🏖️🏄🚣 Serving a holiday village that has seen better days, Playa Chelem scallops the Gulf in neat scoops of shell-scattered sand and is overlooked by little stucco cottages. The fusion of the Gulf of Mexico and the Caribbean sea here yields lovely blue water pocked with the stumpy remains of wooden piers. Swimming is very pleasant; windsurfing and fishing are good. Camping would be cramped with no privacy. ~ Located 14 kilometers west of Progreso.

PLAYA CHUBURNA 🏖️🏄🚣 This long, lazy stretch of sand slopes down from shrub-covered dunes crested by little beach houses and shady palms. Serving a sandy-trailed beach community, the narrow beach continues for about 50 kilometers west along the Gulf to the once-bustling port of Sisal, where henequen was shipped by the ton. Do not attempt the roller-coaster sand road from Chuburna to Sisal in a passenger car. Playa Chuburna has small restaurants. Windsurfing and fishing are good, and swimming is very good in the beautiful turquoise water. ~ Located 20 kilometers west of Progreso.

▲ Camping is possible on Playa Chuburna, but cramped and rather public. The beach-camping situation is better a few kilometers down the beach.

A visit to either or both of the fishing villages that flank Parque Natural del Flamenco Mexicano de Celestún on the west coast of Yucatán state makes a good daytrip or overnight excursion from Mérida. To reach Sisal, take Avenida de los Itzaes out of Mérida, following the old route to Uxmal through Umán, turn west at the highway junction in central Umán and take Route 281 west to the fair-sized town of Hunucmá, a distance of 29 kilometers. From there, Route 25 takes you 24 kilometers north to Sisal.

If you stay on Route 281 for 63 more kilometers, you'll reach Celestún. On the way to Celestún, you'll pass the picturesque, crumbling Spanish colonial hacienda of Bella Flor. Both Sisal and Celestún feel isolated and have good beaches. Celestún is larger and has more tourist accommodations; Sisal is somewhat closer to Mérida and has historic ruins.

Sisal and Celestún

SIGHTS

◀ HIDDEN

Founded in 1811, **Sisal** was the main shipping port for the Yucatán Peninsula in the 19th century. Henequen, the rope fiber that was the Yucatán's main cash crop in those days, was known in other parts of the world as sisal because it was shipped from this port in huge quantities. Early explorers such as John Lloyd Stephens first set foot on Yucatán soil at Sisal, as did the Empress Carlota and her entourage on her 1865 visit to the Yucatán, during which she visited Maya ruins and tried unsuccessfully to rally local support for her husband, Maximilian, Mexico's only French ruler. Today, the ruins of a big abandoned customs house and some warehouses dwarf the town's modern structures. It's hard to believe that the town's short little pier could ever have served as a shipping center. The town seems to sleep in the daytime and liven up a little after dark, when the small fleet of open wooden fishing boats head offshore to cast their nets for shrimp.

Some visitors may find that Sisal, with its magnificent sunset vistas, fits their vision of a perfect undiscovered beach hideaway.

Resort development plans for Sisal have been announced and postponed repeatedly over the years, and the village remains a sand-blown remnant of past glory. The town's main industry is shrimp cultivation—raising Pacific white shrimp in tanks to supplement declining shrimp catches in the Gulf of Mexico. Sisal is separated from the mainland by a stagnant estuary, which locals call the "petrified forest" because of the islands of dead mangroves. The area is a wintering ground for countless thousands of Canada geese.

Although it is much smaller than Progreso, **Celestún** is rapidly becoming a popular beach resort where people from Mérida go to escape the heat of summer. Celestún is surrounded by the mucky, sulfurous-smelling wetlands of **Parque Natural del Flamenco Mexicano de Celestún**, the largest of the natural areas along the Yucatán Gulf coast that have been set aside to protect flamingos.

To see the flamingos, hire one of the fishermen in the village or at the bridge over the estuary. Here, even more than in Río Lagartos, the locals can make more money birdwatching than catching shrimp, and because Celestún is within easy daytrip distance of Mérida, many more people come to see the flamingos here than at the natural parks on the north coast. Flocks of the big pink birds gather along the estuaries of the Río Esperanza, just north of the village, especially during May and June. Early morning is the best time to see them in flight. A two-hour excursion costs around $40 for four people.

LODGING

Except for a members-only duck-hunting club outside of town, lodging in Sisal is plain and cheap. The **Balneario Las Felicidades** has 13 dark, basic rooms, as well as camping palapas where you can hang your hammock on the beach and a moderate-priced, family-size casita with full kitchen facilities. Other, even more spartan, hotels are found along Avenida 6. There's no phone service to Sisal, so it's impossible to make reservations or find out about lodging availability. On winter weekdays, you'll have your choice; indeed, you may find that you're the only visitor in town. ~ Avenida 6 No. 104, Sisal. BUDGET TO MODERATE.

Celestún has an abundance of small beachfront hotels along Calle 12. The best of them is the modern, two-story **Hotel María del Carmen**. All 12 bright, clean, tiled rooms have sliding glass doors that open onto balconies where you can watch a giant red sun sink into the Gulf and the lights of the small shrimp boats that work the shoals a half mile offshore in a long line until dawn. The hotel lobby has a good collection of books in Spanish on the wildlife and archaeology of the Yucatán, and the manager hands out complimentary copies (in English or Spanish) of the magazine from Pronatura, the Mexican environmental group that helps safeguard and study Parque Natural del Flamenco Mexicano de Celestún and other natural parks and biosphere reserves around the Yucatán. ~ Calle 12 at Calle 15, Celestún; 9-916-2051. BUDGET.

AUTHOR FAVORITE

If you don't like seafood, avoid Celestún, a quaint fishing village where there's absolutely nothing else to eat. Personally, I find the stone crab claws, octopus ceviche and shrimp in garlic sauce absolutely irresistible at palm-thatched beachfront eateries like **La Palapa**, where the same family catches the seafood, cooks it and serves it fresh from the sea. This restaurant and bar caters to tour groups when they're in town and seems cavernous the rest of the time. The specialty of the house is crab claws. ~ Calles 12 and 11; 9-916-2063. MODERATE.

Located nine kilometers north of the village is Celestún's only upscale resort, **Hotel Eco Paraiso**. This European-owned inn has 15 large cabañas with palapa roofs, tile floors, rattan furniture and floral accents. Set in a grove of coconut palms, the cabañas have views of the gulf and three miles of virgin beaches covered with sea shells. There's a swimming pool, a jacuzzi and a clubhouse shaped like a sunken ship. Lodging packages include meals and tours of the area including Celestún Estuary, Uxmal and Kabah, and a hacienda; bike tours can be booked separately. This hotel is a clone of another Eco-Paraiso in Playa del Carmen, and week-long vacation packages divided between the two coasts are available. ~ 9-916-2100, fax 9-916-2111; e-mail ecoparaiso@ prodigy.net.mx. MODERATE TO DELUXE.

DINING

During the winter off-season, finding a place to eat can be a problem in Sisal, since many restaurants are open limited hours or only on weekends. **Balneario Las Felicidades** has a palapa restaurant on the beach where meals are available year-round. ~ Sisal. BUDGET TO MODERATE.

As in Sisal, the winter off-season brings limited operating hours at Celestún's restaurants. A number of zesty little seafood restaurants are scattered along the beach, and the menu consists of shrimp, octopus and stone crabs at each and every one. A typical decent, unpretentious place is **Restaurant Lupita**. ~ Calles 10 and 7, Celestún. BUDGET. Another is **Restaurant La Playita**. ~ Calle 10, Celestún. BUDGET.

If you crave something other than fresh-caught seafood, you'll find a few hole-in-the-wall *taquerías* around Celestún's central plaza, three blocks east of the beach.

BEACHES & PARKS

PLAYA SISAL Fishing boats parked on the beach make much of the beach an obstacle course of ropes and nets close to town, but the farther you walk from the center of the village, the more open and empty the white sand is. There's no shade.

▲ Camping is permitted.

PLAYA CELESTÚN Fronting the dusty fishing village, the long white beach of Playa Celestún curves north along the Gulf of Mexico toward the flamingo sanctuary. The north end of the beach is best for shell collecting—scallop shells and big conches. Along the village beach stand armadas of little fishing boats bristling with *jimbas* (cane poles), used to catch the local specialty, octopus. Hurricane season brings a brisk north wind; otherwise, the sand, sea and palms sway in a pleasant lull. Swimming is lovely in the opaque green water. Windsurfing, boating and fishing are great.

▲ Camping is good north of the village.

Outdoor Adventures

FISHING

Gulf waters swarm with tarpon, grouper, red snapper, mackerel and sea bass. A few kilometers west of Puerto Progreso, **Servicios Acuático en la Peninsula de Yucatán** provides boats and fishing tips. ~ At the harbor in Yucalpetén.

A poor man's alternative is to stop in a fishing village such as Río Lagartos, Sisal or Celestún and hire a local fisherman to take you to the good fishing spots. You'll usually find plenty of eager would-be guides, since tourist charters pay better than catching fish. You may even learn some ingenious angler's tricks. Expect to pay about $25 an hour or $200 a day.

WIND-SURFING

Generally smooth waters and prevailing winds that parallel the coast make the waters along the north coast from Dzilam de Bravo to Sisal outstanding for windsurfing. Finding a sailboard for rent can be problematic, however. Some beachfront hotels in the Yucalpetén area rent them, and independent entrepreneurs appear with rental sailboards and occasionally sea kayaks on the beach at Celestún on busy weekends.

DIVING

Arrecife Alacrán (Scorpion Reef), a circular coral reef more than 20 miles in diameter, lies some 70 miles off the north coast. The distance is such that only the most intrepid scuba enthusiasts attempt the trip, and there are no dive shops or organized trips along the north coast. Fishermen from Dzilam de Bravo, Progreso and even San Felipe/Río Lagartos go there, though, to net colorful tropical fish for export to U.S. pet shops and to harvest the abundance of shellfish. If you have your own gear, it is often possible to arrange a trip to the reef on a local fishing boat. The same is true of the smaller **Arrecife Madagascar**, off the coast near Sisal.

Transportation

CAR

Carretera Kantunilkin, off Route 180 a few kilometers east of Nuevo Xcan on the Quintana Roo–Yucatán state line, is the main thoroughfare to Isla Holbox. **Route 295** runs from Valladolid through Tizimín to Río Lagartos. **Route 27** traces the coastline from Dzilam de Bravo to Progreso. **Route 281** leads to Celestún; Sisal is off Route 281 via **Route 25**.

AUTHOR FAVORITE

Flocks of flamingos in flight are an unforgettable sight, but I get as much of a kick out of watching the annual spring ritual of birdwatchers descending by the tens of thousands from all over the world to observe the mating games and nestbuilding at the vast flamingo breeding grounds of Yucatán's coastline at **Parque Natural Río Lagartos**, **Uaymitún** and **Parque Natural del Flamenco Mexicano de Celestún**.

Two passenger ferries, one in the early morning and the other in the **BOAT**
early afternoon, depart daily for the one-hour trip from Chiquilá
to Holbox, the equally small village on the island. The fare is about
$3. For a small additional fee, you can leave your car near the ferry
dock and the harbormaster will keep an eye on it.

Several buses a day go from Valladolid to Tizimín, but only the one **BUS**
that stops in Tizimín around 11 a.m. continues to Río Lagartos.
At other times, a few *combis* travel from Tizimín to Río Lagartos
and nearby San Felipe.

Buses leave Mérida's central bus station (Calle 69 at Calle 68)
for Progreso every 15 minutes from 6 a.m. to 9 p.m. There are also
ten buses a day to Celestún—about one every two hours.

Local buses leave the Progreso bus station every half hour and
go to Yucalpetén. ~ Calle 29 No. 151.

▼▼▼▼▼▼▼▼▼▼▼▼▼▼▼▼▼▼▼▼

Addresses & Phone Numbers

Emergency number (Progreso) ~ 060
Police (Progreso) ~ 9-935-0026
Progreso Tourist Office ~ Calle 80 between Calles 25 and 27,
   Progreso; 9-935-0104

TEN

Uxmal and the Hill Country

Only a scattering of people live today in the Puuc region of southern Yucatán state, but during the Late Classic period (A.D. 600–900) this was the most densely populated part of the Yucatán Peninsula. Although none of the Puuc sites, not even Uxmal, approached the size of the great cities to the north such as Chichén Itzá and Izamal, there were so many centers along this 30-mile stretch of sierra that the Puuc was like the Greater Los Angeles area. Small and moderate-sized communities, each with its own patch of fertile farmland among the rugged hills, grew so close together that they formed a single giant megalopolis with complex political ties and shared styles of art and architecture. The population is estimated at 150,000 to 200,000 at its peak, making this hill country the second-largest community in the Americas. Yet it seems to have had no centralized government until the last decades of the Classic period, when Uxmal suddenly grew into the dominant administrative and ceremonial center in the region.

Puuc means "Hills" in the local Maya language; the region's Spanish name is *La Sierra Yucateca*. This hilly region fills the western interior of the otherwise flat Yucatán Peninsula between Mérida and Campeche. Ever since 800 B.C., this rolling terrain has held the best farmland in the Yucatán because earth washes down from the forested hilltops to collect as rich topsoil in valleys below. Yielding two corn crops a year, the Puuc still supplies most of the grain for Maya Mexico.

The only problem with living in the Puuc hill country, now as in the past, is the lack of water. There are no lakes or running streams in these hills and no cenotes like those that supplied water for Chichén Itzá and Dzibilchaltún. The ancient occupants of Uxmal and other Puuc centers dug huge underground cisterns called *chaltunes* to catch and hold rainwater, they irrigated their farmlands with a network of reservoirs and canals, and they covered their temples with huge stone masks of Chaac, the Maya rain god.

Beyond Uxmal and a short distance past the ruins of Kabáh, a paved, un-numbered road called La Ruta Puuc winds eastward through the hills to sites such as Sayil, Xlapak, Labná and the spectacular Grutas de Loltún.

Today, the part of the Puuc where the ancient Maya lived is virtually empty. The Indian population was driven out of the hill country or wiped out during the 19th-century War of the Castes, and when the Maya returned to the area they settled in towns and villages along the road that is now Route 184, between Muna, in Yucatán, and Felipe Carrillo Puerto, in Quintana Roo (formerly the 19th-century Maya capital Chan Santa Cruz). The majority of all Yucatecan Maya people today live near this 136-mile highway route. You can visit major Maya towns such as Ticul on a shortcut return trip from the Puuc Zone to Mérida.

The whole Ruta Puuc, from Kabáh to Oxkutzcab, is 41 kilometers long; allow plenty of time, however—preferably a full day—for sightseeing en route. If possible, allow a minimum of two days to explore Uxmal and the other major ruins along the Ruta Puuc, spending the night at Uxmal or Ticul. The best plan is to visit the Ruta Puuc ruins on Sunday, when admission to all archaeological sites is free. Otherwise, entrance fees to Uxmal, Labná, Sayil, Xlapak and Loltún Cave add up to more than $25 per person. (*A word of caution:* In Maya villages, it's the custom for all the men to get extremely drunk on Sunday afternoons. There's no real danger, but weird, unsettling encounters can result, especially if you don't speak the Maya language.)

Uxmal

To tour Uxmal and the other Puuc Maya sites, head south from Mérida on Route 180. At the town of Umán, continue south on Route 261 until you reach Uxmal. Uxmal is 78 kilometers from Mérida, 61 kilometers from Umán. The drive from Mérida takes about two and a half hours.

Many ruins buffs consider Uxmal to be the finest, most purely Maya site in the Yucatán. Like Chichén Itzá and other centers in the region, it was occupied for much of its history by people of Toltec descent, but its ornate facades covered with complex geometric patterns and graceful sculptures of finely cut stone blocks bear little resemblance to the grandiose and somewhat sinister designs of Chichén Itzá. If Chichén Itzá can be compared to ancient Rome, then Uxmal, with its subtly perfect architectural proportioning and ornamentation finely balanced between simplicity and complexity, is like the city-states of Classical Greece. Unlike Chichén Itzá, nothing at Uxmal suggests militarism, human sacrifice or other dark forms of blood lust. Uxmal, one cannot help but feel, must truly have been a place of intellect and ceremony, of science and spirit, just as local legend suggests.

Although Uxmal was never lost and was still used as a ceremonial center when the Spanish conquerors arrived in the mid-1500s, almost nothing is known about its early history except that it was founded in the 7th century A.D., at the height of the Classic period. (Recent analysis of pottery found at the site indicates that Maya people were living there centuries before the first existing structures were built.) In those days, an educated ruling class of priests and nobles extracted taxes in the form of agricultural products and labor from the uneducated peasant farmers and erected ceremonial centers that grew to become the central plazas of Maya cities.

We know very little of Uxmal's history because the few monuments or hieroglyphic records found at the site are so badly eroded that they cannot be read. The city's emblem has been identified in stone inscriptions throughout the Classic Maya world, indicating that it must have been among the most influential cities in the empire once upon a time; yet unlike almost all other major Maya sites, we do not even know the names of its original rulers.

The last date inscription at Uxmal corresponds to A.D. 907. The people who had built the city abandoned it soon after that for reasons unknown; recent discoveries suggest that the abandonment occurred during a time of prolonged drought, which the Puuc region with its large population and absence of cenotes could not survive. Some evidence indicates that Nahuatl people from central Mexico occupied the site immediately afterwards, suggesting also that a military invasion may have put an end to ancient Uxmal. Beginning around the year 1400, Uxmal was used as a ceremonial center by the Xiu dynasty, a Nahuatl-influenced Itzá Maya clan, whose descendants continued to rule Maya towns including Mani and Oxkutzcab through the entire Spanish-colonial era until the early 19th century. The Xiu clan's version of the history and mythology of Uxmal was recorded by Fray Diego de Landa and others and in the family records that the Xiu kept through 1685. But neither Landa nor the Xiu knew much about Uxmal's ancient origins. The only fragments of the city's early history that we know today are cloaked in fantastic, often contradictory legends that have made their way down to us through the centuries. Like Chichén Itzá and Mayapán, the ancient city of Uxmal comes complete with an elaborate collection of fairy tales that may, just possibly, contain grains of truth.

The local Maya people continued to use Uxmal's ancient temples for religious ceremonies even after the Spanish Conquest. It was the discovery of these secret rituals that inspired the auto-da-fé at Mani, in which Spanish inquisitor Fray Diego de Landa smashed 5000 Maya "idols" and burned nearly all the Maya books in existence. Centuries later, in 1841, when explorer John Lloyd Stephens first visited Uxmal, he recorded that the local people would not stay at Uxmal after dark because they believed that the snakes and gods on temple facades came to life at night.

Grouped on a broad plateau, the ruins of Uxmal cast a low silhouette above a flat jungle landscape—not the towering rainforest you encounter to the south in the Lacandón and Petén regions, but a tangle of undergrowth with a few tall trees. Back in the 1970s, a forest fire raged across the land surrounding Uxmal, burning most of the trees to ashes. Though arid conditions mean the forest is slow to grow back, the land surrounding Uxmal grows more lush each year. Iguanas of impressive size can often be seen basking among the ruins.

SIGHTS

Before you reach Uxmal, you'll come across **Hacienda Yaxcopoil**, an old henequen plantation that is now open to the public as a museum. Admission.

Upon entering **Uxmal** (admission), you come first to the **Pyramid of the Magician**. This unique, oval-shaped pyramid is 117 feet high and 178 feet wide at the base. The main stairway to the upper temples is exceptionally steep, so most people who climb it cling to the chain that was originally fastened to the center of the stairway as a handhold for Empress Carlota, the wife of Emperor Maximilian of Mexico, for her visit in 1865. Looking at the Pyramid of the Magician from a distance, you can see how newer temples were built over older ones. The name *Uxmal*, from Maya words meaning "Built Three Times," probably refers to the three levels of temples here. The pyramid actually contains five

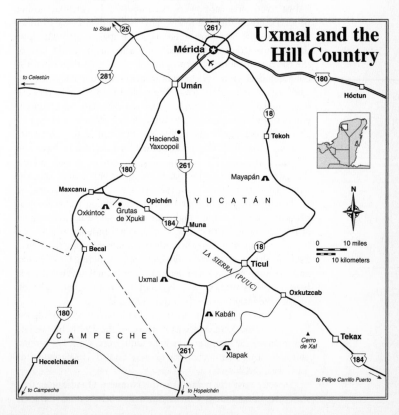

Uxmal and the Hill Country

temples, constructed at different times—one at ground level, three more on a platform two-thirds of the way up the pyramid, and a fifth one at the top. Rocks filled the lower temples when archaeologists began the restoration of Uxmal. During the excavation they cleared passages to expose the facades of two of the buried temples and opened them to the public, but Temple I, at ground level, was sealed after Hurricane Hugo because water damage was weakening the pyramid's interior. A passage from the east side leads into Temple II. The pyramid builders left the front of Temple IV, the latest of the second-level temples, exposed when they buried the rest to build the summit. The facade of Temple IV was built in the style of the Chenes Maya ruins in northern Campeche (see Chapter Thirteen), which is quite different from the Puuc style of the two earlier temples on the same level and the later temple above them.

One of the largest cities in the Yucatán, Uxmal had about 25,000 residents at its height.

According to a tale first recorded by John Lloyd Stephens in the 1840s and still told by tour guides today, Uxmal was built by a dwarf with magical powers. A *curandera*, the spiritual mother of all Yucatecan healers today, hatched the dwarf boy from an egg she had bought from some magical beings of the night. One day the boy struck a forbidden gong, and this upset the lord of the town tremendously. A prophesy had foretold that when the gong sounded, a boy "not born of woman" would replace the ruler. The lord condemned the dwarf boy to death but offered a reprieve if he could accomplish three seemingly superhuman tasks of mathematics, sculpture and architecture. One of them was to build a great pyramid in a single night—the Pyramid of the Magician. The boy passed all three tests, yet the lord decided to have him beheaded anyway. Through trickery, the boy contrived to have the old lord executed in his place. The dwarf boy then became the new lord of Uxmal and built the city whose ruins we see today.

Despite the legend that the Pyramid of the Magician was magically built in a single night, the number of successive temples at the site indicates that it was constructed little by little over a period of about 400 years. According to another legend, the Toltec-Maya leader Quetzalcóatl-Kukulcán, after rebuilding Chichén Itzá and founding Mayapán, ended his life at Uxmal and was buried beneath the Pyramid of the Magician. So far, however, archaeologists have found no tomb in this pyramid.

The first archaeological project undertaken at Uxmal, the Pyramid of the Magician was restored in the 1940s by the late Franz Blom, the explorer whose headquarters, Casa Na-Bolom, you'll want to visit if your travels take you to San Cristóbal de las Casas, in Chiapas.

Directly past the pyramid is the **Nunnery Quadrangle**, four structures surrounding a main plaza. An early Spanish explorer gave the ruins that name because he thought they looked a lot like a Spanish convent. Actually, nobody is quite sure how the buildings were used. The 74 cell-like rooms are too cramped to have been the homes of nobility, and there are too many for them to have been quarters for resident priests. Some archaeologists theorize that the Nunnery Quadrangle was actually a sort of university campus, just as the old legend claims—perhaps a military academy, a seminary for priests or a school for the children of the ruling class. Others think it may have provided housing for visiting dignitaries participating in ceremonies in the central quadrangle. Today, only swallows occupy the dark, vaulted rooms of these ruins, ceaselessly darting back and forth across the plaza.

The ornamentation on the Nunnery Quadrangle facades includes some of the most magnificent stonework in the Maya world. The intertwining stone rattlesnakes that decorate the oldest structure, the **North Building**, were probably ancestors of the plumed serpent Kukulcán. Long before Quetzalcóatl crossed the Gulf of Mexico to the Yucatán, the rattlesnake symbolized divinity and power to the Maya. The masks that cover much of the facade are of Chaac, the rain god, who is an overwhelming presence in all

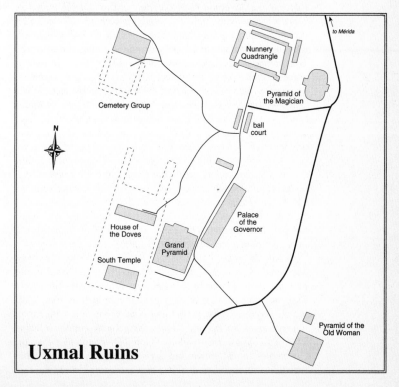

Uxmal Ruins

of the Puuc Zone's ruins. A curious feature is the series of seated human figures, bound like prisoners.

The **South Building**, lowest in elevation and second oldest, is simpler, its facade dominated by a geometric lattice design. Look over the eight interior doorways for stone carvings of Yucatán huts, looking just as they do today. This decorative device seems to have been the rage for a few years back then. The ceilings of two rooms bear red handprints, perhaps the signature of the architect.

The **East Building**, also subdued in its decoration, is the best preserved of the four. The owl-head motif at the roofline is usually understood by Maya archaeologists to symbolize death, but what it means in this context is a mystery.

Grandiose ornamentation decorates the **West Building**. Major features are lavishly rendered giant snakes and male nudes. A throne with a feather canopy is carved over the middle doorway. Seated on the throne is an old man with the body of a turtle, perhaps symbolizing the same lord who resided in the **House of the Turtles**. This small structure, near the Palace of the Governor, south of the ball court, has a row of turtles carved on its facade.

The Uxmal structure most admired by archaeologists is the **Palace of the Governor**. Experts agree that this magnificent palace was the last structure built at Uxmal, between A.D. 900 and 915. It was probably the home and offices of Uxmal's last ruler. Doorways precisely aligned with the path of the planet Venus, as well as sculptural symbolism, suggest that the ruler or his architect was a master astronomer. The palace, 318 feet in length, contained 24 rooms. The frieze on its upper portion was constructed in three layers—a latticework background made from 20,000 identically carved stones, an overlay of geometric fretwork, and a third layer of sculptures depicting persons, gods and animals. Over the central doorway is an empty headdress of long plumes; the face of the ruler who wore it crumbled or was destroyed long ago. Including this image, five rulers are memorialized on the frieze. Other sculptures on this amazing facade personify the planet Venus or glorify astronomers. Modern archaeoastronomers have discovered that at Venus's southern solstice the bright planet aligned perfectly with the central doorway of the palace, the jaguar throne in the courtyard and a temple on a hilltop five miles away.

Southeast of the Palace of the Governor is the most recently excavated structure at Uxmal, the **Grand Pyramid**. On top of this pyramid is the **Temple of the Guacamayas**, so named because of the many unusual stone blocks carved to represent parrots. Maya builders of the Classic period had filled the temple with rubble in preparation for burying it and raising the pyramid to a higher level. This would have made the Grand Pyramid taller than the Pyramid of the Magician, but for some unknown reason, construction was abandoned. When archaeologists cleared the rubble away, they found the giant Chaac mask that you can see in the back room of the temple.

Two other large pyramids stand at Uxmal—the partially restored **Cemetery Group** temple, with its strange skulls-and-bones ornamentation, to the north of the Grand Pyramid, and the unexcavated **Pyramid of the Old Woman**, the oldest pyramid in the area, to the southeast.

Down a forest trail, a third of a mile south of the Pyramid of the Old Woman, are the tumbled-down remains of the **Temple of the Phalluses**, one of several places at Uxmal where early visitors found giant stone monuments that symbolized erect penises—to some, anyway. When she visited in 1865, the Empress Carlota of Mexico expressed shock at all the phallic symbolism at Uxmal— and she wasn't the only one. Until the 1940s a group of more than a dozen of the statues used to stand not far from the Palace of the Governor. Tourists' complaints that Uxmal contained far too much indecent art resulted in the monuments being pulled from the ground and dragged into the woods, where vandals later destroyed them. One of the forbidden monuments found at the Temple of the Phalluses is on display at the visitors' center museum; there is also an old photo of them in the Explorers' Club exhibit upstairs in the Pirámide Inn in Pisté, near Chichén Itzá. Recently, archaeologists have suggested that the alleged phalluses may actually have represented psychedelic mushrooms or symbolized soil fertility.

Perhaps the strangest-looking structure at Uxmal is the **House of the Doves**. Once a ruler's residence, it has collapsed completely, leaving only a bridgelike support wall and the lofty, jagged remnants of a roof comb. This palace formed one side of a ceremonial plaza. The unexcavated ruins of the other buildings that surrounded the plaza are in poor condition.

AUTHOR FAVORITE

I expected the **sound and light show at Uxmal** to be hokey— some artificial spectacle giving the ruins a theme-park atmosphere after dark. When I finally did go, the play of colored lights and shadows on the magnificent facades of the Nunnery Quadrangle permanently enhanced my appreciation of ancient Maya architecture, and the mood was just right. Don't miss it! The show is presented nightly, in Spanish at 7 p.m. and in English at 9 p.m. Impressive narration blends myths and legends about the ancient city with recent archaeological revelations and reveals the symbolic content of the stone carvings. Dramatic, colored spotlights focus attention on sculptural details. Admission.

LODGING Several upscale "archaeological hotels" near Uxmal provide the only tourist accommodations in the Puuc Zone. The most ambitious, the **Lodge at Uxmal**, is the most recent project of the Barbachanos, the Yucatán's first family of tourism, whose patriarch started guiding ruins tours in 1921. The lodge's gate is 100 feet from the ruins entrance—so close that the top of the Pyramid of the Magician rising above the nearby trees serves as a constant looming reminder of the ancient past. The lodge's 40 rooms are in five buildings, each two stories high with a palapa roof and a covered verandah, scattered among tall trees, manicured lawns, two swimming pools and a tennis court. Simplicity is the theme inside the guest rooms, with their red tile floors and plain yellow walls. All the guest-room furnishings at the Lodge at Uxmal, including the beautifully carved doors, are handmade by local craftspeople from mahogany and other forest hardwoods. Bedspreads and wall hangings are likewise the handiwork of Maya artisans. All rooms have air conditioning, ceiling fans and satellite TV; suites are available with king-size beds and private jacuzzis. ~ Route 261, Km. 69 9-971-2102, fax 9-976-2102, or 800-235-4079 in the U.S.; www.mayaland.com, e-mail mayaland@diario1.sureste.com. ULTRA-DELUXE.

Accommodations, complete with swimming pool, can be found at **Rancho Uxmal**. The 20 guest rooms have private baths and hot water. There is also a campground for RVs and tent or hammock campers. Rooms have ceiling fans and some have air conditioning. ~ Route 261, Km. 70; 9-949-0526. BUDGET.

The **Villa Arqueológica**, run by Club Med, is one of a chain of hotels that the Mexican government built at major ruins in the late 1970s. This hotel does not offer the games and organized activities that Club Med is known for, but it does present an audiovisual show about Uxmal and has a good library of English-language books about the Maya and other pre-Hispanic Mexican civilizations. Other facilities include a courtyard swimming pool and tennis courts. Guest rooms are bright and modern. Air conditioning. ~ Route 261, Km. 76; 9-976-2018, fax 9-976-2020, or 800-258-2633 in the U.S.; www.clubmedvillas.com. DELUXE.

AUTHOR FAVORITE

Each of the four upscale "archaeological hotels" around Uxmal has its own distinctive character. My favorite is the **Misión Inn Uxmal**, far enough from the archaeological site to give me a panoramic view of temple pyramids towering above the surrounding forest from my room's balcony. The rooms are large, attractive and ultramodern, with big private balconies. Palms and a pretty lawn surround the swimming pool. Ceiling fans. ~ Route 261, Km. 76; phone/fax 9-924-7308. MODERATE TO DELUXE.

Across the highway from the ruins, the older **Hacienda Uxmal** is full of colonial elegance. Although under the same ownership as the Lodge at Uxmal, the atmosphere is entirely different. The 79 large guest rooms are old-fashioned, with massive handcarved furniture. Some have bathtubs. Outside the rooms, tiled verandas set with divans and plants overlook the beautiful swimming pool. Air conditioning or ceiling fans. ~ Route 261, Km. 80; 9-976-2012, fax 9-976-2010, or 800-235-4079 in the U.S.; www.mayaland. com, e-mail mayaland@diario1.sureste.com. DELUXE.

DINING

In the visitors center at Uxmal, the full-service **Restaurant Yax Beh** serves sandwiches and light meals during the hours when the ruins are open. Prices are higher than you'd pay in Mérida but lower than at restaurants in the neighboring hotels. ~ MODERATE TO DELUXE.

The four upscale archaeological hotels offer guests a choice of rates—the European Plan (without meals) or the Modified American Plan (including dinner and breakfast). Their restaurants are open to the public, too.

Las Palapas, the restaurant at the Lodge at Uxmal, features a changing menu of Yucatecan and Mexican traditional cooking, served by Maya women in embroidered *huipiles* to the accompaniment of a guitar trio. ~ DELUXE.

The excellent restaurant at the **Villa Arqueológica** specializes in Continental cuisine prepared for the palates of European visitors. ~ MODERATE TO DELUXE.

The hacienda ambiance couldn't be more romantic at the restaurant at **Hacienda Uxmal**. There's a varied menu including Yucatecan specialties as well as American and Continental selections. ~ DELUXE.

The restaurant at the **Misión Inn Uxmal** offers a limited but frequently changing menu—usually a choice of chicken, pork or fish prepared in regional style. ~ MODERATE.

Under a big thatched roof, the restaurant at the **Rancho Uxmal** serves a similar selection of chicken, pork or fish entrées à la Yucateca. ~ BUDGET.

SHOPPING

Tourist shops are beginning to spring up along Route 261 between Umán and Uxmal. While there's nothing special about the curios on sale at the roadside **Mercado Central de Artesanías los Pájaros**, out back there's a large private zoo with cages of regional birds like pheasants, toucans, parrots and loros, as well as a tame javelina.

A little farther south in the village of Muna, a **women's cooperative** set up a market for locally made *huipiles* of white cotton with elaborate embroidery. This market has continued to grow over the years and offers some of the best *artesanía* shopping in the region. Among purveyors of other crafts, Maya potter **Martín Morales** creates quality reproductions of polychrome pots from Uxmal and other ancient sites at his studio. ~ Calle 13, Muna.

The archaeological hotels around Uxmal have shops where local crafts workers sell high-quality, pricey handcrafted items. Beautiful carved wooden replicas of sculptures from all over the Classic Maya world are available at the **Misión Inn Uxmal**; at the **Villa Arqueológica** there are exquisitely detailed stone reproductions of Maya art.

At the Uxmal visitors center you will find a Mexican government **gift shop** that carries fine arts and crafts from all over the country as well as a branch of the **Librerías Dante** bookstore chain stocked with a large selection of books on the Maya people and Yucatán's ancient ruins in Spanish, English and other languages. Outside by the parking lot, a number of vendors sell T-shirts and other low-priced souvenir items.

La Ruta Puuc

Following the "Ruta Puuc" signs on the highway beyond Uxmal, you can reach a series of smaller Maya ruins—Kabáh, Sayil, Labná and the cave at Loltún—that date back to the same era as Uxmal. Some structures at each site have been nicely resto red since the area was opened to tourism with the paving of the road in 1978.

The beautiful reddish orange hue of the stonework at Kabáh, Sayil, Labná and almost all other Puuc sites was not the natural color of the limestone, and the Maya did not paint the structures that color. Rather, iron oxide in the dirt stained the ruins as they lay buried during the centuries before excavation began in the Puuc Zone during the 1950s.

SIGHTS

Kabáh (admission), just 32 kilometers by road from Uxmal, is thrown in as an added attraction on most guided tours that run from Mérida. Expect to encounter other visitors there, sometimes by the busload. Thanks to its newfound popularity, the site is undergoing extensive restoration. In fact, on one recent visit it seemed as if entire buildings had suddenly sprung up where only grassy knolls strewn with stone rubble had been before. Workers were scrambling everywhere in the ruins. Roof combs were appearing on buildings that hadn't even had roofs a few years ago. New stone is being quarried to rebuild undecorated walls; in fact, the incongruity of freshly cut masonry at a site more than a thousand years old makes the site seem somewhat artificial at first impression. Kabáh's restored area is sure to keep growing in the years to come.

The most impressive building is the **Palace of the Masks**, the facade of which is entirely covered with about 250 representations of the hook-nosed rain god, Chaac. Each mask consists of 30 individually shaped blocks of cut stone. Indentations on both sides of the nose on each mask may have been used for burning incense or holding torches. In their entirety, the Chaac masks constitute a massive monument to the force that has always meant life or death to the people of the Yucatán.

On the other side of the highway from the ruins entrance, a road leads back past the lofty, rubbled remains of the **Great Temple** to the **Arch of Kabáh**, the gate to the city in ancient times. From the foot of the steps on the far side of the arch, a raised *sacbé* paved with white limestone once ran straight through the forest for a distance of four and a half kilometers to Uxmal. The road continued for another four kilometers to Labná. Now the ancient road runs about 650 yards to a small, plain, ruined temple. Beyond that point, the forest has overgrown everything. A sometimes-faint foot trail continues to trace the old *sacbé* route. If you follow it for a way into the forest, you will gain a deeper appreciation for how much work constructing and maintaining these roads involved. The Maya people had no beasts of burden or wheeled vehicles, so the main reason for the *sacbés* must have been to keep a clear route through the jungle for religious processions and commerce.

Although the site may seem deceptively small, archaeologists have determined that there are at least 80 unexcavated structures at Kabáh.

Midway between Uxmal and Kabáh, where a paved shortcut to Ticul turns off, is **Santa Elena**, the only inhabited town within the archaeological zone. Local guides (ask around for Emilio Santos Camal, reputed to be the best in the area) can show you a number of unexcavated ruins nearby. The best is **Nohpat**, located along the ancient *sacbé* that ran between Uxmal and Kabáh. Nohpat was once a city as large as Kabáh, but it is now so overgrown and decayed that only a clutter of old quarried stones distinguish the Maya pyramids from natural hills. If you want to try hiking or jeeping there on your own, take the unmarked, rough dirt road that leaves the highway two and seven-tenths kilometers west of Santa Elena and goes 4 kilometers south to the ruins site. (*Note:* This road is too rough for standard-clearance cars.) The best thing about this site is the deep forest that surrounds and obscures it.

The ancient Uxmal–Kabáh *sacbé* can also be seen at the site named **Sacbé**, a small site with vaulted temples and some well-preserved stone facades constructed in classic Puuc style. It is located five kilometers from the highway on another bad road that turns off a little more than a kilometer north of Kabáh and curves around through the jungle in a long arc (keep right at the fork in the road). If it hasn't been cut back recently, the last part of the road can be so overgrown that you won't be able to follow it easily or turn around, so be sure to ask the caretaker at Kabáh about the road's condition before setting off in search of these ruins on your own.

Other ruins in the area include **Mul-Chic**, a small site with a six-tiered pyramid one kilometer south from the highway on a

◀ HIDDEN

road that starts a half kilometer west of the Santa Elena turnoff and is too rough to drive but short enough to walk. Another hard-to-reach site is **Xkampon**, on the other fork of the road to Sacbé. It's a ten-kilometer jeep trip followed by a kilometer-long forest hike to the few structures still visible at the site.

HIDDEN ►

Follow the "Ruta Puuc" sign, taking the east (left) fork in the highway five kilometers beyond Kabáh. Another five kilometers will bring you to Sayil. It's five and a half kilometers more to Xlapak and another three to Labná. These ruins are beyond the reach of most tour buses; though some van tours now cover the entire route in a rushed one-day trip, rental car is the best way to go. The paucity of tour buses means you will encounter few other tourists here. You may even find that you have the ruins all to yourself.

At **Sayil**, only two structures have been restored out of 75 known to lie hidden under tree-choked earthen mounds at the site. Admission.

The main restoration is **El Palacio** (The Palace), an exquisite three-story building about 233 feet in length. It has 50 double-chambered rooms as well as patios, porticoes and galleries. Sculptures of mythological beings on the cornices of El Palacio include a huge Chaac mask—complete with teeth—and several "diving gods."

Behind the palace you can see a catch basin about 33 feet in diameter that was designed to funnel rainwater into an underground *chultún* (cistern). Farther along you will find a small, ruined pyramid called **El Mirador** (The Lookout), topped by a temple with a tall, intact roof comb. Stay on the foot trail that continues beyond the pyramid and you will come to a big sculpture of a nude male figure with exaggerated genitals, thought to be a fertility idol used in Postclassic Putún Maya rituals.

The significance of the "diving god" at Sayil is the subject of endless speculation. The same motif is found at Tulum, built 500 years after Sayil on the other side of the Yucatán Peninsula; it is not found elsewhere in the Puuc Zone. Ufologists point to this landlocked diver as "evidence" that humanoid extraterrestrials visited the ancient Maya people—diving down to earth from the

AUTHOR FAVORITE

sights

My perception of the Yucatán was forever changed the first time I went down into the Maya "underworld"—the endless maze of limestone caves just beneath the ground at **Grutas de Loltún**, where indigenous people lived in the dawn of time, held sacred rituals (and still do) and hid from Spanish soldiers. Among the items discovered here are a giant stone head and a mastodon skeleton. See page 326 for more information.

sky. A more conventional explanation is that "diving gods" were people who, like Mayapán founder Hunac Ceel, dived into the depths of sacred cenotes seeking enlightenment.

This is also the place to arrange tours to some of the Ruta Puuc's hidden sites, since the top guide in the area, Miguel Uc Medina, is the caretaker at Sayil. One of the more archaeologically significant such ruins is **Sodzil**, four and a half kilometers south on the unpaved road that runs through Sayil. Inside one of several low temples at the site you can still make out fragments of thousand-year-old murals depicting a royal procession. By the way, *Sodzil* means "Place of the Bats." You'll see why.   ◀ HIDDEN

Another intriguing place for a quick visit is **Gruta de Chac**.   ◀ HIDDEN
First explored by John Lloyd Stevens, who gave it a lengthy description in *Incidents of Travel in Yucatán*, the cave is famous among archaeologists because large caches of Maya polychrome pottery have been found in the deepest recesses of the cave. Without climbing ropes and plenty of spelunking experience, visitors can only go a little way into the .6-mile-long cave before reaching the first frightening drop-off, where a rotting fragment of rope ladder dangles into the abyss. ~ On a short trail from the main road three and a half kilometers west of Sayil, not far from where the Ruta Puuc turns off Route 261.

The next ruin down the paved main road is **Xlapak**. The only structure there, besides a few rubble heaps, is a single temple restored by INAH (Instituto Nacional de Arqueología e Historia) in the 1960s. Although the temple is nothing special either in size (one story, nine rooms) or decor (columns, geometric patterns and Chaac masks), the original masks were well preserved, and the restoration was so painstaking that the place looks almost like new. If you're pressed for time on the Puuc Route, this is the one to skip; otherwise, it makes for an enjoyable pause between the larger complexes at Sayil and Labná. Admission.

Labná seems to be the most peaceful and contemplative of the Puuc Zone ceremonial centers. Admission.

The **Palace of Labná** is similar to the one at Sayil but longer—52 miles. Its most remarkable sculpture is a human face emerging from a serpent's jaws. Many experts think it symbolizes astronomy, the art of science—the practitioners of which were priests, who dominated Maya culture during the Classic period. Another interpretation is that the gruesome reptilian jaws are those of the crocodile, symbol of the underworld where ancient Maya leaders were believed to go when they died. The Chaac mask flanked by human figures on the palace facade is one of the largest masks of the Maya rain god ever discovered. Over the central doorway of the palace is a hieroglyphic date that corresponds to A.D. 869.

A restored *sacbé* leads from the palace to the **Labná Vault**, the largest and finest example of a Maya arch ever found. Over the entrances to the rooms on each side of the arch are sculptural representations of Yucatecan huts like the ones the Maya people of the region still live in today. Fragments remain of the elaborate roof comb that topped this grand gateway. Through the arch is **El Castillo** (The Castle), a steep pyramid with a temple on top. One half of the temple is crumbled to rubble, while the other half is miraculously intact right up to the lofty roof comb.

If you see only one cave in the Yucatán, make it the awesome **Grutas de Loltún**. The network of *grutas* (caves) forms a long cavern, the limits of which have not been fully explored. The largest-known limestone cavern in the Yucatán and certainly the most beautiful, it has been used by the Maya people since before the dawn of history. There is evidence that cave-dwelling ancestors of the Maya lived here at least 4000 years ago. During the Classic period, chambers were used for rituals to establish contact with the underworld. As recently as 1850, Maya people of the area lived in the caves to hide from Spanish soldiers during the War of the Castes.

The cavern displays plenty of stalactites, stalagmites and other strangely shaped minerals as it leads room by room to a "lost world" where daylight pours through a hole in the ceiling, allowing trees to take root inside the cave, and vines drip down from the earth's surface high above. A large flat area may have been used for ceremonies, with stalactites that ring in perfect tune when struck. Magical paintings cover the walls. The palpable sense that people have been using the place since Old Testament times gives the place a haunted feeling. Explorers who have ventured deeper, beyond the big room where tours turn back, have returned to claim that a mysterious force seems to guard the cavern's innermost recesses. Visitors are only allowed into the caves with a tour guide. Regularly scheduled tours run about every 90 minutes from 9:30 a.m. to 3:30 p.m. Guides are usually available to take you on a private tour at other times for a more substantial tip. The guides work for tips only, so plan to pay a few thousand pesos in addition to the charge for admission to the caves. Admission. ~ To reach the cave, continue on the Ruta Puuc highway for 15 kilometers past Labná and turn left onto the four-kilometer entrance road to the caves.

LODGING & DINING Lodging and restaurants are nonexistent along the Ruta Puuc, but they can be found at both Ticul (17 kilometers north of Oxkutzcab) and Uxmal (37 kilometers north of the Ruta Puuc turnoff).

SHOPPING Shopping opportunities are minimal; on busy days, somebody may come around the ruins' parking lots with hammocks and bags of oranges; otherwise, there are no souvenir vendors. Women selling embroidered *huipiles* or other handicrafts can sometimes be found around the village square in Santa Elena, but most of the local artisans' work is sold in Mérida.

All along the Ruta Puuc from Uxmal to Grutas de Loltún there are hardly any signs of modern-day inhabitants. It is

Maya Towns of the Sierra

easy to see how early explorers in these hills could have formed the erroneous belief that the people who built the cities and ceremonial centers of the Puuc Zone later vanished mysteriously. The truth is that within a generation after the Spanish Conquest, an estimated 90 percent of the Maya population of the hill country died from European diseases to which they had no natural immunity, such as smallpox, influenza and measles. The few survivors regrouped in old towns a short distance to the north.

Most visitors to the Puuc region turn around after visiting Grutas de Loltún and retrace their route back to Route 180, either to head back to Uxmal or Mérida for the night or to continue south toward Edzná and Campeche. If you continue instead for ten more kilometers beyond Loltún, you'll come to Route 184. Heading west on this highway, a 38-kilometer drive through Ticul brings you back to Muna, which is an hour south of Mérida and also on the most direct route to Oxkintoc and points south.

Oxkutzcab (pop. 25,000), where the Ruta Puuc meets Route 184, is a very old town with bicycle-choked streets around a large public market that offers an interesting glimpse into the economic life of the Yucatán interior. This is the center of a rich agricultural zone where most of the vegetables and fruits sold in the public

SIGHTS

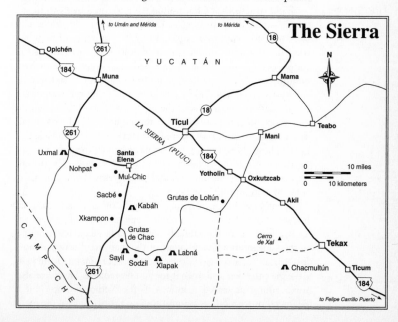

market at Mérida come from. Local farmers bring their produce here and sell it in wholesale quantities to other Maya entrepreneurs, who take it to the city to resell at higher prices. Orange orchards and tobacco fields surround the town. The massive 17th-century church in the center of town contains one of the few ornately carved Spanish colonial altarpieces in the Yucatán that survived the destruction of churches during the Mexican Revolution. The Virgin Mary stands at the center of the *retablo,* surrounded by St. Francis, the four evangelists and Annunciation and Nativity scenes, amid a whole array of other religious images.

Before you turn back toward Mérida, consider a side trip to the little-known ruins at Chacmultún. To get there, first drive southeast to the busy, modern Maya town of **Tekax**, 32 kilometers from Oxkutzcab. Though Tekax dates back to ancient times, with a big mission church and hermitage that still show damage from the War of the Castes, when it was used as a Mexican Army fortress, and the Mexican Revolution, it only became an important town in the 1970s, when a federal irrigation project, called the Plan Chac after the Maya rain god, transformed the surrounding countryside into some of the best sugar cane– and orange-growing land in the Yucatán. Take the paved road past the cemetery for six kilometers to the village of Kancab, then turn at the Zona Arqueología sign and drive another three and a half kilometers to Chacmultún. The drive takes you past the summit of **Cerro de Xal**, the highest point in the state of Yucatán, 820 feet above sea level.

HIDDEN ►

Eight structures at **Chacmultún** were restored by INAH (Instituto Nacional de Arqueología e Historia) in the early 1980s. The back road to the ruins was paved in 1991, in hopes of popularizing the site and attracting tourist dollars to this part of the state. So far, however, hardly anybody has come to see Chacmultún, mainly because it is too far to be a practical daytrip possibility from Mérida. Tekax has little to offer in the way of accommodations, so just about the only way to work Chacmultún into most itineraries is to spend the night at Ticul or Uxmal. Three separate groups of cleared structures stand on hillside terraces. The architecture is reminiscent of Labná, from the vaulted palace rooms to the niches representing Maya huts. The overall impression is very much like Kabáh a few years ago, at an earlier stage of restoration. Admission.

What sets Chacmultún apart from the other sites in the area is a series of faded mural paintings depicting a royal procession. They are in one of the vaulted rooms of a large palace structure in the **Chacmultún Group**, west of the main road down a short forest trail. A locked gate protects the mural remnants from vandals; the caretaker will open it for you on request. There are also some poorly preserved paintings in the **Xetpol Group**, half a kilometer down a different forest trail on the east side of the road.

On Route 184 between Oxkutzcab and Ticul, watch for the remains of two magnificent stone mission churches—**Yotholin**, whose grand facade has more bell openings than any other church in the Yucatán, and, a little farther, the picturesquely ruined **Xocnaceh** at Hacienda Granja Xocnoc.

Sixteen kilometers northwest of Oxkutzcab is **Ticul**, the area's largest town with a population of about 40,000. Most of the inhabitants of the town and its surrounding villages are direct descendants of the Xiu Maya people who lived around Uxmal in Postclassic times, though they are probably not related to its original builders. There is a large public market where both food and folk art are sold, and a big, partially ruined Spanish-colonial mission church that dates back to A.D. 1625.

A "must-see" for visitors who are interested in Spanish-colonial history is the church at **Mani**. Now an insignificant village occupied by people whose ancestors lived in ancient Mayapán, Mani ranked among the most important towns in the Yucatán during the 16th century. It was the capital of the Xiu Maya empire, which spanned the Puuc Zone and much of the Yucatán interior when Francisco de Montejo arrived and decided to build his personal hacienda here. At about the same time, Maya ruler Tutul Xiu converted to Catholicism and offered the town as a site for the greatest mission church in the Yucatán, which was built in 1549. It became the seat of the Spanish Inquisition in the Yucatán, presided over by the notorious Fray Diego de Landa. The inquisition culminated in 1562, when Landa flew into a rage upon learning that pre-Christian rituals were still being practiced in secret at Uxmal and other ancient Puuc ceremonial centers. In a shocking auto-da-fé in the atrium of the church at Mani, Landa destroyed more than 5000 Maya "idols" and all the Maya books his priests could find. Though tour guides often exaggerate and claim that thousands of Maya books were burned during Landa's reign, reliable historical sources

AUTHOR FAVORITE

The tranquil Maya town of Ticul is considered the capital of Maya cuisine because its restaurants were the first to serve Yucatecan home-style cooking to non-Maya visitors back in the early 1960s. While some Ticul restaurants now have locations in Cancún and Mérida as well, **Restaurant Los Delfines** keeps bringing me back to Ticul because it is long-established, still totally local and serves unusual seafood dishes. Try the *chiles rellenos con camarones*—chile peppers stuffed with shrimp and fried. ~ Calle 27 No. 216, Ticul. BUDGET.

put the number at 27 books, leaving only four in existence today. Though it served as the headquarters for the missionary effort in the Yucatán for only 12 years before the much grander church at Izamal was completed, Mani's church is still in use and contains perhaps the finest collection of Spanish-colonial religious art in the Yucatán, including works of genius by an anonymous 16th-century artisan known only as the "Master of Mani." ~ Located about 15 kilometers off the main highway along a paved road north of Oxkutzcab or another one east of Ticul.

If you detour from Route 184 (or sometimes even when you're trying to stay on the main highway), finding your way through the Maya towns in this area can be difficult. Roads lead to the town plaza and leave you there without a hint as to how to find the road to the next town. Few road signs or highway numbers are posted. You will have to ask directions frequently. Hardly anyone understands English in these parts, and even travelers who are fluent in Spanish may have trouble with the local dialect.

Navigation problems, together with livestock, playing children and *triciclos* in the roadway, make travel very slow. On one recent trip through the interior, I spent eight hours in practically nonstop driving to get from Ticul to Chichén Itzá, just 100 kilometers away as the crow flies, or 200 kilometers by road. Still, glimpses into the everyday lives of rural Maya people made the trip worthwhile. Turkeys and pigs wander nonchalantly in and out of whitewashed Yucatán huts, and men dressed all in white pedal along with women, children and bundles of firewood balanced on the rear fenders of bicycles.

LODGING   The easiest plan is to use your Uxmal hotel as a home base for exploring the Puuc hill country. Tourist facilities are almost nonexistent in the towns and villages beyond Labná and Loltún. For visitors who seek really cheap lodging, Ticul, a mainly Maya town of 40,000 people, has the only hotels in the area. The best accommodation there is the **Hotel Bougambillias Ticul**, about three kilometers from the center of town on the highway to Mérida. It has off-street parking and 20 dark motel-style rooms. Ceiling fans. ~ Calle 23 No. 291, Ticul; 9-972-0761. BUDGET.

Acceptable lodging is also available nearby at the **Motel Cerro Inn**. The grounds are nicely shaded with palm trees. The ten guest rooms are motel-style units minimally furnished with double beds and absolutely nothing else, but they have private baths. Room rates are in the very low budget range. Ceiling fans; one room has air conditioning. ~ Calle 23 No. 292, Ticul; 9-972-0260. BUDGET.

In the town center of Ticul is the 15-room **Hotel Sierra Sosa**—noisy and not as nice as the other hotels in the area, but even lower in cost. ~ Calle 26 No. 199; 9-972-0008. BUDGET.

DINING

Visitors passing through Ticul will want to try **Los Almendros,** famed throughout Mexico for its excellent Yucatecan cuisine. The restaurant has been franchised in Mérida, but this is the original. *Poc-chuc,* the orange-and-onion pork fillets popular throughout the Yucatán, were invented in this unpretentious, family-run restaurant. ~ Calle 23 No. 207 between Calles 24 and 26, Ticul; 9-972-0021. BUDGET TO MODERATE.

SHOPPING

A large part of the Maya population in the Puuc region earns money by making tourist goods such as hammocks and Panama hats, but these items are all taken to Mérida for sale, so it takes a lot of searching and bargaining to buy them locally. Ticul is the center for two manufacturing industries that supply the whole Yucatán Peninsula: reddish-brown ceramic pottery, often painted with ancient Maya designs, and shoes. Stroll around town and you'll find more *zapaterías* (shoe shops) than any other kind of store. Maya women in Ticul and surrounding villages make embroidered *huipiles,* both hand-stitched dresses and the more affordable ones embroidered by sewing machine; while most of these, too, are sent to Mérida for sale, some can usually be found at the public market. Another local handicraft is filigree jewelry. Most pottery studios and *artesanía* shops are located along Calle 21 between Calles 32 and 40.

Oxkintoc

INAH, the Instituto Nacional de Antropología e Historia, the Mexican government's archaeological agency, excavated and partially restored Oxkintoc, the "newest" ancient Maya ruin, between 1986 and 1991. It was opened to the public the following year—a great addition to the growing lineup of accessible ruins in southern Yucatán state. Oxkintoc is so centrally located (65 kilometers south of Mérida, 107 kilometers north of Campeche city, and 48 kilometers northwest of Uxmal) that it makes a good daytrip from any of these areas.

NO ORDINARY HILL

Before Oxkintoc was excavated a few years ago, the Labyrinth was almost entirely buried so that it looked like just another forested hill. John Lloyd Stevens, describing his visit to the site in 1842, wrote that the local people believed the Labyrinth to be a natural cave used by leprechaun-like supernatural beings called *aluxes.* According to another legend, a Maya tunnel used to lead all the way from Oxkintoc's Labyrinth to the city of T'ho, site of modern-day Mérida. No trace of any such tunnel has ever been found, and the story seems improbable since Mérida is about 75 kilometers away from the site.

Oxkintoc was occupied for a remarkably long time—from 300 B.C. to A.D. 1100. A carved lintel here bears the oldest hieroglyphic date yet found in the Yucatán, corresponding to the year A.D. 475. The ancient city covered an area of about two square kilometers and was probably larger than Uxmal in its heyday. Among the more than 200 structures found here are 12 pyramid mounds and numerous smaller temples, of which only a few have been restored. Oxkintoc is far away from any other Maya sites; its architectural and artistic style is unique. Sculptures of interest include several carved stelae and door lintels, as well as columns shaped into nearly three-dimensional statues of unidentified human figures. While excavating the site, archaeologists found three royal tombs containing jade masks, a jade plaque carved with hieroglyphs, and manta ray spines. Sculptures at other sites in Chiapas show Maya rulers using the spines to self-inflict pain by piercing the tongue or the penis. The best artifacts found at Oxkintoc are now displayed upstairs in Mérida's Museum of Anthropology.

SIGHTS

The centerpiece of the ruins at **Oxkintoc** (admission)—though by no means the largest of the structures there—is the **Labyrinth** (known to the locals as *Satunsat*, Maya for "Lost-and-Lost"), a three-tiered temple whose original function is unknown. Almost unique in the Maya world (the only known similar building is at Yaxchilán, Chiapas), it has a single entrance at ground level on the west side. A maze of claustrophobically narrow passages lead up, down and around through the interior, eventually making their way up to the partially collapsed top level as well as into the limestone depths below (be careful not to disturb the myriad sleeping bats that hang down from the low ceilings).

HIDDEN ▶

HIDDEN ▶

If you loved the Grutas de Loltún, you'll like the **Grutas de Xpukil.** These caves are natural, and it's easy to believe that *aluxes* live in it. Trees teeming with birds grow inside the entrance, bats slumber in the inner recesses, and Maya skeletons and artifacts are found inside. The narrow caves go on and on, with ladders and ropes to take you between levels. The caretaker of Oxkintoc guides two-hour tours of the caves, which his father discovered half a century ago. ~ A few kilometers east of Oxkintoc via either the ruins road or another unpaved road that runs south from the nearby village of Calcehtoc.

Oxkintoc and the Grutas de Xpukil should be seen on a daytrip from Mérida, Uxmal, Ticul or Campeche. No food or lodging is available in the nearby villages.

Visitors to Oxkintoc are within 25 kilometers of **Becal,** where *jipis* (Panama hats) are made in underground caves. The cool temperatures and steady humidity of the caves make the fibers used in the hats pliable for shaping and weaving. A Panama hat is so pliable that you can wad it up and cram it into your pocket, backpack or suitcase, and, when you pull it out later, it will spring right back into shape. Although the hats are Yucatecan, they became known as Panama hats because American fortune seekers bound for the gold fields of California bought these hats to keep the tropical sun at bay on the overland trek across the Isthmus of Panama. In the center of the village, a unique stone monument depicts three giant Panama hats. Along the highway, a row of roadside stands offers thousands of the hats for sale at much better prices than you'll find in Mérida. ~ The village is just off Route 180, over the state line in Campeche.

Transportation

CAR

To get to Uxmal from Mérida, head south on **Route 180**. This highway is an extension of Avenida de las Itzaes, the *periférico* that goes around the western perimeter of Mérida. Once you get past the town of Umán, where the highway branches three ways in a confusion of signs at the central plaza, **Route 261** to Uxmal is easy to follow. If you come to Hacienda Yaxcopoil you'll know you're on the right highway.

Beyond Uxmal and a short distance past the ruins of Kabáh, a paved, unnumbered road called **La Ruta Puuc** winds eastward through the hills to sites such as Sayil, Xlapak, Labná and Grutas de Loltún. It turns off Route 261 five kilometers south of Kabáh and goes 36 kilometers east to intersect Route 184 and across the Yucatán Peninsula, passing through Opichén, Muna, Ticul and Oxkutzcab. Motorists will find gasoline available in Ticul and Oxkutzcab.

Mani is about 15 kilometers east of Ticul on a paved side Oxkutzcab.

BUS

There is no bus service along the Ruta Puuc. Buses go from Mérida to Uxmal once an hour during the day on their way to Campeche. Several buses run daily between Mérida and Felipe Carrillo Puerto along Route 184, stopping in both Ticul and Oxkutzcab en route. *Combis* run intermittently between the towns of Ticul and Mani.

ELEVEN

Campeche

Tourism is less important to the economy of Campeche than orange groves or Cemento Maya factories. In fact, fewer people come to explore the magnificent rainforest and amazing Maya temples of the Campeche backcountry in a whole year than check into Cancún hotels on an average day. This is particularly remarkable when you consider the state's amazing archaeological wealth. Here you'll find pyramids taller than the ones at Chichén Itzá and fascinating abstract sculpture unlike anything else in the Maya world. Because most of these ancient architectural masterpieces are located along back roads and foot trails through the rainforests that cover 60 percent of the state, seeing them yourself always makes for a memorable adventure. Recently the Mexican government has paved the roads into a number of previously inaccessible sites and marked the turnoffs with big green-and-white signs—yet the tourist trade they seek hasn't materialized. When you visit any of the Maya sites described in this chapter, you can expect to find yourself pretty much alone there. Campeche isn't for everybody. Its dearth of tourism translates into occasional small discomforts, and from time to time visitors may find themselves sleeping in places and eating things that they would just as soon avoid under normal circumstances. But the rewards you gain in experience are more than worth the hardship. In addition to the rainforest and the haunting Maya ruins of the Zona Chenes, Edzná, Calakmul and the Xpujil area, Campeche presents such oddities as the peninsula's largest Spanish-colonial fortress, the mysterious island where the ancient Maya buried their kings, the longest stretch of coastal highway on Mexico's Gulf coast and a state capitol built in the shape of a flying saucer.

▼ ▼ ▼ ▼ ▼ ▼ ▼ ▼ ▼
Zona Chenes

The Chenes people, south of the Zona Puuc, designed and decorated their forest ceremonial centers in a style that was utterly unlike anything found in what is now the state of Yucatán. When you drive through the old-looking archway on a lonely hilltop that marks the Campeche state line, you enter a different world of Maya art and architecture. Most Chenes centers share the same characteristics: facades covered with stucco sculptures in ornate, twisted, nongeometric patterns that symbolized the various gods of the Maya pantheon; curved corners adorned with stacks of Chaac masks whose hooked noses may have been used to hold lanterns; and, most striking of all, a large central doorway that forms the mouth of a huge visage of Chaac that covers the facade. Look for the huge teeth lining the door lintel and the eyes above; structures covered by these huge masks are sometimes called "monster-mouth" temples. Remember the sculptures at Uxmal that showed a human face emerging from the jaws of a monster? Imagine the show Maya priests could put on by appearing from the gaping mouth of one of these monsters in stone. The temples were brightly painted, and some even had secret passages where a person could sneak into the back of the temple unobserved and appear by surprise.

The **Zona Chenes** is best visited en route between Uxmal and Campeche city or as a daytrip from either place. These little-known ruins are situated almost the same distance between the two cities. Soon after you cross into the state of Campeche you will pass through a small Maya village called **Bolonchén de Rejón**. A short distance south of the village a turnoff on the right takes you to **Grutas de Xtacumbilxunán**, an extensive cave network. Here, in times of drought, ancient people climbed all the way down to a series of subterranean cenotes, each of which is said to be a different color. Expert spelunkers can make the trip to the cenotes and back with a local guide in two days. Casual visitors can see colorful limestone formations in the upper level of the caves in about two hours.

SIGHTS

◄ HIDDEN

Located about 90 kilometers from both Uxmal and Campeche, **Hopelchén**, a long, winding Maya town of about 30,000, is the center of the Chenes realm. It's an odd town, where it's not easy to find anyone who speaks Spanish, but several thousand German Mennonites live and farm side-by-side with the Maya in apparent harmony. Although several magnificent archaeological sites lie within an hour or so of Hopelchén, the concept of tourism has not caught on here. There are food stores, a pharmacy and a bank with an ATM, as well as a single spartan little hotel with a restaurant. Don't count on finding gas here, even though maps show a Pemex station. There is one, but the building is a crumbled ruin and fuel—when available—is dispensed from an elevated tank using a length of garden hose. The only reliable Pemex station in the whole region is at Xpujil, more than 180 kilometers to the south.

A well-marked paved road just north of Hopelchén goes about 40 kilometers past the minor ruins of **Nocucich**, where two un-

◄ HIDDEN

HIDDEN ▶ usual freestanding square towers rise above the forest canopy, to the remnants of **Santa Rosa Xtampak**, a large Classic-period Maya city that dominated the Chenes from about A.D. 650 to 850 and had a population of 10,000 to 12,000 at its height. The most impressive of several large buildings at the site is the three-story, 40-room, elaborately decorated **Palacio**, which John Lloyd Stephens called "the grandest structure that now rears its ruined head in the forests of Yucatán." It is one of the most complex multilevel temples in the Maya world, with a maze of internal staircases. The Universidad Libre del Sureste in Campeche began restoring the Palacio in 1991, and the work continues today. The site could not be reached easily by passenger car until the government built the paved road in 1998. Admission.

For more jungle excursions to hidden ruins, turn off Route 261 at the town of Hopelchén and follow a paved road that takes you 41 kilometers south to the village of **Dzibalchén**. This large, isolated Maya town has a *Modulo de Información Turística*—a tourist information stand—on the central plaza. It's usually unoccupied, but as word spreads that there's a tourist in town, someone will be along, ready to guide you through the area's back roads and hidden ruins.

HIDDEN ▶ You don't need a guide for the short drive from Dzibalchén to **Hochob**, a small but well-preserved ceremonial center. Near the southern village limits of Dzibalchén, a road across from the cemetery turns off west to the even smaller village of Chenko; following the markers from the center of the village, turn left and then left again around the plaza to the mostly paved ruins road. Hochob consists of eight buildings around a plaza on a natural plateau that is the highest point in the area. It was cleared in 1982 and 1983; at that time the two best-preserved structures were partially restored while several others were excavated and stabilized. On the north side of the plaza, the **Palacio Principal** has intact stucco designs that form a Classic Chenes monster mask flanked on both sides by limestone latticework. On the opposite side of the plaza are three pyramid temples; the one farthest to the east, known only as **Structure 5**, is topped by a little square temple. The temple itself and a portion of the steep stairway to it have been restored, while the towering roof comb and most of the pyramid base have only been stabilized. Admission.

HIDDEN ▶ Another side road from Dzibalchén runs east through the forest for about 22 kilometers to the next village, **Iturbide**, where the ruins of **Dzibilnocac** feature an unusual rounded pyramid that looks like a miniature version of the one at Uxmal, with a small temple on top that has Chaac masks on the corners and beautifully preserved stucco work on all four sides. The same archaeologists who did the work on Hochob excavated and stabi-

Text continued on page 340.

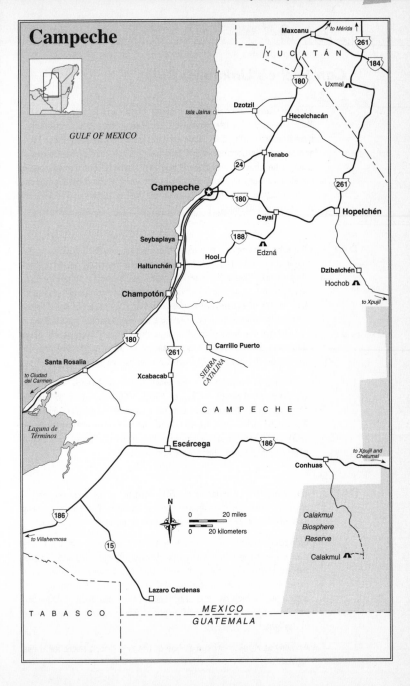

Campeche

GULF OF MEXICO

Maxcanu
to Mérida
261

Y U C A T Á N

180

Uxmal

184

Dzotzil

Isla Jaina

Hecelchacán

Tenabo

24

261

Campeche

180

Cayal

Hopelchén

Seybaplaya

188

Edzná

Hool

Haltunchén

Dzibalchén

Hochob

Champotón

to Xpujil

180

Carrillo Puerto

261

Santa Rosalia

SIERRA CATALINA

Xcabacab

to Ciudad del Carmen

C A M P E C H E

Laguna de Términos

Escárcega

186

to Xpujil and Chetumal

Conhuas

186

N

0   20 miles

0   20 kilometers

Calakmul Biosphere Reserve

15

to Villahermosa

Calakmul

Lazaro Cardenas

T A B A S C O

MEXICO

GUATEMALA

Five-day Getaway

Campeche's Unknown Ruins

Eastern Campeche has as many major Maya ruins as any place in the Yucatán—and a lot fewer tourists. Until recently, most of these sites have been closed to the public or inaccessible by passenger car. Now access is easier but food, gas and lodging are rare commodities in Campeche's backcountry. Since you may never be out this way again, here's a strategy I've found to work for visiting the most Campeche archaeological sites in one trip—total driving distance: 574 kilometers (about 350 miles).

DAY 1
- If you're starting this trip from Mérida, begin early. If you spent last night at Uxmal, a leisurely breakfast and midmorning departure will do fine. Take Route 261 south across the Campeche state line (usually marked by a military checkpoint), and continue for about 40 kilometers to **Hopelchén**, the village at the center of the Chenes archaeological zone. Since there are hardly any accommodations in the village, the best plan is to visit the ruins of **Nocucich** (page 335) and **Santa Rosa Xtampak** (page 336) today and see the others on the return trip from Campeche city tomorrow.

- Returning to Hopelchén, drive west on Route 261 for 42 kilometers, then turn south on Route 188 for 18 kilometers to the big Maya ceremonial center of **Edzná** (page 340). Later, returning to Route 261, drive west for 43 kilometers to **Campeche city** (page 342). Stroll the plaza and surrounding historic district; this city is pretty by night and unbearably hot by day.

DAY 2
- Take time to visit **Fuerte de San Miguel** (page 345) on the hill above Campeche, then leave the city the way you came, heading east on Route 261 to Hopelchén, a distance of 85 kilometers.

- Turn south on the paved but unnumbered Carretera at Xpujil, taking time to visit the Chenes sites at **Hochob** (page 336) and **Dzibilnocac** (page 336). Keep in mind that it's a two-and-a-half-hour drive from the Dzibilnocac turnoff at Dzibalchén to the next village, Xpujil, which has the only accommodations around. The road goes through the Calakmal Biosphere Reserve and is best driven in daylight.

- Arriving at Xpujil, check in at one of the two hotels there for three nights.

DAY 3 • Visit the Maya ruins surrounding Xpujil village: ancient **Xpujil** (page 358), **Becán** (page 358), **Chicanná** (page 357) and, if you're feeling adventurous, **Hormiguero** (page 360) or the **Río Bec** sites (page 359). Spend the night in Xpujil again.

DAY 4 • Get an early start. Fill your tank at the Pemex station six kilometers east of Xpujil—it's the only one on this entire highway. Then drive out to the remote site of **Calakmul** (page 361) in the Calakmul Biosphere Reserve. Plan to return by dark and spend the night in Xpujil.

DAY 5 • Top off your gas tank again before starting out. Drive 100 kilometers east, crossing into the state of Quintana Roo, to the intersection with Route 307. Along the way are **Kohunlich** (page 223) and other sites. Turn left and drive 114 kilometers north to Felipe Carrillo Puerto, where the highway splits three ways—Mérida, Valladolid or Cancún.

lized the temple, known as the **Palacio Principal**, in 1982 and 1983. Surrounding Dzibilnocac are at least seven other pyramids that have not been cleared or excavated. Admission.

HIDDEN ►   **El Tabasqueño**, the other worthwhile site in the area, is deep enough in the forest that visitors can't reach it on their own. The caretaker at Hochob guides private or group tours to this site; other guides operate out of Chenko, the village near Hochob. The road to the ruins is less than two kilometers from the main road between Hopelchén and Dzibalchén. After that, it's a mile-and-a-quarter uphill walk to the ruins. There are two structures: the **Templo-Palacio** temple, with its monster-mouth facade, and **El Torreón**, a square tower 16-and-a-half-feet tall. The ruins suffered near-destruction in a 1995 hurricane, and restoration efforts have recently begun.

LODGING   Hopelchén has the only hotel in the region, the **Hotel Los Arcos**. It has saggy beds and private bathrooms with solar-heated water. ~ Hopelchén; 9-812-0123. BUDGET.

DINING   A dozen or so food vendors hawk their wares from carts around Hopelchén's central plaza, but the only sit-down restaurant is the modest little eatery in the **Hotel Los Arcos**. ~ Hopelchén; 9-812-0123. BUDGET.

Edzná

If you treasure solitude among the ruins, or if you want to visit a major Maya city that nobody back home has ever heard of, Edzná is one of the best options. Thanks to its out-of-the-way location, 50 kilometers southeast of Campeche, few travelers visit Edzná. Take Route 188, off Route 261, south seven kilometers to reach this wonder.

SIGHTS   Dating back to the Late Classic period, around A.D. 633–810 (based on hieroglyphic dates carved on stelae), **Edzná** was a large, prosperous center ideally located at the crossroads between trade routes from the Puuc hill country, the Petén and the southern lowlands. If Edzná had been located much nearer to Cancún, or even Mérida, it would now be overrun with tourists. In fact, there are no visitors' accommodations in the vicinity of Edzná. It is best seen as a daytrip from Campeche city, 60 kilometers away. Admission.

The name *Edzná* means "House of Grimaces," referring to the masks that once graced the roof comb of the **Temple of Five Levels**, the site's largest pyramid. Though the best masks have been removed to museums, leaving a rather plain facade with badly weathered remnants of jaguar and serpent motifs on each level, the temple's height and steepness make it impressive. It stands about 128 feet high—taller than either Chichén Itzá's Castillo or Uxmal's Pyramid of the Magician—and overlooks a broad acropolis. It is unlike other Maya temple pyramids in that each of the lower four levels contains rooms that appear to have been residences of rulers or priests. A passageway runs beneath the stairs on the first level to an inner temple within the pyramid. Mysterious hieroglyphs carved into several steps on the broad central stairway are still legible if not translatable. The 20-foot roof comb on top of the rather plain temple at the pyramid's apex is similar to those seen on some temples at Palenque. Imagine what Edzná must have looked like when the stone walls of its temples were covered with ornate stucco sculpture and painted in bright hues of red, yellow, blue and brown.

In front of the Temple of Five Levels, the **Plaza Central of Edzná** covers an area of 177,000 square feet—three times the size of a football field—and is elevated 22 feet above ground level. As a feat of earth moving, the raised plaza was an even more formidable construction project than the pyramid. At the center of the plaza is a ceremonial platform, and at the far side of the plaza a grand stairway 330 feet wide goes up the side of a long pyra-

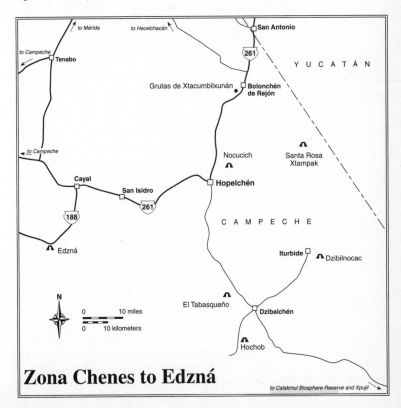

Zona Chenes to Edzná

to Calakmul Biosphere Reserve and Xpujil

mid crowned by what was probably a government administration building, now called the **Temple of the Moon**. Two other structures, known only as the **Southwest Temple** and the **Northwest Temple**, mark the corners of the plaza.

The restored part of Edzná was once the center of a city that covered about three-quarters of a square mile. At least five smaller complexes on the outskirts of this major site, including a recently discovered ball court, await excavation. Several stelae carved with hieroglyphs have been found around these outlying sites, though the ones that have not been removed to museums are broken or so badly weathered that they cannot be read.

Unlike the buildings at most ancient Maya sites in the Yucatán, those at Edzná did not have stone roofs. Instead, the original roofs were thatched—large-scale versions of the palm-thatched roofs still used today on traditional Yucatán huts. Another feature of Edzná that interests archaeologists is the extensive system of Maya irrigation canals and reservoirs that surround the center. Little by little, future archaeologists will reveal more of this ancient city. Meanwhile, we must be content to ponder the scrub-covered man-made mounds throughout the area and wonder what new mysteries they conceal.

Campeche (City)

The port of Campeche (pop. 175,000), capital of the state of the same name, has a unique and fascinating history but few tourists. It's not that the city is "undiscovered"; it's just that most travelers don't spend much time there if they can help it, instead speeding through town en route to Palenque and points west. It is 193 kilometers southwest of Mérida (a shortcut into the city on Route 24 saves about 20 kilometers) and 377 kilometers northeast of Villahermosa. The fairly limited hotel and restaurant scene discourages visitors from staying long, and the dearth of tourists, in turn, discourages new or improved hotels and restaurants. It's too bad, because the city's past has left it scattered with so many fascinating historic places that in 1999, UNESCO declared it to be a Human Cultural Heritage Site. The population of Campeche city today is about three-fourths Maya Indian, and one often gets the feeling that the populace is content to live among the decaying ruins of Spanish colonialism, a civilization as bygone as that of the ancient Maya.

SIGHTS

Campeche originated as the Maya village Ah-kin-pech, a name that means "Place of Ticks." In 1517, the river inlet at Champotón, south of Campeche city, became the first place in Mexico where a Spanish expedition set foot on land when explorer Francisco Hernández de Cordoba realized that the "island" he was trying to sail around was not an island at all. He was driven off by hostile Maya warriors. The area between Campeche and nearby

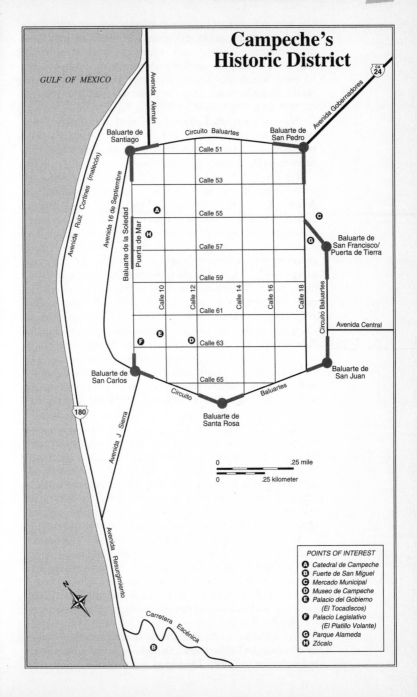

Campeche's Historic District

GULF OF MEXICO

Avenida Alemán

Avenida Ruiz Cortines (malecón)

Avenida 16 de Septiembre

Avenida Gobernadores

CA 24

180

N

Baluarte de Santiago

Circuito Baluartes

Baluarte de San Pedro

Calle 51

Calle 53

Ⓐ

Calle 55

Ⓒ

Baluarte de la Soledad

Puerta de Mar

Ⓗ

Ⓖ

Baluarte de San Francisco/ Puerta de Tierra

Calle 57

Calle 59

Avenida Central

Calle 10

Calle 12

Calle 14

Calle 16

Calle 18

Circuito Baluartes

Calle 61

Ⓕ Ⓔ

Ⓓ

Calle 63

Baluarte de San Carlos

Calle 65

Baluarte de San Juan

Circuito

Baluartes

Baluarte de Santa Rosa

Avenida J. Sierra

0   .25 mile

0   .25 kilometer

Avenida Resurgimiento

Carretera Escénica

Ⓑ

POINTS OF INTEREST

Ⓐ Catedral de Campeche
Ⓑ Fuerte de San Miguel
Ⓒ Mercado Municipal
Ⓓ Museo de Campeche
Ⓔ Palacio del Gobierno
   (El Tocadiscos)
Ⓕ Palacio Legislativo
   (El Platillo Volante)
Ⓖ Parque Alameda
Ⓗ Zócalo

Champotón was where subsequent Spanish invasions of the Yucatán hit the beach, including Montejo's ultimate conquest three decades later.

In the years that followed, the city became an important outlet for exotic woods used as dyes. As it grew and became more vulnerable to pirate attacks, a massive wall was erected in 1686 for the then-staggering sum of $3300. The **Puerta de Mar** (Door of the Sea) and **Puerta de Tierra** (Door of the Land), a pair of huge stone portals at opposite ends of Calle 59, are the most poignant remnants of the wall, which was torn down after several centuries to let the stifling city breathe again.

For a look at the biggest, boldest example of the contrast between the historic and ultramodern in Campeche, walk south down Avenida 16 de Septiembre between the Puerta de Mar and Baluarte de San Carlos. Where the wall used to be, the two main buildings of the state capital district prove that the ancient Maya have nothing over modern Campecheans when it comes to creating architecture that will leave sightseers scratching their heads for centuries to come. The **Palacio del Gobierno** (Government Palace) is nicknamed *El Tocadiscos* (The Jukebox) for its massive open facade of decorative concrete blocks, its absolutely weird roofline and its garish mosaic attempt to summarize the whole history of Campeche on the front of a government building. Next door, the **Palacio Legislativo** (State Congress) carries the nickname *El Platillo Volante* (The Flying Saucer) for obvious reasons.

Though most of the old wall is gone, the *baluartes* (bulwarks) of Campeche's fortress remain intact, so you can trace the old wall by following the boulevard Circuito Baluartes from one bulwark to the next, all the way around the sides and back of the old city. The fortifications enclosed an area of 40 square blocks, and walking around it, you will see how seriously the city takes its historical preservation efforts. Everything inside the mostly imaginary wall of the old city is, well, old. But it is a historic district devoid of funds to restore it, and many buildings seem to be waging a battle against decrepitude—unsuccessfully. Outside the invisible wall, everything is somebody's idea of modern, with lots of Mediterranean-style tile roofs and experimental architecture.

Walk the narrow streets, alluringly lit at night with Spanish lanterns, and explore the ponderous *baluartes* and pretty plazas. Start at the **Baluarte de San Carlos**, the first fort in Campeche, built in 1676. It formerly served as a dungeon and today houses the **Museo de la Ciudad**, where you'll find historical photographs, a model of the old city and a collection of model ships. ~ Calles 8 and 65.

Proceed down to the **Baluarte de la Soledad**, which houses the **Museo de las Estelas Mayas**, an outstanding collection of stelae and sculptures from Edzná and other sites in northern Campeche, including Isla Jaina, the sacred Maya burial island 45 kilometers to the north along the most isolated stretch of the Gulf coast. Admission to the museum. ~ Calle 8; 9-816-8179.

The old fort **Baluarte de Santiago** now contains a lovely botanical garden, **Xmuch'haltun**, full of hummingbirds and stone pathways. ~ Calles 8 and 49; 9-816-6829.

A few blocks west stands the rambling **Parque Principal** in the shadow of the moldy 16th-century **Catedral de Campeche**. Go have a look at the amazing sarcophagus near the altar, encrusted with silver bells, angels and a figure of Christ. ~ Calles 10 and 55.

Campeche has so many churches it seems to have one foot in Heaven. One is the old **Iglesia de San Francisco**, where the son of conquistador Hernán Cortés was baptized. ~ Located along the *malecón* at Calle Mariano Escobedo. The **Museo de Campeche** occupies the former cathedral of San José. This hulking, weather-streaked stone shell now shelters a display of artisans' work. ~ Calles 10 and 63; 9-816-1424.

It's a short walk from the Museo de Campeche to the delightful **Parque Alameda**, a triangular garden just beyond the Baluarte de San Francisco. Surrounded by castlelike ramparts and posts, Alameda welcomes strollers with its molded benches and shade. **Puente de las Mercedes**, at the north end, is a small, white bridge guarded by snobbish stone dogs with their noses in the air. ~ Avenida República and Calle 55.

Campeche's best sightseeing highlight is **Fuerte de San Miguel**, which leans out over a hillside and is rimmed by moats once filled with skin-searing lime. In 1771, this fort was the ultimate in defensive technology with its massive walls, drawbridge and moat, turrets and narrow entranceway enclosed between curved walls that prevented the use of battering rams. The fort put an abrupt halt to the violent sieges that had plagued the city for generations. After its completion, pirates immediately stopped attacking Campeche. The fort was used only once, in 1842, when General Santa Anna used it to defend the city from revolutionaries fighting for the Yucatán's independence from Mexico. From the battlements, you can see the fort's twin, the **Fuerte de San José el Alto**, holding the high ground on the north side of the city;

AUTHOR FAVORITE

sights

Every once in a while a view comes along that begs to be a setting for one of those ads that features diaphanously dressed fashion models poised in picture-perfect places. I see the colonial battlements of **Fuerte de San Miguel**, with its cannons overlooking turquoise gulf waters, as one of those views. See above for more information.

currently under restoration, it houses a small exhibit of boats and armaments. ~ Take Carretera Escénica up the hill from Avenida Resurgimiento toward the south end of town.

Fuerte de San Miguel now houses the **Museo Regional de Campeche**, an archaeological and historical museum that includes pirate lore and Maya art. In recent years, Mexico's federal government has been cycling its touring exhibits, which generally include some of the finest pre-Columbian artworks on earth, through this museum in an effort to boost tourism. Regardless of what's showing, the view from the parapets is worth the trip. Not only can you see the whole city below, old and new, but from the cannon-lined ramparts you can easily visualize the fearsome pirate attacks that terrorized this isolated colonial outpost for centuries. Admission.

Near the southern entrance to town on Route 180, a huge stone figure, called **Monumento Resurgimiento** (Revival Monument), rises between the lanes—a torso with a torch held high for democracy, a Latin Statue of Liberty.

HIDDEN ▶

Crocodiles and songbirds thrive around the **Hampolol Wildlife Station**, a pristine 250-acre wildlife reserve. Walking trails lead through the low jungle and marshes, and a modest visitors center offers a look at the research and conservation programs underway in the area. ~ Located 14.5 kilometers north of Campeche city on Route 24.

LODGING

Campeche has a number of upscale hotels that cater to tour groups and visiting politicians. These are about the only hotels in the state where you will find in-room phones, TV sets, air conditioning and deluxe prices. At the other extreme is an abundance of depressing hotels in the rotting old buildings of the old city, budget-priced at around $10 a night. There is almost nothing in between.

The best hotel in town is the **Del Mar Ramada Inn**. The U.S.-based Ramada chain took over this location of the bankrupt El Presidente, which used to set the standard for luxury accommodations in Mexico. With 120 spacious rooms, modern decor and balconies overlooking the water, it has much to offer and seems to cater primarily to international bus tours en route to Palenque. The amenities include a swimming pool, restaurant, bar, playground and even a popular disco. Air conditioning. ~ Avenida Ruíz Cortínes 51; phone/fax 9-816-2233. DELUXE.

Across the street, the 103-room **Hotel Baluartes** offers significantly lower rates than the Ramada. Modern and square, set in an unexciting parking lot with its back to downtown and its face to the *malecón*, the Baluartes has ample rooms, many but not all of them recently refurbished (ask to see your room before renting it), with hanging wicker lamps, carpets, color TVs and big pic-

Feasting with the Dead

The city of Campeche is a great place to experience El Día del Muerto, the Day of the Dead. Stroll the spooky moonlit streets of the old city on the night of November 1, when the *zócalo* is filled with people dressed in elaborate Maya *traje*. A free, colorful extravaganza of folk dancers and musicians takes center stage in the plaza, surrounded by altars full of flowers and baked goods, including *pibipollo*, a large Maya tamale pie reserved only for this holiday. Delicious as they may look, these offerings are not to be eaten by the living. They are for dead ancestors, whose spirits come in the night to "eat the souls" of the food. Afterward, the food is ceremoniously disposed of like the mortal remains of a deceased loved one. Don't worry, though—there's also plenty of food for living people to savor during this annual feast with the dead.

The most popular holiday in Mexico, El Día del Muerto is a mostly happy time for honoring the memory of ancestors, celebrating their spiritual return, and remembering that death, inevitable as it is, need not be feared. The celebration originated with the Aztecs of central Mexico, where it was presided over by the goddess Mictecacihuatl (pronounced pretty much the way it's spelled). With the Spanish Conquest, missionaries allowed the celebration to be held on All Saints' Day and All Souls' Day (November 1 and 2), since it seemed similar to celebrations of All Hallows' Eve, or Halloween, in some European traditions.

Among the Maya, however, El Día del Muerto has an additional meaning: it incorporates Uayéb, the five unlucky days preceding the new year. The Maya calendar has 18 months, each 20 days long, each presided over by a different god or goddess who gives the month its unique character and protects certain types of activities. But Uayéb, the leftover five days after the end of the last month, is godless, leaving humans unprotected from evil spirits.

Even today, Uayéb is observed in some traditional villages by clearing a ceremonial road beyond the outskirts of town, in a different direction each year. An idol or altar is placed at the end of the road to distract evil spirits while the local shaman performs augeries in the town center, along with rituals to counteract bad predictions.

Because Uayéb has been merged with El Día del Muerto throughout Maya Mexico, its celebration is more public and more solemn than elsewhere. It lasts a full five days, during which nearly all shops and offices are closed.

ture windows with views of the Gulf. For extras, there's the restaurant/bar, nightclub, pool, café and terrace. Air conditioning. ~ Avenida Ruíz Cortínes; 9-816-3911, fax 9-816-2410; www. baluartes.com, e-mail baluarte@campeche.sureste.com. MODERATE.

Another of the few waterfront hotels is the **Alhambra** at the southern end of the *malecón*. This big pink hotel has 98 modern rooms with satellite TV. There is a swimming pool as well as a restaurant, bar and disco. The hotel is right across from Campeche's public bathing beach and a block away from the scenic drive to the hilltop fortress of San Miguel, an ideal spot from which to watch the sunset. Air conditioning. ~ Avenida Resurgimiento 85; 9-816-6822, fax 9-816-6132. BUDGET.

Among the numerous low-cost inns in town is the **Hotel Campeche**, overlooking the old city's *zócalo*. The setting, in the heart of the city's atmospheric historic district, couldn't be better; the guest rooms couldn't be plainer. But then, they cost less than $10 a night. ~ Calle 57 No. 2; 9-816-5183. BUDGET.

DINING

Campeche is a shrimp-boat port, so *camarones* (shrimp) and other seafood specialties abound here. The local seafood institution, **Restaurant Miramar** faces the Puerta del Mar. This old colonial building is full of romantic touches: black Spanish lanterns, golden glass doors laced with grillwork, beamed ceilings. Its atmosphere outshines its cuisine, which includes the popular *cangrejo moro* (stone crab), fish soup, squid and *pan de cazón* (shredded baby shark, a Campeche specialty). ~ Calle 8 No. 293-A at Calle 61; 9-816-2883. MODERATE.

One of the most attractive eateries on the Campeche coast is the shiny, colonial **Restaurant Marganzo** in the middle of the

AUTHOR FAVORITE

Campeche city is known throughout Mexico for its distinctive seafood dishes. Having encountered *mariscos estilo campechano* on menus from Santa Fe to Puerto Vallarta, I never pass up a chance to eat seafood at **La Pigua**, where most *campechano* cuisine is first introduced to the public. (Can you resist the shredded baby shark tostadas?) Located outside the old city walls, two blocks north of the Baluarte de Santiago, La Pigua is considered Campeche's finest restaurant. Lush greenery completely fills the view through the big picture windows, creating a junglelike atmosphere, setting the stage for plates piled high with crab claws. The chef blends imagination and tradition to come up with entrées such as pasillo chiles stuffed with shark meat and shrimp battered in shredded coconut. For dessert, try the *chicozapote* mousse, made from a sweet local fruit. ~ Avenida Miguel Aleman 179, Campeche; 9-811-3365. MODERATE.

block near the *zócalo*, across from the baluarte. Marganzo features regional seafood dishes in a setting accented by black-and-white tile, arches and ceiling fans. There is a nightclub upstairs. ~ Calle 8 No. 262, upstairs; 9-811-3898. MODERATE.

A real find for travelers suffering from a veggie shortage, the **Yax Kin Restaurante** offers a mainly vegetarian menu, using fresh ingredients washed in purified water. They assure patrons that everything they serve is *"de origen 100% natural"*—the Mexican equivalent of "organic." ~ Calle 55 No. 56; 9-816-0842. BUDGET TO MODERATE.

One of the city's few all-night cafés, open from sundown to sunup, is the indoor-outdoor **Cafetería Le Jardín** in the Hotel Baluartes. Locals and international travelers alike gather in air-conditioned coolness around the white wrought-iron tables to enjoy coffee, pastries and ice cream with a view of the parking lot (and the *malecón* beyond). ~ Avenida Ruíz Cortines; 9-816-3911. BUDGET TO MODERATE. Also in the Hotel Baluartes, the full-service **La Almena** restaurant is long, narrow, light and airy; its menu is so blandly international that it offers a comforting cure for culture shock. ~ MODERATE.

For an authentic Mexican eating experience, try **La Parroquia**. Open 24 hours a day, it serves cheap, filling *comidas corridas* (daily specials) and Campeche specialties such as *colados*, a regional variation on tamales. ~ Calle 55 No. 8; 9-816-2530. BUDGET.

SHOPPING

Tops on the Campeche shopping scene is the **Plaza Comercial Ah-Kin-Pech,** the city's only American-style indoor mall. What makes this mall remarkable is that it's the only place in the state where you can find all the same stuff that a KMart sells back home. ~ Avenida Pedro Sainz de Baranda between Calles 51 and 49.

Campeche does have a row of shops along Calle 8 where souvenirs are peddled. One good shop is **Artesanía Típica Naval,** which carries bottled exotic fruits like *nance* and *maranón*. ~ Calle 8 No. 259; 9-816-5708. **El Coral** has Maya replica figurines. ~ Calle 8 No. 255; 9-816-3285.

Another collection of shops, **Exposición y Venta Permanente de Artesanías,** occupies the old Baluarte de San Pedro. Locally made craft items—indigenous dresses and hammocks, as well as baskets and Panama hats woven from *jipijapa* palm fronds—are for sale. ~ Avenida Circuito.

The **Casa de Artesanías Tukulna,** operated by a state economic development agency, offers a selection of textiles, furniture and crafts made in outlying villages. ~ Calle 10 No. 333; 9-816-9088.

The federal government's **Casa de Artesanías** features quality arts, crafts and clothing from local villages and from around Mexico. ~ Calle 55 No 25.

Powerful odors assail the senses at the **Mercado Municipal,** a labyrinth of indoor stalls tumbling over with food, baby chicks, good-luck soaps, handicrafts and posters of pop personalities and Jesus. ~ Avenida Gobernadores.

NIGHTLIFE   Pirates loom large in the historical sound and light show presented every Friday at 9 p.m. at the **Puerta de Tierra**, which is located at the back of the old city. Admission. ~ On the east end of Calle 59 between Calle 18 and the Circuito Baluartes.

Overnight tourists mingle with politicos and rich kids at the town's three main nightclubs. **Disco Atlantis** is located in the Del Mar Ramada Inn. ~ Avenida Ruíz Cortinez 51; 9-816-2233. **El Olones**, in the Hotel Baluartes, offers live contemporary music on Friday and Saturday nights. ~ Avenida Ruíz Cortínes; 9-816-3911. The **Jet Set Bar** is located at the end of the *malecón*. ~ Plaza Comercial Ah-Kin-Pech.

BEACHES & PARKS   **PLAYA BONITA** 🚶 🏊   If the city of Campeche ever had a beach, it was replaced by the pirate-proof seawall centuries ago. Locals escape the heat at Playa Bonita, on a small cove south of town. It's friendly but lacks beauty. Backed by a line of palms and a big recreational pavilion, the thin sand is littered with bottle caps and stones. Facilities include lockers, showers and baths, refreshments and palapa shelters. Swimming is calm and gentle, but there is possible contamination from the nearby thermoelectric plant in Lerma. A seaside trail leads south for a few miles to a nicer, less-accessible beach called San Lorenzo. ~ To get to Playa Bonita, take the marked turnoff 13 kilometers south of Campeche on Route 180, just past the town of Lerma.

▲ Camping is not safe at Playa Bonita.

▼▼▼▼▼▼▼▼▼▼▼▼▼▼▼▼
Campeche's Gulf Coast

The shore of northern Campeche is so swampy that no road goes near the more than 39 kilometers of coastline between Parque Natural del Flamenco Mexicano de Celestún and Campeche city. Along this inhospitable segment of the Gulf coast lies a small limestone island that provides one of the strangest glimpses of the ancient Maya world. Isla Jaina, 45 kilometers north of Campeche city on the most inaccessible part of the Gulf coast, was used as a burial island for Mayan nobility. The number of royal tombs that have been found on the island and the riches they contained are without equal in the Maya world. The finds included thousands of pieces of carved jade, the most precious material of the ancient Maya, which was imported from Guatemala. There were also beautifully painted ceramic vessels that once held food offerings of chocolate or *atole* (finely ground corn meal).

Just who was buried there is one of the mysteries surrounding Isla Jaina. Some scientists believe it was the ruling class of the

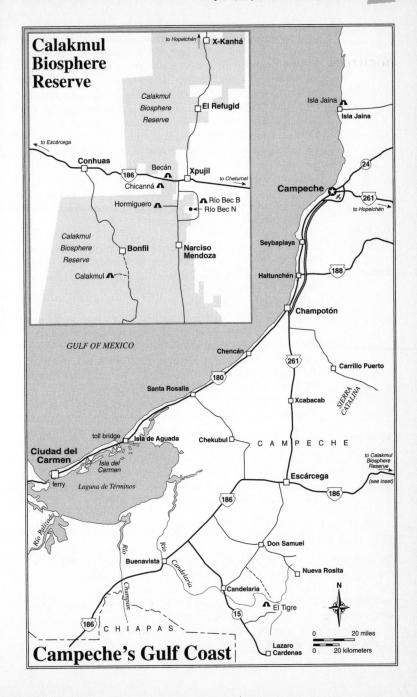

Calakmul Biosphere Reserve

to Hopelchén
X-Kanhá

Calakmul Biosphere Reserve

El Refugid

to Escárcega

Conhuas

186

Becán

Xpujil

to Chetumal

Chicanná

Hormiguero

Río Bec B
Río Bec N

Calakmul Biosphere Reserve

Bonfil

Narciso Mendoza

Calakmul

Isla Jaina

Isla Jaina

24

Campeche

261

to Hopelchén

Seybaplaya

Haltunchén

188

GULF OF MEXICO

Champotón

Chencán

261

Carrillo Puerto

180

Santa Rosalia

Xcabacab

SIERRA CATALINA

toll bridge

Isla de Aguada

Chekubul

C A M P E C H E

Ciudad del Carmen

Isla del Carmen

ferry

Laguna de Términos

to Calakmul Biosphere Reserve

(see inset)

Escárcega

186

186

Río Palizada

Río

Río Candelaria

Don Samuel

Buenavista

Nueva Rosita

Champan

Candelaria

N

El Tigre

186

C H I A P A S

15

0   20 miles

0   20 kilometers

Lazaro Cardenas

Campeche's Gulf Coast

Puuc region, 39 kilometers inland. The Zona Puuc was the only area with a sufficiently large ruling class in its separate centers to account for all the burials here, and sufficiently interconnected to have produced the pottery and figurines found at Jaina in a unified artistic style. Wherever these privileged people ruled in their lifetimes, carrying their mortal remains to Jaina must have meant long and difficult expeditions. This part of the coast was as inaccessible in ancient times as it is today, and there's no sign of Maya settlement for 27 kilometers in any direction.

In making their funeral arrangements, the ancient Maya rulers seem to have been more concerned with the offerings sent to the underworld along with their corpses than with the grandeur of their tombs, for unlike the ostentatious status-symbol structures found in Maya town cemeteries today, the tombs of Jaina were marked by small, unremarkable temples.

SIGHTS

HIDDEN ▶

The Mexican military guards **Isla Jaina** to prevent looting. Until 1993, no visitors were allowed except archaeological expeditions approved by INAH (Instituto Nacional de Arqueología e Historia). The island is now open to the public in a new drive to attract tourism to Campeche.

You can book an all-day **boat tour** to Isla Jaina at the tour agency in the lobby of Campeche's Ramada Inn or Hotel Baluartes. The tour is costly. If you wish to go to the site by boat on your own, you must first get a permit from the Mexican Department of Tourism at their office in Campeche. ~ Avenida Ruíz Cortinez, Plaza Moch-Couoh; 9-811-9200, fax 9-816-6086.

The character of the coast south of Campeche city is far different from the coast to the north. The 124-mile segment of Route 180 between Campeche and Ciudad del Carmen is the longest stretch of coastal highway anywhere on the Mexican Gulf coast. If you are heading toward Villahermosa, this highway is shorter than going through Escárcega on Route 186 and much more scenic, though it takes considerably longer because of the time you spend waiting for ferries.

SPIRITUAL SOUVENIRS

The artifacts for which Isla Jaina is most famous are small, delicately wrought clay figurines. They are hollow, and when a person blows into the hole in the back of one, it whistles. Each one has an individual character. The prevailing theory is that each figurine depicted the deceased person with whom it was buried, though it could also represent someone the deceased hoped to symbolically carry with him on his journey to Xibalbá, the Maya underworld.

Route 180 runs a surprisingly hilly course for the first 12 and a half kilometers to the traditional fishing village of **Seyba Playa**, which occupies one of the most attractive locations along this part of the Gulf coast. The highway passes turnoffs to sandy shores for another 12 and a half kilometers to **Champotón**. This large town has colorful hillside charm and a history that goes back to pre-Hispanic times, though the waterfront reeks of dead fish parts. From Champotón to Ciudad del Carmen, the busy highway seldom loses sight of the sea.

You have to pay to get on or off **Isla del Carmen**, which is linked to the mainland at its northern tip by an expensive 3.25-kilometer toll bridge that is the longest in Mexico, and at the south end by a car ferry that runs across the mouth of the lagoon to the mainland several times a day. From there it's a 93-kilometer drive through soggy terrain to the town of Frontera, Tabasco; from Frontera it's an hour to Villahermosa (see Chapter Twelve).

Isla del Carmen is a long, narrow sandbar between a lagoon and the open sea, much like Isla Cancún. And like Ciudad Cancún, **Ciudad del Carmen** was transformed in the early 1970s from a dirt-poor, laidback fishing village to a booming new city. The similarities end there, however. The industry that transformed Ciudad del Carmen was not tourism but oil. Seventy percent of Mexico's oil production comes from oil wells offshore or in the Tabasco wetlands across the lagoon. During the city's development, the population has grown to nearly 250,000, making it the largest city in the state and third-largest on the Yucatán Peninsula. The sudden growth has created animosity between the *carmelitos* (natives of the island) and the *estranjeros* (foreigners—not *norteamericanos* or Europeans, but newcomers from other parts of Mexico assigned by Pemex to work here). The oil company workers generally enjoy a much higher standard of living than the long-time locals, and the two groups rarely mix. The unwelcoming attitude is one reason Pemex workers view Ciudad del Carmen as an undesirable place to relocate in spite of the reasonably nice beaches.

About 365,000 barrels of oil a day are shipped from the supertanker port at Ciudad del Carmen. Though the oil business has obscured the fishing-village charm this town must have had in earlier days, it has brought the kind of middle-class prosperity that supports good restaurants and a fun beach scene despite the black goo that sometimes washes up with the surf.

Downtown, a number of buildings recall Ciudad del Carmen's small-town colonial heritage. The **Museo del Ciudad** was originally built as a hospital in 1898 and converted into a museum in 1998. While part of the building is still being renovated, its halls contain exhibits on the town's history, Gulf Coast pirates and ancient Maya civilization in the area. Admission. ~ Calle 22.

A more ornate 19th-century building houses the **Centro Cultural de la Ciudad del Carmen**, where arts and *artesanía* from Campeche and other parts of Mexico are exhibited, as well as traditional Maya *traje* of the island and surrounding area. ~ Calle 24 at Calle 27.

Within walking distance of downtown, the **Barrio Guanal** is the city's historic district, established by the island's first seven non-Indian families in 1722. The whitewashed houses are built in Mediterranean style, with red tile roofs and window balconies. Contemporary buildings in the area are required to conform to the historic 18th-century style.

General Ignacio Zaragoza Park offers a quiet retreat in the center of the city. Set in the park, the **Parroquía de la Virgen del Carmen** dates back to the U.S. occupation at the end of the Mexican War in 1846; it was designed by American Commodore Perry, who would later attain fame as an Arctic explorer.

Isidro Verdejo takes visitors on boat trips through the mangrove jungle on the lagoon side of the island, an ideal place for birdwatching. ~ 9-382-1425.

Ciudad del Carmen's small **zoo**, with about 200 animals representing 12 local species, is located at the north end of the island near Playa Norte.

Laguna de Términos, the body of water that separates Isla del Carmen from the mainland, was declared a protected area in July 1994. The 1,800,000-acre reserve, which also encompasses the wetland deltas of the Candelaria, Chumoan and El Palizada rivers on the mainland shore, supports a diversity of ecosystems. Wildlife in the reserve includes manatees, tapirs, whitetailed deer, wild boars, crocodiles, caymans, ducks, iguanas, green turtles and hawksbill turtles. The mangrove jungle that fringes the lagoon is a major breeding ground for shrimp and oysters. Guides can be arranged through hotel travel desks in Ciudad del Carmen to take visitors on motor launch tours of Laguna de Términos.

LODGING

Between Seyba Playa and Champotón, the **Tucan Siho Playa** offers beachfront accommodations in a 19th-century hacienda, pink on the outside with even brighter pink inside, complemented by bold green and blue accents in its 74 guest rooms and suites, most of which have king-size beds. The guest facilities include a large swimming pool, gardens, a private beach, a restaurant and a small disco. Air conditioning. ~ Route 180, Km. 40; 9-223-1200, fax 9-223-1203; e-mail aurora-e@hoteles-tucan.com. DELUXE.

Champotón has a number of small hotels near the waterfront. The **Snook Inn** was designed with American anglers and hunters in mind. It has 20 motel-style rooms with TVs and a swimming pool. Air conditioning. ~ Calle 30 No. 1, Champotón; 9-828-0201, fax 9-828-0059. MODERATE.

Left: Dressed in local costume, this girl wears a traditional huipil, a colorfully embroidered blouse.

Below: Daily markets display such fresh fruit as papaya, mango, pineapple and melons.

The "Sound and Light Show" dramatically highlights the sculptural details at Uxmal's Nunnery Quadrangle.

The **Hotel Géminis**, just up the street, has TVs in some of its 24 rooms; it also has a pool. Both hotels have views of the Gulf and the Río Champotón. Some rooms have air conditioning. ~ Calle 30 No. 10, Champotón; 9-828-0008, fax 9-828-0094. BUDGET TO MODERATE.

Ciudad del Carmen has a full range of hotel accommodations, from basic beds to full-line resort lodging. Top of the line, the **Holiday Inn Ciudad del Carmen** is located near the airport and oriented toward a business travel clientele. Each of its 160 spacious guest rooms and suites has a modem line and VCR as well as a private balcony overlooking the pool area. There's a complete business center with secretarial services, video conferencing capabilities, computers and lots of other amenities you may not want to think about while you're on vacation. ~ Calle 31 No. 274, Ciudad del Carmen; 9-381-1500, fax 9-382-0520, or 800-009-9900 in the U.S.; e-mail holiday@mail.hinncmemx.com.mx. DELUXE.

Besides the giant prawns and oysters that are caught along this part of the coast, a local seafood delicacy is baby hammerhead shark.

The elegant **Eurohotel** has 92 bright, modern guest rooms including 12 suites. This place has all the amenities—reliable hot water, in-room phones and cable TV, plus a swimming pool, restaurant and disco. However, it is a long way from the beach. Air conditioning. ~ Calle 22 No. 208, Ciudad del Carmen; 9-382-1030. DELUXE.

A better bet for resort comfort is **Los Sandes,** a red-roofed two-story complex a block from the beach. The hotel presents blank walls to the street; its 62 spacious and comfortable though rather bland rooms face an interior courtyard with a swimming pool. ~ Avenida Periférico at Justo Sierra, Ciudad del Carmen; 9-832-2400. DELUXE.

For low-priced lodging, a good place to go is the **Hotel Acuario,** two blocks from the busiest part of the Gulf Coast beach and within easy walking distance of downtown. The simple rooms have solar-heated water. Ceiling fans. ~ Calle 51 No. 60, Ciudad del Carmen; phone/fax 9-382-5995. BUDGET.

Along with crustaceans and mollusks, duck is featured on many menus during the spring hunting season. Shrimp cocktails and other light seafood fare are served at a number of *cocktelerías* on the lagoon around Playa Manigua and Playa Caracol.

DINING

A good place to sample seafood is **La Red**, an open-air restaurant under a tile roof where you can savor the ceviche while looking out over the lagoon beyond the car ferry dock. ~ Calle 20, Ciudad del Carmen; 9-382-0544. MODERATE.

If you're weary of the steady Gulf coast diet of shrimp, head inland a couple of blocks to **Cactus**, a simple restaurant with dining under a tiled portal, open 24 hours. The specialty here is beef, served with Mexican and Californian wines. ~ Calle 31 No. 132, Ciudad del Carmen; 9-382-4986. MODERATE.

The finest dining in town is at the **Piamonte**, the dining room at the Eurohotel. The restaurant features lobster and shrimp from the Gulf of Mexico, as well as tasty Italian pasta dishes. The contemporary, almost minimalist Continental ambience is geared toward a business clientele in the daytime. Soft music sets the stage for a more romantic mood after dark. ~ Calle 22 No. 208, Ciudad del Carmen; 9-382-3090. DELUXE.

Ciudad del Carmen has more South American restaurants than other Yucatán Peninsula cities. For Argentinean-style steaks—thin-sliced and tender—try the **Bar Antonio**. ~ Calle 28 No. 78; 9-382-3662. If spicy Brazilian food is more to your taste, there's **Espeto–Restaurante Brasileiro**. ~ Calle 56 No. 324; 9-382-4465.

SHOPPING   The local handicraft specialty in Ciudad del Carmen is lamps, flowers and other decorative items made of fish scales. Otherwise, the city offers little to tempt shoppers. The main downtown shopping mall **Plaza Camel** has a few quality jewelry stores such as **Albricias** (9-382-4853) as well as several fun shops. **Splash** (9-382-0014) does hand-painted T-shirts and lets you design your own; it also sells a lot of practical everyday items and imports from the United States. ~ Calle 22 No. 148. **Plaza del Mar** is another mall. ~ Calle 35 No. 2 at Calle 20; 9-382-0297.

NIGHTLIFE   Ciudad del Carmen supports a jumping little disco scene. One of the hot spots is **Bahía 56**, near the beach. Weekends only. Cover. ~ Calle 56 No. 294; 9-382-4465. Downtown, you'll find **Umma-Guma**. ~ Calle 26 No. 206 at Calle 55; 9-382-0102. These clubs both attract an exuberant young crowd on weekends with live music. Or shake your booty, if you wish, at the **Club Skiros**, just off Avenida Periférico, two blocks south of the Los Sandes hotel. Sexy disco sounds left over from the 1970s draw a somewhat more mature clientele than you're likely to find at the other two clubs. ~ Calle 31 No. 248; 9-382-4870.

BEACHES & PARKS   SEYBA PLAYA The beach at this fishing village is small, secluded and idyllic. Balneario Payucan rents lockers and lounge chairs and sells refreshments. Camping is prohibited. ~ Located just south of the village of Seyba Playa.

ISLA DEL CARMEN Lined with coconut palms, the main beach runs along Isla del Carmen's western shoreline, becoming less lively and more meditative farther north. On the lagoon side, **Playa Caracol** is a good snorkeling area; you can rent snorkeling gear and other water-sports equipment there, and it has changing rooms and a palapa bar. Camping is unsafe. ~ Isla del Carmen's main beaches lie along Avenida Periférico, the circle drive that follows the sandy western shoreline and then loops around to the lagoon side of the island and Playa Caracol.

Midway between the noisy, unappealing truck-stop town of Escárcega and Quintana Roo's capital at Chetumal, Xpujil is the only village along the otherwise un-

Xpujil and the Calakmul Biosphere Reserve

populated route. Its population has grown to about a thousand, though the government plans to open up land here for as many as 5000 homesteaders. Most of the people living in the area are Chol Maya who have recently moved here from the lowlands of Chiapas, where overpopulation has joined forces with traditional slash-and-burn farming methods to destroy vast areas of the Lacandón rainforest. The Chol feel little cultural connection with the Yucatec Maya and speak a different language; most are evangelical Christians. A raw, frontier excitement pervades the area—as well as a nagging sense of impending environmental disaster. Given the government's decision to bring population into the area, whether the largest remaining rainforest in Mexico will be cleared by family farmers or preserved depends on whether the villagers can develop other sources of income—particularly ecotourism. The state of Campeche has mounted a major effort to put the Xpujil and Calakmul Biosphere area on the tourist map, though the shortage of lodging and restaurants in the area suggests that boom times may be a while in coming. The government recently broke ground on an ambitious highway project that will link Campeche city directly with Xpujil, bypassing Escárcega and somewhat shortening the drive.

Certainly the most "undiscovered" destination in the Yucatán today, Xpujil is in the midst of a concentration of large, little-known Maya ruins from the Río Bec culture. These elaborately decorated ruins hold great interest for archaeologists, but until quite recently they were too far away from modern civilization for many travelers to visit. In 1993, the local roadside restaurant

AUTHOR FAVORITE

When I was a kid, one of my favorite ways to while away a fourth-grade arithmetic class was to daydream about discovering a mysterious lost city deep in a tropical forest teeming with wildlife. If you find the thrill of discovery lacking at Chichén Itzá or Uxmal, make an expedition to the ruins of ancient **Calakmul**—a daydream you can reach in a rental car. See page 361 for more information.

built half a dozen wooden cabañas out back, so for the first time visitors can spend a few days exploring the ruins and the surrounding rainforest.

SIGHTS   Several of the largest ruins are just off Route 186. Approaching the Xpujil area from the west, the first ruin is **Chicanná**. The name *Chicanná* means House of the Serpent Mouth, which is also the name of the most completely restored structure at the site. The facade of this temple is a Chenes-style monster mask almost exactly like the one at Hochob, which was separated from these southern sites by more than 39 kilometers of uninhabited jungle. Most archaeologists believe the mask represents Itzamná, the Maya sun god. Admission. ~ Off Route 186, 500 meters south of the highway.

Although Chicanná was not discovered until 1966, it has been the focus of three major excavation and restoration projects, the latest begun in 1991. Today, four temple groups can be seen. They are connected by trails that lead through dark forests under a dense canopy of leaves. Several temples have monster-mask fronts as well as tall decorative roof combs.

Becán, two and a half kilometers east of Chicanná, was inhabited from A.D. 550 to 1200. Temples at Becán once stood as much as 115 feet tall. Long stairways reach the tops of two pyramids and command a view of the forest for miles around. The ruins of ancient Xpujil thrust above the treetops about four miles to the east. The most unusual feature of Becán is the mile-and-a-quarter-long moat that once surrounded the city and is still visible today. All the Río Bec cities were built with defensive features much like those of medieval European castles, suggesting that wars plagued the region during the early part of the Classic period. The political situation seems to have stabilized eventually; around the end of the 7th century A.D., the people of Becán started using their moat as a trash pit. Most of the buildings that stand here today date from the 8th and 9th centuries, when the region was at peace. A dozen temples surrounding three large ceremonial plazas have been excavated and stabilized or restored since the mid-1970s, and the work is still going on. Admission.

The ancient city of **Xpujil**, believed by many archaeologists to have been the capital of the region in the Late Classic period, is on the outskirts of the present-day village. Maya people have continuously inhabited Xpujil since around A.D. 400. Although an archaeological survey conducted in the 1970s shows that the city of Xpujil covered an area of several square miles and had at least four large building groups, to date only the structures of **Group I** have been excavated and consolidated. They are one of the best examples of the architectural feature that is unique to the Río Bec zone: massive towers disguised as pyramids with as many as 12 tiers. Stairways too steep to climb lead to false temples adorned with stucco masks and lofty roof combs. The ancient Maya used a technique, known to modern movie-set designers as "forced perspective," to make Xpujil's towers look much taller than they actually were. Admission.

Between Becán and Xpujil, the highway crosses a narrow strip of protected rainforest that connects the two vast expanses of the **Calakmul Biosphere Reserve** that lie a few miles north and south of the highway. The reserve is intended to save a portion of the Petén rainforest on the Mexican side of the border, where so much of it has already been burned off for farming. Established under UNESCO's Man and the Biosphere program, the reserve adjoins Guatemala's Maya Biosphere Reserve north of Tikal National Park and Belize's smaller, hard-to-reach Río Bravo Conservation Area on the northwest border. Supporters of the Mundo Maya concept, hoping to improve the region's economy by developing ecotourism, envision the three reserves as a single international park, which they refer to as the Maya Peace Park.

Camping among the Río Bec ruins is possible if you really trust your mosquito repellent.

At the reserve's northern boundary is the tiny village of X-Kanhá. Several sites at least as impressive as Chicanná, Becán and Xpujil are found in the southern part of the reserve. Chol Maya homesteaders who live along the reserve's boundary have been recruited to serve as caretakers, accompanying anybody who goes to the ruins. Travel is limited on the roads south of Xpujil, which run all the way to Guatemala and are regularly patrolled by the Mexican Army. In good weather, a passenger car can usually manage the roads to Hormiguero and the Río Bec sites, though few signs mark the way through the maze of little back roads along the edge of the reserve. You can save wear and tear on your rental car and your nerves by taking a **guided tour** with one of the guides who offer ruins trips from the local hotels and from Rancho Encantado on Laguna de Bacalar, about 120 kilometers to the east.

Among the best adventures going in the Yucatán today is a guided all-day trip to **Río Bec**, which is only about 15 kilometers south of Xpujil but takes more than two hours to reach on a narrow four-wheel-drive road through the jungle. The archaeological zone sprawls over 19 and a half square miles, completely overgrown by jungle, and the ruined structures are difficult to find without a knowledgeable guide. Río Bec is not a single site but a series of at least 20—some a single building, others a group of temples around a central plaza—five of which are worth the formidable effort required to see them. Trying to see all five sites on the same trip is not realistic, however, because it takes about eight hours to hike the forest trails that link the main sites. Any daytrip

◄ HIDDEN

to Río Bec should include **Río Bec B**, which has a temple with a tall roof comb flanked by two nearly 55-foot-tall towers disguised as pyramids. It is the only structure at Río Bec that has been completely cleared and stabilized. Of the other possible side trips, the best in my opinion is **Rio Bec N**, where the central temple looks almost exactly like the one at Rio Bec B did when archaeologists found it in 1973.

HIDDEN ▶ A shorter daytrip into the biosphere reserve, involving almost as much rough road driving but less hiking, is to **Hormiguero**, where there are two temples. **Structure II**, nearest to the road, is a favorite among archaeologists because it combines Río Bec–style fake pyramids and Chenes-style monster-mouth facades more completely than any other ruin in the region. A short trail through the forest brings you to **Structure V**, a small but elaborately decorated temple on top of a mound that was once a small pyramid. The tunnels in the base of the mound, from which Hormiguero (Ant Hill) got its name, were dug by looters before Carnegie Institute archaeologists located the site in 1933.

HIDDEN ▶ A small palace and steam baths known as the **Bird Mask Temple** illustrates just how much must still await discovery in this dense forest. It was first seen in 1967 by an archaeologist who, unfortunately, was lost himself. He photographed the temple with its ornate facade and tall roof comb and published the photograph along with an account of his discovery, estimating the location to be about 25 miles southwest of Xpujil.

Twenty-four years later, a local woodcutter told archaeologists that his nine-year-old son had found an old stone house in the woods. When the archaeologists saw it, they realized they had rediscovered the missing Bird Mask Temple. It is within walking distance north of the village of Xpujil—and only about 750 yards from the main highway. But you still need a guide to find it.

In the Maya language, *bec* means "elm"—one of the nearly 700 tree species that make up the forest around Río Bec and Hormiguero. In both areas, the diversity of tree and plant life in the practically primeval jungle is as fascinating as the ruins themselves. While some of the region's flora is the same as that found in old woodlands of the southeastern United States, much is tropical and as exotic as anything you could hope for in a rainforest experience. One tree that is encountered frequently—trails are laid out to lead to them—is the sapodilla, an economic mainstay for villagers in the region, who tap it for *chicle*; its fruit, which has a sweet taste similar to *flan* (custard), is a regional delicacy as well as a favorite food of spider monkeys and coatimundis. Another cash product harvested in the local forests is pepsin, which is used as a digestive aid in remedies such as Pepto-Bismol. In earlier times, the most lucrative tree in the region was the lofty *caoba*, or mahogany. Hundreds of thousands of these rainforest giants were cut in the southern Yucatán Peninsula and Central America, shipped to Europe and sold there for as much as $30,000 per tree. Today, though they are rarely found in parts of the forest that can be reached by road, great stands of mahogany still exist deep in the biosphere reserve, where they are protected by law.

Besides its *cohune* palm trees, palmettos and myriad climbing and hanging vines, much of the exotic look of Campeche forests can be attributed to their colorful orchids, bromeliads and other epiphytes, which grow in the branches of trees and never touch the soil. But not only small plants grow in the high branches. The tiny seeds of the strangler fig tree are deposited by birds in the high branches of other trees, and by dropping fine tendrils to the forest floor, they take root. The tendrils thicken to become a whitish trunk that wraps around the host tree, engulfs it and, over a period of about 20 years, kills it.

The gumbo limbo tree provides the Maya with a powerful natural anti-biotic used to prevent infections and cure certain fevers.

The Maya people who make their homes in this forest believe that the lush environment provides a natural solution for every problem encountered there. The *chechén*, or poisonwood tree, and the *chacah*, or gumbo limbo tree, are a commonly cited example. The poisonwood tree can be spotted by the black sap that oozes from its trunk and exposed portions of its roots; the poison, which causes instant, painful burns to the skin and can be fatal if it touches an open cut, is in the sap. Fortunately, the peeling, copper-colored bark of the gumbo limbo contains an antidote for the poison. Local people believe—and it appears to be true—that a gumbo limbo tree grows within a few feet of every poisonwood tree.

The Calakmul Biosphere Reserve is named for the ancient Maya city of **Calakmul**, located about 55 kilometers southwest of Río Bec in the heart of the reserve and reached via a paved but badly potholed one-lane road that leaves Route 186 at the tiny village of Conhuas, 58 kilometers west of Xpujil and 97 kilometers east of Escárcega. You pay a fee at the turnoff for the use of the road into the reserve, and another fee to enter the archaeological site itself. Driving to Calakmul is half the adventure. From the turn-off at the main highway, expect the drive to take between two and three hours. It's unlikely that you'll see another vehicle—more likely that you'll see a coatimundi or forest fox dash across the road, or a tree full of *oropéndolas* or toucans. Leave your car in the small parking lot at the end of the road and walk for a kilo-meter along an ancient Maya *sacbé* through the forest. Suddenly you reach a clearing and find yourself surrounded by the pyra-mids and palace of Calakmul.

◀ HIDDEN

Although Calakmul was discovered in the 1930s, excavations did not begin until 1984. Only then did archaeologists begin to realize how vast the site really was. It covers 27 square miles, and more than 7000 structures have been identified there so far. Experts now believe that Calakmul was the largest city in the Classic Maya world; population estimates range from 60,000 to as many as 200,000 inhabitants at its peak between A.D. 600 and 800. Hints about Calakmul's history are only now beginning to surface, and archaeologists now believe that it was the "capital" of an alliance of cities that also included El Mirador on the Guatemalan border and Uaxatún just north of Guatemala's Tikal National Park. Together, the allied cities vied with Tikal for political, military and economic control of the Petén rainforest. At least 118 stelae have been found here so far—more than at any other Maya site. Many have been defaced, and centuries of erosion plus decades of acid rain have obliterated the faces of many of them; but the hieroglyphs along the outside edges of the monuments remain legible and may one day provide the most detailed historical record of the Classic era in the rainforest that lies at the center of ancient Maya civilization.

References to Calakmul have been identified in hieroglyphs at many other sites, including Palenque and Yaxchilán in Chiapas and Naranjo, Caracol, Piedras Negras, El Peru and Dos Pilas in Guatemala. In 1994, scientists discovered a 10th-century royal tomb containing a body mummified using a method previously unknown in the Maya world and similar to the technique used in classical Egypt. In 1985 the vaulted crypt of a 7th-century noble was found beneath one of the many temples. It contained 2000 pieces of jade, the most precious of Maya treasures, in the form of jewelry and an elaborate mosaic burial mask.

At other deep forest cities like Tikal, the central plaza is cleared and sometimes planted with grass. But at Calakmul, a minimum-impact approach keeps the central plaza covered with tall trees and thick vegetation. The forest has been cleared for only a few feet away from the partially restored pyramids and palaces, making them hard to photograph. From the ground, a wide-angle lens can't take in the immensity of the largest pyramid—at 175-feet, one of the tallest in the Maya world. To find great photo possibilities, you have to climb to the top, where you get a sense of the ancient city's size and layout as you look across the sea of greenery at many more unrestored pyramid mounds, each a temptation to hike farther into the tall forest festooned with orchids and teeming with wildlife. Don't lose sight of the fact that the long drive back to Xpujil is much longer in the dark, so watching the sunset from one of those amazing temples three or four kilometers up a jungle trail is a temptation you may want to pass up.

Literally hundreds of smaller Maya ruins, most of them unexcavated and many inaccessible by road, dot the nearly uninhabited jungle south of Route 186. In the unlikely event that you find yourself spending more than a single night in Escárcega, an interesting ruin to visit is **El Tigre**. To get there, take the unpaved road that heads south from the main highway about two kilometers west of town. After about 25 kilometers, bear east on a smaller road, passable only during the dry season, to the village of Nueva Rosita, where locals can direct you to the ruins. Originally called Itzamkanak, the site was a Postclassic Maya town that was still inhabited at the time of the Spanish conquest. Many historians believe that this out-of-the-way spot is where conquistador Hernán Cortés killed Aztec chief Cuauhtemoc, sacrificing him in Aztec style. The ruins are at the edge of the wetlands that surround a large lake known as Laguna Salsipuedes. (A common name in the nether regions of rural Mexico, *salsipuedes* is Spanish for "leave if you can.")

◄ HIDDEN

In the Xpujil region, the **Restaurante y Cabañas El Mirador Maya**, on the west edge of the village, has 14 guest units including thatched-roof huts with shared baths, rustic tin-roofed cabins and a few motel-style rooms with varnished hardwood trim and modern plumbing. There are no TVs or telephones, but a swimming pool is under construction. ~ Route 186 Km. 159, Xpujil; phone/fax 9-832-9163. BUDGET.

LODGING

Nearby, the newer, equally basic **Hotel Calak Mul** offers 14 plain rooms situated on a hillside, but not high enough to isolate them from the noise of the truck traffic on the highway. ~ Route 186, Km. 153, Xpujil; 9-832-9162. BUDGET.

AUTHOR FAVORITE

My top choice for lodging in the state of Campeche is the **Chicanná Eco Village**—partly because you gotta admire the optimism it takes to open the only luxury resort in the state's remote southeastern rainforest, and partly because the location is an archaeology buff's fantasy come true. This jungle lodge has 28 rooms in two-story stucco buildings with palapa roofs. Each unit has a living area and separate bedroom with king-size bed or two double beds, and a patio or balcony with a view of the Xpujil ruins. There are no TVs or phones, but the lodge does have a pool and jacuzzi surrounded by lush flower gardens, as well as a full restaurant, coffee shop and bar. Make reservations through the Ramada Inn in Campeche city, which owns and manages the resort. Ceiling fans. ~ Off Route 186, Km. 144 at Zona Arqueológico Chicanná; reservations: 9-816-2233 in Campeche city, fax 9-871-6075; e-mail diro_62@uol.com.mx. DELUXE.

In an area that is otherwise completely devoid of accommodations, the new **Puerta Calakmul** offers rustic jungle lodge-style accommodations in thatch-roofed huts at the junction where the road to the Calakmul archaeological zone turns off the main highway. As this book goes to press, facilities are rudimentary, though the likelihood is that the plans for a full-service restaurant, more guest lodgings and other amenities will become a reality soon as more visitors find their way to the Yucatán Peninsula's least-known major Maya site. ~ Route 186, Km. 96; 9-894-1588; e-mail calakmul@amtave.com. MODERATE.

DINING

Restaurante y Cabañas El Mirador Maya offers a basic menu of roast chicken, tortillas and black beans, tropical fruit and beer. Save-the-rainforest posters and maps and photographs of the region's Maya sites cover the restaurant walls. ~ Route 186 Km. 159, Xpujil; phone/fax 9-832-3304. BUDGET.

Otherwise, dining options in Xpujil are limited to the kind of indoor *comedores* where locals sit at long, plain plywood community tables and speak Maya while feasting on fat little tortillas and stew containing a strange assortment of turkey parts—a memorable intercultural experience for those with strong stomachs and no self-consciousness. Very inexpensive (and worth every penny).

Transportation

The city of Campeche is on **Route 180**, the main highway linking Cancún and Mérida to the major cities of central Mexico.

CAR

Hopelchén is located on **Route 261** between Uxmal and Campeche. South of Uxmal on Route 261, 42 kilometers beyond Hopelchén, is the intersection of **Route 188**, which leads to the archaeological zone of Edzná.

From Champotón, head due south on Route 261 for 80 kilometers to Escárcega, where the main highway from Mexico City forks—one way to Campeche and Mérida, the other to Quintana Roo. From Escárcega, **Route 186** runs just about due east through tall forest for a distance of 270 kilometers to Chetumal and the Caribbean coast.

Expect to be stopped at Army checkpoints anywhere along Route 186, especially at Xpujil near the Quintana Roo–Campeche state line. The government's main concerns are smugglers dodging customs (Quintana Roo is a free-trade zone, while Campeche is not) or carrying guns (the highway is just a few miles from the roadless Guatemalan border). But tourists are subject to arrest if they're found in possession of drugs during a security check.

AIR

Aeroméxico operates daily flights from Mexico City into Campeche's small airport. ~ 9-816-6656.

BUS

Buses come and go constantly at Campeche's main terminal. Buses arrive from Mérida at the rate of more than one an hour around the clock, from Villahermosa 15 times a day, and from Mexico City eight times daily. ~ Avenida Gobernadores 289; 9-816-2802.

Two second-class buses a day from Campeche (one at 8 a.m. and one at 2:30 p.m.) pass through Hopelchén on their way to Edzná. Buses going from Mérida to Campeche that take the long route through Uxmal stop in Hopelchén.

Ten second-class buses a day (five each direction) pause for passengers in Xpujil en route between Escárcega and Chetumal. Although several first-class buses also run along this highway, they don't stop. No buses go to the Calakmul Biosphere Reserve.

▼▼▼▼▼▼▼▼▼▼▼▼▼▼▼▼▼▼▼▼

Addresses & Phone Numbers

Campeche State Tourist Office ~ Plaza Turistica, Avenida Ruíz Cortínez, Campeche; 9-811-9202, fax 9-816-6068

Cruz Roja (Red Cross) ~ Avenida Resurgimiento, Campeche; 9-815-2411

Emergency number (Campeche city only) ~ 060

Hospital General ~ Avenida Central y Circuito Baluartes, Campeche; 9-816-0920

Policia ~ Avenida Resurgimiento, Campeche; 9-816-2329

Internet access ~ Excalibur Cybernet & Boutique, Calle 8 No. 402, Campeche; 9-816-3367

TWELVE

Beyond the Yucatán

Once the Maya ruins of the Yucatán capture a traveler's imagination, they don't let go easily. Several fascinating options present themselves to those who wish to explore more widely in the ancient Maya world. If you have a passport, it's easy to venture into Belize from Chetumal, in Quintana Roo, and visit Maya sites such as Lamanai and Altun Ha. For complete information, read this book's companion volumes, *Hidden Belize* by Catherine O'Neal (Ulysses Press, 2001) and my own *Hidden Guatemala* (Ulysses Press, 2000).

The ancient ceremonial centers of the Lacandón rainforest in lowland Chiapas, a natural side trip from Campeche, are among the most awe-inspiring and unforgettable Maya sites to be found anywhere. Palenque, in particular, is certainly the most beautiful ruin in Mexico and arguably the quintessential sight of the whole Maya world. The river journey to Yazchilán, hidden deep in the jungle, may well be remembered the adventure of a lifetime.

Villahermosa

Villahermosa (pop. 550,000), capital of the neighboring state of Tabasco, is the gateway to Palenque for air travelers from the U.S., Mexico City or Mérida. For motorists coming from the north, passing through Villahermosa is unnecessary, but anyone wishing to see the great anthropology museum and the outdoor display of giant Olmec heads there will find the city an easy daytrip by car from Palenque. Villahermosa is situated just 140 kilometers west of Palenque in the heart of Mexico's oil-producing region. Too commercial to be charming, Villahermosa is nevertheless graced with wide boulevards and a modern park with a unique Olmec sculpture garden.

The origin of the Maya civilization is connected with an even more ancient group, the Olmec people. Some anthropologists believe that the first Maya were direct descendants of Olmecs who migrated from Veracruz to colonize Chiapas and the Yucatán Peninsula. Others think the Maya civilization resulted from the influence of Olmec ideas on more primitive Maya people living along the Pacific coast of Chiapas and Guatemala.

Exactly who the Olmecs were is one of the great mysteries of New World archaeology. Some Olmec art depicts two separate races: one with Polynesian characteristics—thick lips, broad noses and oriental eyes—and the other with Semitic features and beards. While there is evidence that the Olmecs lived in the region at least as early as 8000 B.C., their civilization flowered suddenly around 1200 B.C. and lasted until 300 B.C. No Olmec burial remains have ever been found, and their dwellings were swallowed up by swamplands millennia ago. All that is known about the Olmec people comes from their art, which includes giant stone heads (the head was a great source of power for the Olmecs), round clay pyramids, sculptured altars and finely carved jade jewelry. The jaguar god, later revered by the Maya as the symbol of earth and night, first appeared in Olmec art. The Olmecs developed a form of writing and the foundation of the calendar system later used by the Maya and other Mexican cultures.

Parque La Venta, a beautiful park that weaves along La Laguna de los Ilusiones, has bridges, lookout points, a columned promenade and a zoo. ~ Off Paseo Tabasco and Boulevard Grijalva. It also has an unusual **outdoor museum** that resembles a sculpture garden. Three massive, Polynesian-looking heads stare eerily out of thickets of tropical foliage. The 25-ton heads were hewn out of basalt dragged 99 miles from the nearest mountains to La Venta, an Olmec ceremonial center, more than 3000 years ago. Twenty-five other Olmec monuments in the outdoor museum include stelae, altars and a tomb. All were discovered in an oil field in the Tonalá Swamps 80 miles northwest of Villahermosa. Admission. ~ 9-314-1652.

SIGHTS

Another Villahermosa must is the **Museo Regional de Antropología Carlos Pellicer Cámara,** one of Mexico's finest museums. Poet Carlos Pellicer Cámara organized its fine collection of Olmec, Totonec and Maya artifacts. The museum also contains representative pieces from Aztec, Mixtec, Teotihuacán, Totonec and Zapotec cultures, as well as from archaeological sites in the states of Colima and Nayarit. Admission. ~ Periferico Carlos Pellicer 511; 9-312-6344.

Villahermosa's newest visitor attraction is **Yumká,** a 250-acre animal park located 16 kilometers east of town near the airport. Jungle and lakeshore habitats are home to native birds and animals of eastern Mexico, and a savannah allows grazing room for giraffes, antelope and other exotic species from Africa and Asia. The animals roam free; the human visitors view them from safari-like tour vehicles. Admission. ~ Ranchería Las Barrancas; 9-933-5601.

LODGING
The nine-story **Hyatt Villahermosa**, located along Route 180 on the north side of the city near the Tabasco 2000 shopping mall, is convenient for motorists and offers all the comforts of an American-style business travelers' hotel, including a swimming pool, two lighted tennis courts and a children's playground. The 209 guest rooms are spacious, with contemporary furnishings and cable TVs that receive English as well as Spanish channels. ~ Avenida Benito Juárez 106; 9-935-1234, fax 9-935-3073, or 800-233-1234 in the U.S. DELUXE.

The new luxury leader in Villahermosa lodging is the **Calinda Viva Villahermosa**, located just a block from Parque La Venta. Its 240 spacious guest rooms have Mexican tile floors and bright, modern decor, with two double beds and a host of amenities such as hair dryers, coffee pots, steam irons and minibars. Sliding glass doors open onto balconies with city views. There's a swimming pool, a spa and a complete business center. Air conditioning. ~ Avenida Ruiz Cortines at Paseo Tabasco; 9-935-1856, or 800-900-0000 in the U.S.; e-mail reservas@calinda.com.mx. DELUXE.

The award-winning **Hotel Maya Tabasco** is a contemporary five-story hotel with 160 large, comfortable rooms. Each is appointed with red carpets, colonial furniture and blue-tiled baths. The staff is exceptionally friendly. ~ Boulevard Ruiz Cortines 907; 9-934-4466, fax 9-932-1133, or 800-221-6509 in the U.S. DELUXE.

Located between the Río Grijalva and the small Plaza de Armas near the state capital complex, the **Hotel Plaza Independencia** has 89 simple, spacious rooms with TV and in-room phones. Some top-floor rooms in this six-story hotel have balconies with views of the river. There's a swimming pool. Air conditioning. ~ Calle Independéncia 123; 9-932-1299, fax 9-934-4724; www.hplaza.indepcia.com.mx, e-mail hplaza@nexus.net.mx. MODERATE.

There are plenty of clean, basic, very inexpensive hotels near the city center, especially along Calle Madero. The **Hotel Palma de Mallorca** stands out from the rest simply because it offers air-conditioned rooms—a must in the steamy climate of the Tabasco lowlands. Air-conditioned rooms cost almost twice as much as those with ceiling fans. ~ Calle Madero 510; 9-932-0144. BUDGET.

DINING
The most highly regarded restaurant in the city is **Los Tulipanes**, located near the Museo Regional de Antropología Carlos Pellicer Cámara. Tabasco has its own regional cuisine that is distinctly different from that found in the Yucatán, and this is the ultimate place to try it out. Fresh seafood in spicy sauces is the focus of the menu; empanadas (grilled meat or fish pies) are another house specialty; and of course, what would an upscale Mexican restau-

Beyond the Yucatán

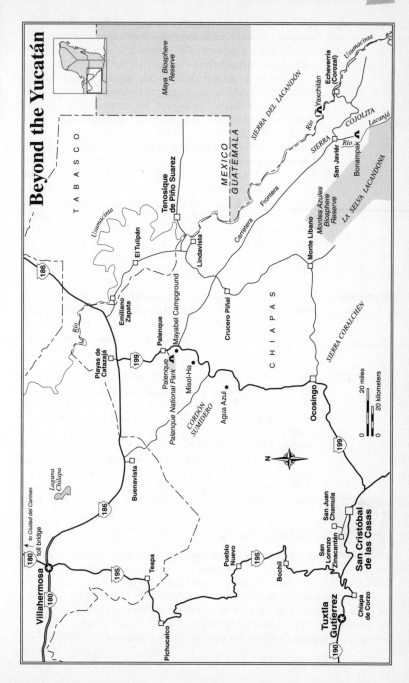

rant be without a selection of American-style beefsteaks? The atmosphere is white tablecloths and candlelight in the evening, more casual at lunchtime. The Sunday brunch here is legendary. ~ Periférico Carlos Pellicer Cámera 511; 9-932-9209. DELUXE.

A downtown prize is the sparkling, air-conditioned **Galerías Madán**. Booths and carpet are part of its Americanized look. The menu features banana splits and hamburgers, plus Mexican dishes—and the food is good. ~ Avenida Francisco Madero 408; 9-932-1650. BUDGET TO MODERATE.

Veggie lovers in Villahermosa soon find their way to **Aquarius Centro Vegetariano**, an all-vegetarian restaurant near Parque Juárez that features a range of Mexican and *norteamericano* dishes served in simple, comfortable surroundings. ~ Avenida Franco J. Mina 309; 9-934-2537. BUDGET TO MODERATE.

Small but elite, **El Guaraguao** specializes in empanadas *pejelagarto* (empanadas filled with alligator fish) as well as other regional dishes from Tabasco. The few tables fill quickly in this popular spot, so go early or make a reservation. ~ Calle 27 de Febrero 947; 9-932-2155. MODERATE TO DELUXE.

SHOPPING   For browsing, the downtown **pedestrian mall** has attractive boutiques, though not many crafts. ~ Along Avenida Francisco Madero.

For indigenous art, try the **artisan's shop** at the Museo Regional de Antropología Carlos Pellicer Cámara. ~ Malecón Carlos Madrazo.

NIGHTLIFE   The hottest dance club in town, **Disco Dasha** draws a young, well-dressed crowd, especially on weekends, when the cover triples to about $15 for men, $10 for women, which includes all you can drink. ~ Tabasco 2000; 9-936-2174. **Disco Ku Rock House** is a lively new contender on the dance club scene. ~ Avenida Augusto Sandino 548; 9-935-9431. **Snobs Disco** is a hopping deluxe club that draws a young crowd. ~ Excelaris Hyatt Hotel, Avenida Benito Juárez 106, Colonia Linda Vista; 9-933-4444.

If a jazzy drink is enough action, saunter over to **Carlos 'n Charlie's** and enjoy live tropical music amid bullfight decor. Bull-

AUTHOR FAVORITE

They are a mystery I could never pass up—so ancient and unexplained that some of my New Age friends claim they were refugees from Atlantis. They vanished hundreds of years before the rise of Maya civilization, leaving behind giant stone heads weighing 25 tons, carved from boulders that were transported 100 miles, and smaller figurines depicting an apparently different, bearded race. Find out about the lost Olmec civilization at **Parque La Venta**. See page 367 for more information.

PALENQUE 371

fights are held seasonally at the neighboring Plaza de Toros. ~
Plaza de Toros; 9-933-4260.

The most romantic place to relax after dark is **Los Guaya-
canes**, a beautiful bamboo-roofed restaurant-bar attached to the
Museo Regional de Antropología and overlooking the Río Grijalva. ~ Malecón Carlos Madrazo; 9-932-9285.

PLAYA PARAÍSO 🏊 Appropriately named, this beautiful beach
is the Gulf Coast's own little piece of paradise. Ten miles long,
with sand almost white against a dark forest of towering coconut palms, it stands at the end of a very circuitous route north of
the delightful tropical village of Paraíso. A large, modernistic pavilion dominates the sand like a ladino Sydney Opera House,
bouncing with salsa tunes on Sunday. You won't find many tourists here. ~ Located 107 kilometers northwest of Villahermosa.

**BEACHES
& PARKS**

Palenque was made famous by American adventurer
and travel writer John Lloyd Stephens during his first
expedition to Central America in 1837. Actually, for
nearly 70 years before Stephens' arrival, Palenque had been known
to Spanish explorers, who had removed some of the best sculptures and hieroglyph panels and sent them to King Charles III of
Spain. It was Stephens, however, who captured the public's imagination with a series of books recording his adventures. Stephens
astonished the reading public with his detailed 90-page description of the wonders of Palenque, his attempts to buy the site, and
his desperate retreat from the site when his illustrator companion,
Frederick Catherwood, fell gravely ill with a fever. The events
formed the climax of Stephens' two-volume *Incidents of Travel in
Central America, Chiapas and Yucatán*, an instant bestseller when
it was published in 1841. Catherwood's 35 detailed drawings of
Palenque for the book are widely reproduced as prints and sold
in tourist shops throughout the Yucatán today.

Several years before Stephens and Catherwood "discovered"
Palenque, Jean-Frédéric Maximilien, Comte de Waldek, a gentle-
man artist from Austria, lived among the ruins for two years.
The count, who was 64 years old when he arrived in 1832, lived
with his local Indian mistress first in the small temple now called
the Temple of the Count and later in a compound of huts below
the Temple of the Sun. Count Waldek's many paintings of Palenque, always depicting the ruins in a romantic golden glow, were
captivating but wildly inaccurate. Eager to support his convic-
tion that the Maya culture had its roots in the ancient civilizations of the Mediterranean, the count filled his paintings with
stylistic details borrowed from ancient Egypt and Greece. He
also imagined Hebrew, Hindu and Roman artistic influences.

Even today, Palenque remains one of the most romantic and
mysterious of the Maya "lost cities." Much of its mystique

Palenque

comes from the overabundance of theories about its origins. The pagoda-like architecture of the palace and artistic similarities to temple friezes in Cambodia have led some to see a link between Palenque and the Buddhists of Southeast Asia. Others have convinced themselves that Palenque was inspired by the Egyptians, Greeks, Hebrews or Romans. More recently, researcher Erich von Däniken has asserted that the relief sculpture on Lord Pacal's stone sarcophagus depicts an "ancient astronaut," supporting his theory that the Maya world was inspired by visitors from outer space. Somehow, explorers have often felt uncomfortable with the obvious truth that the classic magnificence of Palenque was conceived in the minds of "primitive" forest people.

Travelers who come to Palenque after visiting other major Maya sites such as Chichén Itzá and Uxmal will see the differences in art, architecture and environment immediately. The more you travel in the Maya world, the clearer it becomes that each ancient Maya ceremonial center was unique, displaying the singular genius of a great leader or dynasty. Most rulers, like the dwarf magician of Uxmal or the god-king whose plumed serpent emblem lurks everywhere in Chichén Itzá, remain cloaked in legend. At Palenque, however, archaeologists know exactly who built the palace and temples, including exact dates of birth and death and even what they looked like and how they dressed.

Although small temples at the Palenque site were used for worship as early as A.D. 400, this remote outpost of Maya civilization only became a major ceremonial center in the year A.D. 615, when Lord Pacal, one of the greatest charismatic leaders in Maya history, ascended the throne at the age of 12. Under the rule of Pacal and his two sons, Chan Bahlum II and Kan Xul II, Palenque bloomed for a hundred years and then vanished as jungle overran its temples, pyramids, palace and ball court. By the year 720, all construction had ceased, and by 800 the city had been abandoned forever. Yet the Lacandón people, Maya descendants who live deep in the rainforest of western Chiapas, still make religious pilgrimages to hold ceremonies in these temples.

As political tensions ease in Chiapas, the ruins at Palenque are receiving more international visitors than ever before; of course, the number of vacationers who visit Palenque are only a tiny fraction of the tourism figures for Chichén Itzá or Tulum. The most pleasant time to visit, and perhaps the most beautiful, is in the early morning, when a soft jungle mist drifts ghostlike through the ruins.

SIGHTS   At the ruins of ancient **Palenque** (admission) you'll find a clustered array of architecturally exquisite temples surrounding a 1300-year-old royal palace, one of the most remarkable structures in the Maya world. Elaborate stucco sculpture was a specialty of Palenque's artists, and well-preserved examples can be found both inside and outside of several structures, along with traces of the bright red paint that once set off the city against the deep green walls of jungle.

Tucked into a pocket on the side of the Tumbala Mountains, which rise suddenly from the flatlands to the cool, remote high country, this most sacred of ancient Maya ceremonial centers consists of three compact clusters of buildings, some of which have been restored, and a number of other mounds on the edges of a jungle clearing. In ancient times, the temple complex of Palenque extended for at least four miles up and down the banks of a small river, now known as the Río Otolum.

The **Temple of Inscriptions** stands to your right as you enter the ruins area. At 75 feet, it is the tallest structure at Palenque. The roof comb, now nearly gone, is thought to have added another 40 feet to its height. Although this stepped pyramid set into the hillside is no rival in size for the grand pyramids at Chichén Itzá and Uxmal, it holds a couple of surprises that have made it one of the most famous ancient Maya structures. Climb the steep stairway to the top. From there, you can see a great distance over the lowlands to the north and get the best view of the labyrinthine palace directly below. On the front of the long temple are a series of carvings that depict a Maya nobleman in formal dress holding a child. They probably represent Lord Pacal and his heir, Prince Chan Bahlum II.

Inside the temple, the walls are filled with three huge panels of hieroglyphs. They are not very legible today. Fortunately, even

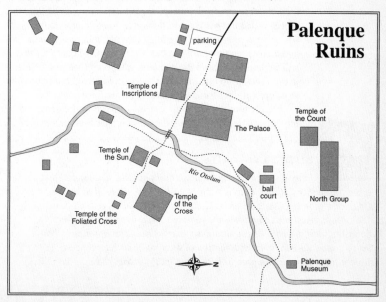

though they doubted that anyone would ever be able to make sense of the Maya glyphs, American explorer John Lloyd Stephens and his artist companion, Frederick Catherwood, painstakingly recorded them all in 1841, before time, tourism and air pollution had taken their toll. Many archaeologists have dedicated their lives to translating these particular inscriptions, and today they are understood to contain a genealogy of Lord Pacal and a history of the major events during his reign.

Another secret of the Temple of Inscriptions remained hidden for more than a century after Stephens and Catherwood surveyed Palenque. In 1948, Mexican archaeologist Alberto Ruz Lhuiller chanced to notice that the floor inside the temple was slightly higher than the platform outside. Searching for an explanation, he discovered that one of the floor flagstones had holes in it that could be used to lift it. Under the stone was an opening filled with rock and rubble that turned out to be a secret stairway.

Ruz spent four years hauling rocks out of the stairway. When he finally reached the bottom, which was lower than the ground level on which the pyramid stood, he found eight corpses. They were young men buried there to guard the mortal remains of Lord Pacal himself, who lay dressed in ceremonial garb and jade ornaments in a sarcophagus under a five-ton slab of rock. Carved on the slab was one of the most spectacular bas-relief sculptures ever found in the Maya world.

The bones and treasures were taken to the National Museum of Anthropology in Mexico City, but the sarcophagus can still be seen by descending the steep, slippery stairway down narrow, green-walled passageways to the tomb. According to experts, the bas-relief depicts Pacal descending into the underworld on a "foliated cross," a powerful symbol from Classic Maya times that is still a common sight in the highland villages of Chiapas. Believers in the "gods from outer space" theory could be right: if you squint your eyes, it does look a lot like an ancient astronaut.

Pacal's tomb was the first royal Maya burial discovered by modern archaeologists. Since then, others have been found at Tikal,

AUTHOR FAVORITE

sights

I sense a living link to Maya spiritual practices whenever I enter the former Catholic church in the highland Maya village of **San Juan Chamula** near San Cristóbal de las Casas. The clergy were banished in an 1869 revolt; crucifixes and pews were removed. Today fresh pine needles cover the floor, incense fills the air, and supplicants sip liquor while praying to god/saints—all revealing a glimpse of what may have happened in ancient Maya temples. See page 377 for more information.

Guatemala, and Copán, Honduras, while at Palenque more than a thousand burials of lesser personages have been discovered within the ceremonial complex. But no other Maya tomb yet found can rival the splendor of Lord Pacal's.

Past the Temple of Inscriptions is Palenque's most fascinating building, known simply as **The Palace.** It was built one addition at a time over more than a century as the royal residence of Lord Pacal and his clan, who are represented in stucco friezes throughout the complex. The palace is an intricate maze of a ruin, with inner courtyards, dank vaulted galleries, porticoes, underground passageways, a five-story tower and pagodalike roofs. You can spend an hour or more just poking around in this structure.

Many archaeologists believe the tower of the Palace was built as an astronomical observatory. On the winter solstice, the sun, when viewed from the tower, sets directly behind the Temple of Inscriptions—into the tomb of Lord Pacal.

The Palace contains 176 separate fragments of painting and sculpture. Most of the sculpture at Palenque, except for hieroglyphs, were done in stucco, which the artist made by mixing finely powdered limestone with water to make a paste similar to modern concrete. It allowed artists to do more elaborate high-relief work than was possible with limestone. Unfortunately, the jungle's dampness destroys stucco quickly, leaving modern visitors to marvel at the remaining fragmentary examples and speculate on what the city must have looked like when all the sculptured friezes were intact and painted bright yellow, blue and green against the city's red walls. What has endured at Palenque and especially at the Palace is considered to be the finest decorative architecture of pre-Hispanic America. The delicately rendered facial expressions in the friezes speak to us today with all the power and passion their creators put into them.

The main footpath beyond the Palace takes you past Palenque's small, partially buried **ball court** and a multilevel cluster of little buildings known as the **North Group.** Located just west of the North Group is the **Temple of the Count,** where in the 1830s Austrian artist Jean-Frédéric Maximilien, Comte de Waldek, lived while working on his romanticized paintings of Palenque. You will understand why the count called this structure home when you see the picture-perfect view of the main ruins from its doorway.

At the end of the main trail, just beyond the North Group, is the **Palenque Museum.** The central exhibit is a huge tablet of hieroglyphs originally found in the Palace. At the top of the tablet, a relief carving depicts Lord Pacal, his wife, Ahpo-Hel, and their second son Kan Xul. This 7th-century family portrait was probably made when Lord Kan Xul ascended the throne long after

A Short Trip to the Maya Highlands

No grand tour of Maya Mexico would be complete without a visit to the Chiapas highlands, home to the most traditional and colorful Maya groups, the Tzotzil and Tzeltal people, who speak different languages from the Yucatecans—and from each other. The highlands feel a lot like Guatemala, and no wonder; Chiapas was part of colonial Guatemala for nearly 300 years. In Palenque, you're 191 kilometers from San Cristóbal de las Casas, the heart of the highlands, following Route 199 the whole way. Take your time on this spectacular mountain highway.

MISOL-HA AND AGUA AZUL   Leave Palenque early, allowing time to enjoy two fabulous natural water parks en route. At **Misol-Ha** (admission), 20 kilometers from Palenque, a waterfall plunges 100 feet into a picture-perfect pool where you can take a swim in a rainforest setting. Located 26 kilometers farther on, more than 500 waterfalls at **Agua Azul** (admission) spill between large limestone pools, making it the most popular swimming spot in the state. Climbing higher into the mountains, you'll pass through **Ocosingo**, a large Maya town where you're likely to find an Army checkpoint. From there, it's an hour's drive through pine forest to San Cristóbal de las Casas.

SAN CRISTÓBAL DE LAS CASAS   Hotels in San Cristóbal offer colonial ambience at affordable rates. Pick a place on the *zócalo*, such as the Hotel Santa Clara (9-678-1140) or the hotel Ciudad Real (9-678-0187), both with budget-to-moderate rates. Spend the late afternoon soaking up San Cristóbal's special charm. Unlike in the lowlands, the sidewalks roll up early here. Among the city's sights are the lively **public market**, the magnificent **Santo Domingo Church** and the hilltop **San Cristóbal Chapel**, reached by 244 stairs that are more challenging to climb than

his parents' deaths. The museum also contains stucco sculptures, jade jewelry and the only stele found at Palenque.

Across the river, to the east of the Temple of Inscriptions, a group of three temples stands out against the surrounding forest. These are the **Temple of the Cross**, the **Temple of the Foliated Cross** and the **Temple of the Sun**. From a distance the three structures appear to be rather small. The two lofty and delicate-looking roof combs that remain intact seem larger than the temples they crown. It is only as you walk into the plaza between the temples that you realize their massive scale. They are set on high pyramids that were once stuccoed and painted but are now buried and covered with grass. All three temples, representing a "holy trinity" of gods who

any Maya pyramid. Then there's **Casa Na-Bolom**, the home of the late
Franz and Trudy Blom, the husband-and-wife explorer team who restored
Uxmal and photographed the Lacandón Maya people of the rainforest;
now a Mexican government museum and cultural center, Na-Bolom
contains the world's largest library of books about the Maya and hosts
Lacandón Indians visiting the city. Start back by 2 p.m. to return to
Palenque before dark.

HIGHLAND MAYA VILLAGES   Tour some of the Maya villages on the outskirts of San Cristóbal, such as the dramatically tradition-bound **San
Juan Chamula** and its colorful neighbor, **San Lorenzo Zinacantán**,
a village whose economy revolves around flower-growing. You can go on
your own, but a knowledgeable guide is a big help here. Mercedes Hernández Gómez, who has a stand on the plaza, can be reached through
the tourist office (9-678-0665); she organizes all-day village-to-village
treks. *Do not bring a camera to any of these villages!*

A safety note: Tourists avoided this region after the 1994 Zapatista rebellion. Soon,
though, young activists (referred to by the previous Mexican government as *turis-
tas revolucionarias*) came to work with the Indians, or at least show their support.
Today there are more gringos in the region than ever, and there have been no incidents involving foreign visitors. If there were trouble in the air, the army or the
locals would warn you away from it. Prospects look good for a peace settlement
soon. For an update before you go, check with Palenque's state tourism office. ~
Calle Jiménez and Avenida Cinco de Mayo, Santo Domingo Palenque; 9-345-0760.
For another slant on the situation, check with rebel leader Subcomandante Marcos,
who maintains a powerful presence on the World Wide Web. Start with the official
Zapatista home page: www.utexas.edu/ftp/student/nave. Other large pro-Zapatista
websites include www.zapatistas.org and www.ezln.org.

were believed to be the ancestors of Palenque's royal family, were
built simultaneously in honor of Lord Pacal's successor—his older
son, Chan Bahlum II—when he ascended the throne in A.D. 683.

The eastern temple group has provided speculative thinkers
with clues hinting that foreigners from across the ocean might
have influenced the building of Palenque. Relief sculptures in the
Temple of the Foliated Cross are strikingly similar to some found
at Angkor Wat in Cambodia. Flower motifs in the temple sculptures resemble nothing so much as the lotus, an Asian plant that
was unknown in ancient Mexico. Large, sculptured stone crosses
found inside two of the temples even led some early scholars to
believe that medieval Christian missionaries built Palenque.

A relief panel to the right of the doorway to the Temple of the Cross is the oldest-known picture of a person smoking a cigar—just like the hand-rolled ones used today by the Lacandón Indians, descendants of the people of Palenque.

It is worth your time and energy to venture into the back-country of **Parque Nacional Palenque** during your visit. Although the park is not large, it preserves the only remnant of virgin rainforest in Chiapas that is accessible by paved road. The main route into the forest is a trail that follows the west side of the river from one park boundary to the other. If you take the trail downriver past the museum and staff residences, you will come to a series of waterfalls with idyllic little pools for swimming. After a couple of steep descents down rock faces, the trail meets the main road near the Mayabel campground.

For a longer hike, take the trail that runs south along the hillside above the river for about four miles to an Indian village, where local people live by subsistence farming on fields they created by slashing and burning the rainforest, much as farmers did during Palenque's heyday. The Palenque backcountry, with its towering ceiba trees and hanging vines, is one of the last places in Mexico where the throaty cries of endangered black howler monkeys still ring through the forest. Hundreds of small temple-like structures were erected in this area, some still visible near the trail. Those that have been excavated have proven to be tombs—another mysterious hint about Palenque's unique status in the ancient Maya world.

The predominantly ladino town of **Palenque** (pop. 30,000) near Route 186, about seven kilometers from the archaeological site, was called Santo Domingo until the ruins became a famous tourist destination with the discovery of Pacal's tomb. Its name has been changed to Palenque on maps and train and bus schedules. Locals still use the old name; you can quickly win new friends with remarks like *"Mucho gusto Santo Domingo"* ("I like Santo Domingo a lot"). To avoid confusion with the ruins and respect local tradition, many people refer to the town as "Santo Domingo Palenque."

The western side of town, where the bus stations and most hotels are located, has only a few streets. Along a rugged ravine called *la cañada* that fills the northwest quarter of the town, many of the houses have no road access and are reached by steep footpaths. Proceed west along Avenida Juárez to reach the long, narrow concrete plaza in front of the church. Past the plaza, the upper end of town is residential in character. Stroll through a few back streets to see all the little urban farmsteads teeming with pigs, turkeys, goats and even burros, right in the middle of town.

LODGING   Unlike Chichén Itzá, Uxmal and Cobá, Parque Nacional Palenque does not have any luxury tourist accommodations within walking distance of the ruins. The only place to sleep at the park is the funky **Mayabel Campground**, which has tent and RV campsites, palapas for hammock campers and a few very basic motel-style rooms, as well as a small restaurant. The hillside campground is surrounded by rainforest on three sides, and a trail leads to nearby waterfalls and small Maya ruins. ~ BUDGET.

The nearest jungle lodge to Parque Nacional Palenque is the **Chan-Kah Ruinas**. The resort is midway between the ruins (too far to walk up the steep road, though it's a nice sunset walk back down) and the town of Palenque. Minibuses run back and forth along the ruins road constantly, so you will never have to wait more than a few minutes for a ride either to town or to the ruins. The charge is just a few cents. The 28 guest accommodations are spacious, modern duplex units scattered throughout the lush, landscaped grounds around a series of river-fed swimming pools. The huge, thatched-roof, open-air main building houses the lobby, restaurant and spacious sitting areas. ~ Km. 3 Carretera a las Ruinas; 9-345-1100, fax 9-345-0820. DELUXE.

> The management at Chan-Kah Ruinas claims that the water that fills its swimming pools comes from a mountain spring that was sacred to the ancient Maya for its miraculous restorative properties.

The same owners also operate the **Hotel Chan-Kah Centro**, a hotel near the main plaza in Santo Domingo Palenque. The bright, modern rooms have private baths, and there is a large second-floor terrace. Ceiling fans. ~ Calle Hidalgo 15; 9-345-0318, fax 9-345-0489. MODERATE.

In the countryside on the outskirts of the town of Palenque, you'll find the region's most luxurious lodging, the **Hotel Misión Palenque**. This member in the familiar chain of upscale Yucatán hotels offers guest rooms with televisions and phones. Facilities include a swimming pool and tennis courts. The hotel provides guests with free shuttle service to the ruins. This is also the largest hotel around, with 160 rooms. Air conditioning. ~ Route 199; 9-345-0241, fax 9-345-0300. DELUXE.

There are dozens of smaller hotels in the commercial district and west side of the town of Palenque. Those on the main streets offer low rates but generally spartan accommodations and can be noisy. If you wish to stay in town, your best bet is the Cañada area, secluded in a forested ravine just a few blocks from the center of town. The nicest of the little lodges here is **Hotel La Cañada**, ◄ HIDDEN
Guest accommodations are in cottages that were originally built for archaeologists during the restoration of the Palenque ruins. Most have bathtubs. Ceiling fans. ~ Calle Merle Green; 9-345-0102, fax 9-345-1302. BUDGET.

Visitors to the Palenque ruins have two options for lunch or dinner nearby. One option is the small thatched-roof restaurant at

DINING

Mayabel Campground, just inside the national park entrance. The simple, filling fare features tacos, pizza and such along with delightfully cold soft drinks and beer. ~ BUDGET.

Halfway between town and the ruins, the full-service restaurant at **Chan-Kah Ruinas** offers well-prepared chicken and fish dishes in a quiet, casual atmosphere with a touch of tropical elegance. Prices are much higher here than they would be in town. ~ Km. 3 Carretera a las Ruinas; 9-345-0318. DELUXE.

In the town of Palenque, one of my favorites is **Restaurant Girasoles,** an unassuming checkered-tablecloth café that offers a good selection of conventional Mexican dishes. This is about the only restaurant in Palenque that opens before 8 a.m., and breakfast specialties include *chilaquiles* (leftover tortillas cooked with chile, chicken and cheese—a tasty Mexican favorite) and the best cup of coffee in town. ~ Avenida Juárez 189; 9-345-0383. BUDGET.

Another low-priced restaurant that is frequented by a mixed clientele of locals and tourists, the **Restaurant Maya** serves delicious standard Mexican fare, including great tamales wrapped in banana leaves—a specialty that's not found in Mexican restaurants as often as you'd expect because these deceptively simple-looking portions of stuffed corn *masa* are time-consuming to make. ~ Avenida Independencia at the plaza; 9-345-0042. BUDGET.

Probably the nicest restaurant in the town of Palenque is **La Selva,** next door to the Hotel La Cañada. Hidden in a junglelike setting within walking distance of Avenida Juárez and the *zócalo,* this place offers fine dining in a self-consciously tropical atmosphere. Waiters dress in flamboyant regional style and ceiling fans spin incessantly. Try the *pigua,* a large freshwater shellfish that is caught in the local rivers and cooked like lobster. ~ Calle Hidalgo; 9-345-0363. MODERATE TO DELUXE.

Local innkeepers—at least those without restaurants on the premises—recommend **La Chiapaneca,** located a short distance out of town on the road to the ruins. Tropical greenery makes an

AUTHOR FAVORITE

Perhaps the most interesting "curios" I've ever come across in Maya country are the colorful **handmade arrows** sold at the ruins and town of Palenque by Lacandón Indians who live in the surrounding rainforest. Bartering with these strange, stone-age people in their long white gowns and incongruously shiny black shoes is a memorable experience. See page 381 for more information.

ideal setting for regional specialties such as *pollo Palenque,* chicken and potatoes stewed in an onion-and-tomato sauce. ~ Carretera Ruinas, Km. 1; 9-345-1771. MODERATE.

SHOPPING

The most distinctive souvenir items sold around Palenque are the handmade arrows of the Lacandón Indians who live in the surrounding rainforest. The arrows have brightly colored tail feathers and assorted styles of chipped stone and sharpened bone tips. When they are used for hunting, the tips are dipped in poison. Sets of arrows that have actually been used (though probably not poisoned) sell at a higher price than those originally made for the tourist trade, though they don't look much different. The arrows are usually sold in splayed bundles of 5 to 15 that can be pulled together for carrying, then fanned out to hang on your wall back home. White-garbed Lacandones sell them by the parking lot at Palenque ruins.

Several shops and vendors' stalls in the town of Palenque offer reproductions of Lord Pacal's sarcophagus and other sculptures from the Palenque ruins in a variety of media, from leather burnings and plaster of Paris castings to wood carvings and limestone sculptures. Palenque is full of highly skilled craftspeople who have been making these reproductions for years, and the workmanship is often quite fine. A good bet for quality arts and crafts is **Casa de Artesanías Chiapaneca.** ~ Avenida Juarez, one block from the plaza.

BEACHES & PARKS

MAYABEL CAMPGROUND 🏃 🛶 Set at the boundary of Parque Nacional Palenque, this informal campground is adjacent to a small Maya ruin and a fantastic series of waterfalls and jungle pools for swimming. Drinking water and central restrooms are just about the only facilities here. A steep short-cut trail leads up to the ruins of Palenque, and the cow pasture across the road sprouts psilocybin mushrooms. ~ Located on the road to Palenque, three kilometers before the ruins entrance.

▲ There are four crude, unfurnished camping cabins, 18 palapas for hammock (and mosquito net!) camping, and an indeterminate number of tent sites.

Bonampak and Yaxchilán

Many ruins enthusiasts say that Yaxchilán is their favorite Maya site— better than Palenque, Copán or Tikal. Yaxchilán is the Maya ceremonial center most recently opened to public view. The adventure of getting there, of discovering as if for the first time the ruins of a once-great city deep in the jungle, makes a trip to Yaxchilán and the smaller outlying site of Bonampak one of the most memorable experiences on the Maya Route.

Situated deep in the Lacandón rainforest on the Guatemalan border, Bonampak and Yaxchilán were accessible only by private-charter bush planes flying out of Tuxtla Gutiérrez and Villahermosa until 1985. That was the year the Mexican government responded to worsening social violence in Guatemala (which had driven more than 40,000 Maya villagers over the border to refugee camps in Mexico and erupted in clashes with Guatemalan soldiers on the Mexican side of the Usumacinta River) by building a 287-mile unpaved *carretera frontera* (border highway) along the entire border between Chiapas and Guatemala. The road also served to open the border region to settlement. Today, visitors who go to Yaxchilán by plane see a dramatic border panorama—pristine, impenetrable rainforest on the Guatemala side; cleared agricultural lands on the Mexican side.

SIGHTS

The border "highway" makes it possible to travel most of the way to Bonampak and Yaxchilán by minivan tour or private car. The unpaved road is good enough for passenger cars as far as the trailhead for Bonampak and all the way to Corozal, the departure point for the boat downriver to Yaxchilán.

A road under construction will someday take tourist traffic right up to Bonampak and Yaxchilán. In the meantime, whether you get there by private car, tour van or flightseeing plane, the trip to Bonampak is about ten kilometers on a rough road that often washes out, followed by a hot hike through the jungle.

HIDDEN ►

Bonampak is set in the foothills of the mountain range that separates the Lacanja and Usumacinta river valleys. The tropical rainforest that shrouds the hills gives the ruin an atmosphere of mystery and great age. The site is made up of a small plaza surrounded by a group of buildings, most of them crumbled into mounds of stone rubble. When archaeologists "discovered" it in 1946, Bonampak was still being used ceremonially by the Lacandón Indians who lived in the surrounding forest, descendants of the people who built the temples between A.D. 200 and 900. Archaeologists found elaborately carved stelae and charted all the structures at the site except one, which was so hidden by tangled greenery that early expeditions overlooked it, even though it was in the heart of the complex. Later the same year, United Fruit Company photographer Giles G. Healy found his way into the hidden building, which was dubbed simply **Building 1**. The works of art concealed inside would revolutionize scientists' ideas about ancient Maya civilization.

Three chambers inside Building 1 contain panels of frescoes. Painted on surfaces of wet limestone cement, the whole array, containing some 270 human figures, was completed in just 48 hours. Now, 1200 years later, the frescoes are by far the best-preserved known examples of Maya painting. Once brilliant in their hues, they have faded badly since their discovery, but reproductions have been installed for comparison. (Other copies of these famous paintings can be found in the Museum of Anthropology in Mérida, the Regional Museum of Anthropology in Villahermosa, the National Museum of Anthropology in Mexico City and the Hotel Bonampak in Tuxtla Gutiérrez.)

The Bonampak frescoes tell the story of a raid and sacrificial ceremony. In the first room, nobles dressed in jaguar-skin robes and elaborate headdresses, carrying richly decorated scepters, organize their warriors for battle as musicians and masked dancers perform a processional that may have been a kind of war dance. The painting in the central room shows the raid itself, armed warriors of Bonampak swooping down on a rival village. Despite the bloodthirsty brutality evident in the painting, the limited weaponry of the Bonampak army suggests that the main purpose of the raids was to maim and take prisoners, not to kill. A smaller painting in the same room shows a group of prisoners being led before the lord of Bonampak for judgment. In the third room, we see one of the prisoners being sacrificed on the temple steps while his fellow prisoners plead for their lives. The favored method for killing prisoners of war appears to have been hacking off their heads with a big stone knife.

One-day airplane tours of Bonampak and Yaxchilán, which are very expensive, can be arranged at the airport in either Santo Domingo Palenque or San Cristóbal de las Casas.

Before the paintings were found, experts and laypeople alike generally believed that the Maya were a peaceful, morally superior people who lived under the benign rule of philosophers and who found spiritual guidance by studying the mysteries of time and the universe. Any evidence of human sacrifice at other sites, especially Chichén Itzá, could be explained away as evil influences imported from central Mexico by the Toltecs. But now, deep in the rainforest where no Toltec ever ventured, the Bonampak frescoes revealed a savage world where warlords ruled over a rigid caste system and slaughtered neighboring communities to enhance their own prestige—in other words, a society not much different from the one Cortés found in the Aztec empire some 700 years later.

Since the discovery of the Bonampak murals, archaeologists have found other evidence of warfare among the Maya cities in Classic times. Scholars who have reconstructed Maya history from hieroglyphs have learned, for instance, of a long-running conflict between Tikal and its neighboring city of Uaxactún that reshaped the power structure throughout the Petén every time a general devised a new combat tactic. What no one knows is whether mass violence was widespread in ancient Maya society or limited to a few anomalous times and places.

After all, the Bonampak murals were painted in 48 hours out of the 700-year history of this small, remote settlement on the western outskirts of the vast Maya empire. Few other artworks of the Classic period in Maya history deal with military subjects.

Could Bonampak have been some kind of outlaw stronghold when the paintings were made? Or could Building 1 have been a temple of some strange religious sect? Once, hundreds of temples throughout the Maya world must have contained such murals, now lost to the ravages of time. Would they have corroborated the Bonampak view of Maya civilization, or would they have shown us that the Maya world was one of greater cultural diversity than we realize? As is usually the case in Maya archaeology, the discovery of the Bonampak frescoes raised more questions than it answered.

Animals depicted in ancient Maya paintings such as those at Bonampak include owls, cougars, serpents, monkeys, tapirs and various birds.

When you return from Bonampak to the main road, you're less than 21 kilometers south of Yaxchilán as the crow flies. But to get there, you need to drive east for an hour to the town of **Corozal** (Echeverría), a small port across the Usumacinta River from a remote area of the Petén in Guatemala. Van tours and independent adventurers traveling by car spend the night here. (Bring your own food and camping equipment. Tourist facilities are probably inevitable in Corozal's future, but today they do not exist.) In the morning, visitors take a motorized launch from Corozal to Yaxchilán, about a 45-minute trip down a river as smooth as glass and deep green with algae, flowing between solid walls of jungle.

HIDDEN ►

Yaxchilán was a major ceremonial center during the same period as Palenque to the north and Tikal to the east. Building began here around A.D. 200. The city reached its highest development under two lords, Jaguar Shield and his son Bird Jaguar, in the 700s. Although Yaxchilán was deserted around A.D. 900, like other lowland Chiapas sites it is still used for religious rituals by the Lacandón Maya people who inhabit the surrounding rainforest. According to anthropologist-photographer Gertrude Blom, who spent years among the Lacandones, they believe that their chief god, Hatchak'yum, lives in the ruins of Yaxchilán.

The Lacandones are the last nomadic, un-Christianized tribe in Mexico. They fled into the jungle 400 years ago to save their independence and have avoided contact with Spanish colonial and ladino influences ever since. They are probably descendants of the people who built the magnificent ceremonial centers of Yaxchilán and Palenque. Many experts believe that studies of Lacandón spiritual practices—as described by Gertrude Blom, who lived among the forest people for extended periods of time—offer a unique window into the belief system of the ancient Maya. Sadly, the world that the Lacandones have known for more than a millennium has nearly vanished. Population pressures, slash-and-burn farming techniques and timber operations are destroying the Chiapas rainforest at an alarming rate.

Although we think of Yaxchilán today as one of the loneliest places in the Maya world and one of the hardest to reach, 1200 years ago it was a big, busy port city. Boats were the fastest and easiest transportation mode in the ancient Maya world, and the Usumacinta was its longest navigable river. Yaxchilán's strategic position made it a key commercial center from which trade routes reached the Petén, the Maya highlands and the lowlands around Palenque.

Disembarking by the **main plaza**, which spans about 1000 feet along the river's edge, one can easily imagine the clamor and commotion that must have characterized the busy, colorful waterfront in bygone days. Adjoining the plaza are two ball courts, several low platforms that may have been marketplaces and the ruins of structures that were probably residences and warehouses.

The ruins of Yaxchilán cover an area larger than those at Palenque, though only a few structures have had any restoration work so far. A total of 86 stone buildings have been identified at the site. The dense tangle of giant trees and choking vines has been cleared away to expose the tops of about 40 structures whose foundation mounds remain buried.

Unlike almost all other Maya sites, Yaxchilán is not organized in a square oriented to the paths of planets. Because the terrain, along a gooseneck in the river, is on a slope, the city is built up from the main plaza in a series of terraces.

A long stairway climbs more than 200 feet from the main plaza to the site's showpiece ceremonial temple, called **Structure 33**. The dominant temple at Yaxchilán, it has a long roof comb decorated with a sculpture of a seated god. From the temple's level, a stairway to the south continues even higher—to **Structure 41**, on a hilltop 360 feet in elevation, making it much higher than any manmade pyramid in the Maya world. The third major area consists of **Structure 44**, on a separate hilltop to the west. This unexcavated ruin was a complex labyrinth of rooms and courtyards similar to the Palace at Palenque or the North Acropolis at Tikal. A series of five monumental stelae stands in front of Structure 44. Some of the best examples of the sculpted lintels for which Yaxchilán is famed can be found over three doorways, and the doorsteps are carved with rows of hieroglyphs.

The art of Yaxchilán rivals almost anything at Palenque, and the secluded rainforest setting far from the roar of tour buses makes it all the more magical. At Yaxchilán, limestone lintels, stelae and interior and exterior walls were carved with hieroglyphic inscriptions, portraits of royalty and many dramatic scenes that seem to be windows into the dark side of the ancient Maya spirit. Warfare, captivity and ritual bloodletting are common themes, as are symbolic representations of sacred visions. Priests' visions, induced by psychoactive plants and self-inflicted pain and depicted as curling, smokelike rays in friezes at Palenque and Yaxchilán, are central to ancient Maya religion. Take a close look at the lintel sculpture from Yaxchilán that has been reproduced on the Mexican 20-peso note. It depicts a woman driving a stingray's spine through her tongue in a ceremony performed in order to evoke visions, symbolized by the smokelike patterns coming from her head. Was Yaxchilán known in the Maya world as a place of prophecy, as tour guides claim?

Sculpture seems to be strewn everywhere in Yaxchilán, in broken fragments so alien and fraught with symbolism as to defy 20th-century understanding. The only disappointment at Yaxchilán is that there is never enough time to spend poking around in the hills and ravines for more artistic enigmas to puzzle over. As long as the only access to the city is by hired boat and no lodging is available in the vicinity, visits will be limited to a few brief hours. Some day, when the road to Yaxchilán is completed and archaeological hotels begin to spring up nearby, future travelers will be able to linger at Yaxchilán for days on end—but never again with the solitude that can be experienced there today.

Unlike the art found at other known Maya centers, many relief sculptures at Yaxchilán are of women, suggesting that they may have been rulers or priests.

For more than a decade, the Mexican government promoted a plan to develop a series of dams on the Usumacinta River that would have flooded Yaxchilán. The plan has been abandoned (for now).

Note: Although the idea of continuing on the border "highway" beyond Yaxchilán to Lagos de Montebello and Comitán may seem intriguing, it is feasible only if you have a high-clearance vehicle and several extra five-gallon cans of gasoline. The journey cannot be made in a single day, and no food, lodging or designated camping is available anywhere along the route. Beyond the tiny settlement of Boca Lacantún, the "highway" through the jungle becomes sort of vague and theoretical in places.

LODGING You spend the night in a hammock in a **Quonset-hut dormitory**—the only tourist accommodation around—in the border outpost of Corozal, where the boats depart for Yaxchilán. Inquire in Santo Domingo Palenque at Viajes Toniná. ~ Avenida Juárez 105; 9-345-0384. BUDGET.

Transportation

CAR To reach Palenque from the Yucatán, take **Route 186** southwest from Escárcega for 184 kilometers to Villahermosa, situated west of Palenque at the junctions of Routes 186, **195** and 180. From there, go 101 kilometers southeast on Route 186 to the **Route 199** intersection. Go south for 26 kilometers on Route 199. The archaeological zone is 8 kilometers beyond town on a paved road.

The **Carretera Frontera**, the unpaved military road that follows the Guatemalan border at a discrete distance, is used daily by civilian motorists and tour vans on their way to Bonampak and Yaxchilán. The road goes to within 10 kilometers of Bonampak, where you turn west at a marked junction to the village of San Javiér and then south to the ruins. Future plans envision a paved road that will take tourists all the way to Bonampak. In the meantime, the last several kilometers of the road to the ruins are rough enough so you should expect to hike unless you have a four-wheel-drive vehicle.

AIR

Visitors from the United States, Mexico City or Mérida land at **Carlos R. Perez Airport** in Villahermosa. It's serviced by Aerocaribbean, Aeromexico and Mexicana.

BUS

There are 14 buses a day from Campeche to Villahermosa and four a day from Palenque (the bus station in Palenque is on Avenida Hidalgo at Cinco de Maya.)

One rather run-down first-class bus goes direct to Palenque from Mérida via Campeche, three slow second-class buses depart from Escárcega, and six first-class buses depart from Villahermosa. All buses run daily.

There are no buses to Corozal. To reach Yaxchilán, you must park in the little river port of Corozal (also called Echeverría) and take a power launch downriver to the ruins. The boat trip takes about 45 minutes to get there, but the return trip against the current takes twice as long.

▼▼▼▼▼▼▼▼▼▼▼▼▼▼▼▼▼▼▼▼▼▼▼▼

Addresses & Phone Numbers

Centro de Salud y Hospital General (Palenque) ~ Avenida Juárez; 9-345-1443

Clínica Air Médica 2000 (Villahermosa; english-speaking medical clinic) ~ Paseo Tabasco 114; 9-933-1933

Cruz Roja (Villahermosa) ~ Avenida General Sandino, Col. 1 de Mayo; 9-315-5555

Emergency number (Villahermosa) ~ 060

Oficina de Turismo (Palenque) ~ Avenida Juárez at Calle Abasolo; 9-345-0760

Oficina de Turismo (Villahermosa) ~ Tabasco 2000; 9-316-3633

Policia (Palenque) ~ 9-345-1844

Policia (Villahermosa) ~ 9-315-2633

Internet Access (Palenque) ~ Internet Café, Calle Independencia; 9-345-0934

Internet Access (Villahermosa) ~ Internet Zona Luz, Calle Aldama No. 404-C; 9-312-9659

Index

Lodging Index

Dining Index

HIDDEN GUIDES

Adventure travel or a relaxing vacation?—"Hidden" guidebooks are the only travel books in the business to provide detailed information on both. Aimed at environmentally aware travelers, our motto is "Where Vacations Meet Adventures." These books combine details on unique hotels, restaurants and sightseeing with information on camping, sports and hiking for the outdoor enthusiast.

THE NEW KEY GUIDES

Based on the concept of ecotourism, The New Key Guides are dedicated to the preservation of Central America's rare and endangered species, architecture and archaeology. Filled with helpful tips, they give travelers everything they need to know about these exotic destinations.

Order Form

HIDDEN GUIDEBOOKS

____ Hidden Arizona, $16.95

____ Hidden Bahamas, $14.95

____ Hidden Baja, $14.95

____ Hidden Belize, $15.95

____ Hidden Boston & Cape Cod, $14.95

____ Hidden British Columbia, $17.95

____ Hidden Cancún & the Yucatán, $16.95

____ Hidden Carolinas, $17.95

____ Hidden Coast of California, $18.95

____ Hidden Colorado, $15.95

____ Hidden Disneyland, $13.95

____ Hidden Florida, $18.95

____ Hidden Florida Keys & Everglades, $12.95

____ Hidden Georgia, $16.95

____ Hidden Guatemala, $16.95

____ Hidden Hawaii, $18.95

____ Hidden Idaho, $14.95

____ Hidden Kauai, $13.95

____ Hidden Maui, $13.95

____ Hidden Montana, $15.95

____ Hidden New England, $18.95

____ Hidden New Mexico, $15.95

____ Hidden Oahu, $13.95

____ Hidden Oregon, $15.95

____ Hidden Pacific Northwest, $18.95

____ Hidden Salt Lake City, $14.95

____ Hidden San Francisco & Northern California, $18.95

____ Hidden Southern California, $18.95

____ Hidden Southwest, $19.95

____ Hidden Tahiti, $17.95

____ Hidden Tennessee, $16.95

____ Hidden Utah, $16.95

____ Hidden Walt Disney World, $13.95

____ Hidden Washington, $15.95

____ Hidden Wine Country, $13.95

____ Hidden Wyoming, $15.95

THE NEW KEY GUIDEBOOKS

____ The New Key to Costa Rica, $18.95

____ The New Key to Ecuador and the Galápagos, $17.95

Mark the book(s) you're ordering and enter the total cost here ⇨ [   ]

California residents add 8.25% sales tax here ⇨ [   ]

Shipping, check box for your preferred method and enter cost here ⇨ [   ]

❏ BOOK RATE   **FREE! FREE! FREE!**

❏ PRIORITY MAIL/UPS GROUND   cost of postage

❏ UPS OVERNIGHT OR 2-DAY AIR   cost of postage

Billing, enter total amount due here and check method of payment ⇨ [   ]

❏ CHECK   ❏ MONEY ORDER

❏ VISA/MASTERCARD _____ EXP. DATE _____

NAME _____ PHONE _____

ADDRESS _____

_____

CITY _____ STATE _____ ZIP _____

MONEY-BACK GUARANTEE ON DIRECT ORDERS PLACED THROUGH ULYSSES PRESS.

ABOUT THE AUTHOR

RICHARD HARRIS has written or co-written more than 20 other guidebooks including *Hidden Baja*, *Hidden Colorado*, *Hidden Southwest* and *AAA Hidden Highways Northern California*. He has also served as contributing editor on guides for John Muir Publications, Fodor's, Birnbaum and Access guides and has written for numerous magazines including *Four Corners*, *Ritz-Carlton*, *Southwest Photographic* and *Southwest Profile*. He is past president of PEN New Mexico and an officer and director of the New Mexico Book Association.

ABOUT THE ILLUSTRATOR

GLENN KIM is a freelance illustrator residing in the San Francisco Bay area. His work appears in many Ulysses Press titles, including *Hidden Southwest*, *Hidden Tahiti* and *Hidden Belize*. He has also illustrated for the National Forest Service, several Bay Area magazines, book covers and greeting cards. He is now working with computer graphics and having lots of fun.